POETRY AFTER AUSCHWITZ

JEWISH LITERATURE AND CULTURE

SERIES EDITOR, ALVIN H. ROSENFELD

Marc Chagall, French, born Russia, 1887–1985, *White Crucifixion,* 1938. Oil on canvas, 154.3 × 139.7 cm. Gift of Alfred S. Alschuler, 1946.925. © 2002 The Art Institute of Chicago / Artist's Rights Society, New York / ADAGP, Paris. All Rights Reserved. Used by permission.

POETRY AFTER AUSCHWITZ

Remembering What One Never Knew

Susan Gubar

INDIANA University Press

Bloomington & Indianapolis

For Barbara —
With warm wishes
for you complex &
rich life!
Susan

PUBLICATION OF THIS BOOK HAS BEEN SUPPORTED IN PART BY DONORS TO THE INDIANA UNIVERSITY PRESS JEWISH STUDIES AND HOLOCAUST STUDIES FUND.

PORTIONS OF THIS BOOK HAVE APPEARED OR WILL APPEAR IN THE FOLLOWING: "POETS OF TESTIMONY: C. K. WILLIAMS AND JACQUELINE OSHEROW AS PROXY-WITNESSES OF THE SHOAH," IN *MAPPING THE ETHICAL TURN: A READER IN ETHICS, CULTURE, AND LITERARY THEORY,* ED. TODD F. DAVIS AND KENNETH WOMACK, 165–91 (CHARLOTTESVILLE: UNIVERSITY PRESS OF VIRGINIA, 2001); "PROSOPOPOEIA AND HOLOCAUST POETRY IN ENGLISH: SYLVIA PLATH AND HER CONTEMPORARIES," *YALE JOURNAL OF CRITICISM* 14, NO. 1 (SPRING 2001): 191–215; "JEWISH-AMERICAN WOMEN WRITERS AND THE RACE QUESTION," IN *THE CAMBRIDGE COMPANION TO JEWISH-AMERICAN LITERATURE,* ED. MICHAEL KRAMER AND HANA WIRTH-NESHER (FORTHCOMING); AND "EMPATHIC IDENTIFICATION IN ANNE MICHAELS'S *FUGITIVE PIECES:* MASCULINITY AND POETRY AFTER AUSCHWITZ," IN *GENDER AND CULTURAL MEMORY,* ED. MARIANNE HIRSCH AND VALERIE SMITH, SPECIAL ISSUE OF *SIGNS: JOURNAL OF WOMEN IN CULTURE AND SOCIETY* 28, NO. 1 (AUTUMN 2002) (FORTHCOMING).

THIS BOOK IS A PUBLICATION OF

INDIANA UNIVERSITY PRESS
601 NORTH MORTON STREET
BLOOMINGTON, IN 47404-3797 USA

HTTP://IUPRESS.INDIANA.EDU

Telephone orders   800-842-6796
Fax orders   812-855-7931
Orders by e-mail   IUPORDER@INDIANA.EDU

THE PAPER USED IN THIS PUBLICATION MEETS THE MINIMUM REQUIREMENTS OF AMERICAN NATIONAL STANDARD FOR INFORMATION SCIENCES — PERMANENCE OF PAPER FOR PRINTED LIBRARY MATERIALS, ANSI Z39.48-1984.

MANUFACTURED IN THE UNITED STATES OF AMERICA

LIBRARY OF CONGRESS CATALOGING-IN-PUBLICATION DATA

GUBAR, SUSAN, DATE
POETRY AFTER AUSCHWITZ : REMEMBERING WHAT ONE NEVER KNEW / SUSAN GUBAR.
P. CM. — (JEWISH LITERATURE AND CULTURE)
INCLUDES BIBLIOGRAPHICAL REFERENCES (P.) AND INDEX.
ISBN 0-253-34176-0 (ALK. PAPER)
1. AMERICAN POETRY — JEWISH AUTHORS — HISTORY AND CRITICISM. 2. ENGLISH POETRY — JEWISH AUTHORS — HISTORY AND CRITICISM. 3. AMERICAN POETRY — 20TH CENTURY — HISTORY AND CRITICISM. 4. ENGLISH POETRY — 20TH CENTURY — HISTORY AND CRITICISM. 5. WORLD WAR, 1939–1945 — LITERATURE AND THE WAR. 6. HOLOCAUST, JEWISH (1939–1945) IN LITERATURE. 7. JEWISH POETRY — HISTORY AND CRITICISM. 8. JUDAISM IN LITERATURE. 9. JEWS IN LITERATURE. I. TITLE. II. SERIES.
PS153.J4 G78 2003
811'.5409358 — DC21   2002004291

1   2   3   4   5   08   07   06   05   04   03

THIS BOOK IS DEDICATED WITH ADMIRATION

AND LOVE TO MY MOTHER,

LUISE DREYFUSS DAVID

Who will immortalize our troubles? . . . A catastrophe that becomes part of poetry . . . spreads among the people and is transmitted to future generations. A poet who clothes adversity in poetic form immortalizes it in an everlasting monument. And this monument provides historic material from which future generations are nourished.

Who will write of our troubles and who will immortalize them? Where is the folk poet of Polish Jewry, who will gather all the tragedy in our lives and perpetuate and guard it in the reliquary of his tears?

Poet of the people, where art thou?

— CHAIM A. KAPLAN, *Scroll of Agony*

Today people know
have known for several years
that this dot on the map
is Auschwitz
This much they know
as for the rest
they think they know.

— CHARLOTTE DELBO, *Auschwitz and After*

CONTENTS

ILLUSTRATIONS

PREFACE

I ask my reader's pardon for the ignorance and the presumption everywhere evident on the pages of this book, ignorance and presumption oddly entwined in my project. While doing my thinking about the verse written in English about the Shoah, I found myself taking all sorts of volumes off library shelves: books on prosody, Jewish theology, biblical narratives, German history, trauma studies, the medium of photography, Yiddish translation, the psychology of torture, aesthetics and ethics, political investigations into fascism, the sociology of bureaucracy, postmodernism, and so on. The poets seemed to be sending me in ever-widening circles, far-flung territories, where I was forced rather painfully to confront my own inadequacies. Why persevere in such abjection — especially since it was bound to produce a marred, inadequate critical work? Well, that's where the presumption — a pedagogical one — set in. As I discovered poet after poet struggling to keep cultural memory of the Holocaust alive, I became upset with the currently available anthologies, critical works, and courses on the Shoah, all of which appeared uninflected by the verse on which I was stumbling. If no one knows about these texts, I worried, would they simply slip into oblivion? Of course, I had another option: putting together a collection of verse. Although such a volume should eventually come into being, it seems too soon to canonize a tradition very much in the making. Instead, I decided to chance speculations that are meant to be provisional, not definitive, an impetus for further study by others. This is what I hope *Poetry After Auschwitz* will inspire. Not nightmares.

In 1996, the year I began writing portions of this manuscript, I became oddly obsessed with quilting. My first completed project was an Amish quilt, dark — even stark — panels of solid colors hand-sewn together in a geometrical design pronounced "nautical" by Don Gray, the infinitely patient man who shares his life with me. But even as I concentrated on perfecting the tiny running stitches that hold batting and backing to the pieced top, I had begun cutting bright patches of fabric for what became a cheerfully mild blanket (deemed "good-natured" by Don) for dear friends who were expecting a baby after having lost their beloved first infant at her birth. Then a ring quilt for one of my two daughters. There was something hectic about the patching and the stitching, which were not interrupted even by calluses and puncture wounds that merely sent me to the drugstore in search of finger cots. Musing about designs and textiles, borders and templates, I wondered what this mania had to do with the Holocaust materials I was studying during this same year, and the next, and the next. That work, too, was done in patches, indeed in swatches of time much more oddly and recurrently interrupted.

I would draft a chapter, but put it away for months on a back shelf of my study closet. I'd send out an article to a journal, then withdraw it from consideration. When asked to participate in a conference or forum, I might compose a response and then refuse the invitation. Once an eminent person in the field was kind enough to offer himself as a reader of work in progress, yet I temporized. Never could I bring myself to offer an undergraduate or graduate course devoted entirely to the subject of my inquiries, though I made sporadic attempts to bring some of the ethical concerns about art into pockets of preexisting courses. Did the innocence of fabric, the prettiness of color, and mindlessness of stitchery offer a kind of antidote to the shocking cruelty of the material I was handling as a scholar? Certainly, on the many nights when I understood myself to be falling into a nightmare about starving inmates shivering under surveillance towers, I would struggle in my sleep to instruct myself to think about quilts instead. Invariably a day spent studying poetry would be followed by dreadful dreams, rarely staved off by attempts to switch to the quilting channel. With relief I turned to putting together a book of my essays on feminist criticism, which effectively stopped the composing of these pages for months. Always, though, it was the verse that drew me back — its mysterious reluctance to illuminate, coupled with its flickering, fitful bursts of meaning.

Had the poets focused on syllabic counts, line breaks, stanzaic patterns, grammar, and rhyme in an analogous attempt to distance themselves from a disorienting subject? About her early poetry, Adrienne Rich has written that "formalism was part of the strategy—like asbestos gloves, it allowed me to handle materials I couldn't pick up bare-handed" ("WWDA" 40–41). Though I hardly want to compare myself to a creative writer like Rich, as a teacher I have found formalism a strategy to handle materials otherwise too painful to touch. I think it can help students in the same way: protecting them — through discussions of how meaning is made and unmade — from scenes and subjects too toxic to approach directly. I remember how angry a number of my undergraduates got at Claude Lanzmann after they saw some footage from *Shoah:* he was manipulative, a bully, they exclaimed, "forcing those survivors to dredge up such ghastly memories." Easier to handle, this rage against the director, than the suffering evident in his witnesses or the emptiness and silence of filmed landscapes that cannot but demonstrate how the pain of the past remains unfilmable. Like the tedium of that empty and silent footage, the formal experimentation of verse about the Shoah required me to suspend evaluation, at times. I did not want to reject outright poems that might originally strike me (or my reader) as boring or out-rageous, fragmented or tendentious. Non-Jews writing about Jewish suffer-ing, Jews picturing the Holocaust through a Christian lens, nursery rhymes about the villains, dramatic monologues in the voices of the dead: many of the works I discuss in this book are likely to offend.

Indeed, the very concept of exploiting the Shoah as a subject or pretext for art strikes even (especially) the authors of Holocaust literature as ob-scene. Yet this revulsion against and repeated return to the aesthetic are precisely what characterize the production of Holocaust poetry. So my only criterion for choosing the verse that I decided to highlight remained a rather ineffable one: namely, its marks of aesthetic ambition or historical seriousness. This means that the pages that follow do not deal with many volumes of verse composed as a therapeutic response to the catastrophe, as heartfelt and personal reactions to the disaster. While I read and reread the verse most rigorously engaged in aesthetic, ethical, and historical inquiries, I often took refuge in the shelter poets found, in formal techniques that seemed to require weird names: proxy-witnessing, anamnesis, antimorpho-sis (works dependent on visual distortion), prosopopoeia (or personifica-tion), and anti-elegiac lamentations. The terms seem clunky, archaic, but they helped me organize a mass of material not previously mapped by liter-ary historians. Throughout the eight chapters to follow, I aimed for a bal-ance between close, extended analyses of individual poems that struck me as particularly resonant and more sketchy overviews of (or mere references to) literary production that could facilitate future scholarship. In no way, then, can this study pretend to be a survey covering the entire corpus of Holocaust verse. Nor does it offer capacious theoretical models for under-standing trauma in general. For, like most of the poets who confront the Shoah as a historical cataclysm in culture, I repeatedly found that the speci-ficity of details I was encountering stymied and humbled answers to gener-alized questions.

Because the majority of the poems I discuss have been accorded hardly any critical attention at all, I sometimes worked without the safety net of other critics' assessments, so I had to hazard readings that remain tentative. Although the high-wire or tightrope act came to mind at times, a schooling in spools provided lessons that stood me in good stead (or so I hope), as I tried to juxtapose poems in pronounced configurations that would display their commonalities and disparities, to keep the movement of each chapter shapely by not indulging in too intricate stitchings on my own responses, to foreground the authors and their words by hiding the seams of my own critical methodology. A Luddite loathing of machinery led me to eschew (or, at least, attempt to pare) academic theorizing that (I feared) would normalize verse that was challenging precisely because of its eccentricities. Yet, of course, the effort to enter into a conversation with other scholars inevitably provoked such speculations.

At first glance, the subject of this volume might seem like a departure from my earlier scholarship. Despite my sense of ignorance and presumption in the undertaking, though, I found myself bringing the approaches and vocabularies I had developed in earlier books to this new subject. When I worried about somersaulting from women's literary history to African American literary history to the aesthetic repercussions of a primarily Jewish experience, I took heart from Frantz Fanon's attention to the interconnections between anti-Semitism and discrimination against people of color as well as from Simone de Beauvoir's introduction to *The Second Sex*, where she meditates on the interconnections between misogyny, racism, and anti-Semitism, on the ways in which " 'The eternal feminine' corresponds to 'the black soul' and to 'the Jewish character.' " Just as important to me was the proviso she added: "True, the Jewish problem is on the whole very different from the other two — to the anti-Semite the Jew is not so much an inferior as he is an enemy for whom there is to be granted no place on earth, for whom annihilation is the fate desired" (xxiii). Clearly, what has impelled all my work is a love of literature and an absorption with its ability to display and disarm mechanisms of Othering. Gender and race enter my purview here when I believe they can strengthen our understanding of the aesthetic and ethical repercussions of the Shoah, although one of my most surprising findings (explicitly engaged only in my concluding chapter) is the prominence of women writers' contributions to Holocaust literature. I hope that in this book I have managed to deploy approaches indebted to women's studies and African American studies without straining after facile analogies that would flatten out the specificity of quite divergent manifestations of societal subjugation.

Books get written for a variety of reasons: this one is meant to pay tribute to my mother and to a group of poets whose publications have been neglected by literary critics and the reading public, even that portion of the public concerned with Holocaust remembrance. Both my mother and the poets substantiate Walter Benjamin's belief that "*Memory* creates the chain of experience which passes a happening from generation to generation" (*I* 98). I hope that *Poetry After Auschwitz* will fasten links on this chain. Especially helpful to my work on it were those residential fellowships that functioned as retreats. For three months in 1999, I profited from a Rockefeller Foundation Fellowship, the supportive fellows and staff at the Virginia Foundation for the Humanities, and the sense of camaraderie fostered by Roberta Culbertson. Like others who have been privileged to receive a residency at the Rockefeller Center at Bellagio, I am most grateful to the Rocke-feller Foundation and to Gianna Celli, who in May 2001 gave me the gift of an expanse of tranquil days in one of the most beautiful places in the world to pursue a project that inevitably brought its own grief in tow. During the 2001–2002 academic year, Princeton University's Center for Human Val-ues, along with a Laurence S. Rockefeller fellowship, made it possible for me to interact with people from a plethora of fields who enriched my approach to the subject. Throughout this period, from near and far, excellent re-search assistance was rendered by Johanna Frank.

During the years it took to complete this book, a number of artists pro-vided suggestions, encouragement, and permission to reprint their mate-rial. Among them were Karen Alkalay-Gut, Jorie Graham, Bernie Horn, Dori Katz, Shirley Kaufman, Irena Klepfisz, Gregory Orr, Alicia Ostriker, Mira Schor, Charles Simic, Tom Sleigh, Maura Stanton, Kirtland Snyder, David Wojahn, and Jeffrey Wolin. Conversations and correspondence with friends, students, and colleagues enriched the project. To those who so generously found time to write letters of support, to respond to queries, or to read and critique work in progress, I am deeply indebted. My naming them here hardly repays my debt: Elizabeth Abel, James Ackerman, Patrick Baude, David Brakke, Linda Charnes, Ralph and Libby Cohen, Dyan Elliott, Jonathan Elmer, Mary Favret, Shoshana Felman, Geoffrey Hartman, Car-olyn Heilbrun, Susannah Heschel, Marianne Hirsch, Barbara Johnson, Her-bert Marks, Alyce Miller, Andrew H. Miller, Nancy K. Miller, Jahan Rama-zani, Alvin Rosenfeld, Kieran Setiya, Steven Weitzman, Niza Yanay, and Froma Zeitlin. At Indiana University, an exceptional group of graduate students stimulated much of my thinking, especially Johanna Frank, Anna Meek, Phil Metres, Adam Rovner, Jeremy Shere, Robin Silbergleid, Tyrone Simpson, Alison Umminger, and Becky Wood. At Princeton, an exceptional group of undergraduates, under the vigilant tutelage of Froma Zeitlin, wid-ened my perspective. I gave the book to Indiana University Press as a retire-ment present to its former director, John Gallman, and Janet Rabinowitch has my gratitude for steering it through production, as does Alice Falk, dear friend and copyeditor par excellence.

As always, the members of my community and family in Indiana and New York provided the support without which I could never have completed this book. The University's assistance was facilitated by the administrative gener-osity of Kenneth Gros Louis, Kenneth Johnston, Kumble Subbaswamy, and George Walker. To my pals and playmates — Shehira Davezac, Ilinca John-ston, Jack Lyons, Cassie and Ben Miller, Jan Sorby, Jayne Spencer — I owe much of the fun and festivity in my life. Julie, Susannah, and John constitute an invigorating extended family. About Kieran, I can hardly express my pleasure at welcoming him with open arms, though he knows how many of his suggestions have shaped my thinking. Despite my own absorption in the disturbing composition process, Mary Jo Weaver has been steadfast, providing ballast in innumerable communications. The best of all possible daughters, Marah and Simone give me the gifts of their exuberant intimacy, for which I am perpetually thankful. Only Donald Gray knows what he contributes to the life of my mind and body, my heart and soul.

This book is dedicated to the most courageous of women, my mother. Although I have been known to tease and torment her, I composed this book as an act of admiration and love. Her integrity, humor, and perseverance continue to inspire her children, grandchildren, and friends.

ABBREVIATIONS FOR CITATIONS

AA	*Art from the Ashes,* ed. Lawrence Langer
BL	*Beyond Lament,* ed. Marguerite M. Striar
BR	*Blood to Remember,* ed. Charles Fishman
GH	*Ghosts of the Holocaust,* ed. Stewart J. Florsheim
HP	*Holocaust Poetry,* ed. Hilda Schiff
TL	*Truth and Lamentation,* ed. Milton Teichman and Sharon Leder
TR	*Telling and Remembering,* ed. Steven J. Rubin

Many of the foreign-language poems discussed are cited from the anthologies above. In citations of these and other texts, whether single-authored books of verse or scholarly works, page numbers are inserted parenthetically in the text. The initials of titles are used to differentiate works by the same author; all can be found, with full bibliographical information, in the works cited at the end of the book.

All biblical citations (to chapter and verse) come from *The HarperCollins Study Bible,* New Revised Standard Version, ed. Wayne A. Meeks.

POETRY AFTER AUSCHWITZ

1

THE HOLOCAUST IS DYING

When I consider the mass murder of Europe's Jews, the words I find forming in my mind seem ominous, yet self-evident; alarming, but true: the Holocaust is dying. How can this be? How can one of the most catastrophic events in modern times — if not *the* most catastrophic event in modern times — be dying? What does it mean to say we turn to the disaster now with heightened awareness that it is dying? Most dramatically, of course, those individuals who personally survived the Shoah are dying out; their painful yet requisite testimonies are drawing to a close. At the start of the twenty-first century, all but the youngest to live through the wholesale expulsions, the ghettos, the mass executions, the deportation centers and transports, the cattle cars, the concentration camps, the death pits have been buried in other countries, given the rituals and markers denied so many of their lost families and friends. I will return to this important shift in post-Holocaust time, but first I want to underline a point many others have intuited, a point more disturbing in its way: namely that the Shoah has always been dying. To some degree, it has always been closed or forbidden to memory.[1]

Throughout the late forties, the fifties, and the sixties, the Holocaust was dying. After the war, the French government's obstruction of the trials of

Vichy officials, the removal of Jews from civic positions in Poland, the liquidation of Jewish cultural organizations within the USSR, the proclamation
at the German Evangelical Conference that the genocide was a spiritual call
on Jews to accept the divinity of Christ — all these events bespoke a dismissal
or denial of the disaster (Cohn-Sherbok 209–21). Neither the social scientists nor the psychologists or theologians of these countries broached the
subject matter of the Shoah in a sustained intellectual enterprise. Both on
the Continent and in the United States, prominent philosophers avoided
the topic as assiduously as did leading literary and historical writers.[2] Given
incredulity about or indifference to earlier reports of the calamity, guilt
engulfing viewers of newsreels and photographs about the liberation of the
camps may have contributed to the idea that humanists needed to consider
the universal condition, that any scrutiny of the particular (Jewish) experience would be construed as parochial or self-incriminating. Hollywood
movie producers eschewed the subject altogether, while the only European
film documentary about the genocide avoided mentioning the Jews.[3] In
London, the Imperial War Museum's growing installations about the Second World War made hardly any reference to the murder of the six million.
Swiss bankers continued to invest Jewish moneys, and Polish landlords continued to own Jewish properties. The German company Topf of Wiesbaden,
which had designed and assembled the Nazi ovens, operated under its original name, building crematoria for civilian use until the mid-1970s, the
decade when Kurt Waldheim, a former soldier in the Waffen SS, served as
secretary-general of the United Nations. In the 1980s, Austrians elected
him their president.

Just as distressing, the children of survivors scattered around the globe
suffered the anguish of parents whose "horror . . . prevented them from
talking either about the dead, or of anything but the dead — as if life itself had
been confiscated by those disappearances." What in a later study the French
psychologist Nadine Fresco would consider the raw edges of "wounds of
memory" pained parents and their offspring, plunging them into "the void
of the unspeakable" (419). In his influential work on catastrophic experiences, Robert Jay Lifton documented "decreased or absent feeling either
during or after trauma," a protective "numbing" that sealed survivors in
speechlessness (interview by Caruth, 134). According to Aharon Appelfeld,
what had happened "was so gigantic, so inconceivable, that the witness even
seemed like a fabricator to himself" (86). Michael Berenbaum, a director of
the U.S. Holocaust Memorial Museum, used the fate of Lot's wife to explain
the survivors' antipathy to introspection: "a person cannot afford to look
back while fleeing" (qtd. in J. Miller 15). Anguish, traumatic numbing,
uncomprehending shock at the surreal proportions of the horror, and a
heroic resolve to rebuild a fractured life beyond the shadow of death's
kingdom may have contributed to the dying of the Holocaust in the forties
and fifties. But the Shoah was also being killed by anti-Semites, who dis-

avowed the atrocities or blamed them on the victims; and by a number of assimilated American Jews as well as some Israelis who sought to craft an identity outside of bigotry, worrying that any attention to the disaster would bring further harm to Jewish people.[4]

Highly effective if only because of the multiple motivations of diverse populations, the conspiracy in the forties and fifties to nullify the Holocaust was brought to public attention and defeated by the first generation of Holocaust studies advocates. The period between 1959 and 1963 serves as one signpost for this transition because in those years *The Diary of Anne Frank* premiered as a movie, Elie Wiesel's *Night* appeared in translation, and the Eichmann trial was reported around the world from Jerusalem; 1967 is another because the victory of the Six Day War "miraculously" unburdened the American Jewish community "of its commitment to subordinate, even to *repress* the death camps" (Morgan 158). From the seventies on, the pioneers of this field — Elie Wiesel and Saul Friedlander, Lawrence Langer and Alvin Rosenfeld, Raul Hilberg and Yehuda Bauer, Terrence Des Pres and Emil Fackenheim — explored the significance of those voices we now associate with the Holocaust canon: Charlotte Delbo, Primo Levi, Anne Frank, Jean Améry, Tadeusz Borowski, Dan Pagis, Paul Celan, Nelly Sachs. Just as important, the emphasis first-generation scholars placed on the value of remembering led to the establishment of archives, memorials, and museums around the world.

Yet as these learned thinkers themselves at times intuited, the Holocaust was still dying throughout the seventies, eighties, and nineties. Was it paradoxically imperiled by their very insistence on keeping it alive as a singular event in history — not merely unprecedented but inexplicable and unrepresentable? For if the earlier period threatened to erase the Shoah in a killing silence, the first generation of Holocaust historians buried it in the European past by claiming it could not be compared to any other phenomenon or should be approached only by those personally involved. Primo Levi emphasized the uniqueness of a Nazi system that he called "a *unicum*" (*DS* 21), that Zygmunt Bauman believed "stands alone, [bearing] no meaningful comparison with other massacres" (32): "To generalize or universalize the victims of the Holocaust is not only to profane their memories," my friend and colleague Alvin Rosenfeld has argued, "but to exonerate their executioners" (*DD* 160). For Saul Friedlander, "the 'Final Solution,' as a result of its apparent historical exceptionality, could well be inaccessible to all attempts at a significant representation and interpretation" (*MHE* 113). According to Claude Lanzmann, too, "the absolute horror" of Auschwitz and Treblinka "cannot be compared to anything" and "is not transmissible" ("HH" 307, 310). Berel Lang made the most absolute declaration when he claimed that all "figurative representation" of genocide "will diminish the moral understanding" of it (*AING* 150). About the composition of literature and in particular the production of verse, which is the subject of this book, the 1949 judgment of Theodor Adorno was taken to be as axiomatic as the biblical commandment against graven images: "To write poetry after Auschwitz is barbaric" ("CCS" 34). Even as the word "poetry" expanded and contracted in meaning — it was understood to signify any and all forms of representation, poetry as a genre, or aesthetic work about the Shoah — the sentence sometimes was taken to be an admonition (beware of writing poetry), sometimes a directive (poetry ought not be written), sometimes simply a diagnosis (poetry cannot be written).[5]

The fundamental logic that seems to encase the Holocaust in silence or singularity and that prompted Adorno's renowned dictum cannot be dismissed as draconian, for art itself — once manipulated by the Nazis as an accoutrement of torture — proved to be implicated in the problem of the "Final Solution."[6] That Germany's extraordinary cultural capital had made it centrally representative of Western civilization hardly inspired confidence in the ethical power of creativity or the moral influence of those monuments of unaging intellect many of its citizens so venerated. Literary responses to the Holocaust might seem particularly preposterous after the contamination of German signaled the failure of language, indeed the spoiling of the very concept of language. Even the best-intentioned aesthetic and pedagogic presentations would fail to convey the full horror or might anaesthetize audiences grown callous about a closed set of recycled artifacts that could be said to reap their own commercial gains from grievous losses. Indeed, anyone who participates in the academic field of Holocaust studies inevitably confronts the danger of "consuming trauma" (the phrase is Patricia Yaeger's), converting grievous suffering into rhetorical pleasure or professional profit in much the manner of those creative writers faulted for finding artistic gratification in imaginative responses to the Shoah.

But if only the reports of those who personally witnessed the destruction of the Jewish people can be judged meaningful, if efforts to make the event consequential by and for those born after it are deemed a profanation of the dead or an exoneration of their murderers, then the Holocaust is doomed to expire. "Even our insistence on the exceptionality of the Shoah may become an isolating maneuver," Geoffrey Hartman has warned, "rather than purely and strongly an acknowledgment" ("BD" 331). The argument for singularity could easily "become diversionary," Dominick LaCapra explains, "in that all events are both comparable and singular or unique, and the historical question concerns the nature and function . . . of comparisons that delineate a specific configuration of similarities and differences" (*HMA* 55). According to Naomi Mandel, a self-congratulatory "rhetoric of unspeakability explicitly effaces the 'drastic guilt' of post-Holocaust culture, a culture that must confront its identity as the product of the presence of the Holocaust in its history" (223). No matter how well-intentioned, the first generation of Holocaust scholars threatened to eradicate the Shoah by stipulating that the bankruptcy of analogizing or generalizing meant only those personally victimized could speak for or about the event.

Acceptable genres included documentaries, testimonials, diaries, and histories — eyewitness accounts — but not poetry, fiction, drama, or visual works composed by those who had watched documentaries, heard testimonials, and read diaries or histories. A number of artists and critics felt that an "avid policing of representation" overvalued verisimilitude and authenticity (Flanzbaum, "BWIT" 273) or that survivors sometimes too jealously insisted "on their exclusive rights to the Holocaust" (Kertész 267). Identity politics kept too tight a rein within Jewish studies on who could address the disaster and how they should do so. (Might this emphasis on authenticity have contributed to what Philip Gourevitch decried in the *New Yorker* as "the stealing of the Holocaust," efforts of an imposter like Binjamin Wilkomirski to produce counterfeit testimonies and in the process become "memory thieves"?)[7] To the extent that assaults were mounted against those who deviated from the standard line, critical responses felt somehow prescribed or programmed. In particular, the concerted effort to bring gender into Holocaust studies has met with considerable opposition, springing from many people's wariness about deflecting attention away from the Nazis' determination to exterminate all of Europe's Jews and thus obfuscating the vulnerability Jewish men and women shared.[8] Faulted for serving "propagandistic" purposes, feminists came under attack for analyses of women's experiences in the ghettoes and camps, studies that were said to insist "on a macabre sisterhood with the dead Jewish women of Europe" (Schoenfeld 45, 46).

Initially scholarship probably had to make the claim of singularity to counter a grotesquely willed obliviousness. We owe to the first generation's meticulous exertions the deliverance of the Shoah from its imminent extinction. That many of the forms created retrospectively *did* fail to honor the dead or blame their murderers by glossing over the particularity and opacity of the evil unfortunately substantiated the claim that the Shoah is not transmissible. Whereas silence first threatened to eradicate memory, whereas next an insistence on singularity censored who could speak and in what cadences, a third method of killing the Holocaust surfaced during these same years in a proliferation of sometimes facile or banal reconstructions that fashioned the past to suit ideological and economic agendas of the present. Just as the memory of the Holocaust was being interred with the aging generation who were its immediate witness, TV programs and bestselling novels, fictionalized biographies and popular films jeopardized that history by commodifying or fetishizing events that continued to recede further from view.

After the movie version of *Anne Frank*, 1979 serves as a punctuation mark for this third phase of shrouding the Shoah in a blanket of media images, because in that year the television series *Holocaust* appeared; some would view 2001 as another because in that year Mel Brooks reinvented his 1968 film *The Producers* for the Broadway stage. In her review of *Schindler's List* (1993), the *New York Times* film critic Janet Maslin worried that the "Holocaust threatens to become unimaginable because it has been imagined so fully." (Might this commercialization have contributed to the "consuming [of] trauma," to "the stealing of the Holocaust" by "memory thieves," or to a related phenomenon Geoffrey Hartman calls "memory envy" — that is, one generation's jealousy of an earlier generation's recollections ["WVT" 230]?) Regardless of how they are judged on their individual merits, there can be no question about the public attention garnered by award-winning productions from *Sophie's Choice* (1982) to *Life Is Beautiful* (1998).

At the turn of the twentieth century, some feared that the multiplication of images in popular culture threatened to turn what originally shocked into schlock, or so warned an unsettling recycled jingle: "There's no business like Shoah business." A host of books argued that Holocaust memory deformed Jewish religious identity, truncated Jewish sympathy for other victimized groups, justified Israeli military aggression, or milked German guilt for materialistic gains.[9] Although the injunctions "never forget" and "never again" continue to prompt the documentary excavations of archivists and curators, whose work presents artifacts not invented so much as rescued from the ruins, many of these same people worry that imaginative accounts of the atrocity by people personally uninvolved in it would exploit the Shoah for sensational or self-interested purposes and thus reduce it to an assimilable and frightfully admissible (or repeatable) phenomenon. A Holocaust industry desecrates the dead.

Still, if the Shoah expires with those whose living it endangered, if memory is interred with the eyewitnesses, many of these same people dread that it will be reborn at some sinister future time, in some unforeseeably repulsive place. Despite the difficulties of knowing how to speak *of* the dead, how to speak *to* the dead, how to speak *for* the dead, what the dying of the last Holocaust survivors at the turn of the century teaches us is the necessity of keeping the Holocaust alive — now through the exertions of those who never struggled within its ghastly regimes. Not that one can construct a clean, complete break between the generations affected by the Holocaust or, for that matter, between factual and fictive responses to it, since the messiness of history and literature blurs all such hard-and-fast distinctions.[10] In any case, though, "the criterion for representing the Holocaust cannot just be propriety or awe as would be appropriate in the face of a cult object," Andreas Huyssen has declared, adding that given its ubiquity as a trope in Western culture as well as its multiple representations, "there cannot be only one way of representing it" (256–57). In addition, the argument of radical singularity or uniqueness will not sustain the exertions of those second-generation artists and scholars who feel they *have* to create analogies, installations, metaphors, performances, and portraits to evoke an ever more distant atrocity that occurred before some of them were born. Turn-of-the-century belatedness means that these figures and symbols must powerfully resist not only pervasive forces of cultural amnesia but also those who would capitalize on the calamity. "The past can be seized only as an image which flashes up at the instant when it can be recognized and is never seen again," Walter Benjamin has explained; "every image of the past that is not recognized by the present as one of its own concerns threatens to disappear irretrievably" (*I* 255).

WHY POETRY MATTERS

Twenty-first-century artists and scholars who address the Holocaust will be more diverse than their predecessors in regional, ethnic, and religious affiliation and in the media as well as the methodologies they utilize. Understanding that their work occurs during the inexorable dying of the Holocaust, such thinkers will nevertheless strive to make the present see the past as one of its crucial, ongoing concerns so as to ensure it will not disappear irretrievably. Those of us who know that the Holocaust is dying should discern the ways it can be recognized and felt in the present; we must keep it alive *as* dying. Since not-writing about the Shoah would constitute a Nazi victory, one way to evade indulging in self-serving forms of recollection involves taking seriously the idea that our stake in the fates of the murdered must be considered along with the stake they have in us.[11] Because fascist rhetoric turned Jews into parasites, vermin or germs or poisoners to be exterminated, perhaps we will evade too vacuous or too lurid, too theatrical or too theoretical, too glib or too sanctimonious a tone by keeping steadily before our eyes the sinister potential of our own rhetoric to imperil the humanity of its subjects.

Oddly enough, given Adorno's injunction against it, poetry serves an important function here, for it abrogates narrative coherence and thereby marks discontinuity. By so doing, it facilitates modes of discourse that denote the psychological and political, ethical and aesthetic consequences of the calamity without laying claim to experiencing or comprehending it in its totality. In an effort to signal the impossibility of a sensible story, the poet provides spurts of vision, moments of truth, baffling but nevertheless powerful pictures of scenes unassimilated into an explanatory plot and thus seizes the past "as an image which flashes up at the instant when it can be recognized and is never seen again." According to Benjamin, images (not stories, which tend to recount the past so as to account for it) put the "then" of the past into a dialectical relationship with the "now" of the present, constitute a critique of the myth of progress, and promote mindfulness about how the past continues to exist as an outrage in the present.[12] More recently, Saul

Friedlander has worried whether "an event like the 'Final Solution' allow[s] for *any kind* of narrative, or does it foreclose certain narrative modalities? Does it perhaps escape the grasp of a plausible narrative altogether?" ("FS" 18). That the Nazis set out to murder not individual Jewish people (charged with specific beliefs or acts) but a corporate collectivity (any and all Jews everywhere) abrogates the individualized "agency that shapes literary plot," Berel Lang believes (*AING* 147). In search of an alternative to a silence that would breed amnesia, Rachel Adler has pointed to "Lament's capacity to represent a pre-narrative or non-narrative state [which] gives it a unique capability to preserve what is irreducible and inexplicable about evil, curbing narrative's tendency to assign causes and meanings, to use storytelling to mend the unmendable" (167).

Verse can violate narrative logic as completely as does trauma itself. When psychologists of trauma explain the significance of the flashback in the later lives of the injured, they view it as a form of recall that recovers a past so horrific *at the time* that it cannot be fully taken into consciousness. What subsequently return, years after the distress, are excruciating experiences so agonizing that they could not be integrated into what the psychologist Pierre Janet called "narrative memory" (Van der Kolk and Van der Hart 160).[13] Like the flashback unassimilated into a story about the past (and like a photograph from the past), poetry can present images that testify to the truth of an event as well as its incomprehensibility — or its limited comprehensibility as a piece of a larger phenomenon that itself still defies understanding.[14] Like symptoms in the aftermath of trauma, lyrical utterance often announces itself as an involuntary return to intense feelings about an incomprehensible moment. But recollected in relative safety, if not tranquillity, such a moment rendered in writing allows authors and readers to grapple with the consequences of traumatic pain without being silenced by it.

Not plausible reparation, explanation, or closure, but the fracturing of a present understood to be shot through with haunting chips of the "wreckage upon wreckage" that still is the past (Benjamin, *I* 257): politically inspired lyricists aspire to this historical work in their attentiveness to the Holocaust. Maybe this is why Seamus Heaney has argued that "The redressing effect of poetry comes from its being a glimpsed alternative, a revelation of potential that is denied or constantly threatened by circumstances" (*RP* 4). The concept of revelation surfaces in Joseph Brodsky's view about what distinguishes poetry from other forms of literature as well, for he believes verse taps three kinds of cognition — analytical, intuitive, and the "prophetic mode" of revelation — while "gravitating primarily toward the second and third" (58). In this perhaps mystic manner, Heaney (considering the imagination as an agent that puts us in touch with what has not but could have happened) and Brodsky (viewing the imagination as an instrument of alternative forms of thinking about what happened) appear to feel that the best poets fulfill Benjamin's definition of the most adroit historian: "Only that historian will have the gift of fanning the spark of hope in the past who is firmly convinced that *even the dead* will not be safe from the enemy if he wins. And this enemy has not ceased to be victorious" (*I* 255).

However, poetry about the European cataclysm has gone largely ignored. Books of testimonials (and scholarly assessments of eyewitness accounts) abound, as do novels (and critical books about fiction). Not only films but also commentaries on them have proliferated. In addition, histories, photographic collections, philosophical treatises, and theological tracts have multiplied. Why no appraisals of verse — particularly verse composed in the English language?[15] The recent publication of a number of anthologies that include poetry — *Ghosts of the Holocaust, Blood to Remember, Truth and Lamentation, Holocaust Poetry, Art from the Ashes, Telling and Remembering,* and *Beyond Lament* — has now facilitated a possible critical assessment.[16] But none has been forthcoming, possibly because of widespread academic disregard of verse; probably because the reasoning behind Adorno's injunction undermined the reputation of poetry about Auschwitz, making it taboo; perhaps because of the other issue I am raising, namely that such verse has been composed predominately by nonparticipants.

"Elie Wiesel, Paul Celan, Nelly Sachs can touch the horror with authority," Harold Bloom has averred, "but British and American writers need to avoid it, as we have no warrant for imagination in that most terrible of areas" (257). Although in the next chapter we will see exactly how difficult it is to locate a distinct line demarcating Wiesel, Celan, and Sachs from British and North American writers, scholarly study, thus far primarily devoted to the events of 1933 to 1945, has quite rightly concentrated on the creative works produced by those who lived through them. Yet despite Bloom's caveats, the proliferation of Holocaust poems in English turns our attention not away from those events but toward their reverberations as they affect a series of generations searching for a means to keep alive the urgency of continuing to confront a past as it passes out of personal recollection. The "warrant for imagination" consists, then, in a psychological, ethical, and historical need to remember what one never knew.

Faced with the brutalities of history, of course, literature has rarely been effectual. In his elegy "In Memory of W. B. Yeats," W. H. Auden put it this way: "poetry makes nothing happen" (*SP* 80). The "efficacy of poetry is nil — no lyric has ever stopped a tank," Seamus Heaney agreed (*GT* 107). Earlier, in one of the first protests against fascism by a non-Jew in English poetry, Ada Jackson drew attention to the futility of her own verse about the genocide of the Jews in a line she placed in the middle of her page without final punctuation: "While you read they die" (22).[17] Exactly this revulsion against the frivolity of verse infused the Columbia University literature student Lucy Dawidowicz when she heard a professor droning on about the poetry of William Wordsworth in 1937, as the European Jewish world was being decimated: "What is Wordsworth to me at this time?" the future historian of *The War against the Jews* wondered, determining to visit the imperiled centers of Yiddish culture in Poland (qtd. in Rosenbaum 374–75). Still, as Heaney explained decades after the war, within the rift between the horror of the killings that occurred and what we would have hoped or assumed might have happened, even self-confessedly impotent poetry (like that by Ada Jackson) manages to hold "attention for a space, functions not as distraction but as pure concentration, a focus where our power to concentrate is concentrated back on ourselves" (*GT* 108).

And, as Ron Rosenbaum has shown, Dawidowicz's literary critical training in the "subtextual ambiguities" of Wordsworth shaped her brilliant insights into Hitler's use of " 'esoteric language' and euphemism to create the *false* impression of hesitation and calculation, a false impression that concealed an unswerving, relentless, decades-long determination to exterminate the Jews" (380, 373). Obviously, the point here is not that Hitler was like Wordsworth, but that Hitler's regime depended on the deployment of elaborate rhetorical conceits and deceits (in rallies, speeches, songs, governmental documents and programs) about which artists have always been supremely conscious. Whether or not one agrees with Joseph Brodsky that a person with literary taste is "less susceptible to the refrains and the rhythmical incantations peculiar to any version of political demagogy," the effort of contemporary poets to tap the "colossal centrifugal energy" of language can instruct readers about what is wrong with our ordinary everyday languages and with demagogic discourses: namely "that they corrupt consciousness with their easiness, with the speed with which they provide one with moral comfort, with the sensation of being right" (49, 57, 54).

Because it discloses the linguistic crisis inaugurated by the Third Reich but also because it marks time as "the imagination press[es] back against the pressure of reality" (Heaney, *RP* 1), verse as a genre plays an important role in demarcating the consequences of the phenomenon Geoffrey Hartman eloquently noted when, shifting his critical gaze from Wordsworth to the Holocaust, he described how the passage of years renders forgetting and remembering equally difficult, even for those personally embroiled in the past: "An event like the Shoah, a political mass murder targeting for extinction an entire 'race' of defenseless non-combatants, . . . cannot now, after the event, be taken into mind without a severe disturbance. . . . *I cannot forget any more than I can truly remember*" ("IDV" 17, 22). The "precision with which poems deal with time," according to C. K. Williams, can provide access to a calamity that can neither be forgotten nor remembered, for the "moments of a poem are very intense, very discrete and vivid; you're moved through them, and through time, in a formal way, with a kind of double consciousness that makes you very aware of other realms, the moral, the ethical and political." No doubt aware that poetry has often taken as its inspiration the mother of the Muses, Mnemosyne (Memory, whose ancestor is Forgetting), he goes on to describe the mental state that verse evokes: "It's like being in a church, or in prayer. . . . you're attentive to your consciousness" ("I" 130). Like the songs inserted into biblical narratives, twentieth-century poems about the Shoah use a kind of interpretive insistence, a sustained "act of attention," to respond to or analyze preexistent literature; to fill in lacunae in the historical record; to curse evil or praise good; to witness against wrongdoing; to caution against ignorance and amnesia, which result in unteachability; and to underscore the central significance of what is deemed to be a decisive convulsion in culture.[18]

The resistance of verse to narrative closure and the prayerlike attentiveness it fosters enhance its ability to "engage with states that themselves would deprive us of language and reduce us to passive sufferers," as Adrienne Rich has suggested (*WIFT* 10). A commitment to poetry's ability to "break open locked chambers of possibility, restore numbed zones of feeling" (xiv), informs Rich's attempt to "severely parse" Adorno's drastic statement against poetry after Auschwitz:

> Adorno, a German Jew who lived for many years as a refugee in the United States, may have forgotten the ancient role of poetry in keeping memory and spiritual community alive. On the other hand, his remark might be pondered by all poets who too fluently find language for what they have not yet absorbed, who see human suffering as "material." (141)

Charles Bernstein agrees with Rich: "In contrast to — or is it an extension of? — Adorno's famous remarks about the impossibility of (lyric?) poetry after Auschwitz, I would say poetry is a necessary way to register the unrepresentable loss of the Second World War" (217). In a 1987 Nobel lecture to which the poet Irving Feldman would return, Joseph Brodsky added his assent: " 'How can one write poetry after Auschwitz?' inquired Adorno. . . . 'And how can one eat lunch?' the American poet Mark Strand once retorted. In any case, the generation to which I belong has proven capable of writing that poetry" (55). Even after devastation, Brodsky and Strand remind us, the human activities (of eating lunch, of writing poetry) necessarily go on. Brodsky, who views the analytic, intuitive, and revelatory modes of cognition at work in verse writing as "an extraordinary accelerator of consciousness," believes that "the generation born precisely at the time when the Auschwitz crematoria were working full blast, when Stalin was at the zenith of his godlike, absolute power, . . . came into the world" to "continue what, theoretically, was supposed to be interrupted in those crematoria and in the anonymous common graves of Stalin's archipelago" (56, 55).

Prefaced through its epigraph by Brodsky's quotation of Strand, the opening of Feldman's poem "Outrage Is Anointed by Levity, or Two Laureates A-Lunching" takes issue with the idea that it is absurd to worry about either writing poetry or eating lunch after Auschwitz, making it clear that the Nobel laureate's assertion — "In any case, the generation to which I belong has proven capable of writing that poetry" — depends on verse inexorably, obsessively haunted by the legitimacy of Adorno's logic:

> *In any case,* (or, as our comedians say,
> "But seriously, folks"), has Adorno's question
> been disposed of, interred beneath the poems
> written since Auschwitz? — rather than raised again
> and again like a ghost by each of them? (48)

Feldman, angered by Mark Strand's levity and resorting to the self-mockery of a stand-up comedian like Lenny Bruce or Mort Sahl, goes on to lambaste godlike bards spewing pearls of wisdom about Auschwitz, even as he insists that poets tap an outrage anointed by levity to keep the significance of "Adorno's question" alive. Beyond poetry's ability to draw attention to the inanity of the poetic — and by extension, literary culture's — enterprise, the fact that verse is read only by a small audience has paradoxically liberated some writers to use it for their most private, self-incriminating thoughts.

Does the societal marginality of poetry — how often does it pay for lunch by getting bought by Hollywood directors or staged on Broadway? — set its aesthetic attentiveness beyond commercialized ventures that merely exacerbate efforts to eliminate the Shoah from public consciousness or, for that matter, to retain it there in debased, melodramatic formats? Because, as Jahan Ramazani puts it, the "exceptional figural and formal density" of verse mediates experience in "a less transparent medium" than that of prose; the opacity of its allusions and figurative devices, rhythmic and stanzaic patterns, symbols and paradoxes allows poets to manifest aesthetically the representational crisis all artists, teachers, and scholars face in their approach to the Shoah (*HM* 4). Even though lyric poetry itself can be melodramatic and debased, what Ramazani calls the "richly conflictual relation between postcolonial poets and the English language" remains resonant for authors dealing with both the incongruity of the English language in foreign, European contexts and the jarring dissonance between, on the one hand, lyrical forms expressive of personal feelings and, on the other, events never personally experienced (*HM* 13). Just as important, poetry after Auschwitz displays the ironic friction between the lyric's traditional investment in voicing subjectivity and a history that assaulted not only innumerable sovereign subjects but indeed the very idea of sovereign selfhood.

Finally, the rigorous linguistic vigilance and originality of poetry enable it to step into the cognitive crisis inaugurated by the Shoah. Because the facts bearing the traces of Auschwitz were destroyed "as much as possible," according to Jean-François Lyotard, "Its name marks the confines wherein historical knowledge sees its competence impugned" (*D* 57–58). Lyotard, whose speculations uncover the grim interface between the reasoning of those who insist on the Shoah's inaccessibility to representation and those who deny its ever having occurred, crystallizes the denier's logic this way: "in order for a place to be identified as a gas chamber, the only eyewitness I will accept would be a victim of this gas chamber; now . . . there is no victim that is not dead; otherwise, this gas chamber would not be what he or she claims it to be. There is, therefore, no gas chamber" (3–4).[19] When the wrong suffered cannot be signified in accepted or extant idioms, new idioms must be found to express how what remains to be said exceeds what can presently be articulated. By providing "idioms which do not yet exist," poets of the disaster prove that "the silence imposed on knowledge does not impose the silence of forgetting, it imposes a feeling" or a constellation of feelings (13, 56). Sometimes through the originality of their thinking or the veracity of their truth-claims about history, more often through stylistic decisions that affect tone and stance, writers who deploy the more expressive, less representational forms of verse convey a range of feelings that forestall "the silence of forgetting."[20]

In my original title for this book — "Poetry *Nach* Auschwitz" — I planned to use the interruption of a foreign word to signal the struggle of presenting what has not been, could not have been seen by British and North American writers determined to find sufficient authority to prove that the Holocaust existed and inflicted grievous harm. Indeed, at their most audacious, some of these literary men and women invent the voices of eyewitnesses of the gas chamber at the very moment their speakers understand it to be what they claim it to be. Yet the decided gap between the ghastly "then" of genocide and the safe "now" of retrospection, the frightful "there" of atrocity and the secure "here" of reflection made the English word "after" a more appropriate sign of the repercussions of composing at a geographic and temporal removal from the calamity. The phrase "after Auschwitz" in my title is meant to redirect Adorno's prohibition — usually interpreted as a warning against or forbidding of imaginative representation in general — back to the ramifications of his specification of poetry, in particular poetry about Auschwitz. In addition, my title's translation of Adorno is meant to indicate that the verse about Auschwitz I study is as much inflected by American and British literary history as it is by the Bible or by Yiddish, Polish, German, Romanian, French, and Hebrew responses to the Shoah.

TWO ILLUSTRATIVE POETS

Mobilized against the forces of fascism, the contemporary verse to which I will turn in subsequent pages — dedicated, as it is, to the local, the particular, the specific — resists the tendency to trivialize the Shoah by drawing from it banal, complacent, or palliative lessons. To the objection that such provisional or exact words could not possibly attain the aesthetic grandeur of works from earlier times, it is instructive to remember the ideological underpinnings of evaluative judgments. Schooled in wariness by a disaster that made artists suspicious about the moral efficacy of art, W. H. Auden once explained that

> A society which was really like a good poem, embodying the aesthetic virtues of beauty, order, economy and subordination of detail to the whole, would be a nightmare of horror for, given the historical reality of actual men, such a society could only come into being through selective breeding, extermination of the physically and mentally unfit, absolute obedience to its Director, and a large slave class kept out of sight in cellars. (qtd. in Jones 48)

Rarely "good" poems in Auden's sense of the word, often composed out of a revulsion at "the aesthetic virtues of beauty, order, economy and subordination of detail to the whole," Holocaust verse uses the awkwardly *un*poetic nature of its subject to inaugurate a *non*cathartic artistry of disaster. Should one conflate poetry with the conventional lyric—with brief utterances of intensely personal feelings about intimate experiences—verse that engages the alien discourses of literary and cultural criticism, journalism, photography, legal proceedings, and the idiosyncratic cadences of strangers touched by the Shoah may not seem to be poetry at all. Scarcely the happiest of mortals, hardly the skylarks whom Percy Bysshe Shelley imagines singing to cheer solitude with sweet sounds, the authors of this tradition nevertheless do strive toward Shelley's goal: to make the imagination an instrument of moral good.

Two quite recently published poems, one about the victims and the other about the perpetrators, can serve as illustrations here, for they filter their authors' realization of the extent of the calamity through their perplexity about how to approach that subject, given our ever-growing sense of its remoteness as well as the inappropriateness of poetic or cathartic reactions. A jeremiad that transmutes into an unraveling lamentation at its close, Feldman's "Outrage Is Anointed by Levity, or Two Laureates A-Lunching" swerves from its opening affirmation—that "Adorno's question" has been "raised again / and again like a ghost" (48) by poets writing after Auschwitz —into loathing, specifically a revulsion against self-satisfied creative posturing that helps explain the extreme measures risked by many of the writers in this tradition. Has Auschwitz made the act of writing poetry as archaic, trivial, and self-serving as "A-Lunching"?

Whether or not he misreads Strand and Brodsky, Feldman conflates poetic expression and eating lunch after Auschwitz, first, to emphasize the absurdity of hoping to find a proper way to do either; second, to express outrage that levity would demean as inconsequential the need to find a proper way to do both; and third, to consider the fundamental equivalency of these two activities as suspect modes of "consuming trauma." Wondering "how one *can* eat one's lunch after Auschwitz," Feldman catalogues how not to:

14

NOT, let it be said, *fearfully*
Certainly NOT *despairingly*
Therefore NOT *painfully*
NOT forgodsakes *starvingly*
NOT *weepingly*
NOT *resignedly*
NOT, please, *horribly, hideously, moribundly!* (48)

Capitalization and italics make all these directives stagy, ironically reducing the composing or consuming of poetry and lunch to a mere shtick.[21] Should one "*bizarrely*, encounter / difficulty in eating lunch after Auschwitz" (48), the poet sarcastically includes a list of adverbs that will do the trick.

Beginning with "HEARTILY and CHUCKLINGLY," he tries out "LOVINGLY, SAVORINGLY" and "INNOCENTLY, because like, man, I didn't do it—I mean, I wasn't even there!" until he arrives at "RIGHTEOUSLY, since poets *must* keep up their strength if they are to prove capable of writing poems 'after Auschwitz,' " and finally "GENEROUSLY, since one is eating (whether *they* know it or not) for others, for civilization itself. / One is (to put it in a nutshell) *lunching for Auschwitz*" (49). A barrage of hyped-up verbiage enables Feldman to ridicule all high-minded efforts to justify lunching or versifying after Auschwitz as activities undertaken somehow "for" Auschwitz. If one composes poetry or consumes lunch "CHARMINGLY, assuring one's food of one's civil intentions," Feldman sneers, "Then it will *wish* to be consumed by one" (49): the Shoah has devolved here into a thinly veiled pretext for ingesting and digesting food for self-aggrandizing thoughts. Not merely satirizing Mark Strand, the author of "Eating Poetry," Feldman hints that both Strand's and Brodsky's breezy dismissals of Adorno's claims are "Out to Lunch" (the original title of early drafts).[22]

Feldman has nothing but a fine excess of scorn for laureates fattening themselves on words of wisdom about and after Auschwitz. As these banqueting "godlings" up on a "noble dais" in "hog heaven splat down their pearls on us, / So outrage is anointed by levity" (49). But that levity is checked in the final stanza of this poem, where the words "poem" and "silence," "cannot" and "nevertheless" interrupt and interrogate each other in a column of words that refuses the coherence of grammar and forces the hyperloquacity of the first part of the poem to devolve into gibberish:

— this page
I write and
the silent
who couldn't cannot
whom silence

and I
cannot what nevertheless
I nevertheless
how can I
write (50)

Lamenting all the voices silenced in the Shoah, Feldman writes the words that refuse to be silent about this silence, which (though spoken about) remains definitively unspoken, unspeakable. The indecency of poetic quips after the enforced silencing of so many voices, the offensiveness of *bons mots* savored at the literary award ceremonies bestowing prizes on the ruined bards issues in sarcasm about the inefficacy and complicity of art as well as the breakdown of language impotent to redress the wrongs it addresses.

That, as is true of this powerful poem, much verse has appeared late in the twentieth century and has not yet been anthologized in the various collections of literature seeking to keep memory of the Holocaust alive helps explain why so few people know that this tradition exists. Jacqueline Osherow is a good example of a turn-of-the-twentieth-century writer not generally anthologized in the extant collections of Holocaust verse. Like Feldman, Osherow has not devoted all or even most of her poetic attention to the Shoah, and in this regard they typify many of the other poets discussed in the later pages of this book. Although they approach the Holocaust in a few of their more perplexing works, they never aspire to become "laureates" of the Shoah, to consume or be consumed by what would dwindle into the "material" of an oeuvre. (This is the reason why my table of contents could not be organized around a succession of authors.) Like Feldman's "Outrage Is Anointed by Levity," Osherow's "Villanelle from a Sentence in a Poet's Brief Biography" does not fit into the generic categories deployed in subsequent chapters of this book. Together, therefore, both works serve to emphasize how provisional and limited those categories are. Varied in technique, extant poems about the Shoah as well as those yet to be composed will undoubtedly continue to expand critical taxonomies, drawing attention to the intellectual poverty resulting from recent scholarly neglect of verse in general, and of Jewish American and Anglo-Jewish verse in particular. Osherow's formalism, distinct from Feldman's freer forms, also demonstrates the diversity of verse approaches to the Holocaust. For she eschews a poetics of ruin, often depending on strict "metrical rules that forbid automatic responses," that "force us to have second thoughts, free from the fetters of Self" — as Auden once phrased his defense of formalism ("SII" 47).

Yet although Osherow deploys elegantly structured forms, her "Villanelle from a Sentence in a Poet's Brief Biography" is just as stymied by stutters as Feldman's final stanza. In a work very much in the tradition of Elizabeth Bishop's "One Art," Osherow meditates on a single phrase presumably found in a headnote or biographical entry about an older writer, a phrase repeated in each of its six stanzas—"*In '42 he was conscripted to work on trains*"—so as "to figure out what this entry means." Exactly who this poet is, exactly what dictionary of biographies she has consulted, exactly which trains he worked on and where: the documentary framework remains obscure, perhaps because Osherow refrains from sanctimoniously pointing a finger of blame at a particular individual so that she might instead address the larger issue of culture's culpability; her focus on culture may also explain why she uses the high artifice of the villanelle form. As she recalls the situation of Dutch workers, who "wouldn't work *their* trains," Osherow sardonically explains, "They found out that *work makes you free*"[23] (*DMP* 35). This last italicized reference to the infamous motto over the entrance to Auschwitz inevitably brings to mind other debased words that we translate as "Final Solution" or "selections" or "action" or "showers." If the German language was corrupted, Osherow seems to ask, did the more generalized Enlightenment ideal of language as a mode of mastery, a signature of individual identity, also suffer a fall? Given the Dutch workers' refusal to work the trains and the subsequent death that was those workers' common fate, the passive voice of the biographical note about the poet she is investigating ("*he was conscripted*") raises questions about the occlusion of agency and responsibility (conscripted by whom and why and how?) that the recurrences of the villanelle revisit in its series of sorties.

Despite or perhaps because of the admitted inefficacy of passive or active resistance, the words "work" and "free" have been thoroughly perverted in the Shoah, harnessed to what Arthur A. Cohen calls "a kind of cauterization of conscience by the use of metaphor and euphemism; . . . in official Nazi language the extermination of Jews was precisely that—the disinfectant of lice, the burning of garbage, the incineration of trash, and hence language never had to say exactly what acts its words commanded: kill, burn, murder that old Jew, that middle-aged Jew, that child Jew. Language," Cohen emphasizes in a passage pertinent to Osherow's inquiry, "created its own rhetoric of dissimulation, and conscience was no longer required to hear accurately—a phenomenon not unique in Nazi Germany, but, indisputably, a consequential aspect of its discipline" (7–8). To assess the consequential fallout of Nazi discipline on the highly disciplined nature of poetic form, at the end of her villanelle Osherow goes on to concede in her own carefully plain, determinedly literalist lexicon that "trains // Weren't that busy" until a year or so later:

> But the next line says, *after the war,* which means
> That he was still at it in '43,
> '44, '45. . . . In Czechoslovakia, trains
>
> (What did he do? Run switches? Check the lines?)
> Were as instrumental, let's face it, as Zyklon B.

In '42 he was conscripted to work on trains.
In '42. In Czechoslovakia. Trains. (*DMP* 35)

Characteristically colloquial in her self-interruptions, Osherow often presents herself as an author reading and responding to other writers' lives and works. Here the hypothetical interjections make it seem that the biographical entry has caught her off guard, causing her to worry about the status of poetry, if composed by someone who "*was conscripted to work on trains*" that shuttled the enslaved to the gas chambers. Her own train of thought, her own training in artistry, her own carefully checked lines: have they, too, been tarnished by poetry's or some poets' complicity in the disaster? Put another way, does attentiveness to aesthetic form insulate artists from the ethical repercussions of their own lives? When combined with the pollution of words, the interruption of parenthetical questions, the repeated snippet of quotation, the ellipses, and the inconclusive conclusion with its halted, fragmentary sentences: all raise the specter of Adorno's query about the possibility of poetry after the Holocaust.

Although the villanelle conventionally exploits two rhymes (in its first and third lines) that are repeated alternately until they join at the conclusion — like the words "master" and "disaster" in Bishop's "One Art" — Osherow's final couplet makes explicit her bleak awareness of the impoverishment of the poetic imagination through her refusal to find a sufficient word to rhyme with "trains," even if the absent rhymes of "brains" and "drains" and "strains" may persist in some readers' ears. "Trains," following "*trains,*" drives home Osherow's belief that "There is nothing to be gotten out of writing poetry in America but the poetry itself, and this ought to make us . . . a fairly monomaniacal bunch" (in Barron and Selinger 112). Because the villanelle draws attention to the end word of each line, especially the end words of the last two lines, "Trains," following "*trains,*" marks "The station [which] is not a railroad station" but instead, in the words of Charlotte Delbo, "the end of the line" (4). The need simply to repeat the word seems as sinister as the echoes of "biography" and "guilty," "1943" and "Zyklon B." Focusing not on the casualties but on the people who consciously or not helped the trains run on time to their appointed designations, Osherow enacts a sort of sputtering stall, a spasmodic loss of power that frequently characterizes the quotations, lists, questions, repetitions, and nonsensical rhymes of poets using language to stress its impotence, to enlist verse in a ruin and re-creation of artistry.

Like many (though by no means all) of the poems discussed in this volume, Feldman's and Osherow's verse derives not from any personal witnessing of the Shoah but instead from a concerted effort to grapple with their oblique access to events nevertheless formative in their individual development and in Western culture's unfolding. In an attempt not to forget what they cannot remember, Feldman and Osherow critique seemingly innocuous languages that nevertheless corrupt consciousness by providing a buffer against the moral discomfort induced by contact with the Holocaust. Still, how does their work achieve what Seamus Heaney called the "redressing effect" of verse that reveals an alternative threatened by circumstances, or the "prophetic mode" Joseph Brodsky associated with poetic cognition? How do these two poets fan "the spark of hope in the past" in a manner comparable to that of Benjamin's historian "who is firmly convinced that *even the dead* will not be safe from the enemy if he wins"? By taking the obliteration of personal expression in the past as a mandate for poetic expression in the present, incommensurate though it must be, Feldman and Osherow glimpse an alternative, a revelation of denied potential. But two other and better known poems by Feldman and Osherow provide more obvious instances of verse permitting us to recognize and thus salvage images of the past as crucial concerns of the present.

Less sarcastic, more wistful in a work composed earlier in his life, Irving Feldman presents his task as a quixotic effort to contain the past safely within the frames of a movie that could be rewound to the moment before catastrophe. His often-anthologized "The Pripet Marshes" begins with the poet transporting his Jewish friends to "the *schtetlach* and ghettos" of the Ukraine and setting them to visiting, praying, feasting just one sunlit second before the Germans will arrive. As Sidra DeKoven Ezrahi points out, the transplanted American members of the poet's family are "only the understudies for the real victims, whom the poet never knew" (*BWA* 210). A director of sorts, Feldman imagines his family and friends arguing in a Yiddish replete with "timbres whose unfamiliarity thrills" him as they promenade among the mists of the marshes he has himself never seen. His Whitmanesque catalogue — of uncomfortable Maury, good-hearted Frank, sullen Adele — culminates in the poet's mother, pictured "as merry as a young girl," and his own "brown-eyed son who is glowing like a messenger impatient to be / gone and who may stand for me" (*NSP* 50–53). As they begin to metamorphose into illuminated figures on the brink of some sort of transformation — glimmering, shining, dazzling in their radiance — the poet tries to assert his power: "when I want to, I can be a God." The braggadocio of his defiance — "No, the Germans won't have one of them!" — is belied by the absurdly fragile pillowcase, handkerchief, and shoebox into which he attempts to stuff himself and his people, as he endeavors to carry them away from the motorcycles zooming through the town. Fled is his vision at the end of the poem, when at a Keatsian impasse the poet remains uncertain if he wakes or sleeps: "I can't hold out any longer," Feldman admits. "My mind clouds over. / I sink down as though drugged or beaten" (*NSP* 53).

Whereas Feldman uses his godlike attempt to unravel history in order to posit the possibility of providential intervention in the Shoah and then to face the nonintervention of Deity, Osherow's "Brief Encounter with a Hero, Name Unknown" discerns a possible revelation when she meditates on unlikely and doomed but heroic human intervention in the Holocaust. The opening and closing stanzas of this poem —

> It could have been a matter of modesty
> It could have been the gold sewn in your dress
> You might even have feared for your chastity
> Maybe it was simple recklessness

— provide the blueprint or outline for a series of speculations about a story Osherow's father-in-law "mentioned in passing" about a woman, on her way to the gas chamber and ordered to undress, who grabbed a guard's gun and killed him as well as three others before being murdered herself (*WMT* 17–18). Far removed from the scene, the contemporary poet resorts to a mounting series of hesitant uncertainties, of "perhaps"es and "maybe"s, to sketch a succession of motivations for such an extraordinary act of rebellion, a sequence in which no possible plot can be ruled out since the second-hand anecdote resists closure. Whether the young woman simply could not part with a dress given by a beau or clung to it to hide a pregnancy, whether she had seen "a Western dubbed in Polish" and was inspired by "some hokey John Wayne flourish" or had "been contemplating suicide" or had trained in resistance as a "fighter in the woods" (17–18), Osherow extols a heroism recorded in historical accounts so as to discern a revelation of potential denied by circumstances. In the process she honors the motives of the heroine in the story told by her father-in-law, a resistance as inexplicable as the infliction of the disaster itself.

Bafflement, the need to find words to express feelings about events that must be transmitted even though they cannot be understood, a resistance to closure with respect to consideration or judgment of the events that transpired during the Shoah: here resides the mandate of Holocaust poetry. Both Feldman and Osherow put on display the inadequacy of the poetic imagination, its inability to intervene in or even illuminate a grievous past. In "The Pripet Marshes," the vision of the poet concentrates on the brilliant and the stupid, the sullen and the vulgar surrogates he has catalogued until they are transfigured, illumined, loved. Yet poetic concentration fails: despite Feldman's effort to "cover them in mist," he cannot "take them out" of an overtly ersatz stage set. In "Brief Encounter with a Hero, Name Unknown," the name of the SS guard with the gun, Schillinger, underscores the absent name of the heroic "new woman, ordered to undress," whose act of revenge seems so unlikely to the poet, though "Such things, says my father-in-law, were common" and though "Needless to say, in seconds you had joined" the guards in death (*HMT* 18). Yet although "poetry makes nothing happen," both writers also stress the ongoing need to grasp images of the past that can be recognized as the ongoing concern of the present: Feldman by admitting the frequency of his fantasizing ("*Often* I think of my Jewish friends and seize them as they are and transport them in my mind"

[*NSP* 50]) and Osherow by refraining from end punctuation ("It could have been a matter of modesty / It could have been the gold sewn in your dress"), by repeating her rhymed beginning speculations at the end of her inconclusive musings, and by using the poem to address the "Hero, Name Unknown" directly as "You."[24]

Taken together, "The Pripet Marshes" and "Brief Encounter with a Hero, Name Unknown" meditate on the mysterious absence and presence of Jewish resistance during the Holocaust. If, as Raul Hilberg informs us, "in Russia there was an unguarded escape route to the Pripet Marshes, but few Jews availed themselves of the opportunity" (298), did Jewish flight and resistance fail to materialize because, as Hilberg claims, unprepared Jews lacked a tradition of activist intervention? Or, as Yehuda Bauer argues and Feldman's poem intimates, did resistance take linguistic and social forms of attempting to sustain community and culture, issuing in physical conflict only "wherever there was the slightest chance that it could, which did not happen too often" (165–66)? Or perhaps, as Osherow seems to suggest, might it have occurred but gone not so much unrecorded as disregarded? For example, widely disseminated in testimonials was one account of "a group of Jews from Warsaw who had become American citizens, some of them American born," among them "a splendid young woman, a dancer from Warsaw, [who] snatched a revolver from [Walter] Quackernack, the Oberscharführer of the 'Political Section' in Auschwitz and shot the Referatführer, the notorious Unterscharführer [Josef] Schillinger"; one source adds that "Her deed bolstered the courage of other brave women, who in turn slapped and threw vials and other such things into the faces of those vicious, uniformed beasts — the SS" (Gradowski 549). The narrator of Tadeusz Borowski's story "The Death of Schillinger" feels inclined to believe a *Sonderkommando* foreman's ironic version, where the shot is triggered by the vigilant Nazi officer's having "taken a fancy to" the naked body of a woman with "a classic figure": after the woman shot Schillinger, he kept "groaning through clenched teeth: '*O Gott, mein Gott, was ha' ich getan, dass ich so leiden muss?*,' which means — O God, my God, what have I done to deserve such suffering" (145–46).

Aware (and who could not be?) of the plethora of portraits of Europe's Jews as nothing but piteous scapegoats, Feldman and Osherow relate what might have happened and what did happen within the historical gaps of our knowledge so as to encourage readers to try to imagine, say, your own sister and mother, your own children and friends, back in that grievous setting. Only then, perhaps not even then, will you know even a particle of the shameful impotence that they would have experienced and that the poets must acknowledge about their own visionary efforts; only then will you know how much you do not know about what could have been, what might have been sources of strength. By evoking the dead through unpredictable reinventions of earlier accounts or assessments of the Shoah, Feldman and

Osherow dedicate poetry's formal elements to the task Adorno believed to be the lyric's particular job: bearing witness as an "I," but an "I" whose conditions of knowing constitute an awareness of the radical alienation of subjectivity ("LPS" 39–40).

In both Feldman's and Osherow's texts, entertainment imagery hints at the growing distance of the disaster, the impossibility of conceiving it in terms uncontaminated by the media that have so thoroughly saturated it. Engaged more in simulation than in mimesis, Feldman's speaker, who has "made" the day "sunny" for his "crowds filling the town," implicitly comprehends his directorial decisions as one more desecration of the victims when he uses the words "seize" and "transport" to describe the initial mechanism of his inner fantasy. Not only the allusion to dubbed Westerns with John Wayne but also Osherow's title, which invokes a romantic World War II movie (*Brief Encounter*) as well as a later film about extraterrestrials (*Close Encounters of the Third Kind*), suggest how obscured the past is by layers of its subsequent celluloid representations. With quite distinct postures — Feldman playing hardball with the big boys (Brodsky, God), Osherow musing over the written and verbal authorities she has studiously consulted — self-conscious practitioners of a so-called high art heighten awareness of the risks of distortion taken by popular cultural forms, but without countenancing any delusion that these influential lenses can be disavowed or circumvented. As poetry about Auschwitz so often does, Feldman's and Osherow's works stress their oblique access to remote events and thus implicitly engage what in other texts they and their contemporaries more explicitly contemplate: the ethical ramifications of "consuming trauma," of "stealing the Holocaust," and of "memory envy."

KADDISH

In their work, if only intermittently, Feldman and Osherow identify themselves as Jewish writers; however, non-Jewish poets also assay verse meditations on the Holocaust. Since we do not ordinarily assume that creative writers can only explore themes linked either to their personal experiences or to the more generalized experiences of their ethnic or religious or national group, throughout this book I will be questioning why, on what basis, with what consequences some people argue that only a survivor or a Jewish writer can address the Shoah. Like the approach of the poets I study, my line of thinking in the pages to come swerves away from a consideration of any unique authorial license to grievous material so as to ponder instead the artistic achievement of making that material meaningful for readers who may or may not have a personal relationship to the disaster, may or may not be Jewish. Although, as Amy Hungerford has pointed out, a number of contemporary thinkers associate trauma with language loss, although they also sometimes identify the confrontation with trauma (through the reading of testimonials or the viewing of videotapes) with a transmission of trauma that involves yet another language loss, twentieth- and twenty-first-century poets of the Holocaust recognize their distance from the atrocity as an opportunity to craft linguistic tools that put themselves and their readers in touch with the feeling that the evils of racism inflicted on Europe's Jews during the "Final Solution" are of crucial importance to the human race.

"Imagining What One Never Knew" might, therefore, be a more appropriate subtitle for a book about creative work that rarely confuses writing or reading about the calamity with experiencing it directly; however, I have retained my original subtitle, "Remembering What One Never Knew," because I believe the most scrupulous of the poets strive to braid their and our apprehensions of the Shoah with an earlier generation's memories of a history that continues to demand a personal, ethical response. There is, of course, a way in which a traumatized person must learn to remember an event so horrific that it cannot be fully recalled, but this is a subject one finds treated in eyewitness responses. Primo Levi has explained that even survivors of the Lagers "never fathomed them to the bottom" because "Those who did so did not return, or their capacity for observation was paralyzed by suffering and incomprehension" and thus "We speak in their stead, by proxy" (*DS* 17, 84). Closer to the situation of some second-generation poets are the families of survivors, like the husband of one of Delbo's surviving companions: Marie-Louise says about him, "We never stop talking about Auschwitz. My memories have become his own. So much so I have the distinct impression he was there with me" (Delbo 281). For the poets insistently focus on collecting and circulating events recollected by eyewitnesses. This reliance on earlier testimony, which I will term "proxy-witnessing," brings to mind legal venues of finding a way to testify for those (such as children, or animals, or the dead) who cannot testify for themselves. According to the *OED,* the noun "proxy" signifies substitution: "the agency of one who acts by appointment instead of another"; "a document empowering a person to represent and act for another"; "a person appointed or authorized to act instead of another." As in legislative or political representative bodies, in aesthetic representation the proxy functions as a licensed authority for an absent party. The proxy does not replace, but instead acts or speaks in the place of, another.

In verse, proxy-witnessing can take the form of a reiteration of or reflection on extant testimony; or the imagining of affidavits that might have been made, if circumstances had been otherwise; or the interpretation of evidentiary (visual and verbal) documents. Quotation marks may not appear on the printed page; however, many artists cite eyewitnesses or historians of eyewitnesses, or they create depositions that should have been but could not be made. That a hint of fraudulence wafts around a branch of law related to the problems of hearsay,[25] around efforts to remember what one never knew; a taint of bad faith that could breed counterfeit, spurious records of a traumatic past; the stigma of stealing or consuming or envying the memories of others: this, too, is what the poets sometimes seek to investigate. As my readings of the verse of Feldman and Osherow demonstrated, poets in this tradition often ask us to remember what we never did and never will know about the calamity of the Shoah. Additionally, the subtitle of my book hints that we need to keep in mind what no one, single person during the Holocaust could ever have known, given its massive destructiveness. Through retorts to those people who so distress Delbo, bystanders who "think they know" what the genocide meant or means, poets after Auschwitz ask us to admit what we do not know.

The disjunction between the delight usually associated with poetry and the horror of the Holocaust explains the relative paucity of the literary history being traced here. To be sure, as with any shockingly painful occurrence, much banal verse has been produced about the Shoah, though it seems wrong to dismiss as banal what has to be honored as a sincere expression of grief. Curiously, the more powerful poems that should be better known also sometimes exploit clumsy, under- or overstated languages; at times they seem bogged down in the specificity of details or floundering in false analogies; stymied by stutters or by untranslatable words; thwarted by interruptions, caesurae, and hiatuses marking pertinent but absent documentation; driven to abrupt transitions and authorial hesitations; tangled in loops of ululation; rebarbative.[26] In the effort to tell the truth "slant," as Emily Dickinson once famously described her own circuitous and tangential utterances (J. 1129), such hesitant, stymied, stalled words relinquish the hope of closure or finality. I do not mean to argue that these rhetorical markers signal authenticity in this tradition. On the contrary, many poets writing about catastrophic scenes they never witnessed firsthand would agree with Maurice Blanchot: "If there is, among all words, one that is inauthentic, then surely it is the word 'authentic' " (*WD* 60). Nor do they signal inferiority, since these stylistical eccentricities display the place of the *un*poetic and the *non*cathartic in Holocaust poems — their authors' distance from eyewitnessing, their willed turning from incomprehension of the whole to occasional anecdote, their haplessly ironic participation in conventions of literary culture that have been discredited. These works constitute especially forceful acts of remembering because they are belated, partial, flawed, and yet necessary.

So as to trace this complex enterprise without evading my own vexed relationship to it, I begin on a personal note in the next chapter, "Masters of Disaster," which sets alongside "the principle of discontinuity" (which Lawrence Langer describes as an "impassable chasm" separating victims from their offspring [*HT* xiv]) a complementary principle of ongoingness. Starting with the background of my own family, I consider suicide among so-called survivors as a long-term effect of genocide in order to question when "after Auschwitz" definitively occurred and to enlarge our sense of who has a warrant or license to speak about the Shoah. Through an analysis of Marc Chagall's *White Crucifixion* (which I use as a touchstone through this book), I then argue that reactions to the Shoah — however diverse in origin or genre — remain of one piece, part of a fabric woven with reiterated patterns. The third chapter, "Suckled by Panic," examines the autobiographical verse of child-survivors and children of survivors as well as works about children who did not survive. Taken together, all suggest that women writers in particular express their personal sorrow over *der khurbn* (the destruction) by rendering the rent that severed parents from children and numerous writers from the *mame-loshn* (mother tongue) of Yiddish. If poems about the sacrificed child remonstrate against what Charles Bernstein calls "the grammar of control and the syntax of command" (202), so does verse that uses the partiality of the detail to dismantle any generalized understanding of the Shoah.

The verse considered in chapters 4 and 5 responds to photographs, quotations from trials, and testimonial or scholarly accounts: replacements for actual recollections, simulated artifacts that remain fragmented in the poetic text and thus mutely testify to the incommunicable. While chapter 4 highlights meta-photographic art that broods on the importance of flagrantly inadequate visual evidence, chapter 5 distinguishes the journalistic reporting attempted by documentary poets from the proxy-witnessing of recent authors who stress their baffled efforts to make sense of testimony receding into the past. Powerful as it is, the documentary mode relies on narratives that break off at the moment of crisis, when victims were constrained to give up any accounting of their torments. In chapter 6, "The Dead Speak," I discuss those poets who deploy the rhetorical figure of prosopopoeia: personification of an absent speaker. To fill in the hiatus in evidence on which the Nazis relied, this controversial work — in the service of necromancy, the practice of communicating with spirits of the dead — constitutes an effort to speak for, with, and as the casualties of the Shoah.

The concluding chapters explore why the disaster causes artists to resist yet also repeatedly adopt literary and imaginative methods of keeping it alive in cultural memory. In chapter 7, I consider how Jewish liturgical traditions as well as the nature of the Shoah ruptured the elegiac tradition. Bleak parodies, riddling catalogues, nonsensical singsongs, and mordant arraignments of God reject the usual consolations of mourning and discover little redemptive meaning arising out of suffering besetting not a specific person but an entire people. Finally, in "Poetry and Survival," I interpret one poet's lyrical novel — Anne Michaels's *Fugitive Pieces* — about the empathic imaginative identification motivating poetic proxy-witnessing about Auschwitz. Besides trying to think about how the musicality of verse — the fact that we memorize and recite it — lends it a special role in remembrance, here in my conclusion I begin analyzing how gender profoundly shaped and was shaped by the experiences of men and women in the Shoah, even as gender played a role in interpretive responses to it.

Never complacent, many of the astute authors discussed in subsequent chapters gesture toward their own shortcomings to engage a writing practice composed of foreignisms, fragments, quotations, and decidedly tentative words deployed against the authoritative as well as the authoritarian uses to which aesthetically ambitious writing had been put by cultural institutions that either produced or did not derail the growth of fascism. In his approach to Hebrew responses to catastrophe, Alan Mintz has explained, "It took the Rabbis of the midrash generations before they undertook to interpret the Destruction" (269). I agree with the determination he derives from this fact, namely that literature of the Holocaust "is still very much in the making, although a point will soon be reached when the authority of the survivor's voice will cease to play the role it has until now" (269). I hope to demonstrate that the distance signaled by the word "after" in my title forms a divide between the "then" of Europe's casualties and the "now" of North American and British writers and readers, a lacuna foregrounded by a host of linguistic navigations: translation and archival work that disrupts lyrical form, the inconclusiveness of visual and verbal primary documents not of the poets' own devising, the adoption of uncanny cadences and alien perspectives. Through their negotiations between "then" and "now," the authors studied in the pages to come clarify Adorno's resonant 1957 definition of "the poem as a philosophical sundial telling the time of history" ("LPS" 46).[27]

Telling, not retrieving or salvaging, the time of history: in poetry about the Shoah, the hiatus between "then" and "now," "there" and "here," results in ellipses not only within the genealogies of confessional poets but also between the documentary photograph or testimonial archive and interpretive engagement with it, between dead speakers and living authors, between pre- and post-Holocaust engagement with a traditional genre like the elegy. These breaches characterize the humility of literary men and women aware of the oxymoronic nature of the very idea of "Shoah verse" — indeed, the term would strike most people's ears as absurd, even obscene. In short, what Benjamin claimed about Kafka holds true for Holocaust poets who count themselves "among those who were bound to fail," bound to the very idea of failure and guilt (*I* 129).[28] At the same time, the poets' admittedly overt insufficiencies lay waste aesthetic expectations that might disengage us from or provide recompense for the brutality of the disaster, even as they facilitate anamnesis: the recalling of things past.

Were I to make a list of the authors studied here in terms of the timing of their contributions, it would begin with Anthony Hecht and Gerald Stern, Sylvia Plath and William Heyen; then it would include Jerome Rothenberg and Charles Reznikoff, Michael Hamburger and Dannie Abse, Irena Klepfisz and Adrienne Rich, C. K. Williams and Jorie Graham, Irving Feldman and Jacqueline Osherow, Marilyn Hacker and Anne Michaels. But generic choices, rather than chronologies of birth or publication dates, govern my table of contents. Still, my capacious grouping of writers risks lumping together literary men and women with quite diverse backgrounds and projects so as to consider how they probe precisely the cognitive quandaries narrative seeks to solve; how they draw on the photographed and filmed, verbal and written testimonies of survivors, serving as witnesses of the witnesses, or proxy-witnesses. Though they inhabit diverse national and aesthetic worlds, together they paradoxically put on display the tension between historical reference and imaginative figuration that characterizes all retrospective approaches to the Shoah. Authors of Holocaust poetry create a unique tradition not by disproving Adorno's injunction against the barbarism of poetry after Auschwitz but by dramatizing its pertinence again and again.

All too aware of the vulnerability of the dead — in particular the poignant dependency of those nameless legions who died anonymously, unidentified, unburied, and unmourned — the next generations of Holocaust artists and scholars join the first generation in saying kaddish, even as we all refuse to recite the prayer over the Shoah itself. The syllables "Yitgadal ve-yitkadash sh'mey raba," intoned by the living to express grief, are supposed to be spoken in the midst of a congregation, not alone but with a community of fellow worshipers. So as to sustain a future community of mourners, post-Holocaust artists and scholars transform their farewells to the dead into doubtful invitations, exchanging rites of exorcism for rituals that attempt to reanimate not the dead but our anguish for the dead. When in the sixties Adorno refused "to soften the saying that to write lyric poetry after Auschwitz is barbaric," he nevertheless asserted that "*literature must resist this verdict,*" for "it is now virtually in art alone that suffering can still find its own voice, consolation, without immediately being betrayed by it" ("C" 312; emphasis mine). That the Holocaust is dying — this is a condition which must be acknowledged in our attempt to make sure the calamity of the Shoah never submits to its own demise. That the Holocaust, though dying, is not yet dead — this is the subject of my next chapter.

MASTERS OF DISASTER

"The contemplation of horror is not edifying," Anthony Hecht has cautioned, "Neither does it strengthen the soul" (*CEP* 43). Yet a number of contemporary artists, including Hecht himself, believe as does Jerome Rothenberg that "after auschwitz / there is only poetry   no hope / no other language left to heal" (*K* 14). For Hecht, Rothenberg, and their contemporaries concur with the point the French philosopher Maurice Blanchot makes in *The Writing of the Disaster:* "*When all is said, what remains to be said is the disaster. Ruin of words, demise writing, faintness faintly murmuring: what remains without remains* (the fragmentary)." Composed amid a "*Ruin of words,*" poetry after atrocity recounts "*what remains without remains*" (33): what remains without the physical remains of the individual corpses; what remains when too many remains remain unaccounted for, when no explanatory or redemptive beliefs sustain.

"Never forget," plead Jewish immigrants from a war-torn Europe, enjoining their American descendants to keep the past alive in the future. My own mother — besides compiling photo albums complete with detailed notes — assiduously records her experiences in Fürth, in Hamburg, and finally in New York for her children and grandchildren to read. I am proud (though a bit daunted) to admit that her book currently adds up to more than 530 manuscript pages. Like my mother, some of our acquaintances have traveled back to the scenes of their youth, reconnected with relatives scattered all over the globe, met with the officials of their hometowns, and shared common cause with Jewish men and women from their original regions at get-togethers like the one in the Catskills that served as the occasion prompting this study.[1] Still others have subjected themselves to audio interviews or have themselves pioneered the videotaping of testimonials so as to chronicle their youths in Poland or Germany or Hungary. The Holocaust Museum in Washington, D.C., built out of the fragile hope that memory stands bulwark against repetition, represents the fierce desire of countless survivors to create a solidly material case documenting the unimaginable and in so doing make the world bear witness: "Never forget" means "never again."

But how does one remember what one never knew? For the second generation of refugees — the children of parents exiled from their homelands by Hitler — "never forget" and "never again" combine to create a curious divide between those who lived through painful disruptions, dislocations, deaths and those who did not and therefore may not fully comprehend their significance. This gulf, ruled by what Lawrence Langer calls "the principle of discontinuity," constitutes an "impassable chasm" permanently separating even the most loving parents from their offspring; a divide he uses testimony to "undo" (*HT* xiv). On one side of the widening abyss stand survivors who often censored their own responses to an experience so traumatic as to be inexpressible; on the other, their children who question the imagination's capacity to understand what has not been personally endured. Given the entreaties "never forget" and "never again," however, it is important now as a dwindling number of survivors enter their seventies and eighties to find in art a bridge over the gulf of discontinuity, to entertain the contrary view that not writing (or, for that matter, not reading) poetry after (and about) Auschwitz constitutes an act of barbarism.

Especially as the Shoah recedes into the past, the compassionate lexicons of the imagination can safeguard the transmission of what will soon have been witnessed by no one still alive to give firsthand accounts. Some of the most talented North American and British poets in the postwar period have responded to the intensely paradoxical need to speak about the unspeakable calamity by composing verse that takes as its perplexing subject the ethics of art at the brink of terror, where writers must acknowledge the inadequacy of language incommensurate with what it seeks to record. These poets accentuate their engagement in precisely the philosophical questions that absorb scholars of the Holocaust. Is it morally acceptable to speak at all about an atrocity one did not really know? Is it permissible to use our distance from the events of the Shoah as an enabling conduit of their imaginative reconstruction? And how can writers reconstruct those events without giving them an aesthetic order or finish that makes them assimilable and thus frightfully admissible (or repeatable)?

We will see that the task of remembering what one never knew drives even the most vigilant poets to confront their confusion about why they were drawn to the topic in the first place or even their sense of distress and shame about the indecency of mining what Adrienne Rich called "material" in human suffering. In these introductory pages, then, it is appropriate to admit that the same holds true for the scholar. Like many men and women of letters anxious that they might be reaping aesthetic gain from ghastly losses, cultural historians and teachers worry about professional benefit accruing from the misery of the 1933–1945 period. Should one make an artistic or professorial career out of talking about (or talking about not talking about) the disaster? To put the query most harshly, could it be considered self-serving (a case of credentializing) or self-indulgent (a case of lugubrious sentimentalizing) to "dredge up" suffering about which nothing can be done? Does writing about the Holocaust (or reading about writing about the Holocaust) mean playing "the victim card," cashing in long-ago, faraway Jewish anguish for what it is worth in the competitive game of vying for victim status with other hyphenated groups?

The poets whom I study throughout this volume consistently mistrust their right to speak, even as they attest to the means by which they speak. Their scrupulous scrutiny of their own warrant for composing and their wariness about retrospection manifest how creative analyses of the Shoah resist exploitative rhetoric. At the core of the problem for creative and critical authors stand the questions, Who is authorized to speak, how, and on what basis? Despite all the reasons for hesitation, I believe that those who did not suffer in the Shoah are licensed to write about it because it cannot be confined between the brackets of 1933 and 1945; and because to speak about it is to explore its consequences as well as its presence not as a past event but in the present. In this chapter, I patch together personal, literary, and historical matter to reveal the tensions at work in the concept "after Auschwitz," to subvert any hard-and-fast disjunction between "then" and "now" that would propose that the extermination of Europe's Jewish population definitively ended on a specific date. Because the affliction continues to seep from the "then" into the "now," because even a dying Holocaust persists to inflict pain, I inquire, when is "after"? Despite its rarified sound, this inquiry will nevertheless lead to a logic that contradicts normative notions that only certain people should or perhaps no one can transmit the Shoah. For this reason, though this chapter engages verse only intermittently, it prefaces the following, more sustained interpretations of the forms deployed by literary men and women grappling with a grievous historical cataclysm that their parents may or may not have experienced, but that they usually do not lay claim to have directly endured themselves.

WHEN IS "AFTER"?

"Were your parents survivors?" asked an e-mail correspondent when she learned about my work on the subject of Holocaust poetry. The difficulty of answering such a question with a simple yes or no illuminates some of the complexities negotiated by the artists who are the subjects of the remaining chapters of this book. When my mother considers why she did not discuss the impact of her immigration from Germany until quite late in her life, she confesses, "I didn't consider myself a victim," even though she had been barred as a girl from achieving a longed-for education by the anti-Semitic Nuremberg laws installed in the 1930s. Not incarcerated, she had neverthe-less watched the Gestapo hunting for illegal (communist) documents in her parents' house during an unanticipated search and knew that many of the men from her neighborhood had been rounded up that same night to eat grass in the town square. "Not exactly unexpected," my mother's Post-It note on the draft page of this chapter explained: "it was April 1st, 1933, the official *Judenboykott* Day." Whether found or planted, communist matter could lead to immediate incarceration or murder (accomplished by com-manding Jews to run so it could be said they were "shot while trying to escape").

Her father, a physician, had been spared that night when he displayed himself in his German army uniform to prove he had served as a doctor in the First World War. After my mother began her own family, she fled Europe in 1938 with an infant son she had to deposit in a child-care facility while she worked as a live-in maid in New York City, waiting to see if her husband would be able to leave Hamburg — a feat he achieved later that same year. By the end of 1938, German laws and regulations had expelled Jews from the school system; terminated their tenancy rights; deprived them of driver's licenses; prohibited them from intermarriages; barred them from employ-ing Aryans in their households; forced them to apply for and carry identi-fication cards, as well as passports stamped with a large, red *J;* and stipulated that they be assigned one of a limited number of presumably "Jewish" names, though the prohibitions against telephones and city transportation were a few years away (Hilberg 41–58). My mother was never sure if my father bribed his way out of Germany or crossed the border to Holland illegally since, the same Post-It informed me, "neither your father nor I wanted to talk about details when we met again — and surely not after-wards!" In any case, they had managed to join the ranks of "two out of every three Austrian Jews and one out of every two German Jews [who] had made their way abroad before 1941" (Landau 163). Besides cousins scattered to Israel and Central America and England, my mother left behind those who would be murdered: her deaf and blind grandmother, booted out of an old age home, hauled off to Theresienstadt; uncle Edgar and his wife Liese, deported and *verschollen* (missing, lost without a trace), taken (it was rumored) to a concentration camp, where he would have lived a few months longer than she, being of use as a doctor.

Only in 1943 did my mother and father learn about the deaths of his parents a year earlier. A Red Cross telegram and some sleuth work revealed that my father's mother resisted deportation by taking poison; a solicitous concierge whom my parents called "Beefsteak" — because he was "brown on the outside" (a Nazi), "red on the inside" (a communist) — brought her veronal, a sleep-inducing drug. When her husband, in the hospital for an angina attack, learned the news, he turned his face to the wall. "Turned his face to the wall" became the always repeated phrase to speak the poignancy of the fate of my father's father as well as the dubious state of our knowledge of it. Their graves are still unmarked, my mother confides about her in-laws, wondering if she will ever gain the energy to have a commemorative stone erected in the Hamburg cemetery. How lucky, she could go on to instruct me, that her own parents left in time, first for Palestine and then to join her in Brooklyn. And that Hitler forced her to pursue a much more expansive and intellectually stimulating existence than she could ever have had in the Old World.

Many of my mother's contemporaries tenaciously hold on to what they, too, consider a healthily upbeat attitude toward their history. At the Catskills conference panel for second-generation speakers that inspired my initial approach to this subject, my talk was originally titled "Relating Her Family's Past to Her Present Success" by a buoyant organizer bent on just such a cheering message. With a brusque, no-nonsense skepticism, my brother scoffed at my attending the reunion of families from Fürth and Nuremberg, hooting at the idea that his early experiences of separation from Germany, from our father, and even from our mother (when she had to reside with the families for whom she cleaned) placed him squarely in the category of child-survivor. To my brother's mind, dwelling on the past bespeaks maudlin self-indulgence and bad faith. "Quatsch," he would say, mimicking our father. Rot. Nonsense. Although as *das einzige amerikanische Kind* (the only American-born child) I was raised to represent the promise of a different and luckier way of being, I remain suspicious not only of the conferees' buoyancy and my brother's bravado but of any response based on efforts to segregate the past from the present, to bury the past in the past, or to construct a happily-ever-after ending to it. Indeed, I have begun to wonder if our relatives did weather their war-related experiences. Is the "proclaimed cheerfulness" of refugees "based on a dangerous readiness for death," as Hannah Arendt once claimed (*JP* 57)?

In 1947, when my mother was thirty-two years old, her father committed suicide. In 1960, when I was fifteen, my father killed himself. Writing such sentences down feels like an act of desecration, a cold-hearted violation of my vow to keep both men (but, of course, especially my own father) in the secure privacy of my silent thoughts. I break that promise here to broach the subject of ongoingness, of what my mother now calls "the long arm" of Hitler, of the refusal of the Shoah to remain contained in an encapsulated past. What sadness over dead relatives, missing friends, forgotten traditions, lost ambitions, deserted professions, abandoned languages, forsaken places might have bewildered these two men, broken their trust in the world, or made them despair of themselves? Add to these the shock of downward social mobility, the anxiety of economic insecurity. To be sure, as a formulaic qualifier should immediately admit, any number of personal and physical troubles unrelated to their wartime traumas may have set my mother's father and my father on their common course in Brooklyn, New York, several years and then several decades after the Allied victory in the Second World War. Certainly, too, we know of a propensity toward suicide in German Jewish culture that predated the rise of fascism.[2] Still, my mother had thought her father and husband were not survivors because they had not been imprisoned in concentration camps. Lately we have both begun to believe they were not survivors because they did not survive.

In his dauntingly elliptical reverie *The Writing of the Disaster,* Maurice Blanchot remarks that the person who takes his own life becomes a "master of un-mastery" (70). What un-mastery did my grandfather and father have to master, and why? "The art of losing isn't hard to master," Elizabeth Bishop boasts with the valiant show of a swagger in "One Art." Given an arena in which winning is inconceivable, in which losing is inevitable, the tercets of this poem instruct the poet and her readers to brave the pain of repeated loss by acquiring psychological methods to cope with it. But, as in Blanchot's analysis of the "master of un-mastery" in *The Writing of the Disaster,* the rhymes of Bishop's magisterially formal villanelle keep positing "master" and "disaster" until they chime together in the final couplet (178). Did the men in my family master the art of losing through the disaster of their injurious, self-destructive deeds? Like the poet, after all, they had lost something every year, they had lost farther and faster: keys and hours, places and names, houses and cities and continents. Raising the stakes, playing for keeps, demonstrating their mastery by upping the ante, did my father and grandfather turn losing into a challenging art? "Lose something every day," Bishop coaches her reader, until you are strong and tough enough to lose your love or your lover's life or, perhaps, your own life. According to Blanchot, suicide (like a test or a game or a bet or a poem proving nothing at all) demonstrates "that in death nothing comes to pass and that death itself does not pass" (70). Nothing came to pass for my father and grandfather, and death itself did not pass for those they left behind.

To this day, at the beginning of the twenty-first century, when I consider the autobiographical project that has taken up my mother's attention for the past decade, I cannot decide which is worse: her graphic account of finding her father's body in 1947 or her decision to end her autobiography at the year of my father's death in 1960. In one draft of my mother's chapter on 1947, "Father's Death," she records how she abandoned "lies of a heart attack" and revealed to her beloved stepmother the truth of the suicide. Both women agreed "that Hitler and his cohorts had been the cause of father's decline long ago — had broken his spirit." Several pages ensue after this assertion, trying to puzzle out why it happened, and then an entry appears typed in capital letters surrounded by asterisks: "***HE COULD NOT HELP HIMSELF***." On the next page, despite the admission "resentment would govern every thought of mine for years to come," again appear the words "FATHER COULD NOT HELP HIMSELF." Since my mother remains uncertain about her ability or willingness to describe seeing her husband's corpse in 1960, she has used these pages about her earlier struggle to accept her own father's fate to educate her children on the importance of their becoming reconciled to their father's death.

Despite her hesitations, in a text undertaken for her descendants my mother has recounted more details about the suicides in our family than I have here. Consider all the specifics I have not related, as I do when I attempt to assuage my apprehension about writing anything at all on this subject. Where did these deaths occur? At home, in which room, or on the street, in a work or public place? How — with what devices — was the dying done? With a gun or a knife or a razor, with drugs taken through needles or orally, with gas from an oven or fumes from a car? Who was the first to discover the body and what did it look like? How was the news of death communicated and received? Was an explanatory note found and if so where, saying what? What sort of cover-up was invented, if any, and for whom? Not-telling remains as much an issue in the context of suicide as in the setting of the Holocaust experience. In the case of suicide, a number of factors conspire to foster silence in mourners — all of them eerily pertinent to the silences of Holocaust survivors.

Wouldn't I betray either the dead or myself if I described the violent means or scenes of their ending, since my feelings must remain incommensurate with those of my readers? As inhibiting as the dread of relinquishing, tarnishing, or trivializing precious personal reflections is the sense that a scandalous death can instill shame, a conviction that the secret should be kept lest its disclosure reveal a hidden weakness or failure that brought it about in the first place. Though as a criminal offense suicide may point an accusatory finger at the victim, it can also persuade survivors that they are the guilty party whose failures or inadequacies caused the grievous loss. Just as important, especially when suicide occurs more than once in a family, surviving relatives suspect that any recounting may perpetuate more self-destruction. Unlike family histories of cancer or heart disease, suicidogenic backgrounds may be hidden from children to protect them from a repetition compulsion that would doom them to the same grievous fate (Jamison 169). Finally, suicide signifies a narrative breakdown — not only for the dead person who could not find a viable life story but also for the living who cannot fully explain, understand, justify, or excuse the death. Regardless of suicide notes, grieving relatives experience the finality of death as inaugurating the mystery of what really caused it. The only authority who could tell the tale is gone. Whether motivated by a fear that telling either tarnishes or perpetuates the past, whether prompted by shame or simply by ignorance, the not-telling of survivors of suicide resembles the silence of many Holocaust survivors. In the post-Holocaust context, the death by suicide of those who experienced the trauma of genocide can be interpreted as a ruinous signature of the catastrophe's ghastly aftershocks.

"In 1968, when I was 20, my mother killed herself": why is the figure of the American cartoonist Art Spiegelman drawn wearing a concentration camp uniform in the sequence titled "Prisoner on the Hell Planet: A Case History," a strip originally published in 1973 (figure 2.1)? A glance at the fore edge of the pages in *Maus* (1986), the blackened section that shows when the book is closed, directs the reader's attention to this tale interpolated inside the larger narrative about his parents' incarceration in and flight from Auschwitz. Vladek, Artie's father, has discovered a comic the young man had produced several years earlier, a series of frames about his mother's suicide. Not only Art but also his stepmother, Mala, have responded to the mother's suicide with different forms of not-telling. Though the son drew the sequence, he published it in an "obscure underground comic book" he thought his father would never see. Knowing that the revelation would upset Vladek, his second wife had attempted (unsuccessfully) to keep it hidden from him. Much to Artie's dismay, Vladek himself participates in an extreme form of not-telling when he destroys his first wife's private papers. Spiegelman's autobiography and his biography of his father, like Vladek's interpolated autobiography and his biography of Art's mother, circle round the silenced suicide. When the Shoah continues through the suicides of survivors who do not survive, their offspring are thrown into a maelstrom of sorrow and self-blame.

Beginning with the father's discovery of his wife's body in the bathroom, "Prisoner on the Hell Planet" narrates the son's arrival at the death scene, his tears at hearing about the suicide from the family's doctor, and his dazed misery at having to parent his shocked father before and during the funeral. Although the black-rimmed pages are meant to indicate the interpolated status of this comic-within-a-comic, they also signal the grief that frames their creator's life, sealing him into a very complex form of mourning. For he suffers guilt, fearing that his own resentfully adolescent tugs against maternal intimacy ended his mother's life, as well as anger and resentment: anger because he blames her for abandoning him and resentment because of his dread that he must fill his mother's empty place by becoming his father's caretaker. Yet, as the only section of *Maus* in which characters appear in their human form, "Prisoner on the Hell Planet" hints that the artist

2.1. Art Spiegelman, "In 1968, When I Was 20, . . ." From
Maus I: A Survivor's Tale / My Father Bleeds History by Art
Spiegelman, © 1973, 1980, 1981, 1982, 1984, 1985, 1986 by
Art Spiegelman. Used by permission of Pantheon Books, a
division of Random House, Inc.

recognizes his and his parents' postwar anguish to be qualitatively different from the dehumanizing pain endured during the Holocaust.

Read from the bottom up, the picture in which Art in his concentration camp uniform is left alone with his thoughts displays him focusing on a series of words reflecting his confusion about whom or what to blame for his mother's death: "BITCH" (the tattooed arm of one hand wields a razor against the wrist of the other); "MOMMY!" (she reads aloud to him in bed); "HITLER DID IT!" (starved corpses heaped beside a wall emblazoned with a swastika); "MENOPAUSAL DEPRESSION" (the mother's naked body in the bathtub where she died). Like the striped costume, the self-pitying scream of the imprisoned son's final accusation against his mother — "You *murdered* me, Mommy, and you left me here to take the rap!!" — perfectly captures the artist's mockery at his mordant appropriation of his mother's fate even as it forecasts his future confinement in it (figures 2.2 and 2.3). It also anticipates the final and lone word in the last frame of *Maus*'s first volume — "Murderer" (159) — here hurled not at Spiegelman's dead mother but at his living father. Concluding with Vladek's admission that he burned his wife's notebooks — "After Anja died I had to make an order with everything . . . these papers had too many memories" — this book rings changes on its title, *My Father Bleeds History,* by demonstrating how Vladek has been bloodied by a murderous past that he bleeds for what it is worth, that he bleeds of its worth.

Nancy K. Miller, who views Spiegelman as a prototypical child of Holocaust survivors, has pointed out that the interpolated "Prisoner on the Hell Planet" exposes "the rage of surviving the survivors" (116). At the same time, the infantile narcissism that causes Art Spiegelman to draw himself as an inmate of Auschwitz, like the cartoons that reduce his parents to mice and their fascist tormentors to cats and pigs, shows the adult artist judging his own self-pity with a nice dose of irony; Spiegelman understands himself and his readers to be trapped inside a burlesqued Walt Disney simulation of Europe's past. In the last frame of the "Hell Planet" sequence, the invisible artist is incarcerated not in an Auschwitz landscape but instead in a high-tech American, four-tiered prison block from which another very contemporary voice yells out, "*PIPE DOWN, MAC!* SOME OF US ARE TRYING TO SLEEP!" Artie's mother is a victim of the Shoah, and therefore so is he, and thus he must speak: and what the artist says is that "after" has not yet arrived. He will not let his American peers sleep through what is happening not to mice but to human beings in their midst.

While suicide stubbornly refutes all efforts of its survivors to explain or understand, it can be interpreted as a jarring consequence of genocide in the Holocaust context, or so Art Spiegelman's *Maus* suggests. This may be no less the case when my father's mother poisoned herself and her husband turned his face to the wall than later when my mother's father, my father, and Spiegelman's mother died. Pause to consider Walter Benjamin's decision to swallow lethal amounts of morphine at the Spanish border, bearing

2.2. Art Spiegelman, ". . . But for the Most Part, I Was Left
Alone with My Thoughts . . ." From *Maus I: A Survivor's
Tale/My Father Bleeds History* by Art Spiegelman, © 1973, 1980,
1981, 1982, 1984, 1985, 1986 by Art Spiegelman. Used by
permission of Pantheon Books, a division of Random House,
Inc.

2.3. Art Spiegelman, ". . . You *Murdered* Me, Mommy." From *Maus I: A Survivor's Tale / My Father Bleeds History* by Art Spiegelman, © 1973, 1980, 1981, 1982, 1984, 1985, 1986 by Art Spiegelman. Used by permission of Pantheon Books, a division of Random House, Inc.

in mind the suicides many years after the war of the poet Paul Celan, the memoirist Primo Levi, the critic Peter Szondi, the ethicist Jean Améry, the psychologist Bruno Bettelheim, the novelists Jerzy Kosinsky and Piotr Rawicz, the short story writer Tadeusz Borowski, and the director Andrzej Munk. The calamitous effects of the Shoah spill over beyond the brackets provided by dates like 1933 and 1945, making it a continuing, lasting phenomenon, not a contained event but an unceasing series of casualties. To some, like Maurice Blanchot, such a lethal listing instills "the feeling of incredulity, or fright, which suicide always provokes in us, at the same time that it incites the desire to refute it" (*WD* 69). To others, like Jared Stark, "the list comes to us too easily and prompts insufficient surprise" at events in which the "present collapses into the past" (103).[3]

For forty-eight-year-old Walter Benjamin, who managed to obtain an entry visa to the United States and to trek across the Pyrenees to Spain, time ran out at Port Bou in 1940, when local border authorities threatened to send him back to France and the Gestapo. His companions decided to wait and see, but Benjamin, most scholars believe, took an overdose of morphine; after his death the next morning, the police let all the others through. In her analysis of this calamity, Hannah Arendt emphasized Benjamin's maverick bad timing: "One day earlier Benjamin would have got through without any trouble; one day later the people in Marseilles would have known that for the time being it was impossible to pass through Spain" ("I" 18). However, later biographers believe that Benjamin was disposed toward suicide after two of his closest friends killed themselves during the First World War. In any case, Benjamin could not have been motivated by what Primo Levi sees as the impulses of Holocaust-related suicides decades after the war, who enacted a guilty awareness "that we had not done anything, or not enough, against the system," notwithstanding rational cognizance of the impossibility of resistance. "Are you ashamed because you are alive in place of another?" (*DS* 81–82) is the self-accusation Levi finds rasping within those touched by the Shoah. Did intolerable levels of anguish during the Shoah result "in an indigestible bolus of pain, a sort of time-bomb," as Janet Schenk McCord has wondered (5)?

The disconsolate protagonist of Elie Wiesel's *Day*, the third book that completes the trilogy begun by *Night* and followed by *Dawn*, describes "the tragic fate of those who came back, left over, living-dead" in terms of a psychic amputation: "they haven't lost their legs or eyes but their will and their taste for life" (*NDD* 273). Such a wretched being, he explains, "takes away from joy its spontaneity and its justification. He kills hope and the will to live. He is the incarnation of time that negates present and future, only recognizing the harsh law of memory. He suffers and his contagious suffering calls forth echoes around him" (304).[4] In her soliloquy in *The Measure of Our Days*, Charlotte Delbo's survivor-companion Mado reiterates her alienation from the life she lives after Auschwitz: "It seems to me I'm not alive"

(256); "I'm living without being alive" (258); "They say spiritless people, people with no appetite for living, are not alive" (262); "To live in the past is not to live" (264).

The suicide of the Polish author Tadeusz Borowski (*This Way for the Gas, Ladies and Gentleman*), like that of the Polish film director Andrzej Munk (*The Passenger*), may have — undoubtedly does have — quite distinct meanings, personal causes, idiosyncratic effects. My father's motives cannot be conflated with those of my grandparents, nor should their intentions be equated with those of Art Spiegelman's mother. However, such deaths can be contextualized in terms of a Holocaust haunting that hunts down and blights survivors as well as their families. Instead of composing a note, Paul Celan left behind an underlined "sentence from a biography of Hölderlin: 'Sometimes this genius goes dark and sinks down into the bitter well of his heart' " (Jamison 77). Bruno Bettelheim ended his life with barbiturates on the anniversary of the Nazis' annexation of Austria. Whether he fell or decided to fall down the stairwell of his apartment building on the anniversary of the liberation of Buchenwald, Levi understood that the will to live can, after extreme instances of legalized sadism, become atrophied (McCord 255, 287). Surely Borowski's determination to turn on the gas in his kitchen three days after the birth of his daughter and Celan's decision to drown in the Seine when his son was fifteen years old shaped the children's living as well as the writers' dying.

A child-survivor and poet whose father died in the resistance, Irena Klepfisz knows "that for the survivors with whom I grew up the Holocaust never ended": she depicts her mother frozen in fear of a bomb some twenty years after the war, when plaster falls from a living room ceiling, and recalls a friend who "committed suicide just when it seemed she had settled into her American life." "The Holocaust," Klepfisz decides, "was not an event that ended in 1945 — at least not for the survivors. Not for me. It continued on and on because my mother and I were alone" but it "continued on in the Bronx, on ordinary streets, at the kitchen table. It continued on invisible" (*DI* 65–66). It also continued on invisible for Jerome Rothenberg, recollecting the "Airless boxcars" in which "Each night another one would hang himself" and mourning an uncle who "drank himself blind in a deserted cellar & blew his brains out" after learning his family had been murdered at Treblinka (*K* 16, 3).[5] And for the philosopher Emil Fackenheim, who spurned the concept of "*Wiedergutmachung* ['making-things-well-again,' the unfortunate German word used for material restitution]" (100), in works composed many years after the suicide of his older brother in Berlin in 1941 and his own internment at Sachsenhausen. In 1994, the philosopher Sarah Kofman — whose father perished in Auschwitz and who published extensively on Nietzsche and anti-Semitism — chose the 150th anniversary of Nietzsche's birth as her death date. Aftershocks in the lives and deaths of those who experienced the issue of the catastrophe persist to breed mourning that may not abrogate so much as it stretches and tangles the "principle of discontinuity." Given these repercussions, next to Langer's principle of discontinuity we should place a dialectical principle of ongoingness.

SUICIDE AND GENOCIDE

To consider "now" an aftershock of "then" does not mean conflating the two. For suicide as a postwar consequence of the Shoah cannot be equated with suicide during the Shoah, which has been viewed by some as a heroic assertion of human freedom or martyrdom. However, we will see that even during the Holocaust, suicide could also be interpreted as nihilistic, a collaboration with or capitulation to the perpetrators. When coupled with the silencing it inexorably instates, precisely suicide's volatility in a genocidal context demonstrates the fraudulence of critical efforts to delineate not only "victims" (capitulating to the brutality of the Nazi system) from "survivors" (enduring beyond the affliction), but also "victims" from "heroes" (resisting the disaster), from "martyrs" (protesting through their self-sacrifices), from "accomplices" (colluding with the Nazis), from "bystanders" (withdrawing from the calamity), and from "witnesses" (recording it). This complication in turn subverts any attempt to legislate who has a right to speak about the calamity, even as it exposes the urgency of nonparticipants' efforts to put the "now" of the present into a dialogic relationship with the "then" of the past.

For some of the relatives of Holocaust-related suicides, it may be tempting to interpret suicide not the way I previously delineated it—suicide as an ongoing consequence of genocide—but instead as a heroic retort to Hitler. How many Jewish sufferers in the ghettos and the camps rejected any cooperation with the enemy and put an end to ravenous hunger, freezing cold, killing exhaustion, sadistic humiliations, numbing thirst by refusing to go on?[6] In the section of his documentary volume *Holocaust* titled "Work Camps," Charles Reznikoff includes one account of an incident that implicitly construes suicide as what Claude Lanzmann, in another context, called "the utmost of human achievement" ("OU" 208):

> A woman came with her little daughter
> and S.S. men were there one morning
> and took the child away:
> a mother was forbidden to keep her child with her.
> Later, the woman found out that her child had been thrown into
> the fire
> in which the dead were being burnt,
> and that night threw herself against the electrified barbed wire
> fence around the camp. (59)

To mark worsening conditions in Auschwitz in his pictorial diary, Alfred Kantor placed many pages after his first depiction of the barbed wire fence (under the surveillance of the tower guard) a second drawing of a suicide; Spiegelman's precursor, Kantor uses his caption — " 'she went into the fence' / or: she hit the wire / A common view in Auschwitz" (figures 2.4 and 2.5) — to contrast the linguistic euphemism with the fearful fatality. Neither

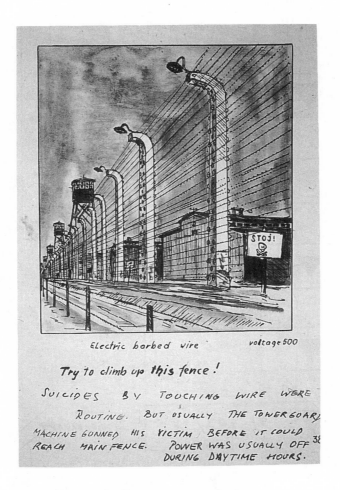

2.4. Alfred Kantor, "Electric Barbed Wire" from *The Book of Alfred Kantor*. Used by permission of Jerry Kantor.

43

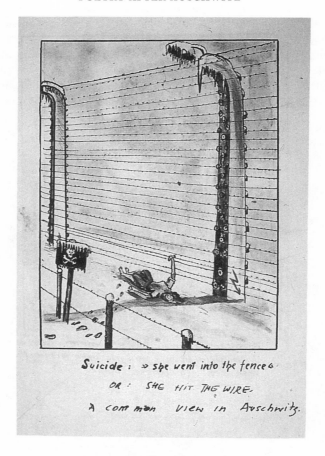

2.5. Alfred Kantor, "Suicide" from *The Book of Alfred Kantor*. Used by permission of Jerry Kantor.

a slave nor an animal can commit suicide, Primo Levi reminds us, for it is a meditated, non-instinctive act involving human choice (*DS* 76).[7]

During the first year of the *Anschluss* that began on March 11, 1938, there were 3,741 deaths by suicide in Austria: " 'The way out for many in Vienna,' observed Sir John Hope Simpson, 'was not emigration, but suicide' " (*Black Book* 129–30). According to Marion A. Kaplan, Jewish suicides in Germany during this period were "a mass phenomenon," for "roughly 10,000 Jews committed or attempted to commit suicide between 1933 and 1943, with the percentages climbing during the deportation years"; in Berlin, some sources suggest "that one-quarter of Jewish deaths" were suicides (180). By mid-1942, "Victor Klemperer had dubbed veronal 'Jewish drops' " (184).[8] A "negative liberty," according to Hannah Arendt, suicide during the period of deportation constituted "the last and supreme guarantee of human freedom": "not being free to create our lives or the world in which we live, we nevertheless are free to throw life away and to leave the world" (*JP* 59). Although at the end of 1939 and then again at the beginning of 1942, Chaim Kaplan praised the "hidden power" that explained why so few people in the Warsaw ghetto killed themselves (131), one of the many so-called *Black Books* about the genocide in Poland noted that

> Epidemics of suicides usually synchronize[d] with waves of deportation or similar acts of oppression. In 1941 five times as many Jews committed suicide in Warsaw as in normal times; at the end of the summer of 1942 there was a new wave of suicides in Warsaw; in Lwow entire families put an end to their lives; in Lublin in March, 1940, 32 suicides were buried in one day. (Apenszlak 189)

In addition, this volume documents the "large number of members of the *Judenrat* [who] committed suicide" when the Nazis began their mass murders (225).[9]

Suicidal acts of eradication, recounted in Lanzmann's film *Shoah,* were chosen by two Jewish leaders — Adam Czerniakow, the head of the Warsaw *Judenrat,* and Fredy Hirsch, a protector of children in Birkenau — after they comprehended their inability to safeguard their wards. Just as the mother in Reznikoff's documentary poem threw herself against the electrified fence as an act of protest against the negation of maternity in the camps, Czerniakow and Hirsch viewed death as a rebuke to the Nazi onslaught against paternal protection within the Jewish community.[10] Despite what Jared Stark calls "the futility of protest suicide" (96), shouldn't Czerniakow and Hirsch be numbered among "Those who asserted themselves by dying," to use a phrase from Anne Michaels's novel, *Fugitive Pieces* (139)? The self-blazing of the Warsaw ghetto has been interpreted by Shoshana Felman as "another suicide"; that is, a "materialization of the desire" not to be inside the atrocity (Felman and Laub 228). Suicide, defined by Felman "as the recognition that what has been done is absolutely irrevocable" (135), acknowledges irreversible losses for which there can be no recuperation or restitution. One could argue further that the suicide stamps as irreversible those losses for which no recuperation or restitution will be accepted. If torture reduces the living person to a fleshly prey of dying (*Sterben*), Jean Améry believed, then suicide constitutes *Freitod,* a voluntary death freely chosen as a radical act proving human liberty (*OS* 128, 147).[11]

Améry's proposition notwithstanding, the concept of *Freitod* devolves in environments designed to eliminate human life. Although Primo Levi thinks of suicide as a preeminently human choice, the circumstances of acute stress that cause some animals to inflict great damage on themselves — overcrowding, confinement, alteration in habitat, sleep loss, elimination of feeding and grooming, changes in physical activity, lack of social or sexual contact — point to the physical roots of a metaphysical sense of unmanageable hopelessness, a disposition toward self-erasure that could not but have oppressed many herded into and then starved within the ghettoes and the camps. Blanchot emphasizes the suicidal person's isolation in a "zone of 'malign opacity,'" where "all relations to himself as well as to the other having been broken, there reigns the irrelation" (WD 32). Such an "irrelation" could be said to replicate the malignant breakdown of human relatedness during the quarantine of Jews caught inside the daemonically efficient mechanisms of dehumanization put into effect by German fascism. Under the "reign" of the irrelation, one need hardly make a "decision" to die since dying was already ordained. "Suicide was so common in Treblinka," according to Janet Schenk McCord, "that at one point the Nazis instituted a special detail of Jewish workers whose job it was to remain awake all night on suicide watch" (17).

Yet this prohibition of Jewish suicides on the part of the Nazis suggests they understood self-destruction as an act of autonomy, a sign of at least spiritual sovereignty. As Inga Clendinnen and as Alfred Kantor's captions have explained, even a choice like that made by Reznikoff's mother "could be negated. Guards were ordered to shoot any prisoners who ran for the electrified fence before they could touch the wire" (Clendinnen 60). Within a genocidal regime, could the assertion of suicide modulate into a pact with the doomed, even though the Torah bans human sacrifice? To refuse human so as to receive deific restitution, to accept one's fate "as a divine decree and to die as a martyr . . . for the sanctification of God's name" has a ghastly place in Jewish history (Mintz 87). Setting aside the unreliable account of Josephus about a mass suicide at ancient Masada, *Kiddush ha-Shem* (sanctification of the Name) later became a form of acceptable martyrdom (McCord 12). In 1096, eleven hundred Jews in Mainz met Crusader demands for conversion with ritual suicides and homicides that they imagined as human offerings, modeled on the Akedah, the story of Abraham's willingness to sacrifice his son Isaac (Mintz 90). Had the shadow cast by the events of 1096 — when the pious became "sacrificial ash on the altar of the Lord" (101) — helped convert self-injury into an ideal of worthiness in the service of God, "a norm of response to catastrophe in the imagination of Ashkenaz" (89) that endured beyond the eight hundred years Alan Mintz judges to be its scope? Engraved on a monument to his memory, the suicide note of Smul Zygielbojm, a Polish Jewish leader, includes the sentence "My life belongs to the Jewish people in Poland and, therefore, I give it to them" (qtd. in J. Porter 58).[12] Perhaps, as John Felstiner has speculated about

Celan's death, "suicide offered a last true way of joining 'With the per-secuted in late, un- / silenced, / radiant / covenant'" (*PC* 55).

Two poems about Holocaust-related suicide—Harvey Shapiro's "For Paul Celan and Primo Levi" and Jacqueline Osherow's "My Cousin Abe, Paul Antschel and Paul Celan"—disagree about whether suicide forges a covenant with the persecuted. "Because the smoke / still drifted through your lives / because it had not settled," Shapiro reasons, Celan and Levi heroically refused to settle, rejected "A coming of terms with man's savagery." Left in a diminished state, we—their timid survivors—never achieve the clarity and compassion of the suicides:

> To understand despair
> and be comfortable with it—
> something you could not do—
> is how we live. (*TR* 169)

The use of a singular verb ("is") for the two acts of apprehending despair and tolerating it discloses the too easy slippage between confronting and becoming inured to desolation. Shapiro's contempt approximates the youthful Benjamin's bleak belief that "the cowardice of the living . . . must ultimately become unbearable" ("MY" 14)—a conviction that loyalty to the dead breeds or even requires disloyalty to the living, making mourning as well as existence itself a shameful disgrace. The "cultural question whether after Auschwitz you can go on living" troubled Adorno as well: "mere survival calls for the coldness, the basic principle of bourgeois subjectivity, without which there could have been no Auschwitz" ("MM" 363).[13]

Whereas Shapiro perceives postwar suicide as an ennobling retort to genocide, this view is complicated when the nihilism of those who take their own lives is taken into account. For, in a gruesome irony, the suicide unwittingly collaborates with Hitler's plan to exterminate the Jewish people. To Osherow, brooding on Celan's poem "There Was Earth Inside Them"—in particular his "brutal" question, "Where did the way lead when it led nowhere?"—suicide constitutes a grievous, not triumphant, rejection of the sanctity of life, at least from the perspective of those who resist its lure (*WMT* 19). Sending regards to Paul Celan from her cousin Abe, who attended the same schools as the poet (then named Paul Antschel), Osherow looks at the picture of their graduation, hears the fates of the few others who managed to evade Transnistria, and attends to her cousin when he interrupts his wife:

> To no one in particular he's quoting psalms,
> Mumbling about the holiness of life.
> *What could have happened?* He is bruised, distraught,
> *What could have made him do a thing like that?* (21)

Although Abe has himself lived through the circumstances that made Celan "do a thing like that," Osherow's cousin chafes at the inexorability of such a fate. Osherow contrasts Celan, defeated in death, with his friend, her be-wildered relative, to speculate on whether suicidal victims of a disaster man-age to master it only by inflicting on themselves the fate cruelly assigned them by their enemies.

Certainly, the German word *Selbstmord,* with its linking of self and murder, suggests as much. According to Freud, too, suicide functions like a disguised murder in which an ego treats itself as object, aiming against itself the hostility that had originally been directed toward someone else. About the death wish, Freud believed that "sadism alone . . . solves the riddle of the tendency to suicide" (252). Elaine Scarry, the author of *The Body in Pain,* thinks that in physical pain, "suicide and murder converge, for one feels acted upon, annihilated, by inside and outside alike" (53). The grieving Art Spiegelman, layering within a single cartoon frame a picture of his mother dying in the bathtub above a heap of stacked corpses, hints that the act of self-murder executes the Germans' job for them, ironically compelling the suicidal survivor to dwindle into a victim, yes, but also an aggressive accom-plice. As objects of Nazi brutality, Jewish people might discharge on them-selves the violence directed against their so-called race or the violence they would, but could not, direct against the destroyers of their so-called race. Self-injury in this context represents adaptive rather than pathological, sub-versive, or spiritual activity: adaptive to the laws of lands pledging allegiance to the "Final Solution."

After Fritz Rosenfelder used his 1933 suicide note to shock Christian friends into an awareness of intolerable persecution, a Nazi publication boasted: "we are pleased with him and have no objection if his racial breth-ren adopt the same method of taking leave" (Kwiet 148). If, as many believe, anti-Semitism was buttressed by the identification of Jews with the betrayer of Christ, then Nazi pleasure at Rosenfelder's leave-taking may have been shaped by the account of Judas Iscariot's act of suicide in the Gospel of Matthew, which signals a penitential admission of his own treacherous na-ture. In his or her mastery of disaster, does the suicide volitionally adopt the part of the apostle who bears the name of the Jewish people and thus his shameful acknowledgment of his own greedy and deceptive nature? Con-sider the multiple resonances of the word "commit" in the phrase "commit suicide": "commit" means placing oneself officially in confinement (the suicide as victim); "commit" signifies entrusting oneself to another or im-posing a moral obligation (the suicide as protestor, bonding with the casu-alties); "commit" implies being responsible for or guilty of a crime (the suicide as accomplice or criminal).

Yet inside frayed feelings of personal loss, to ask such a question — about my own father, for instance, or my father's mother — seems an unpardon-able defilement of their fates. When Lanzmann spoke of the suicide of his sister as "the utmost of human achievement," he sharply contrasted it not only to the "military tradition, to commit suicide," but also to the suicides and attempted suicides of Hitler, Goebbels, Himmler, and Göring, who "just wanted to escape, to *escape justice* and *escape execution,* and to *escape the truth,* and to *escape history*" ("OU" 108). W. D. Snodgrass's *The Führer Bunker* makes clear through the dramatic monologues of his cast of characters that Eva Braun and Hitler, Magda Goebbels and Joseph Goebbels believed such a death "restored" them to their "own Will" (78). One of his Brechtian ditties about "all / Who find they face a blank stone wall" sardonically explains that they

> Can still make one last stand
> Against themselves. You've got to die
> But, though you can't pick when or why,
> You can make sure you perish by
> Nobody else's hand.
> You stay in command. (161)[14]

Since the Nazis controlled the circumstances that led to their suicides (whereas the Jewish victims did not), it would indeed be a calumny to equate the "command" exercised by the Nazi pistol or cyanide at war's end with the mother in Reznikoff's *Holocaust,* throwing herself on the electrified barbed wire fence.[15]

Still, although the motives of Jewish suicides must never be conflated with those of their tormentors, refusing to go on cannot simply be identified with succumbing to or defying the scapegoat role assigned by the fascists — because suicide constitutes an escape from history through an act of self-sacrifice by which the victim who dies also kills. For centuries, after all, suicide has been forbidden by Jewish custom.[16] Suicide does signal a defiance, but one that concedes the impossibility of defiance. Perhaps for this reason G. K. Chesterton believed that the suicide "kills all men; as far as he is concerned he wipes out the world" (131–32). So, though perceived as a protest, Fredy Hirsch's suicide frustrated a planned rebellion: according to Konrad Kwiet, "Czechoslovak Jews in other parts of [Birkenau] had made preparations to respond to the liquidation of the 'family camp' by setting fire to their hutments, thus signalling to other prisoners, above all to the members of the Jewish special squads (*Sonderkommandos*) in the crematoria, who were in the know, that the rising was due to begin" (162–63), an insurrection aborted because of Hirsch's fatal decision. After Adam Czerniakow swallowed a cyanide pill, the Warsaw *Judenrat* disintegrated and was replaced by the collaborationist, "much hated Jewish police" (Bauer 78). Death by suicide betokens criminal, violent actions without a clearly defined, punishable culprit. The "arrogant, hurtful, indiscreet" act of suicide — the adjectives are Blanchot's (*WD* 70) — inevitably conjures up questions of culpability and betrayal. But, given our decent and proper reluctance to blame the victim, whose?

A poem by Dannie Abse, titled "A Footnote Extended," addresses this all-pervasive intimation of a perfidy perpetrated without a specifiable agent. Abse's verse letter to Thomas Szasz, the contemporary British author of an appreciation of the Austrian polemicist Karl Kraus, politely begins by refusing to make any critical judgment of Szasz's book, but then asks that "more attention, please" be paid to one Egon Friedman. Born to Jewish parents in 1878, Friedman responded to anti-Semitic insults and discrimination by changing his name to Friedell; however, since he still found himself mocked, he raised the stakes to master this disaster:

> Tall, he turned the other cheek,
> he converted to Christianity—
> defended the Gospel
> against Mosaic subversion;
> attacked the Jewish Science
> of Psychoanalysis,
> called its practitioners—
> Freud, Abraham, Stekel—
> "underground blood-suckers." (31)

By pandering to the anti-Jewish intellectual climate, Friedman-turned-Friedell won a success that was, of course, only temporary:

> When the Nazis marched
> into Austria
> —strange amphigouri
> of circumstance—
> Friedell, in his bachelor room,
> walked toward the long mirror,
> saw Friedman approaching.
> Whispered Friedman,
> screamed FRIEDMAN,
> and killed himself. (31)

Within the "amphigouri" or burlesque of his fate, the irony of what Friedman's name sounds like underlines the ambiguity of this ending: did he finally free himself from the delusion that his charade could rid him of his Jewishness? did he understand how his assimilationist mimicry advanced the long Nazi trek toward Vienna? The doubling of Nazis marching and Friedell walking, the mirroring of Friedell and Friedman spotlight the inextricable dialectic between anti-Semitic images and Jewish identity in the war years—a dialectic to which apocryphal stories about the Jewish roots of many National Socialists attest. According to one such account, the SS leader Reinhard Heydrich (suspected of having a Jewish father) became so tormented "by the 'Jew within' that one night, in a drunken fit, he stared into a mirror, thought he actually glimpsed the shadowy Jew within somehow *emerge* in his reflection, and promptly fired his pistol into the mirror image, hoping to extinguish it" (Rosenbaum 293). Epidemic suicide rates among Jews in the prewar period may also testify to this gruesome mimetic rivalry between victimizer and victim, bringing to mind Irving Feldman's grim couplet: "*Each man on the street insists he is himself, / but all have in common the same double: Disaster*" (*AUH* 65). And later, during the heights of "the Europe-wide Jew purge (*gesamteuropäische Entjudung*)," a "high degree of assimilation" among secularized Jews correlated with higher suicide rates (Kwiet 158, 164, 166).

Generating a free-floating sense of betrayal, the culprits who caused the violent acts of the last stanza in Abse's poem — the Nazi victory, the suicide — proliferate: to blame are Friedell-Friedman, for internalizing racism; Karl Kraus, for repudiating *his* Jewish origins and bolstering the anti-Semitic climate to which Friedell pandered; Hitler's brand of fascist imperialism, bred on epidemic hatred of Jews; and Thomas Szasz, the current expert on psychoanalysis who writes without a hint of distress that "Kraus sought to identify himself as a master of the German language, rather than as a Jew. For Kraus, this was, I think, a successful solution to the Jewish problem" (8). That German and Austrian Jews attacked psychoanalysis as "a Jewish pseudoreligion" and a "mental contagion" (71) does not strike the anti-Semitic chord for Thomas Szasz that it does for Dannie Abse, who in another poem states: "Auschwitz made me / more of a Jew than ever Moses did" (34). A number of Abse's contemporaries make this same point by underscoring the indeterminacy of death within the genocidal context in contrast to the collusion of later suicides executed within environments of relative safety.

Adrienne Rich explains how Auschwitz made her "more of a Jew than ever Moses did" in *Sources*, a sequence dedicated to her husband, the one "Who drove to Vermont in a rented car at dawn and shot himself" (25), and to her father, who denied his Jewish origins. The assimilated Southern father seems opposed to "the one from the *stetl*, from Brooklyn"; however, the father residing inside "the floating world of the assimilated," built out of a "rootless ideology," resembles the husband, who decided "*There's nothing left now but the food and the humor*" (15, 14, 25). Rich attributes the recovery of her womanliness and her Jewishness to her insight beneath "the power and arrogance of the male" to what resides within both "isolate" men; namely, "the suffering of the Jew, the alien stamp" (15). She then seeks to locate her origins beyond their purview and in "something more than self-hatred" (26):

> The Jews I've felt rooted among
> are those who were turned to smoke
>
> Reading of the chimneys against the blear air
> I think I have seen them myself
>
> the fog of northern Europe licking its way
> along the railroad tracks

to the place where all tracks end
You told me not to look there. (24)

Rich, rejecting a "rootless ideology," affiliates herself with those uprooted against their will. If she is to find a way for herself and others "not to *give ourselves away*" (33), the new identity will never be based on looking away, but on remembering "the place where history was meant to stop / but does not stop," where instead it

only
becomes a different pattern
terrible, threadbare
strained   familiar   on-going. (27)

In trying to detach themselves from the damage done to their own people, Rich's father and husband paradoxically suffered those injuries themselves, becoming the sum of that ruin in a way the despised and endangered never did.

Since self-injury can be interpreted as doing the Nazis' work for them, Roberta Gould adopts a more sardonic tone than either Abse or Rich to take an activist stand against postwar suicide, admonishing survivors haunted by the Holocaust:

don't cut off your wrists as Jim did
don't go mad every year like Renée
don't slice off your finger like Tanya
don't lie in bed afraid of morning
don't smoke yourselves to death
like Daido and Lorraine
don't go sexually dead
obeying the message,
"Work for death
you handcuffed slave
you pest!" (*BL* 273–74)

According to Rich and Gould, the past ironically survives in the acts of those who perpetuate the Shoah by trying to escape through assimilation or self-destruction. Suicide, which means to put a stop to the pattern of annihilation, "only / becomes a different pattern /   terrible, threadbare / strained   familiar   on-going."

A meditation on the Holocaust led Blanchot to think about the suicide's mastery of un-mastery because the proliferation of suicides before, during, and after the Shoah was one of the disaster's disasters. While the suicide may be interpreted as a casualty or resister of, a protestor against, and an accomplice in genocide, genocide nudges each human being closer to suicide, which becomes the only imaginable alternative to murder, albeit one that grotesquely leads to the same futile end. Although for Rich and Gould suicide constitutes a capitulation to a genocidal past, Jacqueline Osherow's "Brief Encounter with a Hero, Name Unknown," which I discussed in the previous chapter, explains how suicide could also be construed as heroic revenge within the camps. Like the mother in Reznikoff's poem, Lanzmann's account of Fredy Hirsch, Abse's Egon Friedman and Shapiro's Levi, Felstiner's and Osherow's Celan can be assigned more than one label in the catalogue of victim, hero, martyr, accomplice, bystander, and witness. Taken together, poets attesting to the consequences of disasters they never knew resist giving one name to the multiplication of suicide and of its indeterminacy during and after the Holocaust.

THE WARRANT

Suicide may indeed be alone in its power to evoke the exceptionality many people attribute to the Shoah, for suicide is perhaps the sole act that can be performed only once in a person's life. Vertiginous in its equivocality yet irreversible, suicide, like the Shoah itself, testifies — the body constitutes evidence — but without a testifier. It can be approached *only* "after" by those who manage not to succumb to its unspeakability. Is this why, although the taking of one's own life is an action, the person who executes it is subsequently conflated with the act — by being termed "the suicide"? The lexical idiosyncrasy of a single deed at the end of an existence establishing an identity means that a type of death metamorphoses into an eerie vocation or profession: we don't speak of "the cancer" or "the heart attack" or "the liver failure," though we talk of "the cook" or "the teacher." But unlike the cook (who cooks) or the teacher (who teaches), "the suicide" has nothing but a posthumous life as the only authority on the suicidal event. If "the suicide" can be said to engage in an action, expression, or profession, what he or she enacts is not self-injury (a suicide does not suicide) but self-censorship. Thus, suicide, like genocide, which deprived the overwhelming majority of those afflicted from communicating for themselves, invokes the mandate of speech after disaster. Both suicide and genocide would go unspoken, were it not for proxy-witnesses.

The act of committing suicide therefore conjures another meaning of the word "commit": to consign for future use or reference, for preservation; to commit the suicide, the genocide to (the safety of) memory, for Auschwitz itself can be approached *only* "after" by retrospective observers who remain external to it. If the receding calamity weeps into the present, if keeping it in mind is one way not to submit to it, then how should it be remembered as it moves into a more remote past? Debates over whether and where and how to memorialize it speak to this problem. So do arguments over who has the right to speak for the murdered, who has the authority to write about such wide-scale devastation, and how they should do so. Because the dead must be remembered in a way that preserves the vexed and finally incomprehensible circumstances of their dying, writings about suicide and about genocide exhibit the tactics and tact proper to such a subject. Wariness, the careful scrutiny of primary and secondary documents: these are the poets' answers to the question of *how* to approach this matter. With respect to *who* can approach it: as with suicide, the unstable meaning and proliferation of death in the Shoah establish an imperative on the part of artists not directly touched by the disaster to convey it. Although nonparticipants will inevitably replace participants as the Holocaust retrogresses into the past, from the very inception of its transmission verse responses have frequently been created by writers at some remove from the calamity.

Among the poets who decried or mourned the event, only a handful can be said to have composed with firsthand knowledge. The manuscript of Abraham Sutzkever, who completed *Faces in Swamps* while hiding in a broken chimney during the occupation of Vilna, was discovered stashed in a ghetto cellar forty-nine years later. Yitzhak Katzenelson, whose *Song of the Murdered Jewish People* appeared one year after his death in an Auschwitz gas chamber, wrote his elegiac epic in Vitel, an internment camp for foreigners in France; a friend managed to place the fifteen cantos in three glass bottles and bury them until after the liberation.[17] Decaying compositions interred with decomposing bodies, a form of "carrion comfort,"[18] retain a privileged, if frightful, place in the Holocaust canon. "Root is what I am, root-poet / here at home among the worms, / finding here the poem's terms" (*AA* 631): Miklós Radnóti's last ten poems were found in his coat pocket after his body was exhumed from the ditch in Hungary where he had been shot in the neck; on paper saturated with his bodily fluids, his poems' terms were literally rooted in the worms.[19] That Radnóti had converted from Judaism to Catholicism, however, made him less representative for some readers than a number of Jewish contemporaries who lamented the horrific fate of the Jewish people, poets never at the scene of the crimes they recounted.

For instance, Urzi Zvi Greenberg, who grieved over his perished family in *Streets of the River*, left Warsaw for Palestine two weeks after the Nazis appeared in 1939; and Nelly Sachs, who deplored "the setting sun of Sinai's people" (*AA* 540), fled Germany for Sweden in 1940. Neither ever beheld what they expressed with keen compassion. Similarly, Jacob Glatstein, who emigrated to the United States in 1914, only visiting Poland briefly in 1934, saw not with his physical but with his mind's eye the "Cloud-Jew" whose sacred assent curling from the crematorium chimneys makes his "lips tremble" in one poem while in another he posits the bruising assertion "God—where You are— / we all disappear" (*AA* 660). In other words, Greenberg (composing in Hebrew from Palestine), Sachs (writing in German from Sweden), and Glatstein (publishing in Yiddish from America) no more described their firsthand experiences than did Primo Levi, who warns that the overwhelming majority of Jews in Hitler's Europe could no more testify about their own end than the dead can ever return to describe their own demise. Remonstrating against *any* writer's presuming to a greater degree of authenticity than any other, in a grim three lines Paul Celan himself cautions,

> No one
> bears witness for the
> witness. (241)

As if meditating on the mystery of these words, Dori Laub has defined the uniqueness of the Holocaust as a historical occurrence that "*produced no witnesses*" (Felman and Laub 80). Not only did observers of the calamity fail to communicate their testimonies to a disbelieving world, but many participants felt so contaminated by it that they could not find any (material or psychological) means to bear witness. According to Laub, then, "*being inside the event . . .* made unthinkable the very notion that a witness could exist" (81). But if the possibility of a victim appealing to anyone outside the event was extinguished, are Sachs and Glatstein to be considered somehow less authentic — or differently authentic — in their responses than Radnóti or, say, Celan because he lost both his parents and endured two years of forced labor before he went on to publish his "Death Fugue"? Should "verbal tombs for a murdered people" (*AA* 555), as Lawrence Langer trenchantly puts it, be judged by their creators' propinquity to atrocity, their veracity to a corporeally endured reality?

Or, as some have speculated, might it be true that only those outside the events could obtain the distance needed to focus on them imaginatively and rationally? Laub seems to suggests as much when he wonders whether it takes "a new generation . . . removed enough from the experience, to be in a position to ask questions" (Felman and Laub 83), a generation that another thinker imagines "bear[ing] the scar without the wound, sustaining memory without direct experience" (Cohen 2). For the French writer Henri Raczymow, whose 1985 novel *Un cri sans voix* (trans. as *Writing the Book of Esther,* 1995) meditates on the suicide of a young woman born during the war and bearing the name of an aunt murdered in Auschwitz, a distinction between the right to speak and the need to do so opens up a space for utterance:

> My question was not "*how* to speak" but "*by what right* could I speak," I who was not a victim, survivor, or witness. To ask, "By what right could I speak," implies the answer, "I have no right to speak." However, as any psychoanalyst will tell you, the time comes when you have to speak of what is troubling you. (102)

Is a nonparticipant's effort to speak for the victims an appropriative act of arrogance, an empathic identification with those desperately in want of a medium of communication, or an urgent compulsion to express feelings, compunctions notwithstanding?

Regardless of how individual readers answer these questions, the degrees of separation that distance Sachs or Glatstein from the Shoah are quantitatively (not qualitatively) different from those that remove later American poets like Irena Klepfisz or Anthony Hecht. Indeed, to the extent that the Jewish child Irena Klepfisz lost her resistance-fighter father in the uprising of the Warsaw ghetto and had to be hidden by a Catholic family in Poland, that the twenty-two-year-old Anthony Hecht (in the 386th Infantry, 97th Division) helped liberate the Flossenberg concentration camp (an annex to Buchenwald), they could be said to have been more personally, physically embroiled in the European war landscape than Sachs or Glatstein. Shifting national boundaries hardly predict or circumscribe individual participation, either. As Radnóti's conversion highlights, religion plays just as equivocal a role as nationality in the history of poetic reactions to the Holocaust. From the beginning of its literary history to more recent times, Jews and non-Jews alike have struggled to fathom the cataclysm from their various perspectives.

Comparably elusive are those generational markers erected by literary historians to organize responses to the Shoah.[20] In other words, the neat lines a demographer might be tempted to draw in order to organize aesthetic reactions to the Holocaust along generational lines are blurred by what I have been calling its complicated ongoingness. Just as shifty are the usual generic categories used by critics to characterize literary forms of representation, since "Holocaust art" presents itself as a contradiction in terms. Spiegelman's insistence that *Maus* be moved from the *New York Times*'s best-selling fiction list to its best-selling nonfiction list and Lanzmann's objection to those who termed his film *Shoah* a documentary reflect these artists' efforts to navigate between objectively recorded testimonial and subjectively shaped narrative, historical facts and inventive arrangements of accounts, as they attempt to draw attention to archival material spliced with authorial and directorial decisions about its presentation. Like many Holocaust poets, Spiegelman and Lanzmann create generically incongruent forms in order "to break down the cognitive and emotional barriers that keep the past safely in the past" (Horowitz 7).

What one *can* sense about the shape of the past as it is rendered in verse, however, is a pause or gap between, on the one hand, the literature composed primarily in Yiddish, German, Hungarian, Romanian, and Polish during and directly after the war and, on the other, that by English-speaking writers who, emerging in the 1960s, developed a tradition that evolved through the turn of the century. The chapters that follow deal with verse written to dispel repression and denial, poetry composed primarily in Britain and North America during the last decades of the twentieth century. A crime without a sufficient or suitable punishment haunts several national literatures, not least of all those produced in English-speaking countries. The warrant to speak or write about it consists precisely in our inhabiting the post-1945 period. What needs to be judged vis-à-vis that work is not any unique right its authors might have to the subject, but the rigor and vigilance with which they engage it.

Irrespective of the motives behind my discussion of suicide, then, this chapter needs to conclude with caution about using suicide as an emblem of the catastrophe, a monition related to any contemptible distortion of my argument that would construe the Shoah as Jewish self-injury. For precisely the *sui* (of oneself) of suicide is inevitably abrogated amid genocide, a term coined in 1944 to describe the killing (*cide*) of a *genos* (a race or kind), violence directed against neither individuals nor personal deeds. Victims were not targeted on the basis of beliefs or possessions or acts or identifications: not in suicide but in genocide "the victim is no longer, except in an accidental physical sense, a person at all," but merely an instance of (specious) biological traits that can neither be affirmed nor denied (Lang, *AIEG* 20). A survivor brooding over Jewish poisonings, drownings, hangings, and wrist slashings, Charlotte Guthmann Opfermann leaves unanswered her unanswerable question: "Were these 'suicides' voluntary, assisted, encouraged, or were they murders?" (44). Her concept of "assisted" suicide evokes the 1938–1941 legalized murder (by gassing or lethal injection) of 90,000 mentally and physically handicapped adults and children in the Nazi euthanasia program that preceded the "Final Solution." So as to situate the poetry in a wider aesthetic contest, so as to illustrate how some forms of art convey the "impersonality and abstractness [which] are the essential features" of a regime that denied individuation and agency to the Jewish people (Lang, *AIEG* 145), I conclude this chapter by turning to a work of art that definitively interprets the Holocaust as an apocalyptic infliction of unmastery.

WHITE CRUCIFIXION

Even the English poems composed at the very brink of the twenty-first century sustain the themes and images that surfaced when violence against Jews in Germany began to escalate. Chronologically, geographically, and generically diverse reactions to the Shoah remain, to a remarkable degree, of one piece, part of a fabric woven with reiterated patterns. English verse remains enmeshed in that larger tapestry crafted not only of poems in other languages but also of testimonials, diaries, novels, photographs, films, and paintings. No single work of art better illustrates this commonality than Marc Chagall's highly acclaimed but controversial painting *White Crucifixion* (1938), for it presents figures, settings, and themes that preoccupy artists working in many different media and countries. Indeed, the shock this work administers typifies the impact of many literary responses that are equally heretical. A Jewish artist using Christianity's Jesus might look like a case of arrogation to the Christian viewer or of apostasy to the Jewish viewer. Especially in the context of the Shoah, one can understand why as sensitive an interpreter as Leon Wieseltier, the son of refugees and author of *Kaddish*, judges Chagall's decision to portray the Jewish people as Jesus "dishonorable," since a "Christian civilization was exterminating the Jews" (469). "Let *him* burn on *his* cross," Sonia Pilcer's survivor-mother seethes, remembering drunken Poles on Christmas and Easter trying to force her to clean the street with her own dress (Pilcer 84). Executed in the year when synagogues and Jewish-owned shops in German cities came under wide-scale attack, the startling central portrait of a Jewish Christ is encircled by the dance of death performed by scattered members of a Jewish community clearly in diaspora (see frontispiece). Because these characters, locales, and activities occupy the attention of Chagall's literary descendants and because the difficulty of distinguishing between honorable and dishonorable representations of the Holocaust haunts postwar writers, his painting serves as a touchstone throughout the rest of this book.

At the bottom of the canvas, the light of the menorah's candles does not reach the woman whose effort to clasp her infant between her hands has been depicted in a way that cuts her off at the waist, a mark of her precarious hold on existence, on the life of the child, on our attention. At the edge, too, are the three figures near the lower left-hand corner: a worshiper attempting to cradle the Torah, a criminalized suspect bearing a sign, and a weeping older man about to fall out of the picture entirely. In flight, all of these characters have nowhere to go except the oblivion that awaits beyond the margin. On the upper right of *White Crucifixion*, a man attempts to salvage a Torah from a desecrated temple, but the scroll itself blazes on the bottom right, a burning book that seems to signify the incineration of faith in religious wisdom and cultural literacy. That the green-coated refugee burdened with a bag — of provisions? possessions? — appears about to be immolated in the flames of the Torah hardly bodes well for his exodus. While the right-hand and bottom borders of *White Crucifixion* emphasize the fearful suffering of isolated individuals, the figures along the left side and at the top of the painting represent communities of mourners and marauders. A battalion of soldiers bearing weapons and wielding red flags ominously tramps out of nowhere to wreak havoc in the name of the nation-state. Or, given the Russian overlay, are these villagers militant resisters, organized to retaliate against a pogrom? On either side of the soldiers appear Jewish victims: immigrants in a boat, whose hopeless gesticulations or swooning exhaustion presage death before their arrival at a haven; whole villages burning, their outcasts camping on the freezing ground; at the very top of the canvas, elders bemoaning, lamenting, cursing, protesting the evil they have witnessed, but to whom can they testify? With flames blazing out on all sides, an infernal circle of shattered beings dramatizes the vertiginous Walpurgisnacht of Kristallnacht (November 9, 1938).

In the childlike simplicity of their folk art shapes, the Jewish pariahs of *White Crucifixion* appear singularly unaffected by the stunning central image of the crucified Jew on the cross, covered with a prayer shawl for loincloth. "Holy without being divine" to one viewer (Roskies 284), this Jesus can neither be touched nor taken down because the ladder falls away from him. Abandoned by a creator nowhere manifest, the central figure could be said to epitomize all the others, though by fleeing from him, they make his sacrifice appear futile. The tallith that should rest on the sage's shoulders seems no less displaced than the overturned chairs of the synagogue, the toppled houses of the ghetto, the fiddle in the snow. Given the golden glow of his flesh vis-à-vis the title of the painting, the rabbi at the center of the picture, caught in the vertical beam of light as well as the stake on which he is hung, appears to be crucified by ideologies of whiteness. Mythologies of the Aryan, Nordic, master race have defiled Jewish life and its sacred symbols. Although some interpreters worry about a Jewish artist borrowing the oppressor's traditions and in the process either betraying a distinctly Jewish legacy or forgiving instead of indicting those Christians who destroyed it, to my mind such a concern sidesteps the impact of the disturbing central image.

Neither redemption nor resurrection appears in this picture of a suffering being who is the Messiah for some, but not for others. For the Christian viewer, worshiping Christ as the son of God, Glatstein's line "God—where You are— / we all disappear" relates to the Messiah venerated while "Cloud-Jews" vanish into thin air. Not a closeted Christian but a Jewish artist addressing non-Jews, Chagall uses the iconography of Christ to force Christians to witness the Holocaust and be found wanting.[21] To Jewish viewers, seeing Jesus as a wise man but not as the embodiment of God, Chagall relates Glatstein's lamentation to the absent One who has deserted the rabbi and his people, as if proposing the revision "God—where we all are— / You disappear." Chagall stresses the Jewish character of Jesus by placing the traditional sign INRI (abbreviating the Latin "Jesus of Nazareth King of the Jews") next to its Aramaic translation on the crossbar: *Yeshu HaNotzri Malcha D'Yehudai.*[22] That the inscription appears in the language spoken during biblical times in Palestine hints that at stake for Jews is the holy word of God; for Christians, the holiness of God's word made flesh. But what difference does this difference make? A redemptive figure—God's son or sage—has been overwhelmed, surrounded by signs of the cataclysm he did not foresee, could not forestall, will not redeem.

For all beholders, a despised and rejected being—in the forsaken silence after the cry—lapses out of consciousness as the world he leaves behind teeters on the edge of chaos. A poem addressed to Marc Chagall by William Pillin illuminates the shocking gravity of *White Crucifixion* by reminding us that elsewhere the artist was "always painting ascensions":

> The ascension of priestly violinists,
> the ascension of white-gowned brides,
> the ascension of purple donkeys,
> of lovers, of bouquets, of golden cockerels,
> ascension into the clair-de-lune. (*BR* 184)

In opposition to "this soaring / out of shanties and cellars," this "wandering in the bluest realm," Pillin contrasts "a thin column of smoke ascending / and after that / no more ascensions."[23] To the extent that the crucifixion prefigures the deaths of all the figures in the picture, no possibility of mastering this disaster appears on the canvas.[24] In *On Suicide*, Jean Améry views "Rabbi Jeshua as an historical figure" and recognizes his "terrifying death as a *suicide en puissance* (potential suicide)," for the crucified man tells humanity, " 'It's all right, for better or worse, pass on, it doesn't matter' " (83–84).

Such an implicitly perverse view may become more meaningful if, as some thinkers have argued, the desperation of, say, Améry or Levi or Celan sprang from their perception of genocide not as an end but merely as the beginning of a disastrous period in history. Or if one factors in the insight of the fictionalized *Judenrat* in Leslie Epstein's novel *King of the Jews*, it was rooted in their outrage — when confronted by a Nazi demand for a certain quota of ghetto inhabitants — that "We will have to kill each other and the last person alive has to kill himself" (197). Several years before the Wannsee Conference at which Nazi officials planned the "Final Solution," Chagall seems as prescient as Walter Benjamin, whose suicide note (reconstructed from memory by a member of the group trying to cross the Pyrenees to Lisbon) stresses the importance of communicating his destiny after his death: "In a situation with no way out, I have no choice but to end it. . . . Please pass on my thoughts to my friend Adorno and explain to him the situation in which I find myself" (qtd. in Brodersen 257). Benjamin's theses in "On the Concept of History," engraved on the monument to his memory at Port Bou, also help explain Chagall's choice of iconography: "It is more arduous to honour the memory of the nameless than that of the renowned. Historical construction is devoted to the memory of the nameless" (qtd. in Brodersen 262).

Regardless of how and when and where they will meet their individual fates or by whose hand, the green-coated refugee and the mother, the immigrants in the boat and the man in the posterboard inhabit "a zone of 'malign opacity' " in which the only available modus operandi is a mastery of unmastery. Denizens of the disaster, they endure "the time when one can no longer — by desire, ruse, or violence — risk the life which one seeks, through this risk, to prolong" (Blanchot, *WD* 40). According to Blanchot, self-destruction "reverses the possibility of impossibility into *the impossibility of every possibility*" (70). Similarly, just as Elizabeth Bishop's poem "One Art" wonders whether losing can become a form of artistry, Chagall's painting serves as a paradigm of aesthetic reactions to the Shoah that designate art itself as a sign of loss, of wasted lives never brought back into being. Neither sweetness nor light, neither pleasure nor learning — the traditional functions artistry serves — provide recompense in the anti-art produced by aesthetic masters of the disaster.

Yet one factor distinguishes Chagall's medium from that deployed by the poets who succeeded him. Nothing is lost in translation from Chagall's disturbing canvas, regardless of where and to whom it is shown. The only script in a modern language — originally the crime of Jewishness emblazoned on the condemned man's billboard — was overpainted by Chagall. Of course there is writing in *White Crucifixion;* however, the ancient Aramaic would have a comparably mystic obscurity for Russians, Americans, and Danes. Unlike paintings, though, poems, which are created in a medium sticky with local specificity, cannot easily be detached from the lexicons or the linguistic conventions of the languages in which they are composed. "Poetry — that is the fateful uniqueness of language," Paul Celan believed, even though he knew his view shackled him to a mother tongue spoken by the murderers of his mother (J. Felstiner, *PC* 170). Like those of Celan, the brilliant and better known poems produced in European tongues appeared first and certainly influenced English writers, many of whom translated their precursors and were inspired by them to produce new works. As we will see, such authors as Paul Celan and Nelly Sachs had a profound effect on their successors. But for men and women of letters who composed Holocaust poems in English, the medium itself emphasizes their linguistic and geographical removal from the catastrophe since, of course, English was one of the few Western languages not generally spoken by guards or prisoners inside the ghettoes, boxcars, camps, deportation stations, gas chambers, mass graves, and law courts that constitute the settings of these poems.

As their linguistic estrangement demonstrates, British and North American poets resemble many other "children of the Holocaust" who, Helen Epstein explains, "were possessed by a history they had never lived" (14). To adopt a term coined by Marianne Hirsch, these writers remain in thrall to "postmemory," which differentiates itself from memory "by generational distance" even as it distinguishes itself "from history by deep personal connection" ("FP" 8).[25] Their remoteness, compared to that of Nelly Sachs, may be quantitative; however, that quantitative difference grows as time passes, space widens, and the Holocaust recedes into the ever more distant past of another continent's history. English-language poets solve the problem of "the principle of discontinuity" and its counterpart, the principle of ongoingness, by foregrounding the challenge posed to representation through a number of strategies, all of which emphasize corporeal absence, aesthetic deficiency, or temporal distance (the "post" in Hirsch's phrase, the "after" in my title) from remote events to which they feel intimately connected. Anglo-American poets' aesthetic mastery of un-mastery exhibits a number of mutations as it admits that the past cannot be changed, but insists that the future can be. The hiatus between "then" and "now," the ruptures in genealogies mourned by confessional poets, the ellipses between the documentary photograph or testimonial and interpretive engagement with it, the gap between dead speakers and living authors: as we will see, these modulations in Holocaust verse constitute the spaces between rungs in a ladder of responses as equivocal about origins and destinations as the one depicted by Chagall, spaces that dramatize the wide chasm between trauma in the past and writing or reading about trauma in the present.

I return to *White Crucifixion* throughout the pages to come because the figures on its surrealistic clock tell a tale about temporality at the place where, the moment when, time ran out for the Jews of Europe. What time was that, which place was that? — this chapter has wondered. In the spot just before midnight or noon, a woman appears on Chagall's watchface, one of the ancients with hands raised in horror. Her uncanny gesture — admonitory? remonstrative? — reminds me of my fourth grandparent: my mother's "real" mother, the mysterious Franziska whose suicide occurred decades before the Second World War, when my mother was only four years old. On a shelf near my writing desk at home I have a sepia-tinted photograph of this being who — for reasons beyond my comprehension — became my muse many years ago. Just as Elizabeth Bishop, when she ups the ante beyond things that "seem filled with the intent / to be lost," writes with no embellishment, "I lost my mother's watch" (178), my mother had at an early age lost the watchfulness of her mother's presence as well as the maternal timepiece upon which she could count her own measure. Just as Bishop's suffering over the breakdown of her relationship with Alice Methfessel must have tapped her earlier devastation at Lota de Macedo Soares's suicide and the still earlier crisis of her mother's insanity, my mother's later losses reverberated with a primal experience of abandonment.

In profile, Franziska smiles enigmatically, shyly, as if caught in a moment of self-reflection not meant to be shared with the camera. Legends abound, if such robust words can be used about a presence remembered only by her daughter and only dimly at that: she was a gifted concert pianist, romantically involved with a fellow musician but forced to make a good match with an up-and-coming doctor, my mother thinks; or, she was depressed by what today is called postpartum depression, by having to take care of her two babies while her husband was away at the front during the Great War, by the contradiction between the staid proprieties of that bourgeois husband and the unpredictable inventiveness of her artistic temperament. Yes, certainly, I concur with my mother's speculations, but her mother's suicide underscores how many of my relatives have succumbed to this fate. And so considered, she cannot easily be contained within an individual narrative.

Did Franziska's arrogant mastery of un-mastery demonstrate the destructiveness of the culture that had formed her and all the rest destined to die? Was she a harbinger of the ruin to come? Framed by her early death, the photograph of Franziska broods mutely over the irrevocability and silencing of disaster. Writing about the silences of the youthful Walter Benjamin — traumatized by the suicides of his best friends in 1914 — Shoshana Felman relates his intellectual trajectory to the vow "to save the suicide from its meaninglessness," to confront how "the traumatized — the subjects of history — are deprived of a language in which to speak of their victimization" ("B" 215, 213). The "Tattered Kaddish" Adrienne Rich composed "for all suicides" was written for Benjamin, for Franziska, and for the others: "Praise to life though ones we knew and loved / loved it badly, too well, and not enough" (*ARPP* 160).

For those of us attempting to acknowledge irreversible losses, poetry refuses and refutes a silencing which would constitute a victory of the forces of evil. Such verse bears the imprint of the parenthetical, italicized imperative in the last line of Bishop's "One Art":

> — Even losing you (the joking voice, a gesture
> I love) I shan't have lied. It's evident
> the art of losing's not too hard to master
> though it may look like (*Write* it!) like disaster. (178)

In the arithmetic of loss — the subtraction of three houses, two rivers, two cities, two lovers — there can be one and only "one art" which may or may not be able to guarantee that the speaker at some future time will be able to believe she has "won" out over her losses. Under the auspices of urgent truth-claims about her odds in that future ("I shan't have lied"), Bishop inscribes her defense of poetry, refuting the homophonic equivalence that might imply such writing can or will right the wrongful calamity. Because of the parenthetical explicative that erupts and interrupts the last line, her repetition of the word "like" informs us, as does so much literature about the Shoah, of the catch in the throat, the stutter on the tongue, the clenched jaw, the gasp of breath that accompanies the effort to express the inexpressible, to admit the futility of analogizing. This is the choked voice uttering what Sarah Kofman called "smothered words": "Knotted words, demanded and yet forbidden," which threaten to "asphyxiate" (39).

Inflected by this stammer, the collaborative achievement of authors who cursed, lamented, and memorialized the Holocaust signals the capaciousness of poetic language, its ability to compel us to experience the urgency of feeling and thinking even at a distance, in fact to make distance the condition of our feeling and thinking about the lethal consequences of racism. In their most moving and, oddly, their most warily tentative works, poets of the Holocaust counter Adorno's judgment by striving to articulate the imprimatur of the incongruous, even at times the unseemly moral imperative of enunciating not one's own but someone else's suffering. And they do so by making the reader fully aware of their own suspicions about the aestheticizing in which they engage. Thus, what sustains their voices is the allusive (even the blatantly illusive) authority of experiences not their own. Without alleviating either grief or guilt, poets of the Holocaust can teach us how to inhabit, at least momentarily, events in history that we can neither escape nor transcend.

3

SUCKLED BY PANIC

Positioned at the bottom of *White Crucifixion* beneath the afflicted teacher, Chagall's mother and child conjure up a long mystical tradition linking Divinity with tender parenting as well as an image of Mary nurturing the infant Jesus. Yet the final cry of a forsaken Christ, his forlorn "Eli, Eli, lama sabachthani?" exemplifies the abandonment of children. Were the mother and baby below him also divided from the infant's father, in their case because he was criminalized (like the man in the billboard) or consumed in flames (like the green-coated refugee)? Viewed from this perspective, the apprehensive woman at the base of Chagall's centrifugal circle may be clutching her bundle out of fear that she will lose her grip — on herself, on the baby cradled in her arms. A *mater dolorosa,* the mother frightened at the inexplicable but imminent rupture of the bond with her child evokes the figure of Sarah in biblical commentary, stunned by Abraham's determination to obey God's commandment — to bind Isaac, lay him on the mountain altar, and sacrifice his living body. Given their implicit promise of a redemptive salvation or wisdom born of painful sacrifices, however, biblical analogues fail to capture the horror of child-survivors, of children of survivors, and survivors of children who feel robbed of the death of the dead, haunted by bruising silences that call into being necessarily disjointed recollections in verse.

The severing of the parent-child bond has become one of the most poignant representational figures used by artists to approach the slaughters of the Holocaust as well as the eradicated future the murdered would have brought into being. When in 1966 the printmaker and survivor Mauricio Lasansky employed only the simplest of materials — lead pencil, earth colors, commercial paper, turpentine wash — to create *The Nazi Drawings,* he began his series with portraits of Nazi killers and then depicted infants howling in unheard anguish. Six feet high, four feet wide, the thirty massive drawings build to a horrific climax in the collage featuring a cruciform shape not unlike Chagall's, but Lasansky moves the mother and child at the bottom of *White Crucifixion* to the central place of affliction (figure 3.1). Now composed of newsprint smeared with blood, the cross resembles any instrument of torture, for an arm (is it the woman's or someone else's?) pulls a string that hangs her upside down on the gibbet. The only legible words in the newsprint, " *'Kill Him,' Germans / Yell at SS Soldier*" can only refer to the baby on her belly. Since Jewish law traces lineage through the maternal line, the dead mother signifies the extermination of Jewish genealogy, the eradication of all those generations of descendants who would never be born.

With her bulging eyes, dangling head, and emaciated legs trussed or shackled like an animal's, Lasansky's mother cannot possibly protect the infant (dead or alive?) clinging to the trunk of her body. Unable to produce milk, the exposed breasts of the persecuted woman offer no nurturance to an offspring who hugs her hips as if to crawl back into the dead womb. If the arm that pulls the string is the woman's, has she decided to kill herself with her child to evade torments to follow? If the arm that pulls the string is someone else's, is she any more or less the instrument of the figure Nelly Sachs called "the terrible puppeteer"?

> Arms up and down,
> Legs up and down
> And on the ash-gray receding horizon of fear
> Gigantic the constellation of death
> That loomed like the clock face of ages. (*AA* 640)

In the baby's later incarnation (figure 3.2), the swollen head and shrunken extremities prematurely age him into a shriveled, bald sufferer transfixed in a silent scream. He resembles the "emaciated skeletons" observed in the Warsaw ghetto, "children swollen with hunger, disfigured, half-conscious, already completely grown-up at the age of five, gloomy and weary of life. They are like old people and are only conscious of one thing: 'I'm cold.' 'I'm hungry' " (Landau 158–59). The tattooed camp number, reiterated at the bottom of the image, is itself the collar or clamp that chokes voice and

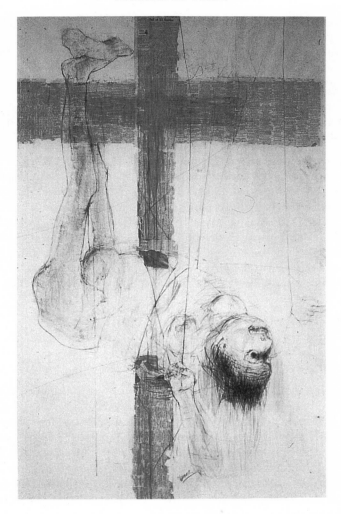

3.1. Mauricio Lasansky, #18 from *The Nazi Drawings*,
75.5″ × 45.5″. © Mauricio Lasansky, Lasansky Corporation,
Richard S. Levitt Foundation.

strangles breath. "O the night of the weeping children! / O the night of the children branded for death!" (*HP*69): Sachs, who in "A Dead Child Speaks" writes of the Shoah as a shocking "knife of parting," portrays a mourning mother whose mind is "torn" and "burnt" as she imagines herself

> Burying her dead child,
> Burying her lost light,
> Twisting her hands into urns,
> Filling them with the body of her child from the air. (*HP*67)

Similarly, the breathless apostrophe of the title and first lines of "O the Night of the Weeping Children!" capture the poet's appalled helplessness at the moment "Terrible nursemaids / Have usurped the place of mothers" so that "Instead of mother's milk, panic suckles those little ones" (*HP*69).

Like Lasansky's and Sachs's, Paul Celan's central image in "Death Fugue" displays the mother usurped, her milk replaced by ghastly panic. Along with his title emphasizing the horror of a camp orchestra being required to play music to accompany grave digging, Celan's opening words stress the surrealism of an enforced swallowing that compels prisoners to ingest indigestible poisons:

> Black milk of daybreak we drink it at sundown
> we drink it at noon in the morning we drink it at night
> we drink and we drink it
> we dig a grave in the breezes there one lies unconfined[.] (*AA* 601)

Within the landscape of darkening air over crematoria, nauseating black milk of cruelty — neither nurturing nor sacramental — is not offered by a maternal breast but administered by a wounding, transcendent male figure, for "death is a master from Germany" (602). At the indistinguishable twilight of daybreak and sundown, at noon and at night, time collapses into the monotony of a forced feeding on sickening dirt, ashes, blood, excrement, carrion, smoke. Celan's German "master" — playing with his serpents, whistling for his Jews, eulogizing the golden hair of Margarete — ghoulishly compels a vampiric draining of grief that turns "ashen" the hair of the black and comely maiden Shulamith (602), a figure of the Jewish people.[1] When the survivor Fanya Gottesfeld Heller contemplated staying in Poland with the Ukrainian who had helped save her life, her gratitude to this man was riddled by a vision of herself "holding a baby to my breast, and my breast and the baby were black with the ashes of their murdered relatives. Black milk came out of my breast" (275).

What might it mean to be transported out of the "horizon of fear" *after* having been "branded for death" as a child? How would it feel to be born to Sachs's maddened mother *after* she had been cut by a grievous "knife of parting" or to be brought up by one of Celan's engorged prisoners *after* he had ingested the "black milk"? North American and British poets employ

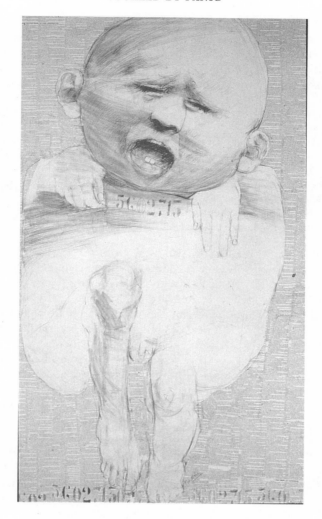

3.2. Mauricio Lasansky, #28 from *The Nazi Drawings*,
82″ × 45″. © Mauricio Lasansky, Lasansky Corporation,
Richard S. Levitt Foundation.

confessional verse to consider their perplexing inheritance as child-survivors and children of survivors. Poets suckled by panic, or imagining babies so suckled, attest to the same confused sense of belatedness that Eva Hoffman articulates in her autobiographical *Lost in Translation,* specifically in a passage describing a family conversation some forty years beyond the war.[2] Responding to a newspaper story about Jews who cooperated with Nazis, Eva's mother — smiling "with her bottomless skepticism" — explains,

> your father's sister was given away by one of them . . . he brought the Germans to the place where she was hiding with her little son. The Jews knew about the hiding places, of course. Your father's brother was hiding with her, and he was on the other side of the wall. He heard the Jew say to the German, "I work well for you, don't I?" Your father's sister was saved that time . . . because she promised to pay them. But by the time she got back with the gold, the child was dead, of course. (252)

Almost half a century and an ocean away from the event recounted, the daughter-listener notes intense reactions to this tale that clarify why it had never been told before. Eva's father goes pale, saying "Let's not talk about these things." Eva herself feels she has done her father "the injustice of not knowing this story," though she can "hardly bear to hear it" or understand "its weight" on his soul (252–53). About her tears over her father's lot, the autobiographer admits, "There's no way to get this part of the story in proportion" because it "could overshadow everything else," and in a curious way did. An acquaintance of her parents' generation once advised her to judge the world by the standard of the concentration camps. However, she believes her own paradoxical task requires a sloughing off of the darkness accompanying her origins but belying her quite comfortable personal condition, for the shadows thrown on the imagination from the source of her life threaten to overwhelm the evidence of her own relatively secure existence.

Many poets of the Shoah, recording its effects on their parents and on themselves, share Hoffman's quandary — namely, her struggle to put into some kind of perspective the disproportionate shadows it casts. What these writers lose in translation when they haltingly tell their families' grim stories they gain in an understanding of moments "which act like time warps permanently trapping all those who are touched by them" (*FW* 192). I will focus in this chapter on Irena Klepfisz — the author of this last quotation — as we consider moving tributes by other child-survivors who mourn the unassimilable deaths of relatives in personal, elegiac poems. But the verse of Klepfisz about living with survivors also directs us to another group of writers: children of survivors who worry about protecting parents whose anguish cannot be integrated into normal existence. Confessional poetry about the Holocaust often contains odd complaints by offspring troubled by their shameful ignorance of the past or resentful about being raised by overprotective parents made depressed by the miseries they endured. Though the shock of parents surviving murdered children cannot be conflated with the tragedy of offspring mourning slain or wounded parents, in either case the "knife of parting" amputates cultural continuity, a psychological and linguistic affliction apparent not only in Klepfisz's meditations on the demise of Yiddish as a mother tongue but also in reflections on wordlessness produced especially by literary women, many of whom express their personal sorrow at the war against the Jews by returning to images of mothers and children suckled by panic. Saturated by grief, the verse discussed in this chapter — whether written by children about dead parents or about parents of dead children — attests to what Jahan Ramazani calls "agonistic mourning" (*PM* 263), the perplexed resentment of the living who chafe at the inexorable burden of bearing the dead.

CHILD-SURVIVORS IN WARPED TIME

In her first volume of verse, *periods of stress* (1975), Irena Klepfisz prefaced a group of her poems about the Second World War with a gruesome tale of her inexplicable origins:

> during the war
> germans were known
> to pick up infants
> by their feet
> swing them through the air
> and smash their heads
> against plaster walls.
>
> somehow
> i managed
> to escape that fate. (*FW* 43)

"Lines like graffiti on a wall," Adrienne Rich calls these two stanzas, praising Klepfisz's "consciousness that, precisely, existence itself is not to be taken for granted" ("I" 15). Klepfisz — born in Warsaw in 1941, hidden by nuns in an orphanage, later passing as Catholic, and eventually brought (via Sweden) to the United States at the age of eight — finds herself "always amazed" at Americans' "certainty / about the past   how it could have been / different," since her experience of losing her father and hiding out with her terrified mother among peasants "who / would have turned us in" convinces her that "you do not know yourselves   you do not know / others" (*FW* 50). For writers in Klepfisz's situation, having lost a parent, homeland, or mother tongue in the Holocaust, the wound of the past consists of silences that will never be broken as well as scenes of death and dying that can never be known. Like Henri Raczymow, whose essay "Memory Shot Full with Holes" presents "memory *as* empty" so as "to restore a non-memory, which by definition cannot be filled in or recovered," Klepfisz describes a familial past that was handed down to her "precisely as something *not* handed down" (Raczymow 104, 103). Bewilderment at being caught up by a discontinuous history, ignorance over the time or place or kind of death suffered by the lost mother or father, anguish at the absence of a grave, guilt over survival — all these factors contribute to the baffled tone of the verse composed by child-survivors seeking solace through recollections and stymied visualizations of the beloved dead.

That a prominently placed poem in her collected works, "Searching for My Father's Body," portrays Klepfisz conducting her search for her father's corpse in the corpus of books about the Warsaw ghetto suggests the futility of the quest because, of course, books contain words, not bodies. And given the capriciousness of what is recorded, even historical accounts are unreliable, for history "depends on who you knew," she explains, "or rather who knew of you" (*FW* 29). Luckily her father's contacts as a freedom fighter in the ghetto ensure that she will find a few details about his past in the indexes of memoirs, information that will furnish the only kind of monument she can hope to obtain. Though she tries to numb herself to the general pain of "strangers' tragedies" by "skimming quickly," a volume without an index means she may "begin to read, despite myself, / and learn a new name, another event, / still another atrocity." Dubious that the research can ever "be done with," she wonders if she will "still insist on carrying / him with me, a thirty-year-old man / who I never knew?" (30). Like the Polish typography used to spell her father's first name and like the italicized quotations from history books embedded in the poem, its footnotes (citing the authors and publication information of the volumes Klepfisz consults) indicate how indigestible the information is, how foreign it remains: not a life or a death but simply archival scholarship, memory reduced to prosthetic words. In stark contrast to the conventional elegiac tradition, where the plentiful paternal inheritance bequeaths power to the poet-successor, Klepfisz's poem underscores how and why other child-survivors feel they have been robbed not merely of an inheritance but more eerily of the death of the dead.

Dori Katz in "The Return" records the growing distance between her father, who died in Auschwitz, and herself, living in the States, as she acknowledges how difficult it is to bear the responsibility of keeping alive his memory:

> The light I turn on to remember you these days
> is small and distant in the dark.
> I go back very deeply for you, and very carefully.
> One false move and I fall off your shoulder
> where I placed myself at three to be carried across
> rain puddles; one inadvertent step and you are gone[.] (*BR* 205)

After putting herself back at the moment of his arrest when there was "No time to say goodbye," Katz describes herself as "Converted," an allusion to her camouflaged Catholicism while being hidden, to the transformation that occurred in her — outwardly "tamed" or obedient but inwardly troubled, a nightly sleepwalker — and also to the mutation of her father, "not Moishe Chaim anymore, not anyone" except the number 177679. Unable to mourn without the certainty of death, the growing young girl escapes into fantasies of reunion with a father lingering for her in a hospital room or on a deserted street. Despite her anticipation that "the dark years" of separation would "disappear," the poet understands herself to have changed places with her father. Whereas he bore the three-year-old on his shoulder, throughout her growing up she has "carried you for years, like salt upon the tongue, / a bitter taste always dissolving, always there" (*BR* 205).

For child-survivors, the absence of a grave and ignorance about a parent's fate mean that living descendants cannot relinquish their attachment to the victims; the dead cannot be laid to rest. Robert Penn Warren's efforts to re-inter his parents psychologically so as to come to peace with their demise — "They must learn to stay in their graves. That is what graves are for" (272) — help illuminate the desolation of children transported to the safety never reached by their unburied parents.[3] Anne Ranasinghe's "Holocaust 1944," which is dedicated to her mother, wonders

> And did you think of me
> That frost-blue December morning,
> Snow-heavy and bitter,
> As you walked naked and shivering
> Under the leaden sky[?] (*GH* 42)

It concludes "I weep red tears of blood. / Your blood" (43). Retrospectively considering her decision to leave her mother in "the desecrated, violated streets / of our conquered city," Gizela Spunberg's "Memories of December" explains that at the time her mother's "was the safe road, mine the dangerous one." Yet the poet is troubled by remorse over her survival: "Did I fail you? Did I betray you by my absence? / Would I have been of any help?" (*BR* 41–42). For Karen Gershon, the line "I was not there to comfort them" leads to the conviction "I must atone because I live" (7). "No sound reached me" is the refrain of "When It Happened," Hilda Schiff's poem about a daughter ignorant of her mother's arrest at the border, then her subsequent journey in a cattle truck to the gas chamber. Schiff concludes with the dreadful logic that what could not be heard in the past resounds in the present: "I was not listening / when it happened. // Now I hear nothing else" (*HP* 137).[4]

The ignorance, regret, and contrition bred by such horrific partings could induce deafness, numbness, and amnesia, or so the verse of Lily Brett demonstrates.[5] In one poem she mourns a youth so shadowed by fear that she cannot hear even the most beautiful music because "for years / I required silence . . . I was waiting / for disaster" (*HP* 126), while in another she registers an anesthetized lack of affect when she records the stunning fact that

> my mother's friend
> patted my cheeks
> and curled my curls
>
> and hurled herself
> from the top
> of a bank[.] (*HP* 124)

In "I Keep Forgetting," despite Brett's remarkable ability to remember trivial phone numbers and gossip, she finds herself constantly needing to consult the books that line twelve shelves in her room:

> I forget over and over again
> that one third of Warsaw
> was Jewish
>
> and in the ghetto they crammed 500,000 Jews
> into 2.4 per cent
> of the area of the city
>
> and how many
> bodies they were burning
> in Auschwitz
> at the peak of their production
> twelve thousand a day
> I have to check
> and re-check[.] (*HP* 138–39)

The unanticipated suicide of the mother's friend and Brett's own loss of feeling, hearing, and remembering reflect in different ways Raczymow's concept of an empty memory "*not* handed down": "There are holes . . . in our genealogy. We have no family trees. At the most, we can go back to our grandparents. There is no trace of anyone before. Whose graves can we go visit? What hall of records can we consult? Everything was burned" (104).

Perhaps the tension between Irena Klepfisz's claims in some works and her subsequent realization of their falsity most poignantly illuminates what it means to try to fill holes in a riddled genealogy. "Solitary Acts," a sequence of poems about her father's sister, employs gardening as a metaphor for imagining growth after transplantation:

> dreaming
> of a perfect garden   of a family tree
> whose branches   spread   through centuries

>of an orderly cemetery   with no gravestones
>missing[.] (*FW* 210)

She who was formed by "many plots of ground" (206) must learn to live with the abrogation of such visions. Klepfisz's word "plots" means graves, of course, cemetery plots either mismarked or missing, but also those multiple narrative plots whose discontinuities punctuate *undzer mishpokhe* (our family). The disjunction between the claims made in "Solitary Acts" — which begins by imagining a scene Klepfisz could not have witnessed, her aunt's 1942 deathbed confession to a priest — and Klepfisz's later admission about the sequence's central factual error stresses the breaks in her lineage. Although Gina Klepfisz was supposed to be buried in a Christian cemetery with an Aryan name, the poems tell us, she revealed her Jewishness to the priest and eventually her body was "rescued from the Christian plot / the only flesh of your family to lie / in a marked grave in the Jewish cemetery": "I cling," the poet admits, "To the knowledge of your / distant grave" (202, 203). Yet the dead woman remains a symbol of the inexplicable "gaping absence" history has become (203), for Klepfisz's later realization that her aunt's body was never actually transported to the new stone carved in the Jewish cemetery — "the grave was never moved (as I erroneously state in my poem 'Solitary Acts' " [*DI* 87]) — highlights how fraught efforts of imaginative restoration remain.[6]

"Gaping absences" in history are the subject of Klepfisz's most ambitious sequence, the long poem *Bashert,* titled with the Yiddish term (meaning "inevitable" or "predestined") that in and of itself speaks of a specifically linguistic loss. What seems inevitable or predestined in this complex series of meditations is the psychological angst induced in the child-survivor suckled by panic. "As a child, I was old with terror and the brutality, the haphazardness of survival" (*DI* 61): before *Bashert* elaborates on this prematurely aged mental landscape, two prefatory sections rely on a formulaic listing that defies the consolation of closure.[7] "*These words are dedicated to those who died*" and "*These words are dedicated to those who survived*" use redundancies that resist any sense of an ending. For those who died, the poet catalogues anonymous numbers who died "because":

>because they played it safe
>because they had no connections
>because they had no faith
>because they felt they did not belong and wanted to die[.] (*FW 183*)

Equally equivocal about those who survived, the poet resists the idea that lessons can be drawn, rules made, axioms derived. Whether death is "a punishment" or a "reward," the "final rest" or "eternal rage" (as at the end of part I); whether life is "a wilderness" or "an awakening," a "struggle" or a "gift" (as at the end of part II), the fate of the dead and the living seems at one and the same time inevitable and indeterminate. *Bashert* insists on the alterity of all the casualties, victims and survivors alike, even as it goes beyond this liturgical framework to ask: After such devastation, how can, *can* living go on?

Four subsequent autobiographical sections, composed of prose paragraphs, answer this question by recording what immigration after the Holocaust signifies to mother and poet, in the process "push[ing] the prose limits of poetry as far as possible" (*DI* 170). In the first, "*Poland, 1944: My mother is walking down a road,*" Klepfisz establishes two major motifs: human existence depends on the fragile fiction of passing as a non-Jew and the equally fragile serendipity of luck. At three years of age, the child Irena has "no awareness that we are playing a part" as orthodox Catholics; however, her ailing mother in search of "some kind of permit" and "carrying her Aryan identity papers" knows exactly how much hinges on a false identity and therefore has "promised herself that never, under any circumstances, will she take the risk" of revealing her Jewishness. Yet "an explosion of yearning" while walking down a road causes the lonely mother "to pierce five years of encrusted history" with another ravenous figure who turns out to be one of Klepfisz's father's teachers: in the midst of the war, "They do not cry, but weep as they chronicle the dead and count the living" (*FW* 189). Unexpectedly, a food package appears after the woman promises "she has contacts." Though the toddler had a life expectancy of only a week, she and her mother "begin to bridge the gap towards life" (189).

Klepfisz's personal history here fits the demographic characteristics distinguishing those deemed Jewish who passed as those called Poles: 69 percent were female, probably because men were anxious that circumcision made them easily identifiable and because daughters tended to be given an "inferior" (Polish, non-Jewish) education compared to that afforded sons (L. Weitzman 201, 204). In this section of *Bashert,* Poland is a world "where no one can be trusted" (Klepfisz, *FW* 189), a minefield governed by permits and faked papers, in which the three-year-old suffers from an oozing ear infection, the thirty-year-old mother from incurable skin sores, the father's teacher from "hunger, the swollen flesh, the infected skin, the rags." Totally isolated, mother and daughter have survived the death of all the other members of their family and can sustain their lives only through the lies made possible by blond hair, blue eyes, and the Polish words in which they pray, ironically, to "the Holy Mother, Mother of God" (187). Like what is spoken, what is eaten cannot nourish: the mother's "terror . . . is swallowed now, like all other feelings," including "her hunger for contact and trust" (187–88). Only cunning suspiciousness can prolong existence in a malevolent no-man's-land. Since nothing but sheer chance brings the father's teacher down the same road as the mother, since only an undeniable "explosion" forces the mother to reveal her identity, no one can take pride in the deliverance, which could not have been planned but simply happens to happen.

The second section, "*Chicago, 1964: I am walking home alone at midnight,*" evokes not only the poet's graduate student days at the University of Chicago but also how during that time she recollected "Elza who is dead" (190). As an eight-year-old left with Polish Catholics during the war, Elza had also been instructed by her parents, "*Never admit who you are!*" and so had vehemently denied her Jewishness until a bribe finally dislodged her from her hiding place and she could be adopted as a war orphan. A loving new family, a fine education, work, marriage — nothing can prevent first depression, then suicide at the age of twenty-five. Klepfisz, kept ignorant at the time by a solicitous mother fearing that she too might succumb to self-destruction, later wonders if Elza missed her fate in Poland only to encounter it in America, trapped in a history that cannot be cheated. The child hidden by passing as Polish had internalized the assumption that Jews mistakenly precipitated their own persecution: in this respect, she lost all ties to her own identity, her own family; thus, when unmasked in America, she found herself deeply alienated from who she was said to be.[8] When the impossibility of counterfeiting without suffering shame and self-division takes hold of the poet's imagination, she decides that "No one simply passes through. History keeps unfolding and demanding a response" (193). The student Irena must have feared, too, that her own efforts at self-fashioning might trap her in Elza's fate. "More than anything," Klepfisz explains in her prose account of Elza's death, "I wondered if our similar backgrounds, similar interests, and the very nature of being a poet indicated that I too would be a suicide. Was it a question of time?" (*DI* 168). Only after she has worked through her grief over the postwar suicide does the speaker of *Bashert* notice her dangerous surroundings: "fringes of rubble" in the Hyde Park ghetto, revealing "vague outlines that hint at things that were." What surfaces, then, is "American hollowness," a perception of "the incessant grinding down of lines for stamps, for jobs, for a bed to sleep in, of a death stretched imperceptibly over a lifetime," and thus "The Holocaust without smoke" (*FW* 193).

As she continues to brood on her relationship between the Old and New Worlds, "*Brooklyn, 1971: I am almost equidistant from two continents*" counterpoints Warsaw with New York City where Klepfisz, now a teacher, appears as the "only white" person in classrooms of black and Puerto Rican students (194). Approaching the age of her father when he was gunned down by the Nazis, Klepfisz records a series of birthdays: her birth (which took place on her father's twenty-eighth birthday), her impending thirtieth birthday (which she associates with her thirty-year-old father's death in the Uprising), and her fourteenth birthday, when she lit a candle honoring murdered children at a Holocaust memorial ceremony in an auditorium filled with "the sound of irretrievable loss, of wild pain and sorrow" (195). The Yiddish names of dead children, called out by "people with blue numbers on their arms," contrast with those of the twenty-eight people in the Brooklyn class-room: not "*Surele. Moyshele. Channele. Rivkele*" but "*Reggie. Marie. Simone. Joy. Christine*" (195). Though not burned, shot, or stomped to death, the poet asserts, the African American and Puerto Rican students in her classes are also ground down, falling behind because of evictions, hospital regulations, sickness, incomprehensible English forms. What she teaches — "Sentence fragments. Pronoun reference. Vocabulary building. Paragraph organiza-tion" (195) — holds out the remedial promise of catching up.

Trapped in a history that cannot be cheated, young people of color have been stymied by a culture that effectively teaches them what the poet and Elza had been told: "*Never admit who you are!*" Klepfisz herself has experi-enced the same tug of self-destruction to which Elza succumbed; however, when she teaches a class composed of students from every conceivable back-ground and must explain who she is, the answer — "A Jew" — educates her to choose neither Europe nor America but instead "the histories of two conti-nents," neither guaranteeing safety (197). Her feeling "of cellular break-down," her wish "to become transparent" like the salt water between Europe and America, is resolved through a definition replacing her earlier self-identification as "the only white"; and "in that moment [when] two vast land masses touch," she feels grounded (*FW* 196).[9] The switch in self-definition — from "white" to "Jew" — accompanies an insight aligned with James Bald-win's that, although "America rescued [the Jew] from the house of bond-age," it *is* the house of bondage for the Negro," who remains "a pariah in his [or her] country" (430, 431). Klepfisz's suicidal wish "to become trans-parent" dissipates as she takes on "muscle, flesh, bone" in an America that "is not my chosen home, not even the place of my birth" (*FW* 196). In Baldwin's terms, she has achieved embodiment after the transplantation of immigra-tion to the United States, but refuses to pay the "price of the ticket," which "was to become white" (xx).

But history has instructed Klepfisz that safety can never be more than temporary, the final section of *Bashert* explains. Trapped in breathless mo-ments during which she feels she "had just tricked someone, but was afraid the ruse would be exposed and I'd be hunted again," the adult matures in the work's conclusion by recollecting Elza hiding behind a Catholic mask but being told by a suspicious Polish shopkeeper that her accuracy about money raised his suspicion that she is "*perhaps a little Jewess.*" Clarifying her ongoing dialogues with the dead, "*Cherry Plain, 1981: I have become a keeper of accounts*" reinvents Elza through a poetic identity dedicated to the idea of accuracy, for Klepfisz becomes a quintessentially Jewish keeper of "scrupu-lously accurate" (*FW* 198) accounts and distinctions. First she looks at de-spised Jewish men — pawnbrokers, Shylocks, merchants — portrayed hag-gling over their coins or demanding their pound of flesh, while they studied legalized bigotry to try to sustain quarantined lives within the prescribed limits; then she turns to detested Jewish women — peddlers, widows, run-aways — presented chiseling for a subsistence, while they begged for their children and "understood the accounts but saw them differently": men whose "zloty, francs, and marks could not buy off the written words *Żyd, Juif, Jüde*"; women "who knew the power of the words *Żyd, Juif, Jüde*" (199). The foreign, repeated label as libel reeks of an obscene international calumny.

Adopting the role of "bookkeeper of the dead," Klepfisz claims as her legacy those old specimens most people assume gone, images she finds in photographs of people ragged at the elbows or ashamed in a coarse wig, figures reduced to absence in an empty landscape:

> The shabby clothes. Buttons missing. The elegant stance. Diamond rings. Gold teeth. The hair being shaved. The face of humiliation. The hand holding the child's hand. A tree. A track. A vague building in a photograph. A facility. And then the fields of hair   the endless fields of hair   the earth growing fertile with their bodies   with their souls. (200)

A breakdown in syntax, accompanied by pauses punctuating and expressing loss, represents the consciousness triggered whenever the eyes of strangers grown "distanced with curiosity" make Klepfisz feel "alien" (198, 200). Types rarely seen any longer, the photographed faces of humiliation can be revived in epiphanic moments through a Whitmanesque self, opening to contain multitudes: she can "shed my present self   and all time merges" (200) through a new subjectivity consisting of a community of presences, as the poet reincarnates the homicidal stereotypes of the past.

In a reverie about Othering, Klepfisz compares Jews in Europe with people of color in America by emphasizing a camouflaging technique (passing), internalization (self-blaming), and scapegoating (the construction of a pariah class). Art Spiegelman's *Maus,* which originated as an effort to present American blacks (not European Jews) as mice, makes ironic the same series of analogies. For although Artie's father, Vladek, has to pass as a Catholic in the first volume, although he clearly internalized anti-Semitic values, although he had been made into a pariah in "Mauschwitz," once in America he engages in the racism that makes him "talk about blacks the way the Nazis talked about the Jews" (1:99). Like *Maus, Bashert* uses its meditations on European versus American styles of discrimination to reject simple solutions to racism. Klepfisz refutes the "melting pot" model of assimilation, in part because she refuses to see emigration to America as an arrival at the promised land, in part because she views ongoing Jewish identification as psychologically crucial to survival. At the same time, by resisting the conflation of whiteness with Jewishness, by establishing analogies between Jews and people of color, *Bashert* complicates multiculturalists' pigeonholing of separate oppressions and ghettoized ethnic identities. A phrase Adrienne Rich has used about herself as an offspring of a Jewish father, a non-Jewish mother—"split at the root"[10]—applies to Klepfisz's attentiveness to Old and New Worlds, past and present. Her epiphany—"I teeter shed my / present self and all time merges"—comes less easily to survivors' children who did not themselves endure the humiliations of the past. Yet they too cope with parents whose message revolves around the lesson Klepfisz's mother learned and taught, that "survival / depends on complete distrust" (*FW* 172).

CONFESSIONS OF CHILDREN OF SURVIVORS

The subject of Klepfisz's anxiously enduring mother with her "mastery of daily survival" (*FW* 204) shifts attention from what it means to be a child-survivor toward what it means to be the child of survivors. While Klepfisz felt her father's and aunt's deaths had been stolen from her, she also portrayed her mother as a survivor robbed of her living. To the elegy about her father at the beginning of her collected volume, *A Few Words in the Mother Tongue*, Klepfisz attached a poem titled "The Widow and Daughter," which depicts the father's death as a fracture in time for his wife and daughter—two who do not "live" after it so much as they "survive" in altered, alienated states. Back in the Warsaw apartment with her youthful husband, the mother sang love songs, read novels, received sisters, dreamed of unborn children, and looked forward to intellectual discussions. The contrast between the expectant, cosmopolitan wife before the war and the anxious, widowed refugee in New York is marked by the three-room apartment with its ivy-covered fire escape:

> To this apartment
> which chained them
> welded them
> in a fatal embrace
> the missing one
> returned at night. (37)

Haunted by her father's ghostly presence, the poet believes the "missing one" to be the crucial link in their confinement, tenaciously clutching at the fire escape, staring out from his photograph on the wall, penetrating every corner of the small apartment. Ambivalence toward the dead father—he is both the heroic legend who fought the Nazis and the deserter who abandoned his family—may account for his pressing between and oppressing the mother and daughter "so when they sat down to eat / they could taste his ashes" (38).

The poem "1945, The Silence" by Burton D. Wasserman can stand for many texts that take as their subject the quandary of writers who identify themselves as the progeny of parents blighted by the war against the Jews.

Wasserman describes how a letter from Poland "seized my mother / Read itself aloud in her quivering / Voice" until "she fell," at which point his weeping father "Emptied its final silence / Into our mouths" (*BR* 97). Though his little sister asks, "Why did the Nazis kill mama's family?" no answers are forthcoming. At the age of thirteen, the poet suddenly "saw my parents / As smaller than life." As if changing places with his mother, the boy helps put his mother to bed at the end of the poem:

> We all carried mother to bed;
> For months after, we tried to reason,
> To love her, to beg — but she
> Would not listen
> Or become part of us again:
> She had become
> The Silence. (97)

Cast down before their child, the parents stricken by the letter look suddenly vulnerable, a waning in suffering that makes the child understand the fragility of the adults and feel the need to protect them. The brittle helplessness and reticence of parents may puzzle children paradoxically taking care of the supposed caretakers.

When not baffled about the inexplicable catastrophe into which their families are plummeted, the confessional poetry composed by North American and British children of European Jews shaken or shattered by the Second World War can take on a tone of exasperation at their needless overprotectiveness. "My father won't talk about the numbers," Gregg Shapiro explains with some vexation in "Tattoo"; "Instead, he spreads himself over me / spilling his protection, like acid, until it burns." To the son, paternal solicitude feels less like a shield or shelter than like a painful torment or burden, as well as a generational barricade:

> We don't breathe the same air
> speak the same language
> live in the same universe
> We are continents, worlds apart
> I am sorry my life has remained unscathed
> His scars still bleed, his bruises don't fade[.] (*BR* 201)

The child parents the parent in Wasserman's and Shapiro's verse because the Holocaust inflicted pain that weakened survivors while effectively muting their ability to express their suffering.[11]

Poets historicizing a generation gap widened by the disaster exhibit varying degrees of remorse and anger that stem from the speechlessness, depression, and paranoia pervading their childhoods. Lending insight into offspring troubled by the impossible burden of making up for an irreparable injury, the psychologist Nadine Fresco — in her case study of eight

Jewish people born in France between 1944 and 1948 — analyzed the damp-
ening effect of a "silence [which] formed like a heavy pall that weighed
down on everyone" in families suffering from the "anachronistic hold of the
present on [an intolerable, inexplicable] past" (418, 420). "Parents explained nothing, children asked nothing. The forbidden memory of death
manifested itself only in the form of incomprehensible attacks of pain."
According to Fresco, the

> silence [of parents] seemed proportionate to the horror that had annihi-
> lated members of their families, while they themselves had escaped. It was a
> horror that prevented them from talking either about the dead, or of any-
> thing but the dead — as if life itself had been confiscated by those disap-
> pearances. It was an impossible mourning, "wounds of the memory" of
> parents frozen in silence, behind their dry eyes. . . . They transmitted only
> the wound to their children, to whom the memory had been refused and
> who grew up in the compact void of the unspeakable. (419)

Jean-François Lyotard's claim that Holocaust art "does not say the unsayable, but says that it cannot say it" (*H*47) furnishes the aesthetic analogue to
the familial silences Fresco views as "an impossible mourning."[12]

The title as well as several poems in Jason Sommer's *Other People's Troubles*
grapples with the psychological and poetic consequences of growing up
within the "void of the unspeakable." "Joining the Story," for instance,
recounts a childhood roped to the violence of a father who "joined / / the
ends of his belt" to beat the tardy boy because "the angry beating / of his
heart was fear" inspired by severe abuse the father had suffered decades
earlier in a labor camp (19). Writing without self-pity about himself in the
third person, Sommer admits:

> Later, he'll want the father to recall the story
> of his little beating, though how can the son enjoin
> him to? He cannot say, On this date my beating
> happened — you frightened your son with your hands
> and your belt. He knows his father's resistance
>
> to memory. His father has forgotten that beating
> when his son, late, took the story from his hands,
> joining it after the worst and without resistance. (20)

In adulthood, the child, who was late merely because he had "forgotten
time," understands his father's willful amnesia and so refrains from asking
what his father "cannot say"; instead, he uses his verse not to chastise his
father but nevertheless to hint that his own childhood beatings com-
pounded the earlier, more horrific abuse suffered by his father. Similarly
attentive to his belatedness, in "Lifting the Stone" Sommer imagines himself a modern Theseus, trying to extract the events of his father's prior life as
if they were huge stones or boulders. Whereas mythic Theseus uncovers his

heroic birthright of sword and sandals under the stones, the excavation of a past the poet never knew proves only his own diminishment: beneath the stones and inside the "rooty dirt," he finds "sword and sandals, but / they are tiny-baby shoes, a toy sword" (22).

The verse of *Other People's Troubles* illustrates a point made by Sonia Pilcer about the second generation: "*Secretly, we believe that nothing we can ever do will be as important as our parents' suffering*" (135). Sommer's long sequence of poems, "Mengele Shitting," ambitiously maps the sense of estrangement instituted by an uncle's declaration that even the poet's name is an eclipsed after-the-calamity construction — " 'You think *that* is your name — *Sommer?*' " — and by his inability to ask what the uncle meant, for

> I was used to the etiquette
> around survivors. Those who'd been through
>
> the European fire could speak or not,
> or any combination of the two. (34)

Exiled from his own identity, the poet recounts stories of his relatives during the Shoah: of his uncle's suicide attempt, which paradoxically ended up as life saving; of his father's perplexity at miming his Jewishness to Russian officers "with no idea of what a Jew is" (38); of his Aunt Lilly whose eyes he cannot meet when he breaks "the etiquette / forbidding anyone to ask for speech / when speech is memory and memory is pain" to ask about the fate of his father's younger brother Shmuel (39). After forty years of silence, Aunt Lilly locates the time frame of Shmuel's death, but not the exact date during the two-day transport to Auschwitz, for "*there was shooting / many times, many times the train would stop*" and "*No one thing happened I could tell from where I was*" (42).

Though the poet wants to believe his works are an offering to those who continue to withhold words from him, he understands his verse to be

> a complicated gift likely to give offense,
> or perhaps no gift at all
> since I hope you'll never see these words.
> Your pardon, Lilly, anyway
> for bringing these things up again,
> also for retelling
> what you know better than anyone,
> out here where others listen,
> as if it were something of my own. (47)

Despite Sommer's anxiety about capitalizing on his relative's memories "as if they were" his own, what he eventually offers her is a just denouement for the "handsome, courtly" man whose gloved thumb jerked her toward the line of those selected for a life-amid-excrement at Auschwitz. If not providence then a grim sense of schadenfreude permeates his recounting of Mengele's physical deterioration after the war, which took the form of bowel problems: "So Mengele shitting would have to lean forward with his precise fingers in his rectum / to guide stools past, sometimes, of course, not stools but a pouring over his hands, / hot as his own insides, bathing him as he should be bathed" (49).

This "symmetry that will pass for justice in its absence" constitutes a telling about "a small hell in the body" that Sommer conceives so as to make his muted relatives "rejoice" (50, 49). At times, though, the "impossible mourning" recorded by children raised by Jews deported from meaning evolves into estrangement from dejected parents and grandparents who never again will trust the world to cooperate with their wishes. Louis Simpson's "A Story about Chicken Soup" captures the confused feelings of Americans who are themselves made small by their shame over not fully assimilating into daily consciousness the disastrous events inflicted on their relatives. Beginning in a tone of decorous etiquette blatantly at odds with the rupture of the Shoah, Simpson explains that the Germans killed his grandmother's family in "the old country," though "I know it's in bad taste to say it" (*BR* 179). Like Eva Hoffman, Simpson needs to slough off the excess darkness cast by haunting presences making "some demand" on him:

> They want me to stick in their mudhole
> Where no one is elegant.
> They want me to wear old clothes,
> They want me to be poor, to sleep in a room with many others —
>
> Not to walk in the painted sunshine
> To a summer house,
> But to live in the tragic world forever.[13] (179)

Children instructed that they should thin their blood of desire or hilarity so as to expect only the hardships of deprivation often express a sense of "growing up haunted," as Marge Piercy puts it in the title of one poem. Looking back on her adolescence in the fifties, Piercy recalls her "grandmother's cry / when she learned the death of all she / remembered." Not only did that outcry make "Fear . . . the underside of every leaf / we turned, the knowledge that our / cousins, our other selves, had been / starved and butchered to ghosts," but those ghosts gathered at the foot of her bed every night to speak to her as a muse would:

> What you
> carry in your blood is us,
> the books we did not write,
> music we could not make, a world
> gone from gristle to smoke, only
> as real now as words can make it. (*TR* 305)

Although for Piercy her grandmother's starved and butchered relatives in-spire the words to make their lost worlds real, other women poets feel hopeless about dealing with the distressing influence of mothers who had suffered through the Shoah, a phenomenon observed by Aaron Hass in his book on the second generation, *In the Shadow of the Holocaust:* "Investigators have reported that communication from parents about their Holocaust experiences affected daughters more adversely—making them more de-pressed, anxious, and withdrawn—than sons" (80).[14]

A number of women poets mourn the madness instilled in mothers made overly controlling by the lingering effects of dread and despair. Two poems by Sari Friedman, for instance, present maternal survivors' apprehension about a malevolent world threatening to their children's well-being, since disaster must always be assumed to be imminent. The hectic mother's voice in "Answering Machine Message" records dreams of the Nazis coming to take her away, tells her daughter how beloved she was at birth, exclaims "You don't know / what they did to babies then," and pleads for a return call (*GH* 103). Bargaining, blackmailing, and guilt-tripping do not diminish the poi-gnancy of the mother's need to reconnect with her alienated American child. The offspring in "Skin" has survived the mother's inexplicable angers as well as her suicide attempt. That "time you tried to kill yourself," the daughter-poet explains, "I dragged you back," though "What was left of you / didn't want to exist" (*GH* 104). Because "I am your American child," an uncrossable fissure divides the mother and her progeny: "I cannot know. / I am not you" (105).

"She is screaming again" is the first line of Hilary Tham's poem about "the daughter of survivors," who is "afraid of this trembling woman / who replaces your mother each night" when "Her dream claws her sleep to shreds" (*BL* 387). "She papers the kitchen with pictures of bodies / tangled like insects in ditches," Lisa Ress explains about her caretaker; "This could be you, she tells me. / I am a child, I say. I am not / supposed to know this" (*BL* 308). BonniLee's "White Candles" and Evelyn Posamentier's "Count-ing Backwards" also express daughterly dread of the burdensome past shared by troubled mother-survivors. In "White Candles," the daughter watches the pacing, cleaning, crying mother, knowing "She was always / inside / bitter" (*GH* 73). Except when reciting prayers over the Sabbath candles each week, the prematurely aged mother engages in pointless ac-tivities to keep herself going: "removing gold speckles / from the formica counters," for example. At the end of the poem, even the singularly peace-ful memory of the candle lighting becomes contaminated by another, more malevolent match:

> I remember
> how the house smelled
> after my mother lit the match

with her head
inside an oven
    filled
        with gas
And the neighbors poured in
the stench
of her private holocaust
causing them all
to remember. (75)

Centered not on a suicidal mother-survivor but on a suicidal daughter of a mother-survivor, Posamentier's "Counting Backwards" begins with a memory of herself at six years of age, being dragged against her will to the synagogue by an Orthodox mother who believed the child "had the head of a thirty year old" (*GH* 115). The next stanza, a recollection of her own "suicide face" at thirteen, contrasts the adolescent's self-absorbed misery with the mother who simply snaps on the radio: "we always ate lunch quietly." The third stanza advances to the older daughter, now sixteen, exposing to her mother "the nightly horror films" playing in her head:

you said that i
thought too much
was influenced by the wrong crowd
didn't really have much to complain about considering
i didn't come from a broken home (or anything like that)

& besides, what did i think the young girls
did in dachau? (115)

Guilty about her comparatively secure lot, how can the maturing daughter complain about her banal problems, given the torments endured by the girls in Dachau? Yet the animosity of the final two lines of "Counting Backwards," presumably spoken in the daughter's mimicry of her mother's cadences, may derive from her counting back to the mother's original degradation, perhaps to her own origins.

Despair and hypervigilance, features of the eerie principle that Fresco calls "substitution," reflect not only the suspicion of survivors that existence has been achieved at the cost of the suffering of others but also the intimation of their offspring that their own births somehow underline the deaths of those who had been killed. At the end of Spiegelman's *Maus,* when the survivor-father says to his artist-son, "It is *enough* stories for today, Richieu" (2:136), he unconsciously illuminates this idea that the living son to whom he is actually speaking (Artie) constitutes an insubstantial simulacrum of the little boy (Richieu) poisoned some forty-five years earlier by an aunt who sought to save him from the death camps. Far from becoming the dead and therefore worshiped son, however, Art must experience the poignancy of his not being Richieu and of his not adequately compensating his parents for the loss of that first child — or so the poets of this experience intimate.[15] Mothers and children share a complex sense of culpability when they understand their presence to underscore the extermination of other relatives, the demise or absence of lost family members.

"In the milk of my mother I could not drink — / were salt tears for her sisters": born amid what her refugee parents considered the relative "haven" of the London Blitz, Karen Alkalay-Gut diagnoses her infant "colic" as an inherited grief; "when I was born I wept, / and could not be comforted / for those who died before my birth" (9). However, this disease — associated with inexplicable infantile rage and pain — lingers on in later life, exasperated by her witnessing the lively tourist industry at German concentration camps:

> Tourists at Dachau read the sign:
> WHILE YOU'RE HERE, WHY NOT
> VISIT ALSO OUR FOLK ART EXHIBIT?
> Now there's another course,
> Holocaustics, someone smirks,
> an "in" subject
> for bored, inured teenagers.
>   My mouth
> remembers eleven aunts and uncles
> gone. (21)

Disturbed not only by the foreignism of the translated ad, with its blindness about what might link Dachau to "FOLK ART," but also by the devolution of the Shoah into tourist and pedagogic industries, educational "courses" into "Holocaustics," Alkalay-Gut turns away from caustic anger in the conclusions of a number of her autobiographical poems, expressing the belief that "When I get old I will speak / Yiddish like my mother" (16), the

> hope I will
> revert to the old tongue —
>
> the prayer shawl of words
> from a world of wholeness. (30)

Lyn Lifshin simply titles one poem about dead siblings "For Years Her Parents Never Said a Word about It" (51). Two babies gassed by Dr. Mengele haunt the mother of another poem by Lifshin, a refugee who responds with rage at an illness threatening her daughter's well-being a number of years after the war; the poem's speaker is first the second-generation daughter and then the daughter miming her survivor-mother:

> No
> drugs in Israel, no
> food, I got pneumonia,

> my mother knocked the
> doctor to the floor
> when they refused,
> said I lost two in
> the camp and if this
> one dies I'll kill
> myself in front of
> you. (*GH* 83)

With characteristic understatement about the ferocity of a maternal love tangled in the knots of a genocidal past, the poet relates her youthful inference that

> once you became a
> mother, blue numbers
> appeared mysteriously,
> tattooed on your arm. (83)

Even more horrified by a maternal devotion so intense that it threatens to annihilate those who inspire it, Judith Hemscheyemer describes a mother who "dreamed we were drowned / Or covered with spiders / Or butchered or tortured" (157) so she "took us all to bed with her." The mother's fearful love, "a prairie fire," roars over her children's horizon, "Burning us out of our burrows." The title of the poem — "The Survivors" — hints that the conflagration the children barely manage to endure is not the Holocaust but what it did to their mother, whose pathologically anxious devotion means

> She had to consume us utterly
> Over and over again
> And now at last
> We are her angels
> Burned so crisp
> We crumble when we try to touch[.] (157)

THE LOST *MAME-LOSHN*

While the plight of mothers like Lifshin's or Hemschemeyer's rings changes on Sachs's and Celan's verse to define the brutality of the Shoah as the perversion of a matrilineage that would have meant a sustained Jewish future, the fact that the mother ordinarily teaches the infant its first words has led a number of women writers to brood over the linguistic consequences of fascist commands severing mothers from their babies.[16] Along with Irena Klepfisz, such poets as Marilyn Hacker and Carolyn Forché, Sharon Olds and Jorie Graham believe that the "knife of parting" wounded language, that "black milk" effected a pollution of the symbolic order. According to these authors, a child "suckled by panic" ingested the inadequacy of symbolization itself: in their works, in other words, divorce from the nurturing protection of the maternal comes to signify not simply a painful relinquishing of intimacy with the first other, the mother, but also an estrangement from signification itself. That refugees from the disaster had to learn new languages in the process of abdicating their native vocabularies, that immigrants were forced to translate their experiences into idioms felt to be perpetually foreign, only underlined the connection between the child's loss of the mother and the loss of the mother tongue, whether it was Yiddish or Polish, German or Romanian. Even more disturbing was the idea that language itself — the ideal of interactive human communication and communion originally generated through and within the coupling of mother and baby — had been nullified by a standard issue, state-based lexicon of command, a spurious but lethal *patrius sermo* in the "Fatherland."

Cynthia Ozick's "The Shawl" can serve as a touchstone here, prefacing the less widely known work of the poets. A very short story that reads like a prose poem, "The Shawl" focuses on female characters first on a forced, freezing march and then incarcerated inside a concentration camp so as to describe the drying up of milk, the cracking of nipples, ravenous hunger, and the emergence of an ardently treasured yet pitiably inadequate "transitional object" to represent the lost breast — specifically, a shawl that mother and child manage to invent as a shared symbol of the nurturance the mother cannot confer, the child cannot receive. Starving and thus unable to nurse her infant, Rosa can merely give Magda a scarf that the infant "sucked and sucked, flooding the threads with wetness. The shawl's good flavor, milk of linen" (4–5). Her lone possession, the shawl becomes "Magda's own baby, her pet, her little sister," a flimsy protection against the other prisoners whose ravenous hungers (Rosa fears) would steal Magda to eat her. Its very capaciousness of meanings reveals the shawl to be the child's first effort at symbolization. By the end of the tellingly brief narrative, when the fifteen-month-old and previously mute child rises on pencil legs to search for the shawl she has imaginatively converted into a surrogate source of sustenance and not only walks for the first time but speaks as well, both signs of her development doom her to destruction, as Rosa watches a "helmet" and "a pair of black boots" hurl Magda toward an electrified fence (9).[17]

Although the tormented Rosa attempts to envision the child as a "butterfly touching a silver vine" (9), the "wolf's screech" ascending on this mother's tongue can be stilled only by stuffing the murdered Magda's shawl into her own mouth. "The Shawl"'s epigraph from Paul Celan's "Death Fugue" draws attention to the ingestion of the indigestible, the swallowed screech of grief that saves Rosa from a bullet but that dooms her subsequent living to a life-in-death conversation with her dead baby. The mother, who has drunk "the milk of linen" and silenced the sounds that would also condemn her to death, tragically becomes the ravenous, abandoned issue of her destroyed offspring. As in Celan's "Black Flakes," the pathetic reversal of the mother imploring her absent child for a thin shawl triggers the textual weavings of Ozick.[18] Recalling Kepfisz's poem about Germans smashing the heads of infants against plaster walls, Magda's fate occurs precisely at that moment when she copes with the loss of her "milk of linen" by speaking a syllable that sounds something like the beginning of her own name, something like a call for her mother. Entering the symbolic order of language sentences the child to death. As the baby's first metaphoric object, then, the shawl represents the murderous defilement of symbolization during the Shoah, the catastrophic assault on meaning making inflicted by it. Unable to supply milk, the shawl cannot replace the nipple but instead becomes a shroud, worshiped in place of the murdered infant by a mother crazed by grief.

Ozick, who affixed the story "Rosa" to "The Shawl" when she published the two together as a book, emphasizes in the sequel the spoiling of all the languages buzzing in Rosa's ear after the hum of the fence's voices growl over the fallen Magda. Like Klepfisz's "The Widow and the Daughter," Ozick's "Rosa" contrasts expectant living in Poland with anxious, depressed surviving in America. In postwar America the bankrupt academic prose of the Holocaust investigator, the immigrant English Rosa uses with her niece, the literary Polish of her letters to Magda, the Yiddish of Florida newspapers: any and all words appear to be "parasites on the throat of suffering" (37). Desperate to convince herself that Magda was not the result of the rapes inflicted by Nazis, determined to believe that Magda lives and prospers, Rosa has become a cantankerous, peevish madwoman. The lyricism of "The Shawl" contrasts with the gruesome humor of the short story "Rosa" because, as the mourning mother herself knows, "Before is a dream. After is a joke. Only during stays. And to call it a life is a lie" (58).[19] Unlike "Rosa," perhaps "The Shawl" reads like a poem because it resides with "during," which "stays." At the end of "The Shawl," when Rosa stuffs Magda's shawl into her mouth so as to stifle a screech that would get her shot, the stilled mother's scream is replaced by the "electric voices" of a fence that begins "to chatter wildly." In place of the baby's pleading call, "Maaa-," Rosa hears what she must resist: commands of "Maamaa, maaa-maaa" that would lead to her own demise. Whether or not it is guilt at disregarding her infant's first cry for help that causes Rosa to interpret the electric voices as a reproach, as Hana Wirth-Nesher has speculated, the loss of this mother's tongue constitutes what Emily Dickinson called an "infection in the sentence" (316, J. 1261) that Ozick's contemporaries mourn as an exile: banished from exterminated native languages, literary women lament their adoption of alien, impotent, or hideously mechanized idioms.

According to Irena Klepfisz, who grew up (like Rosa) as a Polish speaker, what the "knife of parting" amputated was the mother tongue of Yiddish. Klepfisz's frequent use of the caesura—a widened spacing between two words marking a kind of hesitancy or stammer in speech unable to communicate the experience described—visually emphasizes the difficulty of finding the right word in a language learned in later life. An interrupted life, like a broken culture, spells a discontinuity that Klepfisz addresses through bilingual verse that extends her use of blank space on the page. Klepfisz, who was taught Polish by her mother and managed to pass among Polish Catholics precisely because she did not speak Yiddish, mourns Yiddish as what Raczymow calls "a non-memory," by definition beyond recovery. "*Kashes* / Questions," in the sequence "*Di rayze aheym* / The journey home," best illustrates the complexity of navigating between experiences from the Old and New Worlds through the visual columns in two lists kept by this "keeper of accounts"—the left hand in an italicized (implying Jewish) Yiddish, the right in an (implying Christian) English printed in roman type:

> *In velkhn yor?*
>
>   in what year?
>
> *Mit vemen?*
>
>   with whom?
>
> *Di sibes?*
>
>   the causes? (*FW* 220)

The causes and conditions of genocide remain puzzling questions, unanswerable in part because the speaker finds herself at the end of the poem

> *tsvishn fremde*
>
>   among strangers
>
> *oyf der zayt*
>
>   on this side
>
>   *tsvishn meysim*
>
> among ghosts
>
>   *oyf der zayt*
>
> on this side.

In its final two lines, the two languages exchange places but remain separate. Klepfisz mourns the *khurbn* (the destruction) as a perplexing divide for those who find themselves among strangers in English, among ghosts in Yiddish. Within the gap that is a kind of chasm between the inscribed columns, the unassimilable resides: the impossibility of transporting Yiddish as a vital idiom into the English-speaking world, the demise of Yiddish as a living language.

For Klepfisz, as for Jerome Rothenberg, who titled his long sequence of Holocaust poems *Khurbn,* the Yiddish term sounds differently from the Greek "Holocaust"—with its connotations of a burnt but miraculously unconsumed sacrifice offered to God, a word that might be thought to sacralize or sanctify the event as providential.[20] *Khurbn* resonates distinctly, too, from the Hebrew "Shoah" (meaning "desolation") — with its connotations of a link between Zionist claims to a homeland in Israel and the need for a secure refuge from the catastrophe of European anti-Semitism, a logic that also might be thought to interpret the event as propitious. After her use of *Bashert* as a title alerted Klepfisz to the tension between the Continental Jewish experiences she sought to describe and the English language she was employing, she began to realize "how the Holocaust had robbed my generation of the language and culture which should have been our natural legacy" (*DI* 171). Because the success of her passing during the war depended on her fluency in Polish, Klepfisz lost Yiddish as her "*mame-loshn*" from the very start. Yet the "Yiddish word was important, for . . . it resonated with *yidishe geshikhte,* Jewish history, linking the events of World War II with *der ershter un tsveyter khurbn,* the First and Second Destruction (of the Temple)" (*DI* 145).

In a different context, as an anthologist of Native American poetry, Rothenberg has observed that "To submit through translation is to begin to accept the 'truths' of an other's language. At the same time it's a way of growing wary of the lies in one's own" ("P" xviii). In the case of Yiddish, however, those truths and lies either have vanished or are about to perish because this idiom — likened to a "museum" in one of Cynthia Ozick's stories — has been excised from the tongues of the Jewish people: "Of what other language," the narrator of Ozick's "Envy" asks, "can it be said that it died a sudden and definite death, in a given decade, on a given piece of soil?" (42). Klepfisz's writing presents the untranslated Yiddish to accentuate the American reader's need for vigilance with respect to what has not or cannot be spoken in our English lexicon, our American cadences. Although Klepfisz's translations are meant to animate the dead letters, they paradoxically demonstrate how far removed we are from the communities of Yiddish-speaking people who (in the words of Ozick's "Envy") were "Lost! Drowned. Snuffed out. Under the earth. As if never" (51).[21]

Unlike German or French, Yiddish — Jonathan Boyarin has pointed out — "never enjoyed legitimation as a state language, and it has never served as the cultural double of a military power" (*TJ* 120–21). The idiom of a scattered group, a language without a land of its own, Yiddish flourished through the linguistic hybridities invented when disparate, distinct populations throughout Europe interacted. In opposition to normative notions of national idioms, "Yiddish is international. Yiddish is a border-smuggler; it really is a language for transgressors; and that's why they didn't let it live" (199). Klepfisz, who broods over a vernacular shattered into fragments by mass murder and forced dispersal, transliterates phrases to smuggle bits of Yiddish inside the borders of English verse, thereby marking their power but also their impending erasure as well as her own status as "a nomadic polyglot" (Shreiber 282). Yet, demonstrating her inability to write the whole poem in Yiddish, confirming how wrecked the idiom is as a living legacy, Klepfisz uses isolated Yiddish words — no longer in their Hebrew characters—to emphasize their dislocation from the communities that used to speak them, their status now as fossils, specimens, shards of what had been an evolving tradition.[22] For, as Raczymow points out,

> a few words of Yiddish do not constitute a legacy, but merely a remnant, the "next-to-nothing" that remains of what was lost. It is the proof or the mark of the loss—its trace. So a trace remains. In turn, we can lose the trace. Lose loss itself. Lose, if you will, the feeling of loss. And dissolve into nothing. (100)

Refusing to "Lose loss itself," Klepfisz instructs us to consider what is lost in translation:

> Think of it: *heym* and *home* the meaning
> the same of course exactly
> but the shift in vowel was the ocean
> in which I drowned. (*FW* 228)

The poem in which these lines occur, "Fradel Schtock," is a dramatic monologue produced by Klepfisz as if issuing from an actual Yiddish poet who fears getting lost in the "babble" resulting from "using / *alley* when you mean *gesele* or *avenue* / when it's a *bulevar*." Prefaced by an epigraph by Czeslow Milosz—"Language is the only homeland"—the confusion and consternation of Klepfisz's precursor reflect her own sense of linguistic exile. An only child who has remained childless, Klepfisz has found it painful to be told "you-are-the-last-of-the-line" (*DI* 11); however, her bilingual verse—cradling the stillborn mother tongue within her adopted English—represents the "last-of-the-line" for a Yiddish that is incomprehensible except to a dwindling number of native speakers and scholars. Like Klepfisz and Ozick, other contemporary literary women brood on the last-of-the-line by mourning the fate of mothers and children rendered wordless in a diabolical fatherland, bringing to the surface the horrific ways in which the figure of children divorced from mothers remonstrates against lethal forms of legal as well as linguistic authority. Their exceptionally nuanced works of art grieve over the destruction of innocence by focusing on the frightful silencing of children, the ruin of the living languages they inhabited, and the traumatic consequences for the writer who attempts to find a voice to utter the unuttered or perhaps the unutterable.

Espousing elliptical reticence over lies, the opening sequence of poems in Carolyn Forché's complex book, titled (after the figure in Walter Benjamin's essay) *The Angel of History,* frames the destruction of children with a death of language that has devolved into snatches of incoherent memories issuing from difficult-to-apprehend subjectivities. Forché's response to the farmhouse in Izieu, where forty-four children were hidden for a year that ended with deportation to Poland, remains resolutely oblique. After quoting the translated words of Elie Wiesel—"*the silence of God is God*"—she emphasizes her own inability to forge an original, sufficient utterance of her own by reiterating Wiesel's French: "*le silence de Dieu est Dieu*" (5).[23] The fragmentary quotation echoes off the "Hotel-Dieu" near Notre Dame, where her desolate maternal characters reside; reverberates with their real-ization, born out of the abnormality of mothers outliving their children, that "*Le Dieu est un feu*" (7); rebounds against the growing conviction that "*God is insane*" (22); reflects on a birth that makes "God's name *a boneless string of vowels*" (14). Polyphonic and fractured phrases link the ruin not only with a German Jewish refugee and another unnamed woman separated from her child but also with grotesque anti-births, with Gothic rooms "*filled with vultures. / They were hopping about the room, belching and vomiting flesh, / as you saw them at Puerto Diablo and El Playon*" (15). The allusion to "body dumps" in El Salvador here connects the genocide of the Jews with a disaster that dramatizes to Forché contemporary culture's complicity in the ongo-ing history of the Shoah.

What such a shattering of sense means to the composing process is also the difficult subject of Marilyn Hacker's "For a Fiftieth Anniversary," which interpolates a French woman's memory of a wrenching parting from her mother:

> Seventeen then, she's sixty-six, alive
> this year to give her testimonial:
> "Two days after the Fête de la Bastille,
> I mean, two days from when it would have been,
> another year, before the occupation,
> I watched my mother and my brother leave
> — the orders said 'all children under sixteen'
> and 'no unnecessary conversation' —
> on what had been a city bus until
> they gave it a new route, to the Vel d'Hiv.
> I didn't see either one of them again."
> — and the jew squats on the window sill[.] (*WN* 61–62)

The irony of the Bastille celebration reverberates with the last line of this documentary poem, a quotation (repeated in all of its stanzas) from one of T. S. Eliot's more blatantly anti-Semitic works. Depicted as a thieving toady, the image of the Jew functions, according to Hacker, like that of "the Paki or the nigger or the spic" (61), contaminating not only the citizens of all of the unreal cities of Europe but also the language of Anglo-American verse.

Klepfisz's grief over the demise of the mother tongue, Ozick's over the shroud of the symbolic order, Forché's over the Angel of History silenced by the murder of forty-four children, and Hacker's over the corruption of pub-lic signs decreeing " 'no unnecessary conversation,' " of canonical poems in which "the jew squats" — all bespeak the trauma of the Shoah as a linguistic disaster denying mothers and their children the possibility of expressing their anguish. Sharon Olds, who writes in an autobiographical manner and in so doing foregrounds the relationship of contemporary mothers and daughters to those who suffered half a century ago, continues to stress the agony of childhood's end as a language crisis with which the poet must contend, albeit in a manner as mediated as Hacker's interpolated testimonial. Olds's "The Window" begins with a phone call from her daughter, who has just visited a Holocaust site in Poland and finds herself in tears and in a rage that her mother once wrote as a Jew "*when you're not, that's so cheap. You're right,* / I say, *you're so right*" (26).

In the conversation that ensues, the italicized words express the adolescent recounting her nausea at using a bathroom in a barracks she identified as one she had seen in a Holocaust documentary, her dread that "*rooms hadn't been dusted, it was* / *as if everything was left as it was,* / *and some of the same molecules* / *might be there in the room,*" her horror at exhibit cases with heaps of hair, eyeglasses, and the suitcases of those who "*had believed . . . they were going . . .* / *on vacation.*" But what distresses the daughter the most:

> *There were people not*
> *crying, just looking,* and then
> she says there is something wrong with her,
> so much feels unbearable.

The contrast between the daughter "seeing" — actually perceiving and feeling — what others just "look at" fills her with fear that the mother must allay with tender explanations that appear at the conclusion of "The Window":

> I try to tell her that it was not weakness,
> it was love she felt, the holiness
> of each life, and the terror and dread
> of our species. *Yeah, yeah,* she says,
> in the low voice of someone so lately
> the young in the nest, so soon the nesting one,
> within her view the evidence
> of the ark consumed, and no thought of herself
> to distract her, nothing distracts her, not even
> the breathing of her own body as she sees. (26)

Through the innocent transparency of her seeing, the daughter furnishes a window for the mother-poet into her own earlier, though now problematized, identification with Jewish suffering. What the mother — through the daughter's vision and the umbilical cord of the phone — discerns is a landscape behind glass of "human hills and mountains" (26), the intimacies of bodies, needs, and possessions replaced by a "detritus" of hair, eyeglasses, suitcases. Because "so lately / the young in the nest," the daughter takes in the horror of the ark of the covenant "consumed," the sheltering vessel (of the divine promise, of the law, of the boat) provided to humankind by God wasted, incinerated, but also put on display for consumers. Her fear that "*some of the same molecules / might be there in the room*" suggests that — like those observers who look without seeing and, worse yet, like the victims turned into detritus — her own transparency will be clouded over as she grows up, dusted by the film and filth of history. As she matures into adulthood, might she lose her voice on the phone, which reverberates "like water / being forced under great pressure, from densest / stone"; her sobs "like someone swallowing gravel"; her sounding "as if a pebble could talk"? A witness of "the horror of the human," the daughter plumbs the ground of her being at a depth in which human consciousness cannot endure, a bedrock of "the terror and dread / of our species" that the poet may tap but not express as her own.

In one of the autobiographical poems Jorie Graham wrote about the Shoah, an early identification with a traumatized girl furnishes the occasion for coming to terms with her uncertainty about the past and about her present poetic profession. Initially, through its title, "From the New World" emphasizes the poet's distance from the events of the Holocaust, her perplexity at hearing the testimony given in a 1987 Israeli courtroom by John Demjanjuk, a guard at Sobibór accused of being Ivan the Terrible, who had hid out in America. Beginning *in medias res,* the opening lines of the poem —

> Has to do with the story about the girl who didn't die
> in the gas chamber, who came back out asking
> for her mother. Then the moment — the next coil — where the
> guard,
> Ivan, since the 50's an autoworker in Cleveland,
> orders a man on his way in to rape her (*DUF* 106)

— shuttle to a kind of stall or check when the poet directly addresses her readers, worrying about our calloused apathy about such faraway, gruesome events ("Are you there in your stillness? Is it a real place?" [106]) as well as the possibility of shaping poetic form out of them. Although that sputtering stall reflects her greater remove from the catastrophe, Graham's account seems neither more nor less horrific than Lily Brett's recounting of an infant who survived gassing because she was "sucking / quietly / on the breast" from which she is detached by guards before her skull is fractured and she is hurled on a trolley "on / top / of // another / mother" (*BL* 120).

"God knows I too want the poem to continue," Graham admits, detailing her concern about transmuting "the story" of the girl and the guard through the consolation of aesthetic form ("the silky swerve into shapeliness / and then the click shut") as well as the commodification of sincerity on which the genre of lyric may inevitably rely ("will you buy me?" [*DUF* 106]). As the text, using the language of filmmaking to call attention to the poet's splicing of shots, mediates between news stories, artistic perplexities, and personal recollection, the girl who survived gassing reminds the poet of the time in her own childhood when her grandmother, already ill, asked to be introduced to her, declaring "*no, you are not Jorie.*" The young girl locked herself into the bathroom,

> . . . to be held in it as by a gas,
> the thing which was me there in its chamber. Reader,
> they were all in there. I didn't look up.
> they were all in there, the coiling and uncoiling billions[.] (107)

Stripped of her name, the child who was Jorie but not-Jorie eerily understands those who stepped out of their existences when they were inexplicably robbed of their identities.

Not unaware of the differences between the narratives,[24] Graham nevertheless wants to resist any closure that would lock the past into a tidy ending. Throughout, therefore, the locking of the bathroom door echoes with other clamps and clicks, like the earlier click of a well-wrought poem's conclusion: the clicks of the phone her grandfather used when he was "put" into a "Home," never to come out alive; of the clasps of the pocketbook her grandmother grasped when she was "put" into another "Home," never to come out alive; of the camera photographing the Israeli courtroom's witness, screaming "it's him it's him" at Ivan, who had sent the girl who came out alive back in; of "the ending / wrapped round" those who had to step into the gas chamber when the "fable . . . clamps down" (*DUF* 107). The long sentences sprawling over the line breaks constitute what Helen Vendler calls "a poetry of middleness, of suspension," whereby Graham emphasizes her taxing effort to postpone closure, to sustain the urgency of her own "coiling" meditations (Vendler, *B* 80).

The testimony that brings the little girl back out of the gas chamber initiates "something completely new," the poet assures herself at the poem's end; but "*Like* what," she wonders:

> *like what*, I whisper,
>
> *like* which is the last new world, *like, like,* which is the thin
>
> young body (before it's made to go back in) whispering *please.*
> (*DUF* 109)

With the repeated word "like," a "choked-off whimper" (*RP* 184) reminiscent of the one Seamus Heaney hears at the end of Bishop's "One Art," Graham attributes her own doomed search for analogies with the polite word whispered by a motherless girl, as if a modest "*please*" expresses the heinous abnormality of the mother already murdered, the daughter about to be killed. We in the New World ("Are you there in your stillness? Is it a real place?") do not have the last word or, indeed, any word except those based on blatantly inadequate comparisons to comprehend "the fable as it clamps down" (*DUF* 107). Ensconcing the poet in a "region of unlikeness" (the title of the book in which this poem first appeared), the old-fashioned word of courtesy puts the lie to the New World of America and to the promise of finding the new words of a sufficiently fresh language for the miraculously saved but soon-to-be-sacrificed child, since the newness born in the episode is unlikeness itself.

What the German word for please (*bitte*) invokes in the English language (bitter) resounds at the end of Graham's text. Not simply unlikely, the Holocaust is like nothing else: it cannot be taken into consciousness through the usual models of comparison, parallelism, symmetry, similitude, metaphor, resemblance, correspondence. Even the sacrifice of Isaac or of Jesus cannot stand for the senseless murder of 89 percent of Europe's Jewish children. Graham's poem directs attention to the contradiction between the Shoah — an event defying all analogies — and literature itself because, as Alvin Rosenfeld puts it, "Whether we know it or not, we read and understand literature . . . with implicit reference to and analogy with prior texts" ("PHL" 14). To Graham's "*like what,*" the Holocaust presents an acrid region of unlikeness. Rosenfeld derives from this tension between the Holocaust's singularity and the metaphorical impulse of the imagination a "strain of irreality" that often undermines Holocaust literature as well as a "revisionary and essentially antithetical" literary paradigm that causes Holocaust writing to refute aesthetic antecedents, since the aesthetic undermines the authenticity of testimony (21, 22).

Repudiation does figure in the poetry of second-generation poets, whose personal recollections about the dead robbed of their deaths and the living robbed of their livings had to deviate from conventional scripts so as to dismantle the Nazi project to obliterate the genocide by expunging it from history. Haunted by the mute howls of Lasansky's child, second-generation poets record "cries we do not hear" not because they are frozen with fear and exhaustion, as Charlotte Delbo was when she witnessed the condemned shouting in her direction without a sound reaching her, but because, like Delbo, they know these grievous protests came from those whose "vocal cords had snapped in their throats" (34). But Graham's work points beyond repudiation toward two other tropes that play prominent roles in its service. Emphasizing the "strain of irreality," the shots of cameras as well as the testimonial evidence from an Israeli trial in "From the New World" typify the tendency of poetry in English to embed visual and auditory documents into verse that attests to the futility of the poet's imaginative task. For the supremely realistic genres of the photograph and the deposition are felt to be needed — albeit inadequate — records to authenticate the occurrence of a nightmarish rupture in reality. That the camera and the affidavit produce forms associated with legal and medical contexts heightens Holocaust poets' attention to a criminality so heinous as to need continual proofs, a pathology so malignant as to require perpetual treatment.

ABOUT PICTURES OUT OF FOCUS

Remembering the Shoah poses a host of perplexities about the most realistic mode of representation. Besides furnishing precious images of lives later damaged or destroyed, photographs provide indispensable evidence that the inconceivable did in fact occur. Their testimonial value as records of the disaster's multiple calamities consists in documenting the empirical truths of genocide and thus forestalling any who would deny it. But photographic pictures inevitably displace the materiality of the past, decontextualizing a scene from its settings and fragmenting it. And their perpetual circulation can numb viewers made callous by overexposure to a limited set of images. Finally, photography's purported neutrality was contaminated by its complicity in domination. When put to eugenic uses for so-called racial improvement, in other words, Nazi cameras camouflaged or inflicted suffering. All these points have been amply demonstrated by a number of thoughtful intellectuals who, following the logic of Walter Benjamin, understand that the reproducibility of photography (as opposed to the uniqueness of the artwork) enables it to reach a wider audience, to compass more varied classes of subjects, and to serve the state.[1] Although a photograph of Marc Chagall's *White Crucifixion* is mechanically reproduced in this book,

99

the vast majority of books about the Shoah contain photographs of photographs, not of paintings. Beauty or lucidity of design may accrue to a celebrated artist's canvas, housed in a famous museum and signed in colored paint, but truth clings to flimsy copies of black-and-white papers picturing people who actually existed in the specificity of their contingent lives. Photographs and the debates swirling about them therefore play a prominent role in Holocaust remembrance.

Less noted in the conversation about the paradoxes of photography are the contributions of contemporary poets and photographers, although these artists have found various ways to express the affective, emotional consequences of the epistemological and ethical issues tackled by the theorists. By emphasizing the ironic insufficiencies of crucially important Holocaust images, their work dramatizes the hiatus between the "then" of primary documents not of the artists' devising and the "now" of perplexed critical and creative engagement with them. The aesthetic maneuver they employ is what I will term "antimorphosis" in verbal and visual art, which trains us to realize the urgency of keeping in the mind's eye what cannot possibly be presented to us on the page or in the picture. What the artists of antimorphosis demonstrate (in quite various ways) is how to reconcile, on the one hand, our urgent need for the evidentiary photograph and, on the other, our equally urgent need to comprehend the limitations of its value.

Consider, by way of understanding this complex aesthetic tactic, Jochen Gerz's invisible Holocaust memorial as described by James E. Young, one that involved engraving the names of missing Jewish cemeteries on cobblestones that were first removed from a town plaza and then returned, but placed with their engraved face down: Gerz's monument attempts to keep images of the past "out of sight and therefore . . . *in mind*" ("AR" 50). This is close to but not exactly the approach of artists of antimorphosis, who attempt to keep images of the past *partly* or *obliquely* in sight and therefore *in mind*. Unlike *ana*morphosis (an image deformed so that it can be viewed without distortion only from a special angle or with a unique instrument),[2] *anti*morphosis involves artists in the manipulation of visual images so as to critique ocular authority, to hint that an undistorted viewpoint will never be restored. The *ana* ("back" or "again") of anamorphosis signifies an unsettled perception forming anew, an optical correction; however, the *anti* ("against" or "opposite") of antimorphosis balks reformed or resolved perception. Photography described but not exhibited in Holocaust verse, as well as warped or defaced images in photographs, constitutes an occlusion or skewing of the visual that cannot be rectified by an alternative vantage or device. No matter how or how long or from what distance or position you peer at these works, you cannot clearly or fully perceive their pictures. Such qualified images hint that a realistic view of the Shoah eludes us, that our progressive temporal removal fails to put it in a proper perspective. Artists of antimorphosis critique perspectival illusion so as to concede the futility, voyeurism, or complicity contaminating representation in and after the Holocaust. Yet through recirculations framed by their rationales (which, we will see in this chapter, vary in ramification), poets and photographers assert the continual, vital importance of visual documentation of the Shoah.

Edward Bond's "How We See" begins to explain the grounds for skepticism about ocular authority. He claims,

> After Treblinka
> And the *spezialkommando*
> Who tore a child with bare hands
> Before its mother in Warsaw
> We see differently[.]

The contrast between men fighting "for kaiser and King" in "a world asleep in mist" and the Nazis inhabiting a domain "of electric lights cinemas planes and radios" means "We see racist slogans chalked on walls differently / We see walls differently" (*HP* 156). That we see sight differently, too, after the "Final Solution" helps account for the centrality of not-exhibited visual documents in poetry after Auschwitz as well as a reliance on visual distortion in contemporary photography. To gauge more fully why we see sight differently after Auschwitz, factor into the massive propaganda produced by Nazi "electric lights cinemas planes and radios" the later phenomenon that Patricia Yaeger calls "consuming trauma": few events in modern history were as recurrently circulated in visual forms, both "then" (by the Nazis) and "now" (in popular culture). Whereas the fascists employed stills, movies, logos, and posters (as well as the radio, the loudspeaker, and the gramophone) to devalue the importance of print (Gilroy 156–59), artists of antimorphosis question the veracity of the image. To prove the "sexual immorality" of a depraved race, the fascists used whips and guns to produce photographs of Jewish men and women "imitating the sexual behavior of animals"; to demonstrate Nazi benevolence, they staged documentary films of "light-hearted and joyous" ghetto life (C. Kaplan 332, 335). Artists of antimorphosis therefore interrogate the accuracy of visual technologies. Because poets can be expressive rather than mimetic, they are able to communicate feelings, if not directly about the Shoah, about representations of the Shoah. Because photographers can incorporate paint, slides, writing, installation-related setting devices, and darkroom techniques applied to photographs of photographs, they are also able to express sentiments, if not directly about the Shoah, about representations of the Shoah.

A "double operation," according to Allan Sekula, photography's "system of representation [is] capable of functioning both *honorifically* and *repressively*" ("BA" 6). The Holocaust pictures that concern contemporary poets and photographers can be categorized by means of this polarity, with the purportedly neutral documentary located at a sort of midpoint: honorific images, with which I begin, are thought to preserve the selfhood of endangered or destroyed people before they were trapped in the "Final Solution," while repressive images, with which I conclude, derive from genocidal environments that debased the self into a pathologized type of the Other. In both cases, though, we will see that the double operation of antimorphosis—positing a form that is simultaneously thwarted or balked—disturbingly links the honorific with the repressive, the selfhood of the portrayed casualties with their alterity. In images neither overtly honorific nor regressive but supposedly neutral in their evidentiary claims, this double operation also dramatizes photography's positive and negative effects. Theorists of photography have often reflected on the paradox that, on the one hand, photographs contain a mystic capacity to resurrect the deceased; Roland Barthes believed that this "mediator of the truth" creates "that rather terrible thing which is there in every photograph: the return of the dead" (9). But, on the other hand, they also stress that photographic images deaden the living; Susan Sontag felt that exposure to certain images anesthetizes so that "a part of [one's] feelings tighten; something [goes] dead" (*OP* 20). Meditations about honorific, prewar portraits tend to view them as enlivening mediators of the truth, whereas those about repressive, wartime surveillance shots judge them to be deadening simulations. Yet both enlivening mediators of truth and deadening simulations are withheld, bracketed, or partly eclipsed by artists of antimorphosis, as are documentary photographs.

Precious as family albums seem to descendants secure in a present from which they attempt to connect with ancestors fragile in the past, grievous as evidentiary documents and grotesque as mug shots seem to contemporaries secure in a present from which they try to connect with strangers fragile in the past, missing photographs-inside-poems as well as disfigured photographs in installations highlight the necessity of documenting the otherwise unimaginable and the difficulty of doing so, the need to put in its place merely belated, fractured, indecipherable versions of an often enigmatic reality. When poets analyze the not-there photograph, when photographers present the patently doctored, enlarged, or creased and worn picture, they curiously replicate survivors witnessing the indiscernible scenes of an arrested, arresting past so injurious it can neither be fully assimilated at the time nor fully comprehended retrospectively, even though the aesthetic techniques of meta-photographic artists brandish their distance from (their relative safety from) the grievous past. If, as the Bible states about evil, "he is a witness whether he has seen or known of it" (Lev. 5:1), then the obligation to achieve justice cannot be limited to eyewitnesses. At the same time, by recording their own belatedness, their dependency on eyewitnesses, contemporary poets and photographers grapple with the second generation's temptation to steal, consume, or envy memories not their own. Whether they attend to prewar family portraits, post-liberation documentary photographs, or Nazi archives, these artists place themselves and their audience in the position of being—if not the "survivor by proxy" Robert Jay Lifton believed himself to be when he felt haunted by the sources he studied for his book *The Nazi Doctors* (interview by Caruth, 145) — at least proxy-witnesses.

ECPHRASIS

Many poets and photographers, rejecting Nazi-produced photographs of the victims, attend instead to visual archives that date from before the disaster. Their critique of ocular authority derives from the honorific images they seek to keep out of focus and in mind by means of antimorphosis. One reason not to reprint *private* documents — to preserve their impact by dramatizing through their absence from our physical eyes their abiding presence in the mind's eye of the author — illuminates the poignant potency of the not-exhibited photograph for a theorist like Roland Barthes. In *Camera Lucida,* Barthes identifies the medium with grief that he protects by not reproducing pictures that put him in touch with his own sorrow. Barthes writes about his search for a photographic likeness that could serve during the period he mourned the death of his mother, and when he finds such an image he refuses to put it in his book because "For you, it would be nothing but an indifferent picture. . . . [I]n it, for you, no wound" (73). As Barthes intimates, when he explains about the faded picture of his mother that stimulates "a sentiment as certain as remembrance" (70), photography retains a precious record of the real as it once was, as it had to have existed at a time gone by.

Verse descriptions of and responses to precious, unexhibited photographs in Holocaust poetry are instances of what is ordinarily called "ecphrasis" (the verbal description of a specified visual work). The "ecphrastic reading of photographs," according to John Hollander, generally attends to the "*facticity*" of the image (*GS* 293). In the context of Holocaust photographs, however, ecphrastic poets attend less to the facticity of the particular image than to the perplexing contradiction between our reliance in the present on visual documents from the past and their inadequacies of conveyance. Since, as W. J. T. Mitchell puts it, "words can 'cite,' but never 'sight' their objects" (154), the distress of personal grief causes ecphrastic poets of the Shoah to stress that their poems cannot repair the deficits of the visual. Autobiographical poets brood on family photographs taken before the Shoah in a manner that stretches beyond the confines of the confessional mode, for antiquated pictures of missing relatives blight the sentimental illusion that remembrance can sustain genealogical continuity.

In the grip of a protectiveness about cherished portraits that Roland Barthes explained, autobiographical poets use the photographic lack to stand for the eradication of a past of their own. Worrying in "Solitary Acts" if she has "mourned / enough" or "looked at the old / photographs enough," Irena Klepfisz emphasizes how little they tell her about the past:

> And who would say   that I have mourned
> enough   that I have looked at the old
> photographs enough   yellowed and faded
> and the green ink   now a grey dullness
> where Marek   placed the flowers
> on the rubble   where my father's body
> was buried and disappeared   and Marek's head
> looking down   his profile   etched against
> an empty horizon   for there was nothing left[.] (*FW* 205)

Old, faded, dull images of "nothing left" reveal an emptiness that ecphrastic poems formally replicate. Klepfisz goes on to recount once asking her mother if she could have the album that "holds more than most have who are / without a witness"; and when her mother had passionately replied, "this stays here in this apartment / until I die," the daughter-writer "glimpsed again the urgency / to be known" (205). The word "witness" here implies not only that the absent photograph in the poem may function as a marker for those absent ones who died in unmarked places but also that the extant photograph in the album may serve as a witness for the living, one that testifies to the survivor's identity in the present as an extension of an otherwise obliterated genealogy. The mother needs to possess the people portrayed in the album's photographs in order to be impossibly "known" by them and to know herself, since they anchor her to a past from which they say she is torn.

When poets use ecphrasis to describe honorific prewar images of their ancestors, they lay bare the photographic record as what Rosalind Krauss has called "an agent in the collective fantasy of family cohesion" (56). Such an archive or album gives us a simulacrum of Jewish families at the very moment they were being defined as foreign malignancies in the family-nation of the *Volk*. Just "brownish imprints," murdered uncles and aunts in the family album remain unknowable, according to Leo Haber, since "Photos do not show / height or even weight, only depth, and sometimes // the sequestered soul" (*BL* 9). That final shots of soon-to-be-dead relatives picture people still convinced they would have lives left to live shocks Amos Neufeld, too, as he looks at snapshots of his father's family:

> parents, brothers and sisters.
> (The gas and sealed cattle-cars
> are still two years away.)
> They smile. (*GH* 59)

For Haber and Neufeld, the family album illustrates the pitiable innocence of the living-about-to-be-dead faces that prove how little the camera can steal from time. Because flat, fading pictures distance the observer from those so flimsily delineated, Leslie What, contemplating a photograph of the aunt she named her daughter after, suspects she wants "that picture to be black and white. / I want to think it happened long ago and far away / to someone else" (*BL* 311). Obviously dated from a period before the Shoah, portraits within family albums, within the Ejszyszki "Tower of Faces" put together by Yaffa Eliach at the United States Holocaust Memorial Museum, and within historically important published collections — of long-ago marriages and funerals, faraway vacations and graduations, sporting events and business ventures — fail to record the fates of those destroyed in it. Similarly, autobiographical poets can only speculate on the specificity of the destinies of the ancestors whose likenesses they study.

For a character in Irena Klepfisz's play *Bread and Candy: Songs of the Holocaust,* the photographs in Roman Vishniac's extraordinary volume *A Vanished World*—taken during the 1930s, with a hidden camera—speak to a realization that cause and effect "don't apply" in the midst of genocide, that "Logical sequence and development are completely inappropriate" (25). Vishniac, who "knew that Hitler had made it his mission to exterminate all Jews," took over sixteen thousand photographs ("All but two thousand were confiscated") to save a record of Jewish communities he knew he could not rescue, for "The memory of those swept away must serve to protect future generations from genocide" (n.p. [pref.]). Vishniac's book dramatizes a disjunction between cause and effect that bespeaks the abyss between the vanished world that was and the present world that the book's viewers inhabit. Especially when its subjects look back at the spectator, Vishniac's scholars, shopkeepers, and urchins seem to transcend the discursive uses to which they can be put, rebuffing belated narrativizing.

Time may be stopped in these images, but their ambiguities hint that photography — despite its promise to resurrect the dead or oppose temporality with a transfixed moment of being — cannot "break the monopoly which history today has over time" (Berger and Mohr 109). Because the photographic medium frustrates narrative continuity through the still, because its "art of quotation" contrasts with the painter's "art of translation" (111) — the astute terms are John Berger's — the random scene caught on film depends on the happenstance of the moment, rendering the illogic of a quotidian that remains unexplained. Whereas a painterly "translation" announces itself as an imaginative interpretation of reality, the fragmentary "quotation" of a framed photo presents only a fraction or slice of a reality stamped as actual, specific, but bafflingly contingent. Although the veracity of the photo as trace or remnant of the real imbues it with special charisma, not merely its muteness but also its wresting a part from the whole invites interpretive words; such an invitation explains why so many more artists meditate on photographs than on paintings of the Holocaust. Photographic quotation produces the discontinuity that calls out for, yet refutes the explanatory language of the poem. The gaps between shtetl life in the Old World and assimilated existence in the New World only widen with our knowledge of the camera hidden from the eyes of Vishniac's subjects. Their "misunderstanding" (the photographer's word) of the prohibition against making graven images, that photography had not been invented at the time their moral law (the Torah) was composed, and that some of the villagers had never heard about cameras or movies — these circumstances explain why Vishniac himself felt "transported several centuries back in time" during his travels in Eastern Europe (pl. 132), why we today feel they convey us even further back into ancient times.

When we put Vishniac's visual images into a conversation with verbal responses to them, it becomes clear that since the photograph quotes from a specific scene at a particular moment in time, it begs for an interpretation, though it can never be fully explicated by any after-the-fact explaining. Even when the task of filling the lacunae between "then" and "now" presents itself as a moral imperative, the mysterious Otherness of photographic images of people meant to be honored as individual subjects can never be fully voiced by the poet. Increasingly distanced from contemporary writers, Jewish people who would become the victims of genocide are further marked by alterity when pictures feature girls and women to reflect Roman Vishniac's realization that Hitler had targeted for extermination "especially the children and the women who could bear children in the future" (n.p. [pref.]).[3] Kirtland Snyder engages the dichotomy between image and word by bringing the thoughtful interiority of language to the puzzling externalities Vishniac displays.[4] Although the poet uses his suppositions to find some solace in Eastern European people presented not during the Shoah but in the rich ghetto life preceding the "Final Solution," his texts remain perplexed by inexplicable details because of the photographic quotation's irrefutable ambiguities.

Snyder's "Selma . . . A Pot of Soup . . . A Bottle of Milk. Lodz, 1938" (*BR* 28), for instance, considers the dichotomy between pre- and post-Holocaust consciousness with respect to the fates of young girls, in this case directing the reader to scrutinize Vishniac's portrait of a child on the way home from a neighborhood store (figure 4.1). The lines "Look / how Selma holds" appear twice in the poem, asking the reader to consider the milk ("so white! / so cold!") and the soup in the pot ("Can you smell it? Barley!") beneath her shawl ("keeping its warmth / for the walk home"). Though the poet assures us that "Selma's smile / is all we need / to know her happiness," various details in the photograph continue to draw his troubled attention, specifically around the eyes a "swelling / sleeplessness" and on the forehead a mark "that seems / a bullethole — // what of that?" (28). Surely just a

4.1. Roman Vishniac, *Selma was sent to the store for a pot of soup and a bottle of milk. Lodz, 1938.* From *A Vanished World,* 1983 (New York: Farrar, Straus and Giroux). Used by permission.

smudge, another viewer might think about the blemish? scar? scratch? under Selma's hairline. But then other ominous details surface: the cloak too big for her (where is her mother?), the blurry man in the background (what do the posters direct him to do?), the tip of the pot (how full can it be, if she carries the soup without fear of spilling?), the size of the milk bottle (how many must it feed?). The writer's somewhat belligerent and inconclusive "what of that?" punctuates the angry sense of ignorance and impotence that Vishniac's portrait has induced.

Also containing a reference to Vishniac's *A Vanished World* in its borrowed title, Snyder's "City Children at a Summer Camp. Slonim, 1936" evokes the photograph it describes (figure 4.2):

> The naked girls
> lift their arms
> above their heads.
> Are they under
> arrest? (*BR* 25)

With a reminder of the famous photograph of a young boy under arrest during the 1943 surrender of the Warsaw ghetto, Snyder rouses and refutes its terror. While part of that boy's alarm may have derived from the Nazi shooting his picture,[5] the girls (probably unaware that they are being photographed by Vishniac) are only "showering / at the Jewish camp." But the word and act of "showering" at a potentially ominous "camp" are replete with horror for the viewer, a dread that would clearly be unfathomable to Vishniac's unsuspecting subjects. Snyder's belief that they "could be Dresden / dolls" (25) similarly works to draw attention to the marmoreal beauty of the upraised arms and fingers, even as it reminds us how easily such appendages would later be wasted, branded, broken, or burned. Of course, any picture circulating in what Eduardo Cadava calls "the afterlife of the photographed" anticipates mortality, but this shocking effect of the image as a "farewell . . . permanently inflamed by the instantaneous flash of death" (13) becomes heightened, given the dire circumstances Vishniac's children will face. A sign of his discomfort either with his own voyeurism or with the photographer's, Snyder's abrupt conclusion — "No fruit to come, / ever, / from their plump vulvas" (*BR* 25) — emphasizes the disparity between the girls' unself-conscious fleshiness and the viewer's intimation of skeletal, naked girls and women in countless photos like those produced at the Nuremberg trials.

No matter how honorific in intent, Snyder's poems suggest, Vishniac's portraits may invite sentimentality, even prurience, and certainly they seem meager in the information they contain or convey. Although photography freed representation from the class privileges of painting, its mechanical reproductions were responsible for an adulteration of the authentic and singular original into its multiplied versions, as Walter Benjamin first pointed out: what "withers in the age of mechanical reproduction is the aura of the work of art. . . . By making many reproductions [optical technology] substitutes a plurality of copies for a unique existence" (*I* 221). Photographs could be said to deprive Vishniac's subjects of the "aura" of the one-of-a-kindness associated with high art and with interiority. Jason Sommer's

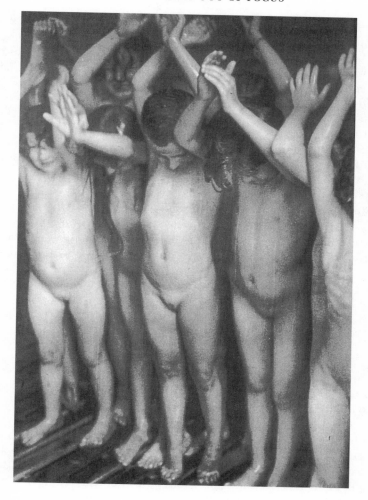

4.2. Roman Vishniac, *City children at a summer camp sponsored by the TOZ (Jewish Health Society). Slonim, 1936.* From *A Vanished World,* 1983 (New York: Farrar, Straus and Giroux). Used by permission.

ecphrastic poem about a 1937 street scene in *A Vanished World* emphasizes how that "aura" can only be faintly recaptured by viewers of the photograph instructed by those who personally knew its subjects in real life and who therefore can assuage the blank misgivings the picture arouses, sustaining our attention in a more than cursory manner, much as the ecphrastic poem itself does. Only those who experienced the pictured places and people of the past can make the photograph meaningful in the present.

Next to plate 123 of *A Vanished World,* Vishniac's caption states: "Every Jewish community adopted its own 'fool,' a mentally retarded person unable to care for himself. All the neighbors would look after him in turn. Rabbi Chaim Yosef (a handkerchief protects his fur hat from the rain) has invited the famous fool Meyer Tsits home for dinner. Mukachevo, 1937" (figure 4.3). Since there are no children in Vishniac's frame, the very title of Sommer's poem, "Meyer Tsits and the Children," brings into focus what the picture excludes, as do the other details related to the poet by his father, who "recognizes for certain" in "the gone world of Roman Vishniac's book" only

> the village idiot of a Munkacs neighborhood,
> Meyer "Tsits," whom they used to tease:
> "Your mother has breasts,"
> the children would say as they passed,
> and frothing with rage he would give chase
> some years before breasts and Meyer were ash. (7)

About the picture of Meyer "contentedly on his way to a meal," the father interprets the expensive sable hat, "a *shtreimel*" protected from the rain by a draped handkerchief, as a clue to the occasion ("it must be *Shabbos*"), while the poet thinks the prosperous burgher "performing his mitzvah" looks "more foolish than the fool." The shortened gait of Meyer and the muff he has made of his coat sleeves recall "the spanceled / steps of a Chinese woman," as Sommer goes on to imagine a background nowhere visible on the page, of stacked firewood and wrought iron entries and rooms "where Hassidim argue passionately" over "the world to come, the Messiah, / and the immortality of the soul" (8). Also invisible is Kertvarosh, "a few blocks / from where Meyer walks" — a cross street where the poet's father welded in a bike shop at the time the photograph was shot, where his grandmother laundered clothes. When "Vishniac clicks his shutter" on Meyer, there are

> no children near to show him
> stripped to his oedipal machinery,
> though here in this moment, as in his rage
> or his final agony, he was incapable of other modes than candor.
> (9)

Because of his father's recollections, albeit conveyed reluctantly, Sommer grasps more about the past and future environment of a mentally incapaci-

4.3. Roman Vishniac, *Rabbi Chaim Yosef and Meyer Tsits. Mukachevo, 1937.* From *A Vanished World,* 1983 (New York: Farrar, Straus and Giroux). Used by permission.

tated person (who would have been among the first "they practiced Holocaust / on") than the subject himself or the photographer could possibly have known. The poem and its author's actions within it seek to steady his, his father's, and our attention: the father "prepares to turn the page" of an image that "is little to him" when of the "dearest faces . . . there are no extant images / outside of memory," but the poet tries to "delay with questions the turning of the page" (10, 11). To do so, he attends to the meaning of the Yiddish word *Tsits,* which means "tits," because the humiliating name conferred by the taunting children signifies to Sommer the "ordinary" cruelties

which have been restored to us at least —
the cruelties of sons and fathers,
cruelties which may be partially redeemed
by forgiveness. (10)

Forgiveness is what he wants his father to ask "for laughing the blank laugh / at those one thinks one never will become," but also what he too must ask of Meyer Tsits "for having made / some part of his life and death / into coin, capital for speculation" (11). Instances of "consuming trauma," Vishniac's photograph and Sommer's poem about the photograph devolve into analogues of the feminizing insult even the fool comprehended:

And to ask forgiveness of Meyer Tsits is to
imagine him restored to faculties
he may never have had,
and to believe for a photographic instant
in the immortality of the soul. (11)

"Meyer Tsits and the Children" has undercut Vishniac's benign caption about the folkloric "fool," whose image in *A Vanished World* is complemented on the facing page with photos of "A merry fool" and "A melancholy fool," both looking more isolated and grotesque than the captions would lead one to suspect; about either one of these or about his father's "village idiot," it certainly cannot be presumed that "All the neighbors would look after him in turn."

A comparable skepticism about mimetic images inspired a series of experiments undertaken by Jeffrey Wolin in a very literary book of photographs. Like Vishniac, Wolin sought to present honorific prewar images; however, like Kirtland Snyder and Jason Sommer, he wanted to address the perplexing insufficiencies of photographic "quotations." Through his deployment of antimorphosis, Wolin realizes both these ends and thereby bears witness to the testimony of survivors. In *Written in Memory: Portraits of the Holocaust*, Wolin uses prose glosses that provide resonant but ultimately skimpy explanations of his pictures, in the process proving that even while poets meditate on visual artifacts, photographers have turned with some urgency toward testimonial forms of writing, extending the traditional caption so as to underline the insubstantiality of the photograph, its inability to convey the full historical specificity of a person's experience. Wolin achieves this by including an earlier, smaller picture, which dates from back "then," within a photograph of "now." On many of the pages of his book, the pre-Holocaust picture-within-the-picture is held by the aging refugee who has chosen it as well as the contemporary American setting in which he or she is photographed by Wolin. These two visual planes of meaning, the smaller and contained prewar photo contrasted with the encompassing postwar image, could be considered two different quotations from a life. When Wolin decided to inscribe a handwritten account to grapple with what happened during the war to people who inexplicably managed to survive it, he employed a technique related to ecphrasis, for these accounts explain in a highly encapsulated manner what the images of the pre-Holocaust picture-within-the-picture mean to the person in the contemporary American setting. These three sets of signification are in turn counterpointed by one more small photograph often included on a facing page: a picture of the survivor at a much earlier time period, before or during or right after the war. The aging survivor looks like a different being, *is* a different person, from the younger self whose traumatic story unfolded decades earlier.

With tentative brevity, the printed narrative negotiates between the "then" and "now" of these doubles.[6] While Wolin's meta-photography consists of three pictorially discrete quotations from three different aspects of his subject's life, the script provides connectives, a fragile narrative bridge between the horrific European past and the American present. Because, as Andrea Liss has pointed out, the words at times "appear as if they are crowding and trapping the pictured survivor," they heighten our sense that each person is engaged in a "struggle against the repercussions of the events" (111). That the writing is done in English with American penmanship means it intercedes not only between the youthful victim and the aging refugee but also between the survivor-subject's story in his or her own words and the artist Jeffrey Wolin's transcription in his own hand. Although originally composed in the third person, the narratives of *Written in Memory* quickly transmute into first-person testimonies that Wolin tape-recorded from his subjects and then excerpted and inscribed on the surfaces of the photographs. What the shift from third to first person achieves is perhaps most strikingly realized in the final portrait of the book, a brilliant instance of aesthetic proxy-witnessing (Wolin bearing witness to the testimony given by the survivor) and one that, in this case, crosses gender lines.

Holding two small (creased and taped) photographs, Jadzia Strykowsky has provided an account almost entirely about them in cadences that remind us of the linguistic switch she had to make when she immigrated to the United States from Europe at war's end (figure 4.4).[7] Given a celluloid tube, "I put there in a poison pill" along with a valuable stone given to her by her mother, but quickly she decided to exchange both for photographs more precious than the release promised by a quick death or the relief provided by a bartering chip. One was a picture of her parents; the other a composite of herself, her brother, and her Zionist platoon leader. Describing how she cut and rolled the pictures to put them in the tube and then hid them in her rectum, she feels herself "lucky" not to be detected. "They had us schlep stones from one place to the other just to wear us out so they wouldn't even have to use a bullet on us," she declares. Only the cherished photos convince her of her humanity: "I am not from stone. I am from people." The abrupt shift to 1978 Skokie, where the Nazis want to march, strikes home.

"Before I smuggled out from the ghetto to join the underground my mother gave me a little celluloid tube and I put there in a poison pill and my mother gave me some valuable stones to put in there... After my capture I was sitting in the cattle car cutting out my pictures, the faces of my mother and the faces of my father. I also cut out a little picture of myself because I wanted to remind myself how I really look. And I had a picture of my brother and me and we were in a summer place the year before the war started. Then I also cut out a picture of my Zionist platoon leader, Icek Rosenblatt, and I cut around the picture of my platoon, Beit-Shan, that we made before we left and I rolled them up all tightly. I left the poison pill, I took out the stones and I put in the pictures. We arrived on a very freezing January evening to Bergen-Belsen. So we went in to get a shower and right before we went in I took my tube and I put it in my rectum. They searched you again in your hair and you had to open the mouth and some of the people they even checked internally, whether they didn't hide any valuables. I was lucky—I passed... It was miserable there. They had us schlep stones from one place to the other just to wear us out so they wouldn't even have to use a bullet on us. And so every day the circumstances got harder and harder. My solace were my pictures. When I came in in the evening I used to unroll them and look at them and say, "My goodness, I am not from stone. I am from people. I am from a family." ... we were in Skokie in 1977 when the situation came out with the Nazis that they wanted to march here. This was already too much. Before that we didn't talk for a few reasons. People did not want to listen. They told us to forget about it, to start a new life, to live here for today, not for yesterday. It's not a question of forgetting—we never, ever forgot. But as I say, we got involved in everyday life and when the Nazis wanted to come here under our windows so to say, that was a little too much and it kind of woke us up and we decided not to let it happen because freedom of speech is not freedom to slander. They legally later on won that they can walk but they got afraid to walk here because they knew that we would never let them get out alive from here... when it was over we started speaking, we started telling our stories.

4.4. Jeffrey Wolin, *Jadzia Strykowsky.* Courtesy Catherine Edelman Gallery, Chicago.

"This was already too much." Because "freedom of speech is not freedom to slander," she and her neighbors awake to a sense of their power: the Nazis "legally later on won that they can walk but they got afraid to walk here because they knew that we would never let them get out alive from here" (Wolin 93).

What moves me about this page of Wolin's book is the fierce repetition of "here" (Skokie is not Bergen-Belsen and Bergen-Belsen will not be allowed to happen in Skokie) as well as the commonplace complacencies of the subject's self-presentation. Someone whose only hiding place was the holes in her own body now displays her possessions and her self-possession: her necklace with its *chai* (the Hebrew word for life); her checkered jacket with shoulder pads; her bifocals, earrings, rings, watch, and manicured nails in contrast to the tiny, faded, and crumpled images she holds before her in frames. What does it mean that even if we read the text attentively and peer closely at the pictures she holds, the figures in them cannot be definitely identified? The parents, the brother, the Zionist platoon leader: none can be discerned. Nor do we know anything about their respective fates. Antimorphosis in this instance teaches us that she knows what we cannot fully comprehend. In quotation marks, the words of Jadzia Strykowsky's testimony constitute the dramatic monologue of a being whose dignity in the face of barbarous violence miraculously survives and triumphs. "My work is the inverse of an illuminated manuscript," Wolin has explained, since "the text is a kind of embellishment . . . for the portrait." Illegible to the viewer but more precious than gems, a better safeguard than suicide to Wolin's subject, personal photographs from the past inspire the stories Jadzia Strykowsky begins to speak only after several decades of silence, words not created by the artist but found and formed by him and thereby imbued with numinous intensity.

SIMULATIONS OF THE UNSEEN

The disjunction between pre-Holocaust artifacts and post-Holocaust responses in ecphrastic works locates the Shoah as the place, the time that was not photographed, where what transpired was perhaps unphotographable. As if exploring the poignant limits of Vishniac's photographic record of shopping districts teeming with beggars, peddlers, water carriers, and vendors, in her long sequence of poems titled *Eastern War Time* Adrienne Rich juxtaposes verse portraits of various girls who enable her to meditate on what was not and cannot be pictured. According to Rich, this is "what you won't believe" (*ADW* 38), the fates of Selma or of the children at the Slonim summer camp after Vishniac had to flee the Continent.[8] In the fifth poem of Rich's sequence, a young girl, who "knows she is young and meant to live," is

> taken on the closed journey
> her pockets drained of meaning
> her ankles greased in vomit and diarrhea
> driven naked across the yard[.] (39)

With her aureole of "pale friz" hair, this girl resembles an American schoolgirl depicted earlier in the sequence, except for her wish to remember "anything textbooks forbidden novels / school songs petnames" that might remind her of who she had been before she arrived at "the operating table / of the famous doctor / who plays string quartets with his staff in the laboratory" (39). Here Rich seems to use her verse as an instrument of optical correction, but toward the end of the sequence she relinquishes faith in finding a proper perspective.

In the next to the last poem in *Eastern War Time*, Rich tries and fails to imagine the chronological sequence after the swarming street life Vishniac had captured in so many Eastern European towns disappeared altogether; that is, after the Nazis had rounded up Jewish men, women, and children; marched them to an assembly point; and forced them on trains to barracks to crematoria, or made them lie down in massive pits where they were shot:

> Streets closed, emptied by force   Guns at corners
> with open mouths and eyes   Memory speaks:
> You cannot live on me alone
> you cannot live without me
> I'm nothing if I'm just a roll of film
> stills from *a vanished world*
> fixed lightstreaked mute
> left for another generation's
> restoration and framing   I can't be restored or framed[.]
> (43; emphasis mine)

Speaking as if for the silent film itself, the poet deals with the curious power and futility of photographs ("You cannot live on me alone / you cannot live without me") for future generations who frame images of realities that will never be restored. Rich's "stills" that "can't be still" of "unkillable though killed" people echoes Vishniac's dedicatory assertion that those he recorded are part of "a vanished but not vanquished world." Whether or not they are stuck into the edges of a literal mirror, "intrusive inappropriate bitter" pictures from the past generate reflections of and on their present-day interpreters.

By emphasizing the blatantly unrestorable character of prewar Jewish society, Shimon Attie heightens awareness of the unphotographable blank Rich's verse locates between pre- and post-Holocaust times. In 1991, after finishing art school in San Francisco, Attie traveled to Berlin, where he found himself walking city streets and wondering, "Where are all the missing people? What has become of the Jewish culture and community which had once been at home here?" (9). Seeking to excavate an unexcavatable past, he collected photographs of Jewish street life during the 1920s and '30s in the Scheunenviertel, the working-class Jewish quarter of Berlin. Then, attempting (but not always able) to match photographic portraits with their original sites, Attie projected insubstantial slide images of these historical representations onto extant urban settings for several days, seeking not a literal reconstruction but an overtly unreal simulation of Jewish life as it once existed. In the final stage of his work, he photographed these installations, which have been collected in a volume with the biblically evocative title *The Writing on the Wall,* to present today's Berlin as a place haunted by transparent images of people "never allowed to become the past through the normal rhythms of gradual evolution and decay—a world whose brutal obliteration has made its very absence a question haunting our lives and practices today" (M. Bernstein 7). As James E. Young cautions about books reprinting Attie's acts of remembrance, they must not be mistaken for the installations of the performed project, "which like the historical events being commemorated are now over" (*AME* 66). Yet such photographs do illuminate a point many historians of the Shoah make: namely that only those endowed with the luxury of hindsight could say that the writing was on the wall for anyone (Jewish or non-Jewish) willing to glance at it.

The photographs of these installations capture fast-fading memories of an impoverished but nevertheless vital German Jewish culture prohibited from emerging into the present and thus unphotographable. At the center of *Joachimstrasse 2, Berlin.* Slide projection of former Jewish resident (ca. 1930), a spectral scholar with a tallith emerges from a building, framed by the contemporary cars on the street (figure 4.5). Like the fossilized remains of an extinct culture or an X ray of the ur-Jew of Nazi propaganda, the figure seems insubstantial, in the process of disappearing, on the verge of being expunged from view. The colors of today's city contrast with the daguerreo-type's browns and sepias, as they do in *Mulackstrasse 37, Berlin.* Slide projection of former Jewish residents (ca. 1932) (figure 4.6). Here construction sites and a technologically up-to-date spire diverge from the writing literally on the wall — "Was der Krieg verschonte" — as well as the two impalpable Jewish children sitting on the curb, uncanny ghosts beamed through the air by a slide projector operating like a time machine.[9] The transparency of the photographed projections calls attention to the phantom unreality of images of people alive "then" and "there" who have no presence "now" and "here," regardless of the optical illusion engineered by the artist. Blatantly ersatz simulations of the past hover on a setting in which they could not exist, do not reside. The irony of the literal writing on the wall consists of "what the war left undemolished" or "what the war has spared": Berlin with its national identity intact, but with a substantial proportion of its population and their cultural traditions extirpated.[10] If the citizens of Berlin could not read the writing on the wall in the past, Attie wants to ensure that they can see it — if only ephemerally — in the present.

Also inspired by a return to a criminal site where visual evidence of a destroyed people had been eradicated, Jerome Rothenberg's volume of poems *Khurbn* opens with an epigraph — "Since the hidden is bottomless, totality more invisible than visible"[11] — that emphasizes the "empty empty" Jewish communities of Europe, which are "lost to us the way the moon is lost to us" (*K*6): "The Absence of the living seemed to create a vacuum in which the dead — the dibbiks who had died before their time — were free to speak" (3), the poet explains. These specters consist of "little ghosts of Lidice"

4.5. Shimon Attie, *Joachimstraße 2*. Slide projection of former Jewish resident, ca. 1930, Berlin, 1992, chromogenic photograph and on-location installation, from the series The Writing on the Wall by Shimon Attie. Courtesy of Jack Shainman Gallery, New York City.

along the road to Warsaw (8); numberless "hapless spirits . . . turned into ghosts at once / the air is full of them" in the forests and fields of Poland (13); and "Dibbik legions [who] perch on trees," for "Once the dibbik was a singular occurrence. It is now repeated many million times as the result of so much early death" (27). Rothenberg's language about the killing fields in Poland responds to the absence of the Jews and the dead memories of their murderers with curses that explain the effect of Attie's installations: "Let ghosts & dibbiks overwhelm the living / Let the invisible overwhelm the visible until nothing more is seen or heard" (35).

Like Rothenberg, Myra Sklarew—returning to the scene of innumerable covered-up crimes—finds "totality . . . more invisible than visible." In a long poem titled "Lithuania," about the Kovno ghetto and Stutthof concentration camp, Sklarew wonders, "if I put my face close / to the photograph, it

4.6. Shimon Attie, *Mulackstraße 37*. Slide projection of former Jewish residents, ca. 1932, Berlin, 1992, chromogenic photograph and on-location installation, from the series The Writing on the Wall by Shimon Attie. Courtesy of Jack Shainman Gallery, New York City.

seems I can enter // there with my body." Yet she understands about the massacre pits filled with dead grandparents, aunts, uncles, and cousins that though "we have seen the pictures, read the descriptions, heard / the testimonies. We know nothing about the killings" (52, 56). Indeed, it is precisely what one cannot see that taints the landscape of the Ponar forest outside of Vilnius when she visits "to remember something I couldn't possibly know" (34). For "Every / hill is suspect, every ravine, every tree. If you put / your foot down . . . you can feel the skull or a bone of someone you knew, someone you almost remembered" (35); visual evidence of the mushrooms, trees, flowers growing over the bucolic vista belies what remains hidden beneath the surface:

> At Keidan in order to cover the cries
>   of the Jews forced to strip at the mouth
> of a mass grave, the Lithuanians started up their tractor

motors. Those not killed by machine guns were buried
    alive. All this was watched by the principal
    of the high school, the mayor, and a young
priest. Afterwards, the Lithuanians told that when
the pit was covered with a bit of earth, the surface
    heaved up and down as if a live pulse

emanated from the mass grave. In order to stop
the heaving of the blood earth, the Lithuanians
used rollers to press the earth down. (40)

When the last section of "Lithuania" begins by asking "What is the nature of the pit which has been made? / With what instruments was it dug?" we come to realize again the obstinate perplexity of the unseen: "How deep is a pit which must hold / 50,000 people? Shall they be murdered facing up / or facing down?" (60).[12]

Attie's transparent apparitions, Rothenberg's "dibbiks," and Sklarew's pulsing field rehearse what was not photographed, what was not photographable. But, of course, some extant pictures, uncontaminated by Nazi censorship or manipulation, do testify to the crimes of the Shoah. Documentary photographs, made by the Allied forces, set out to portray grievous scenes, albeit from an after-the-fact, elegiac perspective; however, Audrey Flack raises questions — for a number of complex reasons — about what can be perceived in such pictures. First, she asks, do documentary pictures of demeaned people only further degrade their subjects, boxing them into the species of Other we call "victim"? Second, what happens when such photographs have been so widely circulated that they lose their shock value and devolve into clichés, unable to inspire empathy for the imprisoned or rage at their jailers? By painting a version of a famous photo from the liberation of the camps and by turning this still into a still life, Flack employs antimorphosis to draw attention to these impediments. As do other practitioners of "fabricated photography," Flack's packaged images "mock the culture with the reductive banality of its simulations," even as they "ask to what extent reality itself is always a kind of ongoing fabrication" (J. Young, *AME* 45). Just as attuned to the lamentable limitations and urgencies of the ocular as Attie, Audrey Flack splices together words and images from before and after the Holocaust so as to show "memory receding in space," as she once put it (78–80).

Flack's color photograph titled *World War II (Vanitas)* (figure 4.7) foregrounds the romance of prewar Europe — candlelight, pastries, a rose, a string of pearls, the butterfly poised on a silver cup and saucer, musical notations — against a backgrounded painting of part of one of the shots Margaret Bourke-White took during the liberation of the camps. Although the contemporary artist has explained that each figure standing behind the barbed wire was carefully copied in her drab palette, the painting's faces

4.7. Audrey Flack, *World War II (Vanitas)*, incorporating a
portion of the Margaret Bourke-White photograph
Buchenwald, April 1945, © Time Inc. Oil over acrylic on
canvas, 96″ × 96″. Courtesy Louis K. Meisel Gallery, New York,
and Collection David N. Pincus, Philadelphia.

seemed to her more like a series of self-portraits than realistic replications of
the original prisoners. Whether the painted photographic image animates
or mortifies its subjects, Flack recycles one of the most famous pieces of
photojournalism, for while photojournalists may not have answered all the
questions, they did supply the single most important evidentiary source of

the Shoah, a calamity that went unheeded because doubted until visual veri-fication proved that the incredible had really happened.

Two contradictory but spliced sentences — "I saw it with my own eyes" and "I could not believe what my eyes had seen" — recur not only in the testi-monials of victims and liberators but also in the responses of photojournal-ists.[13] When Bourke-White, a *Life* magazine journalist of Polish Jewish ori-gins, used her camera to document the unthinkable at Buchenwald, she "did not realize how soon some people would disbelieve or forget"; how-ever, "I had a deep conviction that an atrocity like this demanded to be recorded. So I forced myself to map the place with negatives" (*DF* 77; figure 4.8). In the words of Barthes, the photo as a certification of the actuality of the past means "I can never deny that *the thing has been there*" (76). The act of using the camera to produce evidence draws what Bourke-White called a "protective veil" (*PM* 259) over her mind without which she could not withstand the shock of what she saw. Seeing does not become believing or feeling until the jolt it administers is processed through the passage of time and the distancing of representation.

About the pile of dead corpses that had grown high at Buchenwald be-cause of a coal shortage curtailing Nazi efficiency, Bourke-White explained, "I kept telling myself that I would believe the indescribably horrible sight in the courtyard before me only when I had a chance to look at my own photographs. Using the camera was almost a relief; it interposed a slight barrier between myself and the white horror in front of me" (*DF* 73). A metaphorical shield, a self-imposed "veil" or "barrier" means that the me-chanical eye of the camera provides a crucial reality check for what the human eye cannot take in, although it filters or mediates without recording what Bourke-White felt.[14] A transcription of an interview with Warren Priest, a former surgical technician of the 120th Evacuation Hospital in Buchen-wald, put into poem form by Barbara Helfgott Hyett, explains that the camera could capture more manifest facts than the eyewitness in his distress could apprehend at the time:

> I'm not sure that I could say
> where I was, what I was doing.
> The only thing I have
> is the picture that I know
> I took. I took the picture.
> I had the camera. I had to
> have been there. (99)

Yet, clearly doctored in Flack's repainted version, do Bourke-White's backgrounded inmates take on the look of the callously reproduced after their much-publicized reprintings and retransmissions in countless maga-zines, TV shows, and history books? If, to the youthful eyes of Alice Kaplan, scrutinizing photos used at the Nuremberg trials, the people standing up

4.8. Margaret Bourke-White, *Buchenwald, April 1945*. © Time Inc., 1976.

"didn't look human" (*FL* 29), does Flack register the passage of time during which such recycled artifacts further reified their subjects' nonhumanity? Or, by painting just a few of the photographed figures in Bourke-White's original, does she manage to retrieve their aura, to rectify the unreality of the photograph, to transform a repressive aggregate of alterity into an honorific community of individuals who look back at us as we gaze at them?[15] Perhaps the painted photograph can produce both effects. In either case, an ironic contrast between the decadence of the brilliant Kodachrome of the foreground and the monochromatic deprivation of the calamity has been put on display.

In the still life, Flack sought to use the "sickeningly sweet petit fours" to raise consciousness about the starving prisoners: "Are we not all eating now while humans are starving elsewhere in the world?" (80–81). Set at a few minutes before midnight, the period Flack associates with Walpurgisnacht, the watch recalls Marc Chagall's comparable imagery of time running out in

White Crucifixion. Below it, the burning red candle, "precariously tilted," threatens to bleed onto the Jewish star, drips onto the printed page. Half spent, the candle signals the passage of moments that will tarnish the silver saucer and cup, rot the cut pear, and wither the rose, *memento mori* of time's procession toward death: Edna St. Vincent Millay's couplet — "Night falls fast. / Today is in the past" (335) — comes to mind. At the lower right, a prose passage attests to the "noble vision of redemption" with which the victims bore their "rich sorrow." A Hasidic rabbi is quoted: "Even in the Nethermost Pit one can try to come closer to God." The narrator proclaims, "Disaster did not frighten them. 'You can take everything from me — the pillow from under head, my house — but you cannot take God from my heart.' " For me, the words that Flack found in a book by Roman Vishniac and that "deeply touched" the artist (Toll 66) sound hollow, and the painted photo appears like an air-brushed, cropped, bleached version of what Bourke-White recorded.

Flack's comment that she wanted "the viewer to look at what happened to these people who could see, hear and speak no evil" (Toll 66) comes closer to the impact of *World War II (Vanitas)*. Since the accoutrements of romance appear so colorfully feminine against the black-and-white male denizens of disaster, what seems implicated in the barbaric is the sentimental and nostalgic coffee-klatsch, Haydn quartet cult of *Schmertz* and *Herz* so prevalent in the fascist economy — sickly sweet renditions of "Kinder, Küche, Kirche" to be defended against invasive Jewish aliens. The colorful foreground and drab background hint at an unnerving dialectic between the most cultivated, refined, genteel of Western societies and the unmanning of Jewish men. Although Flack believed that the butterfly represents "the liberation of the Soul, like the Holy Ghost or the dove of Christ" (Toll 81), in the Holocaust context it inevitably invokes Pavel Friedman's "I never saw another butterfly";[16] although the pearls in the foreground contrast with the pain in the background, in the Holocaust context they inevitably invoke Abraham Sutzkevar's "Burnt Pearls" (*AA* 580). Both allusions underscore the relevance of the work's reference to Ecclesiastes 1:2: "vanities of vanities, all is vanity." When Bourke-White's still of a camp liberation becomes Flack's still life, the oscillation between pre-Holocaust and Holocaust images again reminds us of the unseen: the period of time that transpired between quartets and barbed wire, pastry and privation, candles and crematoria. But what I have read as the pre-Holocaust foreground may also register as the post-liberation period invoked by Adorno's poetic injunction against the barbarism of poetry. If that is the case, Flack hints that pre- and post-Holocaust temporality has not been ruptured by the Shoah, that Western culture after the disaster only reiterates the civilization that brought it into being, and that therefore history's clock has been stopped: we will never arrive at a period that could be imagined as existing after Auschwitz.

Flack's conversion of a still into a still life posits the constructedness of

4.9. Pieter Bruegel the Elder, *The Massacre of the Innocents*, 1566 (with studio assistance). 116 × 160 cm. Vienna, Kunsthistorisches Museum.

images of the Shoah as the afterness of "after Auschwitz" thickens. Whereas Flack shot a photograph of her painted version of a Holocaust photograph, Irving Feldman considers a photograph of a famous painting about atrocity, in his case to emphasize the ethical consequences of that growing removal and the detachment it abets. A meditation on Bruegel's sixteenth-century protest against military atrocities in a Flemish village, Feldman's "The Bystander at the Massacre" nevertheless deserves to be read as a Holocaust poem. Bruegel's *Massacre of the Innocents* (figure 4.9) used the gospel story (of King Herod ordering "the massacre of all children in Bethlehem, and its neighborhood, of the age of two years or less" [Matt. 2:16]) to protest violent crimes perpetrated in the Low Countries by King Philip II of Spain. Similarly, Feldman's allusion to Bruegel's title in his own adds several palimpsestic levels.

Thinking chronologically, as the poet emphatically does not, we are moved from the Bible to the sixteenth-century Flemish village (where foot soldiers broke down doors and slaughtered the babies of common people); from Bruegel's painting of the snow-colored cluster of cottages (invaded by the horses and soldiers in their red and black cuirasses and backed by a cavalry troop) to the Jewish American poet's analysis of Bruegel's canvas with its inevitable evocations of the Shoah, to the discussion in the poem of a photographing of the painting and a looking at the photograph of the painting. So many different versions of the massacre of the innocents are what make us bystanders at the massacre, for biblical, historical, painterly, literary, and photographic representations of genocide alienate us from an unmediated sense of the real, the true, the genuine, the sincere, the authentic.[17] Artistic representations created to produce a pleasurable response (related to either the aesthetic design of the picture or the sentimental self-satisfaction of the viewer), painted replacements of actual suffering obscure and betray its specificity. That two versions of Bruegel's painting survive, that the Hampton Court canvas was altered by later retouching and over-painting, and that André Derain chose to produce another version of the massacre of the innocents for his last important work only drive this point home.

What this layering, this palimpsest of levels of meaning, achieves is the poet's subject—namely, the vexed morality of visual and verbal artistry because of its invariable dependence on and escalation of aesthetic distance, or so the first stanza makes clear:

> The bystander at the massacre of innocents
> might have seen his own innocence among the dying
> had not his distance from the spectacle of slaughter
> (Not all that far off, really) given him the space
> to entertain a doubt—while it wrenched time backward
> and made everything appear unalterable and past
> even as everything kept on racing ahead.
> He might not believe or come in time to what he saw.
> (Feldman, *AUH* 14)

The long sustained sentence pulling together the first seven lines, followed by the last sentence in one line, establishes the paradox that representations of the disaster estrange the bystander and thereby blind him to (its depiction of) his own massacred innocence. Viewing what appears unalterably past, the bystander suffers a doubt that induces passivity or paralysis, prompting insensibility or ineffectuality about suffering not only in the past but in the present and future as well. The camera in the hand of the bystander (imagine him in a museum) first allows him to reject the panic and horror of "Murderers and babies and frenzied howling mothers": "when he dropped to a knee to steady the camera / —yes, they could come this far but not a breath farther[.]" Yet, at a later point and repeatedly (imagine him a tourist back at his hotel), "he stabs his finger into the photo / as if to verify something incredible there / or at least to render the illusion palpable" (14).

If we are all trapped in "the spectator's essential doubtfulness," we both know and do not know "that terrible things are going on" (*AUH* 14). Feldman seems to be glossing a passage by Levinas on the irresponsibility of the artist: "The poet exiles himself from the city[.] . . . There is something wicked and egoist and cowardly in artistic enjoyment" ("RIS" 12). In the second part of "The Bystander at the Massacre," Feldman diagnoses our voyeurism as an aspect "of the city-dweller's pastime": an absorbed watching of other people's lives. But the bystander's anguish about his own indifference to "one city burning and another's tinder" means that he hears in "that uproar — our names screaming — always in our ears" (*AUH* 15). The pronoun "our" belies any sheltering persuasion that the bystander can isolate himself from the social scenes at which he gazes. Reminiscent of "The Pripet Marshes," Feldman's catalogue of the denizens of disaster "before the slaughterers came. / Before the slaughterers come" includes each individual "in glowing concentration" and amid scenes not completely consonant with Bruegel's village: "the one of the DOORWAY, the one of the TABLE, / the one of the RESTAURANT WINDOW, the other one . . ." To resist any easy slide from a realization about the simulated phantasms of the disaster to an acquiescence in passivity, Feldman asserts,

> we can have no other way
> but to make our way back
> into the city, into the center
> where what happened is happening now[.] (15–16)

This stubborn rejection of voyeuristic disengagement constitutes part of Feldman's quarrel with W. H. Auden's breezy assessment of Bruegel's masterful paintings in "Musée des Beaux Arts," especially with Auden's claim that the "Old Masters" were "never wrong" (*CP* 79): in an earlier poem that questions Auden, much as a later poem would query Brodsky, Feldman asks, "Sir, respectfully, is it possible / to be *right* about 'suffering'?" (*TM* 34).[18] At the close of "The Bystander at the Massacre," Feldman asserts that it is better to keep stabbing one's finger on the photo to verify "something incredible there" than "not lifting a finger" at all. Acquiescence in voyeuristic indifference breeds evasion, complicity, "the spectator's rage" for "more, quicker death" (*AUH* 16). To be so distanced by representations of atrocity as to reject their reality means being caught up in desiring and bringing about the next catastrophe in all its undoubted and undoubtable reality. A brilliant novel on this subject, *White Noise* by Don DeLillo, presents its academic protagonist ("the most prominent figure in Hitler studies in North America") coming to grips with the realization that "Every disaster made us wish for more, for something bigger, grander, more sweeping" (31, 64). According to Feldman, then, Auden's instructive words about the inevitable indifference of most creatures to suffering in their midst "might well inspire Job / with ruddied fingernails once more to rasp / excruciating music from festers, and boils" (*TM* 34). A "sense of the bystander's ambiguous distance from and proximity to the event," which Michael Rothberg locates as the animating principle of Adorno's and Blanchot's projects (24), goads Feldman in this poem.

Yes, aesthetic looking necessarily proves our detachment from the represented catastrophe; yes, documentary photographs and paintings are simulations of the unreal; yes, we must question our unmediated knowledge of the event; however, Auden's magnanimity about this phenomenon is part of the problem, not the solution. The only bystanders in Bruegel's depiction of bloody slaughter are the reserve troop of cavalry in black cuirasses and a shrugging herald whose embroidered vest incorporates the emblem of the royal House of Hapsburg. As Charles Altieri notes of Feldman's project throughout his writing career, "Even if it is impossible to escape simulacra, it may be possible to so manipulate them that one can use them to express affections or order them so that how they are expressed becomes a shifting from the epistemological to the ethical level, from a concern for reference to a concern for making one's language establish distinctive relations to other persons" ("CS" 68).

AGAINST PHOTOGRAPHY

If artists of antimorphosis frame pre-Holocaust honorific photographs to express affection, if they engage documentary images to insist on their qualified but vital moral worth, those who manipulate repressive Holocaust images do so to deflate their epistemological claims. For poets and photographers dealing directly with Nazi visual documents, which constitute the vast majority of the images that survived from the Shoah, the visible not only hides the unseen and promulgates a morally problematic distancing but also generates factitious, duplicitous testimonies that artists of antimorphosis set out to sabotage. An ambitious poem, Jorie Graham's "History" describes a photographic scene interpreted by the poet but unavailable to the reader of the poem and in the process questions whether photographs — unable to record the invisible anguish of pain (to which they may contribute) — can serve any pedagogic function at all. Partly for this reason, according to Graham, history remains an untellable tale, an unverifiable and receding sequence of scenes, that nevertheless continues to affect us profoundly. To encapsulate the statement Graham is making about efforts to document the history of the Jews visually: it is impossible for the living *to take it in.*

As is not uncommon in Graham's works, "History" opens in the midstream of thought:

> Into whose ear the deeds are spoken. The only
> listener. So believed
> he would remember everything, the murmuring trees,
> the sunshine's zealotry, its deep
> unevenness. For history is the opposite of the eye
> for whom, for instance, six million bodies in portions
> of hundreds and
> the flowerpots broken by a sudden wind stand as
> equivalent. (*DUF* 40–41)

A difficult beginning comes into focus if we assume that the "history" of the title is being personified as that entity "Into whose ear the deeds are spoken." Graham then goes on to define history as "the opposite / of the eye" that too easily equates, say, images of broken bodies and broken flowerpots. Unrelated to vision, so easily seduced by spurious equivalences, are spoken words that establish facts; and "what more / is there / than fact?" (40). The italicized wager that follows —

> *I'll give ten thousand dollars to the man*
> *who proves the holocaust really*
> *occurred* said the exhausted solitude
> in San Francisco
> in 1980 (40)

— is spoken by a Holocaust denier (given the lowercasing), though it remains ambiguous enough to sound like the exasperation of someone attempting to rebut the claims of a Holocaust denier.

Despite her initial caveat about the ocular, in response to those who four decades later question whether "*the holocaust really occurred,*" Graham goes on to provide a fact with her description of a 1942 photographic record of a woods where a mutilated man

> with his own
> genitalia in his mouth and hundreds of
> slow holes
> a pitchfork has opened
> over his face
> grows beautiful. (40)

When history strikes in the life of an individual — the man with genitals in his mouth and holes all over his face — it murderously forces its way in, abrogating boundaries, defiling the body. Now the first few lines take on a more macabre connotation, for if we read this individual (amid "the murmuring trees" and "the sunshine's zealotry") as "the only / listener" who "would remember everything," his calamity suggests a larger scale catastrophe: that only the dead know history.

Graham's antipastoral scene graphically exemplifies Elaine Scarry's conviction that torture reduces the human being to a physicality deprived of any language to utter anguish, the silenced lips and tongue here just a cavity to be raped. The mouth stuffed with genitalia, the holes gaping open and wide all over the rest of the face: how can this man in the photo be said to grow "beautiful"? Ironically, he appears to be surrounded by the innocent beauties of ferns, deepwood lilies, a singing bluebird. Like many pictures, this one includes chance circumstances, pastoral details of ease at odds with the horrific central form. Since photographs "are of the world," Stanley Cavell explains, in them human beings are "not ontologically favored over the rest of nature" (*WV* 37). If the eye of the viewer of the photographic image is so traitorous as to see the mangled face grow "beautiful" and even to be soon caught up by the lilies, the bluebird, and the sky around the mutilated corpse, one can understand the poet's revulsion against the dominion of sight. As in Feldman's "The Bystander at the Massacre" and Graham's other ambitious poems about the Shoah, "History" hints that voyeurism and aestheticism, or simply our remoteness from the disaster, predetermine our failure to take in genocidal atrocity through the eye; in other words, Graham agrees with one theorist that "photography may function most directly to achieve what it ought to have stifled — atrocity's normalization" (Zelizer 182).

Such normalization fails to supply explanations, however. For who are the "Three men in ragged uniforms / with guns" and why do they "keep laughing nervously"? Worse still, which "hand [is] holding down the delicate gun" and whose "hands [are] holding down the delicate / hips" (Graham, *DUF* 40)? The anguish undoubtedly felt at the scene of the crime cannot be photographed, though the laughter can. Readers wondering who shot the fading photograph, for whom, and with what purpose will find themselves instantly discomforted by such conjectures, even as they comprehend the import of its absence from the text. Marianne Hirsch provides the most severe judgment of such pictures: "When we confront perpetrator images, we cannot look independently of the look of the perpetrator" ("SI" 26).

Yet according to "History," neither the eye nor the ear of the living can know the truths of the past, since the conclusion of the poem undercuts Graham's earlier belief — a faith logical in a poet — that sound will save us. About the sound and sense of language, what does it mean to use an adjective like "delicate" to modify "gun" and "hips"? The poet's positing of the efficacy of spoken words over visual images seems ominously challenged by the spurious equivalence of "delicate gun" and "delicate hips," as it had been earlier by such balanced phrases as "For history," "for whom," "for instance" and by the indeterminate vow or wager. She therefore ends "History" with a monitory tale about the destructive power of the historical when it is hidden from view and when its reverberations destroy those who hear it. "Late in the story," a man who cuts firewood without seeing the hand grenade lodged in the pulp of a tree is blinded when the flames in his fireplace produce an explosion that kills his wife. "Now who / will tell the children / fairytales?" (*DUF* 41), the poet asks, reminding us that the ear wants stories that steer us safely home as much as the eye seeks reassurances and resolutions. But what you can't see and what you hear may wound more than what you see. "Watching" the fire one night, "watching it change and change," the family never perceives the violence about to be discharged. A grisly image of the past's hidden but explosive consequences in the present, the grenade lodged in the tree limb answers those skeptics who question whether the Holocaust "*really occurred.*" The ongoing deaths inflicted by the past controvert the death sentence such cynics used to discount history itself.

Disjunction characterizes the four linked time periods of "History": the present of the "I" observer at the start of the poem, the Holocaust denier's wager in 1980, the scene of torture photographed in 1942, and the blinding second the hidden grenade exploded in an Italian fireplace. Inhabiting the present of the "I" at the end, "We read this in the evening / news" (*DUF* 41): Graham underscores the horrors we do not really take in daily, making us "Peeping Toms" of atrocity, as Charles Simic once put it (*UC* 125). Distaste for the ethical numbing this daily intake promotes may instill nostalgia for ceremonies of innocence before the time of media blitzes, maybe those customs of family life in northern Italy before the explosion. But because we all, everywhere, exist "Late in the story," even the fairy tales Jorie Graham wants to believe ruled rural lives beyond the daily tabloids — "The ones where simple / crumbs over the forest / floor endure / to help us home" (*DUF* 41) — evoke scenes of children starved into thin sticks of wood and aged crones thrust alive into burning ovens.

Although the eminently realistic medium of photography provides indispensable evidence that the calamity really occurred, its papery simulations depend on a technology enlisted in sadism. In works that undercut the neutrality and realism of photography, contemporary artists remind us that the fascists stage-managed or censored most of the discredited pictures and films that have survived. These poets and photographers emphasize how Nazi surveillance and state control, which so often involved the click of a machine that "snapped," "shot," "captured," "exposed," "framed," and "aimed" a "shutter" at its criminalized subjects, malevolently undercut the supposed objectivity and transcendence of photography, dramatizing John Tagg's point that "Photographs are never 'evidence' of history; they are themselves the historical" (65).[19] In a story included in Ida Fink's *A Scrap of Time*, a sole survivor of a murdered community, looking at a blurred amateur snapshot (itself "a scrap of time") of her snow-bound "last ghetto," wonders, "who photographed it? And when? Probably right afterwards: the footprints are clear here, but when they shot them in the afternoon it was snowing again" (136). By taking honorific portraits and translating them into horrific mug shots, Christian Boltanski follows Fink in connecting the shooting of pictures with the shooting of people, directly impugning the reputation of photography. He does so by returning to the issue of the invisible: how can the visual artist make the invisible torment of the victims overwhelm the dated optical signs of them that survive?

In installations such as *Pourim Reserve* and *Autel de Lycée Chases* (figure 4.10), Boltanski uses prewar photographs of people who probably did not outlive the disaster; but his enlarging, retouching, cropping, and lighting techniques eerily embody the fate of his subjects during the Shoah, even as they implicate photography itself in the criminality of the "Final Solution." For *Autel de Lycée Chases,* Boltanski recovered a photograph of the 1931 graduating class of a private Jewish high school in Vienna, rephotographed each of the eighteen students individually, then enlarged some of these portraits so as to blur the eyes and extend the mouths into what Ernst van Alphen sees as "empty black sockets" and "grimaces of death" (98). Beyond reminding us that photography played a crucial part in a criminalization of the Jews, one dependent on their devolution from subjects into objects, Boltanski graphically uses devices of the darkroom to replicate the torture of that process. As in torture, what emerges from the darkroom is the mortification of each subject. Since, as exploited by the state, the photograph administers the erasure of the individual's personal identity and privacy, Boltanski employs the deformations of antimorphosis to imply that distortions yield a better, truer (but blatantly spurious) vision because they document the sort of degradation each victim was forced to undergo during the period after their graduation portrait was taken. The bleared features of his subjects seem indeterminate, indistinct, concentrating viewers on what cannot come into focus. Yet does he thereby replicate the genocidal process? What Mira Schor calls "the blur" homogenizes his subjects, makes them indistinguishable, flattens or blots them out.[20]

Placed (for some of its installations) beneath screens of wire mesh and on top of rusty tins, each enlarged picture is lighted by a glaring desk lamp, as if the teenagers are being subjected to a Nazi interrogation. Under the aegis of German surveillance, photography robs each sitter of his or her human dimensions; and the very neatness of the row of portraits, stacked tins, carefully focused lights makes it "difficult to see order in the same way after the war, hard to accept control as a neutral value, . . . hard not to associate systematic operations with the systematicity of the extermination process or peremptory authority with fascism" (C. Bernstein 199).[21] Hard, too, not to see photography itself as well as archival cataloging as contaminated by the disaster. The factitious facticity of photos as well as their power to torment their subjects or mystify their viewers perplexes the poets of antimorphosis. A number of verse meditations therefore subvert photographic images produced for propaganda purposes by testifying to truths below the surface or

4.10. Christian Boltanski, *Autel de Lycée Chases* (*Altar to Chases High School*), 1988. Six black-and-white photographs, 31 tin biscuit boxes, six lamps, 81½″ × 86½″. Courtesy of The Museum of Contemporary Art, Los Angeles. Photo: Paula Goldman.

beyond the fascist frame to reveal what remains staged or hidden on seemingly realistic visual documents that actually served Nazi ends.

One of the stanzas included in the "Ghetto" section of Charles Reznikoff's *Holocaust* makes it clear how fascist photographers participated in the persecution of the Jews by foisting anti-Semitic impersonations on them:

> One morning German soldiers and their officers
> broke into the houses of the quarter where the Jews had gathered,
> shouting that all the men were to come out:
> and the Germans took everything in cupboards and closets.
> Among the men was an old man in the robe — and wearing the
>   hat — of the pious
> sect of Jews called *Hasidim.*
> The Germans gave him a hen to hold
> and he was told to dance and sing;
> then he had to make believe that he was choking a German soldier
> and this was photographed. (26)

Eschewing explanatory frameworks as well as any moral lessons, Reznikoff's *Holocaust* uses particularized scenes in what Charles Bernstein calls "a mosaic of salient incidents" (216). Not simply a record of the Germans' fetishization of visual archives, the verse quoted here documents humiliations inflicted on Jews forced to perform genocidal representations within the carnivalesque freedom from all moral restraint that the rule of fascism bestowed on some of its Aryan citizens.

The right to photograph, monopolized by the Third Reich, itself bespeaks carnivalesque license. In considering the audacious thesis of Daniel Goldhagen — that Germans seeped in an anti-Semitic culture acted not as "isolated, frightened, thoughtless beings performing their tasks reluctantly" (406) but as "Hitler's willing executioners" — Inga Clendinnen deems Nazi photographs of the Hamburg Reserve Police Battalion 101 in Poland "Goldhagen's trump card" (127). Although officially illegal, snapshots of the police cutting Jewish men's beards, hunting Jews in the countryside, and rounding them up at an athletic field display not simply the "Germans' willingness to make an extensive photographic record of their deeds" but also the "pride [they took] in the killings" (Goldhagen 245). Such images, "laid out" so "anyone, as he pleased, could order copies of them," were sent home to relatives like "postcards" of "heroic accomplishments." The dispassionate or ironic comments penned on their reverse side prove to Goldhagen that "The affirmative atmosphere that reigned within the battalion regarding their work took on an almost celebratory, festive quality in the public displaying and sharing of the photographs" (246). In this context, all extant documentary sources remain blatantly contaminated. The framed photo seems less like a memory than a fabrication put in place by an ideology noxious to many poets.[22]

Concerned with what "does not end with the shot / but flows out past its edges" (32), a passage from Stephen Berg's "Memory" warily alludes to compromised optical evidence about the victims of the Holocaust, identifying the snapshots of colluding gentile citizens with the snapped-shut lives of Jewish civilians looked at but deprived of the possibility of looking back and in that deprivation doomed:

> *Photograph:* families looking of all things shy
> cupping their genitals with both hands
> so we will never see — doesn't that mean they
> still knew their own names?
> grouped on the edge of the bottom half of the shot
> that could be of the deep gray ocean
> a pit that does not end with the shot
> but flows out past its edges in the mind
> as they try not to be there by looking as if nothing special
> is going on
> huddling in front of the amateur Sunday photographer's candid
> visor-shaded blank eye. (32)[23]

Given Nazi control over the technologies of production and reproduction, most photographs taken during the Shoah constituted an action in the war against the Jews: the widespread use of photographs to certify identity papers used to quarantine Jews, to document their racial inferiority, to illustrate with scientific precision the before and after effects of operations and experiments performed on them, to record or facilitate the extermination process. Since most extant pictures displayed in museums were taken to demean the victims, the photographic lack in some poems rejects representations of the slain put into circulation by their murderers.

William Heyen's "Simple Truths" moves from the pain and degradation suffered by men and women stripped and shot at close range to our attempts to remember such men and women. Heyen emphasizes the need to look at pictures and films, but also their worthlessness in light of a dangerous complacency such works can instill as they play into a smug sense of our own extrication from celluloid crimes:

> when we see the films of the bulldozed dead
> or the film of one boy struck on the head
> with a club in the hands
> of a German doctor who will wait
> some days for the boy's skull to knit, and will enter
> the time in his ledger, and then
> take up the club to strike the boy again,

the poet explains, "then it is clear to us that this / happened" (*E* 107–10). But the curious syntax of a long poem composed in one sentence — consisting of a succession of seemingly logical steps from "when" to a plethora of "it is clear that" phrases — builds to a climax of rage first against the urgent need of the viewers of such documents to establish their own innocence and then against the paradox that just such an indulgence demonstrates the worthlessness of pictures, condemning their audience to guilt "as we kill them all, as we killed them all" (110).

Insofar as poets such as Reznikoff and Heyen set the photographic record straight, their words could be said to furnish the instruments through which we see the images correctly and thus their poems could be understood as linguistic analogues of anamorphosis. However, in other works (that share more in common with Graham's "History") even a ratification of the falseness of photographs lies beyond the power of writers who can attest only to their own bewilderment. Confounded by an image "from nowhere particular — / books or movies or newspaper / stories," Michael Ryan in "One" describes its subject: a ten-year-old girl, "her neck / inclined like a bather / by Degas," being shorn by sheep shears (39). Wondering "did it ever really happen / to *this* little girl," the poet has "to imagine what I can't / imagine," and in particular he has to imagine exactly what the photograph omits:

> her mother's anguish,
> her father's nightmare terror
> ensnarled with their fear
> for themselves and for each other —
> has she lost them already
> or are they watching her? (40)

Besides providing factitious, tormenting, or inadequate evidence, photographs fail to record the subjectivity of their living subjects, as do poems about such photographs. Stephen Spender's "History and Reality" describes the devastating effects of the disjunction between what the victims perceived and how little can be glimpsed in looking at them on a German Jewish refugee in England who commits suicide after she studies

> Photographs made by the Gestapo —
>
> Jews, her people —
> So various, all one —
>
> Each taken full-face —
>
> The strong — the meek — the sad — the proud.
>
> Hunger had stretched the parchment skin
> Across the contours of the bone —
> Forehead, check-bones, chin.
>
> And in each face there was the same
> Ultimate revelation

Of eyes that stare upon the real —

Some terrible final thing. (*HP* 89)

"So various, all one": composed for propaganda purposes, the Gestapo's images reduce all the victims to one murderous classification of racial difference; they will be sent off to "Be cleansed of lice, and being Jews" (91). Although we can look at the pictorial archive of people captured in this genocidal plot, we do not perceive what they saw or feel what they felt.

Contemporary photographers — aware of arriving "Late in the story," of the unphotographability of pain, of the gap between seeing and comprehending — also use mug shots in the service of visual occlusion. When Aharon Gluska tampered with the mug shots of anonymous camp inmates he found at Yad Vashem and traced back through the museum at Auschwitz to particular names and numbers, he sought to remind spectators how little we discern when we examine pictures of victims. After enlarging these images up to five feet in height and attaching them to canvas, Gluska obscured them by applying several layers of black paint, wiping patches of it away, and placing gel, silk, a glass barrier, or a boxed frame over or around each photograph (Baigell 87). Like burnt cork in minstrelsy, this blackface signals the Otherness of those considered untouchable, Jews demonized as physically deformed and morally depraved (figure 4.11). The corporeal appearance of Jews — their purported inferiority and ugliness — was presumably documented by the Nazis' meticulous photographic records at the concentration camps. To illustrate the point that the Jewish people were not the only ones targeted by the Germans, Raul Hilberg discusses so-called asocials, transferred from prisons to concentration camps because of their "ugliness": in 1944 the decision was made that prisoners ("because of their bodily characteristics") who "hardly deserve the designation human" ("they look like miscarriages of hell") should "be photographed" and "eliminated. Crime and sentence are irrelevant. Only such photographs should be submitted which clearly show the deformity" (269–70). An indicator of caste, photography set out to collapse differences among individual asocial or Jewish victims, establishing instead their collective identity and then their radical alterity from the Aryan race.

Because the supposedly realistic but actually repressive photographs taken at Auschwitz robbed individuals of their individuality, reducing them to types, Gluska eclipses these images to counter their misidentifications — yet not by correcting or righting them. Gluska's revulsion against the bankrupt authority of the mechanical reproduction of the photograph goes beyond its classificatory utility to a critique of its mimetic function. In Nazi propaganda, the Jew signified the mime par excellence: unable to assimilate into the racially superior *Volk,* the Jew supposedly counterfeited an inauthentic, distorted copy of the Aryan citizen.[24] Besides exposing the urgency of stereotyping as one of photography's primary functions, Gluska's repro-

4.11. Aharon Gluska, Untitled, 1993–1994. Mixed media on canvas, 66″ × 57″. Courtesy of Aharon Gluska and Robert Mann Gallery.

ductions call the original a lie, the false copy a belated refuge, thereby impugning the acclaimed mimeticism of the photographic image. To counter the miniaturization of the mug shot, enlargement creates a being of epic proportion.

Gluska's subjects were alive when they were shot at Auschwitz, but his framing device of "corpsing the image" resembles postmortem daguerreo-

138

types.[25] That the eyes appear somewhat untouched, that the face is shrouded in fabric, that some images are placed inside plywood box frames—these emphasize how each appears as if submerged behind the picture's surface, a living corpse entombed in a crypt. Partially hidden by the paint, the smeared faces of Gluska's photographic paintings evoke the tendency of early Jewish artists "to leave facial features blank" because of biblical prohibitions against graven images of God and of the image of God in humanity (Kochan 126). Gluska paradoxically uses a technique ordinarily associated with defamation to preserve the sanctity of his subjects so that the final effect teeters between reliquary (like the Shroud of Turin) and rogues' gallery (of the "most wanted" poster). Martyrs or pariahs in their caskets, his subjects take on the aura of cursed people blessed, blessed people cursed, and therefore, as his title *Identity Pending* suggests, not easily absorbed into the viewer's usual mechanisms of identification.

When Gluska "lays it on too thick," he warns spectators that the casualties of genocide have been papered over with tons of documents in museums, movies, historical reassessments.[26] What Slavoj Žižek would call "a radical opacity" blocks "every essay of interpretation," producing an "illegibility" that forestalls any facile interpretation (151). The deformations of silk, glass, gel, paint—which make it impossible to find a position (as one would with an instance of anamorphosis) for discerning the image in its clear and distinct form—encourage most viewers to position themselves directly before the portrait, accentuating the individuality of each encased being. In contrast to the self-destructive identification sparked in Spender's suicidal refugee by Gestapo photographs (when she starves herself "To become one with her people" [*HP* 91]), the disidentification created by Gluska's portraits wards off a facile sense of familiarity with a doom the victims themselves might not have glimpsed.

In some of his work, Gluska evolves what he calls an "envelope" form that completely contains the enlarged portrait. Bagged in what looks to be black vinyl, the illuminated features of people trashed like garbage peer out at the viewer. When arranged in rows, as in *Six Envelopes* (figure 4.12), they compose a gruesome morgue of the decapitated whose mute communications resemble nothing so much as dead letters sent to those as far away as life. Encased, two-dimensional, and prone, they are packaged, just as the Shoah itself has been. Like sacks of flour or dog food, manure or grass seed, they could be and, indeed, were heaved, stacked, hurled onto conveyer belts first of the Nazis' devising and then of the weighty (though well-intentioned) cultural industry that attempts to keep memory of the Shoah alive. A sort of triple dying is documented here: the death of the human being in the dehumanization of the camps, the literal death of the dehumanized body, the symbolic murder through replacement that representation inexorably exacts.[27] As in some of the other cases of antimorphosis studied here, Gluska's work illuminates what Michael Rothberg defines as the features of "trau-

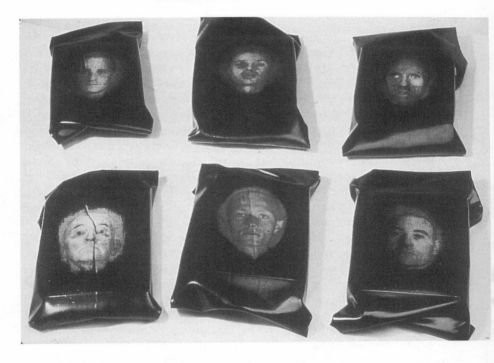

4.12. Aharon Gluska, *Six Envelopes*, 1993. Mixed media on canvas, 13″ × 17″, 11″ × 16″, 12″ × 18″. Courtesy of Aharon Gluska and Robert Mann Gallery.

matic realism" in Holocaust narrative representations: its three components consist of "a demand for documentation" (which he identifies with realism), a "reflection on the formal limits of representation" (which he identifies with modernism), and a consideration of "the risky public circulation of discourses on the events" (which he identifies with postmodernism) (7).

Defamiliarization in antimorphosis guards against making viewers "Peeping Toms of the death chamber," a phrase Simic used to express his worry that "the raw data of history given to us so soon after the event and in such detail" make "each one of us a voyeur": "On the one hand the multiplication of the images of suffering and atrocity, and on the other hand the unreality they bring to our lives with the accompanying suspicion that all that suffering is meaningless, that it is already being forgotten, that tomorrow brand-new sufferings will come" (*UC* 125). As Gluska's body bags intimate, recycled visual representation cannot but rob the Holocaust of actuality. Since truth was stranger than fiction in the fascist economy, according to a number of poets, the artifice of surrealism or film noir conveys the grotesque better than the purported realism of any after-the-fact documentary possibly could; but it also drains the real of its reality.[28] When Dannie Abse devotes a poem to the experience of attending a new Polish film with "images of Auschwitz almost authentic, / the human obscenity in close-up," he presents himself and his wife as "peeping Toms of the death chamber," forgetting that the barbed wire is nothing but a prop, that the victims are merely actors, "as we munched milk chocolate" in the dark (*BL* 478–79).[29]

For the reasons Abse hints at, evidentiary images — no matter how qualified or contaminated — will probably continue to exert more power in the context of the Shoah than invented ones. This is, of course, the reason why antimorphosis played such an important role at the end of the twentieth century, despite our skepticism about the optical. Mira Schor, in one of her scripted works of often multiply traced writing, and C. K. Williams, in one of his meditative poems, undermine any hard-and-fast distinction between honorific, documentary, and regressive photography, factual and fictional images. For Schor's query about the gray blurriness of the past refers to all its extant images (figure 4.13), just as Williams's "Old Man" conflates photographic displays of naked women waiting to be shot and prewar Polish studio portraits with pornography and advertisements so as to confess the obsessiveness of "the unquenchable lust of the eye" (*V* 76). To some extent, Schor's and Williams's evocative works register revulsion at the "lust of the eye," disgust at our desire to gawk at miseries about which (we know) we can do nothing. Perhaps, they seem to suggest, the past *should* remain a blur because, after all, it is and must be out of focus.

In instances of antimorphosis, a photograph from "then" and "there" accords with those who believe that the Holocaust can be presented only through realistic, historical testimonies provided by genuine eyewitnesses; however, the re-representing of the photograph within a contemporary setting of "here" and "now" rejects the idea that late-twentieth-century artists can or need lay claim to verisimilitude or authenticity in responses to events that probably occurred either at their birth or before they were born.[30] "If critics believe that the events of the Holocaust are important enough to bear telling, again and again," Hilene Flanzbaum has cautioned against what she calls "the avid policing" of novelistic and feature film presentations about the Shoah, "then artists must continue to find new ways to tell it" ("BWIT" 276, 284). The poets and photographers to which this chapter is devoted use their work to achieve precisely what she calls for: they "compel viewers . . . to take another look — a deeper look, a more thoughtful look — at the event" as well as the import of its transmission (285).

The haunting silence of photographic bits of paper inspires many of the

4.13. Mira Schor, *Why Does the Past . . . ?*, 2000. Ink and gesso on clay-coated paper, 20″ × 19″. Photo: Ken Pelka, courtesy of the artist.

poems composed by poets about their visits to Holocaust museums and sites, which can here punctuate a tradition based on the magnetism of distrusted ocular evidence.[31] One instance of this quite frequent approach to a pilgrimage (to a concentration camp or the Anne Frank house or a memorial), Jane Shore's "Holocaust Museum" captures the consternation of viewing material remains, real things that seem mutely to testify as circumstantial evidence. Wearing black, the poet files through the exhibits with two friends, Charlotte and Andy, a blind survivor from Warsaw who is accompanied by his German shepherd guide dog, Topper. As she and Charlotte take turns reading aloud to Andy, the poet knows that

> *something* had to break me down —
> the cattle car, the crematorium door,
> the confiscated valises of Jews

> piled high and dramatically lit
> as in a department store display. (93)

But the dramatic lighting of carefully displayed installations threatens to theatricalize the real, turning it into a mere simulation meant to trigger pathos. Perhaps for this reason, not the mountain of shoes in a room oddly smelling "like feet" but a photograph of a girl shot dead and the size of her own young daughter puts a momentary stop to Jane Shore's reading aloud, though she does not know which particular artifact has triggered the tears of her companions.

Ironically, given the frightful use of dogs in the camp, strangers in the museum are heartened to observe Topper, relieved to see amid the "nightmare photographs" something "that wasn't human" (95). The guide dog at the end of Jane Shore's "Holocaust Museum" directs the reader's attention to the same tension between seeing and comprehending that engrossed Sharon Olds's daughter in "The Window":

> Charlotte and I went to the ladies room
> leaving Topper and Andy in the lobby
> by the cloakroom, near a black family
> putting on their coats.
>
> The husband wanted to pet Topper,
> and struck up a conversation
> with Andy. "I see you're blind,"
> He said politely. "Do you understand this
> any better than I do?" And Andy
> shook his head and told him no. (Shore 95)

Does the black man feel emboldened to ask his question because he believes that the blind — unable to color-code categories of being — may be more genuinely insightful than the race-obsessed sighted? Or does his query simply reflect the general notion that blind people have been endowed with spiritual forms of insight? Or maybe the black man simply has to talk, even (or especially) to express his inability to say anything.

No more or less a seer than the sighted, Jane Shore's blind survivor underscores the blinders on all the visitors to the Holocaust museum, reminding us not to confuse the victims with ourselves. A counterpoint of identification forestalled by disidentification is induced by the visual documents deployed by the artists of antimorphosis, the averting of an incorporating identification that can neither be embraced nor disavowed, even in the midst of grief. About a visit to a death camp, Robert Pinsky's "The Unseen" recounts the impossibility of taking in the evidence — "*I cannot look to see*" — and the impossibility of not taking in the evidence: "*We try to take in what won't be turned from in despair*" (*FW* 108). His quandary, which resembles that of many who register for Holocaust studies courses or visit Holocaust museums, conveys an aversion to looking as well as a suspicion about what can be perceived in ghastly documents that always threaten to degenerate into belated simulacra. Representations deploying antimorphosis enable us to confront these perplexities head-on. Like Adrienne Rich — speaking as if for the mute stills on a roll of film — poets and photographers of the unseen intimate that "you cannot live on me alone / you cannot live without me."

5

DOCUMENTARY VERSE BEARS WITNESS

One of the most frequently anthologized Holocaust poems in English, Anthony Hecht's " 'More Light! More Light!' " elaborates on a passage from *The Theory and Practice of Hell* by Eugen Kogan, a survivor of the Buchenwald concentration camp who used his training in sociology to write the book in 1945. That this poem glosses a survivor's testimony—isolating one passage, framing it, substantially revising it—illustrates the importance of factual references in poetry that implicitly dispenses with the imaginative origins of conventional verse and thus heeds Theodor Adorno's dictum. The term "documentary verse" necessarily remains elastic. Few contemporary writers reproduce the exact words of survivors, while many edit, analyze, or partly invent the European sources they invoke to ground their work in historical specificity. "The more narrowly we look into the perplexing lens of Auschwitz, the more painful will the perception be," Cynthia Ozick has explained, adding, "It is moral ease to slide from the particular to the abstract" ("LA" 153). Authors of documentary verse about the Holocaust circumvent moral ease by connecting poetic utterance decades after the Shoah with the particular suffering it inflicted on its individual victims.

Testifying to testimonials of the casualties of calamity, as do the artists of antimorphosis, poets deploying archival material respond to Paul Celan's perplexity that "No one / bears witness for the / witness" (241) by serving as proxy-witnesses. This term does not mean, however, that they conflate the trauma of their subjects with any secondary trauma that might result from writing or reading about their subjects. On the contrary, the work of proxy-witnessing sharply distinguishes itself from that of "poetry of witness," which Carolyn Forché studies because it bears "the trace of extremity" textually (*AF* 30). In stark contrast to poets of witness, poets of proxy-witnessing often acknowledge their belated dependence on after-the-fact accounts of extremities never within their purview. They do so in order to avoid any confusion between victims in the vulnerability of "then" and poets or readers in the safety of "now," to concentrate on the disturbingly specific details of experiences decidedly not their own.

But if, for poet-witnesses of witnesses, documentary sources enable verse to guard against slipping into moral ease, what does such verse lend documentary words? The practices of poetry remove an account from the chronicles that preceded and followed it, facilitate meditation on its significance even when traditional devices for meaning making are baffled, and thereby wrest it for retention from the overwhelming flood of the past. Besides providing "a momentary stay against confusion" (the famous definition of poetry is Robert Frost's [126]), verse can pry new insights out of history by retrieving arresting memories not yet assimilated into banal or clichéd reconstructions in public memorials and popular forms. Put otherwise, poets who excavate eccentric or even trivial details from the calamity counter not only cultural amnesia but also collective memories that lose their potency when they get recycled as packaged commodities. As in much documentary verse, the narrowness of the aesthetic lens in " 'More Light! More Light!' " entails a withholding of some circumstances that clarifies the ethical significance of one of the disaster's many disasters, indicting the traditions of Western civilization that make the poem possible but that failed to prevent or perhaps even enabled the calamity twice remembered (once by the witness, once again by the pondering poet). The humility with which Hecht repeats a flagrantly *un*poetic incident in the Shoah refutes facile theories about its causes and consequences, while generating an attentiveness to the necessity of grappling (again) with the testimonials of survivors.

In its fourth through seventh stanzas, Hecht's " 'More Light! More Light!' " condenses Kogan's testimony (92) about a group of prisoners on quarry detail in the spring of 1944 when an SS detail leader ordered a Polish man named Strzaska to bury alive two Jews.[1] After the Pole refused, he was himself sentenced to their fate — "He was ordered to change places with the Jews" — while the two Jews were forced first to bury the Pole, then to exhume him, and finally to trade places again:

Much casual death had drained away their souls.
The thick dirt mounted toward the quivering chin.
When only the head was exposed the order came
To dig him out and to get back in. (*CEP* 64)

By repeating an eyewitness account (rather than inventing a narrative of his own devising), Hecht acknowledges that personal testimonial provides validation for those imaginative approaches to the Shoah that rest on its truth-claims. Yet the dissonance between his formalism — his rhyming of "hole" and "Pole," his four-line stanzas with lines of five beats, his imagery of "no light" — and Kogan's horrific narrative charges the documentary text with allegorical resonance, as do the poet's excisions.

Just as Kogan's Buchenwald becomes Hecht's more generic "German wood," just as Kogan's Strzaska becomes a nameless Pole (as anonymous as the two Jews in Hecht's poem), the SS man degenerates into a disembodied Luger, glove, riding boot. In several places in his narrative, Kogan provides explanations for the episode that are omitted or amended in Hecht's poem to heighten the scene's enigmatic depravity or to query their adequacy, to highlight unconvincing explanations or inexplicable gaps in the eyewitness account. First, whereas Kogan supplies a motivation for the Nazi command (exhaustion presumably made the Jews worthless as workers), Hecht presents the abhorrent scenario as nothing more than a whim. Second, after Kogan's Strzaska refuses to bury the Jews alive, he lies down in one of several ditches because he is threatened by a "pick handle"; but in Hecht's poem no belaboring or forcing of the man seems to be necessary. Third, although Kogan explains that the Jews then submitted to the order to bury the Pole "in the hope of escaping the ghastly fate themselves" (92), Hecht implies instead that all empathy had been destroyed in the Jews before the time of the event recorded in the poem and they therefore resemble nothing so much as the living dead, even before they are interred alive. Taken together, these and other instances of Hecht's revisions give the episode the hallucinogenic generality of an illogical fable that broods on the meaning of what Kogan faced.

Kogan's sentence "The two Jews now had to lie down in the ditch, while Strzaska was ordered to cover them up" (92) contains the same information as Hecht's "the order came / To dig him out again and to get back in." But the parallelism of this last line, with its repetition compulsion, emphasizes the sadistic game, the nonsensical taking of turns, imposed by "the order" of things on exchangeable beings devoid of any identity except as types classified as victims. Although Kogan describes many prisoners madly working so as not to attract attention to themselves, relieved to be ordered to dig up the buried Jews, and at least minimally palliated (like Strzaska and Kogan himself) by their own survival as witnesses, the crisis of Hecht's isolated trio contains no possibility of rescuing efforts or firsthand recounting. As if to dramatize Dori Laub's reflection on the Holocaust as a unique historical occurrence that "*produced no witnesses*" (Felman and Laub 80), the poem's Pole is shot on top of the grave of the Jews. Burial alive is Hecht's trope for the fate of the Jews not only because so many Jewish people were literally buried alive during the Holocaust but also, as Shoshana Felman has explained, because the "essence of the Nazi scheme" was to make the Jews "essentially invisible" by confining them to hidden death camps, by diminishing their materiality through starvation, and by reducing their dead bodies to smoke and ashes (Felman and Laub 95). That the buried are alive, while the dying lie bleeding unburied: this misrule governs not the original prose but the concluding stanza of " 'More Light! More Light!,' " a title that repeatedly echoes throughout the account of the episode and is used to encapsulate it as well.

Hecht places quotation marks around his title to reiterate what are reputed to be the last words of Goethe, the revered sage who spent most of his life in Weimar, only a few miles from Buchenwald. But of course the exclamation could also be the final cry of the buried Jews at the end of the poem or, for that matter, the last thoughts during the three hours it takes the shot Pole to have his vision put out. That at the end of the poem "No prayers or incense rose up" around the Pole's body — visited only by the "black soot" of the "Ghosts from the ovens" (*CEP* 65) — serves to differentiate him from the Protestant martyrs with whom the poem begins, a frame that definitely moves beyond Kogan's testimony. The sixteenth-century English context that opens " 'More Light! More Light!' " informs readers that torture of the innocent always existed, but that historically it occurred in a setting of religious persecution where suffering attested to the dignity, fidelity, courage, even transcendence of an individual soul calling out to his God, not to the utter senselessness of forced labor, starvation, mass murder:

> Composed in the Tower before his execution
> These moving verses, and being brought at that time
> Painfully to the stake, submitted, declaring thus:
> "I implore my God to witness that I have made no crime." (64)

The first word of the poem marks the contrast between grotesque yet spiritually significant Protestant martyrdom and the torment of the Shoah, for it signals an act of introspection in, for instance, the composing of a spiritual statement that will make the event meaningful for the martyr's followers and will thereby compose *him,* lending him some metaphysical recompense for his suffering.

Although "the death was horrible," those crucified or burnt alive were nevertheless permitted a "pitiful dignity" as they "howled for the Kindly Light." After the rhyming of "dignity" with "tranquility" (*CEP* 64), Hecht takes up the role Alicia Ostriker identifies as that "of an enlightened tour guide" ("*MSS*" 99) by flatly turning (jolting, really) to the landscape of Kogan's account: "We move now to outside a German wood." Hecht's abrupt shift to Kogan's episode juxtaposes, on the one hand, the meaningfulness of death within the "Kindly Light" of the Protestant martyr's spirituality as well as within the rationality of the Enlightenment represented by Goethe's literary work and, on the other hand, the absence of any ethical illumination in the Holocaust. Indeed, motivated by a quest for knowledge, Goethe's Faust trades salvation for wisdom in a swap that seems far more reasonable than the pointlessness of the Nazi pact with the devil that Kogan documents in his *Theory and Practice of Hell*. Did Hecht know that a poem by Goethe about the beauty of death by fire hung over some of the ovens?[2] Both the repentance of Goethe's Faust and the truth telling of the Protestant martyrs have been abrogated by a text about the bankruptcy of traditional paradigms for comprehending evil and suffering. Murdered, not martyred, the Pole in Hecht's parable undergoes the "double dying" Alvin Rosenfeld associates with the Shoah: first, when he becomes nothing but the instrument of the Nazi instrument — when he understands himself to have been robbed (like the Jews) of any moral agency and the light dies in "the blue Polish eye" — and, second, when he is physically killed.

Hecht's dependence on and manipulation of factual commentary typify the practices of a group of poets who deploy testimonial in verse. Like the photograph, the affidavit attempts to bring verisimilitude to what no one wanted to believe at the time, to what inspired in so many Americans during and after the war — even though they had been given a substantial amount of eyewitness information on the atrocities — an "overwhelming incredulity" and "skepticism" about an "enormity" that seemed more like a "wild nightmarish imagining" or mere "propaganda" than an actual event (Lipstadt, *BB* 272–73). Perhaps for this reason, the literary framing of testimonial — like that of the absent photograph — simultaneously questions and stresses the efficacy of unfiltered documentary evidence as a mechanism for conveying truth or fostering empathy. What poetic form achieves over unadulterated documentation (in even that work which most carefully reiterates the testimonial on which it draws) is the charging of words with their utmost meaning, even as verse configurations foreground the poet's reliance on (and at times incomplete understanding of) such testimonials.[3]

The shortness of verse; its deliberate placement of words in lines that do not necessarily accord with syntactic breaks; the use of rhythm or rhyme; the compression of a plethora of details into fewer and therefore more charged terms and images; the reaching for analogies, albeit inadequate ones; the suppression of logical, narrative links: these lead creative writers to take factual material often dubbed "nightmarish imagining" or "propaganda" and, paradoxically, use their imagination to make it more palpably real. Like authors defending themselves against charges of plagiarism, poets of proxy-witnessing attempt to return what they have borrowed "sharper" than they received it.[4] In this regard, the refreshing of testimony relies on verse. Yet by stressing their dependence on recalcitrantly alien eyewitness accounts, poets send readers back to such documents, even as they sometimes implicitly, sometimes explicitly resign their own poems to a belated insufficiency that registers the modesty of their undertaking.

At its least mediated, documentary poetry aspires to the condition of journalistic or legal reportage, reiterating the words of survivors to contest incredulity; however, since even representations that claim to imitate the world also construct versions of it, various aesthetic maneuvers inevitably intervene to complicate the reportorial model. North American and British poets have edited legal depositions; transcribed oral histories; described their reactions to circumstantial evidence and trials; used passages in books about the Holocaust as footnotes, titles, epigraphs, and occasions for ethical speculations; and recorded their reactions to conversations with survivors. To the extent that the most literal, legalistic journalism crops testimony as rigorously as a camera frames experience, documentary poets question the objectivity of representation, just as they emphasize the artifice of presumably factual accounts, the blurring of the line between fiction and fact, and the gender dynamics at work in their interpretive efforts—as well as the bleak pointlessness of such speculations in the face of the suffering of Europe's Jews and the fracturing of those ethical imperatives that made the most orthodox and the most secular of its populace a people.

In their scrupulous vigilance about the specificity of particular and often eccentric experiences, these artists' witnessing by proxy enacts a poetics of anamnesis. Anamnesis: a calling to mind; a remembering of a life before this life; in the context of documentary verse, a recollection of the lives of survivors before the time of their witnessing, the author's composing of the poem, and the reader's confrontation with it. As the Shoah continues to recede into a more distant past, contemporary authors stress the disjunction between documentary sources and their own utterances so that the lacuna between "then" and "now" broadens. By facing the impossibility of remembering what they never knew, authors dedicated to a poetics of anamnesis ask us not to forget what we can neither recollect nor fully comprehend as we ponder what others have recalled.

ORAL HISTORIES

Whether considering victims, survivors, or soldier-observers, the most scrupulously journalistic writers of documentary verse about the Jewish experience in the Second World War severely curtail their own artistic ambition, committing themselves instead to modest repetitions — specifically, repetitions of affidavits — since, as W. D. Snodgrass sardonically put it, "the facts . . . are hard to improve upon" (*FB* 67). As we saw in the case of the photograph described in but absent from the poem, the extensive use of quoted material qualifies the poet's knowledge as merely secondhand while simultaneously delineating truths stranger than fiction. Decisions about line breaks, where the quotation begins and ends, how to embed it with others, whether or not to name the actual speaker, how to translate or condense it: these editorial judgments confine the authorial imagination, reducing the creative writer to a scribe. They therefore formally concede a humbling imaginative exile analogous (but only like a pale shadow or faint echo) to the graver losses described by their speakers. Authors recording what witnesses have written or said relinquish efforts to fictionalize or explain or evaluate those utterances and thereby signal their own aesthetic and moral deportation from stories that are themselves about physical, psychological, geographic, and linguistic dispossession. Expression without conceptualization marks this tradition as "minor," to use the terminology of Gilles Deleuze and Félix Guattari. To the extent that the poetic framers (not exactly authors) of oral histories absent themselves in a kind of disappearing act, they attain one of Deleuze and Guattari's characteristics of minor literature: "There isn't a subject; *there are only collective assemblages of enunciation*" (18).

Perhaps Charles Reznikoff best achieves this aim in his landmark volume *Holocaust* (1975), which consists entirely of quotations from twenty-six volumes of trials compressed into a slender book of 111 pages of verse. Within each section — "Deportation," "Invasion," "Research," "Ghettos," "Massacres," "Gas Chambers and Gas Trucks," "Work Camps," "Children," "Entertainment," "Mass Graves," "Marches," "Escapes" — the voices the reader encounters derive from almost verbatim speeches at the trials (as they appeared in an English translation). Almost verbatim, because Reznikoff omits the names and particular locales of the specific perpetrators and victims, as well as contingent and emotionally responsive details and any extended commentary. The reader situated in a vertiginous moral void takes on the role of judge and jury of the events presented (not of the disembodied, distilled voices that never really become individualized as distinct characters). Trained in journalism and in the law, Reznikoff used his choice of selections to emphasize inexplicable moments of Nazi criminality that would seem preposterous — not merely improbable, but downright impossible — were they not recounted by people who had "been there." Objectivist poetry, according to Reznikoff, abides by the rules of the court of law. "Evidence to be admissible in a trial cannot state conclusions of fact," he explains; "it must state the facts themselves," leaving the "conclusions of fact . . . for the jury and let us add, in our case, for the reader" (*F*8).

The truth-claim made on the title page of *Holocaust* ("All that follows is based on a United States government publication, *Trials of the Criminals before the Nuernberg Military Tribunal,* and the records of the Eichmann trial in Jerusalem") means that each Kafkaesque parable cannot be dismissed as simply a Kafkaesque parable:

The commander of a camp, among his amusements, as in other
  camps
had a large dog
and at the cry of "Jude," that is, "Jew,"
the dog would attack the man and tear off pieces of flesh.
In another camp, the Jews who had just come
kept seeing a dog—
the dog belonged to the S.S. man in charge of "the showers," that
  is, the gas chambers;
the S.S. man would call the dog "Mensch," that is, "man";
and whenever he set the dog on a Jew would say, "Man, get that
  dog!" (73)

Through the repetition of a phrase that emphasizes the urgency of translation-work ("that is"), Reznikoff portrays a topsy-turvy dog-eat-man world
of misnomers in which "gas chambers" has been redefined into "showers,"
"prison" into "camp," "dog" into "man," and "Jew" into "dog."[5] The un-
derstated anecdote, shorn of explicit moral instruction, turns the episode
into a surrealistic insignia—it could be any Jew, a number of SS men, in
various camps—of the destruction of the quotidian. As the word "amusements" resonates with archetypal stories about the early Christians thrown
to the lions and about Daniel in the den, the reader confronts a staged
spectacle whose only payoff for the SS "commander" must be the relish he
takes in his supremely ironic creation of an anti-world, complete with its own
nihilistic lexicon and practices. Even the parasites, germs, and rats to which
Hitler recurrently likened Jews would not be subjected to such bizarre torments, and so Reznikoff's portraits of torture raise questions about the
motivation of their cruel inventors. Folded into the horror of Jews demoted
below animals and toxins is the debasement of dogs trained to inhuman
purposes that only human beings could devise. The discipline of the poet
who denies himself the privilege of moral denunciation or personal revulsion about the material lends Reznikoff's work a stark austerity that refuses
any explanatory paraphernalia as pointless because inadequate.[6]
  Appearing directly under the heading "Entertainment," the verse paragraph quoted above prefaces a collection of poems about camp officers
playing other "games" with prisoners: shooting them in target practices,
putting mice into their trousers after binding the ankles with ropes, making
them stand naked in freezing barrels of water for twenty-four hours. But the
entire volume vibrates with instances of such sadistic "amusements." In the
first section, "Deportation," two SS members of "the entertainment squad"
force a Jewish man "to clean the steps of the entrance" to the Jewish community's closed office: "the water had an acid in it burning his hands"
(Reznikoff, H 13). The only poem in the second section, "Invasion," drama-

tizes an encounter between fleeing Polish Jews and Nazis who strip and beat them, "laughing all the time";

> Then they ordered the Jews to get on their knees
> and sing Hebrew songs;
> the Jews sang the Zionist anthem, *Ha-tikvah*.
> And then they had to crawl through a concrete pipe on the road.
> (17)

"Research," the next chapter, includes one monologue in the voice of a "civilized" defender of the scientific benefits to which the Jews were put "for the good of" the German air force, navy, and army: "to find out the limits of human endurance," the Aryans "wound them and force wooden shavings or ground glass / into the wounds, / or take out bones, muscles and nerves" (21).

Spoken in everyday speech rhythms, the dispassionate reporting of "just the facts" cauterizes even the most awful of actions—of a baby torn apart like "a rag" in the "Ghetto" section (29) —by deleting any mention of the feelings of actors or spectators. After a smiling officer in the "Massacres" section picks out an attractive young woman in a row of people told to undress, for instance, a moment of promise seems to open up: " 'Take a step forward! / Don't you want to live?' " Since it would be " 'a pity / to bury such beauty,' " he tells her " 'Go! // But don't look backwards' "; when she follows his instructions, he shoots her in the back (38–39). Should readers be reminded of other about-to-be-liberated figures told "don't look backward," such as Lot's wife in the Bible or Orpheus trying to bring Eurydice out of Hades, the comparison would only strengthen the deranged pointlessness of the scene, for Reznikoff's young woman has merely been tricked into thinking she belongs among their ranks. Reznikoff forswears such analogues, withholds them, to insist on the incoherence of such unlikely events. Neither a biblical nor a mythic protagonist, the young woman meets her unexpected death within a contemporary urban setting where "There is a street to the boulevard" (39) in clear view. Why would the officer encourage the beautiful woman and her cohorts to hope she might escape, if he was only going to murder her? Psychoanalytic explanations, which attend to an individual's early childhood experiences, seem beside the point, given so many instances of anonymous malignity. Although Reznikoff's book concludes with the rescue of the Danish Jews, the overwhelming effect emanates from depictions of crimes of such senseless and extreme viciousness that one cannot conceive and does not find given an adequate motivation or punishment.

The "amusement" episodes, hardly the most horrific in Reznikoff's book, circle around instances of what Primo Levi called widespread "useless cruelty" that cannot be explained (*DS* 106–107), though explanations inevitably arise. Gratuitously inflicted, such procedures forced the Jewish victims of Reznikoff's *Holocaust* to enact exactly what Levi claimed was their result in the camps — namely, a "caricature" of German military procedures (116). Such a replication of SS behavior led Bruno Bettelheim to accuse inmates of childish regression, whereas it led Terrence Des Pres to defend the use of strategic imitation as a survival tactic (*S*). Given new ranks and serial numbers, housed in sexually segregated barracks and counted at selections, Reznikoff's scarecrows wear their tattered uniforms, exercise in the open yard, undergo physical inspection, and perform their senseless work assignments in an uncanny doubling of their SS tormentors.

> The roll-call went like this: "Attention.
> Cap on. Cap off. Cap on. Cap off.
> Quickly!"
> They spent half an hour doing frog-jumps,
> even in the rain and mud.
> And now and then a man would be taken out of line and sent to
>   the gas chambers. (*H* 104–105)

Of course, the Nazis could have murdered the Jews more adeptly without all these complicated and time-consuming procedures. But if the fascists were to establish themselves as the heroic Super Race of *Übermenschen,* the Jews had to be made to perform as a craven Sub Race. Does the very proliferation of fascist dehumanizing mechanisms suggest that Hitler's executioners really understood Jews to be human beings and thus in need of strenuously debasing rites of passage in what amounts to a theater of cruelty, as Hyam Maccoby has speculated?[7]

In *The Drowned and the Saved,* Levi also reasons that "useless cruelty" served the "highly symbolic" (124) function of lessening German guilt by reducing the Jews to brute matter — animals (herded, branded, harnessed to work, butchered), material (clothing and personal possessions appropriated, hair sold as produce, teeth extracted for gold), dirt (ashes used as land fill, for the paths of officers' barracks) — and thereby expelling them from the human race. Given the jokes, games, and amusements of the Nazis in *Holocaust,* this "symbolic" work, which is produced by the diseased imagination of German fascists, condemns the creative faculty itself and thus grounds Reznikoff's renunciation of any imaginative reconstruction in his own verse.[8] The fascists' reinvention of everyday language, their setting of scenes, and their devising of costumes and highly ironic plots cast them in the thoroughly discredited role of supreme artificer or author. The poet's decision to record cropped versions of testimonies without any other legal framework — no judge, no jury, no lawyers, no verdict, no sentencing — hints that the culpability of the fascist imagination evades subsequent judgments made outside the event. Regardless of *Holocaust*'s juridical sources, such omissions suggest that justice will not and cannot be served.

Barbara Helfcott Hyett uses documentary techniques not to provide testimony in a trial but to perform a kind of postmortem on a stage littered with bodies. Establishing its authority from eyewitnesses on the scene, *In Evidence: Poems of the Liberation of Nazi Concentration Camps* draws its "collective assemblages of enunciation" not from Jewish survivors of genocide but from U.S. citizens, the American soldiers Hyett interviewed and taped some thirty years after their shock at liberating the camps. The voices of often nauseated servicemen enable Hyett to negotiate between the unspeakable plight of the victims, stunned into sickness or silence, and the incomprehension of incredulous civilians back in the States. Retrospective accounts of a succession of enlisted teenagers and their somewhat older officers, her "found" poems circle around the liberators' horror at the abrogation of bodily integrity: a dead man within a freight car "who'd completed the / amputation of his / gangrenous leg with / his own hands" (25); "breathing skeletons. / I used to ask myself / *Is this a man or / a woman I'm speaking to?*" (49); "No cheeks. / No muscles in the chin. Only / skin and lips like paper tapes" (56); "eyes that were sunk / actually halfway into / their heads" (74). Whereas Reznikoff depicts the grotesque mirroring between the Nazis and the Jews, Hyett explores the distressing mimetic rivalry between Nazi and American troops. The Americans, too, talk about containing the prisoners, keeping them away from food, thinking about them as stiffs, mistaking the living for the dead, and terrifying them with retrievers, and thus they unwittingly duplicated the Nazis' roles.

What many of the veterans return to is the indescribable odor in which "was mingled death / and disinfectant, the hallways / jammed, straw pallets, beds / where skeletons lay curled" (74) amid the stench of the ovens:

> You can wipe out
> what you don't want
> to see. Close your
> eyes. You don't want
> to hear, don't want
> to taste. You can
> block out all senses
> except smell. (98)

The ubiquity of the smell convinces the soldiers that people in the "peaceful little / community" across the bridge from the camp had to know: "*Couldn't you tell from / the stench?*" (121). The final poem of *In Evidence* makes it clear how difficult it is to convey the stink of genocide to someone who has not smelled it, yet how important: "*I've been there. / I have seen this. This is real. I still smell the stench*" (158).[9] Different as her speakers are from those of Reznikoff, Hyett just as radically curtails her authorial license, even as she uses *In Evidence* to emphasize the Nazis' reverence for objects over and against their trashing of people, indeed their manufacturing of precious objects out of trashed subjects. The shock of people smelling like lepers or decomposing corpses or the excrement in which they were forced to subsist contrasts with pristine objets d'art, a dissonance that asks us to consider the repercussions of this barbarity on the Christians who perpetrated it:

> A prisoner gave me a boat
> he'd taken from the house
> of Ilse Koch. Ilse Koch,
> the beast of Buchenwald.
> It was a sailboat. *Santa*
> *Maria,* the Madonna painted
> in gilt, the child in gilt,
> three painted crosses, a boat
> with sails of human flesh. (58)

Passages about "Wedding rings, lockets, / actual fillings from / people's teeth" and "filing cabinets / full of baby shoes" (75) display dead objects preserved while moribund people putrefy.

"The first / thing I saw were piles / of shoes, all kinds of / shoes, a pyramid of shoes" (Hyett 19). When one of Hyett's soldier-speakers seems to reappear in W. S. Merwin's prose poem "The Dachau Shoe" as the poet's cousin Gene, Merwin sustains Hyett's perplexity about what it means for Americans to step into the shoes of their predecessors. Here the historical "then" recedes deeper into the past, for the eyewitness does not speak himself but is instead filtered through the poet's apprehension of him. The presumed accuracy of Reznikoff's and Hyett's edited monologues declines, as unreliability escalates. "My cousin Gene (he's really only a second cousin) has a shoe he picked up at Dachau" begins Merwin's text about the futility of a secondhand recounting of a second cousin's effort to preserve a physical article from the past as an object lesson for the future (15). A story about his cousin's efforts to decipher the significance of a shoe he acquired during his time in Germany, the brief paragraphs repeat the words "he explained" or "he explains" twenty-five times. Gene attempts to elucidate why he took the shoe, why he kept it on the mantel, why he fought, why he couldn't stop the murders: the past tense predominates until he has placed the shoe in a cellar drawer, presumably because dust collected on it. As the poem switches to the present tense and it becomes clear that the very profusion of explanations proves the impossibility of finding an adequate commentary, the shoe itself seems less souvenir or trophy and more relic or fetish, shard or fossil.

It stands for loss — the loss of the shoe's mate, the loss of the foot that wore the shoe, the absence of that body from a grave or a history book. Merwin's offhand conclusion — "You really ought to go and see it. He'll show it to you. All you have to do is ask. It's not that it's really a very interesting shoe when you come right down to it but you learn a lot from his explanations" (16) — proves that the shoe does not fit Gene's explanations, that he who never wore it can hardly bear to own it. Multiply removed, the reader—hearing Merwin's account of Gene's reckoning of the ownerless shoe—begins to view the shoe as a symbol of everything stripped away from a human being who remains as anonymous and unknown as the shoe but, ironically, far more mortal, the shoe's sole outliving the cracked soul of its owner. The shoe as remnant of the real seems to carry the promise of the factual; however, since verbal works of art can no more contain actual objects than they can convey smells, the image of Gene's shoe in Merwin's prose poem neutralizes the reality of Primo Levi's experience of the wooden clogs exchanged for shoes that dragged like "a convict's chain" in a realm where "Death begins with the shoes" (SA 34); of Charlotte Delbo's insight that "We pay attention only to our feet" in their oversized clogs, often stolen, leaving frozen toes "bare in the snow" (44). Poems of reportage constitute "a record of what would be lost / if it were not written" and then rewritten again; however, as the author of this phrase, Anita Barrows, concedes in a documentary poem about the Holocaust, "Every poet know this / & knows as well that poetry doesn't save anything" (17).

BANALITY ON TRIAL

In a meditation on a fourteen-year-old boy's experience in Bergen-Belsen, Shirley Kaufman locates another tension in *non*cathartic documentary verse: "The poem wants to get out / of where it is. But is instructed / to remember" (146). Whereas reportorial poets of eyewitness testimony marshal the bare minimum of formal measures to disappear behind the words of "collective assemblages of enunciation," some authors dealing with highly publicized events proffer more formally crafted reactions that instruct us to remember critical analyses of the Shoah. Two verse sequences, one by Denise Levertov and the other by Michael Hamburger, juxtapose allusions to testimonies with scenes of the poets' devising to illuminate the ethical issues examined by Hannah Arendt in the trial of Adolf Eichmann. Under the aegis of Arendt's *Eichmann in Jerusalem,* Levertov and Hamburger grasp the anecdotal source material in a far more literary manner than Reznikoff and Hyett. Although many would take issue with the moral drawn, both poets ask us to feel pity for the pitiless murderer whom they present not as a monstrous perversion of Western civilization but paradoxically as its very embodiment. According to Levertov and Hamburger, Eichmann emerges as the epitome of the civilizing process by which the deployment of violence is divested from any moral desiderata and instead subordinated to an eminently "rational calculus" (Bauman 28). In his banality, Eichmann becomes the legitimate heir of the cultural tendencies at work in the modern, bureaucratized nation-state, the rational and dutiful citizen par excellence.

Yet unlike Arendt, and partly because of the lyrical sequence's capacity to resist narrative closure, Levertov also dramatizes the tensions at work in the "banality of evil" thesis. Not every bureaucrat becomes a Nazi, and the mystery of Eichmann's not-at-all banal capacity for murder remains unaccountable. The three parts of her "During the Eichmann Trial" move backward from the trial itself to the only incident discussed in the trial in which Eichmann was accused of murdering a Jewish boy with his own hands and then further back to Kristallnacht. The tripartite sequence establishes the whole as a series of visceral responses that occurred to the poet "during" the trial, three reactions neither logical nor coherent: first, the remote observer's need to pity Eichmann in Jerusalem almost twenty years after the execution of his crimes; next, the realization that Nazi violence represents not the banality but the personification of evil; and finally, the terror and incomprehension of victims unable to anticipate what would occur. Eventually qualified, the opening section nevertheless makes an effort to break down the "us" versus "them" at work not only in the Holocaust's scapegoating of the Jews but also and more daringly in the post-Holocaust scapegoating of Germans as incarnate evil. Just as the "Final Solution" was an effort to purify Germany of the internal corruption embodied by its polluted Jewish noncitizens, Levertov contends, so juridical solutions to the Holocaust dangerously teeter on the Nazi wrong of *Rechthaberei* (dogmatism, or the quality of obsessively believing oneself in the right), replacing the gas chamber with a glass chamber for pariahs. Unpopular as such a view must have been then and certainly is today, Levertov warns against demonizing German fascists as Nazi monsters because such an imaginative trajectory mimics the translation of (in Arendt's phrase) Judaism into Jewishness: "Jews had been able to escape from Judaism into conversion; from Jewishness there was no escape" (*OT* 87).

In "When We Look Up," therefore, Eichmann in his glass cage becomes a symbol of the isolation of a consciousness rendered incapable of self-reflection. Imprisoned in the booth, as in his solipsism, Eichmann — we are informed in the very first line — "had not looked" and it is this not-looking into the face of the Other or, indeed, into the Otherness of one's own reflected face that breeds murder:

> He had not looked,
> pitiful man whom none
>
> pity, whom all
> must pity if they look
>
> into their own face (given
> only by glass, steel, water
>
> barely known) all
> who look up

to see — how many
faces? (63)

Just as Emmanuel Levinas argues that "The face is an irreducible mode in which being can present itself in its identity," Levertov's text asserts that the secret to understanding the link between the self and the Other depends on the gaze and specifically a gazing upon the face, for (in Levinas's words) "A thing can never be presented personally and ultimately has no identity. Violence is applied to the thing, it seizes and disposes of the thing" (*DF* 8). According to Levinas, "murder is possible, but it is possible only when one has not looked the Other in the face" (10). Eichmann's glass cage, "where we may view / ourselves," therefore tells "us something he / does not know; we are members // one of another" (Levertov 63).

What kept Eichmann from looking up and into the faces of others was not an inherent evil stain within his soul or psyche, but rather the sense of duty on which he prided himself. Reared "to obedience" from the nursery on, Levertov's Eichmann (in lines quoted from the trial's testimony) explains his not-looking into the faces of those marked by yellow stars, for " 'They were cast out // as if they were / some animals, some beasts' " and anyway " 'what would disobedience / have brought me? And // whom would it have served?' " Businesslike and impersonal, Eichmann had worked loyally for the state, disciplined himself to obey its dictates:

"I would not let my thoughts

dwell on this — I had
seen it and that was

enough[.]" (64–65)

Obedience and modesty, ordinarily deemed moral virtues, lent him a sense of forbearance about " 'a spring of blood' " that " 'gushed from the earth.' "[10] Better methods would have to be devised or, he feared, his own people would go mad, although (as Arendt sardonically explains, quoting the humble Eichmann), "Who was he 'to have [his] own thoughts in this matter?' " (*EJ* 114). Although the repetition of the word "pity" suggests that the quality of mercy is strained, Levertov's plea to "Pity this man" intimates that Eichmann's ability to divorce violence from ethics by calculating its social, psychological, and political economy will have to be replicated by those determined to execute him.

The second section of "During the Eichmann Trial," "The Peachtree," elaborates on the only accusation that agitated Eichmann during the trial: the eventually dismissed charge that he had once beaten a Jewish boy to death over some stolen fruit.[11] Whereas the banality of evil thesis implies that all people are capable of the sort of criminality Eichmann exhibited, the identification of Eichmann with the Devil here names Nazism a satanic transgression against humanity. Additionally, the villa garden setting embodies a Nazi distrust of nature that led to fascist efforts to design a perfect societal arrangement, an artificial order that required extensive weeding and pruning.[12] Hitler's July 1941 speech that signaled his determination to murder each and every Jew in German-occupied land was couched in a euphoric vision of transforming Germany into a garden of Eden (Rosenbaum 371). Like a racially pure world, the anti-Edenic orchard with its fruit tree represents Eichmann's ideal Aryan state. Since the Devil owns the entire garden and all its produce, the boy *has* to enter as a plunderer, precisely the role Hitler allotted Jews when he took away their citizenship and limited their food rations to no more than 400 calories daily (*Black Book* 221).

A single yellow, ripe peach "calls" the boy, causing him to reach for the forbidden fruit:

> he cannot withstand desire
> it is no common fruit
>
> it holds some secret
> it speaks to the yellow star within him
>
> He scales the wall
> enters the garden of death
> takes the peach
> and death pounces[.] (66)

Eichmann's determination to keep the fruit for himself merges with his vampiric appetite for Jewish bodies when he "pounces" on the thief-intruder, when trampled yellow juice and red blood flow together beneath the tree. Usually a buttress of anti-Semitism, here the "blood libel" — a scurrilous legend that Jews engage in the ritual murder of Christian children — has been leveled against the Nazis. According to Levertov's parable of the fall, Eichmann's appetite for the peach, for the boy is enormous. The slippage between the boy, the yellow star, and the peach begins with its first description: "yellow and ripe / the vivid blood / bright in its round cheek." If Eichmann resembled a timorous clerk like J. Alfred Prufrock in the first poem, T. S. Eliot's famous line "Do I dare to eat a peach?" haunts this section of "During the Eichmann Trial," lending a pedophilic subscript to the Nazi's desire for the peach's blood, the boy's juice, their round cheeks. Already in the previous section of "During the Eichmann Trial," Eichmann was said to display a fondness for "Yellow / [which] calmed him later" (64).

Just as the German "science of feeding" awarded more food to "higher" races and less to "lower" races, "mister death" devours more than his share:

> mister death who signs papers
> then eats

telegraphs simply: Shoot them
then eats
mister death who orders
more transports
then eats[.] (67)

Comfortably cushioned away from proximity to slaughter, the man who
signs, telegraphs, and orders also confidently and casually consumes " 's
blood" (a term that deletes what Eichmann cannot perceive, God's blood).
Yet to the extent that "The Peachtree" imagines the Jewish boy complicitous
in his own fate, Levertov approaches the most controversial of Arendt's
postulates, namely that Zionist and assimilated Jews alike had "sold [their]
soul to the devil" (a phrase one of the judges leveled against a prominent
Jewish leader [*EJ*42]). As if reflecting on the popular Zionist slogan adopted
as a response to Boycott Day, April 1, 1933 — "Wear it with Pride, the Yellow
Star!" (59) — Levertov implies that the boy voluntarily enters the Devil's
cultivated garden, that his desire for a yellow peach deludes him into believing that he can survive in this terrain and with an internalized identification
("it speaks to the yellow star within him") that dooms him. The grotesque
parallelism between the boy's and the Devil's desire for the yellow fruit hints
at all the disturbing issues of collaboration that led Arendt to condemn
Jewish cooperation with the Nazis and to the subsequent outrage of her
critics. Implicating Jews in responsibility for the disaster, Arendt imagines the
Jews in Nazi-occupied countries as living "in a fool's paradise" about a "legal
solution" to the Jewish problem (*EJ*38–39).

If the first poem's "Pity this man" is confounded by the insatiable, pedophilic "mister death" of Levertov's second poem, such demonization appears equally pointless in light of the incomprehensible terror recorded
in the final verse. The third and concluding section, "Crystal Night," announces a scream accompanied by a shattering of glass, a cracking of bones,
a splitting and splintering of silence that breaks temples and rents veils until,
as in Chagall's title for *White Crucifixion*, Levertov returns to the "white
sound" of the scream, the "white needle" of fear, the "jets of white" flood-
lights, the "white-clouded pantomime" that break all forms of coherence
and clarity,

smashing the windows of history
a whiteness scattering
in hailstones
each a mirror,
for man's eyes[.] (69)

Here, at its shattering conclusion, the glass cage that had metamorphosed
into a mirror splinters into a blinding instrument of torture. As fragile as
glass, grammar breaks down in the face of inexplicable and unbearable

shock. Whereas Arendt insinuated that the Jews and their appointed spokes-men either colluded with the Nazis or failed to organize resistance against them, Levertov's last verse makes it apparent how impossible such charges become in a landscape of alarm. Reduced to inarticulate phrases piled up in horror, the poet stutters— "it is Crystal Night // it is Crystal Night" — to record what Eichmann's own language has repeatedly elided and eluded. According to Arendt, "officialese became his language because he was gen-uinely incapable of uttering a single sentence that was not a cliché"; he "repeated word for word the same stock phrases and self-invented clichés" (*EJ* 48, 49).

This is why Michael Hamburger's sequence "In a Cold Season" takes language as one of the central issues at stake in the Eichmann trial. "Words cannot reach him in his prison of words / Whose words killed men because those men were words," Hamburger begins his five-poem sequence; he repeats the phrase "Words cannot reach" over and over again, linking mind-less linguistic multiplication with Eichmann's propensity to think numer-ically, for people were either words or numbers to Eichmann "And still are numbers though reiterated" (*CP* 129). Words and numbers neither "sob nor whimper," so Eichmann lived in a world inhabited only by words and num-bers. Like all of the officials involved in the "Final Solution," Eichmann was bound by an officialese (*Amtssprache*) regulated by "language rules," which consisted of silences, euphemisms, and lies that would prevent the Nazis or the German population at large from understanding the nature of their genocidal acts (Arendt, *EJ* 85–86). Lucy Dawidowicz also argued that Hit-ler's use of ambiguous words — *Entfernung* (removal), *Aufraumung* (cleaning up), *Beseitigung* (elimination) — could be understood one way (as expulsion) by some of his audience, another way (as extermination) by others. How can the judges in Israel trap a man in words who killed in words and thought in numbers? Eichmann, in his copy of the minutes of the Wannsee Conference (where "emigration" of the Jews was jettisoned for "evacuation" to the East), provided a country-by-country tabulation that would add up to 11 million Jews (Landau 167–68): he included conquered countries with huge popula-tions (Poland with 2,284,00) and small (Norway with 1,300) as well as neutral and enemy nations (Switzerland with 18,000 and England with 330,000). How can the regular numbers of the poet's ten-syllable lines reach "the children, women, men / Who were not words or numbers till they died?" (Hamburger, *CP* 129).

"In a Cold Season" 's second poem invokes a "Muse of the IN-trays, OUT-trays" (*CP* 129) because Eichmann is the hero of the ethos of competency in "our abstract age." Portraying the Nazi as a meticulous manager, Ham-burger satirically invokes memoranda, carbon copies, and file cabinets to certify the conventionality and propriety of this model of a model admin-istrator:

Never lost his temper on duty
Even with subordinates, even with elements earmarked
For liquidation;
Never once guilty of exceeding his authority
But careful always to confine his ambitions
Within the limits laid down for personnel of his grade. (130)

A responsible "specialist in the organization / Of the transport and disposal of human material," Eichmann has had "an exemplary career" (130). The language of moral virtue — self-sacrifice to the greater goal of the organization's efficiency — accords with Ziegmunt Bauman's and Stanley Milgram's view that "moral inhibitions against violent atrocities" can erode when violence has been officially authorized and routinized (Bauman 21). Similarly, the rhetoric of objectivity — dispassionate, meticulous accounting of names and numbers — implicates intellection itself in criminality.

Knowing without feeling is what the bureaucrat accomplishes, according to the third section of this sequence. And words, as well as numbers, helped Eichmann achieve this goal of not feeling anything about people linguistically and mathematically multiplied, divided, subtracted, and reduced. Was it "pride in numbers" that caused Eichmann to say "he would jump with glee into his grave knowing that over five million Jews had been exterminated," as Saul Friedlander has speculated? Did tabulating the growing numbers contribute to "Rausch" [intoxication] stemming "from repetition, from the ever-larger numbers of the killed" (*MHE* 109)? Subverting his own repetitive artifice, Hamburger hints that the incantatory repetition of words and numbers deadens consciousness and conscience. For him, as for other documentary poets, only a "single face" or a "single cry" (*CP* 131) can belie the words and numbers that numb emotion. His own personal history as well as his commitment to those whose fates went unheard and unseen causes him to turn in the fourth poem to the cry he did not hear and the face he did not see on the day his own grandmother was deported.

Like other anti-elegies about the impossibility of writing an elegy (to which I turn in chapter 7), section 4 of "In a Cold Season" emphasizes how little the poet knows about the dead woman he last visited when he was nine years old. Yet richly textured recollections of the specificity of "her little realm" — her lapdog, her three goldfishes, her secretly sharing sweets and the "magic" of a wireless radio with her visiting grandchild — are framed by the more formal stanzas composed in an abstract lexicon about the "exemplary career" man of "No abnormalities" (130–31). Exactly this contrast between abstract terms and numbers, on the one hand, and the specificity of an aging diabetic hiding her sweets in a pillbox, on the other, makes Hamburger's point: whether she was killed "by bullet, gas or deprivation," the ill grandmother "childlike herself and guileless and wise" has been nullified by words and numbers. Knowing she had been forced to "write a postcard to her son in England. / 'Am going on a journey'; and that all those years / She had refused to travel even to save her life" (131), the poet judges his own language fraudulent. It was Eichmann who insisted on the importance of the writing of postcards, which were supposed to sustain the illusion that the murdered were still alive; indeed, he prided himself that in one of his camps "postal communications . . . forwarded directly through the advisor on Jewish affairs" amounted "to more than 1000 letters and postcards" in one month (Erzorsky 70). As Gertrude Erzorsky points out about this so-called *Briefaktion* (letter action), it exemplifies "not the banality, but the *cunning* of evil" (71).

"And yet," Hamburger concludes in his last stanza, "yet I would not have him die" by a word issued from the court's judges. While a death sentence would reach Eichmann to add "one number to the millions dead," his death would subtract "nothing from death," from "Bones piled on bones their only mourners bones / The inconceivable aggregate of the dead" (*CP* 132). Hopeless about getting the sum right, the poet nevertheless counts out the five beats of his astonishingly polished iambic pentameters in a work that ends with a paradoxical affirmation that "words may yet be whole" but only by breaking them, a groundless affirmation attained by an equally quixotic plea for Eichmann's life. Hamburger — fully aware that the most sorrowful or angry words, the most meticulously repeated numbers could neither mourn nor avenge those "Who were not words or numbers till they died" — expresses the futility of his own philosophizing about the impossibility of justice after the Shoah. But since it was rationality (numbers) and language (words) that executed the "Final Solution," perhaps such an irrational conclusion about breaking the words and refusing any addition to the numbers is all that the poet can muster against his ruin. Eyewitnesses attest to the "counting and recounting" during interminable roll calls "until the numbers come out right"; the wearying "keeping track of time" by "keeping track of the dead" and thus worrying "How many days until they add me to the list? Who will remain to take the final count?" (Delbo 101, 257): Hamburger blames the Shoah not on the German nation but on a reduction — of words (names) for numbers (tattoos) — that shapes his own poetic meter.

PROXY-WITNESSES OF MINUTE INCIDENTS

Since the detachment on which Levertov's and Hamburger's Eichmann prided himself had so thoroughly been put into question, recent poets who investigate source materials repudiate the objectivity to which Reznikoff aspired, enlisting neglected details from the receding past in examinations that foreground their subjective reactions. In his introduction to an edited collection of essays titled *Probing the Limits of Representation,* Saul Friedlander begins to examine such overlooked documentation by quoting Etty Hillesum's letter from Westerbork camp in Holland, dated September 2, 1943, which describes as "clownish madness and sadness" scenes related to a revue that was "taking over the whole camp." Although inmates on duty had no overalls, everyone sewed overalls "with little puffed sleeves" for the dancers in the "overall ballet" (1) — until, that is, they were due to leave on the last transport. Friedlander concludes with a speculation that seems pertinent to his volume's title: "documentary material itself often carries the story of minute incidents which seem to escape the overwhelming dimension of the overall catastrophe but which nonetheless express the excess that cannot yet be put into phrases or, differently stated, that leaves an extraordinary uncertainty in the reader's mind, notwithstanding the ultimate significance and total 'concreteness' of what is being reported" (20). Because the ideal of neutrality had been so thoroughly tarnished by the meticulous efficiency of criminals like Eichmann and by the Nazis' manipulation of even the most realistic of media, contemporary poets often abdicate the pretense of objectivity by emphasizing their hapless struggle to apprehend the "minute incidents" that "express the excess" Friedlander analyzes.

From Gerald Stern in "The War against the Jews," a title that cites Lucy Dawidowicz's pioneering 1975 study, to John Berryman in three poems titled "from *The Black Book,*" stanzas that refer to a 1945 publication subtitled *The Nazi Crime against the Jewish People,* literary men and women allude to scholarly work on the Holocaust in order to establish contiguity between imaginative and critical responses to the Shoah. Hardly "news that STAYS news" (Ezra Pound's definition of literature [*ABC* 29]), texts in this tradition sheer away from the objects (like shoes) frequently exhibited in museums and from historically central events (like the Eichmann trial), focusing instead on odd accounts of people not deemed newsworthy. In doing so, these poets counter society's collective memory of the Holocaust, its civic reconstructions of the past, and thereby question the idea of any transcendent or coherent memory. Like Adrienne Rich, whose sequence "Then or Now" attempts "to listen to / the public voice of our time" by quoting from and analyzing the private correspondence of Hannah Arendt and Karl Jaspers, poetic proxy-witnesses try "to remember and stay / faithful to details" (*DFR* 31). Undermining the possibility of attaining a definitive, all-encompassing interpretation of an event as devastating as the Shoah, such proxy-witnesses highlight unexpected or even seemingly trivial experiences that in their very quirkiness put the lie to any deceptive sense that the totality of the Holocaust has been or could be captured.[13]

Two ambitious poems — C. K. Williams's "Spit" and Jacqueline Osherow's "Conversations with Survivors" — focus in quite dissimilar ways on maverick episodes in order to incarnate the shock of criminal violence emerging as an everyday occurrence in the lives of Jewish men and women during the calamity. Williams's abstract theological speculations about the fate of God within the crisis of the Shoah contrast strikingly with Osherow's personal musings on her intimacy with a survivor of Auschwitz, in a divergence that underscores how gender can play a role in proxy-witnessing. For "Spit" deploys biblical exegesis and philosophical modes of inquiry rooted in an overwhelmingly male intellectual history, while "Conversations with Survivors" puts on display the psychological intimacy and specificity of detail often labeled emotive and thus traditionally feminine.[14] With studied detachment, Williams derives from his reading about secular and religious authorities a severely qualified faith in God, whereas Osherow establishes a basis for renewed faith in human worth as she expresses an infectious affection fostered by personal interactions with a seamstress who established a new life as a wife and mother in the United States. Yet what Saul Friedlander called the "total dissonance between the apocalypse that was and the normality that is" (*MHE* 51) makes both Williams's and Osherow's works eerily commemorative. Not simply documentary (because of the blatant inaccessibility of the past), "Spit" and "Conversations with Survivors" stress their authors' inconclusive efforts to grapple with the meaning of events endured by people hindered from directly testifying themselves and whose enforced silencing therefore urgently ratifies the proxy-witnessing of successors.

C. K. Williams attributes his epigraph — "... *then the son of the 'superior race' began to spit into the Rabbi's mouth so that the Rabbi could continue to spit on the Torah* ..." (*SP* 48) — to one of the so-called *Black Books* that proliferated after the war so as to authenticate as documentary fact one form humiliation took. Given the ellipses before and after his quotation, which hint at its decontextualization, "Spit"'s approach to Nazi atrocities gains legitimacy through Williams's willingness to confront the difficulty of comprehending the bizarre account he has perused, a quandary announced by his opening admission: "After this much time, it's still impossible" (*SP* 48). Then the wary writer attempts to imagine the impossible scene recounted in *The Black Book,* but in a language of "probably"s that underscores his distance from it. The incident of the SS man spitting in the Rabbi's mouth so that the Rabbi can continue to spit on the Torah with its "letters blurring under the blended phlegm" (48) exemplifies religious leaders made to dance and sing before being shot or tortured, worshipers herded into synagogues first locked and then set ablaze: these deeds would be accompanied by Nazi declarations that " 'We are fighting against you and against your God! Death to all of you! Let your God show whether he can help you!' " (Apenszlak 227).[15]

Just as aware as his readers of how "many years" have intervened since the event in *The Black Book* occurred and wondering "what is there to say" about it, Williams nevertheless hazards a closer glance. While soldiers impatiently stand by, wanting to "Get it over with," the poet (like the SS man) lingers:

... back there the lips of the Rabbi and the other would have
   brushed
and if time had stopped you would have thought they were lovers,
so lightly kissing, the sharp, luger hand over the dear chin,
the eyes furled slightly and then when it started again the eyelashes
   of both of them
shyly fluttering as wonderfully as the pulse of a baby. (48)

Yet the audacity of words like "lovers," "dear," "shyly fluttering," "wonderfully" immediately plummets Williams into the glum concession, "Maybe we
don't have to speak of it at all, it's still the same." In this first section of
"Spit," the epigraph of *The Black Book* is dramatized, but to what end? Given
the unlikelihood of any higher command preceding the SS man's act,
Williams abjures the idea that the "Final Solution" can be blamed on an
authority-bound personality blindly following orders. The particular form
Jew-hatred takes in "Spit" stresses its irrationality, suggesting, too, that the
Nazi commitment to genocide cannot be explained by recourse to economic or political motivations. For how is the Third Reich strengthened or
protected during a debilitating war by the costly, time-consuming death
industry of the concentration camps or, in this particular case, by an officer
spitting in a rabbi's mouth? Instead, the poet presents the bizarre doubling
of Nazi, "the son of the 'superior race,'" and Jew, the Rabbi of the chosen
people, to establish Nazism as a sect devoted to the annihilation of a competing faith.[16] Instead of the efficient murder of the Jews, their forced compliance in desecrating their own consecrated symbols appears to be the
point. Antithetical belief systems, Nazism and Judaism enter the poem
through the physical union of the SS man and the Rabbi, which hints at a
perverse pleasure at degradation that absorbs the SS man "obsessed with
perfect humiliation" (48).[17]

The Nazi, intoxicated with the power he wields over his victim, flaunts an
amorous intimacy with his prey: "you would have thought they were lovers."
Even the metaphor that likens fluttering eyelashes to "the pulse of a baby"
connects the act of torment with lovemaking, just as spit glues the SS man to
the Rabbi, wedding them face to face in what looks like a kiss. However,
given the "stained beard" (48) clutched by "the sharp, luger hand," Williams's homosocial scene hardly corresponds to the sort of comradely embrace that often figures in poems and stories about *Blutsbrüderschaft,* for
instance between boyish soldiers during the First World War.[18] Instead, it
brings to mind survivors' recollections of sadistic "matadors" in the camps:
one "would throw himself on his victim and lie on top of him, almost ca-
ressingly wrapping his fingers around his victim's throat. To the uninitiated,
it might seem that the two bodies were throbbing in erotic ecstasy, and in
fact the Kapo did have an orgasm at such moments, while his companions
looked on in snickering admiration" (Donat 94). If what in a more innocent

age John Addington Symonds called "the gospel of comradeship" later animated "the manly love" of fascism (3:485), Williams intimates that its spin-off constitutes a sadistic drama of dominance between the phallicized SS man "with his stiff hair and his uniform" and the feminized Jew with his "parched mouth" and "torn overcoat" (*SP* 48). Replete with a Bible, "Spit" 's marriage of heaven and hell, of sacred victim and civic tormentor, occurs inside a moment dedicated to the polluting of the Hebrew Bible. An ejaculation that looks like a kiss but functions as enforced oral sex pays the Jewish Judas back to punish him for his murder of God's son, to disgrace the Jewish people for their stubborn adherence to Mosaic law, although the doubling ironically places the Nazi in the role of Judas, the Rabbi in the part of the Jewish sage.

Spitting on, not kissing, the holy man: Williams's poem illuminates the point Yehuda Bauer makes about Nazism, namely that "it adopted Christian antisemitism without Christianity, which it saw, quite rightly, as a Jewish invention" (43). Did German fascism rely on those gospel scenes in which Judas kisses Jesus to mark and murder him, as Hyam Maccoby has also alleged (36)? The Jewish people's handing over the Messiah to torment meant to many Christians, as George Steiner has explained, that "Judaism eradicated from within itself not only the act of divine election, the 'chosen-ness' by and for God's unique purpose; it tore up from within its own flesh and spirit *the very right to hope*" ("LLM" 58). In addition, by refusing to recognize Jesus as the Messiah, "the Jews have postponed the day of man's salvation, the apocalyptic enfranchisement of suffering humanity and the eternal justice and peace which are to attend the Second Coming" (58). Several repercussions from these anti-Semitic lines of reasoning are drama-tized in the SS man's spitting so that the Rabbi can expectorate on the Torah.

First, the pollution of the book that represents the Jewish faith signifies the discrediting of Jewish refusal to welcome Jesus as the Messiah and there-by dramatizes contempt for a theological monotheism now identified with what Steiner calls "sterility and despair" ("LLM" 58). Second, by using the Jewish mouth as a receptacle for waste, the SS man eliminates Jews from the human community, bringing one step closer the promised salvation that will free humankind from the nightmare of history. Yet how can the polluting Nazi not himself be corrupted by physical contact with the man designated a pariah? Does the Nazi's impassioned embrace attest to an admission of his own guilty desire for the Jew, for the Torah? That Paul, the author of Epistle to the Romans, defined himself as "an Israelite, a descendant of Abraham" (11:1), frames his convoluted response to the Jews: "As regards the gospel they are enemies of God, for your sake; but as regards election they are beloved for the sake of their forefathers" (11:28–29). In any case, the cen-tral event in "Spit" seems "in excess of our frames of reference," to use the words Shoshana Felman employs to describe Holocaust testimony (Felman and Laub 5). Confronting a face-to-face scene that strenuously undercuts the basis of Levinas's and Levertov's ethics, the reader's mind *cannot* settle into understanding.

As the poem progresses, the perversity that occurred during the Holocaust no longer appears "out" or "over" there, but instead seems to be internalized, "twisting and hardening us." Despite his hesitations, the conclusion of Williams's first section turns toward a consideration of "every conceivable torment" that "we make of God," and why "we're almost ashamed to use" these "as metaphors for what goes on in us." However, the poet asserts, "we do anyway"; that is, we do utilize what happened in the war as an analogy for our own capacity for harming and being harmed. Williams adopts *The Black Book*'s account to illuminate the "terror and hatred" within all of us when facing the Otherness of another person. The SS man and the Rabbi locked in his embrace have something to do with "love," something to do with "battle," for "we watch ourselves in love / become maddened with pride and incompletion" (*SP* 48). Here, Williams emphasizes the inseparability of love and hatred, desire and disgust.[19] When God and our souls turn against us, Williams explains, "there is so much terror and hatred" that we try to make the Other "defile his own meaning" in our "struggle to survive each other" (49). The seduction of Nazism, according to Williams, is related to a narcissistic fantasy of striving to tack mortality itself onto the Other so as to assert one's own omnipotence.[20] Williams explores the disturbingly amorous SS man to consider the battle for preeminence he associates with mastery and sadism.

But in the second and concluding stanza of "Spit," Williams swerves from such psychologizing, returning to the theological issues he had initially addressed by flatly introducing "another," seemingly quite different "legend" about Moses choosing a live coal over a diamond and popping the red ember into his mouth "so for the rest of his life he was tongue-tied and Aaron had to speak for him" (*SP* 49). In *Exodus*, the third volume of *Midrash Rabbah*, the tale is explained. Although Pharaoh used "to kiss and hug" Moses, the child's playing with Pharaoh's crown created suspicion among the "magicians of Egypt," some of whom wanted "to slay him and others to burn him"; but Jethro argued that the "boy has no sense" and should be tested (33). After a gold vessel and a live coal were placed before Moses, the angel Gabriel pushed the child's hand toward the coal, which he thrust into his mouth, burning his tongue "with the result that he became slow of speech and of tongue" (34). In the Holocaust context, not only the wish to slay and burn Moses but also the catch-22 of the "test" — either he burns himself or he is murdered — resonates with the persecution of the Jews of Europe. As the SS man's embrace modulates into the Pharaoh's kiss, Jewish chosenness is situated in a tradition where to be guarded by God's guardians means being marked in a peculiarly painful way by the anguish of tongue-tied utterance.

That God burned in the bush and Moses in the mouth made them "cleave together," according to Williams. The scarred tongue of Moses — "it must have been like a thick embryo" (*SP* 49) — recalls the desecrated mouth of the parched Rabbi carrying the weight of the SS man's spit. What Williams's conclusion foresees is the devolution of God into a slobbering, howling force, horrified and diminished by the senseless cruelty of humankind. How could Moses not know

> that all of us were on fire and that every word we said would
>   burn forever,
> in pain, unquenchably, and that God knew it, too, and would say
>   nothing Himself ever again beyond this,
> ever, but would only live in the flesh that we use like firewood,
> in all the caves of the body, the gut cave, the speech cave:
> He would slobber and howl like something just barely a man that
>   beats itself again and again onto the dark,
> moist walls away from the light, away from whatever would be light
>   for this last eternity.
> "Now therefore go," He said, "and I will be with thy mouth." (49)

Although the SS man believes he is making the Rabbi foul the word of God, the SS man himself performs that task by sullying the Rabbi's mouth, where God resides. Williams writes angrily about and against the non-speaking of God in the midst of Jewish suffering — not exactly a silence, but a blaring gibberish that undermines the redemptive potential of poetic language after Auschwitz. Moses' wounded tongue, the Rabbi's dry mouth, the SS man's spit, the turns of the poem itself: did the Shoah occur because of our garbled, maimed expression of whatever possibility Divinity stood for?

If the Rabbi and the SS man wear the human countenance divine, God has been reduced by the Holocaust to a dribbling, bawling replicant of what humanity has degenerated into.[21] The final line of "Spit" also asks, how could even a slobbering, howling God take up residence in the spiteful SS man's mouth? Perhaps the immanence of Divinity is what remains at issue in "Spit," for the Torah insists through Moses' commandments on the central importance not of the Second Coming, not of a heavenly afterlife, but of human righteousness within the world in its imperfect state. Maybe the SS man finds himself locked in a love/hate struggle with Jews not as God killers but as God creators. Does the Mosaic law of the Torah ask too much, so that its worshipers had to be destroyed to deny the validity of their God's rigorous commandments? Repeating a sample of Hitler's table talk — "The Jews invented conscience" — Steiner asks, "for this crime, what forgiveness?" ("LLM" 59). Moses' five books make God inseparable from each human being's duty to act justly in daily life: perhaps this is what the SS man so hates and passionately embraces in the Rabbi and his creed. Or perhaps the transcendence of Divinity is precisely what remains at issue in "Spit."

Jewish monotheism, according to Maurice Blanchot, presents speech as the site where human beings "hold themselves in relation with what excludes all relation: the infinitely Distant, the absolutely Foreign"; language that crosses the insurmountable abyss does not abolish distance but instead maintains it, "preserved in its purity by the rigor of the speech that upholds the absoluteness of difference" (*IC* 127–28). The SS man who spits on the Rabbi's mouth and on Moses' words metamorphoses at the end of the poem into a drooling, bellowing God — spit, spite, and spirit become indistinguishable — to suggest that the proponents of National Socialism sought to annihilate a faith based on the irreducible relation of human speech to "the absolutely Foreign," a mission that damaged Divinity itself. Punishing the Rabbi, excluding Jews from the human collective, the SS man also attaches himself to the Rabbi so as to illustrate Williams's belief that hatred expresses both admiration for and envy of an Other to whom the "I" is intensely bonded. The SS man does not extirpate but instead expresses God perversely, twisted in the chambers of his own flesh. Although the poem refrains from explaining why, what God has become is a sign of our impotent incapacity to articulate righteousness or maintain "the absoluteness of difference."

Williams turns his attention toward people unexpectedly caught up in a disaster never fully comprehended then or now, as does Jacqueline Osherow. Like him, too, she wants to retrieve exactly those memories that have not found their way into Holocaust museums and memorials so as to push against the reductive ways the Shoah has been remembered. One potential antidote to the freezing of memory is close scrutiny of those accidental details that have gone thus far unnoted. For Osherow, these derive from "conversations with survivors" (the title of her volume), whose stories in their specificity and novelty jar us into a new awareness of what common people endured when the unthinkable occurred within an otherwise ordinary life. But in form, tone, and topic, *Conversations with Survivors* contrasts markedly with "Spit." Although Williams uses the long line of free verse to examine theological issues that accrue from his reading, Osherow is fascinated with stanzas of iambic pentameter and the domestic details of private exchanges. Although he analyzes the causes of the disaster, she examines its consequences. Although he decries the psychological and spiritual dynamics of racism, she praises the resiliency of its human targets. Indeed, Osherow rejects the focus of most documentary poets — on the crimes of perpetrators, the punishments of victims — to study and pay tribute to the arts and crafts of survivors.

The prize-winning title poem of Osherow's volume chronicles the impact made on her by her dialogues with a woman named Fany Hochmanova Brown, who had unpredictably fashioned hats at Auschwitz (out of whatever SS women brought her) and then manufactured cloth at a textile factory to which she had been transported (located in an ancestral mansion owned by one Baron Macholt). The hats are made with "Bijoux, dangling cherries, nesting birds / Whatever they'd picked over from the piles / left vacant just outside each crematorium" and, along with what she receives from doing the makeup and hair of her client-guards, she is paid with cigarettes that garner more than gold on the black market, as Fany learns "to *organize.*" While Sam (who eventually would become her second husband) trades jewels (which he finds in the lining of the clothing he delouses) for more prized cabbages, she manages "To find the stray undamaged seconds at Auschwitz / And piece them into minutes, hours, days, / Four decades in America, three sons, / Two side-by-side refrigerators" (22–23) before she dies in a hospital. As the pun on "seconds" hints — both secondhand things and seconds of time — Fany's gift is stitching together a life, despite the "hopeless odds" (23) of Hitler, of cancer.

Eschewing printed sources, Osherow captures Fany recalling her past in a present composed of pill and potion taking, visits to the hospital, betting in Atlantic City, and winning the Pennsylvania lottery when Sam's use of the number tattooed on her arm and the "lucky error" of a cashier who couldn't understand his Yiddish accent earn him more than a thousand dollars. Hats, cigarettes, jewels, cabbages, pills, blood transfusions, lotteries — all the paraphernalia of currency and exchange bespeak Fany's struggle to survive. She herself had been one such commodity "After Ray Brown, maker of banana splits / At an ice-cream parlor in Atlantic City," had paid her passage from Europe "And five hundred dollars to the government / To send her back in case they didn't marry" (24). But by that time she had herself become the wearer of a hat, a tartan tam-o'-shanter, as well as an expert in what Elizabeth Bishop calls "the natural madness of the hatter" (201); Bishop's allusion to Lewis Carroll's Mad Hatter in "Exchanging Hats" seems eminently suited to the antic inventiveness with which Osherow's concentration camp milliner faces adversity. Unlike her sister Dora, Fany had a talent for "making do at Auschwitz," perhaps because she had been the wildest Jewish girl in her Slovak town. This extraordinary vitality is what adds such vibrancy to her descriptions of labor in the camp ("*Making big rocks into smaller rocks*") or of the miraculous train ride (sitting in a passenger train "*like people*") when she was sent to the textile factory (25). Certainly her pragmatic optimism echoes her husband's when he

> breaks in to praise the crematoria.
> *Before that they would make them dig a ditch*
> *And throw them in, pour on kerosene*
> *And light a match* (24)

though the slippage in his "*them*" (prisoners) and "*them*" (corpses) belies his buoyancy. It is evident, too, when an eerily empty factory informs the other girls at *Emmerich Macholt* that the war is over and they proceed to go "crazy" while Fany stays behind, cutting cloth for the "*schmates*" she would wear on her way out of Europe (25–26).

However, at this point in the narrative, the poet begins to equivocate about the relationship between her own stories and those of Fany. First, we are told in splendid anarchic detail about the looting and smashing in which the girls in the textile factory engaged while Fany kept sewing:

> They hurled soup tureens at huge ancestral portraits,
> Plates, cups, teapots, creamers, gravy boats —
> An eighteenth-century trove of heirloom Meissen —
> Shattered on its maiden voyage in air.
> Kitchen knives attacked brocaded sofas,
> Embroidered footstools, bedsheets, goose-down quilts,
> Dinner jackets, evening gowns, fur coats,
> Belgian lace-trimmed hats on porcelain dolls.
> Whole rooms were lost in feathers, shards and tatters
> And others disappeared when gilt-edged pages
> Leapt from books to kindle piles of furniture
> And warm the cheering, gaunt, exhausted girls. (25–26)

The Nazis' preservation of delicate porcelain, ancestral paintings, ornate furniture, expensive toys, and libraries amid the trashing of human beings results in the girls "smashing glass" (25) in a retaliatory mini-Kristallnacht and book burning that Fany did not witness. So evocative of the battle scenes in Pope's *Rape of the Lock,* the piling up of costly plunder turned into a hodgepodge of debris, like the piling up of nouns, issues in the perfect iambic pentameter of the last line, as the mock epic form itself makes a mockery of the heroic ideologies, pageants, and postures of German fascism.

"Fany tells me she was not among them"; however, Osherow chronicles the scene of disorder with obvious delight. Then, the poet wonders how Fany could possibly have seen a pair of Chinese vases crushed on the marble stairs from the vantage of her window. Next, Osherow explains, Fany "doesn't say she didn't join the others" when they hoisted bolts of fabric and flung them off the roof, but "Fany never actually described it," though the poet does (26). Yet about the "Paisleys, tartans, pinstripes, spangles, flowers / Spreading out like momentary tablecloths," Osherow subsequently admits, "It was probably the dull, gray twill of Nazi / Uniforms or stripes for prisoners." Though she could ask Fany's sister, she refrains because "I don't like the facts she tells me" (26). In a curious way, only at this point in the poem, when the poet considers going to a source like Dora, does it seem as if Fany may really be dead. Exceptionally uncanny, the simultaneous aliveness and deadness of Fany that Osherow achieves are heightened by the remembrance of a period when Fany called Sam and Dora to the hospital because she was convinced "Death and being alive were just the same!" (27). Even at her burial, when the rabbi describes "how for years he'd lose his place / In his Rosh Hashanah or Yom Kippur sermon / When he caught sight of Fany, dressed to kill" (28), she seems more animate than her mourners.

In the final two pages, where Osherow begins to explore what it means to be a poet engaged in conversations with survivors, she appreciates Fany's desire to have a scribe, her "Saying *I could not forget this name*" but meaning "*I* should not forget it" (29), her promise to tell all the facts she had never told the ghostwriter of a magazine story about her "Miracle Marriage." Understandably resistant to being turned into Fany's secretary, Osherow confronts precisely the self-effacement that the documentary tradition involves:

> Not that I set out to be a ghostwriter.
> I meant to be a poet, make connections;
> All along I've had an end in mind
> With Fany floating off the hospital roof
> On a bolt of cloth that fleetingly bears wings. (29)

But facts intervene and Osherow must submit to them: "Fany was so sick" . . . "There's nothing I can do; facts are facts" . . . "And even if they aren't facts, I'm helpless / Against a woman . . . Who tells about a pair of man-sized vases, / Some fabric sailing off a roof, a train — " (29). Besides,

> What does it matter that she leaves things out?
> Who is it that doesn't leave things out?
>
> even I, writing now, haven't got the heart
> Not to leave out some of what I know. (29)

The omissions of Fany and the poet hardly qualify but instead foster affection, though Osherow does not conclude by floating Fany away, because the incursion of the apocalyptic into the ordinary necessitates a new aesthetic, "a revised mythology" (30). Instead, at the end of the poem, she dramatizes Fany's return to her hometown in a trope of restitution not of the youth from which Fany was robbed, not of the suffering that she bore, not of the person she had been before the disaster struck or the person she might have become if it hadn't, but simply of those "best things" she had so providently packed away and placed with her most prized customer back in the Slovak town, the "*schmates*" of her youth. Osherow's last line depicts this former customer returning from upstairs with the bat-winged jacket and scoop-necked blouse Fany had stored away: "To hand your ghost a chest of your best things" (30). But if Fany was reduced to a ghost after the war when she was physically alive, she becomes animate after her death in Osherow's verse. In her poetic self-definition — a ghostwriter for this particular ghost — Osherow provides a paradigm for other proxy-witnesses of the Holocaust. By emphasizing how very little we can know about the subjectivity of their

deceased subjects, writers dedicated to a poetics of anamnesis simultaneously evade the charges of appropriation or plagiarism that have plagued
their novelistic counterparts and question the mimetic as well as the expressive potency of art after Auschwitz, turning it toward a more modest, more
historical undertaking. As her "Letter to Rainer Maria Rilke" pays Osherow's respects to the poet, therefore, she clarifies her misgivings about the
consummate artistry he exemplifies: "The enormous thing that now divides
us," she explains, is "so much larger that / To name it is to break the lyric's
rules. / If I write *history*, will you stop reading?" (*CS* 5).

While Osherow as a ghostwriter supplies one resonant figure for proxy-
witnessing, C. K. Williams uses his fable of the "tongue-tied" Moses, his
howling God, and the Rabbi with his spitting "parched mouth" to furnish
another prototype that links the stammering negations, foreignisms, jolting
breaks, admissions of failure, and repetitions of verbal art after Auschwitz to
prophecy. Just as the unclean lips of Isaiah, the demurrals of Jeremiah, and
the mutism of Ezekiel bespeak their defeated efforts to communicate what
in its defiance of ordinary understanding retains a sublime "unattainability,"[22] so the verbal disruptions of the Holocaust poet express not only the
wish to be infused but also the anxiety of being inundated by the Otherness
of the dead as well as by the incomprehensibility of the "Final Solution."
Drawing on documentary materials that call attention to the futility of inventing the terms with which to address the disaster, the incorporated and
translated testimonies of victims and survivors in verse composed in the
English language can neither be thoroughly internalized (ingested) nor
abjured (expectorated). This prophetic "impasse," which Herbert Marks
links in the biblical tradition to Moses' efforts "to renounce his own pre-
rogative in favor of an otherness he is still tempted to disavow" (66, 72),
informs verse about the Shoah that swerves from the personal lyric to derive
multiple meanings from testimony, even when the impossibility of conveyance itself reflects its authors' ambivalence over a wish to address the
material and a terror of misconstruing or, worse yet, blunting its meaning.
Both the "ghostwriter" and the "tongue-tied," spitting prophet address the
perplexing gaps between "then" and "now," "there" and "here" that attend
the poetics of anamnesis.

Conspicuously dissimilar in their engendering of proxy-testimony, Williams and Osherow stretch the poetic enterprise, goaded by the need to
uncover not "news that stays news" but events neither aesthetic nor his-
trionic, and thus absent from literature as well as from Holocaust textbooks
and museum installations. To Rilke, Osherow announces that "for those of
us / Who, just like you, would rather speak of angels / There's a lasting
streak of ash upon the tongue" (*CS* 5–6). According to Williams, too, an
ashy past waits "to receive us," accessible "not by imagination's nets, / but by
the virtue of its being, simply being, waiting patiently for us like any other
unattended, / any other hardly anticipated or not even anticipated — as

much as any other fact rolling in . . ." (*SP* 139; ellipsis his). Holocaust poets who use or allude to archival material deploy the partiality of the particular to protest against universalizing rhetoric. To break the lyric's rules, documentary writers remain in thrall to what Williams seeks to recover in "The Past":

> Not "history" but scent, sound, sight, the sensual fact, the beings
>   and
>   the doings, the heroes,
> unmediated now, the holy and the horrid, to be worked across not
>   like
>   a wistful map, but land. (139)

More tentative, though just as moving in her hesitations, in "Above the Casa del Popolo" Osherow poses a grammatically inconclusive set of questions that describe the anxieties attendant on an aesthetic archaeology studiously willing to accept its liabilities: namely, the possibility that proxy-witnessing cannot possibly produce what one would ordinarily consider a work of art:

> If we do not find our way is it a poem?
> If we not only do not make sense
> But we also don't make beauty in the bargain,
> So absorbed in excavating our details
> That we momentarily forget our purposes
> And then don't dare to make one alteration
> For fear that we'll obliterate our lives? (*CS* 58)

The ambiguous last pronoun here hints that the lives of the casualties emanate the alterity of biographical subjects who have nevertheless been embraced as aspects of the poets' own genealogies. The progress of this chapter — from Reznikoff to Osherow — tracks the ever more insistent presence of the poet and of the artifice of traditional verse as it moves from rendering the anecdote to a speculation on its meaning. Still, against the authoritative, authoritarian uses to which rhetorically ambitious writing had been put by cultural institutions that colluded with the growth of fascism, an Anglo-American writing practice composed of undigested and indigestible facts, inexplicable incidents, decidedly tentative speculations, and admitted omissions refuses to provide aesthetic recompense for the brutality of the Shoah. To counter the numbing amnesia inflicted on its casualties by traumatic injury and on their descendants by our collective overexposure to widely circulated narratives of atrocity, contemporary poets adapt adopted testimonies composed about and by the victims to attest to the survival of their abiding significance.

6

THE DEAD SPEAK

"I died in Auschwitz but no one knows it" (267): both clauses of this sentence from Charlotte Delbo's *Auschwitz and After* dare unintelligibility, since the dead cannot speak and one ordinarily assumes that they can be apprehended as discernibly distinct from the living. Still, it has been heralded as an instance of the phatic language of witnessing (that utters even incoherently so as to be heard) and of the disruptive discourse of art (that proposes meanings it simultaneously dismantles).[1] The extremity of the traumatic events that transpired during the Shoah justifies such a speech act on the part of a survivor composing a memoir about the disconnect between the person she was before the disaster and the person she became after so-called liberation, but we find it much more discomforting when it issues from someone who has not experienced the circumstances that justify it. Yet rather than crafting poems out of documents derived from the disaster, one author infamously and others less notably transgressed across the widening terrain of the "after" into Auschwitz itself. It was a necromantic venture for which they paid the price of notoriety or neglect. By placing their poems inside the calamity's historical moment, by speaking for the dead in the first person, these poets in effect breached Adorno's dictum.

177

Exploitation, larceny, masochism, sensationalism: the terms of oppro-
brium hurled against Sylvia Plath's use of Holocaust material generally accord with George Steiner's distress at any writer boasting "the right to put
on this death-rig" ("IE" 305).[2] In 1962, the same year Plath wrote "Daddy"
and "Lady Lazarus," Adorno qualified his injunction against poetry after
Auschwitz ("C" 312); however, her appropriation of the voices of the casualties still seems outrageous to those who point out the lack of any reasonable affinity or parallelism between Plath's individual suffering and mass
murder. Such readers wonder, how dare she presume to imagine herself as
one of the victims, to arrogate the Otherness of the deceased through a
projection that might be said to profane the memory of people exterminated by the Nazis? To honor the dead, Elie Wiesel has cautioned, the living
must apprehend that "no one has the right to speak on their behalf" (*FKM*
194). Plath's non-Jewishness as well as her lack of a personal stake in the
disaster made her speaking on behalf of the victims appear a desecration.
Plath's adoption of the voices of the imagined, absent dead is hardly anomalous, however. The rhetorical figure of prosopopoeia is also used in some of
the most perturbing poems about the Shoah composed by literary women
and men whose relationships to the calamity vary greatly. Prosopopoeia: the
impersonation of an absent speaker or a personification. This device allowed those poets searching to find a language for the staggering horror of
what had happened to speak as, for, with, and about the casualties in verse
that has been either ignored or disparaged for too long.

Although, as Tadeusz Rozewicz supposes in "Posthumous Rehabilitation," the dead who "see our snouts," "read our books," and "scrutinize our
lectures" cannot or will not exonerate the guilt of the living ("the dead will
not rehabilitate us" [*HP* 170]), postwar poets who felt confounded by Western civilization's guilt over the catastrophic genocide of the "Final Solution"
sometimes attempted an admittedly nugatory but nevertheless shocking
rehabilitation of the dead. Because the victims of the Holocaust did not
have a cemetery, such writers ground their art in exactly the conviction that
Elie Wiesel deduces from this fact, namely that the living must be their
cemeteries (*AA* 141). In the cruel lack of the bodies and of graves to mark
their demise, the poet writes from the perspective of corpses deprived of
coffins, either directly before or directly after they were murdered, speaking
words eerily evocative of the epitaphs carved on ancient gravestones.[3]

Such a shocking reanimation of the dead cannot be equated with the
traditional elegist's attempt to bring a particularly cherished person back
into living memory, to assert the dead person's immortality, or to envision
some union with the dead in a place elsewhere. It does not say farewell to the
dead or envision an afterlife of spirits in a separate realm, be it classical,
Jewish, or Christian. It is not really an example of those authorial meditations on mortality that Jahan Ramazani calls "self-elegies." Nor, as we have
seen, does it form the only (or even the major) poetic response to the

Shoah. Yet, particularly as put to use by Sylvia Plath, it has remained the most noted phenomenon in English verse about the Holocaust, perhaps because the most notorious and decried. Undoubtedly, whether denounced as a usurpation of the dead or praised as an imaginative surrender to them, prosopopoeia in the Holocaust context shapes the most unsettling, disturbing poetry. That the authors who manipulate it summon the posthumous voice to conceive of subjectivity enduring beyond the concentration camp means, however, that they seek to dramatize why and how the anguish of the Shoah does not, will not dissipate. Perhaps the inexorable vacancy, the vacuity, of the anonymous and numerous victims made this project urgent, licensed it, despite its unnerving presumption. Or perhaps historical proximity to irreparable and stunning slaughter plunged some writers into an awareness of the impotence of the normative languages at their disposal.

When facts have been obliterated, as Jean-François Lyotard explained in a passage I discussed in chapter 1, when "the testimonies which bore the traces of *here*'s and *now*'s" were destroyed and "the monopoly over history granted to the cognitive regimen of phrases" was broken by the Shoah, the trope of prosopopoeia allowed poets to step in (where Lyotard would have the historian venture forth) by lending their ears "to what is not presentable under the rules of knowledge" (*D* 57). Massive in its proportions, yet concealed at the time and denied later, the wrong suffered by millions of defenseless noncombatants marked for persecution and extirpation could not be signified in extant words. Therefore "idioms which do not yet exist" needed to be forged to prove that "the silence imposed on knowledge does not impose the silence of forgetting" but instead "a feeling" or a constellation of feelings (13, 56). Lyotard's effort to combat repression issued in his belief that "The shades of those to whom had been refused not only life but the expression of the wrong done them by the Final Solution continue to wander in their indeterminacy" (56).

A retort to Holocaust deniers, the adopted voices of the dead in poetry express the wrong done to one-third of the world's Jewish population by articulating what might have been one shade's consciousness of affliction at the time it occurred or retrospectively after it occurred. Several decades before Terrence Des Pres's 1988 defense of Holocaust poetry, Sylvia Plath substantiated Des Pres's assertion that the imagination confronted by negation "automatically starts asserting itself." Along with such contemporaries as Irena Klepfisz, Anthony Hecht, Randall Jarrell, Charles Simic, Jerome Rothenberg, Adrienne Rich, and Michael Hamburger, Plath implicitly agreed with Des Pres that "We cannot *not* imagine" the subjective alarm and horror that the Shoah must have infused in each one of its individual casualties (*PD* 228).

Whether spoken in the past tense by the dead or in the present by those condemned to a life-in-death, the imaginatively conceived voices of the victims shape the eerie dramatic monologues of Jewish and non-Jewish poets seeking "to smuggle language / from mouths of the dying / and the dead." As Anne Michaels puts it in "What the Light Teaches,"

> What was left but to cut out one's tongue,
> or cleave it with new language,
> or try to hear a language of the dead,
> who were thrown into pits, into lakes— (115–16)

In the aftermath of civilized savagery, the poetic employment of a dramatized first person tends to slide toward "posthumous rehabilitation" even when the voice is supposedly issuing from someone alive, because readers recognize the doom hanging over the scapegoats of Nazi brutality. Many of the dehumanized prisoners lived the half-lives of "*Muselmänner,*" emaciated "non-men" (Levi, *SA* 90), dazed skeletons "ready for the crematorium" (Leitner 128). Whereas immediacy must be forfeited by verse meditations on photographs and by poetic responses to testimonials that constitute modes of proxy-witnessing, poems composed in the cadences of the dead and dying emanate an unnerving invented proximity. At the risk of expropriating the sensibilities of those killed in the Holocaust, English and North American writers who summon up the audacity to write in English from the perspective of the immolated tap the techniques of some of the most important poems composed in Yiddish, German, and Hebrew.

The Yiddish poet Jacob Glatstein's "I Have Never Been Here Before" provides a touchstone for unsettling texts that have definitively entered the Holocaust canon. His efforts to still the "burnt fields, / cartography of cemeteries, / stony silence" of "these last ragged years" fail to stifle the midnight cries of corpses that interrupt his verse:

> Like a tiny candle over each grave,
> a cry will burn,
> each one for itself.
> "I am I" —
> thousands of slaughtered I's
> will cry in the night:
> "I am dead, unrecognized,
> my blood still unredeemed." (*AA* 659)

At times in verse, the " 'I am I' " of "thousands of slaughtered I's" cry out together; at times, alone. Whereas the condemned prisoners in Paul Celan's "Death Fugue" attest to being forced to ingest the "black milk" in a choral refrain, a macabre parody of the beer hall ("we drink and we drink it" [*AA* 601]), the singular dead voice surfaces in the Hebrew poet Dan Pagis's "Autobiography": "I died with the first blood and was buried / among the rocks of the field" (*AA* 586). Quite distinct from the printed (and significantly erasable) words that Pagis's Eve leaves "written in pencil in a sealed railway-car," together these imaginative works constitute if not what in another poem Nelly Sachs called the "chorus of the Unborn" (*AA* 644), then a chorus of the Undead. Albeit blatantly ineffectual at raising the dead, such necromancy illustrates the linkage between mourning and the incorpora- tion of the dearly departed. As Diana Fuss has argued, "To be open to an identification is to be open to a death encounter, open to the very possibility of communing with the dead" (1).

In the less frequently read Holocaust verse composed in English, proso- popoeia has been put to a range of purposes characterized by varying de- grees of imaginative fusion and severance between poets and their vulner- able personae. At one extreme, the trope generates identification with a haunting surrogate figure embroiled in the fate to which writers suspect they would have been consigned, if they had been born at the wrong place, in the wrong time. For a middle group of poets, who present their speakers as distinctively distanced characters, prosopopoeia issues an invitation to living readers to be morally instructed by overhearing the voices of the dead or dying. At the other extreme, the device results in a critique of that luring rhetorical offer by exposing as spurious the very mechanisms of identifica- tion — of projection, of incorporation — that drive this aesthetic maneuver. On both ends of this spectrum stand Sylvia Plath's most famous works, yet her impudent project of posthumous rehabilitation has met with disparage- ment from critics protesting the equation she constructed between a sense of her own traumatized womanhood and Jewish vulnerability in the Shoah, an analogy that is thought to reduce Jewish suffering to an instrument for probing her own psychosexual predicament. Such derogations depend on reading Jewishness as the mere figure of verse "really" about womanhood; but what if Plath is "really" writing about what she claims to be writing about, namely the Holocaust? A reversal of the usual interpretive approach can attend to the uses to which Plath's poems put femininity as a figure of verse analyzing the psychological repercussions of Auschwitz on literature and Jewish identity.

PROSOPOPOEIA AS IDENTIFICATION

I propose a shift in how we interpret Plath not to supplant psychosexual approaches to her most sustained deployments of Holocaust matter, but to supplement them by contextualizing the verse within a literary tradition that thus far has gone disregarded. In other words, this transposition makes sense, given so many of her contemporaries' sense of personal connected- ness to events not experienced firsthand, their visceral but also aesthetic reaction to what Marianne Hirsch has called "postmemory."[4] Like a num- ber of poets in her generation, and not unlike Adorno, Plath viewed the Shoah as a test case for poetry and, indeed, for the imagination as a vehicle for conveying what it means for the incomprehensible to occur. Although

Plath undoubtedly used the disaster to express her personal suffering, in the process she also illuminated the experiences of civilians persecuted under the Nazis' genocidal rule. Given the force of its Holocaust imagery, "Getting There" communicates Plath's horrified compassion for captive shades being hurtled by the onrushing fatality of history toward an irrevocable, incomprehensible death sentence that later observers know only as a hiatus where evidence ought to exist.

"How far is it? / How far is it now?" the poem begins (247), and the first stanza locates its speaker in a train traveling through Russia. The proud "gods" of the willful steel engine Krupp know its destination, while this anonymous prisoner drags her body "through the straw of the boxcars" thinking of bribery, of a letter, of a fire, of bread. The train pumping ahead on its pistons, the blood pumped ahead by its pistons, the plummeting forward of the poem's short lines and their multiple gerunds issue only in a furor of a future, as the poem evokes the furious pace of the Nazis, recalled by eyewitnesses: " 'Out! Out! Everyone! Fast! Fast!' *The Germans were always in such a hurry*" (Leitner 30); "And the furies kept screaming, Schneller! Schneller! Faster, faster, while flailing faster and faster this grain that flowed, ran, ran" (Delbo 36). At the end of the first stanza, which is dedicated to an inexorable driving propulsion toward what the speaker dreads, the train stops where nurses and the wounded appear:

> Legs, arms, piled outside
> The tent of unending cries —
> A hospital of dolls.
> And the men, what is left of the men
> Pumped ahead by these pistons, this blood
> Into the next mile,
> The next hour —
> Dynasty of broken arrows! (248)

This is not the autobiographical Plath writing in *The Bell Jar* about women being reduced to the passive place from which phallic arrows shoot off or in "Ariel" about her personal desire to become an arrow flying suicidally into the red eye of morning. However, the poet's persistent identification does seep into the "I" perceiving the collective emasculation of a "Dynasty of broken arrows" and "dragging my body" through the Russia "I have to get across" (248), if only because of our tendency as readers to equate Plath with her willful but embittered or fearful speakers.[5]

In the second stanza, which also begins "How far is it?," the horror of the boxcar has been supplemented by the horror of a forced march. With red, thick mud slipping on her feet, the speaker experiences the earth as "Adam's side," out of which she rises in agony. Steaming, breathing, "its teeth / Ready to roll, like a devil's," the train metamorphoses into a daemonic engine, as

Plath-Eve confronts a series of "obstacles" amid the thunder and fire of guns, including "The body of this woman," whose "Charred skirts and deathmask" might signify her own double dying (248, 249). Simultaneously at the train stop, on the march, in the cattle car, Plath's persona seeks some silent stasis, but her wish that she were able to bury the wounded and count the dead remains stymied in unachieved futurity: "I shall bury the wounded like pupas, / I shall count and bury the dead," the speaker declares, but "The train is dragging itself, it is screaming— / An animal / Insane for the destination." The end of the poem, sometimes read as a hopeful attempt to imagine rebirth, sounds more disturbing in the context of the Shoah:

> The carriages rock, they are cradles.
> And I, stepping from this skin
> Of old bandages, boredoms, old faces
>
> Step to you from the black car of Lethe,
> Pure as a baby. (249)

At the conclusion to which the poem flies, Plath-Eve arrives at Hades, where forgetfulness courses. Unable to retain a sense of herself or her past—she is stripped of her possessions, her clothing, her previous life, her identity— she too enters the "tent of unending cries." The final solution toward which all events rush transforms Plath's victim into a being as innocent but also as naked and defenseless as an infant. Unlike Whitman's "Out of the Cradle Endlessly Rocking," where the endlessly rocking cradle of waves and of poetic meters consoles by weaving death into life, the rocking cradles of the train's carriages plunge toward the inconceivable "There" not of birth but of oblivion.

Blatantly disturbing in its revision of the "rocking cradle" of Yeats's "The Second Coming" as well (91), Plath's "Getting There" sutures the gap between poet and persona through the same sort of empathy that motivates Irena Klepfisz's project at the conclusion of *Bashert,* a sense of compassion that leads her to become a "keeper of accounts" who can revive the casualties of anti-Semitism when they "awaken in me" (*FW*200). In a number of earlier compositions, Klepfisz adopted the voices of the dead to approach the monstrous particularity of what they must have apprehended in their dying moments. From its shocking opening lines— "when they took us   to the shower   i saw / the rebitsin"—to its conclusion— "my smoke / was distinct   i rose quiet   left her / beneath" (*FW*47)—Klepfisz's "death camp" reminds us how ordinary but also how unknown many of the victims of the Shoah were then and remain now. By providing eyewitness testimony that the gas chamber was used to murder, "death camp" speaks out against Lyotard's Holocaust denier (" 'the only eyewitness I will accept would be a victim of this gas chamber; . . . there is no victim that is not dead; . . . There is, therefore, no gas chamber' " [*D* 3–4]):

when they turned   on the gas   i smelled
it   first   coming at me   pressed myself
hard to the wall   crying   rebitsin   rebitsin
i am here with you   and the advice you gave me
i screamed   into the wall   as the blood burst from
my lungs   cracking   her nails in women's flesh   i
    watched
her capsize   beneath me   my blood in her mouth   i
    screamed[.] (*FW* 47)

Besides visually marking a kind of stammer in speech that cannot communicate the experience described, the pauses punctuating Klepfisz's lines
(here and elsewhere in her oeuvre) recall the theologian Arthur Cohen's
interpretation of the Holocaust as caesura, raising questions about the
Christian and Jewish concept of God and marking the necessity of recognizing the human capacity for evil (58). There is no way to piece together the
lost context of interactions to which Klepfisz's nameless persona alludes: she
remembers the advice of the rabbi's wife, but whether the speaker has
heeded or hated that advice, and what that advice might have been, remains
a mystery. Though we are told about the victim's recollection of her body
being burned, of her feeling the weight of the rebitsin's corpse flung on top
of her, the idea that her smoke "was distinct" at the end or that she has
triumphed by leaving the rebitsin or her own body "beneath" remains a
hollow victory, since the common fate to which the two women have been
consigned overwhelms any grudges that might have existed between them
in life.

As "death camp" demonstrates, another warrant — beyond Des Pres's
"We cannot *not* imagine" (*PD* 228) — for attempting posthumous rehabilitation derives from the blatantly unrealistic rhetoric of prosopopoeia: readers
of Klepfisz's poem know that the author has merely simulated the personification of the dead. For even those poets who strenuously decrease their
distance from the "deathmask" disclose their grating awareness of the inescapable inauthenticity at the core of their oxymoronic undertaking. Bestowing presence onto the absent dead, "*prosopon-poiein,*" Paul de Man's analysis
explains, "means to *give* a face and therefore implies that the original face
can be missing or nonexistent" in an optative fabrication that stresses its
own illusory nature (*RR* 57).[6] The disjunction between "deathmask" and
ventriloquist bears witness to contemporary poets' efforts to confront the
flimsy insubstantiality of the visionary company they keep. In addition, of
course, the English language itself marks not merely British and North
American writers' remoteness from the catastrophe but also the fictionality
of their impersonations.

Klepfisz, feeling haunted by absent, foreign ancestors, undertook translation-work, in particular of the verse of her most resonant Yiddish precursor, Kadya Molodowsky, who (Klepfisz tells us) wrote in her often-quoted poem "Froyen lider" (Women poems) of Jewish women who appear to her in dreams:

> *Es veln di froyen fun undzer mishpokhe*
> *bay nakht in klaloymes mir kumen un zogn . . .*
>
> *(The women in our family will come to me in my*
> *dreams at night and say . . .).*[7]

Quoting Molodowky's lines about her dreams of "*undzer mishpokhe*—our family—the Jewish people" at the end of her book of essays, *Dreams of an Insomniac* (208–209), Klepfisz uses the collection's title to hint that ghostly instructors disrupt her sleep, inducing poetically rich but sleepless nights that issue in verse commemorating her specific family's dead as well as the nameless dead of the Jewish people. When the past tense of "death camp" modulates in other poems by Klepfisz into the present tense, spectral representatives of "*undzer mishpokhe*" express pain in the midst of its surrealistic disruption of their lives.

In "herr captain," the poet intertwines events from various pasts in a palimpsest of sexual abuses endured by the first speaker, a Jewish prisoner whispering to a Nazi captain "i'm not over / used," who metamorphoses into her own or the poet's grandmother revenging herself against a "cossack lover" by slashing his hands with a butcher knife. Violent details remain unexplained for the reader, who cannot sort out which rape story is being told: the sentences "i was pierced / in two" and "my mother floats in well water zeide in mourning tears his red / hair" fuse defilement in the camp and in the shtetl, making it difficult to understand what has happened to whom. The hallucinogenic registers of the poem conflate at the end when the speaker bleakly accepts the man who

> brings me soap
> his boots are shiny
> not like the others   who arrive from the fields
> crusted over[.] (*FW* 45–46)

Klepfisz's personal history, as a child-survivor and the daughter of a father murdered, a mother victimized by Nazi violence, may have contributed to her assuming the license of authoring such discomforting posthumous personae.

Yet other writers—for example, Naomi Replansky and Michael Hamburger—similarly blur the line between poet and persona. Replansky's brief "Epitaph: 1945," for instance, marks the distance between earlier American deployments of prosopopoeia in a classic text like *Spoon River Anthology* (with its community of buried citizens) and the registers necessitated by the shattering devastation of the Second World War, possibly those uttered by a civilian victim of the firebombing at Dresden:

> My spoon was lifted when the bomb came down
> That left no face, no hand, no spoon to hold.
> One hundred thousand died in my hometown.
> This came to pass before my soup was cold. (25)

As in Emily Dickinson's "I heard a Fly buzz — when I died — " or Christina Rossetti's "After Death" ("he still is warm tho' I am cold" [1:38]), the adoption of the voice of the dead insists on the urgency of their perspective.

This is a point Hamburger makes in "Treblinka" through a survivor-speaker who recalls a night that teaches him to reverse normative notions about the value of life over and against that of death. Standing "at the barrack windows," the nameless prisoner and his companions are "Not cold for once," and "Unafraid for once," as they watch a bonfire of corpses flaring "purple and blue and red and orange and gold, / The many colours of Joseph's coat, who was chosen" (*CP* 133). The "radiance" of the "chosen" dead contrasts with the degrading materiality of those doomed to submit to their destinies: "To live with the law" requires inmates "to spit in our own face, / Wipe ourselves out of creation, scatter as dust, / Eat grass, and the dung that feeds grass." What further fuels "thankfulness for death" is a song unexpectedly issuing from another inmate, a former opera singer:

> Eli, Eli . . . his question too in whose name
> Long we'd been dirt to be wiped off, dust to be dispersed —
> Older than he, old as the silence of God. (133)

As is often the case in Holocaust verse, "Treblinka" is based on a documentary source, specifically Richard Glazar's account of "the terrible brightness of the flames" on a night when "one heard nothing except little Edek playing his accordion and the young singer singing *Eli Eli*" (Sereny 193). Taking up the cry of Jesus forsaken on the cross, the opera singer reminds Hamburger's speaker how Christians have for centuries used the crucifixion to justify their punishment of believers in a tradition that predates their own. Whereas the burning dead represent an illuminating "gathering up at last, all our hundred hues / Fierce in one radiance," the diaspora after Treblinka ("Back in a room in a house in a street in a town") constitutes merely a confining, isolating diminishment. Since "everything, anything / Proved good enough for life," the only rationale for living consists in the need "To tell of the fire in the night and briefly to flare like the dead" (*CP* 133). Dying, the living can warm themselves only with the thought of being consumed so as to yield light.

Lest one is tempted to suppose that Raplansky and Hamburger, like Klepfisz, have a more legitimate claim on these grievous subjects than Plath by virtue of their backgrounds, a corrective might be Wiesel's caution that "*no one* has the right" to such speech acts (emphasis mine). It might be useful also to recall that Plath felt intimately connected to European history. The granddaughter of Austrians, Plath was parented in a German-speaking household by a mother and father steeped in German culture: "my background is . . . German and Austrian," Plath explained at one interview. "On one side I am a first generation American, on one side I'm second generation American, and so my concern with concentration camps and so on is uniquely intense. And then, again, I'm rather a political person as well, so I suppose that's what part of it comes from" (Orr 169). Seventeen years after her father's death in 1940, which she associated with the outbreak of the Second World War, the twenty-five-year-old poet composed a work titled "The Thin People," which predicts how haunted she was to become by the Shoah:

> They are always with us, the thin people
> Meager of dimension as the gray people
>
> On a movie-screen. They
> Are unreal, we say:
>
> It was only in a movie, it was only
> In a war making evil headlines when we
>
> Were small that they famished and
> Grew so lean[.] (64)

Although the gray images on a film screen initially appear "unreal," although the speaker assures herself what she has seen "was only in a movie," even at the beginning of the poem there is a slippage between "them" and "us" during a period "when *we* // Were small" and *they* "Grew so lean" (emphasis mine).

Because of this unnerving confusion between the victims and their observer, the "thin silence" of the gray specters constitutes a menace, as they find "their talent to persevere / In thinness" and so enter "Into our bad dreams." Even as Plath chafes at her growing awareness of the world's guilt, she realizes that so "weedy a race could not remain in dreams, / Could not remain outlandish victims," and they therefore eventually populate "the contracted country of the head" (64). From unreal movie screens and nightmare, the starving silent hordes advance into waking consciousness, into the sunlit rooms, and then into the forests, fading cultural and natural worlds, bleaching all realms of color:

> We own no wildernesses rich and deep enough
> For stronghold against their stiff
>
> Battalions. See, how the tree boles flatten
> And lose their good browns

If the thin people simply stand in the forest,
Making the world go thin as a wasp's nest

And grayer; not even moving their bones. (65)

Plath's ghostly troops oddly resemble Charlotte Delbo and her comrades upon their return from Auschwitz, when she and they "become diaphanous, more and more translucent, losing their color and their form" (235); fading into transparent specters, they and she seem to float in the unreality of a suspended weightlessness, a colorless and tasteless insubstantiality. Their experience of gratuitously inflicted privations, humiliations, and pains drained post–concentration camp existence of reality by corroding the bedrock that ordinarily grounds lives: faith in God or goodness, pleasure or knowledge, justice or progress, familial procreativity or imaginative creativity. In their "withering kingship," Plath's skeletal troops constitute a corporate anti-muse who inspire verse less about generation, more about nihilism or anhedonia, for they wear "The insufferable nimbus of the lot-drawn / Scapegoat" (65, 64). Whatever blame might accrue to the victims ("They found their talent to persevere / In thinness") clearly reflects the anxieties they have bred in the speaker's now possessed and obsessed consciousness, a point Plath clarifies in a later poem titled "Mary's Song."[8]

While Hamburger raises the same question of "Eli, Eli" that Chagall posed in *White Crucifixion,* Plath sustains it in "Mary's Song" by surrealistically juxtaposing an opening image of "Sunday lamb," its fat cracking in the hot oven, with "The same fire" that melts "the tallow heretics, / Ousting the Jews" (257). To the mother of Jesus and thus the source of Christianity, the sacrifice of the Christian lamb of God prefigures "the cicatrix of Poland." Perhaps, too, by making "precious" such a fiery sacrifice of the son, the lamb, Christians sanctify the horror of this scar in history which delivers not the bird of annunciation to Plath's Mary but "Gray birds" (reminiscent of the gray "thin people") that "obsess my heart, / Mouth-ash, ash of eye." At the conclusion of "Mary's Song," because of its title the "I" of the mythologized speaker sounds more detached from the poet than the "I" of "Getting There":

> On the high

> Precipice
> That emptied one man into space
> The ovens glowed like heavens, incandescent.

> It is a heart,
> This holocaust I walk in,
> O golden child the world will kill and eat. (257)

The technology that produced space flight also manufactured the glowing ovens of the crematoria that threaten to eradicate Mary's offspring. In the heat and heart of a kitchen where Jesus' fate is grotesquely reduced to that of a Sunday roast, Plath's speaker understands her own complicity in a murderous sanctification of sacrifice that will incinerate her own future, her own hopes for salvation. Just as the Christlike thin people wear "The insufferable nimbus of the lot-drawn / Scapegoat," Mary's last word identifies the sacrifice of the golden (precious, Jewish) child, the communion of the lamb of God with the murderous consumption of innocents and innocence in the Shoah. So it sounds, whether or not readers identify the line "This holocaust I walk in" as a forecast of Plath's decision to gas herself in the oven of her kitchen on February 16, 1963. Any simple equation of Plath's kitchen oven with the crematoria of the Shoah has to be rejected as glib, but the uses to which she put her imagined life and death in the poems give voice to those who suffered larger, more momentous losses. Against the ascension of Christ on the third day, "Mary's Song" counterpoints the tenuous vocalization of verse.

GHOSTLY INSTRUCTORS

Whereas Plath's "Getting There" and Klepfisz's "death camp" provisionally elide the gap between the poet's personal self and the posthumous voice, "Mary's Song" uses a mythological character to widen that gap. Even more pointedly, the works of Anthony Hecht, Randall Jarrell, and Charles Simic stress the chasm between the "there" of the casualties and the "here" of the author, the "then" of the Shoah and the "now" of the reader. That the dead and dying in their poems can verbalize need not mean, as de Man proposed about prosopopoeia, that living readers must be encased in a deadly silence; but it does figure the linguistic discontinuity between Auschwitz and poetry, which broadens in verse that foregrounds the distance between victim and poet by emphasizing the complex and fleeting nature of identification (as Hecht does) or by choosing child-speakers quite obviously hampered by their linguistic and cognitive immaturity (as Jarrell and Simic do).[9]

For these writers, the figure of prosopopoeia holds out the promise of an unsettling empathic identification that connects without conflating the living "now" and "here" to the dead "there" and "then." At an epiphanic moment in Hecht's ambitious sequence of poems, "Rites and Ceremonies," empathic memory moves him from compassion ("when I pray, / I am *there*, I am *there*") to the adoption of the posthumous stance:

> We are crowded in *here* naked, female and male.
> An old man is saying a prayer. And now we start
> To panic, to claw at each other, to wail
> As the rubber-edged door closes on chance and choice.
>   (*CEP* 39; emphasis mine)

But the momentary conflation of "there" and "here" will not be — cannot be and perhaps ought not be — sustained. Hecht quickly relinquishes his brief attempt to enter into a community with those herded into gas chambers, meditating instead on the inefficacy of the poetic imagination in a sustained Holocaust lamentation (which I will discuss more fully in the following chapter on the elegiac tradition). Still, his sardonic reflection that "the little children were suffered to come along, too" inflects two disturbing deployments of prosopopoeia in the Holocaust context, both of which present doomed child-speakers.

Possibly influenced by Nelly Sachs, whose "Dead Child Speaks" is about "the knife of parting" from the mother (*HP* 67), Jarrell and Simic let imagined representatives of the one million Jewish children murdered by the Third Reich talk directly to the readers of their verse. Prefaced with the parenthetical words "Birkenau, Odessa; the children speak alternately," Jarrell's "Protocols" consists of the voices of two children antiphonally describing their entrance into alienating, annihilating experiences — one being squashed in a train that arrives at a factory with a smokestack, the other traveling in a barge into deep water. Jarrell most famously used prosopopoeia in "The Death of the Ball Turret Gunner" to delineate a combat fatality. There he conflated the eradication of a bombed airman with a forced evacuation from the womb: "hunched" upside down in the "belly" of a plane, the aborted speaker posthumously declares, "When I died they washed me out of the turret with a hose" (144). In "Protocols," Jarrell explored the relationship between death and birth for children killed in the Shoah (193). A child who comes to the factory is told by his mother not to be afraid and feels water "in a pipe-like rain, but hot," until he is "washed and dried." Another is held by his mother in a place that "*is no more Odessa*" and "*the water drank me.*" The sardonic title of this poem derides the militarism by which both children arrive at a common fate: "*And that is how you die.* And that is how you die." Whether washed and dried by the mother or held up by her, the children's experiences make a mockery of any solace that would embrace death as what Wallace Stevens called "the mother of beauty" (69).

Switching from Plath's and Jarrell's uncanny present tense to a definitively posthumous modality, Simic's "My mother was a braid of black smoke" associates the trauma of the Shoah with the shock of separation from the mother, death with birth. As if pondering Paul Celan's "graves in the air" in "Death Fugue" as well as Plath's stepping out of the "cradles" of the train in "Getting There," Simic creates a shocking speech act after the crematorium that derives from a consciousness quite distinct from that of the adult poet:

> My mother was a braid of black smoke.
> She bore me swaddled over the burning cities.
> The sky was a vast and windy place for a child
> to play.
> We met many others who were just like us.

They were trying to put on their overcoats with
arms made of smoke.
　　The high heavens were full of little shrunken
deaf ears instead of stars. (*WDE* 3)

The words "bore" and "swaddled" identify the child's death with his birth
into another realm where he abides in his delusion of reunion with his
mother and with his playmates. Evanescent smoke floating across the sky —
all that remains of the remains of child, mother, and many others — troubles
normative ideas about the spirituality and the corporality of the dead.

In a manner reminiscent of William Blake's *Songs of Innocence and Experience*, Simic's verse imagines the child's naïveté — for instance, his contemplating a "braid of black smoke" as the umbilical cord — to emphasize how
inconceivable experience is to the innocent. The child's ferocious desire for
presence propels his image making, his efforts to make substantial not just
the silence of the heavens ("full of little shrunken deaf ears instead of
stars") but also his own dissipating insubstantiality after the crematorium.
As has the Jewish star, celestial stars — images of steadfast eternity, purity,
integrity — have been demeaned or extinguished. Yet powerful as the speaker's quest for meaning is, it hardly serves as an antidote to his fate.[10] The
idea of wind as an inspirational breath of divinity and the ideal of transcendence in this "vast and windy place" are rendered inefficacious, as is the
principle of meaning making as a survival strategy.[11] Since amid and after
institutionalized sadism "the world doesn't end" (the title of the volume in
which Simic's poem appears), what Simic and Jarrell do with the posthumous voice is to conceptualize subjectivity beyond death, thereby intimating
that suffering does not end or fade away like smoke, even though bodies do.
Similarly, although in "Mary's Song" Plath writes that the "thick palls" of
Jews "float / Over the cicatrix of Poland, burnt-out / Germany," she emphatically concludes, "They do not die" (257).

Less the result of a compulsive haunting, the adoption of the voices of the
dead in Hecht's, Jarrell's, and Simic's verse appears to be driven by a moral
duty not to forget those very experiences one could never have personally
apprehended. At times, though, moral duty and involuntary haunting are
hard to disentangle. Jerome Rothenberg's effort to produce "poetry as the
language of the dead" throughout *Khurbn* relies on a quotation from Hiji-
kata about ethical responsibility: "To make the gestures of the dead, to die
again, to make the dead enact their deaths again, this is what I want to feel.
The dead are my teachers & live inside me" (3, 27). Rothenberg's "Di Toyte
Kloles (The Maledictions)" begins with a curse that could also be understood as the sort of plea to which Hecht, Jarrell, and Simic responded: "Let
the dead man call out in you because he is a dead man" (33). A list of
wrathful curses that rhetorically reverses the praise of God in a list poem like
Christopher Smart's *Jubilate Agno* — "Let fools wield power let saints & martyrs root up in a money field of blood" — "Di Toyte Kloles (The Maledic-

tions)" explains the basis of Rothenberg's commitment to a ventriloquism of the dead when an uncle begins to speak in the first person to him: "My face & half my body have vanished & am I still alive? / But the movement of my soul through space & time brings me inside you." After this dybbuk's voice emerges, the uncle discourses in Yiddish to his relative, the poet, and instructive moral duty slips back into an involuntary compulsive haunting: "*Mayne oygen zaynen blind fun mayn khurbn ikh bin yetst a peyger*" (My eyes are blind from my *khurbn* I am now a dead one).[12] By making the poem be what he would not have said himself, Rothenberg alienates the speaker (and reader) from the text in a form meant to disturb or shock.

Also teetering between pedagogy and spectral incarnation, W. D. Snodgrass's "A Visitation" returns to Arendt's portrait of Eichmann in a manner formally (though not thematically) quite distinct from that of Denise Levertov and Michael Hamburger. Snodgrass's epigraph situates the poem in the documentary mode: "*Just as you carried out a policy of not wanting to share the earth with the Jewish people . . . we find that no member of the human race can be expected to want to share the earth with you*" (44); however, the Israeli judges' death sentence prefaces a poem composed as a dialogue in alternating stanzas and perspectives. First, from inside a bedroom on a Detroit night, the poet's persona speaks about the hanged man whose spirit is now turned loose on the world; then Eichmann's ghost speaks back in the first person. Shivering and pale like a dead soldier or lover, the specter at the window longs to be taken back in, not to be outcast; but his urgent pleas go unheeded, met only with disgust. The poet's and the world's decision to scapegoat Eichmann demonstrates to the ghost that he has found his consummation in the poet, the world: "My own love, you're all I could wish to be," Eichmann's spectral voice exclaims, adding "you can look through me" (45). Snodgrass agrees with Levertov and Hamburger, in other words, that the trial replicated on the body of Eichmann an instance of the crime Eichmann had perpetrated against the Jewish people.

At the conclusion of *Eastern War Time*, Adrienne Rich's sequence about the deportation, resistance, and extermination of the Jews, each of the dead speakers is confined to a single line, as she also reconstitutes Hecht's voices "blown away on the winter wind" (*ADW* 45) in an ensemble of speakers who serve less as haunting surrogates, less as teachers, than as diasporic remnants of what had been a people:

> I'm a man-child praising God he's a man
> I'm a woman bargaining for a chicken
> I'm a woman who sells for a boat ticket
> I'm a family dispersed between night and fog[.] (44)

These witnesses need to testify because mimesis cannot provide an adequate reflection of the inexplicably grotesque and undocumented suffering endured by so many. Yet the last lines that conclude her Whitmanesque catalogue of subjectivities — "I am standing here in your poem unsatisfied / lifting my smoky mirror" — attest to the poet's awareness of the insufficiency of the very trope of prosopopoeia she exploits. As some of the living speakers in Rich's chorus demonstrate, when poets reproduce the voices of the dead *before* their demise, the impact of dramatic monologues seems less scandalous, their import more monitory about keeping in mind unrecorded but ghastly historical events, even though their characters' recollections echo off our awareness of their impending mortality and the impossibility of their later testifying about their personal responses to it.

In mourning for her family "in the mass graves of Poland / and in the flames of the Warsaw Ghetto" (2), Emily Borenstein hears their voices crying out to her in *Night of the Broken Glass,* which includes numerous poems voiced by civilians on their way to death. Among them is one titled "Round-Up," which concludes:

> We are ordered to tear up grass
> with our teeth.
> Routed with giant dogs
> we are beaten, driven half-clothed
> through the streets
> while we dream, dream of a piece of wet bread
> or another potato. (23)

Beyond its inclusion of one poem written by the resistance fighter who is its central character, Ruth Whitman's *The Testing of Hanna Senesh* consists of a sequence of poems composed in Senesh's persona that recount her training in espionage, her parachuting into enemy territory, the torments of torture she endured until her death: "I watch myself like a person in a dream / while they invent devices to break me down" (57). Similarly, Stephen Berg adopts the perspective of the French poet Robert Desnos at Buchenwald in "Desnos Reading the Palms of Men on Their Way to the Gas Chamber": "I stumble through the prisoners to hold them, / needing to touch as many as I can / before I go" (*TR* 274). William Heyen's "Passover: The Injections" is spoken by someone awaiting the approach of malevolent soldiers: "We lie down in the fields, / thousands of us, / never mind the rain" (*E* 26).

THE RUSE OF IDENTIFICATION

Unlike some of the poets I have merely mentioned in passing, Snodgrass, haunted by Eichmann's ghost, and Rothenberg, visited by his uncle's dybbuk, suggest less that the living identify with the disaster's dead than that the dead identify with us. In any case, though, all of the poems discussed earlier in this chapter assume some sort of empathic connection between the "then" and the "now," the "there" and the "here," the dead and the living.

Yet in other texts that analyze the link between the posthumous perspective and the critique of humanism brought into being by the Holocaust, the trope of prosopopoeia dramatizes precisely the sorts of empathic imaginative act that the Shoah itself called into question (see Laub and Auerhahn). In the process, it unmasks the rhetoric of identification as a ruse. For if empathy or identification were such a powerful psychic force, how could National Socialism's killing campaign have occurred? One poem by Michael Hamburger elaborates on this point and can therefore serve as an introduction to Plath's highly ironic manipulation of prosopopoeia in her two most famous works. Written from the point of view of a prisoner "Blundering into death" with hideously unsuitable concern for his torturer (*CP* 134), Hamburger's "Between the Lines" focuses on one E. A. Rheinhardt, who is filled with mordant self-derision at his own capacity for an ill-fated compassion, a self-mockery that unmasks identification as nothing but the pathetic delusion of projection.

An epigraph about Rheinhardt's "terrible gaffe" involves a revealing case of mistaken identity: when an elegant but tormented-looking man, speaking cultivated French, came out of an interrogation room, Rheinhardt expressed his concern, only later to be informed that he had been sympathizing with "a Gestapo man." Although this quotation from Rheinhardt's 1944 prison diary gestures toward the more modest documentary mode, in "Between the Lines" Hamburger invents the subsequent reactions of its author. Back in the cell he shares with three others, Rheinhardt's soliloquy records how deeply the incident has changed him. Never before had he laughed in that prison where, even after a food parcel arrived, he drifted away from companionship with the others. But now the other inmates seem "close to me," for the error has demonstrated that the humanistic knowledge on which Rheinhardt prided himself has made him no less feeble — maybe more feeble — than they. Indeed, when Hamburger's Rheinhardt cries "To the killer who cracks my joints: 'Je te comprends, / mon ami . . .' " (134), he discovers how his cosmopolitan education has conspired against him, has deluded him into assuming that a civilized person could not possibly be a Gestapo man.

Ridiculing his own impotent pretensions, Hamburger's persona understands "how one I could not believe in / allows me to blaze like his martyrs" and "how the soul / Anatomists cannot locate even now will rise up" when his "turn comes to blunder again" (134). Skeptical agnosticism notwithstanding, Rheinhardt's faith in humanism has blinded him to the human, even humane face brutality frequently wears. The gallows humor Hamburger reads "between the lines" of Rheinhardt's diary makes this dramatic monologue evocative of Robert Browning's works, but a Browning portrait filtered through the lens of Baudelaire's and T. S. Eliot's doomed doubling with a "hypocrite reader."[13] Hamburger's Rheinhardt, laughing that the joke is on himself, damns his own humanism as a foolish self-delusion that renders him far more vulnerable than the others with whom he shares "the thick stench / From the bucket" as well as "our common attrition by hunger and filth" (134). At the same time, Rheinhardt's hapless projection of his own interiority onto the Gestapo man thematizes and qualifies the act of imaginative identification fundamental to prosopopoeia. As in Rheinhardt's gaffe, the " 'Je te comprends' " informing prosopopoeia devolves into a flaccid delusion.

But, surprisingly, no poet has been more scathingly critical of the figure of prosopopoeia than Sylvia Plath. Even as she exploited the trope in the Holocaust context, Plath emphasized her awareness that imaginative identification with the victims could constitute either a life-threatening trap for the poet or a sinister trip for the poet's readers, as "Daddy" and "Lady Lazarus" demonstrate. Imbued by Plath with a definitively postwar perspective on her own deployment of the voice of the victims ("I think I *may well be* a Jew" [223; emphasis mine]), "Daddy" puts into play not an assumed identification but instead a sustained consideration of what it might mean to say, in a line from a draft of Anne Sexton's "My Friend, My Friend" that probably influenced Plath, "I think it would be better to be a Jew."[14] More self-consciously fictive and qualified than John Berryman's effort in poems and stories to see himself as an "imaginary Jew," Plath's identification illuminates not merely the psychological scenarios that most critics examine but also her brilliant insights into a debilitating sexual politics at work in fascist anti-Semitism.[15] An intuition of this achievement may have led George Steiner, who protested against any author's "right to put on this death-rig," to declare elsewhere that "Daddy" was "one of the very few poems I know of in any language to come near the last horror" and then to dub it the " 'Guernica' of modern poetry" ("DIA" 217).

By highlighting the precariousness of her own identification with the Jews of Nazi Germany, Plath asks us to consider the dynamics of German Jews' vicarious identification with their exterminators. From this perspective, "Daddy" reads less like a confessional elegy about Plath's grief and anger at the loss of her father than like a depiction of Jewish melancholia — the primitive, suicidal grieving Freud associated with loss over a love object perceived as part of the self — and thus a meditation on an attachment to Germany in particular, to Western civilization in general that many European Jews found not only inevitable but galling as well.[16] For Hannah Arendt, Jewish melancholia had to be traced back to "the hopeless madness of assimilationists," a fervent but "insane desire to be changed, not to be Jews":

> Very few individuals have the strength to conserve their own integrity if their social, political and legal status is completely confused. Lacking the courage to fight for a change of our social and legal status, we have decided instead, so many of us, to try a change of identity. And this curious behavior makes matters much worse. The confusion in which we live is partly our own work. (*JP*62)

Arendt's "us" here refers to refugees, trying to transform themselves into exemplary, undifferentiated French or German citizens. Her analysis of the psychological allure and frustration of conformity makes different but related sense in the context of gender.

Through a female speaker who experiences her femininity as a wounding secondariness, Jewishness becomes an amplification of alienation, as Plath measures the costs of adjusting to a hostile culture. In Arendt's terms, Plath's "Daddy" confronts "how treacherous the promise of equality [is that] assimilation has held out" (*JP* 68) for a speaker who understands herself to be a so-called *Mischling*, a mixed-race person, part German and part Jew: "her father," according to Plath, was "a Nazi and her mother very possibly part Jewish" (Newman 65). That her patrilineage is male while her matrilineage is female dramatizes the cultural potency of the Nazis and the societal impotence of the Jews, as the figure of the *Mischling* evokes some of the themes associated with the mixed-race mulatto or the light-skinned passer in African American literature: troubling self-divisions, bifurcated loyalties, sexual ambiguities, but also protean self-fashioning fueled by the fury of being outcast.

Although numerous readers have noted that Plath anathematizes Nazism as patriarchalism pure and simple, they have failed to understand how the dependencies of a damaged and damaging femininity shape her analysis of Jews caught in a genocidal regime. A "bag full of God," a "Ghastly statue," an "Aryan" blue-eyed "Panzer-man" with a "neat mustache," Daddy deploys all the regalia of the fascist father against those robbed of selfhood, citizenship, and language, for the speaker's stuttering tongue is "stuck in a barb wire snare. / Ich, ich, ich, ich, / I could hardly speak" (222, 223). The daughter confronts a symbolic order in which the relationship between the fragile "ich" and the overpowering national and linguistic authority of Daddy frustrates any autonomous self-definition. That, as Jacqueline Rose points out, the English "you do not do" can be heard as the German "you *du* not *du*" (226) heightens awareness of the daughter's vulnerable and blurred ego boundaries, the European Jew's conflicted but nevertheless adoring address, her ardent responsiveness to the lethally proximate society that constructed her. Standing "at the blackboard," the fascist represents the irrational power of rationality, of the arts and the sciences, of culture in the "Fatherland." According to Plath, the Jews chuffed off "to Dachau, Auschwitz, Belsen" suffered the horror of impending extermination along with a crippling consciousness of complicity, if only the collusion of those doomed by a long history of intimacy to love and respect a force dead set against them.

For through a rhetorical strategy itself implicated in the calculus of symbiosis, the poem dares to confront the daughter-speaker's induction into revering Daddy and his charismatic power. Not only does the "black shoe," in which she had to live, become associated with the "black boot" and the "black shirts" of fascism, but we are informed, "Every woman adores a Fascist, / The boot in the face, the brute / Brute heart of a brute like you" (223). The daughter's subsequent decision to make and marry "a model" of Daddy (224) suggests how difficult it may be for a consciousness captivated by the inimical source that shaped it to escape self-destructive forms of thralldom that refigure bonds saturated with the only pattern of attachment known, lexicons of emotion devised by the dead Daddy. Vampiric, the phantom father and his constructed surrogate, the husband who loves "the rack and the screw," have drained the speaker of her creative talents, her currency, her autonomy. The depleted daughter therefore fumes against her appalled feelings of radical insufficiency. Bonded with Daddy and wedded to his surrogate, she rages against the consequences of the blurring of boundaries between herself and the culture they present, a blurring of boundaries between Jewishness and Germanness that many German Jews lamented before, during, and after the Shoah. It was a blurring of boundaries that also absorbed the attention of the many Nazi officials who framed innumerable laws to outlaw *Rassenschande* (race defilement resulting from intermarriage) and to regulate the status of *Mischlinge* of the first and second degree: the former "a person with *two* Jewish grandparents, who did not belong to the Jewish religion, and who had not married to a Jewish person on the target date of September 5, 1935"; the latter with "only *one* Jewish grandparent" (Hilberg 43).

Since the tiny percentage of Germany's population composed of Jews and people with some Jewish ancestry played a relatively important role in business, finance, journalism, medicine, law, and the arts in the twenties and thirties, many German Jews felt shocked at the betrayal of a society to which they had vowed what Saul Friedlander calls "ever-renewed and ever-unrequited love" (*NGJ* 78).[17] During the Weimar years, according to the secretary general of the Central Association of German Citizens of the Jewish Faith, "if there were a Nobel Prize for German sentiments, German Jews would win" (Leo Baeck Institute 34).[18] Reflecting on the decision of Leo Baeck, the famous Berlin rabbi, to sit down and pay his electric bill moments before the SS dragged him off to Theresienstadt, Hyam Maccoby sees his act as exemplifying not passivity but instead many Jews' inability to believe that "this Germany, *which they loved, felt obligations toward . . . , felt gratitude toward*" could have dedicated itself to their annihilation (qtd. in Rosenbaum 335; emphasis mine). How else to explain the "anticipatory compliance" of so many members of the Jewish leadership in German cities, their urging "a conciliatory response *before* being confronted by open threats," first by "trying to anticipate German requirements and orders" and later by undertaking "not only [to contribute] personnel, space, and supplies" but also "the more sensitive task of filling the quotas for the projected deportations" (Hilberg 21, 180)?[19] An inability to conceptualize (really, to admit into full consciousness) the murderous aims of a revered homeland, the pollution of a beloved heritage, and the loss of a citizenship that had signified and certified professional status and security: such grief reeks of the narcissistic wound suffered by Plath's daughterly speaker after she tries to commit suicide, only to find herself instead "pulled . . . out of the sack" and "stuck together . . . with glue" (224).

As the Mother Goose rhymes on "you," "*du,*" "Jew," "glue," "screw," "gobbledygoo," "shoe" accumulate, the poem goose-steps toward the concluding "I'm finally through" that proclaims a victory over the spectral afterlife of the fascist, but only at the cost of the daughter's own life. At the very moment Plath declares she is "through" with her father, the final line suggests that she herself is also and thereby "through" with the poem, with her life story, with her life. Does the rage of Plath's persona signal another, imminent suicide attempt? On the basis of Cynthia Ozick's analysis of Primo Levi's death, one might so surmise: interpreting *The Drowned and the Saved* as Levi's angry suicide note, Ozick claims, "he did not become a suicide until he let passion in, and returned the blow" (*MM* 47). For Plath's speaker in "Daddy," though not for Levi in *The Drowned and the Saved,* the indignation that motivates returning the blow derives from the belief that all German Jews were psychologically, if not genealogically, *Mischlinge.* No longer supported by the fragile link between German and Jew, the outraged daughter knows her "gipsy ancestress" and her "Taroc pack" only confirm her status as a pariah, even decades after the catastrophic engagement with Daddy. Plath's scandalizing feminization of Europe's Jews and Gypsies suggests just how appalling, how shameful would seem, *would be* the emasculation of often intensely patriarchal communities.

Some interpreters of the poem view its conclusion as a ritual murder or exorcism facilitated by the speaker's uniting with a community of people who "never liked you. / They are dancing and stamping on you" (224); however, it is more difficult to kill a phantom than a physically embodied person (Daddy is a ghostly specter from the beginning), and in the context of the Shoah the idea of dancing and stomping "villagers" hardly inspires confidence. Just as Plath's speaker asks herself who she can possibly be without Daddy, European Jewish men and women might well have asked themselves who they could possibly be after the Shoah definitively estranged them from their fathers' lands, their mothers' tongue, their neighbors' customs, and their compatriots' nationality—or so the ghastly number of postwar suicides of survivors-who-did-not-survive intimates.

If identification with the victims who could not disidentify with their tormentors constitutes the trap of prosopopoeia in "Daddy," the trope functions as a trip in "Lady Lazarus," although that is not how the work is usually approached. To those who read "Lady Lazarus" as a poem about Plath's edginess at her own task as a confessional writer, "Dying / Is an art" (245) because her anguished sense of diminishment is what she conveys to her audience, the personal suffering she expresses through her artistry; but this means that dying is also a form of lying, a lying about dying, since the expression of her misery is only a poem, a crafted and crafty effort to gain the attention of readers. A female Lazarus in need of no divine intervention, she brings herself back from death or its brink for the prurient delectation of her fans; a femme fatale like the Lady of Shalott, she weaves and wears her wares in an ecstasy of narcissistic absorption; a lady who is a bit of a tramp, she flaunts and flouts her satanically ambitious dedication to a self-destructive making and unmaking of her aesthetic personae.[20] But what does it mean to factor in this poem's multiple images of the Shoah, and specifically its portrait of the imperiled Jew as a fetishized "master of un-mastery" (*WD* 70), the phrase Maurice Blanchot used to approach the complex subject of Holocaust-related suicides?

The wronged speaker here can liberate herself from "Herr Doktor" or "Herr Enemy" only by wresting the power of persecution from him and turning it against herself. While she advertises the spectacle of herself as miraculous saint and prostituted actress, Lady Lazarus's "music-hall routine" parodies "the trash culture of True Confessions" so as to confess "a commodity status no longer veiled by the aura of the sacred" (Britzolakis 151, 155, 156). As her aesthetic mastery taps the language of the Shoah and thereby capitalizes on the disaster, it demonstrates how that historical calamity has itself been robbed of "the aura of the sacred." The proliferation of roles and of audiences recalls the celluloid horde of newsreel "thin people," who wear the "nimbus of the lot-drawn / Scapegoat." We know that the ongoingness of the torments of the Shoah perpetuated postwar suicides, but did those casualties mutate into mystic scapegoats, whose envied status as paradigmatic victims would in turn generate stars of stage and screen with the "talent to persevere," ersatz survivor-celebrities who commodify trauma?

This is one way to grasp the shock of "Lady Lazarus," for the narcissistic and masochistic speaker has become obsessed with dying, relates to it as "a call." With her skin "Bright as a Nazi lampshade," her foot "A paperweight," and her face "featureless, fine / Jew linen," Lady Lazarus puts her damage on theatrical display through her scandalous suicide artistry (244). Have Jews been made to perform the *Trauerspiel* for a "peanut-crunching crowd" at the movies and on TV, like the striptease entertainer through whom Plath speaks? Does Lady Lazarus's "charge" at making death feel "real" and at "the theatrical // Comeback" (245–46) anticipate a contemporary theatricalization of the Holocaust? Certainly, her vengeful warning that "there is a charge / For the hearing of my heart" (246) evokes the charge — the cheap thrill, the financial price, the emotional cost, the pornographic discharge — of installations, novels, testimonials, college courses, scholarly books, and museums dedicated to the six million.

Because Lady Lazarus's exhibitionism issues in spectators paying "For a word or a touch / Or a bit of blood // Or a piece of my hair or my clothes" (246), her bragging about her expertise at the art of dying — "I do it so it feels *like* hell. / I do it so it *feels* real" (245; emphases mine) — seems to adumbrate the notorious celebrity of a writer like Binjamin Wilkomirski, whose gruesome 1996 best-seller *Fragments* (about a child's experiences in the camps) was praised as "free of literary artifice of any kind" before it was judged to be a fraud.[21] When Daniel Ganzfried argued about Wilkomirski's defenders, "These people talking about suicide will *suggest* it to him," and insisted that "Some of his supporters would love him dead because then it looks like proof that he's Wilkomirski" (qtd. in Gourevitch 66), his remarks gloss Plath's suicide-performer pandering to her audience as well as Blanchot's caution about the contamination of the very idea of the genuine (on which Plath's work broods): "If there is, among all words, one that is inauthentic, then surely it is the word 'authentic' " (*WD* 60). To the extent that the impresario of Plath's stage, "Herr God" or "Herr Lucifer," has reduced Lady Lazarus from a person to an "opus" or a "valuable" (246), the poem hints that even reverential post-Shoah remembrances may be defiled by the Nazi perpetrators, that prosopopoeia will not enable the poet to transcend the tarnished uses to which the past has been, can be, will be put. In the voice of a denizen of disaster, Plath mocks the frisson stimulated by the cultural industry she herself helped spawn.[22]

Revolted by her own dehumanization, Lady Lazarus then imagines triumphing over the murderous Nazis by turning vengeful herself, if only in the incendiary afterlife conferred by the oven:

> Ash, ash —
> You poke and stir.
> Flesh, bone, there is nothing there —
>
> A cake of soap,
> A wedding ring,
> A gold filling.
>
> Herr God, Herr Lucifer
> Beware
> Beware.
>
> Out of the ash
> I rise with my red hair
> And I eat men like air. (246–47)

As it feeds on "men like air" — predatory psychic dictators but also perhaps men turned to smoke — the burning hair, the red rage rising out of the ashes fuels only self-combustion, debunking the idea of transcendence or rebirth at the end of the poem. The lines are incantatory, reflecting Plath's view that the recording or speaking of poems is "an essential ingredient of a good poem," as aspect of her effort to "return . . . to the old role of the poet, which was to speak to a group of people," to "sing to a group of people" (Orr 170–71).

With its ironic echoing of the conclusion of Coleridge's "Kubla Kahn" — "Beware! Beware! / His flashing eyes, his floating hair!" (298) — Plath presents herself as a shaman or prophet and then disowns the identification. "Lady Lazarus" repudiates Romantic wonder at the power of the artist, replacing the magical "pleasure-dome" (297) of his artifice with the detritus to which the Jewish people were reduced, in a speech act that amounts to a caustic assessment of the aesthetic sell-out, the disaster-imposter luminary: "there is nothing there — " (Plath 246).[23] That no consensus exists among contemporary historians about whether the Nazis made cakes of soap out of their victims (though they certainly did "manufacture" hair and skin, rings and fillings and bones) and that many of those incinerated had been shaved of all hair drive home the bitter irony propelling the poem, namely that imaginative approaches to the Shoah may distort, rather than safeguard, the dreadful but shredded historical record.[24] Read in this way, Plath's poems need no longer be interpreted (and then faulted) as statements about the ways in which women experience the masochism, rage, and dread of a vulnerability comparable to that of the Jews persecuted in Nazi Germany. Instead, besides clarifying the ways in which Jewish men and women under fascism suffered a wounding feminization, they enable students to evaluate what it means for a writer to feel impelled to mine material that she knows will necessarily remain discordant with her own situation.

It would seem, from my perspective as a teacher of literature, that even discussions about Plath's psychosexual poetics in "Lady Lazarus" and "Daddy" can deepen understanding of the dynamics of "memory envy," a term Geoffrey Hartman uses to describe a condition "whereby those who have not gone through traumatic experiences adopt those experiences, or identify with them rather than not finding any memories at all, any *strong* memories" ("WVT" 230). In Plath's case, I would modify this definition to argue that "memory envy" can impel a creative writer who *has* gone through painfully strong personal events to adopt historically cataclysmic traumas and in the process illuminate them as well as her awareness of their incongruity vis-à-vis her own quite distinct crises. Reenactments of the calamity, including her own, are indicted, even as Plath issues a warning that they will take a toll.

NECROSPECTIVES

Has the figure of prosopopoeia, so seductive for poets from Jarrell and Plath to Simic and Rich, outlived its functions as the Holocaust recedes into a past that will soon have been witnessed by no one alive to provide firsthand testimony of its atrocities? Or will the imperatives of "postmemory" imbue this rhetorical strategy — which insists on returning to the unbearable rupture of suffering — with newfound resonance once the Shoah can no longer be personally recalled? Given the passage of time as well as the flood of depictions of the catastrophe, the very vacuity of the desecrated (buried alive, incinerated, unburied, dismembered) bodies that licensed the personifications of prosopopoeia may make verse epitaphs seem shoddily inadequate. Plath's taunting sneer — "I turn and burn. / Do not think I underestimate your great concern" (246) — chronologically preceded the highly profitable entertainment industry the Holocaust business has so recently become; however, besides forecasting it, "Lady Lazarus" offers up a chilling warning about the fetishization of suffering with which the figure of prosopopoeia flirts. Indeed, Plath's verse uncannily stages the bases for accusations of exploitation, larceny, masochism, and sensationalism that would increasingly accrue around Holocaust remembrance. In addition, her impersonation of the real victims invariably generates awareness of the spurious representation put in the place of the absence of evidence. Poems that call attention to what Geoffrey Hartman and Jean Baudrillard term our propensity to adopt a "necrospective" deploy prosopopoeia to draw us closer to an event that is simultaneously distanced by their debased status as merely simulated and recycled image-substitutions.[25]

Today, in accord with scholars who stress the exceptionality of the Shoah, creative writers may choose to emphasize the opacity of the disaster, as Jorie Graham does, rather than freight it with voices of their own devising. For we have become exceptionally sensitive to the political and moral problems posed by a trope like prosopopoeia, quandaries articulated by one of the poets who has employed it herself: "The living, writers especially, are terrible projectionists," Adrienne Rich has declared, adding "I hate the way they use the dead" (*ARPP* 113). Anne Michaels calls the effort "to smuggle language / from the mouths of the dying / and the dead" a "suicide mission," because what is rescued cannot be "the old language at all; / only the alphabet the same" and because the "language of a victim only reveals / the one who named him" ("WLT" 115). Yet, addressing the etiology and ethics of prosopopoeia in earlier Holocaust verse, Graham's "Annunciation with a Bullet in It" exposes both the injuries and the urgencies of using the dead and does so by returning to Lyotard's central issue, splicing it with eyewitness testimony taken from Isabella Leitner's *Fragments of Isabella: A Memoir of Auschwitz*. As forecast by its title and its occasion (someone has shot the poet's dying dog, with whom she sits throughout the night), the poem concentrates on shocking moments of inexplicable violence.

In particular, sections 5 through 12 of "Annunciation with a Bullet in It" (*M* 66–77) consist of reprinted passages from Leitner's account of her deportation ("Anyone not up at four a.m. will get a *Kugel*"), the strength she gains in the camps from her three sisters ("*Cipi, Chicha, Rachel, Isabella. We seem to be alive*"), their touching of a newborn baby ("before she is wrapped in / the piece of paper / and handed over to the Blockelteste — "), her fear of carrying a dead body ("the *Oberscharführer* will choose me, I know he will"): all these quotations, sprinkled with foreign words and prefaced by the phrases "Then, she said," do not resemble the language employed by Plath so much as the more modestly documentary works of such poets as Charles Reznikoff and Barbara Helfcott Hyett. But in Graham's poem, the documentary source is immediately followed by another quotation ("Said the angel"), this one expressing the sinister logic of the cynic paraphrased in Lyotard's *The Differend,* a revisionist who has "analyzed thousands of documents" and "tirelessly pursued specialists":

> I have tried in vain to find a single former deportee
>
> capable of proving to me that he had really seen
>   with his own eyes
> a gas chamber
>   TIRELESSLY
> (wingprint in dust) (smoke) the
>
> only acceptable proof that it was used to kill
>   is that one died from it —
> (tirelessly) —
>   but if one is dead one cannot testify
> that it is
>   on account of such a chamber —
>
> there is, therefore, no gas, chamber[.] (72–73)[26]

When history consists of "a rip where evidence exists" or a "stammer between invisibles, / The soft jingling of a chain" (75, 73), can any documentation be found to meet the perverse objections raised by Lyotard's Holocaust denier? To Graham's consternation, what cannot be "seen" in her complex meditation threatens to degenerate into the equivocations of the word "*seem,*" turning the "plaintiff" into a "victim" who cannot find the means to prove the damages incurred (75, 73).[27] Although Isabella Leitner's incorporated testimony focuses, like Walter Benjamin's Angel of History, on a single catastrophe rather than the "chain of events" we observe from a distance, the words of her Auschwitz memoir jingle against those of Lyotard's malignant angel in a sequence that recalls Graham's earlier definition of history as "*the creature, the x,*"[28] a beast "on a chain, licking its bone":

> it is on a chain
>
> that hisses as it moves with the moving x,
> link by link with the turning x
> (the gnawing now Europe burning). (*DUF* 147)

In a retort to Lyotard's revisionist, the adopted voice of one of Leitner's family members at the conclusion of the poem — whose emphatic lie here ("I really really am not hungry" [77]) bespeaks her loving offer of a piece of bread — testifies to her survival in Leitner's and Graham's memory, but only as "A stammer between invisibles" because we know nothing of her fate, nor that of the two sisters in the concentration camp with her. Indeed, in *Fragments of Isabella* Leitner herself has no definitive knowledge of one sister's destiny ("Cipi, Cipi, where are you?"), though she may have been compelled to undertake the death march to Bergen-Belsen; possibly she survived the British liberation (84). Annunciation, with its promise of an emancipating enunciation, has been riddled by such absences, in accord with Cynthia Ozick's protest against any "search for spots of goodness, for redemptive meaning" in the Shoah ("RTD" 279). At the same time, Graham's poem explains why some of her precursors felt compelled to go beyond testimonial evidence, to occupy the "rip where evidence exists," to communicate a "stammer between invisibles." Despite the indubitable fact that the inanimate dead cannot possibly attest to what or who murdered them, imaginatively inhabiting the genocidal hole in annunciation means disproving the deductions of Holocaust deniers. Bloodless, even the words of survivors or photographs of the victims generate only after-the-fact narrativizing that "*the creature, the x*" gnaws, "making stories like small smacking // sounds, / whole long stories which are its gentle gnawing" (*DUF* 146). "How," Graham asks in another poem, "can the scream rise up out of its grave of matter?":

> The war is gone. The reason gone. The body gone. Its
> reason gone. The name the face the personal
>   identity and yet here
> is a pain that will not diminish . . . (*M* 100–102)

An analysis of how to speak about erasure, especially the erasure of voices, "Annunciation with a Bullet in It" subscribes to the philosopher Charles Sanders Peirce's insistence that "a bullet hole is a sign that a gun was fired" (Brinkley and Youra 121). Whereas Graham, like so many other proxy-witnesses, turns the representational tear into evidence, the poets of prosopopoeia — as if inspired by Walter Benjamin's Angel of History, in a passage that Graham quotes elsewhere in *Materialism* (the book in which "Annunciation" appears) — "would like to stay, awaken the dead," though their stutters and caesurae, their foreignisms and fragments prove they know full well that the not-said, the unheard, the unsayable have been buffeted in the storm of time irresistibly propelling them away from the pile of debris growing skyward (*M* 55). Through their invention of the voices of the dead and dying as well as their sometimes explicit, sometimes implicit acknowledgment of the futility of their task, North American and British writers provide images that testify to the feelings of an event as well as its limited comprehensibility as a piece of a larger phenomenon that defies understanding. What persists in the poetry of prosopopoeia is what some might term a fantasy, an abiding faith in the individuality, the autonomous consciousness of each subjectivity touched by a calamity that disproved the powers of individuality and of autonomous consciousness.

Perhaps our discomfort with this body of work — which made it impossible for me to read aloud quite a few of the verse passages quoted here on the two occasions I presented this material at public lectures — perhaps even some of our queasiness or revulsion at Plath's audacity is related to this tension. Possibly our chagrin is incited by the ironies of a trope that expresses personal pain amid genocide: as Berel Lang has explained, "It is precisely the individual consciousness that is denied in the act or idea of genocide — and the imposition of a representation of agency on that subject ... conduces to a distortion that is both conceptual and moral" (*AING* 154). Do literary representations of subjectivity employ characters that contradict the radical unfreedom and impersonality of victims subjected to an abrogated subjectivity and thereby unnerve us? But why should artists honor the point of view of those who denied people individual consciousness — the fascists, certainly not the Jewish victims? And thus maybe our consternation derives from a wish not to recognize even admittedly simulated figures of the past as an abiding concern of the present, a fervent desire to let such figures disappear irretrievably. One of Plath's most recent defenders, Harriet Parmet, argues against her critics,

> It is well to consider that those self-appointed guardians of the culture and destiny of a martyred people — who insist on considering the Holocaust as a unique horror, totally unrelated to any other acts of organized brutality or to any form of personal suffering — are in fact denying the legitimacy of the very process by which events of the past become the shared heritage of humanity. (75–76).

Yet another defense of the project of prosopopoeia derives from a realization that the vast preponderance of Jews who resisted or submitted to imperial domination are dead. "Where [Gayatri] Spivak asks 'Can the Subaltern Speak?' (1988)," Jonathan Boyarin explains, "one item on the agenda for those who would revive a critical Jewish discourse is 'Can the Dead Speak?' " (*SFP* 82). Although he admits "the intuitive answer is no," Boyarin adds that "an underground tradition says that our lives depend on hearing them" (82). Such dependency adds weight to Helen Vendler's supposition that "the lyric is a script written for performance by the reader — who, as soon as he enters the lyric, is no longer a reader but rather an utterer, saying the words of the poem in propria persona, internally and with proprietary feeling" (*GM* xi). Since this is so, there can be no doubt that poets voicing the dead (or readers speaking the lines composed by those authors) uncannily hear themselves in the present moment expressing suffering no longer confined to the fate of long-ago, faraway strangers. A willful "cheat," according to Sharon Cameron, proleptic art (which anticipates what dying or death feels like) "will make its voice heard, will *have* a voice where no voice can really be" (130). By generating unreal images of a past partially obliterated from history, by recording the calamity as a private confession of grave public harm, prosopopoeia enabled poets of Plath's generation to fulfill Benjamin's definition of the most adroit historian, whose "gift of fanning the spark of hope in the past" derives from the conviction that "*even the dead will not be safe from the enemy if he wins. And this enemy has not ceased to be victorious*" (*I* 255).

7

"COULD YOU HAVE MADE AN
ELEGY FOR EVERY ONE?"

The fringes or tzitzit on the prayer shawl draped not on the shoulders but over the loins of Chagall's Jesus symbolize all of God's 613 commandments (Num. 15:39). Within the Jewish tradition of gematria, in which numeric value is assigned to each letter of the alphabet, the word "tzitzit" adds up to 600, to which are added eight strands and five knots to compose the 613. In contrast to this specific sum, the aggregate of casualties (in the boat or the razed ghetto, within the burning synagogue of *White Crucifixion*) appears incalculable, indiscernible in the smoke and snow, the fog and flares. What blocks the poetic imagination are the sheer numbers: how can men and women of letters go beyond confessional and documentary approaches to compose elegies about the countless dead? As if addressing the limits of prosopopoeia's dedication to an individual consciousness as well, Jacqueline Osherow once obliquely asked herself about the victims, "Could you have made an elegy for every one?" Obliquely because the query was patently put to one of her muses, Rainer Maria Rilke, in a verse "Letter" she composed to him and then punctuated with another speculation: "Or would you, in the face of this, have left / Off elegies forever?" (*CS* 9–10). After Auschwitz, would Rilke have had to express a failing, faltering voice stymied by the Shoah's massive assault on the idea of any sovereign subjectivity? Or might he have felt the lure of relinquishing poetry—the most potent effort to incarnate the presence of a speaker with a unique voice—altogether, of leaving off elegies forever?

Historically, the elegy mourns a death that grieves a survivor searching for some recompense, some hint of renewal, and thus it is animated by T. S. Eliot's faith in *Four Quartets* that "We are born with the dead: / See, they return, and bring us with them" (ll. 230–31). As in the years following the First World War, however, in the aftermath of the Holocaust imaginative writers emphasize their decision to eschew any attempt to reverse loss, for they reject or reinvent the usual mandate of the elegiac genre—to ensure through verse the resuscitation or transmogrification of the corpse.[1] Instead they mind the consequences of Cynthia Ozick's protest against any "search for spots of goodness, for redemptive meaning" ("RTD" 279) in the destruction of one-third of the world's Jewish population. Seldom patterned on a quest for redemptive meaning, Holocaust lament deviates markedly from conventional elegiac writing. Rather, it shares much in common with the bleakest sections of the biblical Book of Lamentations, for its authors rarely imagine any resurrection of the dead and often reject conventional forms of solace, insisting on innumerable losses that can neither be understood nor accepted after the passage of time.

Despite the powerful models of redemption in Jewish and Christian traditions, their controlling metaphors "will not be made to work," Ozick has cautioned; "the only thing that the Holocaust can give birth to is further images of itself" (279, 281).[2] For poets who mourn the dead and warn the living of the impossibility of finding meaning in the catastrophic suffering of millions, this task of abjuring the redemptive paradigm has detached the elegy from any of the usual consolations of philosophy or religion or psychology. Their starting point is that of Jean Améry, who believed "there is really nothing that provides enlightenment on the eruption of radical Evil in Germany," an abomination "singular and irreducible in its total inner logic and its accursed rationality," and therefore "all of us are still faced with a dark riddle" (*AML* viii). According to Blanchot, who pushed his own philosophical *Writing of the Disaster* toward poetry through perplexing aphorisms, "silence [should] resound at length, before returning to the motionless peace where the enigma still wakes" (53). To Lyotard, as well, the Shoah feels "like an unresolved problem, an enigma perhaps, a mystery, or a paradox" (*H* 57). Holocaust lamentations in English do not solve the riddle of the Holocaust, but instead keep it unfathomable while lending a semblance of substance to suffering of virtually unimaginable proportions.

Since the beginning of the twentieth century, of course, a deepening pessimism about conventional sources of consolation has informed the elegiac verse of authors dealing with private bereavements over beloved relatives and friends whose deaths resulted from battle, illness, accident, neglect, criminality, or natural catastrophe. If, as Jahan Ramazani has pointed out, "every elegy is an elegy for elegy—a poem that mourns the diminished efficacy and legitimacy of poetic mourning" (*PM* 8), then this is particularly true for those laments over the invalidity of artistic grieving after Auschwitz.[3] Indeed, in the opening pages of his *Poetry of Mourning*, Ramazani's reliance on Geoffrey Hill's "September Song" (as an index of contemporary poets' misgivings about the elegy's tendency to make atrocity aesthetically and historically acceptable) attests to the impact the Holocaust has had on the genre's recent evolution, and more specifically on its authors' suspicion about what Sandra Gilbert calls "the ancient and redemptive narrative of the pastoral elegy." Many late-twentieth-century writers, grappling with personal grief from a position of "unbelief and disbelief," seek "to come to terms with loss" through strategies she enumerates: "first, a meditation on the actual scene of dying; second, a preoccupation with the literal body of the dead one; third, a retelling of the details of the past . . . ; and fourth, a resignation that sometimes involves a hopeful (but often sardonically hopeful or fantastic) resolution and sometimes merely a stoic acquiescence in the inevitable" (" 'RA' " 182–83). But poets confronting the Shoah do not have access to any information about "the actual scene of dying" or "the literal body of the dead one" or "the details of the past." The most forbidding barriers to find a way to mourn consist of the massive number of those killed, for unfathomable reasons and within unknown—indeed unknowable—circumstances and times.

Because Holocaust poets face a gaping hiatus where the past should exist, the formal shape their verse takes differs from those of other elegists, as does their pointed refusal to seek methods of achieving resolution or acquiescence. Whereas recent elegies on the death of a beloved tend to eschew consolation by focusing instead on the physical facts of the dying or dead body, the Holocaust lamentation often contains no corpse at all. There are cadaver parts—extracted teeth, bones, skin in abundance, hair by the wagonload, stacks of remains heaped in piles—but hardly a single being intact, because a crucial aspect of the puzzle of the crime was the mysterious absence of individuals who simply disappeared anonymously not like but as insubstantial smoke, dust, dirt. Whereas most elegies (even anti-consolatory ones) render the intimate responses of the poet mourning a specific dead spouse, parent, child, friend, or mentor whose absence is filtered through the desolation of their lost intimacy, the Holocaust lament rarely contains a single dead person, but instead a murdered people; rarely a surviving companion plunged into despair, but instead an observer-poet shocked and often revolted by his or her detachment from or ignorance of the catastrophic scene.[4] All those social customs and ceremonies invoking the name of the dead—at the deathbed, the coffin, the cemetery, the religious service, the reading of the will or the bequest, the annual commemoration—were annulled for those who died on unknown days, in undiscoverable places during the Shoah. Within the cattle cars crisscrossing Poland, upon arrival at Treblinka, amid the heap of corpses at Buchenwald, and at numerous town squares and courtyards, the Orthodox — knowing there would be no one left behind — recited the kaddish for themselves.

That failure of ritual accounts for the breakdown of any normative relationship between the mourner-poet and the manifold, nameless dead. What replaces the tender bond between the elegiac poet and the beloved dead companion or relative? This chapter concentrates on rancorous satires against inadequate conventions of mourning; enigmatic lists of casualties or indeterminate doggerel about perpetrators; and sometimes futile arraignments of God, sometimes equally futile efforts to play God or God's appointed guardians so as to reverse an irreversible disaster. Fiercely felt Holocaust requiems respond to W. H. Auden's dictum that "poetry makes nothing happen" (*SP* 80) by renouncing efforts either to master grief or to reconstitute the mourning self after the trauma of death. The Holocaust poet seeks to administer shock by activating the appalling desolation of the disaster: not to console the living, not to animate the dead (as in many poems written before the Shoah, especially those composed in Christian contexts), but to counteract our indifference, to foment anguish, or at least to generate a recognition of our limited capacity for being bruised by the calamity that had undone so many. When Leon Wieseltier found the strength to document his year of mourning in the book *Kaddish,* he took to heart an ancient precept in Jewish thinking that also fortifies poets lamenting the Shoah: "There is no prohibition against mourning and there is no commandment to be consoled."[5]

THE INDITED ELEGY INDICTED

Because Adorno realized the nihilism of his prohibition against poetry, he added another sentence to explain its catastrophic repercussions: "And this corrodes even the knowledge of why it has become impossible to write poetry today" ("CCS" 34). Writers of verse often find a mandate for their work by acknowledging such corrosion and countering it, by laying bare the reasons why the composing of poetry after Auschwitz had to become suspect. The self-reflexive state of contemporary verse about the Shoah, then, resembles that of thinking: "If thinking is to be true," Adorno claimed, "it must also be thinking against itself" ("MM" 365). Similarly, some writers believe that if poetry about the Holocaust is to be true, it must also be poetry against itself. Their view takes into reckoning the impact of George Steiner's claim that "the Shoah has eradicated the saving grace, the life-giving mystery of meaningful metaphor in Western speech and, correlatively, in that highest organization of speech which we call poetry and philosophic thought" ("LLM" 61).

According to Michael Hamburger, the midcentury swerve toward a "new austerity" of "anti-poetry" was produced by a total war that shocked poets out of the assumption "that personal feelings and personal imagination will accord with general truths of a meaningful kind"; it infused them with a self-mocking disgust with literariness, a conviction that the aesthetic experience was, as the Polish author Tadeusz Rozewicz put it, " 'a harmless but ludicrous and childish occupation' " (*TP* 247, 249). The Yiddish poet Kadya Molo-dowsky also viewed poetry as simply an "Old, idiotic habit" composed of "letters wearing shoes," the lines running every which way, the strophe closing "with bolt and lock" that "falls upon my head, / More like a stone" than anything else (363). Paradoxically buttressing Adorno's prescription, anti-elegists protesting "what occurred at Linz" inculpate the elegiac tradi-tion itself, judging it to be part and parcel of "the romantic lie in the brain / Of the sensual man-in-the-street / And the lie of Authority" (Auden, *CP* 86, 88). Any reaping of poetic profit from the loss of so many lives inevitably pollutes the process of composition, causing poets to wonder whether thoughts that feel too deep for tears ought not remain too deep for words. As they flaunt emotions dissonant with grief or display an unnerving lack of affect, what anti-elegists mourn is the impossibility of mourning.

So Geoffrey Hill's bleakly inconclusive and terse "September Song," with its epigraph "born 16.6.32 — deported 24.9.42," begins with an admission of the poet's failure: he knows the date of deportation, nothing about the death or death date of the nameless child. The paradoxical status of the pariah — "undesirable" in the state but not "untouchable" by it — means this boy or girl will not be "passed over at the proper time." Within the context of Passover, with its promise of an Angel of Death bypassing inno-cent children, the predictable facts — "Just so much Zyklon and leather, patented / terror, so many routine cries" — are presented through a line break that makes "patented" refer back not only to the gas, patented and sold like any merchandise, but also to the shiny patent "leather," and for-ward to the plain, patent "terror" (*CP* 67). As Derek Attridge explains, "this is poetry that resists the voice, since the visual dimension defies the vocal continuities of the sentences" (369). What such emphasis on the poem as visual text, rather than auditory event, means is clarified in the hesitancy of sentences fractured by line breaks that jar against syntac-tical units and against ludicrously incommensurate elegiac tropes of con-solation:

> (I have made
> an elegy for myself it
> is true)
>
> September fattens on vines. Roses
> flake from the wall. The smoke
> of harmless fires drifts to my eyes. (67)

Although, as Ramazani points out, the line "September fattens on vines" hints at the Shakespearean consolation that "Ripeness is all" as well as the Keatsian relishing of an autumn plump with juiciness before the fall into wintry death, the idea that death constitutes a maturation or consummation is obscenely irrelevant to the disappearance of the ten-year-old, to the harmful connotations taken on by "flake" or "smoke" or "fires." Since all Hill has managed to achieve is a sort of parenthesis, a mere "elegy for myself," he lambastes the insufficiency of his as well as his predecessors' verse and sneers, "This is plenty. This is more than enough" (57). The repeated word "This" refers to the parallelism of killing, writing, and reading, which are all "more than enough" for a poet sarcastic about the efficiency of Nazi as well as his own and our productivity.[6] What Derek Walcott terms the "profit in guilt" contaminates "plenty"—not the fertile "plenty" of harvest but the sterile surfeit of death—when the muse of "this century's pastorals" inhabits a landscape in which "Brown pigeons goose-step, squirrels pile up acorns like little shoes, / and moss, voiceless as smoke, hushes the peeled bodies / like abandoned kindling" (XLI).

For this reason, a number of writers bitterly measure elegiac traditions against genocide to find them wanting. Facing "Load on puffed load, / Their corpses, stacked like sodden wood," Randall Jarrell debunks the futility of elegiac ceremonies in "A Camp in the Prussian Forest" (167–68). Near a wreath plaited for their grave, the poet paints a star he saws "from yellow pine" to "plant the sign / In soil that does not yet refuse / Its usual Jews." The rhyming of "refuse" and "Jews" draws attention to the slippage between a verb meaning "to decline" and a noun signifying the trash of a thrown-away people. Therefore the "white dwarfed star," recalling to his mind how "the breast's star of hope" was "rendered into soap" and fouled by smoke, becomes "a yellow joke." Amid the film of ash and trash, "where men were drunk like water, burnt like wood," the poet considers the "stellification" of the dead in conventional verse, their apotheosis in the heavens, a rebirth that signals resurrection, eternal afterlife.[7] The poem's pun on "pine" (for wood instead of sorrow) mocks the possibility of the metamorphosis of the "puffed load" of corpses "stacked like sodden wood" into a celestial beacon; so, Jarrell concludes, "I laugh aloud" and the wooden "star laughs from its rotting shroud / Of flesh." This gallows laughter at "a yellow joke" marks the entrance of the sarcastic into subsequent elegiac diatribes.

"What differences can contemporary poetry make in our moral thinking?" the critic Charles Altieri explicitly asked in recent years, much as Hill and Jarrell did implicitly in their anti-elegiac elegies. Altieri's answer to his own question, about those artists "extremely wary of making any ethical claims for themselves," is that "the wariness itself [carries] a possible moral weight" (109). Wariness about the moral uplift of memorial rhetoric saturates poetry about the Shoah. When the countless dead appear as misplaced nameplates in James Fenton's "A German Requiem," the poet satirizes post-Holocaust Germany's dedication to "go on forgetting" the genocide of the Jews while it piously eulogizes German citizens' suffering during the war. Juxtaposing smug ceremonies ("the boiled shirts gather at the graveside") with dismay that "so many had died, so many and at such speed," Fenton describes the dismantling of their lives:

> There were no cities waiting for the victims.
> They unscrewed the nameplates from the shattered doorways.
> And carried them away with the coffins.
> So the squares and parks were filled with the eloquence of young
>   cemeteries:
> The smell of fresh earth, the improvised crosses
> And all the impossible directions in brass and enamel.
>
> *
>
> "Doctor Gliedschirm, skin specialist, surgeries 14–16 hours or by
>   appointment."
> Professor Sargnagel was buried with four degrees, two associate
>   memberships
> And instructions to tradesmen to use the back entrance.
> Your uncle's grave informed you that he lived on the third floor,
>   left
> to which one needed a key . . . (*HP* 104–105)

While the debris at grave sites with "improvised crosses" makes appointments for the dead, professionally certifies them, instructs visitors which entrance to use, and informs them the dead will arrive in an elevator, that grisly comedy replaces any recollection of the millions unburied, unmarked. Bathetic German citizens rehearse "what we went through" so as to find mourning rituals that assuage grief and evade guilty memories.

With its allusion to Brahms's *Requiem,* Fenton's work typifies a host of poems that cannot be classified as laments but that nevertheless explain why the anti-elegy evolved, for satirists of the aesthetic condemn the famed arts of German civilization as agents of barbarism. Given the grandeur of Germany's orchestral, quartet, operatic, choral, and lieder traditions, a number of artists illuminate the logic of Holocaust laments by concentrating their rage on and against music.[8] Perhaps the effort to ironize the Nazis' self-aggrandizing uses of music is best illustrated by Louis Simpson's attention to an artistry that buffers people against guilt, helping accomplices to repress any acknowledgment of the disaster.[9] With senseless rhymes that serve to debunk the capacity of verse to produce an anesthetization of the moral faculty, Simpson's "The Bird" takes as its refrain a line from German Romantic poetry—"*Ich wünscht', Ich wäre ein Vöglein*"—sung from the beginning to the end of his life by a man who becomes a concentration camp guard. The sentimental pathos of this dutiful citizen's wish to "fly / Across the sea" makes his mother cry at the start of his life and his children weep toward the end of his life; however, in his middle years his song serves as a death knell to his victims: "They knew that when they heard him / The next day they would die" (*BR* 288). The song of the bird — from verse that Simpson associates with the tradition of Heine, although it probably derives from a poem by Mörike — recalls the Haydn quartet called "The Bird" and by association another that furnished the melody for "Deutschland über Alles." Although the bird in German and English verse signifies the natural transcendence and grace of song, the lyric of Simpson's guard (nicknamed the Bird by the prisoners) resembles the *Wiener Blut* of Strauss that blares on the radio when he arrives at the "fence with towers / On which armed sentries stood" (287). That Simpson's Nazi-bird manages to fly the coop so as to evade justice, that he continues to indulge in the pleasing poignancy of the song: these events ask us to judge the tears produced by art as ludicrous and childish but not harmless, since they insulate perpetrators within a self-serving wallowing in emotions at odds with the bloody waltz of their lives.

Heydrich the classical violinist, Göring the art collector, Goebbels the novelist, Hitler the aspiring painter who wanted to study at the Vienna Academy of Fine Arts: all lurk behind "The Bird," but so does the speculation of George Hersey that the Final Solution consisted of an "artistic racism" (162) that used biogenetic engineering, euthanasia, and mass murder to sculpt the perfected Nordic race of the future. A call for the incursion of ugliness into the aesthetic, Jerome Rothenberg's "Nokh Aushvits (After Auschwitz)" resists the fascists' "artistry of death A stage set / at treblinka ticket window a large clock / the signs that read: change for bialystok" (*K* 18); such elaborate stage settings were produced to create an illusion that set out to delude arriving inmates and observers. The perverse imagination at work in concentration camp settings corroborates the view that artistic consciousness was less a by-product of the Nazi project than its source: not only was the front wall of the Treblinka gas house decorated with the Star of David but at the entrance was hung a curtain taken from a synagogue that bore "the Hebrew words 'This is the gate through which the righteous pass' " (Hilberg 230).

Choreographed SS theatricality in the camps exploited scripted scenes not simply for the purpose of tricking victims but for the titillation of tormentors holding the starring roles. So, for example, the shout "Ivan, water!" at Treblinka was a signal to start the gassing, and a Red Cross car at Auschwitz was used to carry the Zyklon (Hilberg 248). In place of the modernist vow to make the poem new, Rothenberg pledges allegiance to the postmodernist "make it uglier":

> no
> not a moment's grace nor beauty to obstruct
> whatever the age demanded   or the poem

shit poured on wall & floor
sex shredded   genitals torn lose by dog claws
& the ugliness that you were to suffer
later   that they had suffered
not as dante dreamed it but in the funnel
they ran through & that the others called
the road to heaven[.] (18)

To Ezra Pound's "The age demanded an image / Of its accelerated grim-ace" ("Hugh Selwyn Mauberley" 61), Rothenberg posits an infernal death shoot named "the road to heaven."

An important Holocaust lament, Gerald Stern's poem "Adler" draws on the logic informing Simpson's and Rothenberg's critique of the aesthetic in its reproach to Nazi aestheticism amid atrocity. Jacob Adler was a leading actor-manager in the Yiddish theater who wrote a play called *The Jewish King Lear* and died in 1926; he inspired pity and terror in his performances "fifty years / before our hell" during a time when he and his admirers "were buried one at a time, each with his own service, / ... not lined up beside the trucks // or the cattle cars" (*PP* 80, 79). Two death scenes before Auschwitz measure the distance between "then" and "now." Celebrated by the likes of Isadora Duncan and John Barrymore, the dead Adler was himself mourned by people in the streets when his coffin was carried from theater to theater as "he lay in a windsor tie and a black silk coat." And as Lear on stage, Adler lovingly bore the dead, "carried Cordelia around in his arms / he almost forgot his words, he was so moved / by his own grief" (79–80). His specta-tors, too, "were able to weep / and wring their hands for Lear, and sweet Cordelia," whose "life / was the last claim against him — the last delusion," so it could be said to "free" him, or so they might speculate "going back to their stairways and their crowded tables // with real streaks of remorse on their faces — ." The audience's "tears and groans" then served a cathartic purpose at odds with the shock aroused by the dead being "dragged from their places / and dumped on the ground or put in orderly piles — " (80).

Although recalling Adler's Yiddish versions "could make you laugh," post-Holocaust apprehension paradoxically draws the poet back into the earlier Jewish community, for now he experiences the time in which "even Yiddish / becomes a tragic tongue and even Adler / can make you weep" (78). When the Yiddish King Lear regarded his realm stretching "from Sears on the left to Gimbels on the right" (78), translation transported Shakespeare into an immigrant world that in no way decreased his play's power. Indeed, the popularity of the Yiddish *King Lear* with common people could be said to have replicated the eclectic audiences of the original works of Shakespeare at the Globe theater. But the Holocaust after Adler's death functions as a crime against Shakespeare, reducing his Lower East Side audience and his greatest works to mere anachronisms. "If the death camps and mass exterminations allow little opening for the dramatic," Irving Howe once explained, "they also give little space for the tragic" because "In classical tragedy, man is defeated; in the Holocaust, man is destroyed" ("WH" 190).[10] Instead of bemoaning Regan and Goneril's ingratitude, their filial impiety, as the Yiddish audience did ("Daughters, daughters, it cries for the sadness that came / to all of them in America"), the poet sees in the daughters' implacable gaze "hatred reminiscent of the Plains / of Auschwitz — Buchenwald" which would drive Lear "mad / an inch at a time" (*PP* 78). As the poem progresses, Shakespeare's "nothing will come of nothing" eclipses the "serpent's tooth" of his "thankless" children. None of the terms we ordinarily associate with a tragedy like *King Lear*—hubris, nobility, enlightenment, repentance, resignation — could possibly be related to "a match or two" dropped on heaps of "naked bodies" (80). Since such events were conceived in and generated by the rhetorical potency of Nazi speeches, polemics, children's books, novels, poems, and anthems, how could they be represented in speeches or novels, poems or anthems; and what effect do they work on the literature we already possess?

Stern is revolted that

> For the sake of art
> there always was a German or Ukrainian
>
> walking around like a dignified Albany,
> or one made sad repentant noises like Kent
> and one was philosophical like Edgar,
> giving lectures to the burning corpses[.] (80)

Indicting such threadbare playacting, which facilitated the inflicting of suffering, his words bring to mind eyewitnesses' recollections of "a fondness for theoretical argument" in SS tormentors, "a predilection for philosophizing. All of them had a weakness for delivering speeches to the doomed people, for boasting in front of their victims and explaining the 'lofty' meaning and 'importance' for the future of what was being done in Treblinka" (Ehrenburg and Grossman 423). After this accusation, in the next to the last stanza Stern describes the dead "dumped on the ground":

> those with gold in their mouths, and those with skin
> the color of yellow roses, and those with an arm
> or a hand that dropped affectionately on another,
> and those whose heads were buried, and those black tongues — [.]

Intimating that *Lear* itself becomes inadequate as a referent next to these deaths, Stern uses the last stanza of "Adler" to highlight a succession of "as if"s that testify to his skepticism about exactly that faith in the generativity of nature or the ceremonies of innocence to which tragedy and elegy generally subscribe:

> as if there were mountains, as if there were cold water
> flowing through the ravines, as if there were wine cups
> sitting on top of the barrels, as if there were flowers —
> still sang in bitterness, still wept and warbled in sorrow. (*PP* 80)

Given the normality abrogated by Auschwitz, enormous loss swallows song: the final pseudo-elegiac line — "still sang in bitterness, still wept and warbled in sorrow" — contains no subject (grammatical or sensate) doing the singing, weeping, or warbling. Paul Celan's cautionary "No one / bears witness for the / witness" (241) is as pertinent to Stern's conclusion as Dori Laub's more recent reflection on the Holocaust as a historical occurrence that "*produced no witnesses*" (Felman and Laub 80).

Because the elegy was so often favored as a form for mourning deceased poets and thus was exploited to formulate not merely literary genealogies but also artistic ambitions, "Adler" can be interpreted as a statement about a damaging breach in literary history: on or about May 8, 1945 (V-E Day), the vibrant Yiddish theaters on Second Avenue closed down.[11] A self-proclaimed "poet of ruins," Stern has remarked "the loss of the Jews in America, the loss of the shtetl life," noting that he has "wander[ed] around the Lower East Side, and people [have told] me, 'This is where the 20 Yiddish theaters were.' And I weep that I can't go to those theaters" (qtd. in Kelen 112). Different though it may seem, Stern's invention of Adler as a model or muse resembles Alicia Ostriker's adoption of Shostakovich as a precursor. Both mark discontinuities in transnational culture, although Ostriker more overtly sets out to counter what Rothenberg calls "the temptation of the beautiful": "the perpetrators themselves often held to a cult of mindless beauty, while committing the ugliest (because most systematically conceived) of crimes & degradations — as the final issue, so to speak, of a false & lying art" (in Barron and Selinger 144–45). Acknowledging her inability to witness the calamity but rejecting a silence about the atrocity that would ratify the "Final Solution," Alicia Ostriker's "The Eighth and the Thirteenth" establishes a context for thinking about what making art uglier means for artists alienated from artistry.

Subsequently banned by Stalin, Shostakovich's Eighth Symphony memorializes the siege of Leningrad, whereas his Thirteenth was inspired by Yevgeny Yevtushenko's "Babi Yar," itself of course a response to the thirty-five thousand Jews massacred in a Kiev ravine.[12] Ostriker begins with an account of herself drinking wine and the "somber" Eighth Symphony "To the vile lees" (*TR* 350). Amid "a ring" of oboes, an "avalanche / Of iron violins," she envisions Leningrad, where three million dead were "stacked .. Like sticks until May's mud"; however, "the music continues. It has no other choice," though forbidden as unpatriotic by Stalin. After a quotation from the composer's notebook that sets art against the perversion of tyrants, Ostriker slips the Thirteenth Symphony into her car's tape deck, as she broods on the Kiev Jews made to undress and march:

The living ones,
Penises of the men like string,
Breasts of the women bobbling
As at athletics, were told to run
Through a copse, to where
Wet with saliva
The ravine opened her mouth.
Marksmen shot the remainder
Then, there, by the tens of thousands,
Cleverly, so that bodies toppled
In without lugging. (*TR* 351)

As if impelled by Des Pres's "We cannot *not* imagine" (*PD* 228), the "music's patient inquiry" ("the music continues. It has no other choice") contrasts with the poet's heart and mind, which abort in the face of atrocity (*TR* 352). According to Ostriker, the music's endurance to a full chorus ("The immediate reverse of Beethoven. / An axe between the shoulder blades / Of Herr Wagner") is precisely its justification; "*Art destroys silence,*" she writes, quoting Shostakovich again. To those who informed him that art speaks more nobly about beauty, Shostakovich proclaims in his notebook: "*you won't catch me with that bait. I'm like Sobakevich in* Dead Souls: *you can sugarcoat a toad, and I still won't put it in my mouth. // Most of my symphonies are tombstones.*" Artists dedicated to creating tombstones for the numberless, anonymous dead seek the discordant effect that Ostriker finds in Shostakovich's music: "The words *never again* / Clashing against the words / *again and again*" (*TR* 352).

"KEIN WARUM"

Whereas some poems protest the complicity of art or beauty in relation to the Shoah, others put its impotence on display. Whereas the inadequacy of aesthetic traditions of mourning distresses satiric anti-elegists, others nudge the elegy toward enigma by recycling preposterous questions, surreal personifications, catalogues, and nonsense so as to enact the failure of artistic expression. They do so in a manner illuminated by a moment in one of Primo Levi's memoirs. Convinced that "we, the survivors, are not the true witnesses" (*DS* 83), Levi recorded his early consternation, during his "first long day of limbo" at Auschwitz, when a guard responded to his queries about why he was not allowed to break off an icicle to slake his thirst with the announcement, "There is no why here." Given the guard's now famous logic — "in this place everything is forbidden, not for hidden reasons, but because the camp has been created for that purpose" (*SA* 29) — verse seems especially well suited to confront this riddling "no why here," and Levi's use of a quotation from Coleridge's "Ancient Mariner" as an epigraph for *The*

Drowned and the Saved is apt: "Since then, at an uncertain hour, / That agony returns: / And till my ghastly tale is told, / This heart within me burns" (vv. 582–85). Identifying with the Ancient Mariner, Levi hints that he is propelled to repeat his story over and over again to people who must be forcibly made to listen to what will certainly alarm them, to what they may attempt to deny. Like the Ancient Mariner ("Water, water, every where, / Nor any drop to drink" [191]), the parched Levi faces his icicle. He understands how the tautological nature of the guard's saying resonates with Coleridge's tale about the inexplicable opacity of sins that cannot be justified, excused, defended, or understood; thus the "kein warum" frames the significance of unanswerable questions in Holocaust lamentations that devolve into prattle.

Confronting the collapse of the "why," the unanswerable questions of William Heyen's "Riddle" punctuate a topsy-turvy, macabre nursery rhyme modeled on "Who Killed Cock Robin?":[13]

> From Belsen a crate of gold teeth,
> from Dachau a mountain of shoes,
> from Auschwitz a skin lampshade,
> Who killed the Jews?
>
> Not I, cries the typist,
> not I, cries the engineer,
> not I, cries Adolf Eichmann,
> not I, cries Albert Speer. (*E* 36)

Heyen's grim tale revolves around the shock of people reduced to things, bodies divided into parts, the organic demoted to the inorganic, the animate debased to the inanimate. In ghastly bookkeeping that mocks the Nazis' daemonic efficiency, Heyen balances the objects that constitute the only remains of what remains of the Jews — "a crate of gold teeth," "a mountain of shoes," "a skin lampshade" — against "the typist," "the engineer," "Adolf Eichmann," and "Albert Speer" repeating their monotonously predictable chorus line of moral abdication. So overwhelming is the incomprehensible "riddle" of what happened to six million people that Heyen modesty limits himself, asking not "why" (which, Toni Morrison has reminded us in a different context, remains "difficult to handle") and not "how" (which, Morrison explains, can serve as a refuge), but only "who."[14] Yet even this humble inquiry into agency (and thus responsibility) ends in hesitation and moral perplexity: a crime, victims, but who is the culprit and how, where, when will the punishment come?

An offhand reference to specific victims — "My friend Fritz Nova," whose father "swallowed gas," and "My friend Lou Abrahms," whose brother was "beaten and starved" — prefaces the activities of anonymous groups of "some" men close to but then more remote from the suffering, though all are equally implicated:

Some men signed their papers,
and some stood guard,

and some herded them in,

. . . .

and some cleared the rails,
and some raised the cattle. (36–37)

Violence authorized and routinized by bureaucratic procedures eroded the moral inhibitions of individuals, licensing collective acts of violence. By focusing attention on the assignment of blame, "Riddle" enters into a conversation with scholarly interpreters of the Shoah who either attribute responsibility to a collectivity (religious or ideological or political systems of discourse, for instance) or hold the intentions of specific individuals accountable (the Nazi elite, say, or noninterventionist Allied officials). These two interpretations of history, often called "the functionalist" and "the intentionalist" accounts of the "Final Solution," have been the subject of much controversy; however, Heyen asks us to worry instead whether the collusion of those actively administering the genocidal policy and of unwitting citizens pacified by religious or ideological or political systems may have materialized the calamitous events.

The need to assign blame so as to find some form of redress or revenge results only in imponderables — "Were they Germans? Were they Nazis? / Were they human? Who killed the Jews?" — that ultimately incriminate us all in a humanity less benign, orderly, and caring than the physical world operating apart from human intervention:

The stars will remember the gold,
the sun will remember the shoes,
the moon will remember the skin,
But who killed the Jews? (25)

The conclusion of Heyen's "Riddle" departs from the bravado of W. H. Auden's "Stop All the Clocks" —

The stars are not wanted now: put out every one;
Pack up the moon and dismantle the sun;
Pour away the ocean and sweep up the wood.
For nothing now can ever come to any good ("TS" 32)

— so as to abjure even Auden's farcically bombastic invocation of finality. Heyen's sardonic parody of childish, chanting stories (in tales such as "The Little Red Hen" and "Stone Soup") exploits the caustic rhymes of "shoes" and "Jews," "engineer" and "Speer" to hint at the senseless repetition compulsion of the evil at work in the Shoah and in the eminently sensible yet equally outrageous efforts to evade responsibility for it afterward.[15]

In the postwar period, poems not directly lamenting the Shoah also use nursery rhymes and nonsense verse to put poetry on exhibit as a "ludicrous and childish occupation" or an "Old, idiotic habit." Elizabeth Bishop's meditation on Ezra Pound's incarceration, for instance, deploys Mother Goose cadences comparable to those of Heyen so as to stress the driving propulsion of illogical, yet inexorable disasters let loose in and after the Second World War. In "Visits to St. Elizabeths," the fascist poet and a Jew in a newspaper hat come to inhabit the topsy-turvy world of a hospital for the mentally ill, the madhouse that gives the text its title. Bishop derives her stanzaic structure here from her ur-text, "The House That Jack Built," which interpolates the promise of sowing what one reaps, of sunrise, of religion, and of marriage within a rigidly hierarchical plot about atomized beings, all isolated within their own lines and lives:

> This is the farmer sowing the corn,
> That kept the cock that crowed in the morn,
> That waked the priest all shaven and shorn,
> That married the man all tattered and torn,
> That kissed the maiden all forlorn,
> That milked the cow with the crumpled horn,
> That tossed the dog,
> That worried the cat,
> That killed the rat,
> That ate the malt
> That lay in the house that Jack built. (Opie and Opie 231)

Similarly, Bishop's "Visits to St. Elizabeths" measures temporality after the war, the time served by the impounded Pound, in terms of a hodgepodge of autonomous, anonymous casualties, each encased in his senseless activities:

> This is the soldier home from the war.
> These are the years and the walls and the door
> that shut on a boy that pats the floor
> to see if the world is round or flat.
> This is a Jew in a newspaper hat
> that dances carefully down the ward,
> walking the plank of a coffin board
> with the crazy sailor
> that shows his watch
> that tells the time
> of the wretched man
> that lies in the house of Bedlam. (135)

Doggerel assists Bishop in depicting the treadmill of habitually recycled routines through which those irreparably harmed by a gruesome war that sent them to the insanity ward seek escape but find no respite. The recurrent word "that," where one syntactically would expect a "who," and the series of human beings, where one would expect a succession of animals, paradoxically roboticize those doing time in a manner hardly therapeutic. Because in the original Mother Goose rhyme the sown corn devolves into the malt eaten by the rat killed by the cat that had been worried by the dog tossed by the cow, in Bishop's hospital the soldier and boy, the Jew and sailor and man — though locked in their separate grooves — seem linked by more than their proximity in confinement. Was the Jew's dance of death choreographed in the anti-Semitism of the *Cantos,* of the radio broadcasts from Italy, produced by the tragic, honored poet whose laurels bespeak his cranky cruelty and thus win his wretchedness? Did "the wretched" Pound, who "lies in the house of Bedlam," earn his fate through the "lies" that turn the newspaper into a hat?

Positioned at the end of each stanza in the place of the killed "rat, / That ate the malt," what remains of Pound putrefies the madhouse of culture. The heady liquor never brewed that fueled his imagination fouled his songs. Thus Pound's poisonous poetic gifts emerge as the antithesis of the generosity of Saint Elizabeth, a figure who founded hospitals for the poor and needy, who gave bread that God converted into roses. But that "St. Elizabeths" also alludes to Bishop's first name may remind some readers of the famous lines "you are an *I,* / you are an *Elizabeth,* / you are one of *them*" (from "In the Waiting Room," *CP* 160); and in that case the title of her nonsense poem might impugn her own verse in the asinine, even cannibalistic cadences of those maddened by what one prewar book called *The House That Hitler Built* (Roberts). But, of course, the puzzle of what Pound did to the Jews, what the war did to Pound, and what Americans did to Pound after the war has a more limited, less global perspective than verse that takes the Holocaust as its central subject. That "Pound never asked for forgiveness" is "unforgivable" to Gerald Stern, who admires Pound's "sensitivity to language," yet finds his verse "flawed" because its author was himself flawed by "disgusting, vile, abhorrent, unforgivable" Jew-baiting (Pacernick 11).

Perhaps no poem better exemplifies the effort to exhibit the rubble of the poet's own tools — the failure of metaphor — than Gerald Stern's "Soap," which shockingly dramatizes the irreversible devolution of Nazi sense into genocidal non-sense by re-personifying victims de-personified by the Nazis. An extreme instance of prosopopoeia, "Soap" ascribes human identity to inanimate things so as to allegorize the devastating consequences of Nazi linguistic power in an approach similar to that of Roberto Benigni's film *Life Is Beautiful*— specifically when a father feigns incredulity at the rumors his son has heard in the camp: "Buttons and soap. Right. And tomorrow morning I'm washing my hands with Barthlomew and buttoning my jacket with Francesco." Although contemporary historians disagree about whether or not the Nazis actually made soap out of the fat of Jewish bodies, "Soap" — composed during a period when this belief was widespread — witnesses the abrogation of normative notions of the real and the probable in order to drive home the religious and aesthetic crisis inaugurated by the Shoah.[16] Yet Stern began writing the poem "in a little store in Iowa City that was selling soap," when he felt "horrified by the kind of graceless accumulation of soap for its own sake"; so the poem also touches on the same issues of stealing or consuming the disaster that Sylvia Plath and Irving Feldman analyzed in relation to American responses to calamity.

"Soap" 's shocking opening lines — "Here is a green Jew / with thin black lips, / I stole him from the men's room" — turns on Jarrell's "yellow joke" of people manufactured into soap. What should purify and sweeten the body pollutes the woman shopping for a Christmas gift (" 'I think I'll go in and buy a Jew,' she says. / 'I mean some soap, some nice new lilac or lily' ") as well as the speaker who purchases a "black Romanian" to "use for hair and beard" (*PP* 49). Because the Nazis dehumanized people into objects, Stern personifies objects, using the sort of metamorphosis usually found in Ovid's myths and Grimms' fairy tales. The poem thereby draws attention to a Holocaust afterlife in which the incorporeal soul is reduced to corporeal soap and is thus incapable of the spiritual rescue ordinarily obtained through prayer. Not only the Nazis but the Holocaust industry seems responsible for this commodification since "a Dane, who gave good comfort / and sad support to soap of all kinds" displays it as merchandise: "She puts one under my nose all wrapped in tissue, / and squeezes his cheeks" (49). As if confronting not a fairy-tale or mythic character transfigured into a tree or a swan or a river but an actual human being manufactured into a disposable object meant for the bodies of people, the poet (who bows "to hide my horror, / my grief, sometimes the soap is so thin / the light goes through it" [50]) conflates victims with soap to conceal his horror and express a grief that cannot be processed through the usual meditations on the details of each victim's particular thoughts, actions, manner of living or dying.

That Germans literally made Jews into soap (or that many people were convinced they did so), that Nazis tricked gas chambers out as showers and deemed eugenics a hygienic way to cleanse pollutants (Jews, Gypsies, homosexuals) from society, that Holocaust remembrances sell replications of the victims in films and television shows to demonstrate how morally pure and clean audiences can become through such contacts: all these phenomena sap this poem of its metaphoricity, though Stern's Jews do not feel or think or act like soap. On the contrary, they hold their noses, feel buried, dream, or remember other places, other times. How can one conceive of meeting "a piece of soap on Broadway, a sliver really" (50)? As if illustrating George Steiner's claim that "the Shoah has eradicated the saving grace, the life-giving mystery of meaningful metaphor" ("LLM" 61), however, soap the casualties remain — "sometimes I meet two friends / stuck together the way those slivers get" (*PP* 50) — because they seem destined to perform the slippery disappearing act of commodified objects of exchange.

Stern's gruesome presentation of a person as a decomposing cleanser concludes with his reflection on a "counterpart" born in 1925 Poland who was "turned to some use in 1942":

> His color was rose
> and he floated for me for days and days; I love
> The way he smelled the air, I love how he looked,
> how his eyes lighted up, how his cheeks were almost pink
> when he was happy. I loved how he dreamed, how he almost
> disappeared when he was in thought. (*PP* 50)

Like others of his generation, Stern felt "guilt as an American Jew . . . who, if I'd been in Europe, would probably have been dead" (qtd. in Pacernick 2), and so he imagines his European double, a "little brother" who "may have fought a little, piled / some bricks up or poured some dirty gasoline / over a German truck" before he became a "ghost" in "the place I have forgotten" (*PP* 51). Not a spirit rising in its ascension to blessedness; only a floating, vanishing "rose"-colored bar: unlike the soul, the soap will achieve neither immortality nor posterity. Profoundly disorienting, Stern's surrealistic conflation of soul with soap meditates on what Wieseltier calls "history's insult to the Jews of Europe": "They were denied the compliment of apocalypse" (77). The sanity of personal sanitation, the sanctity of a cleanliness next to godliness, goes on. Only the millions of victims perished in obscene travesties of hair, skin, and tooth care, of showering.

The buoyancy of soap as it dissolves heightens the inane pathos of assuming that because this malleable double "died instead of me," he/it can in any way die redemptively "for" the poet. Though Stern wants to believe that his doppelganger "from the other / world" has "come back," he/it has only returned to "see what hell is like" (*PP* 51). The poem's anguished, angry conclusion — "the odor of Irish Spring, the stench of Ivory" — proves that the poet's tentative efforts to imagine the soft, serviceable, melting soap as a tough avenging being fail. Wishing this adamantine Being "could / even prick his agate arm or even weep / with those crystal eyes — oh weep with your crystal eyes" (51), Stern feels nothing but bewilderment. Whatever aestheticizing products are employed to disinfect a disaster permeating the places Stern finds himself (Iowa, Pennsylvania, New York City) some forty years after the Shoah, they constitute nothing more than a whitewashing or a soap opera, doomed efforts to cleanse ourselves of a polluting dehumanization. When the tenor and vehicle of metaphor collapse, when people are not treated as soap or dirt but are literally turned into soap or dirt, the Holocaust lamentation produces a formal analogue to the reflections of many Holocaust scholars on the singularity of a disaster impervious to analogy.

Stern's "Soap" may strike some readers as heretical, or simply repellant; however, he insists on the irreparable dehumanization effected by the Shoah as well as its linguistic fallout, and in a tone captured by the title of Irving Feldman's "Outrage Is Anointed by Levity." The riskiness of manifesting poetry's inanity may explain why some Holocaust verse seems mind-numbing, self-subverting, unteachable because unlovable, and thus easily dismissed. In baffled works that refuse to produce a coherent creation about destruction, William Heyen adheres to a radical humility, ruled by the unacceptability of replacing the dead with memorializing rhetoric. A non-Jew of German ancestry (some of whose relatives were Nazis), Heyen worries, "if I had been born in Germany in 1920 instead of Brooklyn in 1940, might I not have aspired to membership in the SS?" ("UC" 128). What he attempts to disrupt is the gruesome complacency that the Holocaust has inspired in bystanders and observers who blinded themselves to their own contamination in the ethical collapse it signified. As in his "Riddle," recapitulation and interrogation fuel the rage of "My Holocaust Songs," three bitter stanzas dedicated to and illustrative of linguistic deterioration. In the first, the listed victim responses, ranging from the rebellious to the acquiescent, retain their impenetrability to our judgment:

> Some split SS backbones with axes,
> but who can praise them?
> Some filed like sheep into the corridors of the swastika,
> but who can blame them?
> Some found smoke's way to the cosmos,
> but who can see them?
> Some rose earth's way to grass and pond-pads,
> but who can know them? (*E* 105)

Dead Jews — active avengers as anonymous as the passively resigned, the cremated as unknown and unmarked as those tossed into pits — mark the gaping wound of a vertiginous moral vacuum that issues in the second stanza in a brutal set of couplings that dramatize what "Aryanization" means:

> *dead Jew hat on German head,*
> *dead Jew violin in German ear,*
> *dead Jew linen on German skin,*
> *dead Jew blood in German vein,*
> *dead Jew breath in German lung,*
> *dead Jew love in German brain.* (105)

A grammatically symmetrical hodgepodge of things jostle against incommensurable body parts; emotions are syntactically treated as the equivalent of artifacts. Linear, syntactic, and rhythmic parallelism seems to exert a sort of leveling or ravaging of distinctions. An instance of anaphora, the emphatic repetition of the words "in" and "on" draws attention to each quite different utterance and the ways in which it becomes clamped into the same structure of assertion.[17] In the progression from the first to the last line, Jewish possessions, bodily traits, and passions have been plundered, evacuated of meaning, and appropriated, thereby ironically infusing the German with what he steals: at the end of this stanza the German has been possessed by the dead Jew's being.

Letting the fallen vocabulary of anti-Semitism contaminate the verse, Heyen does not write about "Jewish" breath or love because the Jew has been demoted from a person to a loathed attribute in a process of "Aryan-ization" that ironically leads to the "Judaization" of a *Judenrein* Germany. Much as Sartre had claimed, the anti-Semite, seeing in the Jew his own projections, extirpates what he then is condemned to embody. Or does the repeated word "in," as well as the emphasis on a monolithic "German" character, point in the direction of Daniel Goldhagen's thesis that Germany was "pregnant with murder" before Hitler came to power, gestating with an eliminationist anti-Semitism (75)? The compulsive recurrence of italicized but syntactically unconnected phrases drains the language of vitality to stress its mechanization. The third stanza extends this meditation on linguistic futility by speaking the poet's pleading injunction that song, baffled by its stammering singer's inability to praise, blame, see, or know the murdered, should lapse yet return, "the bleeding / notes, break down, break down again, my songs" (Heyen, *E* 106).

Perhaps because the "American mind in particular . . . is unsympathetic to any forecast whose dominant image is an obstacle instead of a vista," as Lawrence L. Langer has argued (*AH* 6), authors of Holocaust verse composed in English rail against their impotence in the face of injustice, their incomprehension in the face of the unexplainable. Wanting to "walk away from twenty-two / graphic centuries of kill-the-jew" because she cannot answer the question "Why?," Maxine Kumin decides "In the Absence of Bliss" that she would not willingly die for any orthodox faith, "Not for Yahweh, Allah, Christ, / those patriarchal fists / in the face." However, lack of faith leaves her in a quandary:

> Bliss is belief, but where's
> the higher moral plane I roost on?
> This narrow plank given to splinters.
> No answers. Only questions. (*TR* 182)

Yet even in the presence of faith, the absence of bodies dismembered into parts, starved into skeletons, or gassed or burned or buried alive can create rage along with perplexity. "Where shall I seek you?" A. M. Klein asks in his "Elegy" for a namesake; "There's not anywhere / A tomb, a mound, a sod, a broken stick" (*TL* 435). Also punctuated by unanswered and unanswerable questions in death's dominion, "To the Six Million" by Irving Feldman counters a sense of emptiness with a series of inquiries: "who is the god rising from death?" "Is it I who am missing?" "Survivor, who are you?" "Should I have been with them?" "Can my death live?" "What can I say?" "What can I say?" "Dear ones, what can I say?" (*NSP* 53–58).

KVETCHEN ZIKH MIT GOT

Just as hopeless about solving the riddle of "why," Harvey Shapiro ponders the "where" of Divinity in his sardonically titled "Ditty": "Where did the Jewish god go? / Up the chimney flues" (*TR* 166). Similarly, in her haunting "Elegy," with its quotations from Claude Lanzmann's survivors, Carolyn Forché considers the question "To what and to whom does one say *yes*?" (*AH* 69). Her only answer, another query, is borrowed, this time from Paul Valéry: "If God were the uncertain, would you cling to him?" Possibly a lament on the suicide of Paul Celan, Forché's "Elegy" engages not only Celan's scathing self-scrutiny — "*Dein Gesang, was weiss er?*" ("Your song, what does it know?") — but also the "verbal arraignment of divinity," which Celan's most recent translator, John Felstiner, sees as "the source of Judaism" and of his verse: "*kvetchen zikh mit got,* the Yiddish saying has it" ("SBS" 391, 398).[18] I use Shapiro's and Forché's gripings with God to broach verse that addresses an all-pervasive spiritual crisis by demoting the Deity in a ditty, blaspheming in irate prayers, railing against a broken covenant, or fantasizing about repairing the harm by usurping Divinity so as to unravel an improvident history. Poems that view the Holocaust as a wreckage of faith — trust in God's word, in God's covenant with the Jewish people — undertake a hopeless unmaking of the disaster in a manner congruent with Yiddish and Hebrew verse impelled by a principle of reversal or undoing.[19] Like so many authors in the tradition I am tracing in this book, writers who arraign God interrogate the notion that catastrophic suffering can either be understood (as punishment for sin) or be accepted (as passage toward enlightenment).

Such poets follow in the wake of Job, chafing at "God [who] gives me up to the ungodly, and casts me into the hands of the wicked" (16:11). A deity without compassion who abandoned to unimaginable violence the people to whom a sacred promise had been made: this offense can issue only in an indignant protest poetry — surrealistic because without any political recourse to speak of, and because of its reliance on discourses of impiety distinct from, but related to, the howl of rage at "cosmic disorder and covenantal rupture," which Rachel Adler finds in the Book of Lamentations (167).[20] The anguished figure of mother Zion in Lamentations, a personification of the devastated city, serves as a prototype for poets denouncing God as the author of affliction, with the rhetorical consequence that appeals to the destroyer for intervention seem doomed.[21]

Inconsolable, Zion demands a hearing, a witnessing in the Bible:

> O Lord, behold my affliction,
>   for the enemy has triumphed! (1:9)

> Look, O Lord, and behold,
>   for I am despised. (1:11)

Look and see
if there is any sorrow like my sorrow
   Which was brought upon me,
which the Lord inflicted
   On the day of his fierce anger. (1:12)

Cry aloud to the Lord! (2:18)

The shocked outcries (of its author and of his acquaintances) that punctuate Chaim Kaplan's memoir about the destruction of Warsaw's Jewish communities also reproach inexplicable suffering: "Great God! Are you making an end to Polish Jewry?" he entreats (54); and "A simple old woman asks me each day: 'Why is the world silent? Does Israel have no God?' " (85). Needless to say, such remonstrances, issuing from eyewitnesses to atrocity, differ rhetorically from the reproaches of poets writing from a geographical and temporal remove; however, Zion's stubborn insistence on calling God to task for innocent suffering continues to sustain voices that refuse to lapse into silence, despite God's unresponsiveness. Although this tone is related to the religious doubt evident in pervasively Christian elegies from "Lycidas" to *In Memoriam*, we will see that writers who wrestle with Divinity nevertheless tap some of the features of traditional Jewish prayers. Even the kaddish, which never mentions the dead but instead exalts Divinity, informs verse about the victims, if, as Wieseltier claims, the "kaddish is not so much the praise of God as a prayer *for* the praise of God" (28; emphasis mine).

At first encounter, though, what seem like sacrilegious prayers — teetering on curses — implore Divinity for a divorce so as to free Jews from the designation of "the chosen people." "Merciful God," one of Kadya Molodowsky's Yiddish *khurbn-lider* (destruction poems), begins with a blasphemous grumble that infuses its title and opening phrase with sarcasm: "Merciful God, / Choose another people, / Elect another" (353). With "no more prayers" and "no more blood," she nevertheless pleads, "No more laments for us, / No more dirges / In the old, holy books." In place of what has been, Molodowsky wants "another country" altogether because "with babies, we have paid / For every letter of your Ten Commandments" (353). Better to have other peoples given the prophecies, better to have un-bookish Jewish shepherds and blacksmiths, if the legacy of literacy and law requires such payments. Her final prayer, a sort of throwaway afterthought or last-minute request — "And do us one more favor: / Merciful God, / Deprive us of the Divine Presence of genius" (355) — links scholarly ingenuity, imaginative endeavor, scientific discovery with a replication of God's creation, sinister in its intimation of another cycle of destruction.

The shock of abjuring Divinity — if the Shoah signifies what it means to be chosen, who would possibly want to be chosen? — surfaces again at the start of "Havdalah," a poem whose title is taken from the Hebrew word for the candle-lighting ceremony that concludes the Sabbath: "God of Abraham, / Make us a second Beginning." The unmaking of a universe that "drove / Our people to the slaughter-shops" (409) — a sterile replacement universe without sun, wind, sea, mountains — constitutes a rejection of God's creation: "We renounce beauty," she vows and "We renounce the praise-song. / May Einstein not leave an heir." This barren second genesis need have only "a strip of sky" and a star shining once a year to be greeted with "Amen and amen," if it arises "Without the world of the Germans, / Without the science of blood." Is this the "orphaned amen" forbidden in the Talmud, an amen spoken after an unheard blessing (see Wieseltier 467)? The poet's assenting answerability to a God who did not create this "second Beginning" protests the unanswerability of the God who did create those who invented "the science of blood." Not exactly the unstitching of language attendant on nonsense poems, Molodowsky's verse instead pleads for the undoing of creation and of the Jewish people's relationship to Divinity.[22]

Whereas Molodowsky imagines herself breaking the covenant with God, Dan Pagis, writing in Hebrew, blames God for the breach. One of Pagis's most famous verses imagines running the reels of the movie of the Holocaust from the end to the beginning so as to right its wrongs. What better way to undo, to wipe the slate clean, to exonerate the living and the dead, than by imagining history as a movie and working the film backward so as to reverse the damages done? "Everything will be returned to its place," the impresario-speaker magisterially assures those who "cry blue murder as always." Not only will the scream go back into the throat, the gold teeth back into the gums, the smoke back into the chimney, and the skin back over the bones so "you will have your lives back," but even the yellow star will be torn from the chest and emigrate into the sky (27). In "Draft of a Reparations Agreement," the poet bleakly jokes at the sham of reparations, given the irreversible losses suffered. If we take the godlike speaker to be God (what other being could make such promises?), how seriously should the divine promise be taken? The covenant broken in the Shoah (with innocent people who will never get back their property, teeth, skin, or bones) hints that earlier promises have also only been drafts, that the proposed future contract between God and the Jewish people will remain just as drafty.

Less bellicose than traditional "law-court argument prayers," Pagis's poem implicitly "calls God to task for His lapses of duty which result in suffering and injustice" (Laytner xv). In verse composed in English, some poets take up the ancient belligerent cry — "Where Are Your Miracles Now?" (Laytner 156) — to challenge God to account for inactivity in the face of martyrdom. An exception to this tradition and therefore useful as a contrast, Naomi Replansky's "The Six Million" lays the burden of blame squarely on humankind and thus reads like a conventional sermon:

> They entered the fiery furnace
> And never one came forth.
>> How can that be, my brothers?
>> No miracle, my sisters.
>> They entered the fiery furnace
>> And never one came forth. (7)

Unlike martyrs cast into the fiery furnace, fallen in the lions' den, or enclosed in blocks of ice, the six million "died at the hands of men, / The cold that came from men, / The lions made like men, / The furnace built by men" and so there was "No miracle to spare them": "Only men could shield them, / From the cold hands of men" (7). Although no "lightning struck the killers," no "rain drowned out the fires," Raplansky places the responsibility not with the Deity but with the brothers and sisters to whom she preaches.

Not so those poets who follow in the wake of Anthony Hecht's ambitious verse sequence, "Rites and Ceremonies." The anguished outcry "where were your miracles then?" reverberates throughout Hecht's invocation of the words of the Psalmists, Job, Isaiah, Matthew, Herbert, Hopkins, and Eliot, which he uses to question not only the durability of the poet's identification with the dead, not only the efficacy of the poetry of supplication, but also the power and glory of "Father, adonoi, author of all things":

> Lord, who, governing cloud and waterspout,
>> o my King,
> held me alive till this my forty-third year —
>> *in whom we doubt* —
> Who was that child of whom they tell
>> in holy lauds and threnes?
> whose holy name all shall pronounce
>> Emmanuel,
> which being interpreted means,
>> "*Gott mit uns*?" (*CEP* 38)

The lowercase "adonoi," the interruption of italicized doubt, the German translation of Emmanuel, and the question mark that follows it undercut the most noble biblical language, just as Hecht's fragmentary refrain "Out of hearing" (42–43) later punctuates the lines he quotes from Herbert: "O that thou shouldst give dust a tongue / To crie to thee, / And then not heare it crying!" (43). Since "Gott mit uns" was inscribed on the belts of some Nazi soldiers, the line "*in whom we doubt* — " takes on profound bitterness. "It is as if," Peter Sachs explains, "this insistent and unassimilably 'broken verse' were the timeless voice of poetry itself lamenting the limits of its efficacy" ("AH" 86). Such "broken verse" links Hecht's unheeded prayer with the unheard voices of those dying in the gas chamber when "the rubber-edged door closes on chance and choice" (39).

Sarcasm about the role played by the Catholic Church (" 'Above all, the savings of lives,' whispered the Pope") and about the Gospels ("And the little children were suffered to come along, too") builds in the second section of Hecht's sequence, as the poet considers various miseries endured in ancient times by Christians. "Was it a judgment?" and "If it was a judgment" and "How could it be a judgment" serve as a refrain in this "Fire Sermon" on how in the past Christianity made sense of cruelty, deemed it "Not a judgment": namely, through rites and ceremonies in which the cause of Christian suffering was assigned to the Jews, who were then forced to confess to "poisoning the wells" and "platforms [were] erected . . . And the Jews assembled upon them, / Children and all, and tied together with rope" (40–42). In a barren, wind-swept landscape, the poet's calls melt into oblivion: "And let my cry come unto thee. / Hide not thy face" (43). Beginning with the warning that "The contemplation of horror is not edifying, / Neither does it strengthen the soul" (43), the next section recounts the carnival of "Bull-baiting, palm-reading, juggling" on the race day in the Corso, a pagan ceremony, where once again the sacrificial appear shuffling "shyly at the starting line" (44) — in this case twenty young men who "have said / Through many generations, long since dead, / 'If I forget thee, O Jerusalem, . . . '" (45).

So as not to reject but instead to quarrel and plead with Divinity, the last section of "Rites and Ceremonies" interprets a central text on the promise of the covenant in Isaiah: "If the Lord of hosts / had not left us a few survivors, / we would have been like Sodom, / and become like Gomorrah" (1:9). Hecht concludes with "Words for the Day of Atonement," a Yom Kippur prayer for the "very small remnant" of Jewish people left (all that distinguishes the chosen people from the inhabitants of Sodom and Gomorrah), when his "Rites and Ceremonies" struggles to make peace with the justification of the judgment in the Sabbath service. As "the child screams in the jellied fire," Hecht proposes that "our present concern" must focus on the purposes for which that "very small remnant" was saved (45). He then attempts to affirm his faith — "The soul is thine, and the body is thy creation"; "The soul is thine, and the body is thine"; "O deal with us according to thy name"; "O Lord, for thy name's sake we plead" — by imagining the "saved and saving remnant" in "a later day" when again "compassed about with foes" (47). Only at this future moment of time may his vision eventuate: a reverie of the "remnant" unburnt by the fire, unkindled by the flame, and "calling on thy name / In the hot kilns and ovens" to receive "thy care" as "they shall turn / To thee as it is prophesied, and say, / *He shall come down like rain upon mown grass*" (47). Renewing consolation remains a promise, a prediction, and thus jars with the Sabbath service's weekly declaration: "Thy justice is justice everlasting and thy law is the truth. Thy justice, O God, is very high, who hast done great things: O God, who is like unto thee! Thy justice is like the great mountains; thy judgments are a great deep, O Lord thou preservest man and beast."

Composed some twenty years after Hecht had seen the concentration camps, "Rites and Ceremonies" returns to the Jewish source, "*Kvetchen zikh mit got,*" as does Jerome Rothenberg's *Khurbn* when he takes as his maxim Job 16:18 — "O Earth, do not cover my blood; / let my outcry find no resting place" —which he places in Yiddish at the beginning of "Dos Geshray (The Scream)": "*Erd, zolst nit tsudekn mayn blut / un zol nit kayn ort zayn far mayn geshray*" (*K* 11). To register his distance from but also his sense of connectedness to the atrocity, Rothenberg begins this poem with an admission of his own ventriloquism:

> "practice your scream" I said
> (why did I say it?)
> because it was his scream & wasn't my own
> it hovered between us bright
> to our sense always bright it held
> the center place[.] (11)

Here, and throughout the entire volume, the poet uses obscenity, lowercase letters, abrogated syntax, caesurae within lines, and deleted end punctuation so as to reiterate the nonverbal shrieks wrung from victims of the Shoah. To "bear witness to the death of metaphor" (25) entails the production of repetitive outcries that echo those of Zion in the Book of Lamentations, as they do here at the end of "Dos Geshray (The Scream)":

> the word still spoken by the dead
> who say   my khurbn
> & my children's khurbn
> it is the only word that the poem allows
> because it is their own
> the word as prelude to the scream[.] (12)

Whereas Molodowsky and Pagis mock the worthless words of the broken contract between God and the Jewish people, Hecht and Rothenberg dramatize the spiritual and linguistic crisis this break ushered into being. "Who believes now? Who cries, 'merciful God'? / We gassed God in the ovens," May Sarton exclaims in the section of "The Invocation to Kali" devoted to the concentration camps (21). Some of these poets' successors — fully cognizant of their own broken, impotent words — respond to the strain on their faith by putting on display their efforts to out-God God. Such an impersonation of Deity, seeking to right the wrongs of the past with a bravado that bespeaks futility, is exemplified by Irving Feldman's declaration "when I want to, I can be a God" in "The Pripet Marshes" (*NSP* 52), which resonates with Pagis's sarcasm and which certainly in turn inspired later texts by William Heyen, Robert Pinsky, and Jacqueline Osherow. In "I Dream of Justice," for instance, Heyen promises to reverse an improvident history: "You who are Jews, take back your teeth. / You who are shorn, take back your hair" (*E* 47). And in "The Children" (*E* 116–18), his repeated admission "*I do not think we can save them*" punctuates a dream about being in Germany, two years after Kristallnacht, at a hospital where "I carry a child under each arm, / down stairs, out to my car" (117). Although many children "huddle in my car. / We have left the city" (117), at the end of the poem the poet bleakly admits, "Later, something brutal happened, of course," as he awakes to the knowledge that all the children were "of course" murdered. But the dream itself prompts thankful prayer: "For one night, at least, / I tried to save the children, / to keep them safe in my own body, / and knew I would again. Amen" (118).

About a visit to a death camp, Robert Pinsky's "The Unseen" hinges on a comparable fantasy of godlike celluloid power turned impotent. Touring the "low brick barracks; the heaped-up meticulous // Mountains of shoes, toothbrushes, hair," which the poet names "the whole unswallowable // Menu of immensities," he and his companions

> felt bored
> And at the same time like screaming Biblical phrases:
> *I am poured out like water; Thine is the day and*
>
> *Thine also the night; I cannot look to see*
> *My own right hand . . . (FW* 107)

This odd combination of ennui and enraged lamentation triggers a recollection of a "sleep-time game, / A willed dream" the poet had never before remembered. It consisted of a "Passionless inward movie" in which he was granted invisibility as he roamed through the camps killing the man holding the poisonous crystals, bludgeoning the commandant's collie, raining blood and water down in "a blurred finale" (108).

What the visit with its recollection achieves is the termination of this fantasy of superpower; never again does Pinsky conceive of himself as omnipotent, "doing / Justice like an angry god to escape insomnia." When he relinquishes the idea that anyone could do anything heroic within the setting of the camps, he turns in a moving conclusion that evokes Celan's "black milk" and Wiesel's *Night* to "swallow" the "whole unswallowable // Menu of immensities":

> And so
> O discredited Lord of Hosts, your servant gapes
>
> Obediently to swallow various doings of us, the most
> Capable of all your former creatures — we have
> No shape, we are poured out like water, but still

We try to take in what won't be turned from in despair:
As if, just as we turned toward the fumbled drama
Of the religious art show window to accuse you

Yet again, you were to slit open your red heart
To show us at last the secret of your day and also,
Because it also is yours, of your night. (108)

Gagging as he takes in "what won't be turned from in despair," the poet of "the unseen" acknowledges the unbridgeable gulf between his visible powerlessness and the indiscernibility of God's heart. As Alan Mintz has explained, "lamentation . . . can be understood as a record of man's struggle to speak in the face of God's silence": "In the covenantal relationship, the discourse of lamentation is the discourse of Israel; consolation is God's" (41). By dramatizing the absurdity of their efforts to provide consolation, to out-God God, the poems composed by Feldman, Heyen, and Pinsky reiterate the boundless wrack and ruin faced by the agonized maternal Zion ululating in the Book of Lamentations.

Martin Amis, in the novel *Time's Arrow* (1991), also experimented with the idea of rewinding the past to a point before the disaster, reversing time in a series of regressions that sabotages the idea of providential progress and horrifically links genocide back to genesis. But since such a replay does not rewrite so much as reify the determinism of the past, another option is a leap into the future like that taken by Hecht at the end of "Rites and Ceremonies" and by Jacqueline Osherow in a shorter, more recent poem titled "Ponar": "In the world to come, the forests won't have secrets," Osherow surmises, so "the people in Ponar will brush off the dirt / And return to the twenty-seven libraries / And sixty study halls of the Vilna synagogue" (*CS* 42). As in the passages of consolation Mintz studies in the Hebrew Bible, the promise of redemption may unfold within historical time or at the end of time, after history has run its course. If the poet plays God to bring about this ambiguous moment, then all the destroyed recipes and murals of the uneducated and the educated can be envisioned drifting through the "air itself, weighted down with ash," to "make each leaf a tiny mirror / To shine, in miniature, an unclaimed face" turning gold (43). Yet the ashes weighting down the air and the face unclaimed mark the vision as blatantly unrealistic. Job's ardent wish — "Oh that my words were written! / Oh that they were inscribed in a book!" (19:23–24) — is paradoxically attained in the Bible's account of his story; however, the print culture consisting of "the twenty-seven libraries / And sixty study halls of the Vilna synagogue" vanished along with the people of Ponar in the soil, leaves, sand, mud of the forest floor: not graven in rock forever, the leaves of inscribed books were literally turned into leaves of grass. In "Ponar," Osherow seems to be driven by the desolation in Lamentations — "Gone is my glory, and my expectation from the Lord" (3:18) — to protest against the devolution of Genesis, the reversion of humanity in the twentieth century from God's living "breath of life" back into "dust from the ground" (2:7).

Like some readers of the Book of Lamentations, aware of the thunderous divine silence before Zion's appeals, Osherow returns to the void this non-response creates and fills that abyss with the supreme importance of a textual heritage that has always refused to gloss over it. God's nonresponsiveness is evident in the Shoah, as in Lamentations; however, Jewish texts (ancient and modern) have resolutely grappled with its consequences. Although the contemporary poet knows all too well that her creation cannot breathe life into the dust of the disaster, Osherow's *Dead Men's Praise* repeats prayers — biblical verses to which she may not be able to lend full credence — as evidence of the worth and wealth of Jewish traditions in danger of demise. As in "Ponar," the fate of scholarship and of religious learning concerns Osherow in her moving "V (Psalm 37 at Auschwitz)," one in a sequence called *Scattered Psalms,* consisting of thirteen verse attempts at commentary or midrash. Instead of grasping at an obvious analog — for instance, Psalm 44:22–23 (with its plaint, "for thy sake we are slain all the day long, and accounted as sheep for the slaughter. / Rouse thyself! Why sleepest thou, O Lord?") — Osherow broods on one of the psalms of retribution: "Fret not yourself because of the wicked, / be not envious of wrong doers!" (37:1). After imagining the arrival at a concentration camp of a schoolboy "who'd started heder at three, / After licking a page of letters smeared with honey," Osherow wonders,

> could he have tried,
> Before his slow death from starvation,
> To bring himself a little consolation
> By reciting all those psalms inside his head? (*DMP* 60)

But bits of Psalm 37 float through the poet's, the imagined boy's mind with a discordant effect. The young man's need to say kaddish for a pious father gone to his death after the trauma of the cattle car, for instance, clashes with David's promise that "*Just a little longer and there will be no wicked one; you'll contemplate his place and he'll be gone*" (60). In a turnaround aimed directly against the idea that the Bible could furnish any recompense in Auschwitz, Osherow admits of her youthful student, "Maybe all the psalms had left his head. / He'd contemplate *their* place and *they'd* be gone" (62; emphases mine). Similarly, the psalmist's assertion that he had "never seen a righteous man forsaken or his children begging bread" (37:25) issues in the caveat that "begging was of little use at Auschwitz: / There, you had to have something to trade — " (61). For the reader sent back to the original psalm, other lines take on an even more hollow ring because in the Bible it is "the enemies of the Lord" who "vanish — like smoke they vanish away," whereas the righteous are meant to be assured that "The Lord helps them and delivers them" (37:20, 40). And so as to underline the absurdity of her own reverie and its basis in her remoteness from the disaster, the poet quotes her father-in-law's eyewitness countertestimony: *"Psalms, I didn't hear"* (62). As for the model of David's heroism, who can conceive of "A slingshot at Auschwitz" (63)?

Yet, despite the abundant ironies, Osherow wants to do much more than scoff at either David or Psalm 37. She willingly abandons as ludicrously inadequate her initial surmise ("Let's forget about my scholar with the shovel — / I'll admit it; he had no thought of a psalm — " [64]); however, the contemporary psalmist concludes her meditation by thinking of the many religious people who had to stand and wait . . . for hair to be cut, teeth extracted:

> I know it sounds crazy, but couldn't one of them —
> Not that it matters, they all died anyway —
> But still, so many people, and enough time
> For reciting what the dying are supposed to say
>
> (*Hear, O Israel,* et cetera) *and* a psalm.
> Or not even a whole psalm. Just one line.
> All those people waiting. Couldn't one of them
> Have mumbled to a brother, a father, a son
>
> (The women, of course, were on another line
> And this was not a psalm they would have known)
> *Just a little longer and there will be no wicked one;*
> *Just a little longer . . . he'll be gone.* (64)

"All those people waiting" evokes numerous accounts of the condemned at extermination camps "waiting their turn" ("their naked feet . . . frozen into the ground") sometimes "for hours at a time" when, for example, a "gassing mechanism broke down" (Sereny 149, 165). Lines of self-mockery ("I know it sounds crazy"), diffidence ("Not that it matters"), flippancy ("*Hear, O Israel,* et cetera"), awareness of the constraints of the inherited tradition ("not a psalm [the women] would have known") nevertheless issue in the "But still" of her consoling supposition about the Orthodox and the solace they might have received from the reassurance in Psalm 37 that injustice apparent everywhere cannot reign forever. Though a literalist, Osherow finds in a line of verse "something to hold onto as a dream" (63).

Since many Jewish scholars prescribe the recitation of the kaddish after the reading of a psalm, the Jewish prayer for the dead brackets Osherow's sequence that enlists Psalm 37 in the paradoxical act of mourning a tragedy whose possibility it foreswore (in, for example, its promise that "*there will be no wicked one; you'll contemplate his place and he'll be gone*" [37:10]). Yet neither the psalmist nor the poet who nourishes herself with faith in the legacy of honeyed words should be held to account for what could not possibly be foreseen. The eleventh poem in *Scattered Psalms*, which explains why, comes from verse the Yiddish poet Jacob Glatstein had used — "We received the Torah on Sinai / and in Lublin we gave it back. / Dead men don't praise God" (*BR* 171) — to hint that praise remains the work of the living, exacted by the dead: *because* dead men do not praise God, the living must do so for them, to keep them in living memory. The "stubborn bravado" of "its delirious proof / of itself" transforms this potentially acrid phrase into a key to unlock the meaning of "the annoying epithet *chosen*" in a manner that explains the audacity of the entire sequence: "chosen for this / tenacious language, / to be the *we* / who get to say this word / and live forever" (*DMP* 80). If, as Robert Alter has argued, the "quintessential biblical notion" is "the nexus of speech that binds man and God" — "God speaks the world and man into being, and man answers by speaking songs unto the Lord" (*ABP* 212) — the audacious woman author who dares to begin her *Scattered Psalms* with "a song of Jacqueline" and to conclude it with a *hallelujah!* chorus raises her voice to manifest her responsiveness and responsibility to Jewish lore and learning.

Prophecy and ghostwriting combine in Osherow's books to sustain the dream of a concluded kaddish: "For the soul an ascension, for the Jews a redemption."[23] As if meditating on Lyotard's wandering shades "in their indeterminacy" (*D* 56), prophecy and ghostwriting in Anthony Hecht's short poem "The Book of Yolek" yoke the lament to the documentary mode so as to answer in a qualified positive the query Osherow posed to Rilke, which began this chapter. I therefore conclude it with Hecht's attempt to make an elegy for just one, as he broods on the moral obligation of allowing oneself to become and remain haunted by a single avatar of what in " 'More Light! More Light!' " he called "Ghosts from the ovens" (*CEP* 65). Dedicated to a kind of reverse exorcism, "The Book of Yolek" exemplifies the necromantic imperative of Holocaust verse in its attempt to plant the ghost of the dead into the psyche of living readers. Like Osherow, Hecht refuses to succumb to the incomprehensibility of the Holocaust, which he fully admits, instead emphasizing what can and cannot be achieved through poetic mourning. Although, like the biblical Book of Job, "The Book of Yolek" instructs the reader in the inexplicable suffering of the innocent, it also protests against the restoration of normalcy after the passage of time. Life may go on, Hecht hints, but it cannot or should not be the same after such a cataclysm. No longer relegated to the historical past, Yolek inhabits our future, or so the poet promises.

Profoundly moved by an account of murdered children that appeared in the *Anthology of Holocaust Literature* (1968) edited by Jacob Glatstein, Israel Knox, and Samuel Margoshes, Hecht associated it with the famous photograph from the Warsaw ghetto "of a small boy, perhaps five or six, hands raised, bewildered, while behind him, uniformed, helmeted soldiers level their rifles at him" (in Barron and Selinger 82). In the documentary source composed by Hanna Mortkowicz-Olczakowa, the narrative of Janosz Korczak's decision to accompany the children in his ghetto orphanage to death stresses its author's distance from the event, her reliance on a host of witnesses with quite different recollections: "some say" one thing, "while others say" something else about what the children wore (134–35); "It is possible" that the teacher held the children's hands, but "Did they sing?" and, if so "Was it really this song" (135, 136)? Hecht's Yolek is mentioned only in a list of those marched to their deaths: "little Hanka with the lung trouble, Yolek who was ill" (137). According to Gitta Sereny, "There are so many stories about Dr Korczak and his little orphans—so many contradicting each other as far as bare facts are concerned—that the exact date when he and these children were killed cannot be ascertained" (259).[24] Given its murky documentary origins, Hecht begins "The Book of Yolek" by emphasizing his even greater remoteness from the event, by describing a pastoral "camp / In the deep bronze glories of declining day" that recalls an earlier spot of time during summer camp when "you got lost on a Nature Walk" (*TM* 73).

About this Wordsworthian childhood scene, the poet concedes, "More than you dared admit, you thought of home: / No one else knows where the mind wanders to" (73). Then his mind wanders to a different home, a different camp, through another of Hecht's purposely flat transitions (to emphasize the wrenching distance between the poet "here," "now," and a foreign past "there," "then"). A simple date—"The fifth of August, 1942"—prefaces an account of that hot morning's events:

> They came at dawn with rifles to The Home
> For Jewish children, cutting short the meal
> Of bread and soup, lining them up to walk
> In close formation off to a special camp. (73)

Thinking back to the shambling five-year-old sent to the "electric fences, the numeral tattoo," as well as the "small, unfinished meal" and the enforced "terrible walk" (73), the poet who has been describing himself in the second person now allows that pronoun to encompass the reader as well in a conclusion that functions something like a foretelling, something like a prayer, something like a curse.

"You will remember," he predicts, "Wherever you are, Yolek will be there too, / His unuttered name will interrupt your meal" (74). In the final, three-line stanza of "The Book of Yolek" Hecht advises his reader to think of Yolek in the form of a humble stranger who will return:

> Prepare to receive him in your home some day.
> Though they killed him in the camp they sent him to,
> He will walk in as you're sitting down to a meal. (74)

Like Elijah in Passover tradition, Yolek will reappear at a ritual meal that presages some sort of regeneration, at which the poem's form hints as well.

For the sestina — six six-line stanzas followed by a three-line envoi — depends on recurrence, specifically a repetition of the first stanza's innocuous-sounding end words ("meal," "walk," "to," "home," "camp," "day") in all subsequent lines. According to Hecht, "the form, by its insistent repetitions, lends itself particularly well to an obsessiveness, a monomania, a kind of hypnotic fixation on some idea or feeling" (in Barron and Selinger 82). An insistence on shape, indeed on "technically binding, and in some ways severely limiting" forms, links Hecht's project here to Osherow's, for (he explains) rigorous forms require and display an "obsessiveness" that also "characterizes the 'Final Solution,' as well as the Jewish need to remember, to memorialize, to honor in spirit and in grief" (83).

Just as victims of the Holocaust experienced their lives cut into sections — before the ghetto and boxcar, at the concentration camp, after for those who survived — Hecht and his readers will enter the future with two lives, one before and one after the reappearance of the haunting, hungry ghost-child. Impotent anger that nothing was done to save Yolek makes Hecht wish for the return of this phantom guest; however, the poem also suggests we can do nothing for Yolek now, just as he could do nothing for himself back then. Though it reads like a conventionally consoling resurrection, Yolek's awaited reappearance brings with it only the mystery of thousands of other children whose individual living and dying were swallowed by the incomprehensible evil of the Third Reich. The poem's foreign epigraph — "*Wir Haben ein Gesetz, / Und nach dem Gesetz soll er sterben*" — hints that the German "law" that "he must die" had not been circumvented in the past, but may be transgressed in the future by the uncanny return of Yolek, because "Wherever you are, Yolek will be there too." If we "Prepare to receive him," Yolek's past will punctuate our future consciousness. Not to rescind but to protest the German death sentence on Europe's Jews, Holocaust poets assure their readers, "Wherever you are, they will be there, too."

"People say," Haim Gouri has worried, "that time is on the side of the murderers, that the memory of the extermination of the Jews in the German death factories will be obscured and fade away, that only historians will concern themselves with it." The verse I have been discussing disproves the skeptics, proving instead what Gouri himself believes — that "the extermination of the Jewish people in the middle of the twentieth century will affect the course of culture and will be significant for the coming generations" (160) — for the poems I have examined in this chapter try to assume the futurity of their themes' importance. The past displaying itself in contemporary art shields the dead, reminds us of our ignorance about them, and conveys their fate from the vulnerability of a history easily sanitized, bowdlerized, or forgotten into the realm of living memory, of prophecy vigilantly opposed to the nightmare repetitions of cultural amnesia. Yet just as the poets of satiric anti-elegies and enigmatic nonsense verse admit the inadequacy of their own languages, the authors who wrangle with God concede the failure of the imagination to conceive either a rescuing in the past or a restitution in the present. Still, memorialized at the conclusion of Lyn Lifshin's *Blue Tattoo,* the injunction of one Auschwitz prisoner to another — "If you resist until / you leave this hell, / tell the world about us. / We want to remain / among the living — / at least on paper" (67) — has been honored, if only in the flimsy, fragile paper life of Holocaust literature.

POETRY AND SURVIVAL

If the tradition I have traced in the preceding pages tells us less about the death industry at Auschwitz than about the distrust in God, humanity, science, art, and language it induced, out of what faith could such verse be composed? From where, in other words, might the motivation for writing poetry after Auschwitz spring? Does it originate, *pace* Joseph Brodsky and Mark Strand, in the fact that we have no choice but to live and breathe, eat and create after Auschwitz; or is there some other ethos at work? In the numerous memoirs that have been published since 1945, all idealisms stumble or crumple, except those related to inexplicable instances of caregiving, generosity, responsiveness achieved despite grave personal danger. *Fugitive Pieces,* a novel by the contemporary Canadian writer Anne Michaels, begins with such a saving act when a Greek archaeologist named Athos discovers an "Afterbirth of earth," a famished seven-year-old hiding from the Nazis in a bog bed. At great risk to himself, Athos adopts Jacob in the course of smuggling him out of Poland. Exactly why and where the excavator finds the strength of his conviction to help this "dirty Jew" (13) remains mysterious, although the rest of the narrative charts the boy's subsequent evolution as a reader and writer so as to consider the role the imagination can play in fostering the sort of compassion that animated his savior.

In Shelley's *Defence of Poetry,* the imagination is imagined as a muscle that needs to be used. To be "greatly good," according to Shelley, people "must imagine intensely," putting themselves "in the place of another and of many others" so the "pains and pleasures of [the] species become [their] own" (759). With disuse, this "instrument of moral good" atrophies (759), as it doubtlessly did throughout the Shoah in the hearts and minds of most bystanders and perpetrators and even of some victims and survivors. Yet with rigorous workouts, it can make the heart and mind more flexible about where the parameters of the self reside, or so *Fugitive Pieces* suggests. For when Athos as a sort of "godfather" rescues Jacob, the muddy boy (clinging to Athos's body like "a blister tight with fear") internalizes the sister whose horrific disappearance haunts him from the moment the Nazis broke into his house and murdered his parents: "We were Russian dolls. I inside Athos, Bella inside me" (20, 14). Adoption, Michaels's metaphor for empathic imagination, offers Athos and Jacob roles that involve neither coercion of nor submission to the Other. Under extraordinary circumstances, such an act attenuates those rigid ego boundaries — based on class or nation, race or gender, age or sexuality — that ordinarily persist in separating us from each other.

Although psychoanalytic thinkers from Freud to Lacan have viewed identification as a violent appropriation of the Otherness of another, the concept of empathic imagination proposes fleeting and fallible but less coercive forms of identification. The verse I have discussed derives from the poets' dedication to flexing their own and their readers' faculty to imagine or adopt experiences they could never have had or known. In Shelley's words, "Poetry strengthens that facility which is the organ of the moral nature of [humanity], in the same manner as exercise strengthens a limb" (759). Albeit ephemeral and chancy and emphatically after-the-fact, empathic imaginative identification explains the artifice of a tradition of verse that can continue to edify teachers and students — as can the undermining of identity politics that, I will speculate, necessarily informs such identification. I will use *Fugitive Pieces* to summarize the traits of this evolving tradition because Michaels's fictional portrait of the poet as a survivor elucidates the survival of poetry after Auschwitz.[1]

A retort to Adorno's injunction, *Fugitive Pieces* accords with the view held by many poets that after the Holocaust it is barbaric *not* to write and read literature so as to counter fascist ideologies of Aryan supremacy with altered definitions of humanity. Virtually every character in Michaels's novel is a writer of one sort or another, and most become devoted readers of each other's works. Refugees from gruesome and inexplicable violence, her protagonists understand the fatal failure of the arts and sciences in the Shoah, periodically retreat into silence, but return to studies crammed with books, manuscripts, and letters, as if to validate her belief that "We like to think language is nothing without us, but in the end, it's we who beg it back" ("CL" 14). Like the poets, then, Michaels believes that genocidal manipulations of language and learning cannot possibly be contested by a repudiation of language and learning. And also like the poets, Michaels underscores her distance from the disaster, her attempt to imagine suffering never experienced firsthand, in her case by writing through and about male witnesses and victims.

The disjunction between Michaels as a woman writer and her masculine subjects dramatizes her effort to replace the concept of sympathy, which supposes affinity among people, with the mechanisms of empathy, with its recognition of disparity. Similarly, the condition Michaels's most resilient characters attain in her plot is related to what Dominick LaCapra has called "empathic unsettlement," a state that "involves a kind of virtual experience through which one puts oneself in the other's position while recognizing the difference of that position and hence not taking the other's place" ("TAL" 699, 722).[2] Michaels's staging of "empathetic unsettlement" explicitly inside the fictional world of the novel and implicitly through its creation enables her to consider the virtues of empathy women have been traditionally acculturated to develop, and to suggest they might be learned by all people seeking alternatives to pernicious psychologies of domination.

By cutting back and forth between narrative episodes in this lyrical novel and the verse I have discussed in previous chapters, I want to suggest that the idea of "empathic unsettlement" helps explain the stance the poets take toward their subjects, the themes they address, the forms of their verse, and the sorts of effect poetry after Auschwitz can have on its readers. Additionally, I hope to clarify the gender dynamics at work in the aftermath of the Shoah and in creative responses to it. Coming, as it does, at the end of a book about the grim failures of culture during an unprecedented evil, my argument in capsule form sounds idiotically sanguine, though it will be severely qualified as its focus is narrowed into a decidedly retrospective and aesthetic realm: the historical trauma of the Holocaust issued in more empathic ways of being and knowing for literary men and women determined to use proxy-witnessing as a means of cultivating identifications that at least imaginatively traverse racial, sexual, national, and historical barriers.

But first, I will define empathic imagination by using Anne Michaels's figure of adoption, and then I will consider how that figure clarifies the impact of the disaster on gender. The "strange coupling" that occurs when Athos hides Jacob under his coat in occupied Poland and then back in his house on an occupied Greek island derives from the conviction that "We must carry each other. If we don't have this what are we . . ." (13, 14). The child as an "Afterbirth of earth" squirming out from the ground because "No one is born just once" or as "a blister tight with fear" against Athos's "solid body," as well as their "strange coupling" and their trying to "carry each other": all convey the two-in-oneness of adoption as a sort of pregnancy, as does Jacob's feeling "We were Russian dolls, I inside Athos, Bella inside me" (5, 14). In these initial scenes, the "I" neither absorbs the "not-I," nor is it usurped by the "not-I." Not aggressively coercive, not passively submissive, adoption exemplifies an empathic identification that joins the "I" and the "not-I" in responsively interactive forms of subjectivity.[3] Later, as it relates to Jacob's ongoing attachment to his lost sister, the heterogeneity of a subjectivity created by such forms of adopted but not fully internalized Otherness will be conceived in terms of invisible fingers tapping on the far side of the thin "vibrating membrane" between the living and the dead (31).[4] Besides transposing (without restoring or replacing) the murdered family into a nonbiological lineage and supplanting a rational, autonomous ego with an emotive, interpersonal psyche, the two-in-oneness of adoption at the start of *Fugitive Pieces* can be understood as a blurring of the boundaries between Jew and non-Jew, victim and witness, the dead and the living.

In stark contrast to such reciprocity stand the acts of Nazi annihilation that punctuate *Fugitive Pieces:* the murder of Jacob's family, the destruction of the excavated ancient city of Biskupin (so as to obliterate "proof of an advanced culture that wasn't German" [104]), the extermination of the Greek Jews. During an adulthood dedicated to a quest for a renovated language, Jacob will discern from his scholarly investigations that Nazi torture hinged on a misnaming of humans as "*stücke*" (pieces), which encouraged the tormenters to annihilate any signs of humanity that might spawn compassion and thereby derail their efforts to cleanse the world of debris, filth, clutter.[5] Whereas empathic imagination is figured as pregnancy, birthing, and nurturing, Nazi genocide depended on a nullification of empathy that is related to the sort of hypermasculinity incipient in the concept of a "master race" of "*Übermenschen.*" By engaging such figures, Michaels illuminates an analysis of gender politics at the core of responses to Auschwitz. In accordance with Virginia Woolf's belief that fascism produced a portrait of "Man himself, the quintessence of virility" (*TG* 142), men and women of letters believe that "Genocide does not happen because of the special nature of males, nor is it going to be prevented by the special nature of females" (R. Smith 329); however, they have stressed the fact that genocide has been committed primarily by men operating under the aegis of a cult of supremacy.[6] "Domination," according to Chaim Kaplan, was an "outstanding psychosis of Nazism" (92).

Though at times verse satirizes this cult, more often the poets demonstrate how it robbed Jewish men of authority. From Adrienne Rich deciphering "the suffering of the Jew, the alien stamp," beneath "the power and arrogance" of her father (*S* 20) to Jorie Graham's raped corpse in "History"; from Barbara Helgott Hyett's American soldiers wondering "*Is this a man or / a woman I'm speaking to?"* (44) to C. K. Williams's spat-upon rabbi; from Sylvia Plath's daughter of "Daddy" to Gerald Stern's vanishing bars of soap: Nazism is seen to subscribe to a grotesque despotism that re-genders all Jews female or de-genders the casualties. Such works elaborate on Elie Wiesel's pronouncement that at Auschwitz "not only man died, but also the idea of man" (*LT* 190). According to men and women of letters, whose lamentations reiterate not the righteous piety of the "suffering man" in the Book of Lamentations but the piteous protests of the maternal Zion, the Shoah discredited authoritarianism as well as authoritative deployments of language, whether public or private, nationalistic or individualistic, sacred or secular. Stern's "The Jew and the Rooster Are One," a revision of Elizabeth Bishop's World War II poem "Roosters," clarifies this point. Whereas Bishop's screaming cocks resemble bomber pilots in their cockpits, Stern's bedraggled painted bird appears "grotesque . . . in an armchair," still "golden underneath his feathers / with freckles of blood" (*TT* 265–67). His "head / hanging down, the comb disgraced, the mouth / open as if for screaming," the rooster, who had strutted and screeched at the dawn of time, ends up "a ripped-open Jew . . . organs all on show, . . . tethered to a table" and "slaughtered" inside the commodiously upholstered house of culture (265). The opening two lines of "The Jew and the Rooster Are One" — "After fighting with his dead brothers and his sisters / he chose to paint the dead rooster of his youth" (265) — make manifest the painter's, the speaker's disillusionment with the rule of the roost.

Toward the conclusion of *Survival in Auschwitz,* a book whose original Italian title translates literally *If This Is a Man,* Levi wrote, "To destroy a man is difficult, almost as difficult as to create one: it has not been easy, nor quick, but you Germans have succeeded" (150). Many of his successors investigate patrilineal plots because the Holocaust shattered the patriarchal communities of Europe's Jews. Male survivors — even if they inherited the patronymic — could never become the heirs of their fathers' places, properties, or positions and instead had to invent a line of inheritance quite distinct from the one denied them in the process of dehumanization. In the context of the impact of the Shoah on the history of gender, what does it mean that the concept of paternal authority was thoroughly contaminated in the "Fatherland," where Jewish fathers were denied such paternal designations as "*be-getter, name-giver, law-giver, castrator, provider, protector, redeemer*" (Brenkman 190)?[7] Since in a shockingly unanticipated manner the "Final Solution" sentenced women and children to death, what did it mean to Jewish men that they could not safeguard their mothers, wives, and sisters?[8] With the patronymic replaced by the figures of an entry number, Primo Levi understood, a man in the camps "is no longer a man" (*SA* 42). As the survivor Richard Glazar put it, describing "the kind of joke" Ukrainian guards at Treblinka enjoyed (bringing a whore to a prisoner so as to display his impotence), "Many of us young men ceased to have any sexual feelings whatever; . . . during all the time we were in Treblinka, and for long afterwards, [we] were men in name only" (qtd. in Sereny 237).[9]

The Shoah — displaying the malignance of mythologies of supremacy — signals a cataclysmic break in the history of masculinity that wrecked the figure of "Man himself, the quintessence of virility." Again, the consequences of adoption in *Fugitive Pieces* provide a framework through which to consider what sort of masculinity might survive in the wake of the demise of "the idea of man," for Michaels explores the intersubjectivity Athos induces in Jacob after their escape from Poland and through an education that fosters empathic ways of being and knowing in the young boy.[10] Multiple scenes of instruction facilitate Jacob's growth toward a masculinity devoid of authoritarianism, even as they explain its repercussions in literary history. The idea of being carried by or carrying an adopting or adopted other informs Michaels's considerations of the ethical functions served by a literary education. Indeed, perhaps the reading process affords the most important entrée to "empathic unsettlement" in this novel because reading generates an intersubjective form of being-in-relation with Otherness, but without the threat of an actual, living other.

As Jacob's gums bleed and his teeth loosen from lack of food, books supply escape routes from the terrors of the past, the dangers of the present. Reading establishes a time-out-of-time for a traumatized consciousness in quest of its own cessation: a modus operandi for those needing to elude their own circumstances, to suspend self-consciousness. Only a lucky few can use books to excavate the past, to find in reading, as Jacob does, a way to make time "buckle" (30) or to "pleat time" (Michaels, "WLT" 112). Through books, the boy manages to inhabit his own "now" and the narrative's invisible "then," his own "here" and the story's mystic "there," gaining him entrance into "parallel image[s]" (*FP* 18) as he discovers that "Every moment is two moments" (138, 140, 143). Jacob's time travels through reading (framed by Athos's tales about the palimpsestic accretions in geological and archaeological formations) recall the layering of successive temporalities in verse: the reader's experience of the poem; the poet's composing of it; the interpolated event that is recollected or a witness's representation of a still prior period.

By putting on display the tenacity with which the past grasps the present, poets after Auschwitz pleat the "here" and "now" of their imaginings with their families' or their evidentiary sources' "there" and "then." Undertaken in the service of recalling what others knew, of anamnesis, most of the formal devices I have enumerated buckle time, bringing two moments together: confessional and documentary verse, ecphrasis and antimorphosis, prosopopoeia and lamentation engage the empathic imagination in conveying the dead past of a foreign place into the living present of our native minds. Like Jacob, whose personal history convinces him that "we're never ourselves until we contain two souls" (189), poets use their studying to interrupt self-consciousness with the experiences of prior lives in other worlds through forms that therefore become double-voiced or dialogic. Consider, for instance, Carolyn Forché and Jorie Graham quoting Walter Benjamin, Jacqueline Osherow conversing with her storytelling relatives or with Fany Hochmanova Brown, Irena Klepfisz composing in a mother tongue not her own or citing passages of books about the Warsaw Uprising, Anthony Hecht reiterating Goethe's last words, Kirtland Snyder and Jason Sommer responding to Vishniac's volume of pictures, Charles Reznikoff and Barbara Helfgott Hyett reordering the line endings of the testimonies of casualties and soldiers, Alicia Ostriker excerpting Shostakovitch's notebooks.

Like reading, learning a foreign language allows the adolescent Jacob to imagine and embrace ways of being quite distinct from his own. Jacob, literally unhoused at the start of his history, exhibits in his multilingual progress the "extra-territoriality" that, according to George Steiner, registers language's "unhousing" after the upheavals of war and exile ("E").[11] When the narrative takes Athos and Jacob from Athens to Canada and thus into linguistic unsettlement, English as a third or fourth language requires Jacob to incorporate foreign phrases into an already hybrid, culturally amalgamated consciousness. Fluent in Greek, haunted by the loss of Yiddish and Polish, Jacob expresses himself in a lexicon at several removes from his mother tongue. His diasporic progress answers the question, how can a literary tradition be crafted out of a rupture, a hole torn in culture, and then reconstituted through the fragile hyphen connecting Jews to new national and linguistic places?

Jacob the polyglot epitomizes the transnational, transgeneric nature of art after the Shoah, when Yiddish actors and German philosophers, Hebrew poets and Flemish painters, French historians and Russian composers function as precursors and sources for English writers who view, as Czeslaw Milosz did, not a single national idiom but language itself as the only homeland. At home in no nation or religion, Jacob dwells among a plethora of ancient and modern texts to which he returns as author, collaborator, commentator, and translator. Such devoted practices — "ontologically and historically at the heart of Jewish identity," as Steiner reminds us in a different context ("OHT" 7, 5) — mean "No one is born just once"; however, rebirth remains textual in Michaels's work, where the resonantly named Bella never is reborn. It takes the same position in much Holocaust verse as well, where bi- or multilinguistic moments abound, often through the eruption of foreign words, sometimes italicized, sometimes not: Sommer's "*Tsits,*" "*Shtreimel,*" and "*Shabbos*"; Plath's "ich ich ich ich"; Michael Hamburger's "Je te comprends"; Forché's "*Le Dieu est un feu*"; Klepfisz's contrast between "*heym*" and "home"; Hecht's "*Wir Haben ein Gesetz*"; Jerome Rothenberg's "*Erd, zolst nit tsudekn mayn blut*"; Osherow's "heder"; Graham's "*Kugel*" and "*Ober-*

scharfführer." Sometimes, though, foreignisms in immigrants' accented, non-standard English mark the linguistic diaspora, as in the words spoken by Jeffrey Wolin's subject, Jadzia Strykowsky. The outburst of foreign words or foreignisms marks the marginality of English, its limited capacity to convey the Shoah in its own (German or Yiddish, Polish or French) terms.

No wonder that Jacob believes translation performs "a kind of transubstantiation; one poem becomes another" (109) because, like poetry, translation facilitates a migration and mutation related to the adoption of a not-known that abides unaltered, intact: "The poet moves from life to language, the translator moves from language to life; both, like the immigrant, try to identify the invisible, what's between the lines, the mysterious implications" (109). Unable to "seek by way of silence," Jacob finds in his linguistic alienation a way to shape English to his own urgent needs by living "a breath apart," like "a touch-typist who holds his hands above the keys slightly in the wrong place, the words coming out meaningless, garbled. Bella and I inches apart, the wall between us. I thought of writing poems this way, in code, every letter askew, so that loss would wreck the language, become the language" (111). Attentive to sound as a "mysterious implication" of sense, Jacob's subsequent verse writing places bits of the past into a form; yet an enigma about those fragments remains. Something missing from the pattern and unredeemed, some word that is "askew" reminds Jacob of stubbornly incomprehensible loss.

In Holocaust verse, the allusion to or quotation of an earlier source constitutes the adoption of a not-known that abides, if not unaltered or intact. Loss often wrenches the language of poetry about the Shoah through a medial metrical pause, what I have called a "stall" or "stutter," marking lines inflected by the impossibility of saying what needs to be said about the "Final Solution," which Adorno viewed "as an objective historical caesura" (Weigel 164). Similarly, the ellipses between documentary evidence (often incompletely rendered) and interpretive responses to it encourage readers to realize the failures of the living author to grasp stable truths about the past. In poems about photographs and poems composed from legal documents, we have found the interiority of perpetrators and victims inaccessible: the wishes, motives, feelings, ideas of people pictured before or during the Shoah or witnessing afterward at trials remain resolutely oblique, their individual psychologies beside the point or simply unknowable. Through the discordant tension between historical data and imaginative responses to it, between the literal and the literary, poets after Auschwitz ponder what can and cannot be learned about the disaster. As if to assuage Charlotte Delbo's fear that people "think they know" (138), the verse writers I have characterized as wary in their humility resemble Michaels's Jacob when he records the genocide of the Greek Jews by punctuating his account with the litany "I didn't know" (*FP* 45–46).

Not only Jacob's aesthetic strategies but also his psychology can help us speculate about the sources of inspiration shaping Holocaust literature, sources related to the intimacy that trauma can establish between the living and the dead. After the death of Athos, Jacob's creative efforts depend on his connectedness to his lost sister, as the stories he composes shift from fictive reconfigurations of his own abandonment to reconstructions of Bella's progress toward death. While studying the Shoah, seeking Bella's spirit in the place of degradation and yet attentive to torments he knows he cannot know, Jacob decides, "It's there that the new Adam must raise himself, must begin again" (167). In quest of renewed lexicons, this new Adam will understand what was abrogated when "the German language annihilated metaphor, turning humans into objects" (143). Feeling the fingers of Bella and the hands of the dead Athos on his own skin teaches the adult Jacob to translate humanistic or androcentric faith in man into "faith" pure and simple, if only in the "body . . . flooded with instinct" (168–69). Through his changing perceptions of his muse, Jacob understands that Bella resembles other ghosts: "She whispers; not for me to join her, but so that, when I'm close enough, she can push me back into the world" (170).[12] With the knowledge that "*To remain with the dead is to abandon them*" (170), the survivor as poet is ready to abandon the dead so as to remain expressively, imaginatively with them.

Through Jacob's evolution, then, *Fugitive Pieces* suggests that the Shoah established empathic relationships between the living and the dead that inspired the creation of verse, even as it transformed gender identity for some survivors. Although Jacob's recurrent awareness of Bella's fingers tapping on the other side of a wall cannot be conflated with the incandescent "androgynous" imagination praised by Woolf in the literary genius (*ROO* 98), his conscientiousness about maintaining this double consciousness relates to bearing, adopting, carrying the dead as an alien presence creating sometimes cacophonous, sometimes harmonious counterpoints within the psyche. A challenge to, even an assault on any conceptualization of the self as autonomous or authoritative, grief over painful loss proves how firmly the self is attached to another. For this reason, the mourner feels himself vulnerable to the comings and goings of a ghost or specter whose visitations cannot be controlled. Jacob does not think about the ghostly Bella "I can push her back," but instead feels "she can push me back . . ." (170).

Haunted by the annihilation of their families, especially by lost children, Jewish men and women had a common stake in reestablishing broken genealogies in the postwar period and thus invested themselves in a re-masculinization of men, a re-feminization of women shattered by their inability in the calamity to be men and women. Because this investment occurred not only after Nazi fascism demonstrated the moral bankruptcy of models of heroic mastery but also amid the fissuring of the autonomous psyche caused by grief over lost loved ones, re-gendering unfolded under the auspices of an eerie promise, namely the emergence of a post-patriarchal masculinity.[13]

For Michaels, such a masculinity beyond masculinism arose out of a rupture in culture that discredited the Enlightenment's faith in the superiority of mind over matter, spirit over body, culture over nature, and thus implicitly queried the dominance of men over women.[14] For some Jewish men, historically distanced from militaristic definitions of non-Jewish manhood by centuries of anti-Semitism, the injury of the Shoah interrupted and thereby paradoxically strengthened cross-gender identifications that were not disavowed; becoming a man therefore no longer meant repudiating femininity. Whereas a number of thinkers believe that men become male by disowning, distancing, or disparaging the feminine,[15] Michaels uses her plot to consider the role siblings play in an erotic imaginary complicated by cross-gender identifications that are interrupted and thus sustained by historical cataclysm.

Many autobiographical accounts of the Shoah record their authors' sense of being haunted by murdered relatives. "Remembering is a branch of witchcraft; its tool is incantation," Ruth Kluger declares in a passage of her memoir, *Still Alive,* that explains the "companionable ghost" to whom she writes her own verse as well as the dybbuks that trouble survivors who feel more intimately connected to the dead they left behind than to the living with whom they reside (69, 191).[16] Kluger's belief that "To conjure up the dead you have to dangle the bait of the present before them, the flesh of the living, to coax them out of their inertia" dovetails with a conviction she shares with Michaels that, as Kluger puts it, "our minds forget what our hearts won't remember" (69, 167). But biographical background on first-generation writers propelled toward cross-gender identifications by the deaths of brothers and sisters, mothers and fathers would be less pertinent to the tradition of Holocaust verse than the ghostly hordes we have encountered in the necromancy of Feldman and Forché, Rothenberg and Shimon Attie, Plath and Osherow.

A recent poem by Marilyn Hacker analyzes the psychological impetus of this necromancy, even as it links the modification of masculinity in the Shoah with a cross-gender identification comparable to Michaels's. Indeed, the second-generation American woman poet seems as haunted by a boy within her as Jacob is by the girl within him. "The Boy," which can be read as an elegy for the boy Hacker might have been — if born in Paris, say around 1932 — imagines her counterpart looking out of the window, having been brought to some realization about his Jewishness and his masculinity by an insult, or so the second stanza suggests:

> (Because he flinched, because he didn't whirl
> around, face them, because he didn't hurl
> the challenge back — *"Fascists?"* — not *"Faggots"* — "*Swine!*"
> he briefly wonders — if he were a girl . . .)
> He writes a line. He crosses out a line. (*SC* 13)

Hacker conjures up a boy-self whose masculinity has been put in doubt by his flinching at a racial jeer. When "boys shouted '*Jew!*' across the park," this youthful student who is and is not Hacker finds himself jolted out of taking his own subjectivity for granted as a sort of "unmarked" or "neutral human" and into an awareness of himself as marked — remarkable or branded; so the boy begins to grapple with the labels "That got you killed in 1942" (14).

In a prose explanation of this work, Hacker clarified her sense of herself as both the woman writer and the schoolboy: "I'm not sure which of us, he or I, thought first that the other identity of 'boy' 'girl' 'man' 'woman' might be as mysteriously fluid as the name and notion 'Jew' — an insult or a proud blazon depending on the context, something that could be flung out as one and accepted as the other" (in Barron and Selinger 78). About her alter ego, a boy "who'll never be a man," the poet knows he would have been sentenced to death by an arbitrary, imposed attribute of his identity that could be a source either of pride or of shame, "if it shows." Visible marks of difference, Hacker reasons, make a disturbing "code" — "he must puzzle out the code" — which is inconsistent with the woman poet's confession that there is a "boy in me."[17] Because she imagines a boy-self whose evolving sense of masculinity is fissured ("he wonders — if he were a girl") by lethal racism, "The Boy" illuminates the fractured psyche of Michaels's central character. At the same time, Hacker's cross-gender identification explains why, although the poem predicts the boy's death, she hopes in the prose gloss that he "may one day reject the stone tablets of gender in the same spirit as he questions what it is that makes him 'a Jew' " (78).[18]

It would be presumptuous to generalize about all the authors discussed in this book that they were goaded into cross-gendered, transhistorical imaginings because of the split within the self produced by the powerful bond the Holocaust mandated between casualties of the disaster and witnesses, even those at greater remove.[19] Yet the common formal strategies of men and women of letters suggest that they do share this motivation. Mourning lost relatives, Klepfisz and Sommer grapple with comparable cleavages in their genealogies; recycling the words of victims and bystanders, Hyett and Reznikoff rely on parallel documentary techniques; shocked by the magnitude of evil, Levertov and Hamburger depend equally in their approach to the Eichmann trial on the perspective provided by Hannah Arendt. Like Hacker, C. K. Williams identifies with a doomed person of the other sex, in his case (and that of many other writers) Anne Frank.[20] Both Jeffrey Wolin and Audrey Flack use meta-photography in a proxy-witnessing that crosses gender lines, with Wolin quoting and picturing female survivors, Flack quoting and picturing male prisoners. Different though they are, all these artists use the imagination to communicate their efforts to empathize with those harmed in the disaster. Especially those who create dramatic monologues in the voices of the victims provide evidence for Michael Taussig's belief that because poetry is "the most mimetically nuanced form of verbal representation and expression," it makes possible "unsentimental" communions with the spirits of the dead (310).

It seems significant, however, that women's contributions are so obvious.[21] Does the project of discrediting authoritarian discourses account for the conspicuous contribution of literary women in this evolving canon, a prominence I had not expected to find when I began collecting verse about the Shoah for this book? Given the ease with which I could list an equal number of men and women of letters, it is apparent that women have played a significant role, as they have in many religious and social contexts related to grief and mourning.[22]

In other respects, too, gender differences have profoundly influenced stance, tone, and generic decisions, a point implicit in the discussion of the verse of Irving Feldman and Jacqueline Osherow in chapter 1. For, whereas Feldman's "Outrage Is Anointed by Levity" engages in a sort of ferocious rap, as its author takes on Joseph Brodsky and Mark Strand in the agonistic cadences of Mort Sahl and Lenny Bruce, Osherow's "Brief Encounter with a Hero, Name Unknown" sounds more like a melodic balladeer's poignant recounting of a folkloric legend. We have seen that the overwhelming number of autobiographical works about childhood's end were composed by literary women. Although both daughters and sons of survivors inhaled what in one novel's title Thane Rosenbaum called "second hand smoke," the daughters' verse expresses far more anxiety about the effects of the Shoah on mothers and maternity than the sons'. Among the satiric anti-elegists, however, not one woman did I find. In the production of texts deploying the voices of the dead or dying, the gender of the author usually correlates with the gender of the speaker. What seems more important, though, is that both male and female artists decry genocidal fascism's cult of virility, even as their work originates from empathic imaginative acts.

Michaels hints through her female characters' capacity for responsive listening that women have been better socialized to experience intersubjective feelings that originate outside the self.[23] With her hair "glossy and heavy" like Bella's (176), Jacob's wife Michaela — endowed with the feminized patronymic of her author's name — manifests intersubjectivity when, "her heart an ear, her skin an ear," she "is crying for Bella" so that Jacob dreams of Bella sitting beside Michaela while "tears stream down Michaela's face" (182). If survivors who claimed to live so as to give testimony actually tell their stories in order to live, Michaela embodies "the role and the responsibility of the listener . . . to be the empathic and responsive witness whom the survivor so desperately searches for" (Laub and Allard 808–809). To the extent that Michaels's female characters become repositories of memories not their own, they represent the connection between post-traumatic mourning, healing retrospection facilitated by witnesses of witnesses, and highly conventional forms of feminine caregiving.[24] Perhaps this nexus accounts for the abundance of women historians, philosophers, novelists, and poets in the evolving post-Holocaust canon.

No claim is being made by any of these writers that empathy is female or that empathic imagination is prophylactic, capable of preventing the Shoah or constituting a viable solution to the perplexities of its aftermath. Martha Nussbaum writes about "the thinner empathy," considering its difference from compassion, because she realizes that in and of itself " 'empathy' is not sufficient to motivate good action" ("ER" 67). A fraught emotional state generally possible only for some and for others only through and in aesthetic contexts, "empathic unsettlement" may have paradoxically bequeathed rigidly conservative gender roles in the postwar period, when the ruin of "the idea of man" placed unique burdens (of silence and nurturing) on women. Nor could it rescue eroticism or citizenship, both having been canceled throughout the disaster, from dwindling into legislated privileges easily annulled, brittle fictions that tended to be regarded as utilitarian as they were subordinated to the major aim of continued survival. In Michaels's coda to her novel, these caveats qualify Jacob's story when he is adopted as a mentor by Ben, the second-generation narrator of part II, who is not a survivor but a child of survivors. Given Ben's upbringing by parents traumatized by the shocking failure of empathy apparent in the perpetrators' (and, indeed, the world's) treatment of the Jews as a subhuman species, the novel ends in equivocation about the possibility of his achieving an empathic identity.

Pervasive anxiety coupled with repression of its sources in dead siblings, paternal suicide, and the draining of eroticism from heterosexual relations (viewed less as a pleasure than as a restorative for the injury endured by survivors) seems a far more predictable offshoot of trauma than "empathic unsettlement." Through Ben's stagnation within a family with "no energy of a narrative . . . , not even the fervour of an elegy" (204), *Fugitive Pieces*'s coda emphasizes the second generation's perplexity at the stranglehold of an incommunicable trauma on a present life that feels enigmatically diminished. Only after the death of his parents does Ben discover a photograph of his father and mother with an infant and a little girl — on its back "a spidery date, June 1941, and two names. Hannah. Paul" (252). Like Jacob, Ben has suffered the loss of siblings, though his knowledge of them is belated and simulated. As the successor of a father who weeps while dutifully consuming food because his personal tragedies have made it unclear whether he should "stuff himself, or starve" (214), Ben inherits a perplexing paternal legacy that buckles at his father's suicide. Suffering from insomnia after his wife's death, the father, "suddenly able to answer the dilemma of hunger that had plagued him so long," swallowed an entire bottle of sleeping pills (256).

Yet the coda of *Fugitive Pieces* does make Ben Jacob's heir by virtue of an act of proxy-witnessing that gestures toward this central maneuver in second-generation poetry after Auschwitz. After Jacob's death, Ben's quest for Jacob's notebooks leads to their discovery. That the first line Ben reads in the notebooks — "*Time is a blind guide* . . ." — is the first line of *Fugitive Pieces* suggests that the excavated books constitute part I of the novel, making Ben as collaborative in Jacob's posthumous publication as Jacob had been in Athos's (283, 284). For Jacob's first sustained act of authorship issued through a sort of ghostwriting: after Athos died without finishing *Bearing False Witness,* a book about the Nazi destruction of the excavated ancient city Biskupin, Jacob completed it for him, bearing true witness to his mentor. Composing "for" and "with" the other — without entertaining the delusion of becoming the other — involves fostering relationships between the visible "now" and the invisible "then," the palpable "here" and the impalpable "there." Jacob's apprenticeship as a publishing author and Ben's recovery of Jacob's notebooks hint at the crucial role that post-Holocaust proxy-witnessing plays in preserving memory, as well as its poignant inability to provide adequate knowledge of or recompense for the dead. Michaels places herself in the role of proxy-witness too: the novel's opening dedication ("for J") and its prefatory paragraphs (about the "Poet Jakob Beer . . . struck and killed by a car in Athens in the spring of 1993," who had "begun to write his memoirs") frame the first section as an actual autobiography of a real survivor that historical exigency caused to go unwritten until the task was adopted by the woman author who ghostwrote it for him. By citing the works or creating the words of others, by dramatizing their own inability to know, poetic proxy-witnesses after Auschwitz attenuate the mastery, the authority of their own authorship.

Given the impasse of authoritarianism, is it any wonder that most men and women of letters are drawn to forms that cradle earlier testimony and in the process grant their own belated insufficiency? The proxy, who remembers what someone else knew, adopts evidence that remains another's so as to elect a lineage based more on volitional consent than on hereditary descent. For the proxy, as she individuates her own responses and merges them with another's, the Other is both remote and proximate. By means of empathic imaginings, the proxy-witness seeks not to incorporate but instead to corporate an Other, if only retrospectively. Because the poets believe that we stand in danger of losing a sense of the loss of many, they eschew prosaic cognitive discourses and use instead the more hesitant forms of expression inspired by what are felt to be fugitive origins. "Every recorded event," Jacob the survivor believes, "is a brick of potential, or precedent, thrown into the future. Eventually the idea will hit someone in the back of the head. This is the duplicity of history: an idea recorded will become an idea resurrected" (161).

Through their excavation of and communion with earlier testimony, Jacob and Ben typify the attempt of many contemporary creative writers, visual artists, and scholars to witness the witnesses in a manner that displays how post-Holocaust proxy-witnessing will continue to foster memory of the Holocaust during the period when there will be no survivors alive to attest for themselves. The inter-identifications of Athos and Jacob mesh with Ben's definition of his scholarly work as a biographer: "The quest to discover another's psyche, to absorb another's motives as deeply as your own, is a lover's quest. But the search for facts, for places, names, influential events, important conversations and correspondences, political circumstances — all this amounts to nothing if you can't find the assumption your subject lives by" (222). The phrase "to absorb another's motives" draws attention to the ways in which empathic identification could, of course, be distorted so as to appropriate or obliterate the Other, whether lover or native informant or foreigner or (as in this passage) simply another person's life in the past. What *Fugitive Pieces* suggests, however, is that perverted forms of empathy do not delegitimize efforts to conceptualize the empathic imagination within frameworks that take into account and defuse its potential for symbolic violence amid those disparate power relations it seeks to traverse.[25]

Though at times literary men and women recognize the danger of recycling the images of others, their acts of reiteration intimate that, as Shelley believed it could, the imagination enabled them to take these heartless images to heart. A comment of Michaels seems particularly salient about the ways in which Jacob's and Ben's trajectories illuminate not simply the creation of poetry after Auschwitz but also its potential effects on readers: "It's probably no coincidence that when we speak of memorizing something, we refer to it as learning by heart" ("CL" 15). Her view accords with C. K. Williams's repetition of Walt Whitman's conviction that "the profoundest service" provided by poems consists in giving readers "*good heart* as a radical possession and habit" (*PC* 28). For readers and for writers, poetry has been the most habitually memorized of compositions — because of its relative brevity, but also because of its compression, precision, and musicality. In *Fugitive Pieces,* fifteen-year-old Bella exemplifies empathic identification when playing the music of Beethoven, Chopin, and Brahms. The passionate instrumentalist memorizes the score by taking its measures into her own being, while simultaneously giving its creator a new vehicle of expression. The physicality of Bella's fingers practicing timing or phrasing on the piano links such empathic learning directly to the body, to a fleshly memory in the muscles and on the skin. Like those medieval faithful who believed that what the soul held steadfast would be somatically imprinted (engraved on the body), reciters of verse sometimes feel physically changed by the rhythmic words that curiously inhabit them.[26] "Poetry attaches itself to consciousness in a way no other language experience does," Williams has argued, pointing out that a poem can "stay in memory" the way a novel cannot (*PC* 130). Bella's reviving the spirit of Beethoven and Jacob's commitment as well as Ben's responsiveness to poetry have everything to do with "the lyric's fixity of its own present," which (like the instrumentalist's performance) "may be described as that moment in which all past moments (potentially) coincide with consciousness" (Cameron 133–34).

Through artistry, Jacob attains the realization that "History is amoral: events occurred. But memory is moral; what we consciously remember is what our conscience remembers" (*FP* 139). Like the idea of being "unmoored" in the moment, the shift in verbs is crucial here, for the present tense signifies what Michaels (in a chapter title) calls "the gradual instant." Whereas history relegates the past to the past, Jacob's ghostwriting replenishes ongoing memories of Bella's existence. Vis-à-vis trauma, empathic reading and writing and reciting collapse time, making of every moment a second moment through parallel images that serve an ethical function in literature, as in liturgy:

> It's Hebrew tradition that forefathers are referred to as "we," not "they." "When we were delivered from Egypt. . . ." This encourages empathy and a responsibility to the past but, more important, it collapses time. The Jew is forever leaving Egypt. A good way to teach ethics. If moral choices are eternal, individual acts take on immense significance no matter how small: not for this life only. (Anne Michaels, *FP* 159–60)

In a related meditation on empathy, Cynthia Ozick, who considers the annihilation of "the distinction between Then and Now" a sort of "Anti-History," suggests that the Exodus "demands memory, and then converts memory into metaphor; 'Because you were strangers in the land of Egypt,' " Egypt becomes "the great metaphor of reciprocity" through which we "imagine the life of the Other." As Ozick concludes, "Metaphor is the reciprocal agent" that "makes possible the power to envision the stranger's heart" (*MM* 270, 279).

Perhaps here resides the link between the empathic imagination and the magnetism of lyrical fiction. Fiction: since the eighteenth century, characters in novels have drawn readers into "a kind of virtual experience through which one puts oneself in the other's position while recognizing the difference of that position and hence not taking the other's place," to quote LaCapra's definition of "empathic unsettlement" again. Lyrical fiction: if, as it is impossible not to suspect, the fugitive pieces of a subjectivity based on empathic identification can be experienced only fleetingly; and if the intangible, the invisible, the unseen of grievous absence remains a primary responsibility for the living imagination, as many of the writers suggest, then the sounds of intimate voices that stop and start in fragmentary bits and parts may be best suited for such an undertaking. The discontinuities and stutters of repetition, the cutting of connectives found in ordinary prose, the blank spaces between stanza-like chapters, the recurrence of mysterious maxims, the clustering of rhythmic image patterns, the elaboration on and analysis of extended metaphors: all these facets of *Fugitive Pieces* testify to an

Otherness that can neither be fully incorporated nor externalized, neither owned nor disowned — only haltingly, sporadically adopted.

Less hesitant, more hopeful than some of the lines of verse composed in the tradition I have been studying, Athos's mystic maxims — "it is your future you are remembering" (21) — nevertheless exemplify the sometimes hyperbolic, sometimes epigrammatic utterances of poets and even some critics who (like Adorno with his koan-like fiat) make memory moral by collapsing time into parallel moments, by mining the syntax of "the gradual instant":

> Dear love, Auschwitz made me
> more of a Jew than ever Moses did (Abse 34);

> Praise to life though ones we knew and loved
> loved it badly, too well, and not enough (Rich, *AARP* 160);

> The bystander at the massacre of innocents
> might have seen his own innocence among the dying
> (Feldman, *AUH* 14);

> Words cannot reach him in his prison of words
> (Hamburger, *CP* 129);

> My mother was a braid of black smoke (Simic, *WDE* 3);

> I turn and burn.
> Do not think I underestimate your great concern (Plath 246);

> We cannot *not* imagine (Des Pres, *PD* 228);

> *dead Jew violin in German ear* (Heyen, *E* 105);

> Wherever you are, Yolek will be there too (Hecht, *TM* 74).

Not through mimeticism or comprehensiveness or logic, but through intense articulations that reverse, stall, rend, compress, flash back, abridge, retard, or predict historical events and thus violate temporality, poets after Auschwitz abrogate sequential temporality. Thus they drive home the paradoxical remoteness of the past (the subject of my first chapter) as well as its proximity (the subject of my second chapter). To the extent that it confounds normative notions of chronology, viewing time less in linear than in spatial terms (as, for instance, the circle in Adorno's definition of the poem as a sundial), poetry after Auschwitz helps readers understand perhaps the most perplexing revision of Adorno's directive. In *Vicious Circles*, Blanchot muses, "No matter when it is written, every narrative from now on will be from *before* Auschwitz" (69; emphasis mine). Despite the poets' commitment to discontinuity and their resistance to closure, Blanchot's word *récit*, meaning "account" or "story" (fictional or historical), encompasses a number of the poets' projects. Though, in order to make a place for commemorative

Holocaust verse, I contrasted it to prose narrative in my opening chapter, such a hard-and-fast distinction cannot, of course, be sustained, as I implicitly concede by concluding with *Fugitive Pieces*. And, by demonstrating that literary efforts to confront Auschwitz are confounded by it, the poets concede their own failure to arrive at forms qualitatively transmuted by the disaster. Thus, they hint that Western civilization has not yet arrived at the temporal domain of the "after" or the geographical domain beyond "Auschwitz."

What can be made from the fact that some of the quotations I have reprinted exhibit marked elements of formalism? Abse's opening and Simic's closing spondees, Plath's internal and end rhymes, the symmetrical balancing of "Words" and "words" in Hamburger's line and of "innocents" and "innocence" in Feldman's sentence, Rich's and Hecht's variations on iambic pentameter: these recall the tendency of many of the poets discussed in earlier chapters to ground free verse in conventional patterns or to deploy intricate verse forms. Perhaps because freer free verse tends to be associated with the delights of expansiveness, freedom, flight, or adventure, poets dealing with the rigid constraints imposed by a historical calamity seem drawn to the rigor of structured forms. Invested with the dignity and ritual that still make verse a preferred choice for readings at weddings and funerals, meter informs readers that they are "not experiencing the real object" being imitated but are encountering "instead that object transmuted into symbolic form" (Fussell 12). Besides linking poetic expression more to mediated than to realistic rhetorics, conventional forms such as riddles, anaphoric catalogues or chants, villanelles, psalms, nursery rhymes, sestinas, couplets, and aphorisms facilitate the ancient mnemonic function of a body of verse that repeatedly returns to a relatively meager cluster of images: trains and tracks, showers and soap, brandings and burnings, thrown-away children and the living dead, discarded shoes and extracted teeth, barbed wire and ovens, heaps of hair and ashes and bodies, broken glass and Zyklon gas, smoke and stars. The formalism evident in some of the lines of verse I have quoted subverts normative notions that a higher degree of craft invariably decreases a text's emotional effect.

At least in part, such formalism has an impact because, as Williams puts it, in verse "the struggle with form . . . actually enriches the expressiveness and effect of content": "Poetry induces mind into involving itself entirely into an awareness of its formal striving, and in doing so it demands that mind realize as much as it can its entire nature, not only its intellectual or moral capacity" (*PC* 133). Thus some of the authors in the tradition traced in these pages contest the assumption of many scholars of the Shoah "that Holocaust writing characteristically 'aspires to the condition of history' " or that it invariably purports to realize "historical authenticity" (Lang, "HGTH" 19). Unlike the transparency of realistic modes of discourse, poetic incantation or performance seeks to make the aesthetic apparent as it intensifies moral, intellectual, and sensory awareness. Meter and syntax, tone and musicality contribute to what Seamus Heaney identifies as poetry's "unpredictability . . . and its need to go emotionally and artistically 'above the brim' " (*RP* 192). "Rather than betraying the historical matter or obscuring its moral import," Sidra DeKoven Ezrahi explains about Celan's most often recited and formally rigorous work, "the performed poem may actually be the only possible conduit to what cannot be faced without mediation" ("SM" 274). Such logic elucidates Czeslaw Milosz's prediction about his war-torn city in his *Treatise on Poetry:* "And for your disasters this is your reward: / As a sign that language only is your home, / Your ramparts will be built by poets" (15). What makes some verse a viable defense or fortification is poetry's capacity to traverse "the division between the living and the dead, creating thereby *a state of living-death* that will bring the poet into full flood and language into its mimetic birthright" (Taussig 310).

How strong are those ramparts? Can we judge the quality of the verse produced by and about the Shoah? Much as classicists call "poetry" what little was preserved from antiquity, of whatever description, scholars countering *damnatio memoriae* (the Roman term for a conscious obliterating of memory) may wish to retrieve words irrespective of any judgment of their quality or may feel that we are too close to recent aesthetic efforts and thus cannot yet evaluate them.[27] Some readers may take issue with my refusal in preceding chapters to fault poets for overidentifying, misusing, or sensationalizing the materials they adopted, but I have withheld judgment so as to learn as much as I could from the poets' daring invocations. Notwithstanding the fragility of verse ramparts, even those built by strong writers, the poems I have been studying throughout this volume amount to fugitive pieces of verse impelled by empathic identification and composed by writers dedicated to resisting idealizations of "Man himself, the quintessence of virility."

Proxy-witnesses after Auschwitz — crisscrossing lines composed in the present with the records of the past — enact a partnership between the living and the dead that Olga Levertoff consecrated in a poem her sister, Denise Levertov, placed at the close of *A Sorrow Dance.* In Levertoff's "Ballad to My Father," the hallowed dead "from concentration camps, and yes, from gas chambers; / from thousand years' ghettoes, from graves old and new," arrive at a moment Michaels would call "the gradual instant" to dance a Hasidic dance at the pious father's dying:

> "Yáchchiderálum, pútzele mútzele:
>   faster and faster the measure we tread!
> Your hand in my hand, your foot to my footzele —
>   partners for ever, the living and the dead!" (93)

The "death-dance of one holy Jew" sanctifies the father's fierce devotion to "*an end of strife for eternal life for behold I make all things new*" (94), a vow that brings me back to a final look at Marc Chagall's portrait of the sorrowful *danse macabre* swirling around a Jesus on the boundaries of Judaism and Christianity, a Jew who was the first Christian for some as well as the rabbi who taught Judaism for others.[28]

The labor of poets after Auschwitz who carry the silenced into language illuminates the swelling belly only partly hidden by Jesus' tallith-skirt in *White Crucifixion,* a being not only Jewish and Christian but also male and maternal. Divinity as mother has Jewish roots, whereas Jesus as mother has Christian sources.[29] Within an iconography saturated by centuries of Christian anti-Judaism and by a dangerous valorization of suffering as elected and elective, the rounded bulge or blister around the crucified figure's navel suggests that empathic modes of being and knowing have been put at stake, as have the lives and cultures of a people in diaspora, some of whom were destroyed by Christians in the name of Christ.[30] On the circumference that encircles the smaller circle on the pregnant Jesus' body, the experiences of the expatriated casualties may be adopted by the martyr but cannot become his own flesh and blood; they are fugitives from him, fragments foreign to him. Although it remains impossible to imagine what crowning the death of the idea of man might possibly portend, the Shoah has given birth to images of itself delivered by its artists.

What does the adoption of the dead by the living, of the historical past by the imaginative present, tell us about debates over whether the Shoah can be represented at all and, if so, by whom? "In poetry more than in other forms," Berel Lang believes, "the tension that separates these two impulses [of historical authenticity and imaginative figuration] is unremitting," and he uses this point to argue that poetry "reveals more clearly both *the occasion and the impossibility* of the project undertaken by all the genres of imaginative writing about the Nazi genocide — at once to incorporate and to forego history" (*AING* 140; emphasis mine). Significantly, however, this scrupulous scholar, who can stand for all those who claim that the calamity cannot be transmitted or ought not be represented, cites the reciting of the Exodus from Egypt in the Haggadah ("When we were delivered from Egypt") as an instance of a morally efficacious form of encouraging empathy, much as Michaels and Ozick do:

> It is one thing to hear or to read an account related by someone else; the act is quite different for the person who recites the story, who speaks and hears the events in his own voice. Even then, of course, the narrator does not create the event; but his voice, the at once literal and metaphorical voice that sounds the words, takes on the shape of its subject, much as a hand does with its grasp. The voice here becomes the expression of its subject, not its source or cause. (xii–xiii)

The same sentences could be written about Holocaust verse. Despite his insistence on documentary or historical approaches to the Shoah, over and against imaginative ones, Lang sees in the expressiveness of speaking with, for, as, or to another the possibility of a transhistorical identification, albeit one he does not grant to non-Jews.[31]

I believe that the effort to devise rules to legislate which modes of representing the past are acceptable and which unacceptable, and of policing who can and who cannot undertake them, will be thwarted by the ingenuity not only of poets but also of filmmakers, novelists, visual artists, curators, and scholars. I would therefore revise Lang's sentence to argue that poetry reveals more clearly than do other genres both *the occasion and the imperative* of incorporating and forgoing history, the project at the center of Holocaust art. What Jorie Graham writes about the verse produced by William Heyen remains true of an entire tradition. "In the strongest poems, . . . one feels what one needs to feel: the battle between the desire to transform and the resistance of the facts; the frailty and perhaps even the immorality of those horrifying facts becoming a story" ("TTD" 30). Poets after Auschwitz emphasize how, at a specific moment of time, their ostensibly private responses to earlier public events are mediated by the high and low cultural formations that have shaped representations of the Shoah since 1945.

Whether narrative or lyric, dramatic or satiric, occasional or visionary, verse about the Holocaust engages readers not only in different types of identifications with those who were harmed by it but also with heightened awareness of how precarious or nugatory those identifications may be. Dependent precisely on the idea of disparity, the concept of empathic imagination subverts any notion that only eyewitness survivors or only Jews can approach the subject of the Shoah. According to Anne Michaels and many of her contemporaries, a literary education challenges apathetic disengagement from the past, along with the overinvestment in historical trauma that Geoffrey Hartman calls "memory envy," because, again in Hartman's words, "the aesthetic . . . recognizes the difficulty of accommodating traumatic experience" ("WVT" 230–31). The aesthetic also marks its own constructedness more than do, say, historical or critical or philosophical writings — and much more than do, say, retrospective autobiographical and testimonial writings.

I began this book with a violent chapter title, potentially disturbing or even repellent because of course events do not die, people do, and because of course nothing can keep the past from being buried deeper and deeper by the passage of time. It was a risk taken to illustrate how metaphorical thinking inevitably informs critical writing. Even though, as decades intervene with their own stupefying disasters in tow, it may be impossible to keep the Shoah from declining into just one among numerous horror shows at the cultural multiplex, the particular burden of second-generation artists and scholars consists in taking up the task. To do so, philosophers and historians, theologians and literary critics of the Shoah inexorably rely on precisely the figurative devices poets more explicitly employ as they repeat, respond to, recast the earlier utterances of those harmed by the catastro-

261

phe. Overtly literary, flagrantly rhetorical, poetry makes manifest what may be subsumed, hidden, or effaced in testimonial or historical forms of representing the Holocaust.[32]

A politics based on racial, ethnic, national, or religious categories, a so-called identity politics, has something but not everything to do with the workings of the empathic imagination, which takes as its mandate not sympathy with those similar to us but connectedness with those quite distinct and distanced from us. Identifying *with* does not necessarily mean identifying *as*. This is especially the case because the notoriously porous term "Jewish" can refer to a cultural or a religious identity group, an ascriptive association (based on unchosen, demeaning characteristics) or a voluntary one.[33] Non- and ex- as well as accidental and incidental and part- and pro- and faux- and even (alas) anti-Jews have participated in post-Holocaust literature. Thus, there is no patrolled fence between poetry about Auschwitz and poetry after Auschwitz, between Jewish American or Anglo-Jewish verse and literature in English. Even those poems not directly about the Shoah but composed with cognizance of its centrality as a cataclysm in culture enable us to face what we are often tempted to ignore. They ask us to confront—in the words of the poet Alan Shapiro—"the inertia of our self-complacencies, our labyrinthine narcissisms, our penchant for self-deception, and most of all our utter vulnerability as mortal creatures in an unjust world," as well as "how limited [poetry's] power is to save or console us in the face of extreme or terrible experience" (*LHO* 3).[34]

Although creative writers after Auschwitz register a keen awareness of the postmodernity of our cultural environment, most persist, as Adrienne Rich does, "on asking the questions still being defined as nonquestions—the ones beginning *Why . . . ? What if . . . ?*" They therefore locate their endeavor in the intellectual terrain of the "pre-postmodern": "We will be told these are childish, naive, 'Pre-postmodern' questions. They are the imagination's questions" (*AP* 167). Just as, in order to ponder the severance and fusion of "then" and "now," I asked when "after Auschwitz" definitively occurred, the poets stubbornly insist on the ongoing relevance of "pre-postmodern" and pre-posthumanist concerns, even as they lay bare the post-modernity, the post-humanism of our condition. As Adorno knew it would, poetry after Auschwitz has survived his admonition by elaborating on it so as to protest the implacable horror of the Shoah, in the process realizing the potential he ascribed to the lyric: its capacity to overcome "the power of socialization" through a "pathos of detachment" that makes "manifest something not distorted, not grasped, not yet subsumed" ("LPS" 37).

Because, next to Israel, the United States housed the largest population of refugees from Nazi Germany, it is not surprising that so many American writers found themselves drawn to the subject of the Shoah. Thus a member of the *Sonderkommando* in Auschwitz, Zalmen Gradowski—worrying "Can the dead mourn the dead?"—was hardly anomalous in his plea to readers of his testimonial that they publish it (along with photographs of his family), when he directed them to a friend in the States, one J. Joffe, residing at 27 East Broadway in New York (549). As, along with their peers in Britain and Canada, American authors were drawn to witness the witnesses, their collective voice "protest[ed] against a social situation that every individual experiences as hostile, alien, cold, oppressive" through expressions of "the dream of a world in which things could be different" (Adorno, "LPS" 39–40). The writing that manifests Adorno's definition of "the poem as a philosophical sundial telling the time of history" (46) was apparently predicted by Hannah Arendt. Leonard Michaels once recalled hearing Arendt say after one of her lectures, "We must wait for the poets," and he concurs: "The poets would transform what isn't even anybody's subject—except for victims and scholars—into a language free of all narcissism. They will speak with correct impersonality, which is by no means unfeeling, of the hideous abomination. In this future speaking, we will rediscover our humanity" (11–12).

To legitimize my portrait of poetry as a survivor of Auschwitz and of Adorno's dictum, I would trace its license back to an ancient mandate in the prophetic book of Joel (1:2–3):

> Has such a thing happened in your days,
>   or in the days of your ancestors?
> Tell your children of it,
>   and let your children tell their children,
> and their children another generation.

A short poem by Adrienne Rich, titled "In Those Days," proffers a more ominous permit. Imagining herself at some future time removed from the present moment, just as we are increasingly distanced from the 1933–1945 period, Rich writes with hindsight about her understanding of why we "lost track / of the meaning of *we*, of *you*" (*DRF* 4). From the retrospect of an imagined hereafter, when the present could be remembered as a true past, in a moment after the period after Auschwitz, she explains, "we were trying to live a personal life," and admits, "yes, that was the only life / we could bear witness to." However, "the great dark birds of history" still plunged screaming "into our personal weather":

> They were headed somewhere else but their beaks and pinions
>   drove
> along the shore, through the rags of fog
> where we stood, saying *I*[.]

Can poetic expressiveness counter the deluded solipsism of "we . . . saying *I*" without falling into the snare of "I" saying "we," the trap of a solitary individual laying claim to speak for others and in the process eclipsing them? In keeping with a tradition that brackets voices within voices, texts within texts, I close with Seamus Heaney's affirmative response to this quest in *The Government of the Tongue,* an assertion he makes through Czeslaw Milosz's "Ars Poetica?" (*GT* 167). Although Heaney does not see "how poetry can survive as a category of human consciousness if it does not put poetic considerations first" (166), he goes on to concede, quoting Milosz, that

> The purpose of poetry is to remind us
> how difficult it is to remain just one person,
> for our house is open, there are no keys in the door,
> and invisible guests come in and out at will. (167)

Heaney reconciles his own commitment to "expressive considerations . . . at the moment of lyric conception" with Milosz's "rebuke to the autocracy of such romantic presumption" through the realization that "the greatest work occurs when a certain self-forgetfulness is attained" (166, 168). The words of Heaney and Milosz may quite properly propel us far away from the subject of the Shoah, but then pull us back, if only momentarily. Besides subverting assumptions about the autonomy of the individual, poets teach us the absurdity of limiting our compass to what just one person, in one space, at one moment knew and the importance of discerning what one person hardly or obliquely knew through the comings and goings of others.

When yoked to this imperative, literature that plucks us out of the present to tug us back to the past can do so in the name of an anti-racist or post-race future. A prominent theorist in race studies is not alone in believing that racism's anachronistic but tenacious sway today — even in purportedly anti-racist movements — can be attributed to the distressing fact that "the memory of the Nazi genocide has ceased to form the constellation under which we work" (Gilroy 41). Although, as Chaim Kaplan cautioned, "Historical events do not repeat themselves in their original form" (368), poets after Auschwitz try to keep this constellation in view through the preposterous task of weighing loss on the scales of poetic justice. In the process, as Kaplan prayed it might, poetry guards the disaster in "the reliquary of . . . tears" (79). Like Samuel Bak's painting *Ghetto* on the cover of this book, the artifice of verse after Auschwitz evokes the sobs and shrieks, the outcries and tears of a vanished population, while its cobbled-together edifice stands with all its rubble and breaks, fissures and tears apparent. *Dis* (negative, ill) and *astēr* (star), disaster: as if a star had fallen out of the sky to shatter the very roof of culture, though some of the walls do not fall. With two quite distinct pronunciations of the last word, then, a "reliquary of . . . tears."

NOTES

1. THE HOLOCAUST IS DYING

1. As this first paragraph illustrates, I use the Greek-derived "Holocaust" (burnt offering) and the Hebrew "Shoah" (disaster) interchangeably throughout this book, although sometimes I refer to the destruction of the Jews as "genocide," sometimes as *Khurbn* (the Yiddish word for cataclysmic destruction). Some of the poets' responses to these designations are discussed in my third chapter; for a recent overview of contemporary debates about the drawbacks and strengths of these terms, see Mandel 206–209.

2. Jean-Paul Sartre was one of the few intellectuals to analyze anti-Semitism in *Anti-Semite and Jew* (1946), and Albert Camus's 1956 novel *The Fall* has been read as a reflection on the Holocaust.

3. With the exception of Charlie Chaplin's *The Great Dictator*, which appeared in 1940, no Hollywood representation of the Holocaust was shown on screen until the 1959 *Diary of Anne Frank* (see Avisar 92, 96). *Night and Fog* (1955) famously protested the atrocities without mentioning that most of the victims were Jewish.

4. Mintz explains that between the Second World War and the Eichmann trial, the Palmach generation "committed themselves to the creation of a new Jew on Palestinian soil" and positioned this self-image against "the death of European Jews, who were perceived at the time to have gone to their death 'like sheep to the slaughter'" (10).

5. On the impact of Adorno's phrase as well as the evolution of his own subsequent thinking about it, see Rothberg 25–58.

6. Many others concurred with Adorno's famous pronouncement against literature. Appelfeld pointed out that "Artistic expression after the Holocaust seems repugnant, disgusting. . . . Moreover, art, and not without reason, was linked in our minds with a sphere of European culture of which we had been the victims" (89). See also Gilman's discussion of "The language damaged in the Holocaust [which] was the universal language of humanity, not merely the language of the Jews" (321–22).

7. The term "memory thief" was coined by Edward Alexander many years before the *New Yorker* piece by Gourevitch, who supplies background to such misrepresentations. Related to ersatz survivors are such novelists as Jerzy Kosinski, Helen Demidenko, and D. M. Thomas, who have been accused of either plagiarizing testimony or impersonating participants in or descendants of the disaster.

8. From the 1980s on, numerous books and articles have been published about women in the resistance, the roles of wives and mothers in the ghettoes, the experiences of female prisoners in the camps, and the memoirs some managed to compose. On resistance to feminist approaches to the Shoah, see Lenore Weitzman and Ofer's introduction, 12–16; Lipstadt, "WI?"; Ringelheim, "WH." The argument for and against using gender in the Holocaust context is best articulated, respectively, by Heinemann and by Langer, "GS?"

9. See Rosenfeld's "Assault on Holocaust Memory," which discusses the work of Norman G. Finkelstein, Peter Novick, Michael Goldberg, Philip Lopate, Ward Churchill, and David Stannard.

10. Ernst van Alphen elaborates on both these points throughout *Caught by History.*

11. In *The Reader,* Bernhard Schlink makes a comparable point, arguing that the silence of second-generation Germans would constitute a Nazi victory (104).

12. My understanding of Benjamin was extended by Wendy Brown's lecture at the University of Virginia, February 19, 1999.

13. For a critique of Bessel A. Van der Kolk's theories, see chap. 7 of Leys.

14. I am indebted to Caruth's discussion of Pierre Janet in her introduction to "Recapturing the Past" (153).

15. To be sure, there are many studies of German, Yiddish, and Hebrew responses to the Shoah in verse as well as insightful passages about English and American poetry, which appear in books written by Ezrahi, Langer, Plank, and Rosenfeld and in a few articles by Castle and Young; however, no sustained critical attention has been accorded verse composed in English. After I completed a draft of this manuscript, an exception to the rule appeared: Parmet's useful *The Terror of Our Days.*

16. Only the first two devote themselves exclusively to verse in English. The others integrate American and British verse with poetry in translation, while *Art from the Ashes* excludes all but translated verse. *Telling and Remembering* includes American Jewish poets writing on many subjects, including the Holocaust. When I quote poems from these texts, I cite them parenthetically, using the initials given in the list of abbreviations.

17. See the excellent discussion of Jackson's *Behold the Jew* in Schweik 17–23.

18. The phrase "act of attention" is D. H. Lawrence's term for the poetic exercise (xv). See Steven Weitzman's excellent analysis of the "congeries of disparate scribal behaviors tied to different genres" in the Hebrew Bible (36).

19. The revisionist Lyotard paraphrases is the French author Robert Faurisson.

20. Vendler contrasts philosophers, who "invent the thought of their epoch," with poets, who "invent . . . the *style* of their epoch, which corresponds to and records, the feelings felt in their epoch" (*BS* 7).

21. See a smart reading of this poem by Slavitt (6–9).

22. Hollander interprets early drafts of the poem, paying particular attention to how "Feldman indulges in some rodomontade of rhetorical analysis, in the manner of Hamlet or Hotspur or Rostand's Cyrano" ("CH" 54).

23. Marrus and Paxton view the timing of the Dutch workers' strike of February 1941 as premature: "This was the first massive, open opposition anywhere in occupied Europe to Nazi anti-Semitism. The strike was crushed by overwhelming force, and to an important degree the courageous Dutch opposition continued for years to be demoralized by the brutally effective display of German power so early in the occupation. And the strike had no effect whatever on the substance of Nazi anti-Jewish activity in Holland, except perhaps to worsen the plight of native Jews" (248).

24. In a provocative reading of "The Pripet Marshes," Ostriker locates its power in "its palpable theatricalization of the scenario of holocaust as form of pleasure"; she argues that the poet moves from a masculine imaginative stance, where he acts like

the SS by seizing his friends and transporting them to the disaster, to a feminine one of paralysis ("MNIL" 110).

25. The idea of "survivors by proxy" comes from Lifton (in the interview by Caruth, 145); the term "secondary witness," from LaCapra ("LS" 267). Since the poems I discuss seem more hesitant about deriving authority from witnessing the witnesses, I have used the related term "proxy-witnessing." The question of when and under what circumstances those who cannot testify for themselves can or should be represented by surrogates speaking in their stead opens up thorny issues that are the focus of ongoing discussion in legal circles. If live eye- or earwitness testimony is unavailable, the preference for it may have to be supplemented by admissible hearsay, if juries are instructed on how to evaluate hearsay. See Mueller.

26. My terms here are indebted to Pinsky's analysis of the uses of the "unpoetic" ("RP") and Kristeva's of the uses of the "awkward." They are also informed by Hartman's view of "writing as orphaned speech" in the work of Celan (LS 164). Hartman discusses the fragmentary as well as the avoidances of ellipses in *The Fateful Question of Culture* (111–17).

27. "For Adorno in the late 1950s," Rothberg explains, "poetry has an important mimetic function, one that consists not in reproducing the harmonious narrative of traditional realist forms, but rather in expressing the rifts that realist mimesis represses" (39).

28. In a pertinent passage on the "self-critique" at work in Holocaust fiction, Horowitz explains that "a sense of inevitable failure dogs Holocaust narrative, which varyingly proves ineffective, too effective, or simply besides the point. This failure — and the strategies evolved to mitigate it — connect strongly with the contradictory pulls of language and silence" (40, 43).

2. MASTERS OF DISASTER

1. I am grateful to Frank Harris for inviting me to speak at the reunion of Fürth and Nuremberg refugees and survivors, June 28–30, 1996, at Kutcher Country Club in the Catskills of New York, where this project was first conceived.

2. For a moving consideration of the centrality of suicide in German Jewish life, see Charlotte Salomon's autobiography *Leben oder Theater?* (*Life or Theater?*) as well as Mary Lowenthal Felstiner's comments on a "suicide epidemic" among German Jews during the 1920s (15).

3. Porter adds to this list the Holocaust scholar Terrence Des Pres; the survivor and newspaper titan Robert Maxwell, who organized the first European Conference on the Holocaust at Oxford University; and the literary men Arthur Koestler and Stefan Zweig (52). Recently, scholars have begun to speculate that Benjamin was murdered on political grounds; however, such speculations only underline the indeterminacy of any suicide.

4. In addition, see David Curzon's "The Gardens" (*BL* 375), Evelyn Wexler's "The Suitcase" (*BL* 348), and Marilyn Hacker's poem cataloguing "the absent fathers of my friends" (*SC* 76).

5. The Holocaust also continued on for Gerald Stern, who worried, "How is it that I didn't become a murderer, or at the very least a suicide?" (*GH* 15). About Klepfisz's non-Jewish peers, James Young states, "John Berryman, Randall Jarrell, Anne Sexton, and Sylvia Plath all killed themselves after representing themselves literarily in light of the Holocaust" (*WRH* 127). Simply studying Holocaust documents, Alvarez worried, could rouse self-destructive impulses (28), a view dramatized in Martha Cooley's novel *The Archivist*. Charles Bernstein claims that to acknowledge the Second World War "means to risk suicide and in the process to

politicize philosophy; and if we desire to avoid death and evade politics, repression is inevitable" (196).

6. Before and during selections, one might also ask, how many people's efforts to commit suicide were foiled simply by circumstances? Ida Fink's story "The Other Shore," with its eerie evocation of Virginia Woolf's suicide at the start of the Second World War, describes one woman's unsuccessful attempt to drown herself at a time when there is nowhere to escape (117–22).

Frankl explains that "The thought of suicide was entertained by nearly everyone" in the concentration camps, but he made a firm promise on his arrival "that I would not 'run into the wire.' That was a phrase used in camp to describe the most popular method of suicide — touching the electrically charged barbed-wire fence" (16). The *Muselmänner* or "moslems" of the camps, "countless men and women [who] were murdered in spirit as the means of killing them in body," could be called neither living nor dead but rather seemed like the living dead (Des Pres, *S* 88–89). In a disturbing passage of *The Informed Heart*, Bettelheim claims that entering the gas chamber was a passive form of committing suicide; however, in *Writing into the World*, Des Pres calls this "blame the victim" logic (67–68).

7. This is the view as well of Baechler (42–47), who uses it to argue that "suicide affirms freedom, dignity, and the right to happiness" (51).

8. In the town of Wiesbaden, "fully half the funerals between November 1938 and May 1945 were deaths from suicide" (Opfermann 46).

9. McCord quotes Konrad Kwiet: "Even the most conservative estimate of 5,000 Jewish suicides during the twelve years of the Third *Reich* would indicate that nearly 1 per cent of the 525,000 Jews living in Germany in 1933 took their own lives" (15). Many Holocaust memoirs include scenes in which families discuss suicide as an option: see Denes's *Castles Burning* (52) as well as Heller's *Strange and Unexpected Love* (162, 208, 269).

10. Felman interprets these suicides as "desperate solutions to the impossibility of witnessing, whose double bind and dead end they materialize. To kill oneself is, in effect, at once to *kill the witness* and to remain, by means of one's own death, *outside the witnessing*. Both suicides are thus motivated by the *desire not to be inside*" (Felman and Laub 228). Chaim Kaplan, who wavers between disdain and admiration for Adam Czerniakow, records first the false rumor of his suicide (196) and then the deed, which "earned his immortality in a single instant" (385).

11. Besides Améry's *On Suicide*, see McCord 150 and Stark 98.

12. Jack Porter names him Arthur Zyglboim; however, Sereny quotes Smul Zygielbojm's protest suicide on May 12, 1943: " 'By my death,' he wrote in a farewell note addressed to the president and prime minister of the Polish government in exile, 'I wish to make my final protest against the passivity with which the world is looking on and permitting the extermination of the Jewish people' " (219).

13. See Elliot Richman's "God's Spit" (56–57) as well as the self-destructive characters in William Styron's *Sophie's Choice*, who argue that after the Third Reich suicide has become a legitimate option.

14. To consider suicide in the context of German cultural history — with its fascination over Goethe's Werther and its later absorption in writers such as Nietzsche, Ibsen, and Schopenhauer — is clearly beyond the scope of this chapter.

15. A documentary film that includes a discussion about whether one Nazi doctor's postwar suicide dramatizes the pangs of a guilty conscience so outraged Claude Lanzmann that he believed it should not be shown, lest it exculpate the criminal ("OU" 208).

16. According to one rabbinic text on death, "we do not engage ourselves with [the] funeral in any way [for those who kill themselves]. We do not tear the garments

and we do not bare the shoulder in mourning and we do not say eulogies" (qtd. in Jamison 14). Even today, the general Orthodox practice after suicide is to "do everything in honour of the surviving, . . . but . . . nothing in honour of the dead apart from burying them" (Jamison 14)

17. Gloria Young discusses the structure and imagery of Katzenelson's work ("PH" 552-53).

18. "Carrion comfort" is the title often given to one of Gerard Manley Hopkins's terrible sonnets in which the phrase appears; in the poem, he wrestles with his doubt about God and the fate of his soul.

19. Forché's "Twentieth-Century Poetry of Witness" describes the story (AF 9). "After the war was over, Radnóti's wife was among those who found and exhumed the grave in the village of Abda. The coroner's report for corpse #12 reads: 'A visiting card with the name Dr. Miklós Radnóti printed on it. An ID card stating the mother's name as Ilona Grosz. Father's name illegible. Born in Budapest, May 5, 1909. Cause of death: shot in the nape. In the back pocket of the trousers a small notebook was found soaked in the fluids of the body and blackened by wet earth. This was cleaned and dried in the sun.' " See also Ozsváth.

20. Having published their works at war's end, Sachs, Glatstein, and Celan are anthologized as first-generation poets of the Holocaust; however, Sachs and Glatstein, born in the last decade of the nineteenth century, gained prominence in the 1940s when they were themselves in their forties, whereas Celan was only twenty-seven when "Death Fugue" appeared in its 1947 Romanian version. Most people would associate American aesthetic rejoinders with a later period. For example, Anthony Hecht published his works in the 1960s and '70s, when Irena Klepfisz began composing hers. However, Hecht is only three years younger than Celan, and both men were born early enough to have fathered Klepfisz.

21. See Plank 143. As Mintz has conceded (201), "Christian associations are inescapable" in the most prominent poem composed in Hebrew about the Shoah, Uri Zvi Greenberg's Streets of the River (Rehovot Ha-nahar). Wiesel's comments almost seem to gloss Chagall's canvas: "A symbol of compassion and love to the Christian, the cross has become an instrument of torment and terror to be used against Jews" (qtd. in Horowitz 129).

22. Amishai-Maisels provides crucial readings not only of this painting's use of Christ's image but also of the centrality of Christ in later paintings by Chagall.

23. See also Amos Neufeld's "In the Heaven of Night" (BR 206-207).

24. As if meditating on precisely this catastrophic consequence during a moment of intense personal grief, Elizabeth Bishop—in a draft version of "One Art"—concludes with "He who loseth his life, etc.—but he who / loses his love—neever [sic], no never never never again—" (Millier 237).

25. See also Liss 86 and Marianne Hirsch's subsequent book on this subject (FF).

3. SUCKLED BY PANIC

1. John Felstiner, considering the extremity of the metaphor, sees black milk as "nullifying the nourishment vital to humankind," though it may also refer to a liquid actually given to camp inmates (PC 33).

2. A similar point is made by a character in Elie Wiesel's novel The Fifth Son, an American offspring of European refugees who exclaims, "Born after the war, I endure its effects. I suffer from an Event I did not even experience" (180).

3. In "To Eva," Osherow wonders about the dead, waiting for the resurrection promised by the Messiah: "Does the prophecy include the decomposed, / the grave-

less? Will they come alive as soap / And parchment and blankets or their old selves? / What will happen if the soap's been used, / The parchment printed on?" (*LANY* 50–51).

4. Other poems grieving over a lost relative include Lotte Kramer's "The Red Cross Telegram" (*HP* 18) and Olga Drucker's "The Brooch" (*BR* 212).

5. See Lore Segal's account of partings at the Kindertransport in *Other People's Houses.*

6. For a different approach to "Solitary Acts" as well as *Keeper of Accounts,* see Friedman 237–42.

7. For similar formulaic verse, see, for example, Melanie Kaye/Kantrowitz, "from *Kaddish,*" as well as Catherine de Vinck, "*Kaddish*" (*BR* 367–47, 348–51).

8. Elza's experience accords with those of the children discussed by Langer in "Damaged Childhood in Holocaust Fact and Fiction."

9. Levitt associates the salt water with an "ocean of tears" and Klepfisz's inability to "carry the weight" of the pain of standing in for all the murdered Jewish children (154, 156).

10. See this phrase in Rich's *Sources* (13) as well as her essay of this title.

11. Florence Weinberger's portrait "Survivor" (*BR* 193) and Mike Frenkel's "Quiet Desperation" (*BR* 191) dwell on some of these same matters.

12. See the section titled "I Am Your American Child" in *Ghosts of the Holocaust* for other poems on this perspective, as well as Hass, chap. 4.

13. On survivors as unpleasant, difficult, unlovable people, see Ruth Feldman's "Survivor" (*BR* 135) and Florence Weinberger's "He Wears Old Socks" (*GH* 91).

14. To be sure, Klepfisz acknowledges the power of her mother, who "learned survival / depends on complete distrust" (adding with admiration that "Even today she is still / fierce in her refusal to rely on others" [*FW* 174]), just as Barbara Goldberg admits about her father that she owes him her life: "paranoia's / useful in uncertain times" (*GH* 107).

15. I am disagreeing with the reading of this frame provided by Marianne Hirsch (*FF* 23). See chapter 8 on Anne Michaels's *Fugitive Pieces,* which also focuses on lives eclipsed by anguish over lost siblings.

16. Sandra Gilbert and I discuss literary women's relationship to the "mother tongue" in vol. 1 of *No Man's Land, The War of the Words,* chap. 5.

17. Ozick's Rosa eventually resembles the character in Harold Pinter's play *Ashes to Ashes,* a contemporary woman who is haunted by the memory of holding a baby wrapped in her shawl, a bundle she has to relinquish on a train station platform.

18. See John Felstiner's discussion of "Black Flakes" (*PC* 32).

19. As Yalom has pointed out, the shift from "The Shawl" to "Rosa" is "like moving from the sacred to the profane, from the sanctity of ritual to the banality of daily existence" (435).

20. See Gillian Rose on the word "Holocaust" as a way of thinking about the event as providential in its purpose (27).

21. Hellerstein says about her own translations of Yiddish poetry that they "are intended to bring you closer to a Yiddish poet's exile in her native language, but they inevitably remove the poems further from their source" and thus "perpetuate their exile in our mother tongue" ("IE" 83).

22. See Jacqueline Osherow's "The Yiddish Muses" (*LANY* 37–38) and "Ch'vil Schreibn a Poem auf Yiddish" (*DMP* 3–4), a poem (despite its title's claims) composed in English.

23. Forché's refrain comes from Elie Wiesel's cantata text *Ani Maamin,* a libretto that returns to the figures of Abraham and Isaac. "Ani maamin" (I believe) con-

cludes Wiesel's deeply ironic prayer, hopeless because, as one scholar of Holocaust literature puts it, "the death of the child . . . is the death of the soul" (Patterson 85).

24. I am disagreeing with an otherwise insightful essay by Longenbach (105).

4. ABOUT PICTURES OUT OF FOCUS

1. See Sekula, "OIPM" 11, but also the work of Cadava, Marianne Hirsch, Liss, Tagg, and Zelizer, as well as the other theorists of photography cited in this chapter.

2. The standard text is *Anamorphic Art* by Jurgis Baltrusaitis (1969; trans. 1977), but see Flieger's review of Baudrillard, Lyotard, and Žižek, all of whom rely on the importance of Lacanian anamorphosis or skewed perspective.

3. See Milton on other Jewish camera-bearing chroniclers such as Mendel Grossman and Abraham Pisarek.

4. Of course, Fishman anthologizes these poets without the Vishniac photographs they gloss. See also David Zucker's "Entrance to the Old Cracow Ghetto" (*BR* 29) and Shelley Ehrlich's "Vilna 1938" (*BR* 30). I am indebted to Kirtland Snyder for sending me his manuscript and giving me permission to quote from it. Snyder's "Kristallnacht. Berlin, 1938" and "Sara. Warsaw, 1939" sustain his focus on Vishniac's portraits of young girls.

5. Yala Korwin's "The Little Boy with His Hands Up" directly addresses this photographed boy: "You have seen Death already / on the ghetto streets, haven't you? / Do you recognize it in the emblems / of the SS-man facing you with his camera?" (*BR* 55).

6. Zelizer looks at the "then and now" use of Holocaust survivors in newspaper coverage (177, 187).

7. Wolin explains that eventually he "stayed away from meddling with [his subjects'] words other than choosing them out of their whole story. I also wanted to try to convey the European way they spoke rather than cleaning it up into contemporary English. In every case I sent them the text for their approval — in case they remembered things differently or needed to correct spellings, place names, dates, etc." All quotes attributed to Wolin come from private e-mail correspondence.

8. In *Sources*, too, Rich meditates on visual images: "we are gifted children at camp in the country / or orphaned children in kindergarten / . . . part of a family group / formally taken in 1936" (26).

9. One sees here what Marianne Hirsch calls a "shadow play" of people who did not survive as well as "the distance, the absence, the unbridgeable gap that . . . makes us who we are" (*FF* 267).

10. About Eleanor Antin's installation *Vilna Nights* (1993), Baigell explains, "There is nothing to contemplate other than that sense of loss, of relatives one might have had, of an existence one's family might have led in other, earlier times" (70).

11. The epigraph is attributed to the American poet and translator Clayton Eshleman.

12. That this question perplexed the perpetrators as well is documented by Hilberg, who explains "the sardine method," whereby "The first batch had to lie down on the bottom of the grave. They were killed by cross-fire from above. The next batch had to lie down on top of the corpses, heads facing the feet of the dead. After five or six layers, the grave was closed" (126).

13. See McWilliams on the importance of these sentences in the works brought together in the first U.S. exhibition of contemporary art devoted to the Holocaust, *Burnt Whole: Contemporary Artists Reflect on the Holocaust* (1994).

14. "People often ask me how it is possible to photograph such atrocities. I have to

work with a veil over my mind. In photographing the murder camps, the protective veil was so tightly drawn that I hardly knew what I had taken until I saw prints of my own photographs. It was as though I was seeing these horrors for the first time" (Bourke-White, *PM* 259).

15. For another instance of an artist using anamorphosis on Bourke-White's image, see Lorie Novack's photograph *Night and Fog,* which Marianne Hirsch discusses in "Surviving Images" (31–33).

16. "The Butterfly" by Pavel Friedman (in *I Never Saw Another Butterfly* 33) contains this now-famous line, which has since been used as the title for a book of children's art from Theresienstadt.

17. Altieri uses these concepts from Baudrillard in "Confession and Simulacra" (63–64), where he analyzes Feldman's poems about the sculptures of George Segal. In addition, see Eaglestone's analysis of Levinas's objections to artistic representation.

18. See Schweizer on this quarrel between Auden and Feldman.

19. With its programmatic use of the press, radio, film, and photo industries, some thinkers "understand Nazism as the most pervasive figure of media violence, the most virulent example of the political exploitation of the instruments of modern telecommunications" (Cadava xxiv). See also Gilroy 156–59.

20. I am indebted to a series of conversations with Mira Schor.

21. Nazi use of the camera "to control and intimidate German public opinion and also to harass, humiliate, and segregate the Jewish citizens of Germany" was evident in public displays of German women guilty of sexual relations with Jewish men and in posters announcing boycotts: "Jewish Business. Whoever Buys Here Will be Photographed" (Milton 46–47). See Liss's discussion of objections to Boltanski's morbidity, his too easy substitution of one history for another (39–41).

22. R. M. Cooper's short poem "Eli 1943" (*BR* 73), Esther Camerson's "Exposure" (*BR* 77), and several of Lyn Lifshin's poems elaborate on these same issues.

23. That Berg's volume constitutes a quasi-translation, quasi-collaboration with Anna Akhmatova illustrates yet another way in which authors can signal their distance from historical materials, although about the poem "Memory" he states: "that poem is mostly mine from beginning to end" (65).

24. See Weiner 64 as well as the discussion of the anti-Semitic propaganda in *The Black Book* (41–52).

25. In an essay unrelated to the Shoah, Schwenger deals with photographic images of corpses; however, his term "corpsing the image" seems apt for Gluska's portraits.

26. The quote comes from Boltanski, who explains "that I lay it on too thick" in order to "elicit emotion." Liss cites these words and argues that Boltanski wants "to implicate the ease with which the viewer gets trapped in a universalized quasi-ethereal and quasi-somber nostalgia" (49); but the phrase resonates better for me with respect to Gluska's overlaying of pigments.

27. With the term "triple dying" I am referring, of course, to Alvin Rosenfeld's book on the "double dying" of victims in the Holocaust.

28. Both Ruth Fainlight and Lynda Hull focus on the "unreality" of visual images of atrocity in, respectively, "Archive Film Material" (*HP* 109) and "Street of Crocodiles" (49–53).

29. "Say you're in the mood for a four-star horror show," Marguerite M. Strair sardonically proposes at the beginning of her poem "These Ultimate Survivors"; choose "the truly innovative atrocities of our day: / The Nazi Holocaust!" (*BL* 385). In addition, see "Cinema III" by Christopher Fahy (*BL* 425–26).

30. Consider, too, Arie A. Galles's *Fourteen Stations Suite,* a series of fourteen 47½" × 75" drawings (in charcoal and white conte crayon) based on aerial views of the

extermination camps taken by Luftwaffe and Allied reconnaissance (the last is Babi Yar): within each drawing, one-fourteenth of the Kaddish is invisibly embedded. When Jerome Rothenberg, who began his responses to the Shoah with a poem about Leni Riefenstahl's film *Triumph of the Will* (1935), composed "14 Stations," he based this poetic progress to Calvary on the Hebrew and Yiddish spellings of the camps' names (Galles 118; Parmet 218).

31. See, for example, Maxine Kumin's "The Amsterdam Poem" (*NF* 21–24), Marge Piercy's "The Housing Project at Dracy" (*TL* 236–37), and C. K. Williams's "After Auschwitz" (*R* 8–10).

5. DOCUMENTARY VERSE BEARS WITNESS

1. See also a similar incident involving Russian prisoners of war recounted by Hilberg (119).

2. "Ashes were still / in the room, / and in the far / corner, hanging / above the ovens, / a poem by Goethe, / in German, a poem / about the beauty of death by fire" (Hyett 95).

3. Of course, there can be no such thing as "pure" or "literal" documentation because, as many people have noted, even eyewitness testimonials have a shape that derives from literary structures. On the "utmost" charging of meaning in poetry, see Gioia 20.

4. I am indebted to Cavell's discussion of Henry David Thoreau—who says of an axe he borrowed, "I returned it sharper than I received it"—and of John Milton's justification of borrowing "bettered by the borrower" and thus not accounted plagiarism (*PP* 45).

5. On the translation of "men into beasts" in Holocaust literature, see Langer, *HLI* 166–204.

6. Alter disagrees with this assessment when he equates "the constant repetition of savagery and murder" with the poet's "masochism" (*DI* 132). For a more positive view, see McDaniels's poem "After Reading Reznikoff."

7. "No one wants to torture a germ before killing it. Rats may be massacred, but no one would force them to live through an ordeal of filth and emaciation before they die" (Maccoby 34).

8. Berel Lang explains that protraction, elaboration, gratuitousness, and jokes in the concentration camp setting testify to "an art of evil," "the role of the imagination" and "artistic consciousness of evil at work in the perpetrators of the Final Solution" (discussed in Rosenbaum 215).

9. "If you'd have been there to smell it, / you'd have known what happened" (41): the last line of Heifetz's Appalachian soldier-speaker in "The Liberator" makes the same point in different cadences. Her *Oral History and the Holocaust* also includes a sequence of poems spoken by survivors.

10. This phrase was used by Eichmann during the trial to record his initial shock at a "horrible sight. A ditch had been there [at Lwow], which was already filled in. And there was, gushing from the earth, a spring of blood like a fountain. Such a thing I had never seen before," and so he reported it to his superior (Arendt, *EJ* 89).

11. Levertov appended a note to this poem, indicating that according to the trial testimony the fruit was cherries, the boy was doing forced labor, and Eichmann killed him in a tool shed, not beneath a tree.

12. This emphasis on artificial order is why Bauman argues that "Modern genocide, like modern culture in general, is a gardener's job" (92). See also the reference to Eichmann's "art" in Primo Levi's poem "For Eichmann" (*TL* 444).

13. My thinking here has been shaped by Hartman's caution against "a deceptive

sense of totality" ("BD" 319), as well as by James Young's discussion of "a new generation of memory-artists [who] have made a critique of institutional memory fundamental to their work" (*AME* 10).

14. Needless to say, I am not arguing that women have never produced philosophically abstract verse or that men did not play an important role in the creation of confessional poetry. However, the personal, occasional voice has played a major role in the history of women's lyric production, while the prophetic role of the bard has had a long history in male-authored poetry. I also write that "gender *can* play a role" because it does not always.

15. On the defiling of holy books and places, see *The Black Book of Polish Jewry* (226–27) as well as the other *Black Books*. Although in the poem Williams credits *The Black Book*, another source may be *Scroll of Agony*, where Chaim Kaplan's December 16, 1939, entry describes an incident in Lodz. When, after complying with a Nazi order, a rabbi stopped spitting on a Torah scroll, the Nazi asked why and the rabbi said that his mouth was dry. "Then the son of the 'superior' race began to spit into the rabbi's open mouth, and the rabbi continued to spit on the Torah" (87).

16. For this point, I am indebted to Wayne Booth's lecture on religion at the University of Virginia, Charlottesville, on March 13, 1999.

17. Theweleit points out "the pleasure of object degradation" at work in fascism (*MB* 318).

18. On *Blutsbrüderschaft* in World War I literature, see Gilbert and Gubar, *Sexchanges* (*NML* 2:309–13). On a "hating homophobic recasting of the male homosocial spectrum," see Sedgwick, *BM* 216.

19. See Yanay's pertinent publication on the interconnections of love and hatred in the works cited list.

20. Williams's poem "Combat" is also about the dynamics of fascism within a psychosexual scenario (*SP* 93–99).

21. To Ed Hirsch, Williams describes a "malevolent, or indifferent" god (152–53). In an interview with Keller, Williams speaks of "God as what happens between our psyches" (172).

22. Marks relates Kant's definition of the sublime object (as one "whose representation determines the mind to think the unattainability of nature as a presentation of [reason's] ideas") to the biblical prophets' efforts to convey "nothing more than the fact of conveyance itself" through "negation and tautology" (61, 62).

6. THE DEAD SPEAK

1. See Trezise's analysis of Delbo, which appears in a meditation on Adorno and the unspeakable (58–62).

2. For representative critics who castigate Plath, see Howe 12 and Ezrahi, *BWA* 214. Recent defenses of Plath come from James Young (*WRH* 118, 133), Jacqueline Rose (207), and Parmet (73).

3. For background on prosopopoeia, see Wordsworth 49–62. Although Barbara Herrnstein Smith views all lyrical poems as fictional representations of personal utterances, the speakers of the poems under discussion articulate utterances in implausible, if not impossible speech acts.

4. The effort to read Plath's poems as statements about the Shoah also makes sense in light of her letters, which demonstrate the inextricable interplay between political, historical, and personal experiences (Strangeways 95).

5. On Plath's use of the arrow in fiction and verse, see Gilbert, "FWFM" 251.

6. See Culler's (146) and Johnson's (184–99) related points about apostrophe and animation.

7. Hellerstein analyzes Molodowky's poems ("IE" 67–68).

8. I am indebted here to conversations with Lisa Katz.

9. I am disagreeing with de Man's claim that "by making the dead speak, the symmetrical structure of the trope implies, by the same token, that the living are struck dumb, frozen in their own death" (*RR* 78). I also disagree with de Man's conclusion, that "Death is a displaced name for a linguistic predicament" (81), since, as Santner points out, this proposition "precludes the possibility of distinguishing one victim from other. Furthermore, the historical victim . . . is overshadowed here by an impersonal and apathetic 'dismemberment' at the violent hands of the signifier" (29). On "the discontinuity between the personal self and the voice that speaks in the poetry [of Verlaine] from the other bank of the river, beyond death," see de Man, *BI* 181.

10. Simic is questioning such thinkers as Frankl, whose *Man's Search for Meaning* posits the idea that meaning making furnishes a key to survival. The psychological process of "creating meaningful images" may be "at the heart" of what Lifton and Olson call "*symbolic immortality*" (75), but it furnishes little solace here.

11. Simic's poem addresses an issue described by Ezrahi: "Because human flesh has been metamorphosed into smoke," she has explained, "the temptation of the post-Holocaust imagination is to reground and literalize that which has become abstracted out of existence" (*BP* 145).

12. I am indebted to Parmet's printing of the author's translation of this passage (212).

13. The conclusion of the first section of *The Waste Land* alludes to Baudelaire's preface to *Fleurs du Mal*.

14. The critic who found the Sexton quote in a draft of a poem and brought it to the attention of Plath's readers was Cam.

15. On Berryman, see Flanzbaum, "IJ" 18–32. For an appreciation of "Daddy" and "Lady Lazarus" in terms of Plath's "agonistic mourning" (263), see Ramazani, *PM* 276–82, 285–88.

16. The psychoanalytic background of this discussion is grounded in Freud's *Mourning and Melancholia*.

17. Writing about the centrality of Jews in German culture, one young intellectual explained, "We Jews administer the spiritual possessions of a people that denies us the right and the capability of doing so" (qtd. in Friedlander, *NGJ* 78).

18. A footnote to this quotation in *German-Jewish History in Modern Times* explains that "In fact, five of the nine Nobel Prizes awarded to German natural scientists in the years of the Weimar Republic were given to Jews" (Leo Baeck Institute 34).

19. Chief of the Reich Association of Jews in Germany, Rabbi Leo Baeck explained: "[I] made it a principle to accept no appointments from the Nazis and to do nothing which might help them. But later, when the question arose whether Jewish orderlies should help pick up Jews for deportation, I took the position that it would be better for them to do it, because they could at least be more gentle and helpful than the Gestapo." In Theresienstadt, Baeck decided not to pass on the information he received about gassings because "living in the expectation of death by gassing would only be harder" (qtd. in Hilberg 304). Compliance was not the case only in Germany. Hilberg also examines "the role of the Jews in their own destruction" throughout Russia and the Ukraine, where the "conviction" ruled that "bad things came from Russia and good things from Germany" (123).

20. Many critics have interpreted this poem, but I am especially indebted to the insights of Tricia Lootens.

21. The quote comes from a blurb by Jonathan Kozal on the book jacket, but many other reviewers could be quoted in their praise of the authenticity of *Fragments*.

22. See Friedlander, who views the "frisson" of the Holocaust entertainment industry as a product of "the meeting of kitsch and death" (*RN* 25).

23. See the discussion of Plath's use of a ghostly iambic pentameter in this closing allusion to Coleridge in Gilbert and Gubar, *NML* 3:290.

24. The historians' debate over whether or not the Nazis actually "manufactured" soap out of human fat continues, but many people during and after the war believed that they did so. Perhaps the rumor during the war was related to the terrible smell around mass graves that brought to mind soap factories.

25. Because we live in an unreal present of endless image substitutions, Hartman writes — quoting Baudrillard — that we " 'want to prove we died between 1940 and 1945,' " a period associated with " 'real history' " (*LS* 45).

26. Recently the British revisionist David Irving has claimed, " 'there were never any gas chambers at Auschwitz' " (qtd. in Guttenplan B1, B11).

27. Vendler has analyzed the "formal consequences, for Graham's verse, of the insusceptibility of matter to dependable interpretation" (*GM* 110).

28. The phrase "chain of events" comes from a passage from Benjamin's description of the angel of history that Graham quotes (*M* 55). The creature x appears in one of several poems Graham titles "History" (*DUF* 145, 147).

7. "COULD YOU HAVE MADE AN ELEGY FOR EVERY ONE?"

1. The word "resuscitation" derives from Schenck (11), the word "transmogrification" from Jahan Ramazani, whose personal communications have shaped my thinking throughout this book.

2. Concurring with Ozick at a 1987 conference they both attended, Friedlander concluded that "the most difficult task we face" consists in the decision "precisely *not* to look for redemption in these events" ("RTD" 289).

3. In *Poetry of Mourning*, Ramazani points out that from Thomas Hardy's to Wilfred Owen's verse, poetry has mocked the idea of conventional recompense for the dead in anti-elegiac modes. While I agree with him, I think that the tradition I am tracing escalated the pessimism of the genre after the Second World War and thus altered its conventions.

4. See Wordsworth's discussion of "sympathy[, which] ought to be quickened" by "particular thoughts, actions, images — circumstances of age, occupation, manner of life, prosperity which the deceased had known, or adversity to which he had been subject" (57), all of which are unknown by the authors of Holocaust lamentations.

5. Nahmanides, the thirteenth-century author of *Torat Ha'Adam* (*The Law of Man*), is quoted by Wieseltier (8), whose insights on the history and significance of the kaddish inform the final section of this chapter.

6. See also Hill's "Two Formal Elegies" and "Ovid in the Third Reich" (*CP* 30–31, 61).

7. To Ezrahi, the poem begins "almost jocularly" with "images of mass inebriation ('Here men were drunk'), but the reversal lies in the radical use of 'drunk' not as an adjective but as a passive verb" (*BWA* 184).

8. Dannie Abse's "No More Mozart" (*BL 366*), Peter Porter's "May 1945" (*HP* 171), and Barry Ivker's "Art and Politics" (*BL* 427) link music to genocide.

9. See Alexander and Margarete Mitscherlich's groundbreaking *The Inability to Mourn* on this postwar phenomenon of memory repression in Germany.

10. A comparable point is made in the ghetto dramatization of *Macbeth* in Leslie Epstein's novel *King of the Jews* (245–68).

11. See David Bleich in Barron and Selinger 186.

12. Ostriker discusses the composition of this poem in Barron and Selinger 117–23.

13. "Who killed Cock Robin? / I, said the Sparrow, / With my bow and arrow, / I

killed Cock Robin. // Who saw him die? / I, said the Fly" is how the nursery rhyme begins (Opie and Opie 130). Each animal answers a query about the death and the funeral and the mourning that follows with the phrase "I."

14. I am referring to the opening of *The Bluest Eye,* where Morrison says about her plot (a story of violence against the innocent), "Since *why* is difficult to handle, one must take refuge in *how*" ([6]).

15. In addition, see Anne Sexton's "After Auschwitz" (*TL* 308–309) and Replansky's "Ceremony" (39).

16. To the footnote on this subject in my discussion of the conclusion of Plath's "Lady Lazarus" (chapter 6, n. 24), I add here the macabre fact that the term *Judenseife* (Jewish soap) was apparently used in jokes among German soldiers; the instability of our knowledge about this phenomenon can play a part in our discussions of Stern's text. According to Hilberg, "In Lublin the belief was strong that the Jewish 'resettlers' had been killed and that the fat from their corpses had been used in the manufacture of soap. Now pedestrians in Lublin were saying that it was the turn of the Poles to be used, just like the Jews, for soap production" (215). Hilberg further explains, "To this day the origin of the soap-making rumor has not been traced, but one clue is probably the postwar testimony of the SS investigator Dr. Konrad Morgen," who claimed that Brigadeführer Dirlewanger "made so-called scientific experiments" on girls whose "corpses were cut into small pieces, mixed with horsemeat, and boiled into soap" (243).

17. On anaphora, see Alter, *ABP* 64.

18. On the verse composed by Nelly Sachs and Rose Ausländer, which questions faith in the divine paternity of God, see Bower 43–51, 63–72.

19. On the quarrel with God in Sephardic poetry of the Holocaust, see Levy 31–38.

20. I stress the absence of politics in this tradition, which makes it quite distinct from some Hebrew verse by, for instance, Uri Zvi Greenberg (*Streets of the River,* 1951) and Abba Kovner ("The Key Sank," 1950, 1965), that counterpoints the destruction of the European exile with the security of a separate Jewish state.

21. On the ways in which Zion's expression of suffering has been eclipsed by scholars who emphasize the "suffering man" of chapter 3, see Linafelt 5–13.

22. Hellerstein discusses how "the disintegration or unravelling of written Jewish languages became a figurative enactment of the destruction of the Jewish people" in a number of Molodowsky's poems ("I" 44).

23. This is a traditional couplet said after the conclusion of a kaddish.

24. The film *Korczak* (1990), directed by Andrzej Wajda, deals with the orphanage as well.

8. POETRY AND SURVIVAL

1. Nussbaum uses the phrase "empathetic identification" to discuss the ways in which "the temporary act of identification" associated with pity means "one is always aware of one's own *separateness* from the sufferer — it is for *another,* and not oneself, that one feels. . . . If one really had the experience of feeling the pain in one's own body, then one would precisely have failed to comprehend the pain of another *as other*" ("C" 35). For a more sustained interpretation of this novel in the context of the incursion of feminism into Holocaust studies, see my essay "Empathic Identification." For three quite different but useful readings of the novel, see Bentley; Cook; and Hillger.

2. Drawing on LaCapra, Marianne Hirsch links "postmemory" to the act "of *adopting* the traumatic experiences — and thus also the memories — of others"

("PM" 9; emphasis mine). Landsberg analyzes the ways in which "empathy recognizes the alterity of identification" in her analysis of what she calls the "prosthetic memories" that museums can generate (82). A concern with empathy places Michaels in a line of women novelists Gardiner studies because "empathy is a characteristic that is more 'marked' for women than for men in our culture" (166).

3. Silverman discusses what she calls the "ideopathic identification of absorbing the other" and the "heteropathic" identification that exteriorizes the other; the former is sadistic, the latter masochistic (263–65).

4. When in his 1759 analysis of "moral sentiments" Adam Smith emphasized how the imagination — by creating an image of the person in pain — allows us to "conceive ourselves enduring all the same torments," which "we have thus *adopted*" (9; emphasis mine), he established the basis for Michaels's paradigm. On the class and gender limits of Smith's staging of moral sentiment, see Ellison 10.

5. See Laub and Auerhahn on "failed empathy" (165).

6. On feminists' response to fascism, see the chapter on the Second World War in Gilbert and Gubar, *Letters from the Front* (*NML*, vol. 2), and Martin. But we should keep in mind, as Gilroy points out, that women actively contributed to the genocide of Tutsi and the killing of Hutu opponents in Rwanda in 1994.

7. If we consider the Lacanian Name of the Father in the historical context of the Shoah, it becomes clear that the functions Brenkman clusters around it, which I have quoted, have nothing to do with Jewish men in the Third Reich, where the bifurcation of symbolic fatherhood in the Fatherland and the real-life Jewish father's powerlessness was repeatedly staged.

8. Ringelheim mentions that the "final solution" was "one of the first such events in history that did not treat the female population primarily as spoils of war" and that part of the difficulty of thinking about gender and genocide revolves around the fact that "Jewish men could not protect women and children from the Nazis" ("SGH" 345).

9. To be sure, there are many fictional and eyewitness accounts about brothels frequented by both guards and prisoners in the camps and about prisoners who struggled to maintain love relationships.

10. See both Daniel Boyarin and Kaja Silverman on the baffling sexual politics ushered in by what Boyarin has called an ethos of "unheroic conduct," what Silverman has termed "male subjectivity at the margins." On the history of "tenderhearted manhood" (12) — male authors' investment in "weeping melancholy, suicide, self-pity, weakness, victimization, and sympathy" (19) — in seventeenth- and eighteenth-century portrayals, see Ellison. On the reasons why female values (of nonviolence, receptivity, malleability) historically were instilled in Jewish men to proscribe violence and for an argument that at times this ironically led to their need to assert more power over women within the Jewish community, see Cantor 9, 84, 91.

11. Like Michaels, Lerner believes that "When you lose your language, you lose the sound, the rhythm, the forms of your unconscious" (39); however, precisely such a loss in the second language paradoxically makes it suitable to conveying traumatic feelings, according to Michaels.

12. What Caruth writes about Freud's and Lacan's analysis of the dream of a father who has lost his child holds true for Jacob. The "dead child, the child in its irreducible inaccessibility and otherness . . . says to the [survivor]: *wake up, leave me, survive; survive to tell the story of my burning*" (*UE* 105). But whereas Caruth believes that it is psychoanalysis which transforms the traumatic "failure to have seen in time" into "the imperative of a speaking [about the loss] that awakens others" (108), for Michaels that imperative springs from the imaginative faculty.

13. I am indebted to a series of conversations with Linda Charnes, whose work on Shakespeare illuminates this concept in very different political and social contexts.

14. On the tenacity of the association of women with nature, see Ortner's now classic essay, "Is Female to Male as Nature Is to Culture?" Interesting in this regard is Primo Levi's championing of "matter" over "Man" (*PT* "Iron").

15. Following Freud, feminist psychoanalytic thinkers from Juliet Mitchell and Nancy Chodorow to Elizabeth Grosz have noted that normative male development begins with the boy's need to distinguish himself from the mother by positing her lack or castration as well as his fundamental difference from her. Butler believes "a man becomes heterosexual by repudiating the feminine" and that repudiation springs from "an identification which his heterosexual career seeks to deny": "he wants the woman he would never be"; "She is his repudiated identification" ("MG" 137). I am indebted in my thinking about mourning to Butler's recent work, presented in the lecture "Violence, Memory, Politics" at the CUNY Graduate Center (December 7, 2001).

16. The sibling-muse, Froma Zeitlin has pointed out to me, also plays a major role in Henri Raczymow's *Writing the Book of Esther* (1986), Maurice Gee's *Live Bodies* (1998), and Magda Denes's *Castles Burning* (1997).

17. "The Boy" also illuminates one of Primo Levi's painful recollections: years before the genocide, Levi knew Jewish friends who suffered from Aryan schoolmates jeering "that circumcision was nothing but castration, and we, at least at an unconscious level, tended to believe it" (*SA* 179). Like Sedgwick (*EC* 75–85) and Koestenbaum, Hacker ponders the interstices of differently structured forms of oppression.

18. The revision in "The Boy" of "He writes a line. He crosses out a line" into the final "He writes down something that he crosses out" considers the sexual or racial lines drawn that need to be written and crossed out precisely because of her character's double-crossed life. For Hacker, then, the fluidity of Jewish identity—related to descent as well as assent—serves as a paradigm for making more permeable other identity categories, while the dynamics of anti-Semitism illuminate the mechanisms of other hate crimes. According to Sollors, "Descent relations are those defined by anthropologists as relations of 'substance' (by blood or nature); consent relations describe those of 'law' or 'marriage.' Descent language stressed our positions as heirs, our hereditary qualities, liabilities, and entitlements; consent language stresses our abilities as mature free agents and 'architects of our fates' to choose our spouses, our destinies, and our political systems" (6).

19. In literature about the First World War, the dead brother often functions as a masculine counterpart of women writers' sense of identity (Woollacott).

20. Williams's "A Day for Anne Frank" concludes with the injunction "Come with me Anne" (*NSP* 7).

21. Needless to say, this prominence is not found in many other traditions—for instance, that of the Jewish American novel.

22. On women's unique sense of "alliance and continuity with the dead" as well as their deployment of the elegy, see Zeiger 64.

23. Pinch, in approaching the "cultural association between women and emotion," summarizes feminist debates on this nexus: "Has the association between women and emotion led to a devaluation of emotion? Do women's interests suffer or gain from their association with emotion?" (12).

24. According to Cook, "perhaps the most disappointing aspect" of the novel "is Michaels' consistent tendency to idealize the women her male characters love" (17–18). Writing about war literature in general, Theweleit analyzes an Orpheus myth that places a dead woman in a role as muse that brings into being male couples who replace her procreativity with their own higher creativity: see his "Politics of Orpheus," as well as the uses to which it is put by Marianne Hirsch and Leo Spitzer.

25. See Jonathan Boyarin's discussion of "the triumphalism of empathic participant observation or empathetic historicism" (*SP* 89).

26. I am indebted here to a series of conversations with the medieval historian Dyan Elliott.

27. This sentence derives from a response to my work by the classicist Gonda Van Steen.

28. Although she does not write about Chagall, Heschel describes this Jesus "at the boundary of Judaism and Christianity" (189–90).

29. See Isaiah 49:1, 15, and 66:13, as well as Bynum 110–35.

30. On feminists' approach to the problem of Christian anti-Judaism and on the negative effects of the Christian doctrines of atonement and redemption associated with the cross, see Fiorenza 67, 98–107.

31. Although he proposes "that each Jew should tell the story of the genocide as though he or she had passed through it," Lang adds, "I do not feel able to argue with the same conviction for a gesture of identification by those who look back now on the Nazi genocide and who are not Jews" (*AING* xiv). On Lang, see Horowitz 23.

32. Ezrahi and James Young have been most pointed about the ways in which diaries, memoirs, oral testimonies, and histories of the Holocaust cannot escape literary tropes of representation.

33. My terms here are indebted to a work in progress, titled "Identity Groups in Democracy," by Amy Gutmann, though my use of them should not be taken to represent her views (since she does not discuss the issue I am considering).

34. See also Shapiro's poem "The Basement" about a survivor (*MC* 65–68).

WORKS CITED

Abse, Dannie. *Remembrances of Crimes Past.* London: Century Hutchinson, 1990.

Adler, Rachel. "*Pour Out Your Heart like Water:* Toward a Jewish Feminist Theology of the Holocaust." In *Humanity at the Limit: The Impact of the Holocaust Experience on Jews and Christians,* ed. Michael A. Signer, 161–71. Bloomington: Indiana University Press, 2000.

Adorno, Theodor W. "Commitment." In *The Essential Frankfurt School Reader,* ed. Andrew Arato and Eike Gebhardt, 300–311. New York: Urizen Books, 1978.

———. "Cultural Criticism and Society." In *Prisms,* trans. Samuel and Shierry Weber, 17–34. Cambridge, Mass.: MIT Press, 1981.

———. "Meditations on Metaphysics." In *Negative Dialectics,* trans. E. B. Ashton, 361–65. New York: Continuum, 1973.

———. "On Lyric Poetry and Society." In vol. 1 of *Notes to Literature,* ed. Rolf Tiedemann, trans. Shierry Weber Nicholsen, 37–54. New York: Columbia University Press, 1991.

Alkalay-Gut, Karen. *In My Skin.* Tel Aviv: "Sivan" Israel Federation of Writers' Union Publishers, 2000.

Alter, Robert. *The Art of Biblical Poetry.* New York: Basic Books, 1985.

———. *Defenses of the Imagination: Jewish Writers and Modern Historical Crisis.* Philadelphia: Jewish Publications Society of America, 5738/1977.

Altieri, Charles. "Confession and Simulacra in the Poetry of Irving Feldman." In *The Poetry of Irving Feldman,* ed. Harold Schweizer, 62–100. Lewisburg, Pa.: Bucknell University Press; London: Associated University Presses, 1992.

———. "What Differences Can Contemporary Poetry Make in Our Moral Thinking?" In *Postmodernisms Now: Essays on Contemporaneity in the Arts,* 109–35. University Park: Pennsylvania State University Press, 1998.

Alvarez, A. *Beyond All This Fiddle: Essays, 1955–1967.* New York: Random House, 1968.

Améry, Jean. *At the Mind's Limits: Contemplations by a Survivor on Auschwitz and Its Realities.* Trans. Sidney Rosenfeld and Stella P. Rosenfeld. Bloomington: Indiana University Press, 1980.

———. *On Suicide: A Discourse on Voluntary Death.* Trans. John D. Barlow. Bloomington: Indiana University Press, 1999.

Amishai-Maisels, Ziva. "Chagall's *White Crucifixion.*" *Museum Studies* 17, no. 2 (1991): 139–53.

———. *Depictions and Interpretation: The Influence of the Holocaust on the Visual Arts.* Oxford: Pergamon Press, 1993.

———. "The Jewish Jesus." *Journal of Jewish Art* 9 (1982): 83–104.

Apenszlak, Jacob, ed. *The Black Book of Polish Jewry: An Account of the Martyrdom of Polish Jewry under the Nazi Occupation.* Co-edited by Jacob Kenner, Dr. Isaac Lewsin, and Dr. Moses Polakiewicz. 1943. Reprint, New York: Howard Fertig, 1982.

Appelfeld, Aharon. "After the Holocaust." In *Writing and the Holocaust,* ed. Berel Lang, 83–92. New York: Holmes and Meier, 1988.

Arendt, Hannah. *Eichmann in Jerusalem: A Report on the Banality of Evil.* New York: Viking, 1963.

———. Introduction to *Illuminations,* by Walter Benjamin, 1–58. New York: Schocken, 1969.

———. *The Jew as Pariah: Jewish Identity and Politics in the Modern Age.* Ed. Ron H. Feldman. New York: Grove, 1978.

———. *The Origins of Totalitarianism.* [2nd enlarged ed.] New York: Meridien Books, 1958.

Attie, Shimon. *The Writing on the Wall: Projections in Berlin's Jewish Quarter.* With essays by Michael André Bernstein and Erwin Leiser. Heidelberg: Edition Braus, 1994.

Attridge, Derek. "Poetry Unbound: Observations on Free Verse." Warton Lecture on English Poetry, 13 January 1988. *Proceedings of the British Academy* 73 (1987): 353–74.

Auden, W. H. *Selected Poems.* Ed. Edward Mendelson. New York: Vintage, 1979.

———. "Shorts II." In *Epistle to a Godson,* 47–50. London: Faber and Faber, 1972.

———. "Two Songs for Heidi Anderson" [often known as "Stop All the Clocks"]. In *Selected Poetry,* ed. by the author, 30–32. New York: Modern Library, 1970.

Avisar, Ilan. *Screening the Holocaust: Cinema's Images of the Unimaginable.* Bloomington: Indiana University Press, 1988.

Baechler, Jean. *Suicides.* Trans. Barry Cooper. New York: Basic Books, 1975.

Baigell, Matthew. *Jewish-American Artists and the Holocaust.* New Brunswick, N.J.: Rutgers University Press, 1997.

Baldwin, James. *The Price of the Ticket: Collected Nonfiction, 1948–1985.* New York: St. Martin's, 1985.

Barron, Jonathan N., and Eric Murphy Selinger, eds. *Jewish American Poetry: Poems, Commentary, and Reflections.* Hanover, N.H.: University Press of New England, 2000.

Barrows, Anita. *A Record.* West Chester, Pa.: Riverstone, 1998.

Barthes, Roland. *Camera Lucida: Reflections on Photography.* Trans. Richard Howard. New York: Hill and Wang, 1981.

Bauer, Yehuda. *Rethinking the Holocaust.* New Haven: Yale University Press, 2001.

Bauman, Zygmunt. *Modernity and the Holocaust.* Ithaca: Cornell University Press, 1989.

Beauvoir, Simone de. *The Second Sex.* Trans. H. M. Parshley. New York: Knopf, 1953.

Benjamin, Walter. *Illuminations.* Ed. Hannah Arendt. Trans. Harry Zohn. New York: Schocken, 1977.

———. "The Metaphysics of Youth." Trans. Rodney Livingstone. In *Selected Writings,* ed. Marcus Bullock and Michael W. Jennings, vol. 1, *1913–1926,* 6–15. Cambridge, Mass.: Harvard University Press, 1996.

Bentley, D. M. R. "Anne Michaels' *Fugitive Pieces.*" *Canadian Poetry* 41 (1997): 5–20.

Berg, Stephen. *With Akhmatova at the Black Gates.* Urbana: University of Illinois Press, 1981.

Berger, John, and Jean Mohr, with Nicolas Philibert. *Another Way of Telling.* 1982. Reprint, New York: Vintage, 1995.

Bernstein, Charles. *Poetics*. Cambridge, Mass.: Harvard University Press, 1992.

Bernstein, Michael André. "Shimon Attie: Images as Memory — Memory of Images." In *The Writing on the Wall: Projections in Berlin's Jewish Quarter*, by Shimon Attie, 6–8. Heidelberg: Edition Braus, 1994.

Berryman, John. "From *The Black Book*." In *Collected Poems, 1937–1971*, 154–56. New York: Farrar, Straus, Giroux, 1989.

Bettelheim, Bruno. *The Informed Heart: Autonomy in a Mass Age*. Glencoe, Ill.: Free Press, 1960.

Bishop, Elizabeth. *The Complete Poems, 1927–1979*. New York: Farrar, Straus, Giroux, 1983.

The Black Book: The Nazi Crime against the Jewish People. By the World Jewish Congress. New York: Duell, Sloan, and Pearce, 1946.

Blanchot, Maurice. *The Infinite Conversation*. Trans. Susan Hanson. Minneapolis: University of Minnesota Press, 1993.

———. *Vicious Circles: Two Fictions and "After the Fact."* Trans. Paul Auster. New York: Station Hill Press, 1985.

———. *The Writing of the Disaster*. Trans. Ann Smock. Lincoln: University of Nebraska Press, 1995.

Bloom, Harold. "The Sorrows of American-Jewish Poetry." In *Figures of Capable Imagination*, 247–62. New York: Seabury Press, 1976.

Booth, Wayne. "Common Grounds." Lecture, University of Virginia, Charlottesville, March 12, 1999.

Borenstein, Emily. *Night of the Broken Glass*. Maxon, Tex.: Timberline Press, 1981.

Borowski, Tadeusz. *This Way for the Gas, Ladies and Gentlemen*. Trans. Barbara Vedder. New York: Penguin, 1976.

Bourke-White, Margaret. *"Dear Fatherland, Rest Quietly": A Report on the Collapse of Hitler's "Thousand Years."* New York: Simon and Schuster, 1946.

———. *Portrait of Myself*. New York: Simon and Schuster, 1963.

Bower, Kathrin M. *Ethics and Remembrance in the Poetry of Nelly Sachs and Rose Ausländer*. Rochester, N.Y.: Camden House, 2000.

Boyarin, Daniel. *Unheroic Conduct: The Rise of Heterosexuality and the Invention of the Jewish Man*. Berkeley: University of California Press, 1997.

Boyarin, Jonathan. *Storm from Paradise: The Politics of Jewish Memory*. Minneapolis: University of Minnesota Press, 1992.

———. *Thinking in Jewish*. Chicago: University of Chicago Press, 1996.

Brenkman, John. *Straight Male Modern: A Cultural Critique of Psychoanalysis*. New York: Routledge, 1993.

Brinkley, Robert, and Steven Youra. "Tracing *Shoah*." *PMLA* 111, no. 1 (1996): 108–27.

Britzolakis, Christina. *Sylvia Plath and the Theatre of Mourning*. Oxford: Clarendon Press, 1999.

Brodersen, Momme. *Walter Benjamin: A Biography*. Trans. Malcoln R. Green and Ingrida Ligers. Ed. Martina Dervis. London: Verso, 1996.

Brodsky, Joseph. *On Grief and Reason: Essays*. New York: Farrar, Straus, and Giroux, 1995.

Butler, Judith. "Melancholy Gender / Refused Identification." In *The Psychic Life of Power: Theories in Subjection*, 132–50. Stanford: Stanford University Press, 1997.

———. "Violence, Memory, Politics." Lecture, CUNY Graduate Center, New York, December 7, 2001.

Bynum, Carolyn Walker. *Jesus as Mother: Studies in the Spirituality of the High Middle Ages*. Berkeley: University of California Press, 1982.

Cadava, Eduardo. *Words of Light: Theses on the Photography of History*. Princeton: Princeton University Press, 1997.

Cam, Heather. "'Daddy': Sylvia Plath's Debt to Anne Sexton." In *Sexton: Selected Criticism*, ed. Diana Hume George, 223–26. Urbana: University of Illinois Press, 1988.

Cameron, Sharon. *Lyric Time: Dickinson and the Limits of Genre*. Baltimore: Johns Hopkins University Press, 1979.

Cantor, Aviva. *Jewish Women/Jewish Men: The Legacy of Patriarchy in Jewish Life*. San Francisco: HarperCollins, 1995.

Caruth, Cathy. Introduction to "Recapturing the Past." In *Trauma: Explorations in Memory*, ed. Cathy Caruth, 151–57. Baltimore: Johns Hopkins University Press, 1995.

———. *Unclaimed Experience: Trauma, Narrative, and History*. Baltimore: Johns Hopkins University Press, 1996.

Castle, Luanne. "Mourning the Six Million: The Holocaust Elegy in North American Literature." *Studies in American Jewish Literature* 7, no. 1 (1992): 96–107.

Cavell, Stanley. *A Pitch of Philosophy: Autobiographical Exercises*. Cambridge, Mass.: Harvard University Press, 1994.

———. *The World Viewed: Reflections on the Ontology of Film*. Cambridge, Mass.: Harvard University Press, 1979.

Celan, Paul. *Speech-Grille and Selected Poems*. Trans. Joachim Neugroschel. New York: E. P. Dutton, 1971.

Chesterton, G. K. *Orthodoxy*. 1908. Reprint, New York: Dodd, Mead, 1954.

Clendinnen, Inga. *Reading the Holocaust*. Cambridge: Cambridge University Press, 1999.

Cohen, Arthur A. *The Tremendum: A Theological Interpretation of the Holocaust*. New York: Crossroad, 1981.

Cohn-Sherbok, Dan. *The Crucified Jew: Twenty Centuries of Christian Anti-Semitism*. Grand Rapids, Mich.: William B. Eerdmans, 1997.

Coleridge, Samuel Taylor. *Poetical Works*. Ed. Ernest Hartley Coleridge. 1912. Reprint, London: Oxford University Press, 1969.

Cook, Méira. "At the Membrane of Language and Silence: Metaphor and Memory in *Fugitive Pieces*." *Canadian Literature*, no. 154 (spring 2000): 12–33.

Cooley, Martha. *The Archivist*. Boston: Little, Brown, 1998.

Culler, Jonathan. *The Pursuit of Signs: Semiotics, Literature, Deconstruction*. Ithaca: Cornell University Press, 1981.

Delbo, Charlotte. *Auschwitz and After*. Trans. Rosette C. Lamont. New Haven: Yale University Press, 1995.

Deleuze, Gilles, and Félix Guattari. *Kafka: Toward a Minor Literature*. Trans. Dana Polan. Minneapolis: University of Minnesota Press, 1986.

DeLillo, Don. *White Noise*. 1985. Reprint, New York: Penguin, 1986.

de Man, Paul. *Blindness and Insight: Essays in the Rhetoric of Contemporary Criticism*. 2nd ed. Minneapolis: University of Minnesota Press, 1983.

———. *The Rhetoric of Romanticism*. New York: Columbia University Press, 1984.

Denes, Magda. *Castles Burning: A Child's Life in War*. New York: Simon and Schuster, 1997.

Des Pres, Terrence. *Praises and Dispraises: Poetry and Politics, the Twentieth Century*. New York: Viking, 1988.

———. *The Survivor: An Anatomy of Life in the Death Camps*. New York: Oxford University Press, 1976.

———. *Writing into the World: Essays, 1973–1987*. Intro. by Paul Mariani. Foreword by Elie Wiesel. New York: Viking, 1991.

Dickinson, Emily. *The Complete Poems.* Ed. Thomas H. Johnson. Boston: Little, Brown, 1980.

Donat, Alexander. "Surviving Slave Labor at Maidanek." In *The Holocaust: Problems and Perspectives of Interpretation,* ed. Donald L. Niewyk, 83–105. Boston: Houghton Mifflin, 1997.

Eaglestone, Robert. "From Behind the Bars of Quotation Marks: Emmanuel Levinas's (Non)-Representation of the Holocaust." In *The Holocaust and the Text: Speaking the Unspeakable,* ed. Andrew Leak and George Paizis, 97–108. New York: St. Martin's, 2000.

Ehrenburg, Ilya, and Vasily Grossman, eds. *The Black Book: The Ruthless Murder of Jews by German-Fascist Invaders throughout the Temporarily-Occupied Regions of the Soviet Union and in the Death Camps of Poland during the War of 1941–45.* Trans. John Glad and James S. Levine. New York: Holocaust Publications, distributed by Schocken, 1981.

Eliot, T. S. *Collected Poems, 1909–1962.* New York: Harcourt, Brace, and World, 1963.

Ellison, Julie. *Cato's Tears and the Making of Anglo-American Emotion.* Chicago: University of Chicago Press, 1999.

Epstein, Helen. *Children of the Holocaust: Conversations with Sons and Daughters of Survivors.* New York: Putnam, 1979.

Epstein, Leslie. *King of the Jews.* New York: W. W. Norton, 1993.

Ezorsky, Gertrude. "Hannah Arendt's View of Totalitarianism and the Holocaust." *Philosophic Forum* 16, nos. 1–2 (fall–winter 1984–85): 63–81.

Ezrahi, Sidra DeKoven. *Booking Passage: Exile and Homecoming in the Modern Jewish Imagination.* Berkeley: University of California Press, 2000.

———. *By Words Alone: The Holocaust in Literature.* Chicago: University of Chicago Press, 1980.

———. "Seeking the Meridian: The Reconstitution of Space and Audience in the Poetry of Paul Celan and Dan Pagis." In *Religion and the Authority of the Past,* ed. Tobin Siebers, 253–84. Ann Arbor: University of Michigan Press, 1993.

Fackenheim, Emil L. *The Jewish Bible after the Holocaust.* Bloomington: Indiana University Press, 1990.

Feldman, Irving. *All of Us Here.* New York: Penguin, 1986.

———. *New and Selected Poems.* New York: Viking, 1979.

———. "Outrage Is Anointed by Levity, or Two Laureates A-Lunching." In *The Life and Letters,* 48–50. Chicago: University of Chicago Press, 1994.

———. *Teach Me, Dear Sister and Other Poems.* New York: Viking, 1983.

Felman, Shoshana. "Benjamin's Silence." *Critical Inquiry* 25, no. 2 (1999): 201–34.

———. "Theaters of Justice: Arendt in Jerusalem, the Eichmann Trial, and the Redefinition of Legal Meaning in the Wake of the Holocaust" *Critical Inquiry* 27, no. 2 (2001): 201–38.

Felman, Shoshana, and Dori Laub, M.D. *Testimony: Crises of Witnessing in Literature, Psychoanalysis, and History.* New York: Routledge, 1992.

Felstiner, John. *Paul Celan: Poet, Survivor, Jew.* New Haven: Yale University Press, 1995.

———. "Paul Celan: The Strain of Jewishness." *Commentary,* April 1985, pp. 44–55.

———. "Speaking Back to Scripture: The Biblical Strain in Holocaust Poetry." In *Humanity at the Limit: The Impact of the Holocaust Experience on Jews and Christians,* ed. Michael A. Singer, 391–99. Bloomington: Indiana University Press, 2001.

———. "Translating Paul Celan's 'Todesfuge': Rhythm and Repetition as Metaphor." In *Probing the Limits of Representation: Nazism and the "Final Solution,"* ed. Saul Friedlander, 240–58. Cambridge, Mass.: Harvard University Press, 1992.

Felstiner, Mary Lowenthal. *To Paint Her Life: Charlotte Salomon in the Nazi Era.* New York: HarperCollins, 1994.

Fink, Ida. *A Scrap of Time and Other Stories.* Trans. Madeline Levine and Francine Prose. Evanston, Ill.: Northwestern University Press, 1998.

Fiorenza, Elisabeth Schussler. *Jesus: Mariam's Child, Sophia's Prophet.* New York: Continuum, 1994.

Fishman, Charles, ed. *Blood to Remember: American Poets on the Holocaust.* Lubbock: Texas Tech University Press, 1991.

Flack, Audrey. *Audrey Flack on Painting.* Intro. by Lawrence Alloway. New York: Harry N. Abrams, 1981.

Flanzbaum, Hilene. " 'But Wasn't It Terrific?' A Defense of Liking *Life Is Beautiful.*" *Yale Journal of Criticism* 14, no. 1 (2001): 273–86.

———. "The Imaginary Jew and the American Poet." In *The Americanization of the Holocaust,* ed. Hilene Flanzbaum, 18–32. Baltimore: Johns Hopkins University Press, 1999.

Flieger, Jerry Aline. "The Listening Eye: Postmodernism, Paranoia, and the Hypervisible." *Diacritics* 26, no. 1 (1992): 90–107.

Florsheim, Steward J., ed. *Ghosts of the Holocaust: An Anthology of Poetry by the Second Generation.* Detroit: Wayne State University Press, 1989.

Forché, Carolyn. *Against Forgetting: Twentieth-Century Poetry of Witness.* New York: W. W. Norton, 1993.

———. *The Angel of History.* New York: HarperPerennial, 1994.

Frankl, Viktor E. *Man's Search for Meaning: An Introduction to Logotherapy.* Trans. Ilse Lasch. Boston: Beacon, 1962.

Fresco, Nadine. "Remembering the Unknown." *International Review of Psychoanalysis* 11 (1984): 417–27.

Freud, Sigmund. *Mourning and Melancholia* (1914–1916). In *The Standard Edition of the Complete Psychological Works of Sigmund Freud,* ed. James Strachey, 14:243–58. London: Hogarth Press, 1957.

Friedlander, Saul. "The 'Final Solution': On the Unease in Historical Interpretation." In *Lessons and Legacies: The Meaning of the Holocaust in a Changing World,* ed. Peter Hayes, 23–35. Evanston, Ill.: Northwestern University Press, 1991.

———. Introduction to *Probing the Limits of Representation: Nazism and the "Final Solution,"* ed. Saul Friedlander, 1–21. Cambridge, Mass.: Harvard University Press, 1992.

———. *Memory, History, and the Extermination of the Jews of Europe.* Bloomington: Indiana University Press, 1993.

———. *Nazi Germany and the Jews.* Vol. 1 of *The Persecutions, 1933–1939.* New York: HarperCollins, 1997.

———. *Reflections of Nazism: An Essay on Kitsch and Death.* Trans. Thomas Weyr. Bloomington: Indiana University Press, 1993.

———. "Round Table Discussion" [with others]. In *Writing and the Holocaust,* ed. Berel Lang, 287–89. New York: Holmes and Meier, 1988.

Friedman, Susan Stanford. *Mappings: Feminism and the Cultural Geographies of Encounter.* Princeton: Princeton University Press, 1998.

Frost, Robert. "The Figure a Poem Makes." In *Robert Frost on Writing,* ed. Elaine Barry, 125–28. New Brunswick, N.J.: Rutgers University Press, 1973.

Fuss, Diana. *Identification Papers.* New York: Routledge, 1995.

Fussell, Paul. *Poetic Meter and Poetic Form.* New York: McGraw-Hill, 1979.

Galles, Arie A. "Fourteen Stations Suite." *Response: A Contemporary Jewish Review,* no. 68 (fall 1997–winter 1998): 118–23.

Gardiner, Judith Kegan. *Rhys, Stead, Lessing, and the Politics of Empathy.* Bloomington: Indiana University Press, 1989.

Gershon, Karen. *Collected Poems.* London. Papermac/Macmillan, 1990.

Gilbert, Sandra M. "A Fine White Flying Myth: The Life/Work of Sylvia Plath." In

Shakespeare's Sisters, ed. Sandra M. Gilbert and Susan Gubar, 245–60. Bloomington: Indiana University Press, 1979.

―――. " 'Rats' Alley': The Great War, Modernism, and the (Anti)Pastoral Elegy." *New Literary History* 30, no. 1 (1999): 179–202.

Gilbert, Sandra M., and Susan Gubar. *No Man's Land: The Place of the Woman Writer in the Twentieth Century*. Vol. 1, *The War of the Words*. New Haven: Yale University Press, 1988.

―――. *No Man's Land: The Place of the Woman Writer in the Twentieth Century*. Vol. 2, *Sexchanges*. New Haven: Yale University Press, 1989.

―――. *No Man's Land: The Place of the Woman Writer in the Twentieth Century*. Vol. 3, *Letters from the Front*. New Haven: Yale University Press, 1994.

Gilman, Sander L. *Jewish Self-Hatred: Anti-Semitism and the Hidden Language of the Jews*. Baltimore: Johns Hopkins University Press, 1986.

Gilroy, Paul. *Against Race: Imagining Political Culture beyond the Color Line*. Cambridge, Mass.: Harvard University Press, 2000.

Gioia, Dana. *Can Poetry Matter? Essays on Poetry and American Culture*. Saint Paul, Minn.: Graywolf Press, 1992.

Goldhagen, Daniel Jonah. *Hitler's Willing Executioners: Ordinary Germans and the Holocaust*. New York: Vintage, 1997.

Gourevitch, Philip. "The Memory Thief." *New Yorker*, June 14, 1999, pp. 48–68.

Gouri, Haim. "Facing the Glass Booth." In *Holocaust Remembrance: The Shapes of Memory*, ed. Geoffrey H. Hartman, 153–60. Oxford: Basil Blackwell, 1994.

Gradowski, Zalmen. "The Czech Transport: A Chronicle of the Auschwitz-*Sonderkommando.*" In *Literature of Destruction: Jewish Responses to Catastrophe*, ed. David G. Roskies, 548–65. Philadelphia: Jewish Publication Society, 1989.

Graham, Jorie. *The Dream of the Unified Field: Selected Poems, 1974–1994*. Hopewell, N.J.: Ecco Press, 1995.

―――. *Materialism*. Hopewell, N.J.: Ecco Press, 1993.

―――. "The Terror of Their Days." *New York Times Book Review*, February 10, 1985, p. 30.

Gubar, Susan. "Empathic Identification in Anne Michaels's *Fugitive Pieces:* Masculinity and Poetry After Auschwitz." In *Gender and Cultural Memory*, ed. Marianne Hirsch and Valerie Smith, special issue of *Signs: Journal of Women in Culture and Society* 28, no. 1 (2002).

―――. *Racechanges: White Skin, Black Face in American Culture*. New York: Oxford University Press, 1997.

Guttenplan, D. D. "Is a Holocaust Skeptic Fit to Be a Historian?" *New York Times*, June 26, 1999, B1, 11.

Hacker, Marilyn. *Squares and Courtyards*. New York: W. W. Norton, 2000.

―――. *Winter Numbers*. New York: W. W. Norton, 1994.

Hamburger, Michael. *Collected Poems, 1941–1983*. Manchester: Carcanet Press, 1984.

―――. "A New Austerity." In *The Truth of Poetry: Tensions in Modern Poetry from Baudelaire to the 1960s*, 220–66. London: Weidenfeld and Nicolson, 1969.

Hartman, Geoffrey H. "The Book of the Destruction." In *Probing the Limits of Representation: Nazism and the "Final Solution,"* ed. Saul Friedlander, 318–34. Cambridge, Mass.: Harvard University Press, 1992.

―――. *The Fateful Question of Culture*. New York: Columbia University Press, 1997.

―――. "Introduction: Darkness Visible." In *Holocaust Remembrance: The Shapes of Memory*, 1–22. Oxford: Basil Blackwell, 1994.

―――. *The Longest Shadow: In the Aftermath of the Holocaust*. Bloomington: Indiana University Press, 1996.

———. "On Traumatic Knowledge and Literary Studies." *New Literary History* 26, no. 3 (1995): 537–63.

———. "Witnessing Video Testimony: An Interview with Geoffrey Hartman." By Jennifer R. Ballengee. *Yale Journal of Criticism* 14, no. 1 (2001): 217–32.

Hass, Aaron. *In the Shadow of the Holocaust: The Second Generation.* Cambridge: Cambridge University Press, 1996.

Heaney, Seamus. *The Government of the Tongue.* London: Faber and Faber, 1988.

———. *The Redress of Poetry.* New York: Farrar, Straus, and Giroux, 1995.

Hecht, Anthony. *Collected Earlier Poems.* New York: Alfred A. Knopf, 1990.

———. *The Hard Hours.* New York: Atheneum, 1967.

———. *The Transparent Man.* New York: Alfred A. Knopf, 1990.

Heifetz, Julie. *Oral History and the Holocaust: A Collection of Poems from Interviews with Survivors of the Holocaust.* New York: Pergamon Press, 1985.

Heinemann, Marlene E. *Gender and Destiny: Women Writers and the Holocaust.* New York: Greenwood Press, 1986.

Heller, Fanya Gottesfeld. *Strange and Unexpected Love: A Teenage Girl's Holocaust Memoirs.* Foreword by Irving Greenberg. Hoboken, N.J.: KTAV, 1993.

Hellerstein, Kathryn. "In Exile in the Mother Tongue: Yiddish and the Woman Poet." In *Borders, Boundaries, and Frames: Cultural Criticism and Cultural Studies,* ed. Mae Henderson, 64–106. New York: Routledge, 1995.

———. Introduction to *Paper Bridges: Selected Poems of Kadya Molodowsky,* trans. and ed. Hellerstein, 17–60. Detroit: Wayne State University Press, 1999.

Hemschemeyer, Judith. "The Survivors." In *MotherSongs: Poems for, by, and about Mothers,* ed. Sandra M. Gilbert, Susan Gubar, and Diana O'Hehir, 157–58. New York: W. W. Norton, 1995.

Hersey, George L. *The Evolution of Allure: Sexual Selection from the Medici Venus to the Incredible Hulk.* Cambridge, Mass.: MIT Press, 1996.

Heschel, Susannah. "Jesus as Theological Transvestite." In *Judaism Since Gender,* ed. Miriam Peskowitz and Laura Levitt, 188–99. New York: Routledge, 1997.

Heyen, William. *Ericka: Poems of the Holocaust.* New York: Vanguard Press, 1984.

———. "Unwilled 'Chaos': In Poem We Trust." In *Writing and the Holocaust,* ed. Berel Lang, 122–36. New York: Holmes and Meier, 1988.

Hilberg, Raul. *The Destruction of the European Jews.* Student ed. New York: Holmes and Meier, 1985.

Hill, Geoffrey. *Collected Poems.* New York: Oxford University Press, 1986.

Hillger, Annick. "'Afterbirth of Earth': Messianic Materialism in Anne Michaels' *Fugitive Pieces.*" *Canadian Literature,* no. 160 (spring 1999): 28–45.

Hirsch, Ed. "A Written Interview with C. K. Williams." *Missouri Review* 9, no. 1 (1985–86): 151–62.

Hirsch, Marianne. *Family Frames: Photography, Narrative, and Postmemory.* Cambridge, Mass.: Harvard University Press, 1997.

———. "Family Pictures: *Maus,* Mourning, and Post-Memory." *Discourse* 15, no. 2 (1992–93): 3–29.

———. "Projected Memory: Holocaust Photographs in Personal and Public Fantasy." In *Acts of Memory: Cultural Recall in the Present,* ed. Mieke Bal, Jonathan Crewe, and Leo Spitzer, 9–23. Hanover, N.H.: University Press of New England, 1999.

———. "Surviving Images: Holocaust Photographs and the Work of Postmemory." *Yale Journal of Criticism* 14, no. 1 (2001): 5–37.

Hirsch, Marianne, and Leo Spitzer. "Gendered Translations: Claude Lanzmann's *Shoah.*" In *Gendering War Talk,* ed. Mariam Cooke and Angela Woollacott, 3–19. Princeton: Princeton University Press, 1993.

Hoffman, Eva. *Lost in Translation: A Life in a New Language.* New York: Penguin, 1989.

Hollander, John. "Creative Hate and Lifelines of Love: Some Thoughts on Irving Feldman's Poetry." In *The Poetry of Irving Feldman: Nine Essays,* ed. Harold Schweizer, 47–61. Lewisburg, Pa.: Bucknell University Press; London: Associated University Presses, 1992.

———. *The Gazer's Spirit: Poems Speaking to Silent Works of Art.* Chicago: University of Chicago Press, 1995.

Horowitz, Sara R. *Voicing the Void: Muteness and Memory in Holocaust Fiction.* Albany: State University of New York Press, 1997.

Howe, Irving. Letter to the editor. *Commentary,* October 1974, p. 12.

———. "Writing and the Holocaust." In *Writing and the Holocaust,* ed. Berel Lang, 175–99. New York: Holmes and Meier, 1988.

Hull, Lynda. *The Only World.* New York: Harper/Collins, 1995.

Hungerford, Amy. "Memorizing Memory." *Yale Journal of Criticism* 14, no. 1 (2001): 67–92.

Huyssen, Andreas. "Monument and Memory in a Postmodern Age." *Yale Journal of Criticism* 6, no. 2 (1993): 249–61.

Hyett, Barbara Helfgott. *In Evidence: Poems of the Liberation of Nazi Concentration Camps.* Pittsburgh: University of Pittsburgh Press, 1986.

I Never Saw Another Butterfly: Children's Drawings and Poems from Terezín Concentration Camp, 1942–1944. [Ed. Hana Volavková; trans. Jeanne Nemcová.] 2nd ed. 1978. Reprint, New York: Schocken, 1986.

Jackson, Ada. *Behold the Jew.* New York: Macmillan, 1944.

Jamison, Kay Redfield. *Night Falls Fast: Understanding Suicide.* New York: Alfred A. Knopf, 1999.

Jarrell, Randall. *The Complete Poems.* New York: Farrar, Straus, and Giroux, 1969.

Johnson, Barbara. "Apostrophe, Animation, and Abortion." In *A World of Difference,* 184–99. Baltimore: Johns Hopkins University Press, 1987.

Jones, Richard, ed. *Poetry and Politics: An Anthology of Essays.* New York: Morrow, 1985.

Kantor, Alfred. *The Books of Alfred Kantor: An Artist's Journal of the Holocaust.* Pref. by John Wykert. New York: Schocken, 1987.

Kaplan, Alice. *French Lessons: A Memoir.* Chicago: University of Chicago Press, 1993.

Kaplan, Chaim A. *Scroll of Agony: The Warsaw Diary of Chaim A. Kaplan.* Trans. and ed. Abraham I. Katsh. 1965. Reprint, Bloomington: Indiana University Press, 1999.

Kaplan, Marion A. *Between Dignity and Despair: Jewish Life in Nazi Germany.* New York: Oxford University Press, 1998.

Kaufman, Shirley. "By the Rivers." In *Roots in the Air: New and Selected Poems,* 145–46. Port Townsend, Wash.: Copper Canyon Press, 1996.

Kelen, Leslie. "Explaining, Explaining: A Conversation with Gerald Stern, Part I." *Boulevard* 7, no. 1 (1992): 2–3, 100–115, 193–210.

Kertész, Imre. "Who Owns Auschwitz?" *Yale Journal of Criticism* 14, no. 1 (2001): 267–72.

Klepfisz, Irena. *Bread and Candy: Songs of the Holocaust.* Song translations by Adrienne Cooper and Irena Klepfisz. *Bridges* 2, no. 2 (1991): 13–43.

———. *Dreams of an Insomniac: Jewish Feminist Essays, Speeches, and Diatribes.* Portland, Ore.: Eighth Mountain, 1990.

———. *A Few Words in the Mother Tongue: Poems Selected and New (1971–1990).* Portland, Ore.: Eighth Mountain, 1990.

Kluger, Ruth. *Still Alive: A Holocaust Girlhood Remembered.* New York: Feminist Press, 2001.

Kochan, Lionel. *Beyond the Graven Image: A Jewish View.* New York: New York University Press, 1997.

Koestenbaum, Wayne. "The Aryan Boy." In *Cleavage: Essays on Sex, Stars, and Aesthetics,* 55–63. New York: Ballantine, 2000.

Kofman, Sarah. *Smothered Words.* Trans. Madeleine Dobie. Evanston, Ill.: Northwestern University Press, 1998.

Kogan, Eugen. *The Theory and Practice of Hell: The German Concentration Camps and the System behind Them.* Trans. Heinz Norden. New York: Octagon Books, 1973.

Krauss, Rosalind. "A Note on Photography and the Simulacral." *October,* no. 31 (winter 1984): 49–68.

Kristeva, Julia. "The Pain of Sorrow in the Modern World: The Works of Marguerite Duras." *PMLA* 102, no. 1 (1987): 138–52.

Kumin, Maxine. *The Nightmare Factory.* New York: Harper and Row, 1970.

Kwiet, Konrad. "The Ultimate Refuge: Suicide in the Jewish Community under the Nazis." *Leo Baeck Institute Yearbook* 29 (1984): 135–67.

LaCapra, Dominick. *History and Memory after Auschwitz.* Ithaca: Cornell University Press, 1998.

———. "Lanzmann's *Shoah:* 'Here There Is No Why.'" *Critical Inquiry* 23, no. 2 (1997): 231–69.

———. "Trauma, Absence, Loss." *Critical Inquiry* 25, no. 4 (1999): 696–727.

Landau, Ronnie S. *The Nazi Holocaust.* Chicago: Ivan R. Dee, 1994.

Landsberg, Alison. "America, the Holocaust, and the Mass Culture of Memory: Toward a Radical Politics of Empathy." *New German Critique,* no. 71 (spring–summer 1997): 63–86.

Lang, Berel. *Act and Idea in the Nazi Genocide.* Chicago: University of Chicago Press, 1990.

———. "Holocaust Genres and the Turn to History." In *The Holocaust and the Text: Speaking the Unspeakable,* ed. Andrew Leak and George Paizis, 17–31. New York: St. Martin's, 2000.

Langer, Lawrence L. *Admitting the Holocaust: Collected Essays.* New York: Oxford University Press, 1995.

———. "Damaged Childhood in Holocaust Fact and Fiction." In *Humanity at the Limit: The Impact of the Holocaust Experience on Jews and Christians,* ed. Michael A. Signer, 329–42. Bloomington: Indiana University Press, 2000.

———. "Gendered Suffering? Women in Holocaust Testimonies." In *Women in the Holocaust,* ed. Dalia Ofer and Lenore J. Weitzman, 351–63. New Haven: Yale University Press, 1998.

———. *The Holocaust and the Literary Imagination.* New Haven: Yale University Press, 1975.

———. *Holocaust Testimonies: The Ruins of Memory.* New Haven: Yale University Press, 1991.

———, ed. *Art from the Ashes: A Holocaust Anthology.* New York: Oxford University Press, 1995.

Lanzmann, Claude. "J'ai enquete en pologne." In *Au sujet de Shoah: Le film de Claude Lanzmann,* ed. Bernard Cuau, 211–217. Paris: Belin, 1990.

———. "The Obscenity of Understanding." In *Trauma: Explorations in Memory,* ed. Cathy Caruth, 200–220. Baltimore: Johns Hopkins University Press, 1995.

Lasansky, Mauricio. *The Nazi Drawings.* Designed by Samuel Maitin, photographed by Alfred J. Wyatt. [Philadelphia: Winchell,] 1966.

Laub, Dori, and Marjorie Allard. "History, Memory, and Truth: Defining the Place of the Survivor." In *The Holocaust and History: The Known, the Unknown, the Disputed, and the Reexamined,* ed. Michael Berenbaum and Abraham J. Peck, 798–812. Bloomington: Indiana University Press, 1998.

Laub, Dori, and Nanette C. Auerhahn. "Failed Empathy—A Critical Theme in the

Survivor's Holocaust Experience." *Psychoanalytic Psychology* 6, no. 5 (1989): 377–400.

Lawrence, D. H. Introduction to *Chariot of the Sun*, by Harry Crosby, i–xviii. Paris: Black Sun Press, 1931.

Laytner, Anson. *Arguing with God: A Jewish Tradition*. Northvale, N.J.: Jason Aronson, 1990.

Leitner, Isabella. *Fragments of Isabella: A Memoir of Auschwitz*. Ed. Irving A. Leitner. New York: Dell, 1979.

Leo Baeck Institute. *German-Jewish History in Modern Times, 1600–1945*. New York: Columbia University Press, n.d.

Lerner, Gerda. "Living in Translation." In *Why History Matters: Life and Thought*, 33–49. New York: Oxford University Press, 1997.

Levertoff, Olga. "The Ballad of My Father." In *The Sorrow Dance*, by Denise Levertov, 93–94. New York: New Directions, 1966.

Levertov, Denise. *Poems, 1950–1967*. New York: New Directions, 1983.

Levi, Primo. *The Drowned and the Saved*. Trans. Raymond Rosenthal. New York: Vintage, 1989.

———. *The Periodic Table*. Trans. Raymond Rosenthal. New York: Schocken, 1984.

———. *Survival in Auschwitz and The Reawakening*. Trans. Stuart Woolf. New York: Summit Books, 1986.

Levinas, Emmanuel. *Difficult Freedom: Essays in Judaism*. Trans. Sean Hand. Baltimore: Johns Hopkins University Press, 1990.

———. "Reality and Its Shadow." In *Collected Philosophical Papers*, trans. Alphonso Lingis, 1–13. Dordrecht: Kluwer Academic, 1987.

Levitt, Laura. *Jews and Feminism: The Ambivalent Search for Home*. New York: Routledge, 1997.

Levy, Isaac Jack. *And the World Stood Silent: Sephardic Poetry of the Holocaust*. Urbana: University of Illinois Press, 1989.

Leys, Ruth. *Trauma: A Genealogy*. Chicago: University of Chicago Press, 2000.

Lifshin, Lyn. *Blue Tattoo: Poems of the Holocaust*. Ed. Joseph Cowles. Desert Hot Springs, Calif.: Event Horizon Press, 1995.

Lifton, Robert Jay. Interview by Cathy Caruth in *Trauma: Explorations in Memory*, ed. Cathy Caruth, 128–50. Baltimore: Johns Hopkins University Press, 1995.

Lifton, Robert Jay, and Eric Olson. *Living and Dying*. New York: Praeger, 1974.

Linafelt, Tod. *Surviving Lamentations: Catastrophe, Lament, and Protest in the Afterlife of a Biblical Book*. Chicago: University of Chicago Press, 2000.

Lipstadt, Deborah E. *Beyond Belief: The American Press and the Coming of the Holocaust, 1933–1945*. New York: Free Press, 1986.

———. "Why Is *The Wall Street Journal* Now Devaluing Women's Holocaust Experiences?" *Lilith* 23, no. 3 (1998): 10–13.

Liss, Andrea. *Trespassing through Shadows: Memory, Photography, and the Holocaust*. Minneapolis: University of Minnesota Press, 1998.

Longenback, James. "Jorie Graham's Big Hunger." *Denver Quarterly* 31, no. 3 (1997): 97–118.

Lyotard, Jean-François. *The Differend: Phrases in Dispute*. Trans. Georges Van Den Abbeele. Minneapolis: University of Minnesota Press, 1988.

———. *Heidegger and "the jews."* Trans. Andreas Michel and Mark Roberts. Minneapolis: University of Minnesota Press, 2000.

Maccoby, Hyam. "Theologian of the Holocaust." *Commentary*, May 1982, 33–37.

Mandel, Naomi. "Rethinking 'After Auschwitz': Against a Rhetoric of the Unspeakable in Holocaust Writing." *Boundary 2* 28, no. 2 (2001): 203–28.

Marks, Herbert. "On Prophetic Stammering." In *The Book and the Text: The Bible and Literary Theory*, ed. Regina M. Schwartz, 60–80. Oxford: Basil Blackwell, 1960.

Marrus, Michael R., and Robert O. Paxton. "Western Europeans and the Jews." In *The Holocaust: Problems and Perspectives of Interpretation,* ed. Donald L. Niewyk, 241–51. Boston: Houghton Mifflin, 1997.

Martin, Elaine, ed. *Gender, Patriarchy, and Fascism in the Third Reich: The Response of Women Writers.* Detroit: Wayne State University Press, 1993.

Maslin, Janet. Review of *Schindler's List. New York Times,* December 15, 1993, C19.

Masters, Edgar Lee. *Spoon River Anthology.* New ed. 1944. Reprint, New York: Macmillan, 1962.

McCord, Janet Schenk. *A Study of the Suicides of Eight Holocaust Survivor/Writers.* Ann Arbor, Mich.: UMI, 1995. [Ph.D. diss., Boston University, 1995.]

McDaniels, Judith. "After Reading Reznikoff." In *Longman Anthology of Women's Literature,* ed. Mary K. DeShazer, 873–74. New York: Addison-Wesley, 2001.

McWilliams, Martha. "Order out of Chaos: 'Burnt Hole: Contemporary Artists Reflect on the Holocaust.'" *New Art Examiner* 22, no. 8 (April 1995): 12–17.

Merwin, W. S. *The Miner's Pale Children.* New York: Atheneum, 1979.

Michaels, Anne. "Cleopatra's Love." *Poetry Canada* 14, no. 2 (March 1994): 14–15.

———. *Fugitive Pieces.* New York: Vintage, 1998.

———. "What the Light Teaches." In *The Weight of Oranges / Miner's Pond,* 112–15. Toronto: McClelland and Stewart, 1997.

Michaels, Leonard. "To Feel These Things." In *Testimony: Contemporary Writers Make the Holocaust Personal,* ed. David Rosenberg, 3–12. New York: Random House, 1989.

Midrash Rabbah, ed. Rabbi Dr. H. Freedman and Maurice Simon. Vol. 3, *Exodus.* Trans. Rabbi Dr. S. M. Lehrman. London: Soncino Press, 1939.

Millay, Edna St. Vincent. "Not So Far as the Forest." In *Collected Lyrics of Edna St. Vincent Millay,* 335–39. New York: Harper and Row, 1943.

Miller, Judith. *One, by One, by One: Facing the Holocaust.* New York: Simon and Schuster, 1990.

Miller, Nancy K. *Bequest and Betrayal: Memoirs of a Parent's Death.* New York: Oxford University Press, 1996.

Millier, Brett Candlish. "Elusive Mastery: The Drafts of Elizabeth Bishop's 'One Art.'" In *Elizabeth Bishop: The Geography of Gender,* ed. Marilyn May Lombardi, 233–43. Charlottesville: University Press of Virginia, 1993.

Milosz, Czeslaw. *A Treatise on Poetry.* Trans. the author and Robert Hass. New York: Ecco Press, 2001.

Milton, Sybil. "The Camera as Weapon: Documentary Photography and the Holocaust." *Simon Wiesenthal Center Annual* 1 (1984): 45–67.

Mintz, Alan. *Hurban: Responses to Catastrophe in Hebrew Literature.* New York: Columbia University Press, 1984.

Mitchell, W. J. T. *Picture Theory.* Chicago: University of Chicago Press, 1994.

Mitscherlich, Alexander, and Margarete Mitscherlich. *The Inability to Mourn: Principles of Collective Behavior.* Trans. Beverley R. Placzek. New York: Grove, 1975.

Molodowsky, Kadya. *Paper Bridges: Selected Poems of Kadya Molodowsky.* Trans. and ed. Kathryn Hellerstein. Detroit: Wayne State University Press, 1999.

Morgan, Michael L. "To Seize Memory: History and Identity in Post-Holocaust Jewish Thought." In *Thinking about the Holocaust: After Half a Century,* ed. Alvin H. Rosenfeld, 151–81. Bloomington: Indiana University Press, 1997.

Morrison, Toni. *The Bluest Eye.* 1970. Reprint, New York: Plume, 1994.

Mortkowicz-Olczakowa, Hanna. "Yanosz Korczak's Last Walk." In *Anthology of Holocaust Literature,* ed. Jacob Glatstein, Israel Knox, and Samuel Margoshes, 134–37. Philadelphia: Jewish Publication Society of America, 1969.

Mueller, Christopher B. "Post-Modern Hearsay Reform: The Importance of Complexity." *Minnesota Law Review* 76, no. 3 (1992): 367–423.

Newman, Charles, ed. *The Art of Sylvia Plath*. London: Faber and Faber, 1970.

Nussbaum, Martha. "Compassion: The Basic Social Emotion." *Social Philosophy and Policy* 31, no. 1 (1996): 27–58.

———. "Exactly and Responsibly: A Defense of Ethical Criticism." In *Mapping the Ethical Turn: A Reader in Ethics, Culture, and Literary Theory*, ed. Todd F. Davis and Kenneth Womack, 59–79. Charlottesville: University Press of Virginia, 2001.

Olds, Sharon. "The Window." *American Poetry Review* 27, no. 6 (1998): 26.

Opfermann, Charlotte Guthmann. "Suicides or Murders?" In *Problems Unique to the Holocaust*, ed. Harry James Cargas, 43–50. Lexington: University Press of Kentucky, 1999.

Opie, Iona, and Peter Opie, eds. *The Oxford Dictionary of Nursery Rhymes*. Oxford: Clarendon Press, 1951.

Orr, Peter. *The Poet Speaks: Interviews with Contemporary Poets*. Conducted by Hilary Morrish, Peter Orr, John Press, and Ian Scott-Kilvert. New York: Barnes and Noble, 1966.

Ortner, Sherry. "Is Female to Male as Nature Is to Culture?" In *Woman, Culture, and Society*, ed. Michelle Zimbalist Rosaldo and Louise Lamphere, 67–87. Stanford: Stanford University Press, 1974.

Osherow, Jacqueline. *Conversations with Survivors*. Athens: University of Georgia Press, 1994.

———. *Dead Men's Praise*. New York: Grove, 1999.

———. *Looking for Angels in New York*. Athens: University of Georgia Press, 1988.

———. *With a Moon in Transit*. New York: Grove, 1996.

Ostriker, Alicia. "*Millions of Strange Shadows:* Anthony Hecht as Gentile and Jew." In *The Burdens of Formality: Essays on the Poetry of Anthony Hecht*, ed. Sydney Lea, 97–105. Athens: University of Georgia Press, 1989.

———. "My Name Is Laughter." In *The Poetry of Irving Feldman*, ed. Harold Schweizer, 101–25. Lewisburg, Pa.: Bucknell University Press; London: Associated University Presses, 1992.

Ozick, Cynthia. "Envy; or, Yiddish in America." In *The Pagan Rabbi and Other Stories*, 39–100. New York: Schocken, 1976.

———. "A Liberal's Auschwitz." In *The Pushcart Prize: The Best of the Small Presses, 1976–77*, ed. Bill Henderson, 149–53. Yonkers, N.Y.: Pushcart Book Press, 1977.

———. *Metaphor and Memory: Essays*. 1989. Reprint, New York: Vintage, 1991.

———. "Round Table Discussion" [with others]. In *Writing and the Holocaust*, ed. Berel Lang, 277–84. New York: Holmes and Meier, 1988.

———. *The Shawl*. 1980. Reprint, New York: Vintage International, 1990.

Ozsváth, Zsuzsanna. *In the Footsteps of Orpheus: The Life and Times of Miklós Radnóti*. Bloomington: Indiana University Press, 2000.

Pacernick, Gary. "Gerald Stern." In *Meaning and Memory: Interviews with Fourteen Jewish Poets*, 109–29. Columbus: Ohio State University Press, 2001.

Pagis, Dan. *Poems*. Trans. Stephen Mitchell. Oxford: Carcanet Press, 1972.

Parmet, Harriet L. *The Terror of Our Days: Four American Poets Respond to the Holocaust*. Bethlehem, Pa.: Lehigh University Press; London: Associated University Presses, 2001.

Patterson, David. *The Shriek of Silence: A Phenomenology of the Holocaust Novel*. Lexington: University Press of Kentucky, 1992.

Pilcer, Sonia. *The Holocaust Kid*. New York: Persea Books, 2001.

Pinch, Adela. *Strange Fits of Passion: Epistemologies of Emotion, Hume to Austen*. Stanford: Stanford University Press, 1996.

Pinsky, Robert. *The Figured Wheel: New and Collected Poems, 1966–1996.* New York: Farrar, Straus, and Giroux, 1996.

———. "Responsibilities of the Poet." In *Politics and Poetic Value,* ed. Robert von Hallberg, 7–20. Chicago: University of Chicago Press, 1987.

Pinter, Harold. *Ashes to Ashes.* New York: Grove, 1996.

Plank, Karl A. *Mother of the Wire Fence: Inside and Outside the Holocaust.* Louisville, Ky.: Westminster John Knox Press, 1994.

Plath, Sylvia. *Collected Poems.* Ed. Ted Hughes. New York: Harper and Row, 1981.

Porter, Jack Nusan. "Holocaust Suicides." In *Problems Unique to the Holocaust,* ed. Harry James Cargas, 51–66. Lexington: University Press of Kentucky, 1999.

Pound, Ezra. *ABC of Reading.* New York: New Directions, 1960.

———. "Hugh Selwyn Mauberley." In *Selected Poems,* 61–77. New York: New Directions, 1957.

Raczymow, Henri. "Memory Shot Through with Holes." *Yale French Studies,* no. 85 (1994): 98–105.

Ramazani, Jahan. *The Hybrid Muse: Postcolonial Poetry in English.* Chicago: University of Chicago Press, 2001.

———. *Poetry of Mourning: The Modern Elegy from Hardy to Heaney.* Chicago: University of Chicago Press, 1994.

———. *Yeats and the Poetry of Death: Elegy, Self-Elegy, and the Sublime.* New Haven: Yale University Press, 1990.

Replansky, Naomi. *The Dangerous World: New and Selected Poems, 1934–1994.* Chicago: Another Chicago Press, 1994.

Reznikoff, Charles. *First, There Is the Need.* Santa Barbara, Calif.: Black Sparrow Press, 1977.

———. *Holocaust.* Los Angeles: Black Sparrow Press, 1975.

Rich, Adrienne. *Adrienne Rich's Poetry and Prose.* Ed. Barbara Charlesworth Gelpi and Albert Gelpi. New York: W. W. Norton, 1993.

———. *Arts of the Possible: Essays and Conversations.* New York: W. W. Norton, 2001.

———. *An Atlas of the Difficult World: Poems, 1988–1991.* New York: W. W. Norton, 1991.

———. *Dark Fields of the Republic.* New York: W. W. Norton, 1995.

———. Introduction to *A Few Words in the Mother Tongue: Poems Selected and New (1971–1990),* by Irena Klepfisz, 13–25. Portland, Ore.: Eighth Mountain Press, 1990.

———. *Sources.* Woodside, Calif.: Heyeck Press, 1983.

———. "Split at the Root: An Essay on Jewish Identity." In *Adrienne Rich's Poetry and Prose,* ed. Barbara Charlesworth Gelpi and Albert Gelpi, 224–38. New York: W. W. Norton, 1993.

———. *What Is Found There: Notebooks on Poetry and Politics.* New York: W. W. Norton, 1993.

———. "When We Dead Awaken: Writing as Re-Vision (1971)." In *On Lies, Secrets, and Silence: Selected Prose, 1966–1978,* 33–49. New York: W. W. Norton, 1979.

———. *Your Native Land, Your Life: Poems,* New York: W. W. Norton, 1986.

Richman, Elliot. *Franz Kafka's Daughter Meets the Evil Nazi Empire!!!* Paradise, Calif.: Asylum Arts, 1999.

Ringelheim, Joan. "The Split between Gender and the Holocaust." In *Women in the Holocaust,* ed. Dalia Ofer and Lenore J. Weitzman, 340–50. New Haven: Yale University Press, 1998.

———. "Women and the Holocaust: A Reconsideration of Research." *Signs: Journal of Women in Culture and Society* 10, no. 4 (1985): 741–61.

Roberts, Steven H. *The House That Hitler Built.* New York: Harper and Brothers, 1937.

Rose, Gillian. *Mourning Becomes the Law: Philosophy and Representation.* Cambridge: Cambridge University Press, 1996.

Rose, Jacqueline. *The Haunting of Sylvia Plath.* Cambridge, Mass.: Harvard University Press, 1992.

Rosenbaum, Ron. *Explaining Hitler: The Search for the Origins of Evil.* New York: Harper-Collins, 1999.

Rosenfeld, Alvin H. "The Americanization of the Holocaust." In *Thinking about the Holocaust: After Half a Century,* ed. Alvin H. Rosenfeld, 119–50. Bloomington: Indiana University Press, 1997.

———. "The Assault on Holocaust Memory." *American Jewish Year Book* (2001): 3–20.

———. *A Double Dying: Reflections on Holocaust Literature.* Bloomington: Indiana University Press, 1980.

———. "The Problematics of Holocaust Literature." In *Confronting the Holocaust: The Impact of Elie Wiesel,* ed. Alvin H. Rosenfeld and Irving Greenberg, 1–30. Bloomington: Indiana University Press, 1978.

Roskies, David G. *Against the Apocalypse: Responses to Catastrophe in Modern Jewish Culture.* Cambridge, Mass.: Harvard University Press, 1984.

Rossetti, Christina. *The Complete Poems of Christina Rossetti.* Ed. R. W. Crump. Variorum ed. 3 vols. Baton Rouge: Louisiana State University Press, 1979.

Rothberg, Michael. *Traumatic Realism: The Demands of Holocaust Representation.* Minneapolis: University of Minnesota Press, 2000.

Rothenberg, Jerome. *Khurbn and Other Poems.* New York: New Directions, 1989.

———. "Pre-face" (1971). In *Shaking the Pumpkin: Traditional Poetry of the Indian North Americas,* ed. Jerome Rothenberg, xviii–xxiii. Rev. ed. Albuquerque: University of New Mexico Press, 1991.

Rubin, Steven J., ed. *Telling and Remembering: A Century of American Jewish Poetry.* Boston: Beacon, 1997.

Ryan, Michael. *God Hunger.* New York: Viking, 1989.

Sachs, Peter. "Anthony Hecht's 'Rites and Ceremonies': Reading *The Hard Hours.*" In *The Burdens of Formality: Essays on the Poetry of Anthony Hecht,* ed. Sydney Lea, 62–96. Athens: University of Georgia Press, 1989.

Salomon, Charlotte. *Leben oder Theater? Das "Lebensbild" einer judischen Malerin aus Berlin, 1917–1943: Bilder und Spuren, Notizen, Gesprache, Dokumente.* Ed. Christine Fischer-Defoy. Berlin: Das Arsenal, 1986.

Santner, Eric L. *Stranded Objects: Mourning, Memory, and Film in Postwar Germany.* Ithaca: Cornell University Press, 1990.

Sarton, May. "The Invocation to Kali." In *A Grain of Mustard Seed,* 19–23. New York: W. W. Norton, 1971.

Sartre, Jean-Paul. *Anti-Semite and Jew.* Trans. George J. Becker. 1948. Reprint: New York: Schocken, 1965.

Scarry, Elaine. *The Body in Pain: The Making and Unmaking of the World.* New York: Oxford University Press, 1985.

Schenck, Celeste. *Mourning and Panegyric: The Poetics of Pastoral Ceremony.* University Park: Pennsylvania State University Press, 1988.

Schiff, Hilda, ed. *Holocaust Poetry.* New York: St. Martin's, 1995.

Schlink, Bernhard. *The Reader.* Trans. Carol Brown Janeway. New York: Vintage, 1997.

Schoenfeld, Gabriel. "Auschwitz and the Professors." *Commentary,* June 1998, pp. 42–46.

Schweik, Susan. *A Gulf So Deeply Cut: American Women Poets and the Second World War.* Madison: University of Wisconsin Press, 1991.

Schweizer, Harold. "Lyric Suffering in Auden and Feldman." *English Language Notes* 31, no. 2 (1993): 66–74.

Schwenger, Peter. "Corpsing the Image." *Critical Inquiry* 26, no. 3 (2000): 395–410.

Sedgwick, Eve Kosofsky. *Between Men: English Literature and Male Homosocial Desire.* New York: Columbia University Press, 1985.

——. *Epistemology of the Closet.* Berkeley: University of California Press, 1990.

Segal, Lore. *Other People's Houses.* 1964. Reprint, New York: New Press, 1994.

Sekula, Alan. "The Body and the Archive." *October,* no. 39 (winter 1986): 3–64.

——. "On the Invention of Photographic Meaning." In *Photography against the Grain: Essays and Photo-works, 1973–1983,* 3–22. Halifax: Press of the Nova Scotia College of Art and Design, 1984.

Sereny, Gitta. *Into That Darkness: An Examination of Conscience.* New York: Vintage, 1974.

Shapiro, Alan. *The Last Happy Occasion.* Chicago: University of Chicago Press, 1996.

——. *Mixed Company.* Chicago: University of Chicago Press, 1996.

Shelley, Percy Bysshe. *A Defence of Poetry.* In *The Norton Anthology of English Literature,* ed. M. H. Abrams, 2:752–65. 6th ed. New York: W. W. Norton, 1996.

Shore, Jane. *Music Minus One.* New York: Picador, 1996.

Shreiber, Maeera Y. "The End of Exile: Jewish Identity and Its Diasporic Poetics." *PMLA* 113, no. 2 (1998): 273–87.

Silverman, Kaja. *Male Subjectivity at the Margins.* New York: Routledge, 1992.

Simic, Charles. *The Uncertain Certainty: Interviews, Essays, and Notes on Poetry.* Ann Arbor: University of Michigan Press, 1985.

——. *The World Doesn't End: Prose Poems.* New York: Harcourt Brace Jovanovich, 1989.

Sklarew, Myra. *Lithuania: New and Selected Poems.* Washington, D.C.: Azul Editions, 1995.

Slavitt, David R. " 'So There Were These Two Jews . . .': The Poetry of Irving Feldman." *Hollins Critic* 24, no. 1 (1997): 1–13.

Smith, Adam. *The Theory of Moral Sentiments.* Ed. D. D. Raphael and A. L. Macfie. Oxford: Clarendon Press, 1976.

Smith, Barbara Herrnstein. *On the Margins of Discourse: The Relation of Literature to Language.* Chicago: University of Chicago Press, 1978.

Smith, Lindsay. "The Politics of Focus: Feminism and Photography Theory." In *New Feminist Discourses: Critical Essays on Theories and Text,* ed. Isobel Armstrong, 238–62. London: Routledge, 1992.

Smith, Roger W. "Women and Genocide: Notes on an Unwritten History." *Holocaust and Genocide Studies* 8, no. 3 (1994): 315–34.

Snodgrass, W. D. *The Führer Bunker: A Cycle of Poems in Progress.* Brockport, N.Y.: Boa Editions, 1977.

——. "A Visitation." In *After Experience: Poems and Translations,* 44–45. New York: Harper and Row, 1968.

Sollors, Werner. *Beyond Ethnicity: Consent and Descent in American Culture.* New York: Oxford University Press, 1986.

Sommer, Jason. *Other People's Troubles.* Chicago: University of Chicago Press, 1997.

Sontag, Susan. *Against Interpretation, and Other Essays.* New York: Farrar, Straus, and Giroux, 1966.

——. *On Photography.* New York: Anchor Books Doubleday, 1990.

Spiegelman, Art. *Maus I: A Survivor's Tale: My Father Bleeds History.* New York: Pantheon, 1986.

——. *Maus II: A Survivor's Tale: And Here My Troubles Began.* New York: Pantheon, 1991.

Stark, Jared. "Suicide after Auschwitz." *Yale Journal of Criticism* 14, no. 1 (2001): 93–113.

Steiner, George. "Dying Is an Art." In *The Art of Sylvia Plath,* ed. Charles Newman, 211–18. Bloomington: Indiana University Press, 1965.

———. "Extraterritorial." In *Extra-Territorial: Papers on Literature and the Language Revolution,* 3–11. New York: Atheneum, 1976.

———. "In Extremis." In *The Cambridge Mind,* ed. Eric Homberger, William Janeway, and Simon Schama, 303–307. London: Jonathan Cape, 1969.

———. "The Long Life of Metaphor." *Encounter* 68, no. 2 (1987): 55–61.

———. "Our Homeland, the Text." *Salmagundi,* no. 66 (winter–spring 1985): 4–25.

Stern, Gerald. *Paradise Poems.* New York: Random House, 1984.

———. *This Time: New and Selected Poems.* New York: W. W. Norton, 1998.

Stevens, Wallace. *The Collected Poems.* New York: Vintage–Random House, 1982.

Strangeways, Al. *Sylvia Plath: The Shaping of Shadows.* Madison, N.J.: Fairleigh Dickinson University Press; London: Associated University Presses, 1998.

Striar, Marguerite M., ed. *Beyond Lament: Poets of the World Bearing Witness to the Holocaust.* Evanston: Northwestern University Press, 1998.

Sutherland, Janet, James Hall, and Nancy J. Jones, eds. *Women: Portraits.* New York: McGraw Hill, 1976.

Symonds, John Addington. *The Letters.* Ed. Herbert M. Schueller and Robert L. Peters. 3 vols. Detroit: Wayne State University Press, 1969.

Szasz, Thomas. *Karl Kraus and the Soul-Doctors: A Pioneer Critic and His Criticism of Psychiatry and Psychoanalysis.* Baton Rouge: Louisiana State University Press, 1976.

Tagg, John. *The Burden of Representation: Essays on Photographies and Histories.* Minneapolis: University of Minnesota Press, 1993.

Taussig, Michael. " 'Dying Is an Art, Like Everything Else.' " *Critical Inquiry* 28, no. 1 (2001): 305–16.

Teichman, Milton, and Sharon Leder, eds. *Truth and Lamentation: Stories and Poems on the Holocaust.* Urbana: University of Illinois Press, 1994.

Theweleit, Klaus. *Male Bodies: Psychoanalyzing the White Terror.* Vol. 2 of *Male Fantasies.* Trans. Erica Carter and Chris Turner in collaboration with Stephen Conway. Minneapolis: University of Minnesota Press, 1989.

———. "The Politics of Orpheus between Women, Hades, Political Power, and the Media: Some Thoughts on the Configuration of the European Artist, Starting with the Figure of Gottfried Been; Or: What Happens to Eurydice?" *New German Critique,* no. 36 (fall 1985): 133–56.

Toll, Nelly. *When Memory Speaks: The Holocaust in Art.* Westport, Conn.: Praeger, 1998.

Trezise, Thomas. "Unspeakable." *Yale Journal of Criticism* 14, no. 1 (2001): 39–66.

Van Alphen, Ernst. *Caught by History: Holocaust Effects in Contemporary Art, Literature, and Theory.* Stanford: Stanford University Press, 1997.

Van der Kolk, Bessel A., and Onno Van der Hart. "The Instrusive Past: The Flexibility of Memory and the Engraving of Trauma." In *Trauma: Explorations in Memory,* ed. Cathy Caruth, 158–82. Baltimore: Johns Hopkins University Press, 1995.

Vendler, Helen. *The Breaking of Style: Hopkins, Heaney, Graham.* Cambridge, Mass.: Harvard University Press, 1995.

———. *The Given and the Made: Strategies of Poetic Redefinition.* Cambridge, Mass.: Harvard University Press, 1995.

Vishniac, Roman. *A Vanished World.* With a foreword by Elie Wiesel. New York: Farrar, Straus, and Giroux, 1983.

Walcott, Derek. *Midsummer.* New York: Farrar, Straus, and Giroux, 1984.

Warren, Robert Penn. *The Collected Poems of Robert Penn Warren.* Ed. John Burt. Baton Rouge: Louisiana State University Press, 1998.
Weigel, Sigrid. *Body- and Image-Space: Re-reading Walter Benjamin.* Trans. Georgina Paul with Rachel McNicholl and Jeremy Gaines. London: Routledge, 1996.
Weiner, Marc A. *Richard Wagner and the Anti-Semitic Imagination.* Lincoln: University of Nebraska Press, 1997.
Weitzman, Lenore J. "Living on the Aryan Side in Poland: Gender, Passing, and the Nature of Resistance." In *Women in the Holocaust,* ed. Dalia Ofer and Lenore J. Weitzman, 187–222. New Haven: Yale University Press, 1998.
Weitzman, Lenore J., and Dalia Ofer. Introduction to *Women in the Holocaust,* ed. Dalia Ofer and Lenore J. Weitzman, 1–18. New Haven: Yale University Press, 1998.
Weitzman, Steven. *Song and Story in Biblical Narrative: The History of a Literary Convention in Ancient Israel.* Bloomington: Indiana University Press, 1997.
Whitman, Ruth. *The Testing of Hanna Senesh.* Detroit: Wayne State University Press, 1986.
Whitman, Walt. *Leaves of Grass, and Selected Prose.* New York: Holt, Rinehart, and Winston, 1967.
Wiesel, Elie. *Ani Maamin: A Song Lost and Found Again.* Trans. Marion Wiesel. New York: Random House, 1973.
———. *The Fifth Son.* Trans. Marion Wiesel. New York: Summit, 1985.
———. *From the Kingdom of Memory: Reminiscences.* New York: Simon and Schuster, 1990.
———. *Legends of Our Time.* New York: Schocken, 1982.
———. *Night/Dawn/Day.* London: Jason Aronson, 1985.
Wieseltier, Leon. *Kaddish.* New York: Alfred A. Knopf, 1998.
Williams, C. K. "Beginnings." In *In Praise of What Persists,* ed. Stephen Berg, 267–80. New York: Harper, 1983.
———. "An Interview." By Keith S. Norris. *New England Review* 17, no. 2 (1995): 127–40.
———. "An Interview with C. K. Williams." By Lynn Keller. *Contemporary Literature* 29, no. 2 (1988): 157–76.
———. *New and Selected Poems.* Newcastle upon Tyne: Bloodaxe Books, 1995.
———. *Poetry and Consciousness.* Ann Arbor: University of Michigan Press, 1998.
———. *Repair.* New York: Farrar, Straus, and Giroux, 1999.
———. *The Vigil.* New York: Farrar, Straus, and Giroux, 1997.
Wirth-Nesher, Hana. "The Languages of Memory: Cynthia Ozick's 'The Shawl.' " In *Multilingual America: Transnationalism, Ethnicity, and the Languages of American Literature,* ed. Werner Sollors, 313–26. New York: New York University Press, 1998.
Wolin, Jeffrey A. *Written in Memory: Portraits of the Holocaust.* San Francisco: Chronicle Books, 1997.
Woolf, Virginia. *A Room of One's Own.* 1929. Reprint, New York: Harcourt Brace, 1981.
———. *Three Guineas.* 1938. Reprint, New York: Harcourt, Brace and World, 1966.
Woollacott, Angela. "Sisters and Brothers in Arms: Family, Class, and Gendering in World War I Britain." In *Gendering War Talk,* ed. Mariam Cooke and Angela Woollacott, 128–47. Princeton: Princeton University Press, 1993.
Wordsworth, William. "Essay upon Epitaphs I." In *The Prose of William Wordsworth,* ed. W. J. B. Owen and Jane Worthington Smyser, 2:49–62. Oxford: Clarendon Press, 1974.
Yaeger, Patricia. "Consuming Trauma; or, The Pleasures of Merely Circulating." *Journal X* 1, no. 2 (1997): 225–51. [Reprinted in *Extremities: Trauma, Testi-

mony, and Community, ed. Nancy K. Miller and Jason Tougaw (Urbana: University of Illinois Press, forthcoming).]

Yalom, Marilyn. "Cynthia Ozick's Paradoxical Wisdom." In *People of the Book: Thirty Scholars Reflect on Their Jewish Identity*, ed. Jeffrey Rubin-Dorsky and Shelley Fisher Fishkin, 427–38. Madison: University of Wisconsin Press, 1996.

Yanay, Niza. "The Meaning of Hatred as Narrative: Two Versions of an Experience." *Journal of Narrative and Life History* 5, no. 4 (1995): 353–68.

Yeats, William Butler. *Selected Poems and Two Plays*. Ed. and intro. by M. L. Rosenthal. Updated ed. New York: Collier, 1962.

Young, Gloria. "The Moral Function of Remembering: American Holocaust Poetry." *Studies in American Jewish Literature* 9, no. 1 (1990): 61–72.

———. "The Poetry of the Holocaust." In *Holocaust Literature: A Handbook of Critical, Historical, and Literary Writings*, ed. Saul S. Friedman, 547–81. Westport, Conn.: Greenwood Press, 1993.

Young, James E. "Against Redemption: The Arts of Counter-Memory." In *Humanity at the Limit: The Impact of the Holocaust Experience on Jews and Christians*, ed. Michael A. Signer, 44–62. Bloomington: Indiana University Press, 2000.

———. *At Memory's Edge: After-Images of the Holocaust in Contemporary Art and Architecture*. New Haven: Yale University Press, 2000.

———. *The Texture of Memory: Holocaust Memorials and Meaning*. New Haven: Yale University Press, 2000.

———. *Writing and Rewriting the Holocaust: Narrative and the Consequences of Interpretation*. Bloomington: Indiana University Press, 1988.

Zeiger, Melissa F. *Beyond Consolation: Death, Sexuality, and the Changing Shapes of Elegy*. Ithaca: Cornell University Press, 1997.

Zelizer, Barbie. *Remembering to Forget: Holocaust Memory through the Camera's Eye*. Chicago: University of Chicago Press, 1998.

Žižek, Slavoj. *Looking Awry: An Introduction to Jacques Lacan through Popular Culture*. Cambridge, Mass: MIT Press, 1992.

INDEX

Page numbers in italic type refer to illustrations.

"Above the Casa del Popolo" (Osherow),
176
Abraham (biblical), 46, 65
Abse, Dannie, 26, 49–50, 51, 52; formalism
and, 258; on voyeurism, 141
Adler, Jacob, 215–216
Adler, Rachel, 8, 227
"Adler" (Stern), 215–217
Adorno, Theodor, 11, 12, 262; Benjamin's
suicide note and, 60; definition of poem,
26, 263; on Final Solution as historical
caesura, 248; on lyric's function, 22; on
survival, 47
Adorno's injunction against poetry, 7, 18,
27, 177, 242; "documentary verse" and,
145; incongruity and, 64; nihilism of, 210;
prohibition of graven images and, 4; rupture of temporality and, 124; as taboo, 9
affidavits, 98, 149, 150
African American literature, 196
"After Death" (Rossetti), 186
agency (responsibility), 219, 220
Alkalay-Gut, Karen, 87
Alphen, Ernst van, 132
Alter, Robert, 237
Altieri, Charles, 128, 212
American troops, in Second World War, 155,
244–245
Améry, Jean, 3, 40, 45, 60, 208
Amis, Martin, 234
amnesia, cultural, 7, 11, 73, 146, 176, 239
anamnesis, 150, 175, 246
anamorphosis, 100, 139

Angel of History, The (Forché), 93–94
animals, 44, 46
"Annunciation with a Bullet in It"
(Graham), 202–203, 204
Anschluss, 44
"Answering Machine Message" (S. Friedman), 85
Anthology of Holocaust Literature (Glatstein,
Knox, Margoshes, eds.), 237
anti-Semitism, 41, 48, 51, 160, 183; Christian
and Nazi, 168; disavowal of atrocities and,
2–3; of Ezra Pound, 222; internalized by
Jews, 79; masculinism and, 250; Nuremberg laws, 31; photography and, 134; refuge from, 92; Sartre on, 226; sexual
politics of, 195; in T. S. Eliot's poetry,
94
antimorphosis, 101, 102, 103, 120, 144; contrasted with anamorphosis, 100; defamiliarization and, 140; documentation
of degradation and, 132; empathic imagination and, 246; ideology of the visible
and, 128; proxy-witnesses and, 146
Antschel, Paul, 47
Appelfeld, Aharon, 2, 265n6
Aramaic language, 59, 61
archives, 3, 134
Arendt, Hannah, 32, 157, 159, 161, 192; on
Benjamin's bad timing, 40; correspondence with Karl Jaspers, 165; on Eichmann, 162, 251; on Jewish assimilation,
195–196; on rediscovery of humanity,
263; on suicide, 45
"Ariel" (Plath), 182
"Ars Poetica" (Milosz), 264

301

SUSAN GUBAR

is Distinguished Professor of English at Indiana University. She has co-authored and co-edited a number of books with Sandra M. Gilbert, including *The Madwoman in the Attic,* its three-volume sequel *No Man's Land: The Place of the Woman Writer in the Twentieth Century,* and the *Norton Anthology of Literature by Women.* Her two most recent publications are *Racechanges: White Skin, Black Face in American Culture* and *Critical Condition: Feminism at the Turn of the Century.*

MONTGOMERY COUNTY

Picture Research by
Marta H. and David N.
Kelsey

"Partners in Progress"
by Philip L. Cantelon
Produced in cooperation
with The Montgomery
County Historical Society
Rockville, Maryland

Windsor Publications, Inc.
Woodland Hills,
California

MONTGOMERY COUNTY

two centuries of change

BY JANE C. SWEEN

Windsor Publications, Inc.
History Books Division
Publisher: John M. Phillips
Senior Picture Editor: Teri Davis Greenberg
Editorial Director, Corporate Biographies: Karen Story
Design Director: Alexander D'Anca
Marketing Director: Ellen Kettenbeil
Sales Coordinator: Joan Baker

Staff for *Montgomery County: Two Centuries of Change*
Senior Editor: Jim Mather
Picture Editor: Susan L. Wells
Assistant Director, Corporate Biographies: Phyllis Gray
Corporate Biographies Editor: Judy Hunter
Editorial Assistants; Kathy Brown, Patricia Buzard, Lonnie Pham, Pat Pittman
Sales Managers: Bill Koons
Sales Representative: Smiti Kumar, Diane Murphy
Designer/Layout Artist: Ellen Ifrah

Library of Congress Cataloging in Publication Data

Sween, Jane C., 1931-
  Montgomery County, Two Centuries of Change.

  Bibliography: p. 235
  Includes index.
  1. Montgomery County (Md.)—History. 2. Montgomery County (Md.)—Description and travel.
3. Montgomery County (Md.)—Industries. I. Cantelon, Philip L. (Philip Louis), 1940-   . II. Title.
F187.M7S96 1984   975.2'84   84-20842
ISBN 0-89781-120-8

Contents

Introduction

The Colony of Maryland was granted to George Calvert, first Lord Baltimore, by a charter from King Charles I of England and was named Terra Maria in honor of Queen Henrietta Maria. However, George Calvert died before the charter was signed and he was succeeded in his title and estates by eldest sons through six Lord Baltimores. It was his son Cecil Calvert, second Lord Baltimore, who sent the first 200 colonists to Maryland in two ships, the Ark and the Dove, under the leadership of his brother Leonard Calvert. A celebration for their safe arrival was held on March 25, 1634 on St. Clement's Island in the Potomac River. A large wooden cross was erected and prayers were said by Father Andrew White, one of two Catholic priests who accompanied the group. This date has since been observed in the state as Founders Day and the 350th anniversary takes place in 1984.

The first permanent settlement was made at St. Mary's City on land purchased from the Indians with cloth, axes, hoes, and knives. Father White did much to maintain good relations with the natives and converted many to Christianity. The colony was founded on the principal of religious freedom although Lord Baltimore was a Catholic. Puritans in Virginia, unhappy with religious restrictions there, were encouraged to come to Maryland. The right to freedom of worship was strengthened in 1649 by passage of the Act of Religious Toleration.

The King had given Lord Baltimore the authority as proprietor to make the laws of the colony. But the settlers demanded this right for themselves subject to his approval. The first legislative assemblies were composed of all the freemen of Maryland. As the population increased the legislature was divided into two bodies and the members were elected. The upper house evolved into the Senate and the lower house became the House of Delegates of the General Assembly of Maryland. The seat of the government was at St. Mary's City until 1694 when Annapolis became the capital.

Autumn comes gracefully to Montgomery County countryside. Photo by Dave Kelsey

The Rock Creek Railway started between 18th and U streets in Washington and ran out Connecticut Avenue to Chevy Chase Lake amusement park in the 1890s. Courtesy, Montgomery County Historical Society and LeRoy O. King

Acknowledgments and Dedication

There are three groups who must be acknowledged as responsible for this illustrated history of Montgomery County, Maryland. Their order is chronological and does not imply the importance of their contribution.

The first group to which recognition should be given are the founders of the Montgomery County Historical Society. On June 19, 1944, Mrs. Lilly C. Stone, then an octogenarian long active in civic and patriotic activities in the county, called a meeting of acquaintances with an interest in history. They met at her home, "Glenmore", near Potomac to consider the formation of an organization dedicated to the collection and preservation of records and artifacts and the dissemination of information related to the history of the county. From the 23 present at this first meeting, the society has grown to a membership of over 600.

Secondly, appreciation should be expressed to the succession of diligent and dedicated leaders - the presidents of the Society. They have, through the years, kept the organization alive and functioning. They have given hours of administrative service and have urged the membership to greater efforts. From the list of these elected officers can be singled out Genevieve Wimsatt, in whose tenure this project was undertaken, and Nancy Hafer, in whose second term it became a reality.

The third to receive specific commendation are the volunteers who help with the work of the Society's library.

Some contribute their time on an informal basis by transcribing records, undertaking research, or donating material. Others work scheduled times collecting information and photographs, cataloguing, and serving the public during the hours that the library is open. It is to these regular volunteers whose interest has sustained the library of the Montgomery County Historical Society that this book is dedicated.

The charter had also given Lord Baltimore the right to grant land. At first 1,000 acres were assigned to every colonist who brought five others; if he brought less he was given 100 acres for himself and 100 for his wife and each servant. This land was subject to an annual "quit rent", a tax payable to Lord Baltimore. After 1683 this method was replaced by a system of patents. A warrant was issued for a tract of land. The holder of the warrant had a survey made and filed a certificate with the Land Office. He was then granted a patent giving title to the land.

As settlers arrived "counties" were formed for local government. The original county, St. Mary's, established in 1637, was followed on the Western Shore by Anne Arundel County in 1650. From the upper part of St. Mary's County were formed Calvert (1650) and Charles (1658) Counties. These in turn were divided in 1695 to form Prince George's County. These were the political divisions when the first patents for land were issued and the first settlers arrived in what was to become Montgomery County.

The spectacular Great Falls on the Potomac caused substantial difficulty in early attempts to navigate the river commercially. George Washington was the first president of the Patowmack Company in 1785 and built canals around both Little Falls and Great Falls. Boats traveled in the river except at the falls. Photo by Dave Kelsey

1
Settling the Wilderness

The wilderness was vast and uncharted. It stretched westward along the Potomac River from the mouth of Rock Creek to the mouth of the Monocacy River. The Patuxent River was its northern boundary. These 508 square miles of forest were inhabited only by wandering tribes of Indians and wild animals. One day it would become Montgomery County.

The first visual record of this area was a map drawn by Captain John Smith from his exploration of the Potomac River in 1608. Published in 1612, his map clearly showed landmarks along the river's shores.

The first written account appears in the journal of Henry Fleet, a young adventurer from the Jamestown, Virginia, colony who had accompanied Henry Spelman on the pinnace *Tiger* in the early 1620s to trade with the Indians living near the present site of Washington, D.C. Fleet was taken prisoner by the Piscataway Indians and held for five years. In 1632 he returned and traveled upriver to a place where he could hear the roar of the Great Falls of the Potomac. In his diary he declared that:

This place without all question is the most pleasant and healthful place in all this country, and most convenient for

habitation ... It aboundeth with all manner of fish. The Indians in one night commonly will catch thirty sturgeons in a place where the river is not above twelve fathoms broad. And as for deer, buffaloes, bears, turkeys, the woods do swarm with them and the soil is exceedingly fertile.

At the time of the white man's arrival in Maryland the Piscataway Indians, members of the Algonquin tribes, occupied the eastern shore of the Potomac River. These native villages were associated by a loose federation and each was ruled by a chief, called a *tayac.* Above the falls of the Potomac there is no evidence of permanent Indian settlements, only temporary hunting camps.

Father Andrew White, a Catholic priest who came with Lord Baltimore's settlers to St. Mary's in 1634, described the Piscataways in his *Relatio Itineris in Marylandiam:*

The natives are very tall and well proportioned; their skin is naturally rather dark, and they make it uglier by staining it, generally with red paint mixed with oil, to keep off the mosquitoes, thinking more of their own comfort than of appearances

... *They are clothed, for the most part, in deer skins or some similar kind of covering, which hangs down behind like a cloak. They wear aprons around the middle, and leave the rest of the body naked ... The race are of a frank and cheerful disposition ... they have a keen sense of taste and smell, and in sight too, they surpass the Europeans. They live for the most part, on a kind of paste, which they call Pone, and Omini, both of which are made of Indian corn; and sometimes they add fish or what they have procured by hunting and fowling. They are especially careful to refrain from wine and warm drinks ... except some* *whom the English have corrupted with their own vices.*

These Indians, exhibiting their tribal characteristic of hospitality, were willing to sell their land for a few trinkets. Eventually misunderstandings and confrontations with the settlers led many Piscataway to abandon their fields and villages and to move westward. Their migration took them through and beyond the land that was to become Montgomery County.

This land was also a place where Indians from the north came to camp, hunt, fish,

Above: *Captain John Smith, adventurer and explorer, in describing the new country, declared that "heaven and earth seemed never to have agreed better to frame a place for man's commodious and delightful habitation." From* Scharf's History of Maryland

Facing page: *Captain John Smith drew this map in 1612. Scharf describes Smith's map and account of his explorations as "an account so ample, and a plan so accurate of that great portion of the American continent now comprehended in the states of Maryland and Virginia, that all subsequent researches have only expanded and illustrated his original report." From* Scharf's History of Maryland

and trade. The Susquehannocks and Senecas, more warlike tribes than the Piscataway, roamed southward through the wilderness, camped along the Potomac and its tributaries, and established a trail used in their trade with the Carolina Indians. Their route crossed the Potomac at the mouth of the Monocacy River and was called the Seneca Path.

Fear of these roving Indians caused the Maryland government to form the "Rangers." The name came from their duty of "ranging" the frontier to protect the settlers from the natives. At first the government only designated officers who

were authorized to arm men and impress horses when an alarm was given. This usually resulted in the Rangers' arrival after the damage was done and the attackers had long fled.

The formation of a permanent force of Rangers in 1694 was an improvement. This Act of the Assembly permitted the drafting of men to patrol each neighborhood for several weeks at a time from April 10th to October 15th. The area they were to cover was from the falls of the Potomac to the first draughts of the Susquehanna River. Although the primary objective was scouting for signs of Indians, they were occasionally requested to find runaway slaves and servants. The Ranger had to provide his own musket, shot, and horse, but was paid for the maintenance of this mount.

In 1693 the government of Maryland constructed a fort at the mouth of Rock Creek from which the Rangers traded with the Indians and set out on their patrols. The Rangers personified the indomitable spirit and bravery of these early settlers in a new land. The lives of two of them, Ninian Beall and Richard Brightwell, demonstrate the extraordinary character required to meet the challenges of the frontier.

Ninian Beall, born in Fifeshire, Scotland, was captured during the Battle of Dunbar in 1650, when the Scottish Army was defeated by the forces of Oliver Cromwell. Transported with other prisoners to Maryland, he was indentured to Richard Hall, a Quaker of Calvert County. In accordance with the custom of that time, an indentured servant worked for seven years for the person who paid his passage to the colony. At the end of that time each man was given 50 acres and the tools with which to start his own farm. At the expiration of Ninian Beall's term of

Facing page: *General Richard Montgomery, Irish-born general of the Revolution, "fell gloriously fighting for the Independence and Liberty of the United States, before the walls of Quebec, the 31st day of December, 1775." Montgomery County was named in his honor September 6, 1776. Courtesy, Montgomery County Historical Society*

Right: *This manuscript contains minutes and proceedings of the first court held in Montgomery County at Leonard Davis' Hungerford Tavern "in the first Year of the Independency of the United States of America—1777." Present at the session were Charles Jones, Edward Burgess, William Deakins, Elisha Williams, Sam W. Magruder, Joseph Offutt, and Richard Thompson.*

Below: *The Chickering pianoforte is one of only two original pieces of furniture still in the Beall-Dawson House. Photo by Dave Kelsey*

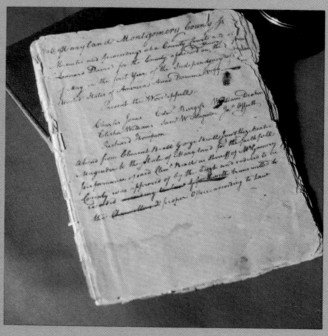

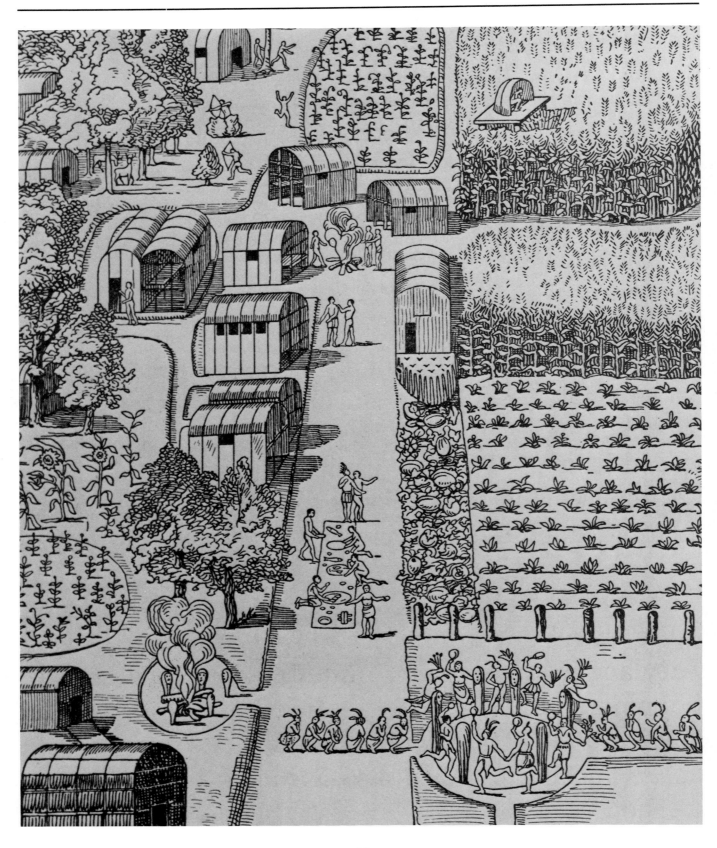

Above: *A Susquehannock Indian warrior is depicted in this 1612 engraving. More warlike than the Piscataway Indians, the Susquehannocks came from the north to camp, hunt, fish, and trade. Engraving by William Hole, on John Smith's 1612 Map of Virginia*

Facing page: *Although no evidence has been found of permanent Indian settlements in Montgomery County, it is assured that villages resembled this drawing of one in Virginia. From Harriot's* Virginia, *1588*

servitude, he started with his 50 acres and continued acquiring land throughout his lifetime culminating in the ownership of more than 25,000 acres at the time of his death. His homestead, "Bacon Hall," stood on the Patuxent River near present-day Upper Marlboro in Prince George's County.

Beall's career with the Rangers was a long one. Between 1668 and 1704 he held all of the ranks between lieutenant and colonel. In 1678 the *Archives of Maryland* record that the Council ordered 30 men be raised for the defense of the plantations and that they be deployed at the discretion of their commander, Captain Ninian Beall. Twenty years later on June 28, 1699, the Assembly records show passage of an Act of Gratitude to Beall stating:

Whereas Colonell Ninian Beall has been found very Serviceable to this Province upon all Incursions and Disturbances of Neighboring Indians and though now grown very Aged and less able to perform, Yet Continues his Resolution even beyond his Ability to do the like Service.

The Assembly went on to direct that three Negroes be purchased as a gift to Colonel Beall.

In 1695 Prince George's County was created from Calvert and Charles counties. The western boundary was vague and included all land in the province to the west. In 1703 Ninian Beall became a landowner on the frontier by taking out a patent on a tract of 795 acres which he called "Rock of Dumbarton." This land formed much of what is today known as Georgetown in the District of Columbia. At his death in 1717 at age 92, Ninian left this property in his will to his son George Beall.

Another outstanding leader of the Rangers was Captain Richard Brightwell. Unlike Ninian Beall, planter and family man, Brightwell was a rugged frontiersman who had traveled into Virginia in pursuit of the elusive Indians. In the course of his patrols he was impressed with the land along the curve of the Potomac River near the mouth of Seneca Creek. There, in 1695, he patented land which he called "Brightwell's Hunting Quarter," 1,086 acres of fertile land and sugar maple trees.

Another early description of part of the county comes from a Swiss adventurer, Baron Christolph von Graffenreid. In 1711 he traveled across the land now known as Montgomery County guided by Martin Charetier, a local surveyor said to be married to a Piscataway woman. Von Graffenreid's purpose was to locate inexpensive land on which to settle Swiss and German immigrants just as he had already done in Pennsylvania and North Carolina. Upon seeing the valley of the Potomac von Graffenreid observed:

We visited those beautiful spots of the country, those enchanted islands in the Potomac River above the falls. And from there, on our return, we ascended a high mountain standing alone in the midst of a vast stretch of country, called because of its form Sugar Loaf which means in French pain de sucre ... After we had come down again from this mountain to a place where there was a very fine spring and good soil, we went to Martin Charetier's where we were lodged and treated after the Indian fashion.

But von Graffenreid's Swiss and German followers did not seem to share his enthusiasm and his settlement never materialized.

EARLY SETTLERS
Land grants, or "patents," were made by the Maryland proprietors, the Lords Baltimore, to the settlers. Each tract was surveyed and given a name. Some of these names were of understandable origin, but others were as unusual as "Wolf's Cow," "Gittings Ha-Ha," and "Bite the Biter." The earliest land grant within the boundaries of what is now Montgomery County was made in 1688. In that year Henry Darnall was granted a large tract which he called "Girl's Portion." It lay on the east side of Rock Creek, and today Silver Spring is located on it. Colonel Henry Darnall had come to Maryland in 1664 and had held various positions in the government of the colony, including Keeper of the Great Seal and member of the Governor's Council.

In 1689 William Joseph was granted two tracts. "Joseph's Park" contained 4,220 acres; today the towns of Forest Glen and Kensington are situated there. "Hermitage" was laid out in the area between what is now Rockville Pike and Veirs Mill Road. This increased Joseph's land holdings along Rock Creek to 8,086 acres. William Joseph also was president of the Governor's Council at St. Mary's.

These grants were followed the same year by "St. Winexburg" to John Woodcock and "Carroll's Forest" to Charles Carroll, Esq., of Annapolis. In 1694 Thomas Brooke obtained a 3,697-acre tract which he called "Dan" (or "Dann"). Before the end of the century Richard Brightwell had patented his "Brightwell's Hunting Quarter," and John Courts, a landowner of St. Mary's County, had patented "Clean Drinking." There were more patents after 1700, but it was not until after 1715 that settlers began to appear. At that time there were no towns and no roads, and this remained the edge of civilization.

Most of the early land grants were obtained by wealthy and influential men who had no intention of living on them or

The "Madonna of the Trail," a landmark in Bethesda, pays tribute to the role of women in the arduous task of settling a wilderness area. Courtesy, Montgomery County Historical Society

or other Produce of the Land, which the Tenants can best spare, at the price current, and give a reasonable Time for making necessary Improvements.

Daniel Dulany

The majority of the early settlers were of English or Scottish descent. They chose to take up these new lands for various reasons. Some were the younger sons of tidewater planters whose family's plantations were usually inherited by the eldest son through the custom of primogeniture. Others were men who had come to the colony as indentured servants, served their time, and were free to own property in their own right. Still others wished for the freedom and adventure of the frontier. Later, Germans, many from Pennsylvania, began settling in the upper part of the county.

One area was settled by the Quakers who remained a tight-knit community. In 1728 James Brooke, a Catholic converted to the Society of Friends, was granted the tract "Brooke Grove." Along with his father-in-law, Richard Snowden, who patented "Snowden's Manor," they owned a great amount of land in the area of Sandy Spring and Brookeville. This was settled by Quakers from Anne Arundel and Calvert counties and later from Pennsylvania.

The typical early farmhouses were of very simple sort. Most were of the type called log cabins, containing one room and a loft. It was not until the latter half of the 1700s that homes of brick and stone appeared. The farm also had outbuildings or "dependencies." There was usually a barn, a spring house, a meat house, and quarters for farm laborers, if there were some. But the most important dependency was the tobacco house. It was in this building that the year's crop of tobacco was

improving them. Much in the manner of today's land speculators, these owners sold the land in small farms (the average was about 200 acres) or leased them to men who promised to make improvements. When Daniel Dulany patented large tracts in the Seneca area as "Middle Plantation" and "Conclusion," he advertised for tenants in the *Maryland Gazette,* the Annapolis newspaper:

I the subscriber, have several Tracts of Land ... which I am desirous to Let for Years, or Lives, upon moderate terms ... I will take the Rent in Tobacco, Corn, Wheat

stored until it could be transported to market. It was on the leaf of this plant that the fortunes of the family depended.

Above: Sandy Spring, located near the Sandy Spring Meeting House, was settled in 1745 by Quakers. The spring can still be found. Photo by Malcolm Walter

Facing page: Georgetown was a thriving seaport long before Washington, D.C., existed, serving as Montgomery County's link to the rest of the world. Tobacco was exported to Europe and items planters could not produce were imported. Library of Congress photo

THE TOBACCO ECONOMY

Tobacco was the primary crop. The leaves were cut, cured, and packed in barrels. These were transported to market, usually by oxen, over roads that history chose to call "rolling roads." Tobacco served as currency; taxes were paid in it; land was purchased by it; rents were paid in it; goods were exchanged for it.

The fluctuation of the tobacco economy, however, made the planter's life an uncertain one. Maryland tobacco was not of the highest quality produced. Prices rose and fell with political as well as economic conditions at home and abroad. Overproduction soon led to regulations. In

1747 the Maryland government passed a Tobacco Inspection Act. It designated warehouses at which this law was to be carried out. One such warehouse was owned by George Gordon on the Potomac River at the mouth of Rock Creek. This was the beginning of a settlement that would become Georgetown, port and center of commerce for the surrounding area.

On June 8, 1751, the Assembly of Maryland appointed a commission consisting of Henry Wright Crabb, John Needham, Samuel Magruder III, Josiah Beall, and David Lynn to lay out a town adjacent to George Gordon's inspection house. They surveyed several tracts and decided that Gordon's 100-acre "Knave's Dispute" and George Beall's "Beall's Levels" were most suitable. Later, part of Beall's "Rock of Dumbarton" was added. The town was divided into 80 lots. The owners of the land were to be paid and, in addition, each could select two lots. The two main streets were High Street (now Wisconsin Avenue) and Bridge Street (now M Street).

The harbor at Georgetown was of sufficient depth to accommodate seagoing vessels. Foreign firms had representatives, or "factors," established there. They purchased tobacco, shipped it to Europe, and imported items that the planters could not produce for themselves. These merchants frequently became wealthy and speculated in land. In view of their wealth, large land holdings, and education, they were often elected to both local and state government offices.

Robert Peter, the first mayor of Georgetown, was one of these men. From Crossbasket, Scotland, Peter came first to Bladensburg and then to Georgetown, representing the firm of John Glassford & Company, one of the largest in the Potomac River trade.

By 1748 Prince George's County had become the most populous in the colony. It was necessary to travel long distances to conduct the business of the county at Marlborough (now Upper Marlboro). As a consequence Frederick County was established by an act of the Maryland assembly on December 10, 1748, with the seat of government at Frederick Town. The area encompassed included present-day Montgomery, Frederick, Washington, Allegany, and Garrett counties. It was informally divided into Upper, Middle, and Lower districts of which the future Montgomery County comprised the Lower District.

THE FRENCH AND INDIAN WARS
The control of the lands west of the Ohio River was the issue that had the greatest effect on Montgomery County during the

French and Indian Wars. The British had treaties with the Indians to protect settlers. The French, however, incited local Indians to ignore the British treaties and harass the frontier settlements. Several times the settlers from the most western parts of Maryland were forced to retreat to more populated areas around Frederick Town for shelter and protection from the Indian raids. A military force under Colonel Henry Ridgely and Captain Alexander Beall was formed in the Lower District of Frederick County to afford protection for the refugees. But eventually British troops under General Edward Braddock marched through Frederick County settlements to meet the enemy.

General Edward Braddock had been ordered to join the British forces in the colonies as their commander-in-chief. In April of 1755 he met the 44th and 48th

Regiments in Alexandria, Virginia, to prepare strategy and gather forces and supplies for a movement against the French. At this point Braddock divided his force. Colonel Peter Halkett and his troops, accompanied by George Washington, were sent to Winchester, Virginia where a new road to Fort Cumberland was nearly complete. Colonel Thomas Dunbar and his men and General Braddock were to go by way of Frederick Town, Maryland.

This Maryland route took them through the entire length of the county. The first day's march from Georgetown on April 20th brought them 16 miles to Owen's Ordinary, later Rockville. The next day they marched along the road now approximating Route 355 to Dowden's Ordinary, a tavern run by Michael Dowden in present-day Clarksburg. There they were delayed by snow. The troops arrived in Frederick Town to find that there was no passable road through Maryland to Fort Cumberland. They crossed the Potomac and arrived at the fort on May 10th.

Braddock's advance was fraught with problems and delays. It was necessary to widen and clear roads to enable such a large army to pass. Food and supplies were requisitioned along the way. Work on the new courthouse in Frederick Town was halted as all available wagons in the area were in use by Braddock's troops. In addition, the army was increased by volunteers and conscripts from Maryland.

The story of Braddock's defeat near Fort Duquesne is well known. The general insisted upon leading his troops into battle in formation while the Indians crouched behind undergrowth and trees. Braddock was mortally wounded and 63 out of 89 commission ed officers were killed or wounded. The assault on the fort was abandoned.

Incidents along the frontier continued

Above: *Frederick, Sixth Lord Baltimore, was the last Lord Baltimore to govern Maryland. He died in 1771 as the clouds of war gathered. Frederick County, established in 1748, was named after him.* From Scharf's History of Maryland

Facing page, top: *General Edward Braddock, commander-in-chief of British troops in North America, was described by Horace Walpole as "intrepid and capable" but "desperate in his fortune, brutal in his behavior, and obstinate in his sentiments."* From Scharf's History of Maryland

Facing page, bottom: *In 1755 General Edward Braddock marched through the county on his way to Fort Cumberland during the French and Indian War. They were delayed by snow at Dowdens Ordinary, a tavern in Clarksburg. Courtesy, Montgomery County Historical Society*

until the Treaty of Paris in 1763 ended the hostilities. It was not long, however, before other events engaged the concerns of the citizens of the county.

Farm life in the early 19th century was hard work, but the citizens of the county developed a way of life that is still evident today. This Woodcut appeared in the Davey Crockett Almanac, 1835-1838. *Courtesy, Montgomery County Historical Society, Library of Congress photo*

2
Laying the Foundations

The following decades were a time of discussion, a time of decision, and a time of change. The thirteen colonies were chafing under the restrictions imposed by the British. Yet there was little to bind the separate colonial governments together. Maryland, like the other colonies, proceeded with a separate course of action until the oppression became unbearable.

The Stamp Act was passed by the British Parliament in March of 1765 while Montgomery County was still a part of Frederick County. This act placed a tax on all legal documents, newspapers, and licenses. The citizens of Frederick County felt compelled to make some sign of protest. On August 29, 1765 in Frederick Town they burned in effigy Zachariah Hood, the Maryland stamp distributor. Hood himself was forced to flee the colony by an irate mob in Annapolis.

When the November term of the Frederick County Court met in 1765 there were no stamps available for Clerk of the Court John Darnall to affix to court papers. So the justices ordered that all proceedings be valid without stamps:

It is the unanimous resolution and opinion of this court that all business thereof shall and ought to be transacted in the usual and accustomed manner without any inconvenience or delay . . . occasioned from the want of Stamped Paper, Parchment or Vellum and that all proceedings shall be valid and effectual without the use of Stamps . . . as no stamps are yet arrived in this Province . . . this Court are of the opinion it would be an injustice of the most wanton oppression to deprive any person of a legal remedy for omitting that which is impossible to perform.

The clerk at first refused to comply, so the court ordered that he "be committed to the custody of the sheriff" for contempt. Darnall then reconsidered his position and accepted the justices' order.

Concerned citizens had formed a Sons of Liberty group under the leadership of Colonel Thomas Cresap. They celebrated the court's ruling with a mock funeral. The Sons of Liberty marched through Frederick Town carrying a coffin with a sign inscribed: "THE STAMP ACT expired of a mortal stab received from the genius of liberty in Frederick County Court, 23rd November, 1765, Aged 22 days." This and similar protests throughout the colonies were instrumental in the repeal of the

Stamp Act on March 18, 1766.

The next oppressive tax levied by the British was the Townshend Act, a bill introduced in Parliament in 1767 by Chancellor of the Exchequer Charles Townshend. It taxed such imported items as tea, paper, lead, paint, and glass. In 1770 it was rescinded with the exception of the levy on tea.

Protest to the continued tax on tea took the form of a nonimportation agreement so widely supported that very little was being brought into the colonies by 1773. Elsewhere this protest resulted in the Boston Tea Party in December 1773 and the burning of the ship *Peggy Stewart* in

This photograph is purported to be the Hungerford Tavern circa 1905. On June 11, 1774, a meeting of citizens from Lower Frederick County (later Montgomery) met at Charles Hungerford's Tavern to discuss the recent Boston Tea Party and events leading up to it. From this meeting came a document known as "The Hungerford Resolves," which expressed support for the people of Boston and urged the breaking off of all commerce with Great Britain and the West Indies. From a 1906 postcard, courtesy, Charles Brewer

Annapolis in October 1774. In Georgetown it was handled by cooler heads. A shipment of tea consigned to Robert Peter of John Glassford & Company and John Ferguson

26

of Cunninghame, Findlay and Company arrived in August 1774. A meeting was held with the two factors. It was agreed that the cargo would be turned over to a committee composed of Thomas Johns, William Deakins, Jr., and Bernard O'Neill, who disposed of it.

The Boston Tea Party so angered the British Parliament that it passed the Boston Port Bill on March 14, 1774, closing the harbor of that city to all shipping. Quickly patriots began meeting throughout the colonies to express sympathy and support for the citizens of Boston. A meeting was called of the inhabitants of Lower Frederick County on Saturday, June 11, 1774, at Charles Hungerford's Tavern. This tavern was located where the road from Georgetown to Frederick Town intersected several other important routes of that time. (The settlement there later received the name Williamsburgh and, later still, Rockville.)

Those assembled selected Henry Griffith as moderator of the meeting. Griffith, an experienced leader, had first represented Anne Arundel County in the Maryland assembly (1768-1770) and, upon moving to this area, represented Frederick County (1773-1774). The citizens expressed their indignation over the Boston Port Bill, their support for the people of Boston, and their endorsement of an end to all commerce with the British in the approval of the resolutions that have come to be known as "The Hungerford Resolves":

Resolved, unanimously, That it is the opinion of this meeting that the Town of Boston is suffering in the common cause of America.
Resolved, unanimously, That every legal and constitutional measure ought to be used by all America for procuring a repeal of the act of Parliament for blocking up

the harbor of Boston.
Resolved, unanimously, That it is the opinion of this meeting that the most effectual means for the securing of American freedom will be to break off all commerce with Great Britain and the West Indies until the said act be repealed and the right of taxation given up on permanent principles.
Resolved, unanimously, That Mr. Henry Griffith, Dr. Thomas Sprigg Wootton, Nathan Magruder, Evan Thomas, Richard Brooke, Richard Thomas, Zadok Magruder, Dr. William Baker, Thomas Cramphin, Jr., and Allen Bowie be a committee to attend the general committee at Annapolis and of Correspondence for the lower part of Frederick County, and that any six of them shall have the power to receive and communicate intelligence to and from their neighboring committees. Resolved, unanimously, That a copy of these our sentiments be immediately transmitted to Annapolis and inserted in the Maryland Gazette.

Signed per Order,
Archibald Orme, Clerk

The First Maryland Convention was held in Annapolis on June 22, 1774. This delegation of representatives from the 16 existing counties quickly agreed to a nonimportation resolution. The matter of a nonexportation policy was, however, more difficult. Maryland was so dependent upon the tobacco trade that such a step might prove disastrous. A temporary measure was reached — exportation would be prohibited provided such a plan should be approved by other colonies. The convention also selected delegates to represent Maryland at the First Continental Congress to be held in September 1774 in Philadelphia.

The Second Maryland Convention met for five days in November 1774 in

Annapolis and then adjourned because of poor attendance. It reconvened on December 8th with 85 members representing all the counties. Henry Griffith, Thomas Sprigg Wootton, Evan Thomas, and Richard Brooke had been chosen to represent Lower Frederick County, but Evan Thomas declined to serve. Among the resolutions passed at this convention was one that organized military units within the counties:

Resolved, unanimously, That a well regulated militia, composed of the gentlemen, freeholders, and other freemen, is the natural strength and only stable security of a free government, and that such militia will relieve our mother country from any expense in our protection and defense ... Such of the inhabitants of this province as are from sixteen to fifty years of age, to form themselves into companies of sixty-eight men; to choose a captain, two lieutentants, an ensign, four sergeants, four corporals and one drummer for each company: and use their utmost endeavors to make themselves masters of the military exercise. That each man be provided with a good firelock and bayonet fixed thereon, half a pound of powder, two pounds of lead, and a cartouch-box, or powder-horn, and a bag for balls, and be in readiness to act on any emergency.

Ten thousand pounds were to be raised by subscription for the purchase of equipment for the militia. Frederick County's quota of this amount was £1,333.

The Maryland Constitutional Convention, held in the summer of 1775, had the overwhelming task of reorganizing the government of the colony. The Lords Baltimore had been the proprietors of Maryland from its beginning until the death of Frederick Calvert, the sixth and last Lord Baltimore, in 1771. The authority of Governor Robert Eden, the second royal governor appointed by the king, passed to the people of the colony.

The delegates to this convention in Annapolis adopted the "Articles of Association of the Freemen of Maryland" as a guide to the administration of the provincial government. The Committee of Safety, consisting of 16 members, was the executive body of the association. The Committee of Observation was the group within each county that carried out the association's policies. This convention had created a de facto government for Maryland.

The announcement on July 4, 1776, of the signing of the Declaration of Independence had made it necessary to frame a state constitution. The Maryland Constitutional Convention, with the Lower District of Frederick County represented by Thomas Sprigg Wootton, Jonathan Willson, William Bayly, Jr., and Elisha Williams, met in Annapolis and produced a constitution that stood virtually unchanged for 60 years. The delegates also voted to support the Declaration of Independence by asserting that "this Convention will maintain the freedom and independency of the United States with their lives and fortunes."

At the direction of the Second Maryland Convention, the militia had been formed. In the Lower District of Frederick County, soon to become Montgomery County, two battalions of militia elected their officers. The Lower Battalion selected Colonel John Murdock, and the Upper Battalion selected Colonel Zadock Magruder as their leaders. Most of the militiamen did not see active duty in these battalions. (The militia was roughly equivalent to the National Guard today.) But a Maryland Battalion of the Flying Camp was organized from the militia in the late spring of 1776 and served until early winter of that year. In July 1776 Colonel Charles Greenberry Griffith took these men to reinforce General George Washington on Long Island, where they served him well at the Battle of Harlem Heights.

Benjamin Latrobe, architect of the U.S. Capitol, frequently visited Montgomery County in the early part of the 19th century. This drawing titled "Out of Robb's Window" was done during a visit to Rockville when he brought his son to recuperate from an illness in the healthy air of Rockville.

BIRTH OF THE COUNTY

Just as this was a time of change for the citizens of the thirteen colonies, it was a time of change for the inhabitants of the Lower District of Frederick County. On September 6, 1776, the Maryland Constitutional Convention passed a bill sponsored by Thomas Sprigg Wootton that divided Frederick County into three parts and created two new counties — Montgomery and Washington. Montgomery County came into being by the following resolution:

Resolved, That after the first day of October next, such part of the said County

of Frederick, as it is so contained within the bounds and limits following, to wit: Beginning at the east side of the mouth of Rock Creek on the Potomac River, and running thence with the said river to the mouth of the Monocacy, then with a straight line to Parr's Spring, from thence with the lines of the county to the beginning, shall be and is hereby errected into a new county called Montgomery.

The two new counties were named for heroes of the day, General Richard Montgomery and General George Washington. This was the first time that a Maryland county had not been named for royalty or a member of the Calvert family — a significant reflection of the new American democratic ideal.

Richard Montgomery, an Irishman, first came to the colonies during the French and Indian Wars as a British soldier. He returned in 1772, after his military duties were over, to settle in the Hudson River valley near Rhinebeck, New York. There he married Janet Livingston, the daughter of the wealthy Robert Livingston. At the outbreak of the Revolution, Montgomery was commissioned as a brigadier general because of his previous military experience. He was in command when the American forces attacked Quebec. His death in that battle on December 31, 1775, made him the highest ranking officer to that time to give his life for the American cause. The following year he was immortalized by giving his name to Montgomery County, Maryland. There are said to be 18 counties in the United States named for him, but the one in Maryland was the first.

The organization of the new county was set in motion by the appointment of seven commissioners: Allen Bowie, Thomas Cramphin, Jr., Henry Griffith, Nathan

Magruder, Zadock Magruder, John Murdock, and John Willson. They were instructed to conduct an election to select the seat of government. The chosen site near the geographic center of the county may have come as no surprise since it was the one that had been used for previous meetings, Hungerford's Tavern. By the time the first court convened on May 20, 1777, however, the tavern was operated by Leonard Davis. A village grew up around the tavern and was known for many years as Montgomery Court House.

Court officials were chosen. The justices presiding at the first court were Charles Jones, Edward Burgess, William Deakins, Elisha Williams, Samuel Wade Magruder, James Offutt, and Richard Thompson. They were appointed by Governor Thomas Johnson with the advice of the Upper House of the Assembly of Maryland. The clerk of the court, appointed by the justices, was Brooke Beall who was "directed and empowered to keep the records and other papers belonging to the Clerk's office at his own House without charge to the County until there is a sufficient publick Building provided for that purpose." Brooke Beall was succeeded by his son, Upton Beall. The sheriff, an important position in colonial times and elected by the people, was Clement Beall. Samuel West was appointed register of wills.

The commissioners were also instructed to purchase a lot not to exceed four acres on which a courthouse was to be built. In 1779 Thomas Owen proposed furnishing a building, as he described, with:

one fire place above and one below Stairs; two Rooms above Stairs to be Seated for Jurys; Tables and Benches to hold Court; the present Goal to be filled in and made secure with a Stove at the Seasons of the year when required; the whole to be completed by November Court next and received as approved of by the Court for three years Rent free.

Tax commissioners were appointed and the county was divided for tax purposes into 11 districts called "hundreds" (a term originating in English feudal times as the area in which 100 men could be brought to arms in support of the lord). These same names had been used in political and tax divisions where the area was all part of Frederick County. The general areas in today's frame of reference were:

Linganor Hundred - Clarksburg, Damascus, Hyattstown
Upper Newfoundland Hundred - Brookeville, Laytonsville, Olney, Sandy Spring
Lower Newfoundland Hundred - Ashton, Brighton, Burtonsville,
Northwest Hundred - Kensington, Silver Spring, Takoma Park, Wheaton
Lower Potomac Hundred - Bethesda, Chevy Chase, Georgetown
Middle Potomac Hundred - Potomac, Rockville
Upper Potomac Hundred - Darnestown, Dawsonville, Seneca
Rock Creek Hundred - Colesville, Layhill, Norbeck
Seneca Hundred - Gaithersburg
Sugar Loaf Hundred - Barnesville, Beallsville, Germantown
Sugarland Hundred - Poolesville

At this time the population of the county was 14,418; 10,000 were white and the remainder were black. By 1790, the time of the first federal census, the population had increased to 18,000 of which about 35 percent were black.

WAR — A REALITY

It is little wonder that some details concerning the formation of the county government were lost in more important events that were occurring. The country was involved in fighting a war, enlisting men, and supplying their needs.

The Second Continental Congress in Philadelphia in January 1775 had organized the Continental Army. Maryland's Thomas Johnson had nominated George Washington as commander in chief. The counties were urged to furnish recruits for the new army and Frederick County had hastened to comply. Two independent companies of expert riflemen were formed with Michael Cresap as captain of the First Company and Thomas Price as captain of the Second Company. These two units hurriedly marched to Cambridge, Massachusetts, a distance of 550 miles, in 22 days, where they joined the American Army.

It was not until January of 1776 that Smallwood's Maryland Regiment was organized. This unit, made up entirely of Maryland men under the command of General William Smallwood, served until December 1776. At that time it was reorganized into six regiments, First through Sixth, and in April 1777 a Seventh was added. Men from Montgomery County served in many of the regiments but were concentrated in the Seventh. Other units had large numbers of Maryland men, but these regiments became known as the Maryland Line — from which comes a Maryland nickname, "The Old Line State." These regular troops, or some part of them, saw action in many of the battles around New York and Philadelphia. Then, early in April 1780, the troops of the Maryland Line were transferred to the southern campaign until the surrender of Cornwallis at Yorktown. As one historian wrote, "These were not mercenary soldiers, but farmers, merchants, mechanics, who pledged their lives to the cause of liberty."

Even though no battles were fought on Maryland soil, it was the patriotic duty of everyone to furnish supplies needed to feed and equip the military. Since nothing was being imported, it was a test of ingenuity to gather together the necessities and then to transport them to the place they were needed by the army. Georgetown became the focal point of efforts in this area. There were located the unsold stores of the British merchants, a concentration of skilled craftsmen, and the means to transport the supplies by way of water.

It was necessary to fulfill the Second Maryland Convention's order that every militiaman be outfitted with a gun, bayonet, lead, and powder. Large numbers of rifles and muskets were purchased from John Yost, the only gunsmith in town, at four pounds each. In 1780, however, Yost moved to Pittsburg. A cannon factory was established along the river above Georgetown. Powder mills were erected in the county and some effort was made to refine crude saltpeter for the manufacture of gunpowder. Companies were established to manufacture clothing and supplies for the soldiers.

Thomas Richardson, a Quaker merchant, was appointed assistant commissary for Maryland at Georgetown. His instructions were to purchase supplies from the counties along the Potomac. He collected grain, cattle, and horses from the surrounding farmland. He saw to it that wheat was ground into flour; that beef, pork, and fish were salted; that cider and brandy were distilled; and that blankets and clothing were purchased. Richardson's duties were increased when the military campaign shifted to the south. George Washington ordered 30 tons of hay and 2,000 bushels of corn as forage gathered at Georgetown for

the wagon trains transporting the artillery and baggage of the army on the move. Montgomery County provided its fair share of these necessities of war.

One segment of the county's population suffered moral anguish in addition to the privations forced upon them. The Society of Friends disapproved of war and violence in any form, but believed that each Friend had to make his own decision in the matter. Several, including Evan Thomas, Richard Brooke, and Richard Thomas, had taken very active roles in the early, pre-Revolutionary unrest. The war led to much soul-searching among the members of the Quaker community.

Some Friends did join the army, compromising their Quaker upbringing. Richard Brooke of "Fair Hill" fought with distinction and attained the rank of colonel. For this he and others were disowned by the Sandy Spring Meeting. Those who decided that war was against their belief also suffered for their devotion to principle. Although they were guaranteed by law their right to refuse military service, they were expected to furnish substitutes or pay a fine.

A preliminary agreement to end the war was signed on April 19, 1783. The country greeted its new independence with celebrations. Montgomery County's festivities during that month were climaxed by a gala dinner with 13 toasts and a ball. They were described in *The Maryland Journal & Baltimore Advertiser*: "An elegant dinner was provided, after which the following toasts were drank, the Hessian band playing the whole time":

● The United States in Congress
● General Washington and the Northern Army
● General Greene and the intrepid Officers and Soldiers of the Southern Army

● His Most Christian Majesty and the Queen and Royal Family of France
● Perpetual Alliance and mutual good Offices between France and America
● The Count de Rochambeau
● The Marquis de la Fayette
● The Chevalier der la Luzerne
● The Ministers of France and America at Paris
● Governor Paca and the State of Maryland
● The Shades of those gallant Heroes who nobly fell in defence of American Liberty
● May Literature, Philosophy, and all the Arts and Sciences meet with every Assistance and Encouragement from the Legislature of Maryland
● The truly virtuous and patriotic Ladies of America, who rejected luxuries, and even the Conveniences of Life, for the Salvation of their Country

The ball held that evening "continued with the greatest decorum and vivacity till 12, when the company dispursed."

The official end of the Revolution, the Treaty of Paris, was signed on September 3, 1783.

PEACE — THE RESULTS

There were many problems to be faced after the victory. One of these was the financial situation in the colonies. The federal treasury was so depleted that bankruptcy was a real threat. Maryland's financial situation was no better.

One plan proposed to restructure the shaky Maryland economy was the sale of property belonging to Loyalists — those who had not signed the Oath of Allegiance during the war.

The Maryland government moved slowly. Charles Carroll of "Carrollton", Thomas Johnson, and Daniel of St. Thomas Jenifer were among those who opposed the confiscation of property and were successful in delaying it. They feared the measure would further increase land speculation and profiteering with the use of "cheap money". Nevertheless, the bill finally was passed. All Loyalists were given the opportunity to come forward before March 21, 1782 and take the Oath of Allegiance that had been taken by patriots in 1778. The valuable property of those Loyalists who refused to sign was seized and sold. Purchase payment was to be in hard currency (the only medium of exchange with any value in the new republic). A few farmer-tenants were able to buy the land they had formerly leased, but most did not have the means to pay.

In Montgomery County large tracts went on the market. One instance of this was the land Daniel Dulany had patented near Seneca in 1731 — 1,913 acres of "Conclusion" and 722 acres of "Middle Plantation." His son, Daniel, who had come into possession of these tracts, had taken the role of a passive Loyalist who, according to historian Aubrey C. Land, "respected his oath to constituted authority [and] who rejected the right of revolution." Although Daniel Dulany II had remained at his home near Annapolis throughout the war, his property was confiscated when the government moved against the "estates of the King's Loyal Subjects."

Economic conditions continued to deteriorate. As soon as the war was over a brisk trade between America and Europe had resumed. There was a great demand for American tobacco after years of scarcity and European manufactured goods were welcome after wartime shortages. But the 1784 glut of tobacco on the market resulted in lower prices, not only for tobacco but for wheat and other grains as well. British companies began to sue for back debts (many incurred before the war) that could

not be paid. Property taxes also remained unpaid for lack of money. County records show a great increase in sheriff's sales of real estate and personal property. Citizens as well as governments had little paper or hard currency.

The economy was not the only problem confronting the farmers of Montgomery County after the Revolution. Agriculture was in a predicament of its own. Those tilling the fertile soil of the area had given little thought to changing their practice of

Above: Built in 1765, this stone house in Georgetown was originally in Montgomery County. A National Geographic article points out that the house stood before Washington, D.C., was even a plan. Photo by B. Anthony Stewart & John E. Fletcher, National Geographic Society, April 1953.

Facing page: Farming in Montgomery County was in trouble during the late 18th century due to soil depletion and outmoded methods. Innovations in farm equipment were greeted with enthusiasm. This wood engraving of a new reaping machine appeared in the Columbian Magazine, in September 1780. Courtesy, Montgomery County Historical Society, Library of Congress photo

planting tobacco year after year. Crop rotation was not practiced and the nitrogen-depleted soil yielded less and less each succeeding year. As the Honorable Thomas Anderson described it in an address on the occasion of the county's centennial celebration in 1876: "In less than a century after this system of denuding and exhaustion began, there were no more forests to clear, and no more land to till. Then succeeded the period of old farms decaying, worn fences, and mouldering homesteads."

A dramatic decrease in population occurred that lasted well into the next century. The young men of the county who might have farmed locally sought land elsewhere. Groups were formed through local ties or family relationships that moved together to new land and founded new settlements. One early migration route was into western North Carolina, where fertile farmland was available. Other routes extended into the territories of Kentucky and Ohio. Still others moved west to settle on lots given them by the government in lieu of army pay.

Another reason for this population loss came about in 1791. After much debate in Congress a compromise was reached between northern and southern factions with the decision to locate the new national capital on the banks of the Potomac River. George Washington came to meet with citizens and inspect possible sites. The merchants of Georgetown did considerable lobbying against Williamsport in Washington County, their chief competitor. On January 24, 1791, Washington announced that the site adjacent to Georgetown was the most suitable.

Maryland donated 64 square miles of land from Montgomery and Prince George's counties. The city was originally laid out as a 10-mile square, but that part given by Virginia was later returned. Montgomery County lost Georgetown, the largest town in the county, but began its position as the neighbor of the nation's capital.

Twenty-five years after its creation Montgomery County had 3,000 fewer people than at the time of the first federal census. Changes were essential if this downward trend was to be reversed.

Brookeville Academy claimed in its 1870 catalog to be a "first-class school, where not only the minds of the pupils will be carefully trained and stored with useful knowledge, but where their manners and morals will be carefully watched over." Courtesy, Montgomery County Historical Society

3

Establishing a Heritage

Montgomery County entered the 19th century with difficult challenges to overcome. Within the new challenges lay the opportunity to build a heritage based on newly won independence and freedom for all people. In the next 50 years Montgomery County citizens established a way of life that survives to this day.

POLITICS AND WAR
Following the Revolution two major political parties had emerged. The Federalist party, with national leaders that included George Washington, Alexander Hamilton, and James Madison, believed that a strong central government would establish order at home and peace with other nations. On the local level the party consisted of conservative, wealthy landowners and merchants. Even after this party lost national popularity, it remained the party in power in Montgomery County.

The Anti-Federalists opposed the Constitution and favored a loose confederation of states and states' rights. Nationally they became the Jeffersonian Republicans and later the Democratic party. Their platform expressed the sentiments of the small farmer and craftsman who feared the power of the wealthy.

Each of the thirteen states was required to ratify the new Constitution of the republic. In the election of delegates to the Maryland Convention in Annapolis in April 1788, the Federalists had a ticket composed of William Deakins, Jr., Thomas Cramphin, Jr., Richard Brooke, and Benjamin Edwards. The Anti-Federalists were represented by Edward Burgess, Lawrence O'Neale, William Holmes, and Henry Griffith, themselves large landowners, who chose to represent the political sentiments of their less affluent neighbors and tenants. In Montgomery County the Federalist ticket won by the margin of 895 to 315. This result agreed with that of Maryland as a whole as the convention supported a strong central government and ratified the new Constitution with a vote of 63 to 11.

The Federalist party had won the national and county elections until 1800. In that year Montgomery County's Federalist candidate for presidential elector, Francis Deakins, won a bitter campaign. Thomas Jefferson, however, carried the presidential election essentially marking the demise of the Federalists on the national level. In Maryland, however, where the Federalists retained power, one young leader was

Alexander Contee Hanson, grandson of John Hanson, president of the First Continental Congress. Along with Robert Goodloe Harper (the son-in-law of Charles Carroll) and Roger Brooke Taney of Frederick County (later chief justice of the Supreme Court), Alexander Hanson was trying to give the party a new image. Hanson was only 22 years old when he founded the *Federal Republican* newspaper in Baltimore in 1808. In 1811 he purchased a house in Rockville located directly in back of the courthouse on Jefferson Street — the name of the street, no doubt, a matter of consternation to the ardent

young Federalist.

Hanson was a still a resident of Rockville when the United States declared war on England on June 18, 1812. Immediately, Hanson editorialized on the unpopularity of the war, declaring that "without funds, without taxes, without an army, navy, or adequate fortifications [this is] a war against the clear and decided sentiments of the nation."

Hanson's point of view elicited a powerful reaction as the newspaper's office on the corner of Gay and Second streets in Baltimore was attacked by a mob. The presses, type, and the frame building itself

Above: *Alexander Contee Hanson, Jr., lawyer, newspaper editor, congressman, and senator, made his home in Rockville. In addition to his other talents he was a leader in the realignment of the Federalist party. From* Scharf's History of Maryland

Facing page: *Black Rock Mill was just one of many mills in the county at the turn of the century. Built in 1815 on Seneca Creek near Darnestown, Black Rock Mill is one of only two mills still standing. Photo by Lewis Reed, Montgomery County Historical Society*

were destroyed in the attack. Publication of the paper was resumed temporarily in Georgetown. Then, on July 26th Hanson and some of his Federalist friends from Montgomery County returned to Baltimore. They armed themselves to protect the new offices, but when the crowd of Baltimoreans spied the guns and ammunition a riot ensued. Hanson and his friends were given police protection and taken to the city jail. But the mob followed and attacked the jail. During the melee General James M. Lingan was killed and several other Federalists were wounded.

In reaction to this violence, the voters elected Alexander Contee Hanson to Congress on March 4, 1813. He served in the 13th and 14th Congresses and resigned in 1816 to fill a vacancy in the Senate created by the resignation of his friend Robert Goodloe Harper. Hanson sold his Rockville property in 1818 and made his home at "Belmont" in Anne Arundel County until his death on April 23, 1819.

The War of 1812 was not a popular war and the Federalists were the outspoken leaders of the opposition. Many Americans were unsure of the reasons for the United States' involvement. Initially, the British naval blockade of the Chesapeake Bay cut trade and shipping. Then, British naval vessels entered the bay and sailed its length and width. They landed at port towns and large plantations to steal, burn, and terrorize the inhabitants. There was little defense for these raids as the new country had only a small regular army. The only protection came from a volunteer militia in each state. The 12 brigades of Maryland militia contained men from lower Montgomery County in its Fourth Brigade and men from the upper part of the county in the Seventh Brigade.

In August 1814, an English force entered the Chesapeake, sailed up the Patuxent River, and landed at Benedict on the 19th. On the 20th, with Major General Robert Ross in command, they began a march northward without opposition. By the time the British reached Bladensburg, a town in Prince George's County on the Eastern Branch of the Potomac (Anacostia) River on August 24th, they were greatly outnumbered and without artillery or cavalry.

The Americans were greater in number but thoroughly disorganized. The militia officers and regular officers argued about who was in command, and the marines under Commodore Joshua Barney refused

Right: *General William H. Winder commanded county troops when Washington was under siege during the War of 1812. Troops gathered at the Montgomery County Courthouse had no food, tents, or supplies of any kind. From Scharf's History of Maryland*

Below: *Known as the Madison house in Brookelle, the home of Postmaster Caleb Bentley served as refuge for President James Madison and his family when the British occupied Washington in August 1814. Courtesy, Montgomery County Historical Society*

to take orders from the army. Brigadier General William Henry Winder was in command of the troops, but President and Commander in Chief James Madison was on the field as was Secretary of State James Monroe. Each was trying independently to position the troops to protect the bridge over the river.

At the time of the British attack, the American troops were still not well situated on the terrain. The battle lasted half an hour. The field "lost all semblance of order" as the American forces broke, turned, and fled "in a tidal wave of defeat." A second line of defense had been drawn up by Barney's marines and Colonel George Peter's artillery. Winder ordered them to retreat, but the Americans fought on until the civilian drivers of their ammunition wagons fled and Barney himself was wounded. The rout was complete. Winder ordered the surviving soldiers to regroup on the heights beyond Georgetown.

In Washington, less than 20 miles away, there was panic. Some citizens had fled to Virginia but most sought safety in Montgomery County. At the President's House, Dolly Madison collected state papers, household silver, and the portrait of George Washington by Gilbert Stuart and departed for Virginia.

The British entered the city. During their occupation they burned the Capitol, the President's House, the Navy Yard, and the treasury and war offices. Homes and stores were sacked. The fires spread a thick cloud of smoke over the city that was clearly visible throughout the county. Fortuitously, nature ended the man-made havoc. General Ross' dispatch described it:

The sky grew suddenly dark, and the most tremendous hurricane ever remembered . . . came on. Roofs of houses were torn off by it, and whisked into the air like sheets of paper; while the rain which accompanied it, resembled the rushing of a mighty cataract . . . The darkness was as great as if the sun had long set . . . occasionally relieved by flashes of vivid lightning.

The storm, which lasted for nearly two hours, dampened the fires and ended the danger of total destruction. General Ross had accomplished more than he had hoped. His troops exhausted, far from their ships, and thoroughly drenched, Ross decided to withdraw. There was no pursuit.

General Winder had reached Tennallytown, three miles west of Georgetown, on the evening of the 24th. The next morning he ordered the remaining troops to assemble at Montgomery Court House (Rockville). Their situation was chaotic. The supply train had gone to Virginia. There were no tents, no food, and no supplies of any kind. Messengers were hurriedly sent to Frederick and Baltimore for bread and salt beef as the soldiers burned the lumber stacked for use in the new home of Clerk of the Court Upton Beall.

The next day President Madison and his wife met briefly in Virginia but at midnight he departed to cross the Potomac and rejoin General Winder at Montgomery Court House. The president's party arrived to find that Winder had left for Baltimore. Unable to overtake Winder the president stopped about 9 p.m. in Brookeville at the home of Caleb Bentley, a Quaker storekeeper and postmaster. Mrs. Margaret Bayard Smith, whose husband Samuel Harrison Smith was editor of *The National Intelligencer* newspaper in Washington, had also fled to the Bentley's. She described Brookeville in a letter to her sister:

The streets of this quiet village, which

never before witnessed confusion, [are] now filled with carriages bringing out citizens, and Baggage wagons and troops. Mrs. Bentley's house is now crowded, she has been the whole evening sitting at the supper table, giving refreshment to soldiers and travellers. I suppose every house in the village is equally full. I never saw more benevolent people.

The following morning news reached Brookeville of the British withdrawal from Washington and the president departed at noon for the city.

The signing of the Treaty of Ghent on December 24, 1814, and its ratification on February 17, 1815, marked the end of the war. The United States had withstood its first major test as a new nation. But even in Montgomery County the popularity of the Federalist party, with its platform of conservatism, pacifism, and pro-British sentiment, declined as a wave of democratic feeling swept the nation.

Along with the revision in party affiliation came an awareness of family domination in county politics. This fact, noted in colonial days in the Beall and Magruder families, became more evident after political parties were formed. In the 1800s it was apparent in the role played by the Peter family, as later it would be in the Lee family.

By 1835 a new courthouse was needed for the offices of the county government. The Maryland assembly authorized the court to raise the needed funds. A brick building in the Federal style of architecture with a central section of two stories and wings of one story on each side was completed in 1840. Later, in 1872, a second story was added to each of the wings.

PROBLEMS AND SOLUTIONS
Soil depletion from tobacco farming became

Above: *This barn stands at "Woodland," Norwood. Although most barns in the county were of frame construction, stone was used occasionally, mainly in areas settled by the English. Courtesy, Montgomery County Historical Society*

Facing page: *Tschiffely Farm shows a typical farm scene. Boyd's* History of Montgomery County *lists close to 900 farmers in the county in 1879. Courtesy, Montgomery County Historical Society*

chronic in the early 1800s in Montgomery County. This, coupled with the fact that transportation had not measurably improved since the arrival of the early settlers, created an urgent situation.

The first efforts to change agricultural methods began in the Quaker community. Quaker farmers experimented with plaster of paris and lime fertilizers, with crop rotation, and with deeper plowing. Results were soon evident. In the 1840s Peruvian guano (bird droppings) was imported and its success as a fertilizer was quickly proved. But the imported guano was expensive and it took several years for the less expensive chemical fertilizers to be manufactured and available.

The Quakers organized clubs to share

information on new farming practices, to discuss agricultural problems, and, occasionally, to publish tracts on the improved techniques. The first was the Farmer's Club of Sandy Spring. The first meeting was held in 1844 at "Bloomfield," home of Richard Bentley, and subsequent

meetings were held at each member's farm. This original club was followed by the Medley's District Agricultural Society in the Poolesville area, the Enterprise Club at Sandy Spring, and others. Both of the Sandy Spring clubs remained active into the 20th century.

The women of the Sandy Spring neighborhood felt the need for a similar organization. Previously the only local aid in home management was Elizabeth Lea's *Domestic Cookery.* In 1845 this local Quaker lady had published a book that contained not only recipes, but also instructions on how to handle servants, cures for various maladies, and household hints. Then, in May 1857 a club for Sandy Spring women, the Mutual Improvement Association, was founded. It is believed to be the third oldest women's club to have met continuously in the United States.

The Montgomery County Agricultural Society was organized in 1846. Its constitution stated its purpose as advancing agricultural interests and improving resources of the county. In September of that year the society sponsored its first "agricultural exhibition" in front of the courthouse. For several years thereafter the fair was held on a lot adjacent to St. Mary's Catholic Church and then moved to a location across the road (now Richard Montgomery High School's football field). Exhibits, competitions, speeches, and music were all part of the annual event. The fair was suspended during the Civil War, but was resumed in 1866. Attendance swelled

Above: The earliest roads in the county are depicted in this 1796 map by Griffiths. Many of these roads today still form a major part of the county's highway network.

Facing page, top: The building of roads was a painstaking and lengthy process, but vital to the development of suburban areas. Samuel McCeney, although a farmer at heart, spent his lifetime building roads in Montgomery County. Courtesy, Virginia Hoffman

Facing page, bottom: Route 28 in Darnestown is depicted here before paving. What is now Route 28 is one of the earliest roads in the county, and was one of the main ways farmers in Poolesville, Darnestown, Dickerson, and Barnesville reached the courthouse in Rockville. Courtesy, Montgomery County Historical Society

with the coming of the railroad and the extension of the streetcar line to Rockville. The Depression of the 1930s, however, put an end to the County Fair and the land was auctioned off in 1933 to the Board of Education to satisfy debts.

Poor transportation made it difficult to move Montgomery County crops to market early in the 1800s. Roads were often barely passable. The Potomac River with its shallow, rocky bed was unnavigable because of its falls. It would take the first half of the 19th century to build turnpikes and a canal.

The earliest roads in the county can be seen on Dennis Griffith's map of 1794. The major route was the one from Georgetown to Frederick. Another was from Georgetown to the mouth of the Monocacy, which became River Road. Originally proposed to connect Georgetown with Cumberland, the plan was never completed. Two other roads connected Montgomery Court House with Baltimore by way of Sandy Spring and Annapolis by way of Bladensburg. Sections of another, Old Baltimore Road, can still be seen today crossing upper Montgomery County. At this time road repairs were made by "overseers of the roads," leading citizens appointed to see that "public roads" were kept passable along the sections in their neighborhoods. The remainder were crude private lanes used by planters to reach the various mills.

The first turnpike was an improved road from Georgetown to Rockville. The Washington Turnpike Company was chartered in 1817; work was completed in 1828. Tolls were charged for various types of traffic, ranging from 4 cents for a horse and rider to 25 cents for a score of cattle or a vehicle with two horses. In 1849 the Union Turnpike Company was organized to build a toll road from Washington to Brookville, an extension of the Seventh Street Pike in Washington. Today this is Georgia Avenue. Later the Washington, Colesville & Ashton Turnpike was constructed northward along the eastern boundary of the county.

The improved roads were heavily used by passenger and mail stages. One of the first stage lines ran between Georgetown and Frederick once a week, but by 1800 it ran twice weekly at a total cost of $3 or for 6 cents a mile. In 1838 it was possible to take the stage every day but Sunday. Additional stage lines ran from Sandy Spring to Laurel and from Sligo to Burtonsville.

One of the most unusual roads built in the county before the Civil War was never intended as a highway. MacArthur Boulevard, originally known as Conduit Road, covers the man-made, brick-lined tunnel built by the federal government to bring the water supply of Washington from Great Falls. Engineers from the U.S. Corps of Engineers began work in 1857 under the direction of the War Department with Montgomery C. Meigs in charge. The aqueduct of red Seneca sandstone that carries the conduit across Cabin John Creek was, for many years, the longest single-span, arched bridge in the world.

The construction of canals was a popular solution to the transportation problems of the early 1800s. The idea for a canal to open trade between the Potomac and the Ohio River Valley came from the old Potowmack Company, incorporated in 1784, in which George Washington was an investor. This company constructed several locks at the falls of the Potomac River but by 1819 was bankrupt.

Interest was revived again with the unquestioned success of the Erie Canal in New York state, which opened in 1825. The Chesapeake & Ohio Canal Company (C & O) was formed and, with federal and state aid, work was begun. On July 4, 1828,

Originally a toll house on the Washington, Colesville, and Ashton Turnpike, Mrs. K's Toll House is now a popular dining spot in Silver Spring. Courtesy, Montgomery County Historical Society

President John Quincy Adams turned the first shovel of dirt in a dedication ceremony for the canal. On the same day in Baltimore, Charles Carroll, the only surviving signer of the Declaration of Independence, performed the same honor for the Baltimore & Ohio Railroad (B & O). The two companies became bitter rivals.

By 1830, two years after it was begun, 20 miles of canal were opened between Georgetown and Seneca. A year later 70 miles of track had been laid and the railroad had reached Frederick. But the B & O did not lie within the boundaries of Montgomery County and was of little help to its farmers. Financial troubles plagued the canal and it reached Cumberland eight years after the arrival of the B & O. All plans for continuing the canal to the Ohio River were abandoned.

The C & O canal ran parallel to the river for 184.5 miles of which 37 miles were in Montgomery County. Building the waterway was back breaking work done with axes, stump pullers, shovels, wagons, wheelbarrows, and horse-drawn scrapers. The usual wage was $10 a month and $20 a month for skilled masons. No slave labor was used. Many of the canal workers were recent immigrants seeking a better life in

Facing page, top: *K.M. Marlow traveled to school in Takoma Park from her home in Four Corners via the Washington, Colesville, and Ashton Turnpike. Courtesy, Virginia Hoffman*

Facing page, bottom: *Construction began in 1857 on the Conduit Road, which is now MacArthur Boulevard. The road covers the conduit used to carry Washington's water supply from Great Falls. Known as the Union Arch, this Seneca sandstone aqueduct crossed Cabin John Creek. MacArthur Boulevard still crosses the creek via this single lane bridge. Courtesy, Library of Congress*

Above: *Transportation was difficult at best in the early 19th century. Stages like this carried passengers from one city to another over primitive roads. Though not in Montgomery County, the Waterloo Inn is typical of the type of accommodations available to the adventuresome traveler. Lithograph by T.M. Baynes, circa 1826, courtesy, Library of Congress*

Left: *Nathan Dickerson Poole, of Edward's Ferry along the C & O Canal, is shown with storekeeper Walter and lock keeper Connell in this 1903 tintype. Courtesy, Montgomery County Historical Society*

Facing page: *St. Gabriel's Church in Potomac was closely linked to the nearby C & O Canal. Canal workers moved away when the canal closed due to heavy flooding in the 1920s. Consequently the church was abandoned and several years later the building burned down. Courtesy, Montgomery County Historical Society*

The Packet was divided into three compartments, a saloon in the middle, the Captain's room in front and the kitchen in the rear. Folding tables were set up at mealtimes in this saloon while passengers were served, then they were removed to give more space. The packet could accommodate about fifty passengers, though it was seldom that so many ... took passage. The saloon had long seats around the sides ... upholstered in red plush and looked very fine.

America. Boom towns sprang up overnight and were abandoned as construction moved on. There were frequent outbreaks of cholera and other diseases. Fueled by whiskey and frustration, fighting frequently broke out among rival factions of the workers.

The C & O Canal, which had been such a hardship to its builders, resulted in a better way of life to the residents of the county. Lockkeepers, who lived in stone houses provided by the canal company, were employed to open and close the locks for the flow of canal traffic. The canal boats carried on an active agricultural trade, hauling the products of the farm and mill to Georgetown and returning with fertilizer and seed. They also carried coal from the mines of western Maryland. Scheduled passenger service was provided by packet boats, and as Alice Darby, daughter of the miller at Seneca, recalled in later years:

Although the canal suffered damage during the Civil War and floods periodically took their toll, it had its best years between 1870 and 1890. A peak of over 900,000 tons of cargo were transported in 1871. The flood of 1889 found the C & O company with insufficient funds to repair the damage. The company was forced into bankruptcy and passed into the hands of bondholders. By 1924 all shipping had ceased. The land was sold to the U.S. Department of the Interior in 1938 and is now a National Historic Park.

COMMERCIAL ENTERPRISE
In the first half of the 1800s, as now, very little manufacturing was done in Montgomery County beyond the everyday needs of the people. There were

harnessmakers, blacksmiths, coopers, and tanners, but their work was not on a large scale. Small, individual industries appear in the records of this era. Edward Stabler of "Harewood" in Sandy Spring was a skilled engraver. His seals and stamps were used by many state and federal agencies. Records indicate that James Brooke had a factory prior to the Revolution where he produced "sea biscuits" for the shipping trade. Whitson Canby owned a pottery factory near Olney. David Newlin operated a woolen mill near Brookeville where blankets were one of the major products.

Triadelphia was the only mill town in the county. The name was derived from the fact that it was established by three brothers-in-law, Caleb Bentley, Isaac Briggs, and Thomas Moore, who had all married daughters of Roger and Mary (Matthews) Brooke. Briggs and Moore, who were surveyors and engineers, laid out the town on the Patuxent River on land Bentley purchased in 1809. It became an active commercial center of about 350 people that produced cotton fabric, bone meal, and lumber. Eventually Briggs and Moore sold out and Bentley retired about 1830. Under new management it became the Montgomery Company. But war, fire, and floods had a devastating effect. The area was inundated by a flood in 1868 and

Above: *Mules provided power for canal boats traversing the 180 miles between Cumberland and Georgetown. A barge is seen rounding a bend at Widewater, 12.5 miles above Georgetown, where the canal follows an old river channel. Photo by John B. Mertie, Jr., courtesy, Dave and Marta Kelsey*

Facing page: *Triadelphia in 1850, complete with Frog Pond and Sycamore Trees, was described by Boyd's* History of Montgomery County *from. . .1650 to 1879: "On the Patuxent River, north-east corner of Mechanicsville District. Soil productive. Products—30 bushels of Wheat, 40 of Corn, and 30 of Oats. Land from fifteen to sixty dollars per acre. Churches, Schools, and Mills. Postmaster, Thomas Lansdale."*

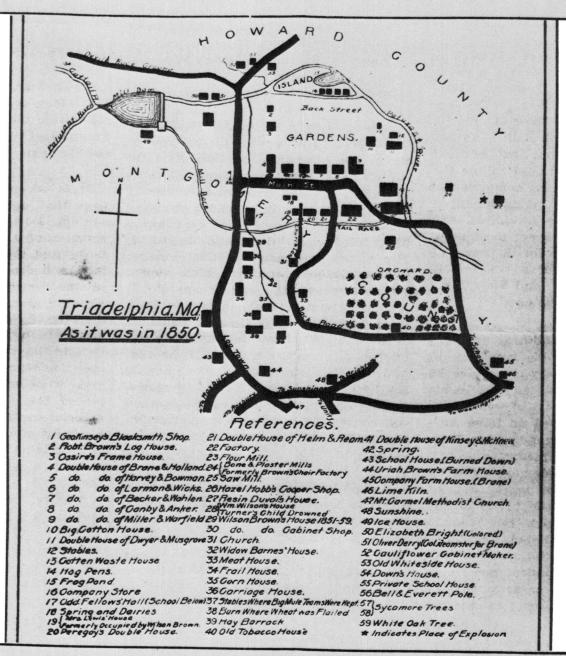

DIAGRAM OF TRIADELPHIA

Triadelphia, Md.
As it was in 1850.

References.

1 Geo.Kinsey's Blacksmith Shop.
2 Robt. Brown's Log House.
3 Ossire's Frame House.
4 Double House of Brane & Holland.
5 do. do. of Harvey & Bowman.
6 do. do. of Larman & Wicks.
7 do. do. of Becker & Wahlen.
8 do. do. of Canby & Anker.
9 do. do. of Miller & Warfield.
10 Big Cotton House.
11 Double House of Dwyer & Musgrove.
12 Stables.
13 Cotton Waste House.
14 Hog Pens.
15 Frog Pond.
16 Company Store.
17 Odd Fellows' Hall (School Below)
18 Spring and Dairies
19 Mrs. Lewis' House Formerly Occupied by Wilson Brown.
20 Peregoy's Double House.

21 Double House of Helm & Ream
22 Factory.
23 Flour Mill.
24 Bone & Plaster Mills Formerly Brown's Chair Factory
25 Saw Mill.
26 Hazel Hobb's Cooper Shop.
27 Resin Duval's House.
28 Wm. Wilson's House Turner's Child Drowned
29 Wilson Brown's House 1851-59.
30 do. do. Cabinet Shop.
31 Church.
32 Widow Barnes' House.
33 Meat House.
34 Frail House.
35 Corn House.
36 Carriage House.
37 Stables Where Big Mule Teams Were Kept.
38 Barn Where Wheat was Flailed
39 Hay Barrack
40 Old Tobacco House

41 Double House of Kinsey & McKnew.
42 Spring.
43 School House (Burned Down)
44 Uriah Brown's Farm House.
45 Company Farm House. (Brane)
46 Lime Kiln.
47 Mt. Carmel Methodist Church.
48 Sunshine.
49 Ice House.
50 Elizabeth Bright (Colored)
51 Oliver Derry (Col. Teamster for Brane)
52 Cauliflower Cabinet Maker.
53 Old Whiteside House.
54 Down's House.
55 Private School House.
56 Bell & Everett Pole.
57 Sycamore Trees
58
59 White Oak Tree.
★ Indicates Place of Explosion

"Sweet Auburn! parent of the blissful hour, thy glades forlorn confess the tyrant's power. Here, as I take my solitary rounds amidst thy tangling walks and ruin'd grounds, And, many a year elaps'd, return to view where once the cottage stood, the hawthorn grew, Remembrance wakes with all her busy train, swells at my breast, and turns the past to pain."
—*Goldsmith, in "Deserted Village."*

Above: *Clopper's Mill took its name from Francis C. Clopper, who was active in trying to bring the railroad to the county. Clopper died before his dream was realized. Courtesy, Montgomery County Historical Society*

Below: *Employees of Seneca Rock Quarry and Stone Mill stand in front of the stone-sawing mill. It was here that the red sandstone was cut into blocks for incorporation into such projects as the Smithsonian Castle, the C & O Canal locks, and numerous bridges. Courtesy, Montgomery County Historical Society*

Triadelphia became a ghost town. Today, it lies completely covered by the waters of Triadelphia Reservoir, formed in 1943 when the Washington Suburban Sanitary Commission built Brighton Dam on the Patuxent River.

Grist mills are known to have existed early in the county's settlement. Every river and creek had at least one built along its banks. These mills were not only the commercial life of their neighborhoods, they were also places for farmers to exchange news and often make purchases and receive mail.

The earliest mills mentioned in records were those owned by James Brooke and Richard Snowden. Joseph Elgar seems to have been a popular millwright who built a

Facing page: *Muncaster Mill Road is named for Muncaster Mill in Norbeck. Courtesy, Montgomery County Historical Society*

mill for himself before the Revolution and later for others in the area. The names of many of these mills exist today only on county road signs such as Bell's Mill Road, Bowie Mill Road, Newport Mill Road, Muncaster Mill Road, and Veirs Mill Road.

Of the many gristmills and sawmills built in the 19th century, only two remain standing. Neither is in operation. Black Rock Mill, built about 1815 by Thomas Hilleary, has been stabilized but its future is unknown. The Hyattstown Mill had a long history since the first was built by William Richards before his death in 1800, but the present one has existed only since 1919.

Stone quarries provided yet another commercial enterprise in the county. Some are still in operation. Historically, the largest was located on the west bank of Seneca Creek at its mouth. Ruins remain of the original quarry, the cutting mill, and the quarrymaster's house. Stone was removed from the quarry and hauled to the adjacent cutting and polishing mill by mules pulling carts over a narrow gauge track. The location on the C & O Canal made for convenient transportation to construction sites in Washington. The distinctive red color makes it easily recognizable in locks on the canal, the old Smithsonian Institution building, the Cabin John Aqueduct, government buildings, and various homes and barns in the area.

OF MINDS AND SOULS

No newspapers were published in Montgomery County prior to 1807. Citizens had to subscribe to a paper from Baltimore, Annapolis, Georgetown, or Frederick. The earliest papers in the county came into being for political reasons and were frequently short-lived. These weeklies put forth party platforms and editorialized on the issues.

The first paper, *The Maryland Register and Montgomery Advertiser,* was published by Mathias E. Bartgis, whose father had a paper in Frederick. It was followed by the *Rockville Journal, The Rockville Courier,* and the *Centinel of Freedom,* each lasting about a year. *The Rockville True American* was established in 1820 by Julius Bingham. This became *The True American and Farmer's Journal* in 1824 and in 1827 was sold to Jesse Leach. A new paper, *The Maryland Journal,* ran concurrently with Leach's paper until they were combined and published by a series of owners until mid-century. *The Maryland Free Press,* the *Farmer's Friend* (a Whig newspaper), and the *Weekly Reporter* (advertised as "neutral in politics") quickly came and went. The *Rockville Journal and Montgomery County Advocate* followed with Braddock and Fields as publishers. On August 11, 1855, the first issue of the *Montgomery County Sentinel* appeared, edited and published by Matthew Fields. This weekly remains one of the major newspapers in the county to this day.

It is not surprising that newspapers were not widely read in the early 1800s. Prior to the Revolution there had been only vague references to schools in the county. Wealthy parents sent their children away to school or employed a tutor. Education was for many years a private concern.

The first successful Maryland legislation in public education was passed in 1825. It provided for a nine-man commission to divide each county into school districts and oversee funds allocated for their use. It was not until 1839, however, when a special act was passed for the "establishment of primary schools in Montgomery County," that progress was made. A manager was appointed for each district, which resulted in schools being established in some areas.

In 1860, of the existing 33 states, only

The log building of the Ridge School in Redland is shown here. 1,074 white children were taught in 30 schools when the countywide system was started in 1860. Courtesy, Montgomery County Historical Society

Maryland and South Carolina did not have a state school system. But in that same year, a county-wide system was established in Montgomery County. A Board of Commissioners of Public Schools was appointed with the authority to hire teachers from those certified, maintain schoolhouses, and designate a course of study. William Henry Farquhar had the title of president of the board, which was later changed to superintendent. A state system was finally established in 1865.

Farquhar's first annual report accounted for 1,074 pupils attending school out of 3,000 white children of school age. They were taught at a cost of $8.10 each in 30

schools that, according to Farquhar, were "such old houses as could be prepared [many being] poor log huts, destitute of suitable desks, seats and other school furniture [and] 15 that have been built during the school year." Teachers were paid according to the number of students, which averaged about $75 per quarter. Parents objected to a fee of one dollar

Chartered in 1809, the Rockville Academy contributed to the education of young men (and women after 1897) of the county for more than 100 years. This 1890 structure replaced an earlier building on the same site and was built with the $15,000 which alumnus Julius West bequeathed to the Academy. This photograph is from a 1906 postcard. Courtesy, Gordon Baker

charged per student according to law, but Farquhar argued that "it throws the expense . . . on those directly interested . . . This one dollar is like the reel on your reaper, cumbrous and troublesome - but the machine won't work well without it."

There were no public schools for black children until well after the Civil War. Black children attended several schools organized in conjunction with black churches — the Sharp Street Methodist Church (1864) and the Mount Zion Methodist Church (1866). They were free to students but without public support.

This left most higher education to private academies. The earliest of these was Tusculum Academy founded by the Reverend James Hunt, a Presbyterian minister. In 1779 Hunt purchased land on which his residence and school were located on the present Greentree Road in Bethesda. The most famous of his pupils was William Wirt, lawyer, prosecutor at Aaron Burr's trial, and U.S. attorney general. A statement in Wirt's biography informs us that "In 1783 I was removed from the grammar school of Mr. Dent in Charles County to that of Rev. James Hunt . . . I was put to board with Major Samuel Wade Magruder, a substantial planter who lived about two miles from Mr. Hunt." He described Hunt as "a man of cultivated mind, liberal study, and philosophical temper. He possessed a good library, a thing uncommon in these days." The school closed in 1787 and the Reverend Hunt died in 1793.

The next institution of higher learning for young men of the county was the Rockville Academy. It was established by an act of the Maryland assembly in 1805 and located at the corner of Jefferson and South Adams streets in Rockville. A charter was obtained on January 6, 1810 that appointed a seven-member board of trustees. They were to hire the principal, teachers, and assistants, who were frequently ministers, to instruct the students "in the vernacular and learned languages, and such sciences and branches of education as they shall think proper and suitable." The trustees were also "to examine the progress of the students . . . in their learning; to hear and determine upon . . . all matters touching discipline and government of the said academy . . . and generally manage the estate and concerns" of the institution. The Reverend John Breckenridge was the first principal followed by Reverend John Mines, who remained for 25 years. A new building replaced the original in 1891.

The Brookeville Academy, established along similar lines, was incorporated by the assembly in 1815. Seven local men formed a board of trustees. School hours were long and vacations short, originally five and a half days a week with a two-week vacation in August and one day off at Christmas. The original stone school building was used until 1868 when the trustees purchased the former home of Thomas Riggs. It was remodeled to include classrooms, accommodations for boarding students, and a kitchen and dining room in the basement. The school prospered until the turn of the century when, as in the case of the Rockville Academy, the public schools became so popular that admissions fell sharply.

There were other later academies, including the Poolesville Academy, Barnesville Academy (or Hays School), Sherwood Academy (which became Sherwood High School), and Andrew Small Academy in Darnestown, whose principal was the minister of the Presbyterian Church for many years. Some of these were coeducational. There were also private schools for girls including the Rockville Female Academy, St. Mary's Institute, the Cottage School, and Briarly Hall.

The Quakers were firm believers in a good education for girls as well as boys. They established several schools in the Sandy Spring area, all of good reputation both locally and in surrounding states. Fair Hill, the earliest, opened on "first second day in the sixth mo. 1820" under the supervision of Samuel and Anna Thomas. They were assisted by Benjamin Hallowell, who was to become a noted educator at his own academy in Alexandria, Virginia. In 1851 it became a school for girls only run by Richard S. and Mary (Farquhar) Kirk and her brother, William Henry Farquhar, but closed at the time of the Civil War. This was followed by other schools directed by Quaker educators — Drumelda (1831), Fulford (1848), and Stanmore (1858).

By the beginning of the Civil War, a good education was available in the county for those white children who could afford it, and a basic education could be had in the public schools. It was not until 1872 that public education for blacks was provided. In that year one school in each district was designated to instruct black students "provided the average attendance be not less than fifteen scholars." By 1900 there was a total of 106 schools in the county, "76 for white and 30 for colored." But these schools were in no way similar in facilities, length of school year, or pay for the teachers. In 1917 Edwin W. Broome succeeded Willis Burdette as superintendent and Andrew D. Owens was hired as the first supervisor for black schools.

The church was not only a source of education but frequently the focal point of family life outside the home as well. There one received spiritual support and social encounters with neighbors. Each of the denominations built a place of worship for their followers.

The Church of England, or Episcopal Church, had become the established church of Maryland in 1692 with the ascension of William and Mary to the throne of England. Marylanders were taxed for the support of the church and the vestries had powerful influence. Piscataway was one of the 30 original parishes formed. John Bradford gave 100 acres to this parish in 1719 for a "chapel of ease," a place of worship for those who lived some distance from the parish church. This became known as Rock Creek Church (near present St. Paul's and Rock Creek Cemetery in Washington). A petition was approved in 1725 to create Prince George's Parish with Rock Creek as the parish church.

There were eventually four churches in the parish. One, of course, was the parish church. The second was a chapel built near Rockville in 1739. The first building of logs and clapboard was replaced in 1808 by a brick structure. In 1822 a new church was built in Rockville, which is the present Christ Episcopal Church. The third chapel was near the Hawlings River "near Mr. Henry Leeke's" but in 1812 this congregation became a separate parish called St. Bartholomew's. A new church was consecrated on May 9, 1819, on land donated by the Griffith family of "Edgehill." This church near Unity was replaced by a new one in Laytonsville in 1909. The fourth, Paint Chapel, though in the parish, was not in Momtgomery County.

Another old Episcopal church, Monocacy Chapel, was built in 1748 as a chapel of ease for All Saints Parish in Frederick County. In 1847 the congregation built a new church, St. Peter's, in Poolesville. The old chapel was virtually destroyed during the Civil War, but the old cemetery remains. These earliest churches were followed by St. John's Episcopal Church in Olney (1845) and Grace Episcopal Church in Silver Spring (1864).

The religious toleration originally practiced under the Lords Baltimore ceased when the Church of England became the official church of Maryland. Catholics were disenfranchised, barred from public office, heavily taxed, and forbidden to hold religious services.

Some devout families, however, remained steadfast in their religion, Daniel Carroll, a Catholic merchant of Upper Marlborough in Prince George's County, purchased a part of "Joseph's Park" that is now Forest Glen in Montgomery County. After his death in 1751 his widow, Eleanor, moved to this sparsely settled area, and it was in her home that mass was said for local Catholics. At her death the estate inventory

contained: "In the Chapel room: 1 Bed and Bedstead, 2 pr Window Curtains, 1 Table, Altar furniture."

Their son John Carroll, a priest in the Society of Jesus, built a small chapel on his mother's property. He then left for Baltimore, where, on November 6, 1789, he was appointed the first Catholic bishop of the United States. In 1808 he was made the first archbishop of Baltimore.

As more Catholics began to settle in the county, they met to worship at five places— Carroll's Chapel at Forest Glen, St. Mary's at Rockville, St. Mary's at Barnesville, a small chapel built by the Waring family on Seneca Creek, and in the homes of the members living in the area of Hawlings River. Until 1866 there was but one priest who lived at Rockville. He went once a month to each congregation, only going to Hawlings River on the infrequent

fifth Sunday.

Church records were begun by the Jesuit Father Redmond, who was also responsible for building St. Mary's in Rockville in 1817. The Barnesville congregation occupied a small church built in 1808 by the parishioners on land donated by Zachariah Knott which stood until July 14, 1900 when it was destroyed by fire. The group that once worshipped in the Waring's chapel began to hold mass at "The Woodlands," the home of Francis Cassatt Clopper. Clopper, although not a Catholic himself, gave land for a church of his wife's religion and St. Rose was completed in 1835. It was named in honor of Mother Rose, the mother superior of the Sisters of Charity. The small congregation near Hawlings River continued to meet in homes until shortly before the Civil War. Land at Mt. Zion was given by the Watkins family for a church that was replaced in 1898 by St. Peter's in Olney.

Many Maryland Presbyterians had their roots in John Knox' Church of Scotland as well as in Scottish soil. In 1683 the

Reverend Francis Mackemie came to Maryland's eastern shore where he found enough Presbyterians to start several congregations. On the western shore, Ninian Beall became an active layman. He gave both financial and moral support in the effort to bring ministers of the Presbyterian faith to the area and establish churches. Early in the 1700s the Reverend Hugh Conn and the Reverend James Orme arrived in Prince George's County.

Occasionally these ministers found their way to the remote location of the Captain John Presbyterian Meeting. One acre of the tract "Outlet" (near the town of Potomac), "where the meeting house now stands" was given to the congregation by Edward Offutt in 1746. In October 1820 measures were taken to provide a place of worship for members living at a distance from the original meetinghouse. The elders

St. Rose's Church in Cloppers was built in 1835 on land donated by Francis Cassatt Clopper with funds donated by Ellen Maria Maher. This postcard dates from around 1910. Courtesy, Montgomery County Historical Society

purchased land at the six-mile mark on the Washington and Rockville Turnpike (now 9400 Rockville Pike) and built Bethesda Meeting House, which took its name from a biblical text — John 5:2. This building burned on November 23, 1848, and was replaced by the present building on the site. The Reverend John Mines came to these congregations from the Leesburg, Virginia, in 1822 and remained for 24 years, serving as both minister and principal of the Rockville Academy.

In 1832 the Presbyterians purchased a lot in Rockville for a new church and the old Captain John Meeting House was abandoned. Other congregations were

organized — one at Brookeville, the basis of the Neelsville Presbyterian Church (1845), one at Poolesville (1847), and one at Darnestown (1855).

Methodism did not reach this part of Maryland until the 1780s when Robert Strawbridge settled in Frederick County. He met with the first members in his home on Sam's Creek and went on to spread the religion of John Wesley throughout the state. The early churches were served by circuit riders, ministers who traveled from church to church on horseback.

The first Methodist congregation in the county was formed in 1783 and the church, Sugar Loaf Chapel, said to be an eight-sided building, was dedicated in 1788. The present Clarksburg Methodist Church, however, claims to be the oldest continuous congregation. Established on June 5, 1783, the members constructed a log church known as Ebenezer Chapel, which was replaced in 1853. Before 1790 a group of Methodists built a log church in the community of Goshen that has twice been replaced. Another old church was one built in Hyattstown in 1804 on a lot purchased from Eli Hyatt.

These churches were all in the northwestern part of the county, where the Methodist religion was strongest. There were, however, other old churches in other areas such as Federal Chapel near Colesville, Concord on River Road, two in Brookeville, and one in Rockville. The first church organized for and by blacks was Sharp Street Methodist Church in 1822 at Sandy Spring.

Early Baptist records indicate that about 1773 a church of that denomination was organized on Seneca Creek by the Reverend Daniel Fristol of Virginia and admitted to the Baptist Association. This was, no doubt, the building referred to in a deed dated 1777 that conveyed property to "a society of people called Baptists" and stated that it was "one acre of ground whereon the meeting house now stands." A new stone church was built about 1817.

Upper Seneca, the second oldest Baptist Church, located near Cedar Grove, is sometime called White Oak Chapel. It was founded in 1805 by Elder Jeremiah Moore who was the minister for 45 years, 10 of

which were in joint ministry with the original Baptist church. The present building was erected in 1888.

While Elder Plummer Waters was minister to the Seneca Baptist Church near Dawsonville, a difference of views arose. According to Baptist records, he was "not only an umcompromising opponent of missionary enterprises, but he also denounced all who sympathized in that work. In 1822 some of the members withdrew and formed a new congregation. Those who remained worshipped as "Primitive" or "Old School" Baptists in their simple form. In 1880 Mr. Nathan Allnutt provided a lot in Dawsonville where a new frame church was built and the old stone building was abandoned.

Those who left the Seneca Baptist Church met on August 19, 1822, and signed a declaration stating that they were "henceforth independent of the church at Old Seneca. And we have determined to form ourselves into a separate and distinct church to be known by the name of Bethel Baptist Church." They decided that the church would have two branches because the members lived so far apart — Lower Bethel in Rockville and Upper Bethel "in the neighborhood of Brother Brewer" near Poolesville. The first Baptist Church in Rockville was built in 1832 at Jefferson and Van Buren streets, where there is still a small cemetery.

Two Christian Churches were founded in the first half of the 1800s. The one at Rockville was started by William McClenahan, the English teacher at the Rockville Academy. This congregation originally worshipped in the academy or at members' homes, but in 1858 the group purchased the old Presbyterian Church on the northwest corner of Jefferson and South Adams streets. The other congregation, in Hyattstown, also met in

Above: *Celebrating the centennial of the Sandy Spring Meeting House are the "Quaker Ladies," representing the old Sandy Spring families of Farquhar, Stabler, Brooke, Magruder, and Russell. Courtesy, Montgomery County Historical Society*

Facing page: *The Zion A.M.E. Church organized for and by blacks in Rockville was razed in the mid 1950s to make way for the construction of Rockville's first shopping center. Courtesy, Charles Brewer*

homes from 1840 until a church was built in 1845.

When the Quaker minister George Fox came to the colony of Maryland he found many who were receptive to the teachings of the Society of Friends. Many of the Puritans of Anne Arundel and Calvert counties were converted and formed the Clifts and West River meetings. As these Quakers moved westward, new meetings were formed.

The early settlers of this county who were of that persuasion originally met in homes, but by 1779 had built a log meetinghouse on land given by James Brooke. This was replaced by a frame one. The present Sandy Spring Meeting House, the third on that site, was built in 1817. Following Fox's exhortation that "God dwells not in temples made with hands, but in human hearts," this was a simple brick

building. Much later two large stoves were installed over the objections of the most orthodox members.

"The Quaker Community" was not a geographic location but a state of mind and family connections. It was concerned with the education of the children and the

cultural enrichment of the adults. Clubs were organized and a lyceum established that brought lecturers who spoke on a wide variety of subjects. Events in the community were chronicled in *The Annals of Sandy Spring.* Although one does not hear "thee" and "thou" in conversation or notice the plain dress in the supermarket, the Quaker religion is still an influence in the area. Their contributions to the county cannot be disputed.

During the first half of the 19th century a pattern of life evolved for the people of Montgomery County. These institutions and accomplishments would become a legacy passed down to future generations. They were a background on which future growth and development would be based.

In July of 1864 General Early made an attack on Washington in hopes of relieving Federal pressure on the city of Richmond. Early found the defenses of Washington too strong to penetrate and decided to withdraw. After their attempt on July 11, they camped in Silver Spring on the grounds of the Blair house. Courtesy, Montgomery County Historical Society

4
War Comes and Goes

Life in Montgomery County during the first half of the 19th century was centered around the home, the farm, and the church. The feeling for a community was stronger than for state or nation. But this loyalty was to change. The terms "secession," "war," "slavery," and "abolition" were frequently heard at meetings and seen in newspapers. Residents of the county would soon be forced to examine their own consciences and take stands on the issues confronting the new Union.

DECISIONS
Bordering the capital of the United States on three sides and situated between states in favor of preservation of the Union and states in favor of secession from the Union, the geographic location of Maryland posed a perplexing problem. Marylanders were divided on the issue of slavery and a choice had to be made.

The economics of slavery in Maryland much resembled that of the Southern states. In 1860 there were 18,322 inhabitants of the county, of which 5,421 slaves and 1,552 free blacks made up about 35 percent. Most slaveholders had only a few slaves. Only 22 percent owned more

than 10 and the Quakers had freed their blacks. Economic factors gave Maryland much in common with states to the south.

The life of a slave has been pictured in many ways. One of the writers who attempted to illustrate slavery was Harriet Beecher Stowe in her novel *Uncle Tom's Cabin.* Her model for Uncle Tom, she claimed, was the Reverend Josiah Henson who was born in Charles County, Maryland. The family was broken up and sold separately. The young Josiah was purchased by Adam Robb, a tavernkeeper in Rockville, but later sold to Isaac Riley, owner of Josiah's mother, whose farm was located on Old Georgetown Road. In 1825 Josiah was sent to Riley's brother in Kentucky from whom he escaped to freedom in Canada. Josiah Henson became a minister and wrote several autobiographies identifying Montgomery County residents and places by name.

Harriet Beecher Stowe drew her characters and pictured life as a slave from these books and several meetings with the Reverend Henson. Her story, first appearing as a serial in the *National Era,* a popular antislavery publication, was acclaimed by some as a novel whose political and humanitarian pleading was for equality and freedom. Others charged it was propaganda for the abolition movement.

The decade of the 1850s had been one of political realignment. The Whigs were no longer a major party and the Know-Nothing party, scorned by Montgomery County's *Sentinel* newspaper, had collapsed. In 1861 the Union party was organized, which endorsed "The Union, the Constitution and the Laws," although it avoided a stand on slavery. The Republican party in the county remained small with Montgomery Blair, soon to become Abraham Lincoln's postmaster general, as its spokesman. The Democrats were still a significant factor in county politics.

Initially, slavery was not the critical issue in events leading to the Civil War. The emphasis at first was on secession from the Union and the avoidance of war.

When the moral and economic question of slavery became an issue, many citizens of the county, particularly in the southern part, were slaveowners with social, economic, and familial ties with the South. Others were proponents of the Union and favored the abolition of slavery. The Quakers of Sandy Spring were the largest and most vocal antislavery group. Following the tenets of their religion they had emancipated their slaves and worked in various ways to help the free blacks.

Politically, the proponents of secession

were Democrats. Led by such men as George Peter, William Veirs Bouic, and William Brewer, they had a strong ally in the *Sentinel,* edited by Matthew Fields. The opposition, predominately Whigs, was led by Allen Bowie Davis and Richard Johns Bowie. Their sentiments were expressed by John T. Desellum, who stated, "I considered, though a slaveholder, that a man's first duty was to his creator, the next to his country."

The election of Lincoln as president in November 1860 brought the slavery issue to a climax. A meeting was called of political leaders at the Montgomery County Courthouse on January 1, 1861, "to confer with each other upon the perilous condition of the country, and to adopt such measures as the exigencies of the times, in their wisdom, may demand." John Brewer, a Democrat, was moderator; John T. Vinson, of the Union party, was secretary.

Preliminary resolutions expressing a commitment to slavery were unanimously adopted, agreeing that:

● Maryland should try every means including concession, argument, and conciliation before leaving the Union.
● Maryland should participate in a convention of border states to protect their rights.
● Slaveholding is a right which the U.S. Government should protect.
● Laws abolishing slavery would be detrimental to Maryland.
● Slavery should not be abolished at Federal installations.
● Free states should not be permitted to pass laws hindering recapture of fugitive slaves.

But the debate grew heated over two other resolutions. The first required the governor to call a special session of the legislature

on the slavery question. The second stated that if the issue of slavery was not settled quickly, then Maryland would withdraw from the Union. A close vote along party lines defeated the first. When the second came to a vote, Francis Miller, a Quaker, was successful in having the resolution

Facing page: Slaves played an important role in the economics of the county. Many slaveowners had strong social, economic, and family ties with the South. Other countians were proponents of the Union and favored the abolition of slavery. This wood engraving appeared in Frank Leslie's Illustrated Newspaper, *October 20, 1866. Courtesy, Montgomery County Historical Society, Library of Congress photo*

Below: Josiah Henson (1789-1883), born a slave in Charles County, Maryland, was brought to Montgomery County as a child. His early life provided Harriet Beecher Stowe with material for her novel, Uncle Tom's Cabin.

tabled. Only one rhetorical question remained — did this meeting of party leaders really represent the feelings of the population as a whole?

Long before the outbreak of war, men of the county had organized military units. The Barnesville Guards, the Montgomery Guards, the Rockville Riflemen, and other groups were armed and drilled. Before long their parades and fancy uniforms gave way to the realities of war. Each man made a choice of allegiance, then marched and fought and suffered privations; some for the South; some for the North.

The Federal government instituted a draft. The first drawing occurred in December 1862, which John T. Desellum of Gaithersburg, a local chronicler of the war, remembered:

When the draught had to be drawn . . . I was earnestly requested to draw the names. I replied it would be putting my character, property and life in imminent danger. But the Country demanded personal sacrifices . . . I drew the names from the box. Then as I had anticipated - from the Pulpit to the grog shop, I was denounced as a Moral Monster, etc. My stockyard was burned and I was ostracised from Society.

It was possible to obtain a substitute for service in the Union army and many county men availed themselves of this. The *Sentinel* listed the substitutes for this and subsequent drafts.

It was found through draft and enlistment attempts, however, that many men had "gone south." They quietly slipped away from the farms and neighborhoods, crossed the river, and enlisted in Southern units. Men from one area often stayed together and fought together. Some men joined the First Maryland Cavalry of the Confederate States (C.S.A.), which was led by Colonel Ridgely Brown of Montgomery County. Others joined Colonel Elijah Veirs White, a native of the Poolesville area. One such group from Poolesville, under the leadership of Captain George Chiswell, called "Chiswell's Exile Band," joined White's command as Company B.

ACTION!
The firing on Fort Sumter in the harbor of Charleston, South Carolina, in April 1861 marked the opening of hostilities in the Civil War. On April 18th the first contingent of Federal troops arrived in Baltimore on its way to Washington, D.C. These 600 men, comprising six companies of regular troops and militia, were protected by Baltimore policemen. They were hissed and booed but there was no violence. The next morning the Sixth Massachusetts Regiment, a regimental band, and units of the Pennsylvania militia arrived. As the railroad cars transporting the soldiers from one station to the other were pulled through the streets, a crowd tore up the tracks. Rioting began when the decision was made to march them through. Four soldiers and 12 civilians were killed.

On April 23 Governor Thomas Hicks called a special session of the Maryland legislature in Frederick as Annapolis was filled with Union troops. Some legislators protested what amounted to Federal occupation of the state. Debate continued on the question of secession as the Federal government made arrests of pro-Southern legislators. It soon became evident that Maryland would remain in the Union.

One of the concerns of the Federal government during the first months of the war was that the rebels would capture Washington. In July l861 the War Department was directed to build forts at important approaches to the city. A

WM. B. SASSCER & CO.,
SUBSTITUTE AGENTS.

he undersigned, having associated themselves together for the purpose of carrying on the

SUBSTITUTE BUSINESS,

Are prepared at all times to furnish Drafted Men from the city and counties at the shortest notice and at the lowest prices.

lso, Exemption Papers Carefully Made Out and Properly Attended to.

GIVE US A FAIR TRIAL AND WE GUARANTEE SATISFACTION.

OFFICE—75 West Fayette Street, (Bible House,)
ROOM NO. 8—UP STAIRS.

perimeter of fortifications 34 miles in circumference was built. Three of these forts were located in Montgomery County for the protection of Chain Bridge and the water reservoir — Fort Ripley, Fort Franklin, and Fort Alexander.

In the summer of 1862, as the Confederates approached the city, it was felt that these small forts were not adequate. Secretary of War Stanton accepted a new plan by Brigadier General John J. Barnard, chief engineer of the Army of the Potomac that called for a ring of forts and batteries connected by rifle trenches and roads. In November and

Many county men availed themselves of a service to provide substitutes for the unpopular draft into the Union army. Courtesy, Montgomery County Historical Society

December of 1862, Fort Simons and Fort Mansfield were built as were batteries Benson and Bailey. In the spring of 1863 the original three forts in the county were combined into one, named Fort Sumner, with an adjacent outwork, Battery Alexander. Of these, only Battery Bailey is still visible in the Westmoreland Hills

Facing page, top: *This street scene is typical of Poolesville. The town saw more soldiers and action throughout the war than any other in the county.* Courtesy, Montgomery County Historical Society

Facing page, bottom: *This view, looking east, shows Darnestown, Maryland. During the Civil War, more than 18,000 men camped near Darnestown. Courtesy, Montgomery County Historical Society*

Below: Harper's New Monthly Magazine *carried a series of "Personal Recollections of the War" by a Virginian. After the battle at Ball's Bluff, he wrote "those who had flattered themselves that the conflict would be 'sharp and short,' that a single victorious and glorious campaign would crush the rebellion, were now disenchanted." This sketch of a signal station in Darnestown accompanied the 1866 article. From* Harper's New Monthly Magazine, *No. CXCVII, October 1866, courtesy, Montgomery County Historical Society*

Recreation Center.

It would be misleading to say that Montgomery County was a major theater of war. But troops of both sides marched back and forth, camped and skirmished, and advanced and retreated across the countryside.

Beginning in June 1861 Federal troops under the command of General Charles P. Stone (then a colonel) moved across the county. Rockville was occupied. Soldiers searched homes for hidden arms and arrested outspoken "secesh" citizens, including Matthew Fields, editor of the *Sentinel.* Stone marched on to Darnestown, Seneca, and Poolesville, leaving detachments at each place to guard the C & O Canal, crossings of the Potomac, and routes to the city of Washington. A military telegraph connected Stone's Corps of Observation with the capital.

Major General Nathaniel Banks was sent to reinforce Stone's troops in August. The North had been defeated at the First Battle of Bull Run and Southern troops were encamped around Leesburg just across the river. Banks' troops were deployed from Offutt's Crossroads (Potomac) to Hyattstown with division headquarters at Darnestown. General Stone was in Poolesville with infantry, artillery, and cavalry camped in and around town. This town continued to see more soldiers and action throughout the war than any other in the county. At this time there were 18,000 men near Darnestown and 20,000 men in the vicinity of Poolesville.

It was from Poolesville that Northern forces set out for an invasion of Virginia known as the Battle of Ball's Bluff. Shortly

Above: This Signal Station Encampment was located near Darnestown during the Civil War. From Harper's New Monthly Magazine, No. CXCVII, October 1866, courtesy, Montgomery County Historical Society

Facing page: An unknown chronicler, probably a Union soldier, drew this sketch of the federal encampment in Poolesville, indicating the 14th New Hampshire and 39th Massachusetts regiments spent Christmas 1863 in Montgomery County, many miles from home. Courtesy, Montgomery County Historical Society

after General George B. McClellan was chosen to lead the Union army, he decided to make a reconnaissance probe toward the Confederates around Leesburg, who were seen as a threat to Washington. The plan called for a main thrust on the Virginia side of the river, but McClellan advised Stone to create a diversion. Colonel Edward

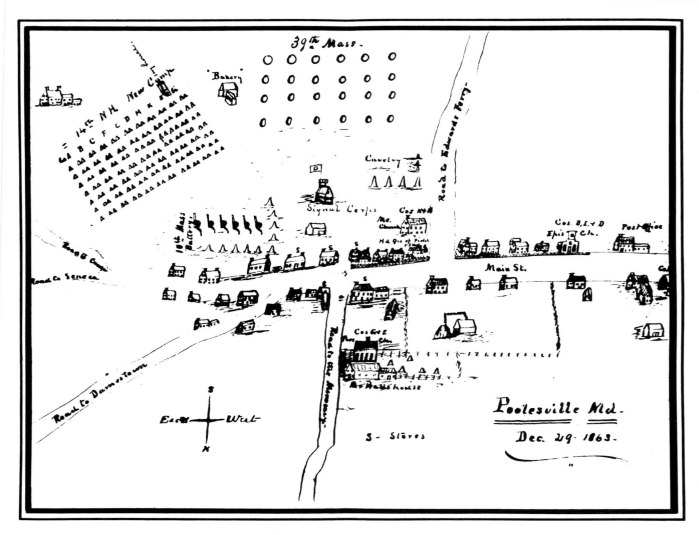

D. Baker, senator from Oregon and no professional soldier, was ordered to undertake this demonstration with 1,700 men.

Harrison's Island lies in the Potomac between Conrad's Ferry (now White's Ferry) and Edwards' Ferry. Across from it on the Virginia shore is Ball's Bluff rising about 75 feet above the river — an awkward place for an assault or a retreat. The men were ferried across in small boats in the early hours of October 21, 1861. Confederate observers discovered their presence and about noon a battle began. The Union troops were completely defeated and Colonel Baker was killed. The only

retreat was over the bluff and into the river. The Union forces' few boats had been sunk or destroyed by enemy fire. Some men chose to surrender, some chose to swim to Harrison's Island, and many were shot while trying to escape. Baker's body was brought back to Poolesville to the home of Frederick S. Poole, where the remnants of his troops came to pay their respects.

As a result of this fiasco the Congressional Committee on the Conduct of the War was formed. General Banks withdrew into winter quarters near Frederick. In the spring most of the remaining troops moved on to other campaigns leaving only a few guards on outpost duty. Militarily all was quiet in the county until fall.

The Confederate forces, fresh from success in the Valley of Virginia and the Second Battle of Bull Run, decided not to attack the strong line of defense south of Washington. Instead they crossed the Potomac at White's Ford (north of White's Ferry) on September 4th to 7th, 1862 and invaded the North. The crossing was observed by Union lookouts on Sugar Loaf Mountain and officials in Washington were quickly notified. Part of Lee's Army of Northern Virginia, the cavalry of James Ewell Brown ("Jeb") Stuart, passed through Poolesville and became involved in several encounters with the enemy. The inhabitants of the town, although most were glad to see the Confederate troops, were described by a contemporary diarist as "greatly terror-stricken, and many women took refuge in the cellars ... some of the missiles passing directly over the houses."

The Union army under General McClellan moved out from Washington on September 9th to place itself between Lee's army and the city. The entire Army of the Potomac spread northwestward through the county by way of River Road, the Frederick Road, and the Brookeville Pike to meet in Frederick. The encounter between the Northern and Southern armies resulted in the Battle of Antietam near Sharpsburg in Washington County on September 17, 1862. This bloody battle forced Southern forces from Northern territory.

Soon after this, in October 1862, "Jeb" Stuart again entered Maryland. His objective was to destroy a railroad bridge near Chambersburg, Pennsylvania, and to seize desperately needed supplies. With 18,000 men he accomplished his mission

Confederate Cavalry leader General J.E.B. (Jeb) Stuart was known as the "eyes of the army." A graduate of the U.S. Military Academy, Stuart resigned from the U.S. Army when the Civil War began and was commissioned a lieutenant colonel with the Virginia infantry. Courtesy, Montgomery County Historical Society, from a Library of Congress photo

and, as he later reported: "After mature consideration [I decided] to strike out for Leesburg as the best route of return ... We reached ... Hyattstown, but found only a few wagons to capture, and we pushed on towards Barnesville." He passed through this town, which had just been vacated by Northern cavalry and advanced to Beallsville, where his scouts encountered Union forces encamped at Monocacy Chapel. The horse artillery held off the enemy while "I made a rapid strike for

White's Ford . . . before the enemy . . . could be aware of my design," he wrote. A member of Stuart's staff and former resident of the area, Benjamin S. White, showed him an old road, almost a path, through fields and woods by which the cavalry reached the ford with a minimum of opposition.

The next invasion of Maryland by Confederate troops followed the Union defeat at Chancellorsville and culminated in the Battle of Gettysburg. This time Lee's Army of Northern Virginia entered Maryland in the vicinity of Hagerstown. Most of the Union troops then in Virginia pursued, crossing at Edwards' Ferry by means of twin pontoon bridges rather than by fording the river. Thus, General Joseph Hooker, soon to be replaced by General George Meade, again interposed Federal forces between Washington and the Southern forces. On June 27th and 28th, 1863, Hooker's headquarters were at Poolesville.

"Jeb" Stuart seized upon this opportunity for yet another ride around the Union army. During the night of June 27th Stuart crossed the Potomac at Rowser's Ford near Seneca to the rear of Hooker's men. Stuart's force drained sections of the canal, captured and burned barges, and destroyed several locks. They then set out for Rockville with Wade Hampton's brigade going by way of Darnestown and the remaining two brigades by River and Falls roads.

Advanced units of Stuart's cavalry encountered a Union supply train of about 150 wagons extended along the pike from Rockville to Darcey's Store (Bethesda), which they easily captured. The Southern sympathizers in town welcomed them; the good Union men went into hiding. Some civilians were arrested, including Judge Richard Johns Bowie; Thomas L. Bailey,

the postmaster; Mr. Moulden, the provost, and John Higgins, along with a few Federal soldiers. Stuart then swept out of town by Old Baltimore Road to Olney and on to Brookeville, where he paroled most of the prisoners. He then moved on to join Lee in Pennsylvania. Tactical historians have credited the delay caused by Stuart's circuitous route and the capture of the wagon train as factors in the outcome at Gettysburg. "Jeb" Stuart arrived too late to be of help to Lee.

In July of 1864 General Ulysses S. Grant's troops were advancing on Petersburg, Virginia. Lee, hoping to relieve the pressure on that city, sent Lt. General Jubal Anderson Early to threaten the city of Washington. Early crossed into Frederick County and on the 9th engaged the troops of Major General Lew Wallace (who would later write *Ben Hur*). Wallace's force of 5,000 men, mainly new recruits, was defeated at the battle of Monocacy in Frederick County and retreated toward Baltimore. Grant remained at Petersburg but sent the Sixth and Nineteenth Corps to defend the capital.

Jubal Early's men marched through Montgomery County with skirmishes along the way. Advanced cavalry units arrived in Rockville and camped on the fairgrounds. The next morning Early himself arrived and ordered his command divided. He had previously sent one brigade, under Bradley Johnson, to cut the telegraph and railroad lines north of Baltimore and, if possible, circle around Washington to free prisoners held at Point Lookout. He now sent another brigade of cavalry down the Rockville Pike to test the defenses at Tennallytown. He led the remainder down the Seventh Street Pike toward Fort Stevens, an important fortification in the defense of Washington.

On the 11th a contingent of Rebels

Left: *General Jubal Anderson Early, graduate of the U.S. Military Academy at West Point, opposed secession, but sided with his home state, Virginia, when the Civil War broke out. After the war, Early returned to practice law in Lynchburg, Virginia. He is shown here in this circa 1862 photograph.* Courtesy, Montgomery County Historical Society, Library of Congress photo

Facing page: *"Silver Spring," home of Francis Preston Blair, was spared by the Confederate soldiers camping there.* Courtesy, Montgomery County Historical Society

deliberately as he got up and was driven away.

That night Early conferred with his aides at his headquarters in Silver Spring. He later wrote: "No attack was made on Fort Stevens ... On the morning of the 12th, it was manifest that the works were so strongly manned that it would have been madness to attempt an assault and I therefore determined to remain inactive in front of them until night and retire." Reinforcements had arrived at the fort. In addition, Early's men had so recently been engaged in battle and then marched the length of Montgomery County that they were in no condition to attack a fort fully manned by veteran troops.

The Confederates moved back to Rockville on the 13th. They spared "Silver Spring," the home of Francis Preston Blair, but the home of his son, Montgomery Blair, was burned. The rear guard, drawn up on Watts Branch, was engaged by pursuing Union cavalry. Bradley Johnson's First Maryland Cavalry pushed them back through the streets of the town in a brisk engagement. Early's men plodded along the dusty road in intense heat to Darnestown and Dawsonville. They stopped at noon at the Seneca Baptist Church near Seneca

moved on the fort. As they advanced, a figure not in uniform appeared. It was Abraham Lincoln, president of the United States. As Asa T. Abbott, a Second Lieutenant in the U.S. Signal Corps, described it in his memoirs:

[President Lincoln] mounted the parapet and stood there ... in a long frock coat and plug hat, a very conspicuous figure silhouetted against the sky ... The officers told him that he had better get down ... but he did not move or make a reply ... Just then a Surgeon came and stood on Mr. Lincoln's left. He had not stood there one half minute before he was shot through the leg. Then Mr. Lincoln got down as

Creek and then pushed on to Poolesville and White's Ford. Arriving near Leesburg, Virginia, a young artillerist in Early's command wrote in his diary: "The march from Washington to this place had been the most severe I have ever experienced."

Union troops were in pursuit of Early and his men. They moved southwest from Fort Stevens and on to River Road. At Offutt's Crossroads, a distance of 15 miles, they paused to rest and then moved on to Poolesville. By that time the Confederates were safely in Virginia.

The county was frequently the target of raids by small Confederate forces. They crossed the Potomac, accomplished their objective, and retreated into the wooded countryside of Virginia. One of the units that frequently appeared was Colonel "Lige" White's 35th Battalion of Virginia Cavalry, especially Captain Chiswell's Company B. They made raids on Poolesville and Edward's Ferry, where they captured prisoners, seized supplies, and destroyed what they could not carry.

Major John Singleton Moseby led his Rangers across the Potomac at Rowser's Ford in early June 1863. At Seneca they surprised Company D of the Sixth Michigan Cavalry near the mill. They burned the camp and chased the Yankees toward Poolesville. The fight along River Road where it crossed Seneca Creek was described by the miller's daughter, Alice Darby:

One spring morning . . . we were awakened by the sharp snap, snap of gunfire, the sound of galloping horses, and the shouts of officers . . . The firing having subsided, we ventured out. Across the road . . . lay five Confederate soldiers, dead or dying. One I recall vividly . . . his pale young face quiet in death . . . We gazed upon these dead men sorrowfully, they were in the flower of their youth. War was getting rather dreadful to us.

There is some question as to whether a raid at Sandy Spring was a military action or that of a band of outlaw soldiers. Some reports indicate that the original purpose was to capture the governor of Maryland. On the night of October 6, 1864, a small band led by Lieutenant Walter Bowie broke into the store of Gilpin and Bentley and stole supplies. A group of local men joined in pursuit and overtook them. The encounter, locally called the Battle of Ricketts Run, disbursed the band and killed the leader.

The civilian population of the county was not without hardships. Occupied as it was by the military of both sides, food and supplies were constantly being demanded: "Foraging (as the soldiers called it) or downright stealing (as the locals called it)." Miles of wooden fences were burned in campfires. Horses were taken as remounts. As Early's troops moved through Gaithersburg, John T. Desellum stated that his "remaining two horses were taken - Stuart's men had previously taken three." Homes were requisitioned as headquarters

for the military. Stores, such as Rannie's at Aspen Hill on the Brookeville Turnpike, were ransacked. Thomas N. Wilson was killed attempting to stop soldiers from stealing his pigs. Slaves used the opportunity to run away. Some sought freedom in Northern cities; others followed the army.

A few Montgomery Countians were arrested for real or believed crimes against the Federal government. Perry Trail was taken into custody charged with recruiting for the Confederacy. Others were accused of aiding or spying for the South or arrested merely for their outspoken sympathies. If the country was divided, Montgomery County itself was the embodiment of that division.

Lincoln was reelected in 1864 and on April 9, 1865, General Robert E. Lee surrendered to General Ulysses S. Grant at Appomattox. Five days later President Lincoln was assassinated by John Wilkes Booth.

A plot was uncovered that included Lincoln's murder as well as that of Secretary of State William H. Seward and the new Vice President Andrew Johnson. Booth's accomplice, George Atzerodt, was to kill Johnson. But several whiskeys could not instill enough courage to complete the deed. The crowd at Ford's Theater, a confrontation with mounted troops, and the knowledge that his coconspirators had fled the city combined to lead Atzerodt to the decision to seek safety at his boyhood home of Germantown in Montgomery County.

Early on the morning of the 15th, Atzerodt trudged into Georgetown, where he exchanged his revolver for cash and caught the stage for Rockville. At Tennallytown he abandoned the stage for a ride to Derwood with a local farmer, William Gaither. He walked from there to the home of his cousin, Hartman Richter, who was glad to give him room and board in exchange for work. Three days later Andrew Atwood, as Atzerodt was known in the neighborhood, was rudely awakened by armed soldiers and taken into custody. Local men had been suspicious and his presence in the neighborhood had come to the attention of military authorities. George Atzerodt was returned to Washington, tried, and hanged on July 7, 1865, for his unfulfilled role in the plot.

Another man charged in the conspiracy was John H. Surratt. His mother had been hanged for her part, but the son, a young courier in the Confederate Secret Service, claimed he was on his way to Canada at the time of the assassination. He left Canada for Europe, but was found and returned for trial. The case resulted in a hung jury and was never retried. Surratt came to Rockville, took a position as a teacher, and married a local young lady. He gave lectures on "an insider's version of the events leading up to the assassination of Abraham Lincoln."

On June 13, 1913, approximately 50 years after the surrender at Appomattox, a bronze statue of a Confederate soldier, a handsome young cavalryman clutching a saber and pistol, was unveiled. Judge Edward C. Peter gave the welcoming address to the 3,000 people attending the ceremony. Funds for the statue had been raised by the E.V. White Chapter of the United Daughters of the Confederacy and the Ridgely Brown Camp of the C.S.A. The inscription on the granite base read: "THAT WE THROUGH LIFE MAY NOT FORGET TO LOVE THE THIN GREY LINE."

The Ridgely Brown Camp of the C.S.A. was made up of veterans of the war who fought for the Confederacy. It was organized with 45 members; in 1910 there were 28 still alive, but the reunion of August 1928 was the last. Commander Elgar L. Tschiffely, then 86, announced that there would be no reunion the following year as he was the only surviving veteran.

POLITICAL AND SOCIAL RECONSTRUCTION

Reconstruction legislation attempted to solve the problems of the war-torn country. The 13th Amendment to the Federal/U.S. Constitution freed the slaves. The 14th and 15th assured blacks full citizenship and the right to vote. The passage of the Reconstruction Act of 1867 was the Federal government's attempt to legislate changes in the nation, the state, and the county. The State of Maryland had passed a Registration Act whereby all citizens who could not guarantee past and future loyalty to the United States would be denied the vote. This affected a large percentage of the people of Maryland. A meeting of Democrats and elements of the Union party, led by William Veirs Bouic, met at the courthouse and called for the repeal of the law. Montgomery Blair, a leader of opponents to the bill, William Thompson and Joseph A. Taney were sent to a meeting in Baltimore on January 24, 1866, which adopted a resolution that stated in part: "the registration law of this state is odious and oppressive in its positions, unjust and tyrannical ... " but the legislature failed to agree demanding that it "ought to be vigorously enforced."

By this time the Democratic party had regained its political power. Conservative Unionists, including Governor Thomas Swann and Montgomery Blair, rejoined the Democrats because of similar ideology, while more radical Unionists looked to the Republican party. A new state constitution was passed in 1867 by a convention

Above: *Famed "Angel of the Battlefield" and founder of the American Red Cross, Clara Barton is probably the county's most famous Civil War veteran. The Barton house in Glen Echo served as headquarters for the Red Cross until 1904 and is now part of the National Park System. Courtesy, Montgomery County Historical Society*

Facing page: *The County Almshouse on Seven Locks Road, Rockville, was later known as the County Home. Providing shelter for the county's poor, the structure was razed in the 1950s to make way for the new County Detention Center. Courtesy, Montgomery County Historical Society*

controlled by Democrats. The new constitution restored the voting privilege to everyone.

The end of hostilities brought into focus the need for another type of reform. The recession that followed the war made evident a need for welfare programs.

The poor and indigent of the county had been cared for by The Trustees of the Poor since 1787. Conditions demanded the need for a new brick almshouse to replace the old frame building on the farm near Rockville. By 1880 there were 40 inmates cared for at a cost of $2,400 per year, including a retainer for a doctor and nurse when needed. Those who were able worked on the farm and in the kitchen.

A Benevolent Aid Society was organized in the county in 1877. Judge Richard Johns Bowie, the president, and other active members were involved in prison reform and other charitable work.

Alcohol abuse was a pressing social problem in the 19th century. Temperance societies, centered in the Methodist church, grew in number and size. After years of debate the question of local option, which allowed voters to decide if alcoholic beverages could be sold within the county, was put on the ballot in the November 1880 election, and prohibition was adopted by a majority of 1,520. Montgomery County remained legally dry for the next 50 years.

On September 6, 1876, between 2,000 and 3,000 people met at the Rockville Fair Grounds to celebrate the centennial of Montgomery County. The objectives of the occasion were, according to Allen Bowie Davis, chairman of the event:

● to bring together all the "old and venerable men of the county that we may have the opportunity of paying . . . all proper honor and respect."
● to bring together as many relics of olden times as possible.
● to gather together "implements of husbandry, household work and handicrafts, such as were used before the day of modern invention."
● to listen to odes and speeches

interspersed with music.
● then will follow an old fashioned picnic.

The *Sentinel* reported that it was an "intellectual treat." It went on to describe the day as "auspicious" and that "by 9 o'clock [the ceremonies did not commence until 11] the village was one mass of people ... The stores were closed, and all were out in holiday attire." The speakers' platform was decorated with flowers and evergreens and over it was worked the motto "In God We Trust" with the figures 1776 and 1876 on each s building was devoted to the collection of antiquities. The newspaper described in detail all the prayers and speeches and musical selections that made up the program. As Montgomery County completed 100 years of its history, the people paused to reflect on the past and to look forward to their future in a reunited nation.

Since before the turn of the century, the Sandy Spring Stage carried passengers and mail between Laurel and Sandy Spring. This glass plate photo was taken in 1916, just before the stage ceased operation. Courtesy, Montgomery County Historical Society

5
From Farmland
to Suburb

The end of Reconstruction initiated a new role for Montgomery County. In the next four decades its farmland was, in places, transformed into the harbinger of the modern age — the suburbs. As the neighboring capital grew so did the communities surrounding it, but with growth came the need for planning and control.

TRACKS ACROSS THE COUNTRYSIDE
New methods of transportation were introduced in Montgomery County in the late 19th century. Turnpikes and canal were supplemented by a railroad and streetcars. With more convenient means of travel, resorts, new towns, and suburban communities flourished.

The first railroad in Maryland is believed to have been built in Montgomery County about 1830. This primitive line consisted of five miles of wooden track laid from a quarry near Sugar Loaf Mountain to a C & O Canal construction site. Cars, in reality wooden platforms on wheels, were pulled by two horses over oak rails without the support of cross-ties — a far cry from the shining steel rails of a later era.

A preliminary survey for a railroad route from Washington across the county was made prior to the Civil War by the Metropolitan Railroad Company. No actual building was started, however, due to the financial depression of 1857. Finally, in 1865 the Metropolitan Branch of the Baltimore & Ohio Railroad was chartered and work began. The route was divided into 42 sections and contracts were awarded for the construction of each.

Section 11 was the first to be built. James Alexander Boyd, a Scottish engineer with a background in railroad, bridge, and dam construction in the United States and Brazil, was in charge of this initial work. He later completed sections 10 through 16, six of the most difficult as they required the cut at Parr's Ridge and the spanning of the ravine at Little Seneca Creek. Boyd moved to the county to be closer to his work and settled for the remainder of his life in the area originally known as Boyd's Station, now the town of Boyds. After establishing a camp for the construction workers, he then built his home, "Bonnie Brae," and ran a successful dairy farm in addition to his engineering work.

By 1873, just over 42 miles of countryside had been graded, trestle bridges constructed over creeks and rivers, and tracks laid. The line, originating in

Washington, ran through the county to
Washington Junction (Point of Rocks) in
Frederick County, where it joined the main
line of the B & O west from Baltimore.

On May 25, 1873, the first train crossed
Montgomery County. The *Sentinel*
reported:

*Well-the Metropolitan B.R.R. is at last
completed and the regular passenger trains
have commenced running. Many ...
assembled at the depot to witness the
iron-horse as he went dashing by ... The
great work has been accomplished, and our
people may bid farewell to slow coaches
and muddy roads - they can now go to
Washington in forty-five minutes at a cost
of sixty cents. This is much gained in time*

Above: *Railroads brought more than people to the
county. Lumber and coal yards sprang up to provide
needed fuel and lumber to the burgeoning economy.
Photo by Malcolm Walter*

Facing page, top: *The coming of the railroad
resulted in Mizell Lumber Yard. Building and
development needed lumber and the easiest way
to get it was by rail. Mizell's was originally opened
in the 1880s as a General Store. Photo by
Malcolm Walter*

Facing page, bottom: *For years, the Baltimore and
Ohio Railroad was a major link in the county to
Washington, D.C., and promoted much development
around its 20 stations within the county. Courtesy,
Montgomery County Historical Society*

ANNUAL
FAIR
AT
ROCKVILLE
◆ MD. ◆
SEPTEMBER 3 TO 6, 1895
GREAT RACES EACH DAY
New Features! Novel Attractions
The Greatest Exhibition of Live Stock, Agricultural
Implements and Farm Products in the State.
ALL DEPARTMENTS FULL AND COMPLETE
THE
B. & O. R. R.
WILL SELL
EXCURSION TICKETS
From Weverton, Frederick, Washington, Laurel and all intermediate Ticket
Stations, for all trains September 3d to 6th, good to return
until September 7th, at
ONE FARE for the ROUND TRIP
With 50 Cents Added for Admission to the Fair.
FOR TIME OF TRAINS SEE REGULAR TIME TABLES.
R. B. CAMPBELL, Gen'l Manager.   CHAS. O. SCULL, Gen'l Passenger Agent.

Facing page, top: *As with all the stations on the B & O, Gaithersburg grew as a result of the railroad's coming. The station was designed by Baltimore architect Ephraim Francis Baldwin and is similar to most of the stations in the county. Courtesy, Montgomery County Historical Society*

Above left: *Derwood Railroad Station on the Baltimore & Ohio line was one of the smaller frame stations designed by Ephraim Francis Baldwin. Courtesy, Montgomery County Historical Society and Janet Manuel*

Above right: *In addition to providing a commuter service, the B & O provided excursions to the Annual Fair in Rockville from Weverton, Frederick, Washington, Laurel, and all intermediate ticket stations. Courtesy, Montgomery County Historical Society*

Left: *Engine Number 635 is shown here in front of the freight station in Gaithersburg in 1890. Sidings at the stops accommodated freight cars for loading and unloading. Courtesy, Montgomery County Historical Society and the Smithsonian Institution*

and money, to the travelling public, while to the farmer along the line, its advantages are incalcuable. Five and six trains have been running daily . . . and after Monday next, twelve trains a day will pass over the road.

There were 20 stops along the line within the county. Stations were built for the convenience of passengers and the handling of freight. Many were built on the same plan; all were designed by the Baltimore architect Ephraim Francis Baldwin. They ranged in size from one-room frame structures to large brick structures with living quarters above for the agent and his family. The larger stations frequently had two waiting rooms — one for ladies and one for gentlemen. Sidings at the stops accommodated freight cars for loading and unloading. Thriving commercial businesses sprang up around the stations in all the communities served by the rail line.

For many years the trip by train to Washington was part of the workday routine for Montgomery County commuters. In 1880 there were 12 trains a day. But with the coming of the automobile, train service was curtailed, and 100 years after the first run there were but three commuter trains and an express with only three stops. In 1973 a one-way ticket from Washington to Dickerson, the farthermost station in the county, cost $2.32.

Though it is hard to imagine today the streetcar was once, for a short period, the most popular form of public transportation. Horse-drawn cars were popular in the nation's cities for some time before the first electric streetcar system was built in Richmond, Virginia in 1888. The new invention was an immediate sensation, and eight months later, Washington, D.C., had a line in operation.

In Montgomery County the first streetcar line was the Tenallytown and Rockville Railroad (1890-1925), sometimes referred to as the Washington and Rockville. The route extended the service of the Georgetown and Tenallytown Railway Company from the District Line at Wisconsin Avenue, past the home of its president, General Richard C. Drum, to Alta Vista on Old Georgetown Road. The original terminus was the Bethesda Amusement Park until its destruction by a hurricane on September 29, 1896. The line was extended to the Rockville Fair Grounds in 1900 and then through the town to the western limit. This company conveyed its rights to the Capital Transit Company and service was discontinued in 1935.

The Glen Echo Railroad (1891-1900) was short-lived. Its route connected the District Line at Wisconsin Avenue with Glen Echo and Cabin John. In 1896 it extended service in the opposite direction to Connecticut Avenue.

The Washington and Great Falls Electric Railroad (1892-1950) constructed a line from Georgetown to Glen Echo parallel to the river. The cars brought patrons to the Chautauqua (1891-1903) and the Amusement Park (1903-1950) located there. The tracks of the defunct Glen Echo Railroad allowed extension of the line to Cabin John and the Bobinger's Cabin John Hotel. The name remained an unfulfilled prophecy as the line never reached Great Falls.

The Rock Creek Railway Company (1892-1935) operated streetcars originating at 18th and U streets, N.W., in Washington, D.C. Within the county they followed Connecticut Avenue to Chevy Chase Lake, an amusement park. All of this was a part of the Chevy Chase Land Company's plan to develop property along

the route. The Kensington Railway Company (1895-1935) began as an extension of the Rock Creek Railway for those who lived beyond the Chevy Chase Lake station. In 1895 both lines became part of the Capital Traction Company, and service was discontinued in 1935.

The Washington, Woodside and Forest

Originally the site of the Chautauqua, Glen Echo developed as a popular amusement park. The trolley became an efficient means of travel and contributed to the general development of the communities along the Potomac River. Photo by Fred Schreider. Courtesy, Montgomery County Historical Society

Glen Power Company (1895-1924), familiarly called the Forest Glen Trolley, had, by 1897, extended the Brightwood Railway Company's line in Washington through Silver Spring to Forest Glen. The residents along Georgia Avenue and the young ladies of National Park Seminary, a fashionable girls' school, could ride to the District Line for five cents and then pay an additional fare on the connecting Brightwood line into Washington.

The Washington and Great Falls Railway and Power Company (1913-1921) finally accomplished what the Washington and Great Falls Electric Railroad had attempted. This company provided service

Above: Picnickers could view the falls at Great Falls by taking a narrow bridge out to the rocks. This bridge has long since been washed away by the rampaging Potomac, as have others which followed. The National Park Service had decided in recent years not to replace the most recent cat walk. Photo by Clifton Adams, National Geographic Society, March 1928.

Facing page: These boys from the Great Falls area proudly show off their possum catch. Although no hunting is allowed within the C & O National Historic Park borders, the surrounding areas are still a favorite for deer hunters and muskrat trappers. Photo by Clifton Adams, National Geographic Society, March 1928.

to Great Falls as a part of a land development scheme west of Bethesda. Tracks began at Wisconsin Avenue and ran parallel to Bradley Boulevard to River Road then across the countryside to the falls.

A recreational attraction was at the end of many streetcar lines, but this was only one appeal in the service. The electric railways provided efficient transportation to the towns along the route and helped to promote new communities. Husbands rode the trolley to work, the children to school, and the wives to shop. Nor did they exist for passenger service alone. Freight Car No. 1001 on the Rock Creek Railway brought food, ice, and store deliveries to patrons. On a more informal basis, Isaac B. Good recalled how, as a young conductor, he would "collect shopping lists from

Above: Not all visitors to the county stayed in fancy resort hotels. A substantial number of city workers set up camp along the Potomac River near Great Falls for the summer. A group of campers are shown here "sprucing up for the office." Photo by Richard M. Stewart, National Geographic Society, March 1928.

Facing page: The Sabbath was not forgotten among River campers as this photograph attests. Families escaped the summer heat of Washington to enjoy camping along the banks of the Potomac. Photo by Richard H. Stewart, National Geographic Society, March 1928.

housewives . . . take them to a store on the way downtown, then pick up the groceries and deliver them . . . on the way back."

Encouraged by the convenience of railroad and streetcar travel, the middle class of Washington, as in other eastern cities, began to spend their summers "in the country." Rooms could be rented by the week or by the month in hotels and boarding houses or a day could be spent at an amusement park. As the popularity of the summer vacation increased, the family might take lodgings for the summer while the husband joined them each weekend.

One of the earliest of the large hotels was the Cabin John Bridge Hotel, which had its beginning as a lunchroom for the construction workers on the bridge. Joseph Bobinger came from Germany and found work as a stonemason. His wife, Rosa, began to cook meals for the laborers and, later, the tourists who came to see this engineering achievement.

The hotel was begun in 1870 and added to until it became castle-like in Germanic taste with 40 guest rooms and two banquet halls seating 100 each as well as parlors, private dining rooms, and a glass showcase for its famed orchestrion. The food was superb. Sweeping lawns extended to the river, where gazebos were frequently used as bandstands. It was here at a banquet for newspaper workers that John Philip Sousa introduced his "Washington Post March." The hotel closed in 1925 and the abandoned building burned on April 6, 1931.

Further up the river at Great Falls, the Crommelin Hotel was built by the C & O Canal Company in 1828 and named for the Amsterdam banking firm that had helped finance the canal project. It had a variety of uses from tavern to grocery store until

its opening as a resort hotel in 1859 for the accommodation of visitors to Great Falls. It attained its greatest popularity as a resort from 1870 to 1890 and is now headquarters for the Park Service and a canal museum.

Two other hotels were part of development companies' land promotion. The Chevy Chase Inn was opened by the

Left: *As Washingtonians flocked to Montgomery County, especially the Rockville and Glen Echo resorts, natives spent their holidays out of town. This group spent the Fourth of July swimming in the Monocacy River. Photo by Malcolm Walter*

Below: *In the late 19th century the Cabin John Bridge Hotel overlooking the Potomac River was a popular summer resort for pleasure parties from Washington who arrived via trolley. Fishing for bass in the Potomac was reported to be excellent. Courtesy, Montgomery County Historical Society*

Chevy Chase Land Company. A trip out Connecticut Avenue to the inn was five cents; the hotel featured "music every evening" and a special "Dollar Table d'Hote dinner, served from 5 to 8." While this kept the inn busy in the summer, it remained empty in winter. In October 1895 the building was leased to a girls' seminary that became Chevy Chase Junior College and the Land Company terminated its summer operation. The college closed in 1950 and the property was purchased by the National 4-H organization as headquarters and a conference center.

The other was, as announced by a stained glass panel over the doorway, Ye Forest Inne. It was part of a grand scheme of the Forest Glen Improvement Company, which had purchased a large tract on both sides of the B & O Railroad tracks in 1887. The sprawling building in a sylvan setting had 32 guest rooms. Rates were $8 to $14 a week or $2 to $2.50 a day. The company hoped that the guests would build summer homes in the vicinity and eventually become permanent residents. But the summer of 1893 was the inn's last and the property was sold to John A. I. Cassedy who opened National Park Seminary in September of 1894.

In Rockville there had been several hotels that were mainly for the convenience of traveling salesmen or those having business with the county court. In the late 19th century the Washington House, Montgomery House, and Corcoran Hotel suddenly found themselves popular as resort hotels. The Woodlawn Hotel was built specifically for the summer trade. It was purchased in 1889 during its construction by Mrs. Mary J. Colley, a Washington hotelier. The hotel, located on eight acres at the western end of town, became the social center of Rockville with dances, teas, musicals, theatricals, and card

parties. But by 1906 the owner was in debt and it was sold to Dr. Ernest Bullard who established Chestnut Lodge, a psychiatric hospital.

There was a hotel in connection with the Bethesda Amusement Park, a three-storied frame building in Queen Anne style, but it was destroyed by fire on October 8, 1894. Other towns had hotels, including the Albany in Washington Grove and the Forest Oak in Gaithersburg. In addition, large country homes took in boarders or "paying" guests. Frequently the same families returned year after year, the young people marrying local residents.

One of the most ambitious land development and resort schemes was that begun in 1889 by the Baltzley brothers, Edwin and Edward. These real estate promoters from Philadelphia purchased land along the river which they named "Glen Echo." They envisioned not the ordinary community, but a "Rhineland on the Potomac" complete with residences resembling castles, similar to their own newly constructed homes. A resort area was also planned, but only one phase of this was built. A cafe, the Paw-Taw-O-Meck, constructed of cedar logs, with public and private dining rooms, balconies, turrets, and a spectacular view of the Potomac, opened for one season in 1890. It was then completely destroyed by fire. The projected hotel, The Monican, was never started.

Then, in 1891, the Baltzley brothers attracted the National Chautauqua to Glen Echo. Chautauquas, originally organized to instruct Sunday School teachers, had become a source of education, culture, religion, and recreation for the general public. On 60 acres donated for the purpose, lecture halls and an amphitheater, with capacity for 8,000 people, were built including a grand organ powered by the waters of a stream beneath the building.

Opening day was June 16, 1891. People flocked to attend lectures and concerts. The Chautauqua was connected to the city by streetcar, although some chose to bring tents and stay for days. But the fascination of the project soon wore off. After a few years of vaudeville-type entertainment, the land was sold in 1911 to the Capital Transit Company, a streetcar line, that turned Glen Echo into an amusement park.

During the next three decades the park attracted thousands on summer days. The Crystal Pool and the Spanish Ballroom were filled. The amphitheater was converted to a "fun house" and the many rides included a roller coaster and a merry-go-round. But 1969 marked the closing of the park due to a number of social and economic problems. Today attempts are being made by the National Park Service to restore Glen Echo's cultural influence as a center for artists.

In 1892 Clara Barton, founder of the American Association of the Red Cross, was

Above: *The Baltzley brothers attracted the national Chautauqua to Glen Echo. The amphitheatre held 8,000 people and had a grand organ powered by the waters of a stream flowing beneath the building. Edwin Baltzley, president of the Glen Echo Chautauqua, was seated on the stage on the day the theatre was dedicated. Courtesy, Montgomery County Historical Society*

Facing page: *In the 1890s Rockville grew both as a resort and as a town. With substantial residential appeal, the need for services grew. In about 1899 Rockville got its first water tower at a cost of about $20,000. This is the tower in a 1906 photograph by Lewis Reed of Reed Brothers Dodge. Courtesy, Montgomery County Historical Society*

attracted to the area by the Chautauqua, which she believed would be "a mighty influence in the land." Her home, built with lumber used in temporary housing for victims of the Jamestown flood, also served as headquarters for the Red Cross from

1893 to 1904 and as a warehouse for their supplies. It is now open to the public by the National Park Service.

A DIFFERENT WAY OF LIFE

The emergence of Montgomery County as a suburb of Washington, D.C., was not solely the result of improved transportation. The population of Washington was burgeoning and local entrepreneurs saw an opportunity for success in their number. Great effort was spent in luring the city dweller to "the country."

The Civil War had turned the capital from a small town into a city engaged in government, politics, and business. Previously government workers had hesitated to move their families to the area as their jobs might be lost in the next change of administration. The Civil Service Act of 1883 is credited with creating a stable population for the city. Soon these federal employees and professionals were

seeking residences outside of Washington but within easy commuting distance. Many who had first been introduced to the appeal of the county by summer resorts and parks now chose to live there.

The commuters, however, who took the train and streetcars into the city, were not all "new people." The city provided alternative employment to working on the farm. Many long-time residents took government jobs or service jobs in the urban area.

New suburban developments began to appear in the 1880s that closely followed the railroad and, later, the trolley lines. At first lots were small and the houses inexpensive, but it was soon realized that more affluent buyers could be attracted. The real estate developer of this era was a man of great imagination (frequently greater than that of his financial backing.) Plats, filed in county land records, subdivided large tracts of farmland with proposed building lots, broad streets, and parks. Exciting brochures, including "How to Get Health, Wealth, Comfort: Peerless Rockville" (1890), "Gaithersburg, Maryland: Its Advantages" (1891), "Glen-Echo

Top: *Montgomery County men served with Company B of the District Volunteers. They rode with Theodore Roosevelt's Rough Riders up San Juan Hill during the Spanish American War. Courtesy, Richard L. Browning*

Bottom: *The Stonestreet sisters, daughters of a prominent Rockville physician, are shown here in about 1877, including Martha, Bessie, Adelaide, Carrie, Edith, and Elba. Courtesy, Montgomery County Historical Society*

Built by a watchmaker, the old Atlantic ran 80 miles on one ton of coal. Phineas Davis won a $4,000 prize as the first to enter Washington after a run to Frederick and Point of Rocks. Photo by Charles Martin, National Geographic Society, July 1938

on-the-Potomac: The Washington Rhine" (1891), and "Takoma Park: The Sylvan Suburb of the National Capital" (1901), extolled the delights of the area. Not only did this development affect the old, established towns, but it also brought into existence new ones and proved the statement in *The Washington Post* in 1889 that "development along the Metropolitan Branch within the past few years has been phenomenal."

Takoma Park, the first new suburban development, was platted in 1883, developed by Benjamin F. Gilbert, and incorporated as a town in 1890. Another that came was the Baltzley brothers' Glen Echo in 1889. The largest and most successful developer was the Chevy Chase Land Company, headed by Senator Francis G. Newlands. According to Newland's biographer, Albert W. Atwood, this company "built out of farmland that great thoroughfare, Connecticut Avenue, . . . and created what probably became the best-known suburb in the country, Chevy Chase." Benjamin F. Leighton, representing a group of Washington investors,

Facing page, top: *In 1912 the development of Bradley Hills, a fashionable new subdivision, led to the building of a new streetcar line to Bethesda as well as new roads. Courtesy, Montgomery County Historical Society*

Facing page, bottom: *Kensington, or Knowles Station as it was once known, developed as a result of the railroad and the promotion of real estate developer B.H. Warner. To the left is a pharmacy and post office, to the right was a local newspaper. Photo by Malcolm Walter*

Below: *At the turn of the century most people were still engaged in occupations relating directly to farming. "Valley View" in Colesville appeared to be typical of the more substantial farms which were the norm. Courtesy, Montgomery County Historical Society*

subdivided a tract on Georgia Avenue and advertised lots for sale in Woodside Park. The Forest Glen Improvement Company hoped to attract residents to that area, while nearby A. S. Pratt & Sons developed Capitol View on the subdivided property of Oliver and Mary Harr. Kensington and Garrett Park came into existence around stations on the B & O line. Henry Copp, earlier involved in Garrett Park real estate, laid out West End Park in Rockville in 1891. The development of Friendship Heights by Henry W. Offutt, Drummond by General Richard C. Drum, Somerset by the Somerset Heights Colony Company (five employees of the U.S. Department of

Agriculture), and Bradley Hills began closer to the turn of the century.

One unique community was Washington Grove. This was chosen by Washington Methodists as the location of their annual camp meeting. The Washington Grove Camp Meeting Association was a stock company in which one share entitled the owner to a tent site and five shares included the privilege of purchasing a lot for a cottage. This town, which originated as a summer community, evolved into an incorporated area with year-round residents.

Interspersed among the suburban communities were the large estates of wealthy Washingtonians. Land along Rockville Pike was a frequent choice but other places in the county were also selected. Some of the elegant homes served as permanent residences but many received only periodic use. Today many of these luxurious reminders of turn-of-the-century wealth are used for schools, foundation headquarters, and cultural centers.

OCCUPATIONS AND SERVICES

Around the turn of the century the average farm was slightly over 100 acres and 90 percent of the people of the county were still engaged in agriculturally related occupations. By World War I farming had virtually been abandoned in the lower part of the county. But suburbs still occupied only a small part of the county's land and about 85 percent remained agricultural.

Mechanization had profoundly changed farming methods. Planters, reapers, bailers and, eventually, the tractor, greatly increased the amount of land one farmer was able to cultivate. Dairying became an increasingly popular usage of land with good transportation and a large local market. Truck farming on small acreage brought the occupation of huckstering into popularity.

During the period after the Civil War a new occupation was pursued by some county residents. Gold was found in several areas, including Sandy Spring, Rockville, and Bethesda, but only at Great Falls were there extensive mining operations. Most credit for the discovery is given to soldiers encamped near this place, although samples from there had been assayed earlier. Some of the men had been prospectors in the California Gold Rush and recognized its presence in the streams. Four returned, purchased land, and formed the Maryland Mining Company. By 1868 they were shipping gold to the U.S. Mint. Since that time a number of mines have been opened, closed, and changed hands, but the Maryland Mine continued to be the largest, followed by the Ford Mine. By 1950, however, all commercial gold mining in the county had ceased.

This period of county history also saw the beginning of private institutions and companies to meet the service needs of the residents. The first had been an insurance company in the Sandy Spring area. The Mutual Fire Insurance Company, patterned after a similar group in Pennsylvania since there were none like it in Maryland, was chartered by the state legislature in March 1848. The first office of the Mutual Fire Insurance Company was a one-room building in Sandy Spring. Many county barns, homes, and businesses were insured, (the home of the first president, Edward

The McCeney brothers attended Maryland Agricultural College in nearby College Park. Standing are George W. and Henry C., and seated is Samuel C. Sam McCeney married Katharine Marlow. Both of their families owned large farms in the White Oak, Colesville, area. Courtesy, Virginia Hoffman

Facing page, top: *County Agent Fred J. Van Hoesen, in his 1918 report on his duties included a photo of a "new" tractor with the following notes: "The speed of the tractor increased the efficiency of the float materially in crushing the clods....The day before this photograph was taken two horse-drawn and two tractor-drawn binders were working in this field." Courtesy, Montgomery County Historical Society*

Above: *By World War I, 90 percent of the people of the county were still engaged in farming. Part of the job of the county agent was to help and advise farmers in ways to improve crop production. Courtesy, Montgomery County Historical Society*

Facing page, bottom: *Montgomery County Agricultural Agent Van Hoesen is shown with a group of future farmers, drawing names out of a hat for the piglets in the box. Courtesy, Montgomery County Historical Society*

Below: *The Mutual Fire Insurance Company was headquartered in Sandy Spring. Directors of the company were unpaid for 18 years until 1866, when they were voted an annual salary of $14.60 and "a dinner and horse feed" provided by the company. Courtesy, Montgomery County Historical Society*

Facing page, top: *With the increase in population and the coming of age of the automobile, service stations adorned the roadsides. This sign proclaiming "D.C. prices" indicates prices tended to be higher in the suburbs in the 1930s. Photo by Malcolm Walter*

Facing page, bottom: *Montgomery County Motor Company in Rockville combined selling Chevrolet automobiles with selling "Pyrofax" gas refrigerators. Photo by Malcolm Walter*

Below: *A sure sign of the burgeoning suburbs is this 1929 ice cream truck based in Kensington. Photo by Malcolm Walter*

Stabler, "Harewood," being policy No. 1). In 1905 automobile insurance was added to their service.

The first successful banking organization in Montgomery County was the Savings Institution of Sandy Spring, founded in 1868 by "26 thrifty and conservative citizens" with Caleb Stabler as president. The office was a room added to the Mutual Fire Insurance Company building. This was followed in 1882 by the Montgomery County National Bank in Rockville, now a part of the Maryland National Bank. In 1891 the First National Bank of Gaithersburg, now merged with Suburban Trust Company, was founded with Upton Darby as president and offices located at Diamond and Summit avenues. The history of the First National Bank of Sandy Spring, formed in 1900, was marred by a sensational robbery in 1920 during which Francis M. Hallowell, the bank teller, was killed. Also in 1900 the Farmers Banking

and Trust Company opened its office for business at Court Street and East Montgomery Avenue in Rockville with William Veirs Bouic as president. Now, at a different location, it is part of the First National Bank of Maryland. These were followed between 1900 and 1920 by the Poolesville National Bank (1907), Silver Spring National Bank (1910), now part of Suburban Trust Company, and the Bank of Bethesda (1919).

The late 19th and early 20th centuries brought an amazing array of new

The first bank founded in Montgomery County was the Savings Institution of Sandy Spring. In 1900 the First National Bank of Sandy Spring was formed. Both banks shared the same building for 72 years and did not formally merge until 1972. Banker's hours are not new, as the hours posted attest. Courtesy, Montgomery County Historical Society

inventions to the United States. The telephone, or "speaking telegraph," as Alexander Graham Bell first called it, was exhibited to the public at the Centennial Exposition in Philadelphia in 1876. John P. Stabler of Sandy Spring saw it and soon devised a short line connecting his home with that of his father-in-law, George E. Brooke, and that of Charles A. Iddings near Brinklow.

In 1891 a group in Gaithersburg headed by Albert Filmore Meem, stationmaster for the B & O, organized the Montgomery County Telephone Company and installed a switchboard in the railroad station. The switchboard was subsequently moved to the home of the operator because the subscribers wanted to use the phone as late as 8 p.m. The Enterprise Telephone Company was organized in Sandy Spring and the first lines were strung in 1894 incorporating Stabler's original three-party line. These private lines were expanded and, with exchange systems, served other communities. In 1906 they were both bought by the Chesapeake and Potomac Telephone Company, which still services the suburban area. In 1895 Samuel Brian, president of the Chesapeake and Potomac, agreed with the mayor and council to bring service to Rockville. The first Rockville telephone was installed in Owens' drugstore. By 1910 there were 1,250 telephones in the county.

Most Montgomery County electricity has been furnished by Potomac Electric Power Company, although a few areas are served by Potomac Edison Company. The early development of electric service closely followed the trolley lines and main roads to communities whose population justified the installation. By 1909 service had been established in Rockville and by 1914 had reached Gaithersburg and Washington Grove. In the next decade service expanded

to include Cabin John, Garrett Park, and Silver Spring.

In its infancy electricity was used primarily for home lighting. But in 1915, 100 incandescent lamps on wooden poles were installed on the streets of Rockville. "Stoves and small appliances came into popular use around World War I." Electricity went on to revolutionize farming and housekeeping in the years before World War II.

The Washington Gas Light Company of Montgomery County was formed and distribution of gas began in Takoma Park in 1894. The Georgetown Gas Light Company was incorporated in 1908 to supply homes in the Chevy Chase area. The Washington Gas Light Company, which had been incorporated in Washington, D.C., in 1848, now supplies all gas service in the county.

Since the earliest days of civilization, fire protection had required community cooperation but suffered from a lack of strong organization. Rural areas were, generally, far behind cities and townships in meeting the need for fire protection. Montgomery County was no exception.

Some of the towns in the county owned equipment. Rockville purchased 100 feet of hose in 1888. In 1894 a group of Takoma Park citizens, alarmed by the increased number of fires, organized the Takoma Park Fire Department with a two-wheeled, hand-drawn hose reel and a gong. A year later Rockville's mayor and council approved the organization of a fire company and purchased additional equipment. Prior to World War I the fire departments in Takoma Park, Silver Spring, Rockville, Kensington, and Glen Echo were all volunteer. Silver Spring was the first to incorporate in 1918.

Law enforcement in the county depended primarily on the services of the sheriff, his

Facing page, top: *Windmills dotted the 1920s Kensington landscape. Used to pump water, many stayed after the advent of electricity. Courtesy, Montgomery County Historical Society*

Facing page, bottom: *The Montgomery Power Company crew is shown here working at Little Falls on the Potomac River in March 1898. Photo by William A. Miller, courtesy, Montgomery County Historical Society*

Above: *Prior to the introduction of electricity to the county, the storage of perishables was very difficult. Ice was cut from ponds during the winter months and stored in ice houses. The ice was packed with sawdust. This is the ice house for Montevideo in Seneca. Courtesy, Montgomery County Historical Society, Library of Congress photo*

deputies, and constables until 1910. That year the legislature authorized the county commissioners to appoint three additional constables to patrol county roads. It wasn't until 1922 that a force was fully established.

There were no hospitals in Montgomery County until the early part of the 20th century. As with institutions of other kinds, the cities of Washington, Baltimore, and Frederick were looked to in extreme cases. It was not until 1907 that the Washington Sanitarium, a small hospital with a capacity of 35 was built in Takoma Park under the direction of the Seventh-day Adventists.

Above: Women supported the Volunteer Fire departments. Here the Kensington Ladies Auxiliary shows off one of Kensington's engines. Photo by Malcolm Walter

Facing page: Fire, long a threat to Montgomery County communities, caused volunteer fire departments to be started in most areas. Photo by Malcolm Walter

In 1916 Dr. Jacob W. Bird opened a five-bed hospital in a rented house in the Sandy Spring area. In 1919, with interest heightened by the influenza epidemic, a stock company was formed and a hospital

built. Dr. Bird was chief of staff at Montgomery County General Hospital until his death in 1959. In 1962 the stock was recalled and it became a nonprofit organization and, at the same time, "County" was dropped from the name. Montgomery General and the Washington Sanitarium were the only two hospitals in the county until Suburban Hospital opened in 1943.

In 1908 the Montgomery County Social Service League, the first in the state outside of the city of Baltimore, was organized. It grew out of a concern for the problems and conditions of the poor. Its stated purpose was "to assist in the care of the poor, of the sick . . . and of the destitute and deficient children of the county; to direct public attention to the causes and prevention of disease and suffering; and to arouse general interest in securing proper provisions for the needy in their homes and in institutions." For the next 27 years this organization, with Dr. Jacob W. Bird as its president, performed these functions until they were taken over by the county government.

POLITICAL ROLES

The Democratic party dominated county politics from the Civil War to World War I, although an occasional Republican candidate would win an election. During this period, however, a division arose in the Democratic party, between "machine" elements, led in the state by Arthur Pue Gorman, and those in the party seeking political reform.

The Peter family, originally machine leaders in the county, broke with that faction and joined Dr. Edward Wootton of Poolesville, William Veirs Bouic of Rockville, and Philip D. Laird, a delegate to the Maryland legislature, in the "anti-machine" group. Spencer Cone Jones of Rockville assumed the local leadership of the other members of the Democratic party.

The reform Democrats were strengthened by the participation of Blair Lee. Lee's involvement reflected a family history of political activism beginning with his grandfather, Francis Preston Blair. Blair was brought to Washington in 1830 by President Andrew Jackson to edit a newspaper, *The Globe,* that would reflect the Democratic administration's views. He became a member of Jackson's Kitchen Cabinet and purchased a home, now the Blair House, across Pennsylvania Avenue from the White House. A short time later he purchased land in the county and built a summer home that eventually became his permanent residence which he named "Silver Spring."

One of his sons, Montgomery Blair, a lawyer, defended Scott in the case before the Supreme Court that resulted in the Dred Scott Decision in 1857. Although slaveholders, Francis Preston Blair and his son, Montgomery Blair, believed in the preservation of the Union and broke with the Democratic party over its platform. They became Republicans temporarily and spent much energy in an attempt to keep Maryland in the Union. For his effort Lincoln appointed Montgomery Blair as

postmaster general. After the war Blair returned to the Democratic Party, was elected to the House of Delegates from the county, but was unsuccessful as a candidate for Congress. In the national election of 1868, he was the vice-presidential candidate on a ticket headed by Horatio Seymour but, although they won in the county by a margin of 1,745 to 199, they lost to Republicans Ulysses S. Grant and Schuyler Colfax.

Francis Preston Blair's daughter, Elizabeth, married Samuel Philips Lee, a member of that illustrious family of Virginia and a rear admiral in the U.S. Navy. Their only child was Francis Preston Blair Lee. Blair Lee, a Princeton educated lawyer, was invited to become a candidate in 1905 for the state senate on the anti-machine ticket and won. In the Maryland assembly he was successful in his efforts toward the adoption of legislation regarding aid to education, regulation of utilities, improvement in the state road system, and revision of election laws. He was unsuccessful in his candidacy for governor in 1911 but was elected U.S. Senator for the district in 1913.

For many years the Republican party was made up largely of Quakers, a few other white families, and the black population. As more voters moved into the suburbs from other parts of the nation, however, many joined the Grand Old Party. Brainard Warner, a developer of Kensington, vied with Thomas Dawson, the Rockville postmaster, for party leadership.

As early as 1880 it became evident that the 1840 Montgomery County Court House was inadequate to house all the functions of the county government. An item in the *Sentinel* that year remarked that:

The court house in its present condition is but poorly suited for the comfort and convenience of the official occupants who are compelled to be in daily attendance, and insecure so far as the preservation of records are concerned in case of fire . . . To overhaul the old court house . . . in our opinion, will cost more than a new [one].

But it was not until 1890 that a building committee was appointed. Frank E. Davis, an architect from Baltimore, was engaged to draw up the plans and a contract for construction was awarded to Thomas P. Johns of Baltimore. A new red brick courthouse was completed in 1891.

The rapid development and progress in the county brought concern to the citizens and government alike. Both long-established towns and new communities grew without county planning, regulations, or codes. Developers or property owners were responsible for their own water and sewer systems, utilities, and streets. Residents of the suburban areas called upon the county school board for relief of overcrowding in their schools. Many students withdrew and enrolled in Washington schools as a result of the board's slow response to public concern.

The terms "up-county" and "down-county" were frequently used to reflect the division of vested interests of the suburban and farming population. Farmers claimed that downcounty residents had "set a new . . . and fictitious value on the land, and large areas have been turned over to him for his home, his club and his park" and that more tax money was going for services and improvements in that area. Suburban residents claimed that all political power was held by old upcounty families. This problem was pushed from the forefront by the onset of World War I, but the local conflict remained to resurface later in the century.

Facing page: *Montgomery Blair (1813-1883) believed so strongly in the preservation of the Union that he broke with the Democratic party over the issue, even though he owned slaves himself. From Scharf's History of Maryland*

Below: *With the population increase came more cars and more trains, sometimes competing for the same space. A road which once crossed the railroad tracks was built above it to avoid accidents. This overpass in Gaithersburg is still used today. Photo by Malcolm Walter*

George Lamar, president of the Board of School commissioners, had originally planned to develop only one high school in the county. Other towns developed their own high schools, and so the Montgomery County High School was known instead as the Rockville High School. The name Richard Montgomery High School was officially adopted in 1925. Courtesy, Ruby Tyler

6
Planning to Grow

Change came even more rapidly during the decades spanning World War I, the Great Depression, and World War II. World events touched everyone's lives. It was during this period that the dramatic increase in population brought many changes to Montgomery County, including the expansion of federal government agencies into the county. New county commissions were established and an increasing number of services provided. These pressures brought about a need for reform in county government.

WORLD WAR I

On April 6, 1917, the day that the United States declared war on Germany, the weekly *Sentinel* reprinted the entire text of President Woodrow Wilson's speech, that concluded, "The supreme test of the nation has come. We must all speak, act, and serve together." The people of Montgomery County did just that.

On that same April 6, Maryland's Governor Emerson C. Harrington ordered a census taken throughout the state to ascertain the number of men between 18 and 45 available for military service. In Montgomery County, a five-man commission was appointed to the task.

When the federal government announced that all males between 21 and 30 were to register on June 5th, 2,475 county men responded. Montgomery County's draft quota was 131 men.

The first 40 recruits were to report to Camp Meade on September 28, 1917. They assembled at the courthouse at 10 a.m. for a brief induction ceremony. Then they were entertained at the Montgomery House, the hotel across the street, where the dining room was decorated with flowers and flags. The *Sentinel* reported that after dinner and speeches, the recruits formed a line headed by the King's Valley Band and "the entire assemblage joining the procession" and all paraded to the depot.

Prior to the war there was a National Guard unit made up of 84 men and three officers. On June 1, 1917, the War Department ordered that it "be recruited up to 150 men" and sent to Camp McClellan, Alabama. At Camp McClellan they became Company K of the 115th Infantry, 29th Division, one of the few National Guard units to remain together overseas with their former officers still in command. The 115th served with distinction throughout the war and their commander E. Brooke Lee returned with honors — the Distinguished Service Cross, a Division Citation for Gallantry in Action, the Belgian Order of Leopold, and two French Croix de Guerre. Montgomery County continued to send young men to the armed services by enlistment and the draft throughout the war. 41 did not return.

Civilians were also called upon to do their part. The slogan "Food Will Win the War" was taken seriously. Governor Harrington's Seven Point Program to the people of Maryland carried recommendations dealing mainly with agriculture:

● *"farmers should cultivate the largest acreage possible.*
● *farmers should consult and cooperate with Extension Service specialists to insure better and larger crops.*
● *those employed in non-agriculture related jobs should assist in obtaining labor, purchasing and transporting implements and supplies, and generally aiding farmers.*
● *farmers should chiefly produce staples, giving them preference over perishable products.*
● *groups should be organized for growing, canning, and preserving food.*
● *vacant-lot and backyard gardening should be encouraged.*
● *the people of Maryland should cooperate in the development of agricultural resources "to meet successfully the conditions which confront us."*

A statewide Council of Defense was organized in June of 1917 to collect information from organizations involved in war-related work. The Montgomery County committee was composed of chairman Otho H.W. Talbott, Thomas L. Dawson, Robert G. Hilton, Howard Spurrier, and R.

Kenneth Waters. A Woman's Section consisted of Mrs. Frank J. (Clara) Wilson, Mrs. William H. (Bertha) Talbott, Mrs. Elden J. (Eliza) Hartshorn, and Mrs. Henry Clinton (Josephine) Allnutt. There was also a "Colored Division" with Mr. Noah E. Clarke as chairman.

A Woman's Preparedness and Survey Commission was set up to make a survey of the "woman strength of the county." It found women were active in knitting sweaters, sending packages to servicemen, and urging people to send books and magazines overseas as "mental food for the National Army." Red Cross auxiliaries were formed. The Woman's Section of the Council of Defense organized a Motor Messenger Service with Mrs. Josiah W. (Margaret) Jones as captain. The Council of Defense in its final report stated that "during the war the women of Maryland rose to new eminence in service and patriotism."

Liberty loans were first mentioned in the *Sentinel* of May 25, 1917, and thereafter the frequent attempts to reach quotas were reported. Robert G. Hilton, president of the Farmers Banking and Trust Company, was appointed chairman of the Liberty Loan Committee for Montgomery County. Certificates as low as five dollars, which yielded interest and matured in five years, were issued. "It is vitally necessary that the American people should practice saving on a large scale during the progress of this war ... This will give every man, woman, and child in America, no matter how small their means, the opportunity to do something to help the government," reported the *Sentinel*.

At the war's end, the Council of Defense stated that "through cooperation and personal sacrifice, the folks at home did all within their power to send food, supplies, and support to the armed forces."

Defense Day Celebration held in Kensington September 12, 1924, brought townspeople out to listen to speeches and singers. Photo by Malcolm Walter

Montgomery County citizens welcomed the Armistice on November 11, 1918, and the men who came home and quietly mourned for those who did not return.

BETWEEN TWO WARS

The population of Washington, D.C., and the suburbs had increased during the war. Veterans returned to a civilian life-style that included homes and families. The postwar boom was reflected in the expanding population, climbing past 35,000 in 1920 and increasing to nearly 50,000 in the next 10 years.

Pressure was put upon the county government by citizens' associations, women's organizations, and civic activists to provide more and improved services. In order to satisfy these demands, the county commissioners created 11 special tax districts in the down-county area that localized the cost of street construction and maintenance, police and fire protection, street lighting, and garbage collection. This protected rural areas from assessment for services they did not use. The first special tax district was Friendship Heights and it was soon followed by sections of Chevy Chase, Oakmont, and Drummond. But even the politicians realized that this was only a partial solution. The county needed long-range, centralized planning.

The Washington Suburban Sanitary Commission (WSSC) had its beginning in a complaint from the District of Columbia concerning the pollution of streams having their origin in Maryland. Public health officials and interested citizens made a study of the problem. As a result legislation was proposed to create a bicounty commission that would control pollution, develop and operate a water supply, and provide a sewage system in Montgomery and Prince George's counties. The plan was drafted by T. Howard Duckett of Prince George's County and backed in the legislature by E. Brooke Lee, a Montgomery County delegate. The WSSC came into being on May 1, 1918.

The three original members of the commission were William T.S. Curtis and Emory H. Bogley from Montgomery County and T. Howard Duckett from Prince George's County. Today there are six members, three from each county. Originally the WSSC served an area of 95 square miles in the two counties. It now includes about 1,000 square miles — most of both counties, except certain municipalities that provide the same services for themselves. The commission indirectly influenced the direction of county development in that later building

followed the construction of water and sewer lines.

The phenomenal growth of the area brought an increasing concern for more planning. Residents had become alarmed at unregulated commercial and residential development. The Maryland-National Capital Park and Planning Commission (M-NCPPC), another bicounty agency, was created in 1927 to meet this need. Its purpose was to guide and plan for the orderly growth of the suburbs in Montgomery and Prince George's counties.

The original commission was composed of six members: three from Montgomery County, Robert G. Hilton, George P. Hoover, and P. Blair Lee; and three from

Above: *Klansmen came from all over the country to demonstrate in Washington, D.C., in August 1925. This camp on Rockville Pike was a source of concern to both black and white countians. Photo by Malcolm Walter*

Facing page: *This young girl from New York proudly displayed her Klan garb. Thousands of Klan families came to the Washington area to demonstrate in August 1925. Photo by Malcolm Walter*

Prince George's County, Irving Owings, George N. Palmer, and T. Howard Duckett. The officers of the chief planner, Irving C.

Root, and his three-man staff were located in an office in the Silver Spring Police Station. Today, there are 10 members of the commission with a regional headquarters building on Georgia Avenue.

By 1932 a plan for regional parks had been adopted. Funding for land acquisition was aided by the Capper-Crampton Act passed by Congress in 1930. This bill, sponsored by Senators Arthur Capper of Kansas and Hugh Crampton of Michigan, authorized federal funds for one-third of the purchase cost of parkland along major streams flowing into the Potomac and Anacostia rivers. Since that time M-NCPPC has developed an extensive system ranging from small neighborhood

Chief Charles T. Cooley was photographed in 1922 in front of Reed Brothers garage. He is posing with the first mounted unit of the Montgomery County police force. Courtesy, Montgomery County Historical Society

parks to large regional recreational facilities.

The M-NCPPC's Department of Planning is charged with formulating the policies and procedures for the two counties' development. It has the power to review and approve subdivision plats, assign street names and numbers, and furnish advisory opinions regarding zoning and land-use plans. The area over which the M-NCPPC has jurisdiction has expanded through the years, until it now includes all of the two counties with the exception in Montgomery County of Rockville, Gaithersburg, Poolesville, and Laytonsville, which have control of land within their boundaries.

Adequate protection of citizens against crime was another popular cause. In order to provide protection the Legislature authorized the county commissioners to create a police force to take over the duties previously handled by the sheriff and his deputies. The *Sentinel* of July 7, 1922, reported the installation of Chief Charles T. Cooley of Forest Glen and his five-man force. Chief Cooley was paid $1,800 a year; the others each received $1,500. Earl

Burdine, the last surviving member of that force, said that he was attracted to the job by the steady pay. "The men were required to have a telephone . . . . With no training in weapons or law, they were sworn in and assigned beats. The officers were given Harley-Davidsons, a .38 Smith & Wesson handgun, a black jack, and a law book." The chief drove a Model T Ford. In 1937 a detective bureau was added. By 1941 the force consisted of the chief and 45 officers; today there are 763 policemen.

Prisoners arrested by the police were incarcerated in an old stone jail built in 1801. It was an awesome structure with walls two and a half feet thick. There were 12 cells and an 8-by-14-foot dungeon in the basement. Whippings and hangings had taken place in earlier days in the stone-walled courtyard.

When a new courthouse was built in 1931, the upper floor was used as a jail until 1961. Overcrowding became a problem with female and juvenile offenders in close proximity to "hardened criminals." Segregation was practiced as far as conditions would permit. When the new Detention Center was opened on Seven Locks Road in 1961, it was described as a national model for county jails.

On the national scene, Herbert Hoover's administration had hardly begun when the country began to slip into a severe economic recession. The collapse of the stock market marked the real beginning of the Great Depression. But Montgomery County was somewhat insulated from the full force. The federal government employed a large percentage of the population in suburban areas. As relief programs were instituted more jobs were created. There was virtually no industry in Montgomery County, so unemployment was not the major problem that it was in other regions. The Depression, however, did halt

the explosive development in the county. Homeowners defaulted on mortgage payments, school expansion was curtailed, and the State Roads Commission took over maintenance of the county's road system. The Social Service League announced in 1932 that it would have to refuse about half of the requests for relief unless further financial aid was forthcoming, whereupon the county commissioners made available the use of their "revolving fund" for welfare work.

The farmers were the ones hardest hit by the Depression. Declining prices for their products resulted in an increase in mortgage defaults, worn-out equipment, unrepaired buildings, and unpaid taxes. The farmers organized to urge legislative aid and tax reductions. The Agricultural Act of 1933 gave subsidies for reduced production of certain crops. The Farm Credit Administration offered short-term loans. Help came but it was often too little too late.

At the height of the Depression a group of farm women, members of the Home Demonstration Clubs sponsored by the Extension Service of the University of Maryland and the U.S. Agriculture Department and led by Miss Blanche Corwin, conceived of a plan whereby they could sell their farm produce to residents of the suburbs. On February 4, 1932, they held their first sale in a vacant store in Bethesda. The project was so successful that it became a weekly event. They organized the Montgomery Farm Women's Cooperative Market, Inc., with 42 members, capital stock, a nine-member board of directors, and a paid manager. By December they had moved into a building at Wisconsin Avenue and Willow Lane and purchased it in 1935. The market is still held on Wednesdays and Saturdays, and provides a mix of farm products, ethnic foods, and crafts.

Herbert Hoover tried to assure Americans that prosperity was "just around the corner." His administration instigated programs for the construction of roads and buildings, but, more importantly, was responsible for the creation of the Reconstruction Finance Corporation (RFC) through which loans were made to railroads, banks, industry, and farmers. The RFC kept many businesses from failing during the Depression that gripped the nation. But dissatisfaction with Hoover's inability to substantially improve the country's economic conditions led the county's Democrats to unite, at least temporarily, in the election of 1932. Franklin D. Roosevelt received 11,805 votes to the incumbent president's 8,257 votes.

Congress gave the new administration the power to assist in the crisis that had caused many banks to fail. On March 6, 1933, President Roosevelt declared a bank holiday that allowed time for reorganization. Those institutions that were in sound financial condition were allowed to reopen. Farmer's Banking and Trust Company in Rockville was open for business again on April 25 and all but one in the county soon followed.

Soon after Roosevelt's inauguration, a "New Deal" began for the people of the United States. Congress passed the Federal Emergency Relief Act, which funded welfare and public works projects. The relief funds were administered locally by the Social Service League. Congress also established the Civilian Conservation Corps (CCC), which gave training and employment to many young men who could not find jobs. Two were located at Cabin John and Garrett Park. Some county boys availed themselves of the opportunity to work for one dollar a day in conservation of natural resources.

The Works Progress Administration (WPA) created jobs for skilled and white collar workers as well as laborers. Under the WPA roads were improved, water and sewer lines were laid, and a number of new buildings were constructed in the county. Murals painted by WPA artists decorated new post offices in Rockville and Bethesda. An inventory of county records was compiled and published. A Writers' Program produced *Maryland: A Guide to The Old Line State,* which included points of interest in the county. Quite an impressive body of creative work emerged from the need to find relief from economic woes.

Despite the depressed economy, the county was in need of a larger courthouse. Additional land was purchased adjacent to the 1891 building, Court Street was abandoned, and the structures on it razed or moved to new locations. The new addition, completed in 1931, was of Indiana limestone and attached to the old red brick structure.

In county politics the number of Republicans had increased with suburban growth but by 1930 still remained less than a third of the registered voters. The anti-organization Democrats, now called Progressive Democrats and led by J. Vinson Peter, conceived the idea that a slate made up of their candidates and Republicans might defeat the Democratic party controlled by E. Brooke Lee.

This Progressive Democrat and Republican "Fusion party" was organized in 1934. At the next election Fusion candidates took votes from the Democrats and were able to gain a majority on the Board of County Commissioners. Lee announced his retirement from politics, citing business pressures, but this was not to be permanent. The Fusionists soon found that three seats out of five on the

Board of County Commissioners was not enough. Democrats had won the state senate seat with Steadman Prescott and continued their domination of the delegation to the Maryland assembly. The Fusionist party's success was short-lived; Democrats regained control of the county in 1938.

Montgomery County's recovery from the Depression was perhaps more quickly achieved than in other places. There were memories of hard times but few of soup kitchens and "Hoovervilles." By 1935 there were as many new building starts as before the decline in the nation's economy. In 1940 the federal government had 7,700 residents of the county on its payroll, by far the largest single employer, but half that many were still engaged in agriculture.

WAR, GOVERNMENT, AND POLITICS

Although war seemed inevitable to many, the attack on Pearl Harbor on Sunday, December 7, 1941, came as a shock to the nation. Montgomery County and the rest of the country made preparations to contribute to the war effort.

On December 12th the 7th Battalion of the Maryland State Guard was mobilized. Colonel E. Brooke Lee was still in command. The Selective Service inducted 158,121 Maryland men into the armed forces during the war, 6,822 from Montgomery County. Many young men enlisted and young women joined to release men for active duty. Of those who served, 316 died defending their country.

Civilian defense organizations reacted quickly. Within a week of the United States' entry into the war, there was a blackout drill under the supervision of Albert E. Brault, executive director of the Civilian Defense Council, in the metropolitan area. The system of air-raid wardens and emergency groups were well trained and efficient. Two companies of Minute Men were formed in Rockville as a "second line of defense" with Judge Steadman Prescott and Allison Chapin, both World War I veterans, as their Captains. Eventually, there were seven companies in the county.

The federal government formed committees and boards with wartime swiftness, the War Production Board, Office of Price Administration, War Labor Board, and Office of Economic Stabilization among them. All had their effect on the county as they exercised authority over wages, rents, prices, and manpower. Ration books and coupons were distributed for a fair division of scarce items. Meat, butter, sugar, canned food, coffee, shoes, and gasoline came under these restrictions. Many manufactured items, including tires and automobiles, were redirected to wartime uses. Factories that produced consumer goods were converted to war material. Rationing and shortages became a way of life to those at home.

Civilians organized to help servicemen and the Allies. The Red Cross was active in forming Blood Donor Units, Canteen Corps, and courses in first aid and home nursing. Scrap metal was collected for recycling. Everyone volunteered to make items for soldiers and collect clothing for war orphans. War bond rallies were held and there was a strong sense of patriotism in investing in bonds and stamps.

Headlines in *The Washington Post* on May 8, 1945, proclaimed V-E Day with "Germany Surrenders Unconditionally," but Fred Vinson, head of the Office of War Mobilization, urged, "Let's stay on the job until both wars are won." And the effort continued until V-J Day was announced on September 2, 1945.

Even before the war, the U.S.

government had begun to relocate, expand, and establish facilities in suburban Montgomery County. The first of these to be built was the National Naval Medical Center. The center, authorized in 1931, had been in existence since 1935 at a location in Washington, D.C. When construction funds were allocated in 1937, more than 80 sites were considered. Tradition states that President Franklin Roosevelt personally chose the Bethesda location. There is a sketch by the president on White House stationery showing that his design for the main building was followed closely. The first building of this large complex was dedicated on August 31, 1942. This facility provides treatment and hospitalization for the personnel and families of the navy, marines, and Coast Guard and is the principal educator of doctors, dentists, and hospital administrators for the navy.

The David W. Taylor Naval Research and Development Center, originally known as the David W. Taylor Model Basin, is located on the tract "Carderock" near Cabin John. The facility was authorized by Congress on May 6, 1936, to replace a 40-year old testing basin at the Navy Yard. The site was chosen for its bedrock base, which assured a firm foundation, its proximity to a water supply, and the fact that it was "remote from heavy traffic, smoke, dust, and noise which might disturb delicate instruments and experiments," yet within a reasonable distance to the Navy Department. The first two buildings, completed in 1939, contained a testing

"Convalescing Yanks replace girl students at National Park Seminary," a 1943 National Geographic *article stated. Walter Reed Army Medical Center moved ambulatory patients to the former school in Forest Glen during World War II. Photo by N. Anthony Stewart, National Geographic Society, September 1943.*

basin, offices, and shops where models were built. The center is primarily concerned with determining speed, power, and hull design of ships. The only residential construction during the war was to provide about 100 "temporary" homes for employees, which are still in use today.

The history of the National Institutes of Health (NIH) in Bethesda began when it was a single institute, part of the public health service, and occupied two buildings at 25th and E streets, N.W. The donation in 1935 by Mr. Luke I. Wilson of part of his estate, "Tree Tops," additional donations by Mrs. Wilson, and purchases by the government have combined to make up this large federal installation. In 1953 the Clinical Center was opened and in 1962 the National Library of Medicine was dedicated. Today, as part of the Department of Health and Human Services, NIH not only conducts its own research, but is also the principal distributor and administrator of federal funds for independent research projects.

The Army Map Service began in 1917 as the Central Map Reproduction Plant at the Army War College in Washington, D.C. It moved to Brookmont, just across the district line, in May 1942. Under the jurisdiction of the chief of engineers, U.S. Army, expert mapmakers at the Army Map Service produce and reproduce maps, catalogue and store foreign and domestic maps, and develop and improve mapmaking.

During World War II the world-famous Walter Reed Army Medical Center faced a severe shortage of space at its Washington, D.C., location. It expanded by transferring convalescent patients to the National Park Seminary in Forest Glen, a former girls' school. By January 1943 ambulatory patients were moved to Forest Glen and given the best in rehabilitation and therapy

in a pleasant suburban setting.

THE CHARTER MOVEMENT

The government of the county was faced with growing public dissatisfaction. Historically, all local laws originated in Annapolis, where they were brought before the legislature, debated, voted upon. These laws were than returned to the county, where they were administered by the five county commissioners. These commissioners were appointed by the governor of Maryland until 1851, when they became elected officials. The Democratic party's nomination for a seat was virtually synonymous with election.

The commissioners were criticized for their informality. Stella Werner, an early member of the government reform movement and later executive director of the Charter Committee, complained that there was "too much rural control" and that "matters seemed to be taken care of before the meeting took place." The commissioners were also charged with vote trading, catering to special interest groups,

Above: *Ken-Gar School, shown here in 1927, was a school for blacks in Kensington. This was one of the schools phased out following the consolidation of black schools in 1949. Courtesy, Montgomery County Historical Society*

Facing page: *Kensington Elementary School stood on Mitchell Street at the site of the present Kensington Armory, until it burned in 1920. Photo by Robert Humphrey, courtesy, Montgomery County Historical Society*

and patronage.

Positive action toward change was centered in the Montgomery County Civic Federation, formed in 1925 by delegates from citizens' associations throughout the county, and the League of Women Voters. A federation study by a committee headed by Allen H. Gardner, a Silver Spring lawyer, resulted in a report that recommended "home rule" and improved administration, as well as a professional study to determine a better form of government.

In 1939 the county commissioners authorized a study by the Brookings Institution. Its 700-page report, which took two years to compile, analyzed all the functions of the county government and suggested improvements. The major recommendation was to take advantage of a provision in the Maryland constitution whereby a charter could be adopted. Local government would then have the power to enact its own legislation and institute home rule.

A charter committee was formed and, following procedures set forth in the Maryland constitution, circulated a petition calling for a charter and a five-member Charter Board to draft it. When the signatures of 20 percent or 8,037 of the registered voters were obtained, the issue was placed on the ballot in the general election of 1942.

The matter became a hot political issue, sharing space in local and Washington newspapers with war news. Both the Charter Committee and the Democratic party named a slate for the Charter Board. The charter proposal was accepted by a vote of 7,826 to 6,032 and all of the candidates endorsed by the county commissioners were defeated.

A charter was drafted during 1943 by the Charter Board, headed by Frederic P. Lee. It provided for:

1. a nine man council, five elected from the districts and four elected at large.
2. a county manager to be appointed by the council.
3. a merit system for county employees.
4. non-partisan elections for county council every four years.
5. provisions for referendum on bond issues.
6. centralized purchasing for a departmentalized government.

This was submitted to the voters at the election of 1944, but well-organized opposition by the Citizens Committee to Defeat the Charter (CCDC) was successful. The plan was defeated by a close margin with 53 percent against and 47 percent for the proposed charter.

Proponents of the new government began

again. They modified some positions, including their intention to remove planning functions from the M-NCPPC. The number of council members was changed. E. Brooke Lee and Lacy Shaw, the Democratic leaders, tried to keep the party neutral, but again there was concentrated resistance to the change. The November 1946 election passed the referendum again so that the question could appear on the 1948 ballot. The charter was finally adopted by Montgomery County voters in the election of November 1948 — the first county in the state to accept this form of government.

The charter opposition, however, did not die easily. The fact that the commissioners had been elected for four years and were now being replaced was being contested in both circuit and appellate courts. Both ruled in favor of the charter. The seven members of the County Council elected on January 6, 1949, were Frederic P. Lee, Thomas C. Kelley, P. Garland Ligon, Dorothy S. Himstead, J. Douglas Bradshaw, Augustus R. Selby, and Dr. Lewis Meriam. Irving G. McNayr was appointed county manager. After nearly 175 years, these were important and substantial modifications in the form of government for Montgomery County.

EXPANDING EDUCATIONAL OPPORTUNITIES

Education in Montgomery County by the turn of the century had begun to reflect attitude changes of the population. The Board of School Commissioners, appointed by the Governor, was enlarged to six members in 1906. In that year the commissioners appointed Earle B. Wood as superintendent to direct the 5,884-student system. He was followed by Edwin W. Broome who served for 36 years.

In 1906 there were three high schools in Montgomery County located in Rockville, Gaithersburg, and Sandy Spring. It was at this time that the consolidation of small elementary schools began. A survey of education made in 1912 reported that "obviously, a one-room, one-teacher school devoted to seven grades, cannot furnish the instruction the majority of parents nowadays wish their children to have." The Home Interest Club, a woman's organization in Silver Spring, requested the closing of one-room schools in Forest Glen, Takoma Park, and Sligo and the establishment of a graded school, Woodside Elementary. The extensive use of busing supported the growth of these larger schools.

The school system was segregated and "separate but equal" was certainly not the case. In this system it was a fact that black school buildings were inferior, school supplies meager, and the books were previously used in white schools. Measures were taken to improve black education. The county constructed "Rosenwald Schools" that met the standards required to receive grants from a fund set up in 1917 by Julius Rosenwald, a merchant and philanthropist.

Along with other inequities, the salary scale for black teachers was much lower. On December 31, 1936, a case was filed in circuit court against Superintendent Edwin W. Broome by William B. Gibbs, a black teacher and acting principal of Rockville Colored Elementary School. *Gibbs* vs. *Broome et al* charged that the Board of Education, as it was now called, had established two systems of public education and that white teachers were paid higher salaries. The petitioner's salary was $612 a year, while a white teacher with comparable training and experience received $1,175. Gibbs, represented by the then little-known Thurgood Marshall, had the backing of the Maryland State Colored Teachers' Association and the NAACP. The suit was settled out of court and adjustments were made to equalize the pay scale.

By World War II there were 16,063 white students in Montgomery County schools. Four more high schools, Poolesville, Bethesda-Chevy Chase, Damascus, and Montgomery Blair, had opened. There were 2,044 black students attending 19 elementary schools and one high school, Lincoln, in Rockville which opened in 1938.

The Board of Education recognized the desirability of a public two-year college in the county to respond to the needs of the returning World War II veterans studying under the G.I. Bill. It was also an opportunity to offer vocational courses for high school graduates. Thus, Montgomery Junior College was founded — the first junior college in the state. Classes began in September 1946 at Bethesda-Chevy Chase High School. Hugh G. Price was appointed dean of the faculty of eight. Since facilities were shared with the high school, classes were held on weekdays from 4 to 10 p.m. and on Saturday from 8 a.m. to noon. Students were enrolled in either a terminal or transfer program, the latter preparing them for admission with advanced standing to a four-year college.

In 1950 a branch of the junior college was opened in Rockville as George Washington Carver Junior College under the segregated school system. In the same year the Board of Education purchased the Bliss Electrical School in Takoma Park and classes moved from Bethesda-Chevy Chase High School to that location. The next major development was the opening of the 87-acre campus in Rockville in September 1965. On July 1, 1969, the name was changed to Montgomery College. Since its beginning the school has grown to include

three campuses — Takoma Park, Rockville, and Germantown — with a student enrollment of 19,000 in 1983. In addition, noncredit classes are held at off-campus locations by the college's Office of Community Services.

The Supreme Court ruling in May 1954 that segregation in public schools was unconstitutional brought significant changes to Montgomery County schools, but without the demonstrations and violence in other parts of the country. An advisory committee of 14 white and 5 black members appointed by the Board of Education reviewed suggestions, reports, opinions, and recommendations from various segments of the population. One plan, favored by many people, was to integrate one grade at a time beginning in the elementary schools. The board, however, did not concur and outlined a plan whereby integration would be accomplished one school at a time. Only rural Poolesville saw organized resistance to the plan.

Montgomery County has more recently responded to the decline in school enrollment by "small school closings." Many schools were built in the suburban area when residential development was occurring there. Today, with the school-aged population declining in the suburbs, schools with minimum enrollments are closing. Simultaneously, population is increasing in formerly rural areas and more schools are needed. With 90,000 students, the Montgomery County school system ranked 19th in size in the United States in 1984.

The shift in school-age population reflects the trend in the county. Today the "up-county" and "down-county" conflict has all but disappeared. The fertile farmland has been replaced by unparalleled urban development.

As the county developed, one of the recurring problems was traffic. This sign nailed to a telephone pole on Connecticut Avenue in 1967 attests to the furor over the question. Courtesy, Montgomery County Historical Society and the Sentinel

7
Visions
From the Present

By mid-century the nation and the county were involved in fast-paced expansion. The county's population skyrocketed to 164,000, almost doubling in the decade of the 1940s. Housing developments, apartment buildings, shopping centers, offices, and corporate headquarters sprang up on what was once farmland. County roads were improved, interstate highways were constructed, and new methods of transportation were planned. The government, recently reorganized, was challenged to plan for and, at the same time, regulate changes.

WHERE HAS ALL THE FARMLAND GONE?

The statement that Montgomery County was the "bedroom community" of Washington, D.C., was widely heard in the 1950s. The phrase was used in a speech before the Montgomery County Publisher's Association in 1945 by the advertising manager of Woodward & Lothrop. He went on to say that "too many of the people work in Washington and sleep in Montgomery County." There was truth to the statement.

After World War II there was a critical housing shortage in the metropolitan area.

The housing need fostered the construction of large developments on Montgomery County farmland. Small and affordable, the homes were perfect for veterans able to pay the $300 "move-in" cost with a 20- to 25-year mortgage and 4 percent financing. Two of the earliest housing developments were Twinbrook (1947) and Veirs Mill Village (1948), located between Rockville and Wheaton. Typical of these and later projects, the Harris Company of New York completed as many as 10 units a day on Veirs Mill Village's 300 acres. Over 1,000 identical 750-foot square, two-bedroom homes were sold for $8,700 each. There was public disapproval of these projects, with the opposition calling them "crackerboxes" and "future slums," but time has proven to be the best rebuttal to these critics.

These early developments laid the groundwork for the more sophisticated "planned" communities of today. Containing a mix of housing types and commercial buildings, Montgomery Village and Rossmore Leisure World are excellent examples of this type of community. The Kettler Brothers, who had been conventional homebuilders, were the first to offer townhouses. They worked closely with county planners and their own consultants

Above: *Land use changed after World War II. Industries related to the building boom proliferated and turf farming came into being. One of the most successful turf farms in the area was the Summit Hall Turf farm of Gaithersburg. This photo shows the farm house before it was taken over for the turf farm.* Courtesy, Montgomery County Historical Society and Joseph Wilmot

Facing page: *This "Montgomery County greeting from a cornshock" came from a February 1927* National Geographic *article describing suburban Maryland. Photo by Clifton Adams, National Geographic Society, February 1927*

to produce Montgomery Village. A self-contained area, it includes parks and a golf course, public schools, a library, shops and professional offices as well as a variety of housing types. Rossmore Leisure World on Georgia Avenue, built by Ross W. Cortese, takes into consideration the needs and desires of the retired or semi-retired resident in its design.

Prior to World War II the few multi-

family units that existed in the county were the garden-type with three stories or less. An early example was the Falkland Apartments in Silver Spring, constructed on 25 acres during the 1930s. But communities were opposed to the postwar apartment buildings. One of the first high-rise buildings, Pook's Hill in Bethesda, waited several years for zoning approval before construction could begin in 1949. In 1940 over 90 percent of the dwelling units were single-family homes. With inflation, rising housing costs, and soaring interest rates, however, young people and the elderly found high-rise apartments to be an economic alternative. By 1960 the number had increased to 54,500 constituting 30 percent of all housing units.

Farms had virtually disappeared from the Bethesda and Wheaton areas by 1950. Construction moved farther and farther into the western part of the county as vacant land became scarce in the lower county. From 1971 to 1972 the number of building starts in Gaithersburg increased by 28 percent as compared to 0.5 percent in Bethesda. The direction of development was determined, in large part, by the arteries of transportation — access to the Capital Beltway (I-495) and I-270 was considered to be a highly desirable feature. An economic recession and a sewer moratorium were only temporary setbacks as growth continued through the 1970s.

The rapid population growth quickly absorbed the existing supply of private low- and moderate-priced housing. This prompted the county government to exercise its authority to enter the field of public housing and urban renewal. The Montgomery County Housing Authority was created to provide funding for government projects and for assistance to the private construction industry for lower priced units. Legislation was passed that

required builders of 50 homes or more to make at least 15 percent of them available at a lower price. An increase in density was allowed in order to compensate for the profit reduction.

As new development came to the county, older black communities became enclaves of substandard conditions surrounded by middle-class comfort. *The Washington Post* dramatically characterized one neighborhood as "a pocket of misery festering in suburban affluence." In the early 1960s, three communities, all situated on land that was given to freed slaves, were singled out for rehabilitation. Efforts in Scotland on Seven Locks Road began in 1965 with the organization of Save Our Scotland (SOS) by residents and white neighbors. Federal loans and grants to the nonprofit Scotland Community Development, Inc., enabled it to provide improved

Above: These business leaders of Rockville were photographed at the first annual outing of the Rockville Chamber of Commerce. The July 29, 1927, Sentinel described the event as "one of the most successful community enterprises ever conducted." Two hundred citizens, escorted by a patrol of county police, three expert mechanics, and a service truck, made the trip to Chapel Point, a well-known resort on the lower Potomac. Photo by Malcolm Walter

Facing page, top: *This Walker Avenue photograph is believed to have been taken from the steeple of Grace United Methodist Church in about 1913. Poles lying in the roadway were probably for electricity, which reached Gaithersburg in 1914. Courtesy, Montgomery County Historical Society*

Facing page, bottom: *By 1945 electricity had revolutionized the way food was stored and marketed. However, this interior of the Soper store in Olney demonstrates that "small townishness" had yet to give way to the march of urbanization. Courtesy, Montgomery County Historical Society*

housing, water, and sewer lines. SOS helped to furnish preschool care, youth employment, summer camp scholarships, and a community center.

Emory Grove near Gaithersburg, had been, in its early days, the site of religious events called camp meetings. In the 1960s the county bought 160 acres where a combination of townhouses, apartments, and single-family dwellings were built. Conditions in this community were substantially improved.

Toby Town on River Road was a century-old collection of homes labeled substandard by the county health department. Scattered over 15 acres and surrounded by the homes of the wealthy, Toby Town was the first area east of the Mississippi assigned a VISTA volunteer.

Temporary measures were taken to improve housing, and, finally, in the early 1970s federal grants allowed the construction of 26 frame homes.

Commercial development has been closely linked with housing development in Montgomery County. Retail business first developed at major crossroads and grew with commercial activity to spread and become "main street." Congestion and parking problems associated with the coming of the automobile forced some merchants to choose sites beyond the central business areas. These were, for the most part, single-use buildings scattered along major roads. The first shopping center in the county, was built in Silver Spring in 1944 by Sam Eig.

Washington, D.C., remained the principal shopping district for the Montgomery County area until the mid-1940s. In 1946, two large Washington stores, Jelleff's and The Hecht Company, opened the first branch stores in Silver Spring, followed in 1949 by Woodward & Lothrop at Friendship Heights. Developers then conceived plans for regional shopping centers and malls. Designed to attract the public to a compact group of stores and shops in an attractive setting with good access and ample parking, Wheaton Plaza opened in February 1960 and Montgomery Mall in 1968. More recent mall openings are White Flint (1977) and Lakeforest (1978).

Meanwhile aging neighborhood shopping centers and main business districts in Rockville and Silver Spring were dying. Urban renewal has been undertaken to revitalize these areas and attract new businesses. Similar projects are being undertaken by other towns across the county. In addition, the coming of Metro Rapid Rail is changing the face and the skyline of these areas.

When urban renewal came to Rockville the entire downtown was demolished, roads removed or rerouted, and grand plans were laid for the rebuilding of a fading town. The Brosius Building shown here was originally built about 1929 and housed at various times the post office as well as the local pool room. Courtesy, Montgomery County Historical Society and the Sentinel

By the 1980s federal employment in the county formed a nucleus of economic stability. Government agencies continued to relocate after World War II — the Naval Ordnance Laboratory on New Hampshire Avenue, the Atomic Energy Commission near Germantown, and the Bureau of Standards in Gaithersburg.

Montgomery County also attracted many divisions and corporate headquarters of national companies. They have found Montgomery County a favorable location for their firms and their employees. Spurred on by the presence of government installations, the high technology industry is the fastest growing industry in the county. Their architecturally innovative buildings have increased activity in construction trades and real estate. There is presently 12 million square feet of office space available and that amount is increasing daily. The work force of scientists and engineers for the high-tech industries along route I-270, said to rival California's Silicon Valley, has been an enormous boost to the county's economy.

As population increased and the network of county roads linking commercial centers grew, vehicular congestion became a challenge. Streetcar lines were discontinued in the county and were replaced by bus service. But these operated primarily in the more densely populated areas close to the city. In more sparsely settled areas the automobile remained the main method of transportation.

Land development has been coordinated with highways and public transportation. The improvement of existing roads and the construction of new highways added to the transportation links between the county and other sections of the metropolitan area. Interstate 270, originally 70 S, opened in the 1950s and is now part of the federal highway system. This limited-access highway serves as a commuter artery and as an attraction for business development along its "corridor." In 1964 the Capital Beltway (I-495), one of the first circumferential highways for a major city, was opened. These roads help to accommodate the estimated 238,000 people who make the daily commute from the suburbs to the city.

The Washington Metropolitan Area Transit Authority (WMATA) was organized in February 1966 and charged with planning, constructing, and operating an improved regional system of transportation. A regional Metro Rapid Rail system was approved in 1968 and is planned to provide a 97-mile network with 18.4 miles of surface and elevated tracks and 12 stations in Montgomery County. The WMATA also operates Metrobuses as part of the metropolitan transit system.

In view of the commercial development and improved intra-county transportation which has occurred in the county, Ioanna Morfessis, director of the Office of Economic Development, stated in January 1981 that "Ten years ago Montgomery County was a bedroom community for Washington, D.C. Today we no longer are. We are an employment center in our own right ... More than 50 percent of our resident work force works here in Montgomery County."

THE GOVERNMENT'S ROLE
In recent years, the county government has been forced to increase its role in planning and controlling development. Charged with drafting a plan for orderly expansion, local officials consolidated previous plans for highways, parks, and schools along with those for residential and commercial growth. Broad policies for conservation, open space, sewer and water systems, and other environmental issues were established in a General Plan adopted in 1964 and updated in 1969.

The plan is based on the concept of "wedges" and "corridors." It recommends that most urban development be channeled along major radial transportation routes. Between these corridors are areas of low density with less intensive uses, with only certain designated "satellite towns" as exceptions. The wedges also contain parks, country clubs, and other types of "green space." Area Master Plans or Sector Plans for 29 planning areas contain more detailed and specific land-use recommendations. These plans propose desirable zoning for each parcel of land and determine road patterns.

The county government also created the Office of Economic Development (OED) to attract new capital investment from the

Writer Gilbert Grosvenor's home "Wild Acres" was credited by the U.S. Department of Agriculture as having the densest bird population recorded anywhere. In 1927 there were reported to be 135 pairs of 24 different species nesting in the five acres adjacent to Grosvenor's house. Photo by Gilbert H. Grosvenor, National Geographic Society, March 1927

private sector and to retain existing business, thus adding to the tax base and creating new opportunities for employment. The agency offers its services to the employer and to the job seeker.

The county participates in the Metropolitan Washington Council of Governments (COG). This organization, composed of 16 local governments, was established informally in April 1957 and is now a nonprofit corporation. COG strengthens cooperation with other jurisdictions as a planning group for mutual problems in the areas of air pollution, transportation, solid-waste disposal, crime prevention, and equal opportunities in housing and employment.

Montgomery County, as other rapidly growing urban areas, is a tapestry of ethnic backgrounds. Original settlers were of a western European or African background. They were followed by immigrants from eastern Europe. As the Jewish population grew in number, the Montgomery County Jewish Community, Inc., was organized in December 1948. They built the first

synagogue, now Ohr Kodesh, on East West Highway on land donated by Sam Eig. More recently the number of Hispanics and Asians has greatly increased. Between 1970 and 1980 the number of foreign-born residents rose from around 7 percent to about 12.1 percent of the population. The educational system has adjusted the curriculum for those to whom English is a second language.

The bicentennial of the country and Montgomery County in 1976 helped to focus attention on historical landmarks in Montgomery County. The M-NCPPC was authorized to identify these sites and in

One of the problems of government is how to deal with mother nature. For many years, flooding of the Seneca River caused a great deal of hardship for those who had cabins or homes on the banks of the river. The county, reluctant to spend a great deal of money for flood control, in the early 1970s prohibited building or rebuilding on the floodplain. Much of the land then became part of the park system. Courtesy, Montgomery County Historical Society, and the Sentinel

1976 published an atlas giving the location of about 1,000. The county Planning Board formed the Montgomery County Advisory Committee on Historic Sites. Its work resulted in a Master Plan and Ordinance adopted in 1979 and the Montgomery County Preservation Commission appointed in 1980.

Nonprofit groups have been formed to aid preservation and research on specific sites and in specific districts such as Peerless Rockville and Historic Medley District. A number of properties have been purchased, stabilized, and resold or adapted to uses retaining their historic value. This has resulted in protection and preservation of much of the remaining visible signs of the county's heritage.

September 6, 1976, was officially designated as Bicentennial Day in Montgomery County, but a year-long series of projects and events accompanied it. Towns were designated Bicentennial Communities, and organizations sponsored their own programs. Montgomery College was the site of the premiere of the opera *Joshua,* composed especially for the occasion. The county government and the historical society joined in producing the film *Montgomery County-Then and Now* and publishing the history *A Grateful Remembrance.*

The County Bicentennial Committee planned a seven-hour extravaganza that marked the day. Entertainment, exhibits, and refreshments at Cabin John Park and the adjacent Montgomery Mall were accompanied by speeches at this celebration. James P. Gleason, the county executive, noted that the county's growth had kept pace with the nation's, both in population and economic development. Other speakers recounted the history and achievements of the government and the people. It is this heritage that will be the foundation for Montgomery County to begin its third century of growth and change.

The town of Laytonsville was primarily a farming village. Boyd's history of the area states that the city "produces 30 bushels of wheat, 25 to 40 of oats, 150 of potatoes, 50,100 of corn, and 1,200 pounds of tobacco per acre." Courtesy, Montgomery County Historical Society and Janet Manuel

8
The Towns:
A History Apart

PROLOGUE

In 1816 the nine post offices in Montgomery County indicated the important population centers of that day—Brookeville, Carrolsburg, Clarksburg, Darnes, Hyattstown, Middlebrook Mills, Montgomery Court House (Rockville), Poole's Store, and Triadelphia. Some have faded to obscurity today.

By 1879, according to Boyd's *History of Montgomery County,* towns having over 150 inhabitants in descending order of size were Rockville, Poolesville, Brookeville, Clarksburg, Darnestown, Gaithersburg, Barnesville, Brighton, Great Falls, Hyattstown, and Sunshine.

Today, there are 13 incorporated municipalities in the county. Rockville (1801); Poolesville (1867 withdrawn, 1888); Gaithersburg (1870); Barnesville (1888); Brookeville (1890); Takoma Park (1890); Laytonsville (1892); Kensington (1894); Garrett Park (1898); Glen Echo (1904); Somerset (1906); Chevy Chase Village (1914); and Washington Grove (1930). Each of the towns has its own distinct history, which provides yet another view of Montgomery County.

BETHESDA

A small settlement grew up during the first half of the 1800s around a store and tollhouse on the Washington and Rockville Turnpike. In 1862 William E. Darcy, proprietor of the store, was appointed postmaster and the community received a name — Darcy's Store. When, in 1871, Robert Franck became the postmaster and the post office was moved, a new name was needed in order.

A short distance up the pike was the Bethesda Meeting House, built by the Presbyterians, named for the biblical Pool of Bethesda that had great healing power:

Now there is at Jerusalem by the sheep market a pool, which is called in the Hebrew tongue Bethesda, having five porches. In these lay a multitude of impotent folk, of blind, halt, withered, waiting for the moving of the water. For an angel went down at a certain season into the pool, and troubled the water: whosoever then first after the troubling of the water stepped in, was made whole of whatsoever disease he had. [John 5:2-4]

It was from this church, built in 1820 and rebuilt after a fire in 1849, that the town received its name, meaning "house of mercy."

The community remained small through the remainder of the 19th century. A blacksmith shop stood at the edge of the Gingell farm at the intersection of Old Georgetown Road and the pike. About a mile away was St. John's Episcopal Church and a school building. An assortment of stores and houses lay between, with what was to be East West Highway a country lane leading to the Watkins farm.

When streetcars arrived and suburban development began, paved streets appeared lined by substantial homes. Drummond, Edgemoor, Woodmont, and Battery Park were among the first subdivisions created. Along the pike toward Rockville were Woodmont Country Club (now the site of the National Library of Medicine) followed by the estates of Luke I. Wilson and Brainard Parker. There was also Merle Thorp's "Pooks Hill," where the Norwegian

Since the Great Depression, the Bethesda Farm Women's Market has provided an outlet for local farm women to sell their fresh produce, baked goods, and preserves to urban dwellers. Today local handcrafters display their wares as well. This photo was taken in 1932. Courtesy, Montgomery County Historical Society

royal family lived during World War II, and Gilbert Grosvenor's "Wild Acres."

Government development in the area began just before World War II with construction of the Naval Medical Center and the National Institutes of Health, the principal research branch of the public health service. These have been followed by scores of other foundations, institutions, and groups related to the field of medicine, fulfilling in a modern way the biblical meaning of the name Bethesda.

BROOKEVILLE
One of the oldest communities in the county, Brookeville was founded in 1794 by Richard Thomas on land acquired by inheritance from the family of his wife, Deborah Brooke. In colonial days James Brooke, a Quaker settler in the area, owned thousands of acres. One of his largest grants was "Addition to Brooke Grove." Deborah (Brooke) Thomas, his granddaughter, inherited the part of this tract that would later become Brookeville.

A town was laid out with 56 lots on two main streets, Market and High, and four side streets. A post office was opened in 1802 with Caleb Bentley as postmaster. In 1814 President James Madison spent a

night at the Bentley home while the British occupied Washington. By this time there were at least 14 houses, two stores, a school, a tanyard, a blacksmith, and two mills belonging to Richard Thomas and David Newlin. Soon the prestigious Brookeville Academy was established.

Many, but not all, of the inhabitants were Quaker. The prosperous men of the town built large homes, many of which remained in the families for generations. The presence of these well-preserved residences lends to the community a feeling of permanence, stability, and dignity.

BURTONSVILLE

In 1825, Isaac Burton, son of Basil and Alice (Duvall) Burton, bought out his sisters' and brothers' share of his father's land. Isaac and his wife, Keturah (Duvall) Burton, were parents of 17 children, ensuring the survival of the Burton name to the present day.

A small community once known simply as Burton's, it lay at the intersection of Old Columbia Road and the road to Sandy Spring. Isaac Burton was the town's first postmaster. An old log schoolhouse, sometimes called Frog Pond School for the nearby marsh, doubled as a church for many years. The local Methodists, anxious to have a real church, were unable to agree whether it should be located at Spencerville or Burtonsville. A compromise was effected — the community that could raise the most funds could chose the Methodist church site. Liberty Grove Methodist Church was built in Burtonsville in 1862.

Today numerous shopping centers, banks, and fast-food franchises replace the general store, blacksmith, and wheelwright shops of the original Burtonsville.

CHEVY CHASE

Today, Chevy Chase is that indefinite area bordered by Bethesda on the west, Kensington on the north, and Silver Spring on the east, and includes a portion of the District of Columbia. The original Chevy Chase, however, was a specific area of 560 acres granted to Colonel Joseph Belt in 1725. Belt called the land "Cheivy Chace," a name first found in "The Ancient Ballad of Cheviot Chase." It tells of an incident in 1388 in which Lord Percy, the English Earl of Northumberland, is determined to hunt the Scottish borderlands of the Earl Douglas without Douglas' permission. Douglas inquires, "Who gave you leave to hunt this Cheviot Chase in the spyte of me?"

The idea of extending Connecticut Avenue as a residential thoroughfare for the homes of Washington's wealthy is attributed to Colonel George A. Armes. Armes is reported to have declared expansively to prospective backers, "Here, Gentlemen, is where you should develop the finest suburb in America." He was joined in his enthusiasm by Nevada Senators William Stewart and Francis G. Newlands. The Chevy Chase Land Company, formed in 1890 with Senator Newlands as president, purchased a total of 1,712 acres including 304 acres of Belt's former land. The company hired urban planners, architects, landscape architects, and sanitary engineers to create a new Chevy Chase. The first four houses were built by members of the board of the company and were designed to be the standard for other homes. Regulations controlled the cost of houses and sizes of lots. No apartments, row houses, or alleys were allowed. The company built a Town Hall that served as the post office, fire station, and as a library and was the site of many of the community's early social and civic events.

The Chevy Chase Club, of which Senator

Above: *Phair & Lindsay were dealers in general merchandise in Spencerville in 1892. Near Burtonsville, Spencerville was a small community of approximately 100. Posters proclaimed an upcoming picnic and tournament in Clarksville. Courtesy, Montgomery County Historical Society*

Below: *Chevy Chase Land Company hoped to develop the route along Connecticut Avenue that was followed by the Rock Creek Railway Company streetcars. At the end of the line was Chevy Chase Lake Amusement Park, offering welcome diversion to city dwellers. Courtesy, Montgomery County Historical Society*

Newlands was first president, is situated on the part of Belt's land that had been purchased in 1815 by Assistant Postmaster General Abraham Bradley. For years land around the club remained undeveloped and the fields were used for fox hunting.

A drive through the community confirms the careful planning that resulted in this extraordinary residential community. A tribute to these efforts is a memorial fountain in the center of Chevy Chase Circle, placed there in 1933, which reads: "Francis Griffith Newlands . . . Founder of Chevy Chase."

CLARKSBURG

An early settlement located on the old Seneca Indian trail and the road from Georgetown to Frederick, Clarksburg is named for Indian trader William Clarke.

Among the earliest settlers was Michael Ashford Dowden, who patented 40 acres in 1752 calling it "Hammer Hill." Two years later he obtained a license to operate an ordinary. It was at this tavern that General Edward Braddock's men stopped on the second night of their march through the county. There is also evidence that Dowden's was a meeting place for the local Sons of Liberty in the 1770s, a stage coach stop, and a place that Andrew Jackson dined en route to his inauguration as president in 1829. Under subsequent ownership it was known as Roberts', Scholl's, and Shaw's Tavern.

About 1770 John Clark (the "e" seems to have been dropped from the name), grandson of the original Indian trader, built a house and general store. Soon lots were laid out along both sides of the road and on April 1, 1800, John Clark was appointed postmaster. Clarksburg reached the height of its commercial development about 1875 with four stores, a printing firm, two hotels, and the usual assortment of craftsmen and tradespeople.

But the construction of the metropolitan branch of the B & O diverted business from Clarksburg. Incorporated in 1894, incorporation was withdrawn in 1938. Many buildings have disappeared along with the maple trees that once lined the main street, now Route 355. A school, built in 1909, is now a museum. Log cabins have grown to large comfortable homes, and stand as a reminder of the days when Clarksburg was a bustling trade center in Montgomery County.

DAMASCUS
"Pleasant Plains of Damascus" was a 1,101-acre land grant surveyed in 1783 for Nathaniel Figman. On February 14, 1814, Edward Hughes purchased 40 acres of the tract laid out 14 lots, and advertised in the *Fredericktown Herald,*

I will sell at public sale ... eight lots in the

new town of Damascus ... There is at this place an extensive opening for mechanics of all the different kinds ... A law of Congress was passed ... establishing a post route through town and an office in it. There are at present two blacksmith shops, a saddler's shop and a store in the place-a tailor, a wheelwright, and a shoemakers are much wanted.

Edward Hughes fought in the War of 1812, leading a militia group from Montgomery County, the Concord Uniform Company. Upon his return he purchased Pigman's land, laid out the town, and became the first postmaster in 1816.

The town was incorporated in 1890 and administered by three elected commissioners who served without pay for the next 24 years. The townspeople requested that this status be withdrawn in order that the streets and roads could be built and maintained by the State Roads Commission.

Today, Damascus remains the commercial center for the communities of Clagettsville, Browningsville, Cedar Grove, Woodfield, King's Valley, Purdum, and Lewisdale.

DARNESTOWN
The name of this town comes from the family who owned the land on which town lots were laid out. William Darne's wife had inherited 2,000 acres, part of the tract "Mt. Pleasant," from her father, Charles Gassaway. Earliest references called this village Mt. Pleasant but soon it was simply Darnes. There was a tavern on the road from Montgomery Court House to the Mouth of the Monocacy run by Andrew Barneclois, a couple of blacksmiths, a wheelwright, and the first store operated by John Candler. A log building west of the community served as a church for several

denominations as well as a school. The Presbyterians, wishing to have their own place of worship, accepted three acres of land from John DuFief and laid the cornerstone of their church on September 14, 1856. After the Civil War the small school held in the church basement was expanded. This was made possible by the generosity of Andrew Small, a contractor who had become wealthy building the C & O Canal. The Andrew Small Academy occupied a large building and the minister of the church was principal until 1892. It quickly gained a fine reputation for both day and boarding students and became the focal point of the town's social activities.

The Civil War brought changes to the village. David Strother, whose sketches appeared in *Harper's New Monthly Magazine* under the name "Porte Crayon," gave a glimpse of local landmarks. A Union soldier penned a description of Darnestown as he found it:

Most of the homes are of the log-and-mud style ... It has three 'country stores' where hardware, dry goods, groceries, boots and shoes, quack medicines, and whiskey are sold in rather small quantities-barring the whiskey as to the small ... A post office was in one of the stores, and before our advent a stage-coach passed through ... but as a whole, the village of one street was of the Rip Van Winkle order ... But Darnestown woke up one day. A division of army grouped itself on either side ... soldiers lounged about ... regiments moved up and down ... orderlies cantered [through] ... at all hours. Trade inflated.

This activity continued throughout the 19th century. Then Darnestown ceased to be a commercial center. Today, there are no stores to sell "quack medicines and whiskey" and only a few of the buildings

Mrs. Bell's Darnestown residence is shown here in October 1866. This sketch accompanied an article on the Civil War in Harper's New Monthly Magazine. *Courtesy, Montgomery County Historical Society*

that once lined the road remain.

GAITHERSBURG

"Deer Park" was an early land grant made in 1723 to Ralph Crabb. The small settlement of Log Town, sometimes called Germansburgh, was established on part of the "Deer Park" tract (near Gaithersburg High School).

Henry Brookes became the owner of the northern part of "Deer Park" and built his home, "Montpelier" (now the site of the IBM building), around 1782 to 1793. Part of Brookes land became the property of Benjamin Gaither through his marriage to Margaret Brookes, Henry's daughter. The name, Gaithersburg, came into use and Log Town lost its separate identity. But at the opening of the first post office in 1851, the name was changed to Forest Oak for an unusually large tree in the town. (This tree was still living and determined to be 175 years old at the time of the bicentennial.) With the arrival of the railroad, the original name returned as the station was called Gaithersburg. The incorporation of the town in 1878 removed any lingering ambiguity as the official name became Gaithersburg.

The last quarter of the 19th century saw great progress in the town. Several churches and both public and private schools were organized. A mill, grain elevator, and two hotels were built. There were numerous stores, one of these, Ward & Fulks, was said to be the largest store in Montgomery County. The railroad played a significant role in the expansion of Gaithersburg commerce and shifted the center of trade from Frederick Avenue to the vicinity of the railroad station.

A meeting of the citizens at Diamond Hall in February 1878 considered the "expediency of incorporating the village," and it soon came about. There have been three forms of government — a board of commissioners until 1898, a mayor and council until 1963, and since then a mayor, council, and city manager.

GARRETT PARK

Garrett Park was named for John W. Garrett, a president of the B & O Railroad Company. In 1886 Henry W. Copp formed the Metropolitan Investment and Building Company and purchased land as a site for a suburban development. This residential community, planned by its developer to recreate an English village, included streets named for places in Sir Walter Scott's novels — Kenilworth, Keswick, Montrose, and Strathmore.

When the town was incorporated in May 1898 it contained 500 acres of land, much of it undeveloped. A decision to limit commercial development controlled growth, and even today there is only one store in combination with the post office.

Further planned development came in the early 1920s with the organization of Maddux, Marshall & Company (later Maddux, Marshall, Moss and Mallory), a syndicate of retired military men. They advertised the community as "the realization of the dreams of the family of small income . . . in an environment fit for millionaires," and offered three styles of five-room bungalows complete with Atwater Kent radio and built-in Murphy bed. As an option there was a garage with a new Chevrolet automobile. About 50 of these "Chevy houses" were sold. These structures were a marked architectural contrast to the turreted, gingerbread Victorian homes of earlier development.

Garrett Park is the only town in the lower part of the county that has been relatively untouched by the encroachment of contemporary change.

GERMANTOWN

Before the Metropolitan Branch of the B & O was built, Germantown was situated at the intersection of the roads from Clopper's Mill and Darnestown about a mile from the present location. This settlement received its name for the large number of German immigrants coming to the area in the 1830s. Jacob Snyder and his family were the first. They were followed by the Metzes, Richters, Stangs, Hogans, and Grusendorfs. There was once a store, a post office, a blacksmith shop, and a school, but little of this original town remains.

The railroad bypassed Germantown and called the nearest depot Germantown Station. A commercial center formed here and by 1880 there were 100 inhabitants. Local merchants were John H. Gassaway,

Richard E. Harris, Horace D. Waters, and Thomas N. Henderson who was also postmaster. Thomas Carlin was the bootmaker and John H. Nicholls made harness. When Dr. William D. Waters was unable to cure patients, they were taken to William L.G. Appleby, undertaker, coffin maker, and carpenter, who advertised a "Fine Hearse with glass sides." During the 1880s a large steampowered mill was built.

But the Germantown of today is not the small farming community of the 1930s and 1940s. "Satellite city," "corridor city," and "town sector zoning" are just a few of the planning terms for this rapidly growing community that is scheduled to see even more growth in the coming decades.

HYATTSTOWN

Hyattstown stretches along both sides of the old road from Georgetown to Frederick, an important highway in early days. In 1798 Jesse Hyatt laid out 105 lots of a quarter-acre each on part of his land. There Henry Poole purchased the first lot, erected a building, and became the first storekeeper. Two of Jesse Hyatt's brothers, Asa and Eli, also lived in the town and the family name was used when a post office was established in 1813.

The Georgetown-Frederick road was the lifeblood of the town. Wagons laden with cargo lumbered through and drovers goaded their herds down "the great road." Both Northern and Southern troops marched along the road during the Civil War and Coxey's Army came down it to camp along the creek on their way to Washington in 1894. Because the road was so well used, the main street was dusty or rutted at times and impossibly muddy at others. It was finally paved in 1925.

As the railroad bypassed the town and freight traffic waned, the Hyattstown economy became dependent on the

surrounding farming community. These farmers, like the inhabitants of many of the old homes which line the road, are descendants of the early settlers of the area.

KENSINGTON

Before the arrival of the Metropolitan Branch of the B & O, Kensington was a farm owned by the Knowles family. After the construction of the railroad, the crossing at Old Bladensburg Road was called Knowles Station, which developed into a small settlement with two stores, a post office, and a blacksmith shop.

In 1890 Brainard Warner, founder and president of the Washington Loan and Trust Company and president of the District of Columbia Board of Trade, invested in 125 acres near Knowles Station for his own summer home and a projected subdivision called Kensington, after the London suburb of that name. Brainard Warner invited his wealthy friends to join him in building summer residences near his own and was active in making Kensington a desirable place to live. He donated land for Warner Memorial Presbyterian Church, built a town hall, and helped to organize the Kensington Railway Company to bring

streetcar service to Kensington. Warner and his friend, Crosby Noyes, owner of *The Washington Post,* newspaper, donated land and money to start the Noyes Public Library. Warner himself became a publisher when he founded the *Montgomery Press,* later owned and operated by Cornelius W. Clum.

Kensington was incorporated in 1894 with a mayor and council. Within a few years it had become a self-contained suburban town with train, streetcar, and automobile providing easy commuting into the city. These characteristics of a suburban town are retained today.

LAYTONSVILLE

The first name to be associated with this area was Cracklintown. The unusual name is believed to have come from an old local tavern with a reputation for cracklin bread. Records of the post office show that John Layton was appointed postmaster at Cracklintown on July 19, 1849, and in August of that year the name was changed to Laytonsville, although a dual designation appears on maps for some years after this.

Laytonsville is located at a crossroads about a mile east of the original Cracklintown. The first house was probably that of the Laytons on the southwest corner. George W. Mobley purchased the northeast corner and opened a general store. The town grew and was incorporated in 1892.

The fertile farmland surrounding Laytonsville was settled early in the county's history. The Riggs, Griffiths, Gaithers, Plummers, and Dorseys had large farms with substantial homes. As late as 1918 a report stated the "80 percent of the land is still owned by the descendants of those persons who had originally settled there." Newcomers have arrived and their homes have been built on these fertile fields. But the heart of the town is still composed of buildings constructed by the early inhabitants.

OLNEY

The town and the election district in which Olney is located was originally called Mechanicsville. Sometime before 1850 the Postal Service demanded that the name be changed to avoid confusion with another Mechanicsville in St. Mary's County. Olney, the name of the home of Dr. Charles and Sarah (Brooke) Farquhar, became the new town's name. Dr. Farquhar was a great admirer of the poet William Cowper, whose home was in Olney, England.

Some of the earliest residents of the area were Richard Brooke, who lived at *Fair Hill,* his brother, Basil, who resided at *Falling Green,* the Waters family whose home was called *Belmont,* and Whitson

Canby who built the house which the Farquhars named *Olney.*

The town, located on a tract patented to Richard Brooke in 1763, was the site of a tollhouse on the well-traveled Washington and Brookeville Turnpike. In the beginning the town's four main corners were occupied by a blacksmith, a wheelwright, Canby's pottery factory, and a store owned by Benedict Duley. Moses Barnsley arrived in about 1806 to work for his brother-in-law William Kelley, the wheelwright. Barnsley continued in Kelley's business until 1840, when his son, William B. Barnsley, took over. The Barnsley family, whose original home was across from St. John's Episcopal Church, remained in the community. Those early inhabitants would be surprised by the development which has transformed Olney in the modern era.

POOLESVILLE
The original boundaries of Poolesville incorporated parts of five tracts: "Poole's Right," "Poole's Hazard," "Joseph's Choice," "Forest," and "Difficulty." The first building was a log structure on Coxen's Road, which was the store and living quarters of John Poole. About 1800 there were four buildings in Poolesville and John Poole's store was one of them.

In 1806 John Poole's uncle, Joseph Poole, laid out six lots on "Poole's Hazard" along Coxen's Road. He deeded one to each of his sons and most of them were eventually built upon. Major George Peter, owner of "Forest," began to sell lots in 1819. Since his land was not on the road, he successfully petitioned to have the old road abandoned for a new right-of-way, which accounts for evidence of two roads that seem to "Y" at the town hall. Peter sold all the land on the south side of the main street as far as Edward's Ferry (Willard) Road. Alexander Whitaker, influenced by

the success of the Pooles and Major Peter, directed in his will in 1826 that the part of his tract, "Difficulty," that lay at the western end of town, be divided into 16 lots and each of his children were to receive two.

By the Civil War, Poolesville was a large town by the standards of the day. Major Peter gave land for a Methodist Church in 1820. St. Peter's Episcopal Church (1847) and Poolesville Presbyterian Church (1849) followed. Major Peter also gave land for a school in 1841. The first fair in the county was held in Poolesville in 1846. At that time, there were about 200 inhabitants and nearly 20 businesses, including several general stores and livery stables, two taverns, and The Merchants Hotel. Some of these 19th-century structures survive to the present day.

Over time the town has annexed more land and provided more services, but the form of government remains the same. The Commissioners of Poolesville consist of five unpaid members, one of whom is selected "president," although he is generally referred to as "mayor." The commissioners have been called upon to make the transition from a country town to a modern community with all the inherent problems.

POTOMAC
Before 1880 Potomac was known as Offutt's Crossroads — the Offutt family being the area's largest landowners. The surrounding farms were on three original patents, "Outlet" and "Clewerwall" granted to William Offutt and "Cool Spring Level" granted to Archibald Edmonston. At William Offutt's death in 1734 his land was left to his 11 children and Edward Offutt inherited "Outlet." Edward married Archibald Edmonston's daughter, Eleanor, and this couple gave land in 1746 for the first place of worship in the community,

The red brick courthouse built in 1891 was the third to be constructed in Rockville and is presently flanked by newer Montgomery County courthouses built during the 1930s and 1980s. Courtesy, Gordon Baker

Captain John Presbyterian Meeting House.

By the time the name became Potomac, a settlement had grown up around the original commercial establishment, a tavern built by Kinsey Gittings about 1820. Both the building of the C & O Canal and the discovery of gold in the area had some effect on the village, but it still remained a country crossroad. As one resident described it about the turn of the century, "there was not a whole lot in the village. There used to be a baseball field on one corner ... and on the other ... a beer joint.

Across Falls Road there were two grocery stores."

In the early 20th century farms were purchased for speculation and fields were turned into estates. The Congressional Country Club opened in 1924 and in 1930 two Washington, D.C., hunt clubs joined to form the Potomac Hunt Club. Today Potomac is a residential area often sought out by those who appreciate fine real estate.

ROCKVILLE

A small settlement here was called Owen's Ordinary when General Edward Braddock's troops marched through in 1755. By 1774 the place was referred to as Hungerford's Tavern. After 1776, at the founding of the county, most people called it Montgomery Court House although it had been officially named Williamsburgh. The Williams family, who owned part of the tract "Exchange and New Exchange," laid out lots adjacent to the courthouse and offered them for sale. By 1798 there were 17 houses and 21 other improved lots. In 1801 the name was changed to Rockville, after Rock Creek, and the town was incorporated.

The town of Rockville was divided into 85 lots on six streets. As the county seat it became the residence of judges, lawyers, and other professional men. Newspapers were published here. Good schools and churches of most denominations were established. Hotels and livery stables did a brisk business especially on court days. Rockville had more stores carrying a greater variety of merchandise than any other town. The commissioners tried to dispel any remaining rural atmosphere by passing an ordinance in 1860 that "no horse, hog, shoat, goose ... or goat shall be allowed to run loose ... under penalty of one dollar." Soon after this dirt streets were paved, sidewalks were laid from the railroad station into town, and eventually electric lights were installed to replace streetlamps. Summer boarders found Rockville a pleasant Victorian town with an active social life for a summer vacation.

SANDY SPRING

James Brooke came to the endless forest of the western wilderness early in the 1700s and made it his home. Descended from Robert Brooke, one of the wealthiest Englishmen to come to the colony of Maryland, James and his wife Deborah (Snowden) Brooke left their comfortable life soon after their marriage in 1725 to build a home on the 800 acres of "Charly Forest." James Brooke would eventually become the largest landowner in the county.

The Brookes were soon joined by Deborah's sister, Elizabeth, and her husband, John Thomas, and then by John's brother, Samuel Thomas, and his wife, Mary Snowden. The Thomases and Snowdens had a background of Quaker tradition and James Brooke had been converted. Meetings were held in their homes until the first log meetinghouse was built; the present one was erected in 1817 on the same site. A spring, the origin of the town's name, is located nearby.

Beginning in 1790 there was a migration of other Quakers from Pennsylvania and Virginia to join those from Maryland in the growth of the community. Many made important contributions to society as educators, inventors, skilled craftsmen, astute businessmen, and advocates of emancipation and women's rights. Isaac Briggs was not only the first schoolmaster and founder of the town of Triadelphia but was also chosen in 1803 by President Thomas Jefferson as a surveyor for the Louisiana Purchase. Thomas Moore

invented the first patented refrigerator. Benjamin Hallowell, a local educator, became a cofounder of Swarthmore College in Pennsylvania, the first president of the Maryland Agricultural College (now the University of Maryland), and was for some years president of the National Philosophical Society in Philadelphia. Others were officers of the Mutual Fire Insurance Company and the Sandy Spring Savings Institution. The entire county profited from the knowledge and accomplishments of this community.

The first post office was established on February 25, 1817, at "Harewood," although there was but one mail a week. A single store was opened in 1819, but there was never a tavern. Life in the community centered around the Quaker meeting, the lyceum, the schools, and in the interrelated families. Not all who lived there were Friends but the religion held influence into the 20th century. Local organizations still contain members of the original families. Sandy Spring Friends School (1961) and Friends House (1967), a retirement home, have been built in the area. As one elderly Quaker expressed it, Sandy Spring is "not so much a place as a state of mind."

At the turn of the century Rockville was a small town with a population of 1,100. But as the county expanded so did its major town. Additional land was annexed, construction boomed, and the status of city was attained. A program of urban renewal replaced the old commercial district with a mall. New government buildings, the Judicial Building and the Executive Building have been erected. Through these many changes, Rockville has performed the various and growing functions as the seat of government for Montgomery County.

SILVER SPRING

The history of Silver Spring began with the

The boundary stone in Silver Spring is shown here marked with a flag. The stone marks the northernmost corner of the District of Columbia. Courtesy, Montgomery County Historical Society and the Washingtonia Room, Martin Luther King Library, Washington, D.C.

arrival of Francis Preston Blair from Kentucky to Washington, D.C., and his search for a site for a summer residence to escape the heat and unhealthy conditions of the city. The traditional story is that Blair was riding through the countryside when his new horse, Selim, shied and threw him. In looking for his mount Blair noticed a spring in which sand and mica appeared to shine like silver. He purchased this property, built a home there in 1842 which he named "Silver Spring," and moved to it permanently in 1854. Today, the spring, marked by an acorn-shaped gazebo, stands in a park amid high-rise buildings near the intersection of East West Highway and Colesville Road, but the water in it is now supplied by the WSSC.

By the time of the Civil War there was a community called Sligo at the juncture of the Washington and Brookeville and the Washington, Colesville and Ashton turnpikes. A tollhouse, a store and post office, and a few homes were surrounded by farms and the estates of the Blairs — Francis Preston Blair's "Silver Spring," Montgomery Blair's "Falkland," and James Blair's "The Moorings" (the only one still standing and now called the Jessup Blair House). After the Civil War, the communities of Woodside, Forest Glen, and Linden came into existence and were joined with Washington by the tollroads, the railroad, and the trolley. With the establishment of a post office in 1899, these towns lost their separate identities and the community was known as Silver Spring.

After World War I Silver Spring began to develop. A bank and newspaper were founded. Sidewalks were laid and streetlights installed with the Woman's Improvement Club paying the electric bill for the first 12 years. E. Brooke Lee, great-grandson of Francis Preston Blair, was responsible for much of the development. Not an incorporated area and without municipal government, it was claimed by 1946 that if Silver Spring were a city, it would be the second largest in Maryland. And it continues to grow with Metro development and high-rise buildings, changing the face of the area once called

Sligo which forms the nucleus of present-day Silver Spring.

TAKOMA PARK
Tacoma is a word of American Indian origin meaning, in various translations, "exalted," "high place," or "close to heaven." This is the name, with a spelling change, that Benjamin Franklin Gilbert gave to the community he planned.

In 1883 Gilbert purchased the Grammer farm, and began to sell lots in his new subdivision advertised as "the Sylvan Suburb of the National Capital." Within

three years there were 16 homes including his own. But Gilbert's involvement only began with the sale of lots. He also built streets and sidewalks and supported community projects with interest-free loans. When the town was incorporated in 1890 at the instigation of the Takoma Park Improvement Association, Mr. Gilbert was its first elected mayor.

In 1893 a fire destroyed the newly built business district, including the first store and post office owned by Isaac Thomas and the Watkins Hotel erected the previous year. That year also saw the construction of Gilbert's 160-room North Takoma Hotel, which advertised the presence of pure spring water in the vicinity. Large homes in a variety of Victorian styles on tree-shaded streets formed a "sturdy nucleus for the greater growth that is coming."

The Seventh-day Adventist Church has had a strong influence on the community. In 1904 the church moved its national headquarters from Battle Creek, Michigan, to Takoma Park. The construction of the general conference building and the Review and Herald building, the publishing branch, were followed by the main section of the Washington Sanitarium, the county's first hospital and the Washington Training

some noted men in the field of electrical engineering, including C. Francis Jenkins, a pioneer in the field of television.

The success of Benjamin F. Gilbert's original venture, based on a combination of a permanent residential area with resort-oriented facilities, resulted in a unique community. The town of Takoma Park is still faced with the perplexities of divergent roles. It now struggles with the challenge of solving the contemporary problems brought about by the influx of residents with a mix of economic and ethnic backgrounds.

The Circle at Washington Grove is the site of the Tabernacle where camp meetings took place when it was a summer camp. Washington Grove is now a small residential community retaining much of the "camp" flavor. Courtesy, Montgomery County Historical Society and Thomas Anderson, Jr.

College, now Columbia Union College.

In 1908 Louis Denton Bliss purchased the North Takoma Hotel, for his Bliss Electrical School. When the building burned to the ground a few months later, Bliss immediately began to build a new campus (now the Takoma Park Campus of Montgomery College). This school produced

WASHINGTON GROVE

The town of Washington Grove includes the 200-acre site chosen by Methodists of Washington, D.C., for their annual camp meeting, an evangelistic and social gathering for church members. Chartered on March 30, 1874, the Washington Camp Meeting Association issued 1,000 shares of stock at $20 per share. The association's business affairs were controlled by a board of directors and an executive committee.

At the first camp meeting, two years before, in 1872, the members cleared a circle, built a platform for the preachers and singers, and laid out six avenues radiating from the circle. On these radiating streets they pitched their tents and later erected their cottages. The Metropolitan Branch of the B & O encouraged the project. The railroad ran excursion trains during the meetings and hauled construction materials without charge when members started to build permanent cottages. Families began to come early and stayed on after the camp meeting was over. Gradually, new structures were added — the octagonal Assembly Hall, an auditorium, and the white frame Albany Hotel.

At the turn of the century, a touch of the secular began to invade the meetings when they became a part of the Chautauqua circuit in 1901. A baseball team of considerable talent was organized to play on the new athletic field and a brass band was formed. Washington Grove became a summer resort.

By 1937 a permanent community was firmly established. The association was abandoned and the town was incorporated. The government, which has a mayor and council, relies on the most direct form of democratic government, the town meeting, with each citizen having one vote on budget and policy issues. The annual meeting is held June at the Assembly Hall of association days, now named McCathran Hall for Washington Grove's first mayor, Irving L. McCathran.

WHEATON

Once known as Mitchell's Crossroads, Wheaton was situated at the intersection of Washington and Brookeville Turnpike and Old Bladensburg Road. Robert T. Mitchell's tavern was on the northeast corner. During the Civil War, this small community saw Jubal Early's troops march through on their way to Fort Stevens and march back in a hasty retreat.

Among the postwar settlers were George F. Plyer and Charles A. Eccleston, former Union soldiers. There is some conjecture as to which of these two men named the newly established post office. Whichever the case, the area became known as Wheaton for General Frank Wheaton, the commander of the defenses of Fort Stevens when it was threatened by Confederate forces in 1864.

Other small towns have existed in the area now known as Wheaton. Leesboro was a settlement on the turnpike toward Silver Spring. Aspen Hill was further out the turnpike and named for three trees near George Gill's store where a post office was located. Enster was beyond Aspen Hill with postal service in John A. Bennett's store. But all of these lost their separate identities and became absorbed in the growth of Wheaton.

As recently as World War II there were only about 29,000 people living in the Wheaton area. With the construction of new housing developments, the widening of Georgia Avenue and Veirs Mill Road, and the attraction of Wheaton Plaza, one of the earliest shopping centers, the population increased to 219,000 in 1970. The Wheaton area was the first to experience the unprecedented growth that came to Montgomery County.

* * * * * * * *

EPILOGUE

While many of the county's towns are a part of its long history, others are relatively new. The residents of both take pride in their community and their county. As new business is attracted to the area, as the county's population expands, and as its government grows to keep pace, an awareness of the heritage of Montgomery County will enable all to participate in the next century of change.

Hyattstown, on the border just inside the county, stretches along both sides of the old road from Georgetown to Frederick. Many descendants of the early settlers in Hyattstown still live in houses along the road, which is now Route 355. Photo by Dave Kelsey

Left: *The Rockville Civic Center Mansion was once the home of Judge Richard Johns Bowie, local Rockville attorney as well as state senator, U.S. congressman, and chief judge of the Maryland Court of Appeals. The Greek Revival style home was built by Bowie before 1840. Photo by Dave Kelsey*

Top: *Although known as the Madison House, fourth President James Madison never lived here. He did seek refuge from the British in the home of postmaster Caleb Bentley following the burning of the Capitol and White House. The house is now a private residence in the quiet town of Brookeville. Photo by Dave Kelsey*

Bottom: *Home of the Montgomery County Historical Society, the Beall-Dawson House was purchased by the city of Rockville. Built in the early 1800s, the house has been restored and maintains the charm of its era. Courtesy, Montgomery County Historical Society*

This Seneca sandstone is from a nearby Seneca quarry shore canal. Most locks in the lower Chesapeake and Ohio Canal, as well as the Smithsonian Institution Building in Washington, were constructed of this red sandstone. Photo by Louis Reed, courtesy, Montgomery County Historical Society, hand-colored by Marta Kelsey

The Chesapeake & Ohio Canal linked the coal-laden hills of Maryland and West Virginia with the seaport of Georgetown, providing western Montgomery County farmers with an easy access to a ready market. Photo by Louis Reed, courtesy, Montgomery County Historical Society, hand-colored by Marta Kelsey

Top: *Rolling countryside of the western county is still primarily farmland, although more and more land is being subdivided into mini-estates and "farmettes." Photo by Dave Kelsey*

Above: *In 1943 the Washington Suburban Sanitary Commission built Brighton Dam to form the Triadelphia Reservoir. Named for the town its waters now cover, Triadelphia provides both water and recreation to county residents. Photo by Dave Kelsey*

Facing page: *Brookside Gardens in Wheaton maintains 50 acres of exotic gardens. Open to the public and dedicated to public education, Brookside offers lectures, courses, and workshops, and a specialized library for horticulture. Photo by Dave Kelsey*

Above: *Golf courses in summer make wonderful cross-country ski areas in winter. Although downhill skiers have to find their hills outside the county, the rolling hills are just right for cross-country aficionados when there's enough snow. Photo by Dave Kelsey*

Left: *Old tombstones in the Monocacy Cemetery are made of red Seneca sandstone. Monocacy Chapel was known as a chapel-of-ease where services were held every few weeks by the parish (Episcopalian) rector so that parishioners in the outlying areas could attend services. The chapel was built in Beallsville sometime before 1748. These tombstones were brought to the chapel from "Mother's Delight." Photo by Marta Kelsey*

Courthouse Square in Rockville is aptly named for the three Montgomery County courthouses. In the center the 1891 red brick courthouse has watched many changes in the face of Rockville. To the right, the 1931 courthouse is currently being renovated. The new Judicial Center can be seen in the background. Photo by Dave Kelsey

Above and facing page: Every Memorial Day, crowds flock to Rockville for a parade. Clowns, high school bands, and fire departments are but a few of the groups who participate in Rockville's annual tribute. Photo by Dave Kelsey

Montgomery County has long been a favorite of "horse people." Many rolling acres of pasture in the county are home to grazing horses. Polo has gained popularity as more and more spectators make their way to Potomac to watch this fast, exciting game.
Photo by Dave Kelsey

Local kids are seen here enjoying a day off from school at the ice-skating rink adjacent to the new Judicial Center and Executive Office Building. County employees often skate their way through lunch. Photo by Dave Kelsey

Top: *The first United States Government facility to relocate in Montgomery County was the Naval Hospital in Bethesda. The complex provides treatment and hospitalization for Navy, Marine, and Coast Guard personnel. Many presidents have been patients there. Photo by Dave Kelsey*

Above: *Formerly a seminary for young ladies, Forest Glen is now an annex of Walter Reed Army Hospital. Ambulatory patients were moved here for rehabilitation and therapy beginning with World War II. Photo by Dave Kelsey*

Facing page: *Facing east, the Washington Temple of the Church of Jesus Christ of Latter-Day Saints looms above the capital beltway. Built in the early 1970s, the building's exterior is sheathed with 173,000 square feet of Alabama white marble. Photo by Dave Kelsey*

9
Partners in Progress
by Philip L. Cantelon

By the time Montgomery County was founded in 1777, the economy of the region was firmly established. The English traditions of land speculation and tobacco farming shifted to colonial successors during the war. Economic and political power became centered in Georgetown, then part of Montgomery County, and the town's merchants invested heavily in county land.

But Georgetown did not become the county seat. Rather, voters tapped property in what would become Rockville. The Montgomery County Courthouse became the focal point of new businesses, and Georgetown, with its vigorous commercial

The Dickerson Power Plant's arrival along the Potomac was greeted with mixed reactions. The tall smokestack looms over the horizon of an otherwise agrarian scene. Farms and industry, however, have managed to live together. Photo by Marta Kelsey

base, became part of the new Federal City in 1791.

Left without a port or ready access to river transportation, Montgomery County remained largely agricultural in the early 19th century. Many farmers shipped their goods by road to Baltimore, but the development of canals and railroads began to change that orientation toward Georgetown. The Chesapeake and Ohio Canal, begun in 1828, held the promise of cheaper shipping charges for county farmers. Within six years the canal had reached Harper's Ferry and significantly boosted the economy for the nearby farmers and businessmen.

The canal initially prospered, but competition from the Baltimore and Ohio Railroad, which ran near the northern border of Montgomery County, drew some commerce back into the Baltimore orbit. However, not until after the Civil War, with the building of the B&O's Metropolitan Branch, did the improvement in transportation bring boom times to the county.

Montgomery County was a quick recipient of growth following the Civil War and Reconstruction in the late 19th century. Suburbs sprang up along the Metropolitan Branch railroad line from Washington through Takoma Park, Linden, Kensington, Brookland, Garrett Park, and Rockville. Land values for suburban property continued to soar as trolley lines stretched out to Chevy Chase where Nevada Senator Francis G. Newlands gave up the silver lodes of his state for the real estate development by his Chevy Chase Land Company. Bethesda, too, took on new commercial vigor.

The population boom in the south also created an agricultural boom "up county." Sales of milk and dairy products became a feature of the local farms, and, in spite of the county's growing suburban character, about 80 percent of its acreage was in farmland in 1920.

A second, and greater, explosion in the Montgomery County suburbs took place after World War I. Bethesda, Chevy Chase, Silver Spring, and Garrett Park all witnessed substantial growth. The housing and commercial growth slowed significantly during the Great Depression only to take on a renewed vigor from the thousands of workers who poured into the region to staff the New Deal and wartime agencies. Indeed, in the three decades after 1940, Washington, D.C., was the second fastest growing area in the nation.

The notion that Montgomery County had become largely a bedroom community for the federal government was correct. And following the lead of the federal agencies, a number of corporations, most concentrating in the areas of research and development and high technology, also moved into Montgomery County, many along the Rockville, Gaithersburg, Germantown, Clarksburg corridor.

As Montgomery County enters its third century, it can view with pride the accomplishments of its citizens and business leaders. The county's prosperity is reflected in its schools, its real estate, its homes, and its vigorous commercial community. The vision of the political and corporate leadership over the years had helped shape the county into an area of comfortable household incomes, high academic training, and continuing economic opportunity.

The organizations you will meet on the following pages have chosen to support this important civic event. They illustrate the variety of ways in which individuals and their businesses have contributed to the county's growth and development. The civic involvement of Montgomery County's businesses, institutions of learning, and local government in cooperation with its citizens, has made the community an excellent place to live and work.

MONTGOMERY COUNTY HISTORICAL SOCIETY

The Montgomery County Historical Society, observing its 40th anniversary in 1984, acknowledges its debt to its founding mother, Lilly Moore Stone. In 1944 this history-minded, 83-year-old activist invited area leaders with similar interests to her home to consider forming an association to preserve records and landmarks of Montgomery County and to disseminate historical information to scholars and the public. By November of that year the Montgomery County Historical Society had written a constitution and elected Mrs. Stone its first president.

Initially, the Society met primarily in private homes. Its first repository for archival materials was a donated desk kept at the courthouse in Rockville; larger artifacts were stored in a member's home.

A permanent headquarters was needed early on, and in 1954 the Society purchased "Glenview," the 19th-century stone mansion of Judge Richard John Bowie, for $100,000. Interest and membership immediately increased, but soon the prodigious management and maintenance costs overwhelmed the organization's enthusiasm and resources. In 1957 the Society sold Glenview to the City of Rockville, which made it the centerpiece of the Civic Center complex.

Fortunately, the Society found another, more suitable property in the Beall-Dawson House on Rockville's West Montgomery Avenue. The City of Rockville purchased the property, with a contribution by the Historical Society applied toward a long-term lease. The Society maintains the interior of the building, while the city takes care of the exterior and grounds. Continuing historical and technical research direct the ongoing restoration and furnishing of the Beall-Dawson House, which was listed on the National Register of Historic Places in 1973.

In 1972 the Beall-Dawson was joined by the tiny frame building that, from 1850 to 1903, had housed Dr. Edward E. Stonestreet's medical office. In its new location it has been restored to its Victorian appearance and furnished as a 19th-century physician's office.

From the beginning the Society has collected Montgomery County documents and artifacts. A large print and graphics collection has also been gradually accumulated. An acclaimed reference library, now housed in a detached frame garage, serves large numbers of researchers.

In its 40 years the Society has arranged lectures on county history; collected, conserved, and exhibited historical objects; placed historical markers; carried on oral history; prepared a guide to local records; jointly sponsored a definitive history of the county; visited historic places; organized a genealogy club; and hosted Civil War encampments. It publishes *The Montgomery County Story* quarterly, provides a monthly newsletter, and operates a museum shop.

In recent years the Society has emphasized educational programs aimed at bringing its resources to an even wider audience. Trained docents present the history of the Beall-Dawson House and its occupants in the context of the history of the county. The library staff seeks constantly to augment the Society's information and facilitate its use by all interested persons.

The Beall-Dawson House, built in 1815, home of the Montgomery County Historical Society.

The Montgomery County Historical Society's Medical Museum, originally built in Rockville in 1850, housed Dr. Edward E. Stonestreet's medical practice. The library currently occupies the frame building in the background.

MONTGOMERY MALL

Regional shopping malls surrounding the Washington Beltway create their own special atmosphere to attract customers to their centers. Such is Montgomery Mall. Opening in 1968, with three major department stores, Sears, Hecht's, and Garfinckel's, and 60 shops and businesses, it has been an integral part of the community ever since.

Montgomery Mall is located on 58 acres of the original 300-acre Weaver Farm. The land was once part of a tract called Magruder's Discovery. Dr. John Solomon, a Miami, Florida, physician, purchased the land for $2,500 per acre in 1950, envisioning the parcel's potential as a strategically located major retail center. In the late 1950s Solomon sold the land to May Centers, Inc., retail real-estate developers seeking a West Bethesda location for a major shopping center. Today the May Centers share a general partnership interest in the ownership and management of Montgomery Mall along with Strouse Greenberg and Company, shopping center developers and lessors, and Linowes and Blocher, a major real-estate law firm.

Development of the mall proceeded smoothly in accordance with the Cabin John Master Plan, which was adopted by the County Council in 1956-1957. Dr. Solomon believed so strongly in the mall's future that he moved to construct and widen Bell's Mill Road (later named Democracy Boulevard), converting it to a six-lane arterial highway at his own expense because the county was dragging its road-building feet.

Phase II of Montgomery Mall's

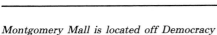

Montgomery Mall is located off Democracy Boulevard in Bethesda on 58 acres, once part of the Weaver Farm.

expansion opened in April 1976 and included a luxurious Woodward and Lothrop addition, and 35 more specialty stores. The entire mall area is now more than one million square feet and is one of the largest of the May Centers' regional shopping centers. With a total of 97 stores, including 4 major department stores, 89 specialty stores, 2 service stations, and 2 tire centers, the facility is varied and comprehensive in the range of goods and services of-

With four major department stores and 89 specialty shops, Montgomery Mall provides a relaxed shopping environment for county citizens.

fered to its customers. Montgomery Mall was the first covered, air-conditioned, two-level mall in Montgomery County and has now added a third wing after being completely renovated in 1982. Phase III, the 1984 addition, features three theaters, a food park, two large sit-down restaurants, and more than 13,000 square feet of retail space.

Although merchandising is the primary purpose of Montgomery Mall, creating a sense of identity with the community and local residents is a very important aspect of its operation. Community ties are so strong that citizens feel possessive about the center and participate often in varied activities occurring there. Major community fairs, displays, and exhibitions are regularly scheduled every month by the mall marketing department with the active participation of the merchants. Events such as hospital week, voter registration, elementary and secondary school art fairs, and charity bazaars are regular events at Montgomery Mall.

Montgomery Mall has a waiting list of retailers desiring space in the center. The steady patronage of old as well as new customers who return time and again to renew their acquaintance with the mall has made Montgomery Mall one of the most successful centers in the area.

HOLY CROSS HOSPITAL

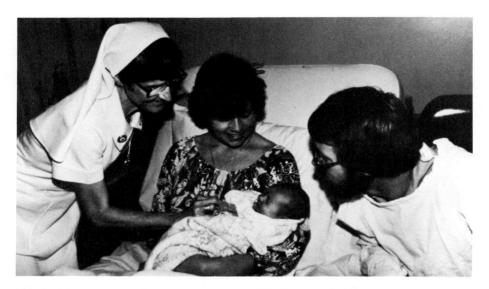

Known for its family-oriented patient care philosophy, Holy Cross Hospital leads all Maryland facilities in its number of new births.

Holy Cross Hospital of Silver Spring has been serving the community since opening as a 226-bed, $9-million facility in January 1963. A need for a hospital in the Wheaton-Silver Spring area was first recognized in the 1940s, when a coalition of neighborhood civic organizations, Allied Civic Group, created the Silver Spring Hospital Association. This group acquired the present hospital site, and after several unsuccessful attempts to raise construction funds, entered into an agreement with the Sisters of the Holy Cross in 1958 for the Sisters to assume full responsibility for developing and administering the facility. The Sisters sought to relieve suffering and restore health in a Christian environment.

Toward those ends the hospital has moved on two fronts. Within the facility itself new instrumentation, new treatment modes, and more sophisticated diagnostic equipment are continuously

implemented. The success of this aspect of patient care of Holy Cross is demonstrated by the fact that the hospital was so highly regarded that in 1963 it was chosen by the Public Health Service to establish a pilot program of coronary-care service to help determine whether it was feasible for a community hospital to provide such care. The program was a great success and has since become a prototype for hospitals throughout the country.

In 1968 Holy Cross developed another innovative program when it began its ambulatory surgery service. By 1983 over 103,000 patients had been served by this program. Another area in which the facility is a leader is in the field of dialysis services.

The hospital tries to provide

health care to the largest number of people possible and operates numerous outreach programs, such as referral services from Columbia Road Health Services, which primarily treats indigent Spanish-speaking patients. The Holy Cross Resource Institute houses an adult day-care program, and Kids In Safety Seats (KISS) was begun in 1983 as an effort to increase the use of child auto restraints. During its first two decades more than 320,000 individuals were hospitalized at Holy Cross; more than 700,000 persons received care in the emergency department; more than 62,000 babies were delivered; and nearly 200,000 people underwent surgery.

Holy Cross Hospital's original building was expanded in 1978 with the addition of a four-story wing which cost $14 million and increased the bed capacity to 450. It also provided new, expanded facilities for a number of medical and administrative departments as well as a new outpatient center.

A $7.75-million expansion and remodeling of the labor, delivery, and nursery areas, as well as kitchen and cafeteria facilities, was begun in 1983 with completion scheduled for the spring of 1985.

An aerial view of Holy Cross Hospital looking southeast, with the Capital Beltway bordering the hospital grounds.

THOMAS W. PERRY, INC.

When Thomas W. Perry encountered him, Francis G. Newlands was a very important individual, even in Washington, D.C.—a city dominated by President Theodore Roosevelt. Perry worked in a lumberyard and Newlands, a Democratic senator from Nevada, had given his name to legislation financing irrigation projects in the West. More important for Montgomery County, the senator was a vigorous land developer and founder of the Chevy Chase Land Company. He thought he could spot success and was willing to bet on Perry. One morning, as the young Kensington native was putting down ballast for the B&O Railroad track, Newlands strode up and told him to go into business for himself.

Newlands was no fool. If he wanted to develop Chevy Chase, one important ingredient would be an ample supply of fuel and feed for the area. In 1910 he offered Perry 50 feet of land on Connecticut Avenue near the B&O tracks. Encouraged by his mother and older brothers, Perry bought the land, eventually acquiring more than two acres. There coal

could be unloaded from the B&O cars and delivered to customers in Chevy Chase, Silver Spring, Bethesda, and northwest Washington, D.C.

In 1917 Perry bought a feed mill in Silver Spring, on the corner of Sligo and Georgia avenues, where the company manufactured feed for local dairy and chicken farmers. Ten years later the land in Silver Spring was sold, and Perry carried feed prepared by General Mills or local Baltimore mills in the mid-1920s. By then a fleet of trucks replaced the horse-drawn delivery wagons, and Perry had become a substantial stockholder in Farmer's Bank and Trust of Rockville. Newlands had not misjudged him.

Thomas W. Perry soon added cement to the growing business and sold it to road contractors who raced to keep up with the demands for better highways in the booming years of the 1920s. Stone from Frederick County

provided a gravel base for the roads; Perry-mixed cement provided the surface. It was natural to add brick, block, and mortar to the expanding inventory to meet the demands of home builders.

Thomas Jr. joined his father in 1947, just as the changing face of Montgomery County was forcing the firm to change too. The growth of the suburbs spelled doom for the feed business as farmland became housing tracts. The last major feed customer was the National Institute of Health, which was feeding cattle, goats, and other animals that had been exposed to the atomic tests at Bikini in the Pacific. As feed faded in importance, Thomas W. Perry, Inc., added lumber and hardware to its fuel oil business, and that segment soon became a major facet of the company.

As the population of Montgomery County moved out along the Interstate 270 corridor, Thomas W. Perry, Inc., moved with it. In the near future Thomas W. Perry, Jr., and his two sons will open a new facility at the Gaithersburg-Montgomery County Air Park.

Thomas W. Perry, Sr., fifth from left, and his staff in July 1927.

STONEYHURST QUARRIES

"We have approximately seven million tons of stone remaining in the ground, and we take out 10,000 to 12,000 tons a year; at that rate, we won't run out of stone for a long time!" says John P. Stone, owner of Stoneyhurst Quarries. The Bethesda business has been in the Stone family for five generations, and the sixth generation is being groomed to continue the operation. Obviously, Montgomery County will be rich in stones for quite some time.

John Moore, a naval captain from Prince Georges County, moved to Montgomery County to farm in the early 19th century. While plowing, he hit a vein of stone called mica schist, well known for its construction properties. Moore believed that the stone was ideal for the Chesapeake & Ohio Canal, then under construction, and offered his assistance in December 1832. He subsequently quarried the rock and built Aqueduct No. 10 and locks Nos. 71, 75, and 76 on the canal. Moore's original quarry was located one-quarter mile from Stoneyhurst's present site on River Road. The original quarry closed in 1975 when the State of Maryland bought it for parkland.

Captain Moore alternated quarrying stone with agriculture; he took stone out of the ground only when someone requested it. Otherwise, he kept busy with farming and with supervising crews working on canal boats. This pattern remained with the family until the early 20th century.

Moore's son, John D.W. Moore, continued the cyclical method of quarrying and farming. At that time the family owned 500 acres and two farms—the Stoneyhurst, on the north side of River Road, including a residence dating to the 1730s, and the Glenmore, near Cabin John. The Moores owned enough property to construct an overland railway from the quarry to the C&O Canal. Oxen pulled the railway cars filled with stone along the wooden track to the canal, where the stone was loaded into boats and shipped.

John D.W. Moore's daughter, Lilly, married Frank Stone, who

(Below) Men breaking stone in the original quarry, which opened in 1832.

(Bottom) Members of the Stone family shown here (left to right) are John P., J. Dunbar, and Katherine, with Captain John Moore's portrait in the background.

Stoneyhurst—the home for which the quarry was named.

took over his father-in-law's quarry business. Before Frank died, he told Lilly to open the stone quarries at full tilt "if times got hard." Frank died in 1918, and by 1919, Lilly—then in her sixties—opened the quarry. The family has been at work full time ever since.

Lilly's first attempt at business was with a stone contractor. The contractor promised not to sell the stone to anyone else, but Lilly found otherwise. She took over the quarry, hired her own workers, and began a sales campaign for the mica schist. Her sales effort was the first and last of its kind; once the stone was in place around the city, word spread throughout the country about its use, versatility, and variety of color. The Stone family has had a steady stream of customers ever since.

Lilly's son, John Dunbar Stone, entered the family business in 1925, after several years of copper mining in Arizona. The quarry provided stone for bridges on Mt. Vernon Boulevard, K Street, and Massachusetts Avenue; for numerous churches

John Dunbar Stone (left) and his mother, Lilly, at one of the Stoneyhurst Quarries in February 1929. Lilly Stone, who died in 1961 at the age of 99, remained actively involved in the business throughout her lifetime.

Lilly Stone oversees operations at the quarry in 1929.

in the area, including those buildings around the National Cathedral-St. Albans, the College of Preachers, and various garden walls; and for many residences in the metropolitan region. John Moore's prediction that hard times needed hard stone proved accurate.

Stoneyhurst's busiest years were those of the Great Depression. The Works Progress Admininstration and the Public Works Administration constructed roads, bridges, parks, schools, dams, and waterways from stone.

Lilly Stone died in 1961 at the age of 99. She remained interested in the quarry until her death, frequently checking general business procedures. Also active in the community, Lilly

was a co-founder of the Montgomery County Historical Society and helped design the Montgomery County flag.

John P. Stone, Lilly's grandson, started working at the quarry full time in 1953. He spent most of his youth at the facility, learning the business from the bottom up. He was a water boy at age 10 and progressed through the ranks of truck driver and driller until he finally took over the full operation.

In recent years the quarry has experienced a minor slow period during which home building decreased. Residential construction now accounts for about 30 percent of the quarry's business, while commercial and government work comprise the remaining 70 percent. Usually the government and commercial to residential ratio is 50-50.

Stoneyhurst Quarries has experienced little in the way of change, whether it be corporate policy or economic climate. According to John Stone, "What's been in practice is still in practice," and this keeps the family business strong.

ROBERT A. PUMPHREY FUNERAL HOMES, P.A.

Four generations of Pumphreys have been serving Montgomery County families for over a century and a half, offering quality attention for funeral needs. The family has been at the forefront of new concepts in funeral services and has developed strong ties to the county and its residents.

In the 1830s William Ellican Pumphrey, a Rockville cabinet-maker, decided to build coffins and enter the "undertaking" business. His firm originated on Main Street, now Washington Street; later, his son, William Ruben Pumphrey, moved the business to its present location in Rockville. The younger Pumphrey concentrated on embalming and stopped making coffins. Because most embalmings and funerals were held in private homes in the 19th and early 20th centuries, the mortician basically needed a means to travel to homes to perform his duties and to transport the bodies of the deceased to cemeteries. To reach his customers more efficiently, Pumphrey expanded his operations to include 14 branch offices, where horses, hearses, coffins, and carriages were stored, ready to respond to any emergency or need.

This need to respond to emergencies led Pumphrey to start an ambulance service that operated much like the pony express, where horses were changed at strategic points along a given route—a route usually leading to the train station. Because the only hospitals were in Frederick and Washington, D.C., ambulances needed to respond quickly so patients could receive much-needed medical attention. Pumphrey would wire ahead to his Georgetown branch, telling them to meet the patient at the train and to take the

patient immediately to the hospital, via the Pumphreys' Georgetown ambulance.

William Ruben, Jr., the third-generation Pumphrey, entered the family business in 1910. When the flu epidemic hit Maryland, just after World War I, he traveled from house to house with an embalming buggy equipped with instruments, embalming fluid, and an operating table. Large farm wagons followed, leaving caskets at the homes of the flu victims. Many of the caskets were only shells, and the families could "trim the casket" or finish the interior as they wished. Because of the large number of deaths, funerals were performed only when there was a break in embalming.

During the 1920s funeral services were held in informal chapels and viewing rooms. However, William R. Jr. believed that funerals should be held in a comfortable, home-like atmosphere and from this idea came the concept of a "funeral home." The new idea needed a new environment, and in 1928 Pumphrey purchased a large, turn-of-the-century home at the corner of Williams Street and West Montgomery Avenue, where the business is still located.

Robert A. Pumphrey, Sr.,

present owner and president, has continued the family tradition of serving Montgomery County's funeral needs. As a child, he began learning about the business and conducted his first funeral at the age of 12. During the past 50 years Pumphrey has witnessed several changes in funeral requests. Funerals, he recalls, used to be held on Sundays. Now cemeteries are closed for burials on Sunday, so funerals are held on other days. Moreover, attendance at funeral services has declined, and viewing of the body the night before burial has become more popular. So, too, is cremation, which now comprises 15 to 20 percent of final disposition.

Robert Pumphrey also has a funeral home in Bethesda. Both facilities have a manager, an assistant manager, and a funeral service staff on call 24 hours a day. In addition, a general manager provides overall supervision for both homes.

Despite the many changes in the funeral service profession, Robert A. Pumphrey, Sr., believes one aspect of his business has remained the same. "Our four generations of service—that's the most important thing."

A late 19th-century carriage used in funeral processions. Photo courtesy of the Montgomery County Historical Society.

W. BELL & CO., INC.

Walter Bell, founder, president, and chairman of W. Bell & Co., Inc.

W. Bell & Co., Inc., a firm dedicated to providing quality merchandise at low prices, began operation in 1950 as a silver wholesale outlet, selling only to embassies, government agencies, and dealers. This "closed-door" policy evolved to an open catalog/showroom of jewelry and fine gifts, employing 1,200 people and serving 18 locations in metropolitan Washington, D.C., Baltimore, Houston, and Chicago.

Walter Bell, president and chairman of the company, has been involved with fine art and merchandise for most of his adult life. After two years at George Washington University, he began working in the auction business with his brother. Bell solicited consigners, estates, and individuals for 16 years, and in the process developed a keen sense for quality products and their prices.

In 1950 Walter and his wife, Dorothy, rented a space above Velatis' candy store at Ninth and G, Northwest, in Washington, D.C., and began a wholesale silver business, selling silverware items to jewelers. Dealers appreciated the outlet because they no longer had to keep tarnishable silver on their shelves.

The company moved locations throughout the 1950s and 1960s, continually expanding warehouse and showroom floor space. However, it stayed near the commercial areas. The first catalog appeared in 1951, promoting sales to such an extent that the 1952 version grew four times in size. By the mid-1950s jewelry, watches, luggage, and small appliances joined silver to adorn the pages of the Bell catalog.

In 1957 the company was incorporated. The sales policy at this time specified purchase only for the intended use of "prizes, trophies, awards, business gifts, premiums and incentives, commercial use, or for eventual export." W. Bell & Co. became

W. Bell & Co.'s headquarters and showroom on Twinbrook Parkway in Rockville.

aware of the need to change its policy, which kept the public out, to one that let the public in. By 1972 W. Bell & Co. decided to change its policy in response to other catalog showrooms springing up in the area. It began selling to the public and became a publicly owned corporation as well.

W. Bell & Co. began to develop skilled staff early in its existence in order to provide the continuity necessary for future growth. Finding the need to reach new customers in the shifting market, the company moved to its present Rockville location on Twinbrook Parkway in 1969, targeting the busy corridor as a high-growth area that fit the company's expansionary requirements.

The Bell family still remains active in the business. Walter heads the operation, Dorothy selects jewelry, and their son, Fredric J., is senior vice-president. W. Bell & Co., Inc., remains committed to providing quality merchandise, thus ensuring that customers receive the finest merchandise for the lowest prices, which represents excellent value to the consumer.

KETTLER BROTHERS, INC.

Milton E. Kettler, Charles L. Kettler, William Forlines, and Clarence E. Kettler (left to right) in the firm's office at 44th and Chesapeake streets, Washington, D.C., in 1962.

For more than 30 years Kettler Brothers, Inc., has been conceiving plans and programs, creating communities and neighborhood facilities, and constructing homes and business environments to enhance the good life that abounds in the Maryland area. Throughout those years Kettler Brothers has remained a privately owned, family-operated company, which banks its success on responding faithfully to the needs of the families it serves.

Today Kettler Brothers is headed by Clarence and Charles Kettler, and their partner, Frank Ewing. (Former partners Milton Kettler and William Forlines are deceased.) The foundation for the brothers' growth in the building business was set by family tradition—Kettler Sr. owned and operated several Washington apartment buildings, giving his sons their first insight into responding to people's housing needs. By the time Clarence, the

youngest, graduated from college with a background in economics and architecture—and an interest in building homes—the older Kettler sons were well experienced in the real estate field. Clarence's first homes were sold prior to completion—success seemed eminent. In 1952 Milton and Clarence formed Kettler Brothers, Inc. Charles joined later to direct the company's general contracting division.

The year 1959 brought the firm widespread recognition with its first major community, Old Farm, in Rockville. It was here that Kettler Brothers established its reputation for blending grand-scale development with environmental sensitivity and an understanding of buyer concerns. It wasn't long before the company aspired to combine its planning skills and development talents into a total living environment. The opportunity came its way in 1961, when the 400-acre Walker Farm in Gaithersburg, Maryland, became available.

As neighboring farm parcels were added to the purchase, the potential for a pioneer community

seemed feasible; thus Kettler Brothers planted the seeds for Montgomery County's first new town—a self-contained, planned community, 25 miles north of the nation's capital, on the rapidly growing I-270 corridor.

Planning for the village began in 1964, with the formation of an experienced planning team, headed by key Kettler Brothers managers and assisted by top consultants in the fields of land use, design, and marketing. Groundbreaking ceremonies took place on February 28, 1966; seven months later the new town became an offical "hometown" when the Crosby family set up housekeeping at Lakeside at Whetstone. The Crosbys still reside in their Montgomery Village home.

Local history played an important part in the character of the new town. Streets and home communities were named after original land grants, such as Lost

Milton E. Kettler, Charles L. Kettler, Frank M. Ewing, and Clarence E. Kettler (left to right) at a reception at Westover Place, 1978.

Knife and Dorsey's Regard; after previous landowners, such as Mills and Walker; or after local pastimes such as gristmilling, such as Watkins Mill.

Since its inception Montgomery Village has been the showcase for Kettler Brothers' varied activities. In the true "hometown" spirit, the company has strived to balance cultural, social, and recreational opportunities, as well as schools, churches, and shopping to fill the residents' needs. While preserving the integrity of the land, Kettler Brothers added natural aesthetic improvements, moving earth to add hills and valleys to the face of flat terrain. Over 50,000 trees have been planted along village roads and pathways, and man-made lakes and ponds are now home for visiting geese and ducks

Kettler Brothers' innovations in Montgomery Village include Montgomery County's first townhouses. Modeled after Washington and Baltimore row houses, the firm introduced the concept as an affordable alternative to apartment living. Since that time, Kettler Brothers has lead the way in local high-density housing design.

The company's community involvement extends well beyond building homes for people. A continual involvement in charitable and civic organizations and business associations occupies a good portion of Kettler Brothers' time. It has been involved in the Bethesda Boys' Club, the Montgomery County

This 300-year-old white oak measured 50 inches in breadth in 1967. Kettler Brothers preserved the tree while developing Old Farm in Rockville. The tree, called "wolf" in the tree trade, became a community symbol.

Chamber of Commerce, the National Association of Home Builders, and the Washington Board of Trade, to name a few. Since 1971 Kettler Brothers has co-sponsored the Harden and Weaver Golf Tournament, donating all proceeds to Children's Hospital, where Clarence has served as a board and corporate member.

In addition, the firm has received special requests for its services. In 1964, 10-year-old Jennifer Lippincott desperately wanted a treehouse. Her own attempts at construction had

Lake Whetstone in Montgomery Village, Kettler Brothers' highly successful planned community.

fallen short. Her solution: write to Kettler Brothers and offer her $25 savings for its expert carpentry. Kettler Brothers honored her request, "forgot" about the bill, and Jennifer was delighted.

Kettler Brothers, Inc., the company known nationally for its trend-setting home building, is equally respected in Maryland, for its dedication to community service and the citizens of Montgomery County.

NATIONAL 4-H COUNCIL

The wholesome-looking youngsters and the gracefully designed Chevy Chase mansion seemed made for each other. Thus, a three-year search for a headquarters came to a happy end in 1951.

When officials of the newly formed National 4-H Foundation were looking for a headquarters during the 1940s, the stately building, erected in 1893 on Connecticut Avenue in Chevy Chase, was for sale. Originally named the Chevy Chase Inn, the facility served the railroad that connected Maryland to the District of Columbia, and housed Washingtonians as a summer

In 1983, 4-H club members attended a meeting at the organization's national center in Chevy Chase.

resort.

In 1903 the inn was sold to the Chevy Chase College for Young Ladies, later known as the Chevy Chase Junior College. After the 4-H Foundation bought the college building and grounds, members from across the nation sent in their nickels and dimes to help pay for the structure. The staff moved into its new headquarters in 1958, and President Dwight D. Eisenhower participated in the formal opening ceremonies on June 16, 1959.

The 4-H movement, however, started at the turn of the 20th century. Agricultural officials found that the best means of educating farmers in modern technology was by showing them what farm children could do in corn and canning clubs by demonstrating modern and more

In 1951 the National 4-H Foundation purchased this building, on Connecticut Avenue in Chevy Chase, to serve as its headquarters. Courtesy of U.S.D.A. Extension Service. Photo by George C. Pace.

efficient agricultural methods.

In 1914 Congress passed the Smith-Lever Act, creating the Cooperative Extension Service of the Department of Agriculture, the 4-H parent organization in the federal government. After World War I, private interests formed the National Committee on Boys' and Girls' Club Work in 1921 to finance, promote, and gain public support for 4-H clubs. At the same time, the organization's symbol, a four-leaf clover, standing for "Head, Heart, Hands, and Health," was created.

After World War II a small international exchange began between 4-H clubs and European farm youths. Edward Aiton, a Department of Agriculture official, promoted the international exchange but failed to obtain support from the National Committee. In 1948 the Extension Committee on Organization and Policy agreed to the Delaware chartering of a "not-for-profit" foundation supporting 4-H. Aiton took leave from the Department of Agriculture to become the Foundation's first director in 1951. He returned to the extension service in 1952 to serve as first director of the newly formed division of 4-H clubs. In 1976-1977 the National Committee merged with the Foundation to form the National 4-H Council.

The center became known for its nationally sponsored events such as its week-long citizenship programs for 14- to 19-year-old 4-H youths from all across the United States. In 1983 some 5,100 members from 44 states participated in these events.

By 1984 the 4-H had offices in 52 states, with one-third of its membership from farms, one-third from the suburbs, and one-third from urban areas.

RACAL COMMUNICATIONS, INC.

Car radios and home-stereo systems pulsate with the latest top-40 hits or gently lull listeners with soft classical tones. However, radio electronics come in many shapes and sizes, and transmit information vastly different from that which is heard on our AM or FM stations.

Racal Communications, Inc. (RCI), is a company that manufactures that "different type" of radio: complex HF (high-frequency), VHF (very-high-frequency), and UHF (ultrahigh-frequency) receivers for military communications and for areas of the world where the creation of general communications networks require long-range transmissions.

RCI is a Rockville-based subsidiary of the United Kingdom's Racal Electronics PLC (REP). The firm originated in England in 1950 with a group of communication consultants specializing in HF radio. Raymond Brown and G. Calder Cunningham led the organization's rapid rise in the industry, lending parts of their first names to the company's title. By the early 1960s the British group sought an outlet in the United States to adapt the Racal equipment to specific requirements for the American market, primarily for military defense.

Racal wanted a metropolitan Washington-area location because of its proximity to the federal government. During its search the company discovered a branch of General Electronics Laboratories (GEL), of Cambridge, Massachusetts, in Silver Spring. GEL specialized in high-frequency radio and seemed perfect for Racal's United States operations. The corporation purchased GEL's Silver Spring facility in 1964, which included the physical plant and equipment, and hired its chief engineer, Harold Herman, to become vice-president of the new REP entity, Racal Communi-

From left to right are Robert Blatt, Herbert White, Jackie Lowry, and George Ruthvin, original Racal Communications, Inc., employees.

Racal Communications, Inc., moved into its new office facility on Research Place in Rockville in 1971.

cations, Inc. As chairman of the main Racal board, Brown headed RCI until 1971, when Anthony Chapman became president.

Throughout the 1960s RCI endeavored to make the equipment smaller and more compact. Equipment size is critical in the electronics field, to such an extent that technical developments often shape industry's direction. Racal's advances in HF communication, such as high-performance receivers, amplifiers, demodulators, and transmitters, set the pace for the electronics industry.

By the early 1970s RCI outgrew its Silver Spring facilities. The firm chose the I-270 high-technology corridor for its operations and moved into its new building, located on Research Place, in 1971. Corporate growth in the early 1970s was consistent, but not dramatic. However, a major six-year military contract, awarded in 1979, spurred RCI's growth to over 300 employees. The company has delivered 5,000 HF receivers to the military since 1979 and will complete orders in 1985.

The banner year, 1979, also brought a new enterprise to RCI, the R.E. Grimm Company (REGCO). Formed by Ralph E. Grimm in the mid-1970s, REGCO specialized in VHF and UHF electronics. Racal Electronics acquired REGCO upon Grimm's death, and the formal merger was completed in April 1984.

As Racal Communications, Inc., entered the 1980s it received a new president, Herbert L. Robinson, and a new management team. They will direct RCI's strategies and goals for the new decade, and oversee the technological change from analog to digital devices.

THE McARDLE PRINTING COMPANY, INC.

The history of The McArdle Printing Company, Inc., one of the area's most successful local firms, reflects Washington, D.C.'s, growth north to the suburbs. Although the company did not move to its present site in Silver Spring until 1968, the benefits of a suburban location were apparent to its owners. The firm is located near the city, where McArdle Printing has many of its accounts, with 70,000 square feet of space. The company sits in a multi-use section of Silver Spring surrounded by apartment buildings, car dealers, restaurants, a shopping center, and the subway. Easy access to neighborhood housing allows many of the bindery workers to walk to the plant.

A family-owned and -operated business since it began in 1947, McArdle Printing is managed by its founders and sole stockholders, Walter McArdle and his brother, Edward. The former is chairman of the board and the latter its current president. During World War II, Walter left New York City to head up the printing of ration books at the Government

The second home of The McArdle Printing Company, Inc., was located at 24th and M streets, Northwest, in Washington, D.C., from 1952 to 1969.

Printing Office in Washington, D.C., and met David Lawrence who operated a printing company in conjunction with publishing *U.S. News & World Report,* as well as publications for the Bureau of National Affairs.

In 1947 Lawrence decided to devote all his energies to publishing the magazine. He sold the bureau to a group of employees and the printing company to Walter, who, along with Edward, built and maintained a solidly profitable business. Interestingly, McArdle Printing's main accounts are still the Bureau of National Affairs and *U.S. News & World Report.* The firm is also the largest newsletter printing company in the area on a daily, weekly, and monthly basis, and one of the largest in the United States. The company also prints much of the promotional material for *USA Today.*

McArdle's first location was at

22nd and M streets, Northwest. In 1969 the company moved to its present location on East-West Highway and Newell streets in Silver Spring, and has been a mainstay of commercial life in Montgomery County ever since. Both McArdles have been actively involved in community affairs, with membership in the Silver Spring Chamber of Commerce and the Economic Development Advisory Council of Montgomery County. Walter has served as the president of the Printing Industries of America, and both brothers have been president of the local trade association, the Printing Industry of Metropolitan Washington. Additionally, Walter was the first president of the Metropolitan Washington Urban Coalition and represented the United States at the U.N. Tripartite Meeting of the International Labor Organization in Geneva, Switzerland, in 1962.

Walter McArdle (left) receiving the National Conference of Christians and Jews National Brotherhood Citation, on March 10, 1977, from Mayor Walter Washington.

QUALITY INNS INTERNATIONAL, INC.

Driving to Florida in the 1930s could be a real adventure. For the weary traveler, the long, dusty drives did not always lead to a clean, comfortable room for the evening. In addition, the young motel industry suffered from an image problem. "Tourist cabins," as the early roadside motels were labeled, were considered disreputable.

To upgrade the quality of motels and the motel industry, seven southern motel operators met in late 1939 to discuss ways to raise standards, attract new business, and increase profits. The group foresaw growth in travel as the United States emerged from the Great Depression, and they wanted to plan their actions accordingly. After the meeting, the owners corresponded with one another and started referring to their properties as "Quality Courts." At a second meeting in Jacksonville, Florida, in November 1940, they formed an association, outlining the prerequisites and standards for membership.

Of the founders of Quality Courts United, as the new organization was called, A.J. (Red) Mackay, Edmund Worth, Gilbert Chandler, Lloyd G. Thompson, and William F. Gorman ran motels in Florida, L. (Bert) Verburg in Fredericksburg, Virginia, and J.F. (Pat) Patterson in South Carolina. The new association prepared a membership solicitation letter and raised $4,000 to publish 10,000 copies of the first free guidebook published by Quality Courts United.

In November 1941 the association held its first annual membership convention in Daytona Beach, Florida, and transferred ownership from the committee to the members and filed for a charter as a nonprofit corporation under Florida law. At that meeting, the members also agreed on the Quality Courts United, Inc., emblem of a gold seal and a blue ribbon to represent excellence.

After World War II Quality Courts United and the motel industry grew steadily. By the late 1950s and early 1960s America had truly become a nation on wheels. The private passenger car replaced the passenger train as the chief means of transportation. Quality Courts completely reorganized, becoming Quality Courts Motels, Inc., a for-profit company to own and franchise motels across the country. The new venture established a full-time professional staff to coordinate policies and operations more effectively. It also began nationwide institutional advertising and a promotional program, developed uniform operating procedures including the recruiting and training of motel personnel, and began constructing and acquiring motels in new geographic areas.

Quality Courts moved north to Montgomery County in April 1968 when a Silver Spring resident, Stewart Bainum, merged his Park Consolidated Motels, Inc., into Quality Courts.

The firm's name was changed from Quality Courts to Quality Inns International, Inc., in August 1972, and the corporate offices moved to 10750 Columbia Pike in Silver Spring. In 1981 Quality Inns International was acquired by Manor Care, Inc., a health care organization operating nursing homes in 44 states and four countries. That same year the corporation divided its lodging business into three distinct chains—Quality Royale, Quality Inns, and Comfort Inns—to attract clientele from the top-, middle-, and budget-price segments of the market. By 1984 Quality Inns offered travelers 70,000 rooms in nearly 700 inns in 11 countries. As one of the largest and fastest-growing lodging chains in the country, Quality Inns International has traveled a long way since its inception with seven motels in 1939.

By 1984 Quality Inns offered travelers 70,000 rooms in nearly 700 inns in 11 countries.

WEAVER BROS., INC.

Any economic history of Washington, D.C., Montgomery County, and its surrounding area would be incomplete without the story of Weaver Bros., Inc., realtors, mortgage bankers, and independent insurance agents. The company's origin is easily traced to a single person, John L. Weaver, who in 1888 formed a real estate partnership known as Barnes and Weaver. In 1898, along with his two brothers, he started a company known as Weaver Bros. Weaver's commitment to and knowledge of real estate, his honesty and fairness in business transactions, and his concern for employees subsequently convinced four other men to make Weaver Bros. their career home.

As Weaver's brothers became less actively involved on a day-to-day basis, he looked for other men to help him. Over the next 30 years he found three men who would, by 1926, be brought into equal partnership. The first one appeared in 1900, when Clarence Dodge was hired as an office boy at the tremendous sum of five dollars per week. Earl M. Mackintosh, another office boy, began work in 1912. The last partner to come to Weaver Bros. during this period was Martin R. West, who had previous mortgage loan experience with American Security and Trust Company.

These four men were instrumental in having the Potomac Savings Bank of Georgetown appointed mortgage loan correspondent for the Metropolitan Life Insurance Company, with Weaver Bros. as co-correspondent, sharing profits with the bank. In 1927 Weaver Bros. was incorporated in the District of Columbia to meet a Metropolitan requirement, and

John L. Weaver, founder of Weaver Bros., Inc.

was named the sole correspondent. The first officers and directors were John L. Weaver, president; Clarence Dodge, vice-president and treasurer; Earl M. Mackintosh, vice-president; Martin R. West, vice-president and secretary; and Edward K. Jones, assistant secretary. Jones, who had joined the firm in 1923, would play a significant role in Weaver Bros.' future.

As correspondent for the Metropolitan Life Insurance Company, the firm was able to bring millions of dollars of outside capital into the Washington area to help finance residential purchases, apartments, shopping centers, and office buildings. In addition to this mortgage loan business, Weaver Bros. conducted a general brokerage business, specializing in sales and leasing of commercial property, management, and insurance.

Although the Great Depression hit Washington in the 1930s, Weaver Bros. remained solidly committed to the metropolitan

area. As the servicing agent for Metropolitan Life, Weaver Bros. bought many loans prior to foreclosure and attempted to resolve stress problems with the borrowers in an amicable manner. It was during this time that the property management department grew in size and importance.

John L. Weaver retired from the presidency of the firm in 1939 and was succeeded by Clarence Dodge, although Weaver remained on the board of directors until his death in 1949. In 1935, at a dinner party honoring his 70th birthday, Weaver recalled that he earned the magnificent sum of $10 per month as an office boy when he first entered the business. To show his role within the company, he traced his nomenclatures, first as Johnnie, then John, then J.L., later "The Boss," and finally, "The Old Man." Also in 1939 vice-president Earl M. Mackintosh was elected treasurer, while Edward K. Jones became a stockholder by acquiring Weaver's shares. At that time Weaver Bros. had 38 employees.

Under the leadership of Dodge, Mackintosh, West, and Jones, the company entered the second expansionary phase with all areas of the business growing. Sales, leasing, and management of commerical properties, always a major portion of the business, increased, as did the insurance and residential property management departments. The most signifcant growth during this phase was achieved in the mortgage loan department with the financing of homes under the Veteran's Administration and the Federal Housing Administration loan programs.

In 1945 the sons of the founders returned home after service in World War II and joined the firm:

Clarence Dodge, Jr., and Earl M. Mackintosh, Jr., in the sales and leasing department, and Martin R. West, Jr., in the mortgage loan department. In 1948 Richard T. West joined Weaver Bros. in the insurance department.

By 1956 the firm had grown to 94 employees and the board of directors had increased from five to eight members. However, the 1950s brought sad days to the corporation as several of its key leaders passed away. In April 1954 Martin West died. Clarence Dodge died in April 1957. Earl Mackintosh, who had been elected president following Dodge's death, became ill and died in July 1957.

However, these men had left their capable friend Edward K. Jones and their heirs to carry on. The new officers elected on July 15, 1957, were Edward K. Jones, president; Clarence Dodge, Jr., senior vice-president; Martin R. West, Jr., senior vice-president and treasurer; Earl M. Mackintosh, Jr., vice-president; and Richard T. West, vice-president.

With Edward K. Jones at the helm, the company entered its third expansionary phase with real estate development becoming an important element of the firm's business. By 1960 the number of Weaver Bros. employees had grown to 127. Realizing the phenomenal growth the organization was undergoing, management began searching for another administrative officer with a background in real estate and finance. They found what they were looking for in the person of Donald G. West, brother of Martin R. and Richard T. West, who had earned a great deal of experience during his seven years as a real estate loan officer at The Riggs National Bank. In October 1961 he became an integral

member of the management team. This third expansionary phase continues today with Weaver Bros. currently employing 365.

During this entire period Weaver Bros. continued its commitment to the metropolitan Washington real estate expansion. In Montgomery County it financed home building and purchases in subdivisions such as Forest Estates, Garrett Park, Hungerford, Calverton, and Parkwood; apartment projects such as Grosvenor Park, Promenade, Summit Hill, and Court House Square; and office facilities such as the Bethesda Air Rights Building, the Chevy Chase Office Building, and the Parklawn Office Building. In 1960 Weaver Bros. financed the Wheaton Plaza Shopping Center, one of the earliest malls in Montgomery County. Today its commercial and residential management divisions manage numerous commercial, apartment, and condominium properties, including the Willoughby in Chevy Chase.

In Prince William County,

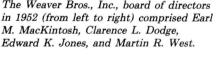

The Weaver Bros., Inc., board of directors in 1952 (from left to right) comprised Earl M. MacKintosh, Clarence L. Dodge, Edward K. Jones, and Martin R. West.

Virginia, Weaver Bros. is currently developing, through its subsidiary Ridge Development Corp., a 3,500-acre residential planned community known as Lake Ridge. At present, 22,000 of the 30,000 expected residents are calling Lake Ridge home.

Weaver Bros. moved to its present quarters in Chevy Chase in 1971 after having resided for over 40 years in the Washington Building, located at 15th Street and New York Avenue, one block from the White House. Descendants of three of the four principals are still actively engaged in the daily operation of the firm: Clarence Dodge, Jr., chairman of the board; Martin R. West, Jr., president; Earl M. Mackintosh, Jr., senior vice-president; Richard T. West, executive vice-president and secretary; and Donald G. West, executive vice-president and treasurer. The third generation has already appeared among its corporate officers in the persons of Martin R. West III and Richard T. West, Jr. Through its corporate officers, Weaver Bros.' commitment to the metropolitan Washington real estate market, which began with John L. Weaver, will continue in the future.

TRACOR APPLIED SCIENCES, INC.

To the passersby on Research Boulevard in Rockville, Tracor Applied Sciences, Inc., stands as the handsome, dark glass building complex set among a tree-studded hillside. The story of Tracor Applied Sciences of Tracor, Inc., however, is a tale of accomplishment in the world of research science. From sonar and ship engineering to the discovery of hazardous materials in children's sleepwear, Tracor, Inc., has made an impact in research science since its 1962 beginning in the county.

Tracor was formed in 1955 in Austin, Texas, when Frank M. McBee, Jr., its current president, started a research science firm with three physicists and an attorney. Associated Consultants and Engineers, Inc., as the enterprise was first known, began business with a $5,000 contract from the Eastern State Petroleum and Chemical Company, now the Signal Oil Company. McBee's firm later merged with the Textran Corporation, started in 1956 and known for its development of a VLF receiver.

The company began operating in Montgomery County when it opened its Applied Technology Division offices in Bethesda. Charles Anderson managed the division, which worked on sonar,

scientific, and analytical studies.

Tracor's operations expanded during its first decade in the county. The Applied Technology Division grew so rapidly in the 1960s that it had to move several times to accommodate its increasing operations. The corporation added a Sonar Projects Office in Washington, D.C., and a laboratory in Rockville by 1965. After Tracor moved to its Research Boulevard site in 1967, it acquired the John I. Thompson Company, an engineering and science consulting firm, specializing in the chemistry, drug, cosmetic, and food industries. Tracor also acquired the Sulzer Electronics Company during the 1960s.

During the 1970s the Systems Technology Division (formerly Applied Technology) grew in size as well as stature, and the division hired its 1,000th employee. National recognition also came to Tracor's Jitco subsidiary for its work in explosive ordnance disposal and later for its literature analysis and analytical support of such federal agencies as the National Institutes of Health, the Environmental Protection Agency, and the Food and Drug Administration. The subsidiary became the publisher of the *Registry of Toxic Effects of Chemical Substances* for the federal government.

In 1974 Jitco became the principal contractor for Bioassay

Testing, the national toxicology program for screening chemicals for toxic agents. This led to the firm's discovery that tris, a flame retardant used in children's sleepwear, produced toxic side effects. This finding led the federal government to ban the use of the substance.

By 1980 Tracor, Inc., with headquarters in Austin, Texas, operated 4 groups in 14 states and 5 foreign countries as a high-technology contractor and manufacturer of advanced electronic systems and scientific instruments.

William C. Moyer, Ph.D., vice-president, Applied Sciences Group.

William M. Pugh, vice-president, Systems Technology Division.

The Systems Technology Division of Tracor Applied Sciences, Inc., is located at 1601 Research Boulevard in Rockville.

ROCKVILLE CRUSHED STONE, INC.

Crushed stone is man's most ancient, yet most modern, building material. Quarried from Rockville Crushed Stone's huge pit, which is 250 feet deep and covers 125 acres, the stone's physical attributes of hardness, durability, and strength make it a versatile construction material. The stone is an aggregate consisting of serpentinite and gabbro. When crushed and sized, this particular stone becomes a major ingredient in asphalt for road surfaces, bases for parking lots and driveways, rip rap and jetty stone for shoreline protection, and railroad ballast, along with other construction uses. In fact, the average Montgomery County home requires 350 tons of stone for direct and indirect use —everything from the home's foundation and driveway, to the sidewalk in front, the roads and parking lots of the nearest school, shopping center, or church.

Since 1955 Rockville Crushed Stone has provided Montgomery County with a local source of stone. Stone is expensive to haul great distances, and the founders saw the need for a local quarry in the rapidly growing Montgomery County area. The majority of the

The Blake Crusher, 1850. This old-fashioned way of crushing stone differs greatly from today's modern methods.

area's interstate highways, major roads, and housing subdivisions were built with this crushed stone. The quarry, at the junction of Piney Meetinghouse and Travilah roads, was originally the site of a dairy farm and cornfield. The first load of stone left the quarry in April 1955 in a small truck. From that point on, Rockville Crushed Stone grew steadily; nearly 500 large dump trucks now leave the quarry on an average day loaded with stone. Over 100 people are now employed, not including

contract haulers.

Rockville Crushed Stone operates on a 300-acre site to quarry, crush, size, wash, and haul the 2.5 million tons of stone removed from the ground each year. Landscaped berms around the quarry reduce the visibility of its operations from the roads. The firm owns 2,500 acres in Montgomery County, including 1,900 acres near Boyds, a site for future expansion.

Rockville Crushed Stone is proud of its community involvement and charitable contributions. The firm is the longest continuous sponsor of four different ages of youth baseball teams in Rockville and has supported local hospitals, and other charities, conservation groups, and Chambers of Commerce. Company officials encourage the quarry's community spirit and direct the firm's path of serving the organizations and individuals of Montgomery County —whether it be in providing quality construction materials, volunteering snow-removal equipment, or buying a 4-H sponsored beef at the county fair.

Before paved roads travel was often difficult. Photo circa 1910.

ASPEN SYSTEMS CORPORATION

Nothing better represents the shift from an industrial to a post-industrial economy than the booming growth of high-tech businesses along the Interstate 270 corridor in Montgomery County. From the southern edge of Rockville to Clarksburg, these new, pollution-free research and development companies dot both sides of the road. Crucial to the success of high technology is information. So it is not surprising that Aspen Systems Corporation, an information management and publishing company, would locate in Montgomery County.

In 1956 Aspen Systems Corporation originated as the Health Law Center of the Graduate School of Public Health at the University of Pittsburgh. A group of lawyers at the Law Center, aided by grant funding, created a compendium of all state laws and regulations concerning the health care and welfare systems as then existed in the United States. This compendium led to the group's next venture, publication of the *Hospital Law Manual* in 1959, the first complete collection of hospital law in the 50 states and Canada, which Aspen is still publishing.

The potential of storing documents on the computer without indexing or prearranging the text became apparent. As part of the university's research some of the source legal information for this book was entered into a computer and, with the cooperation of the mathematics department, the authors developed the concept of a full text-retrieval system. Aspensearch I, the first and largest computer-based text storing and search system, was born. And the entire text of the Pennsylvania legal code became the first full text legal computerized data base.

Subsequently, the original founders left the University of Pittsburgh in 1965 and formed Aspen Systems Corporation. In conjunction with Computype, a pioneering phototypesetting firm, the company published the statutes of the State of Hawaii using the computer to drive its typesetting devices. In the 1960s the firm entered the statutes of all 50 states as well as the United States Code onto a full text data base. In another innovation, Aspen installed the first full-screen display text editing system—Qwik Draft—for legislative bill drafting used by state governments.

By 1973 the founding group left Aspen to enter a law practice. With the change in management and subsequent expansion, especially with information services to the federal government, Aspen moved to the Washington, D.C., area because of its proximity to governmental agencies.

In 1978 Wolters Samsom acquired Aspen, and it is now a wholly owned subsidiary of the Wolters Samsom Group, a publishing and information management company based in the Netherlands and dating back to 1836. With its European affiliation, Aspen now has the capability to serve customers worldwide.

Today Aspen has more than 300 employees, and develops and markets problem-solving information products and services to professionals and managers in business, government, and private practice. These include books, journals, loose-leaf manuals, newsletters, seminars and on-line electronic information services for the health care community, clearinghouses, and library services; data base design and development and computerized information management systems for the federal goverment; automated litigation support services and file management systems for the legal marketplace; and data base publishing systems and information management systems for the publishing industry and other commercial businesses and trade associations.

The corporate headquarters of Aspen Systems Corporation is located at 1600 Research Boulevard in Rockville.

LINK SIMULATION SYSTEMS
DIVISION OF THE SINGER COMPANY

Emergency lights flash menacingly, indicating a problem somewhere in the nuclear power plant. Yet the engineers respond with a collected calm, assured that they can solve the problem. The mood is tense, but panic and fear are absent. The employees in the control room of the plant are entrusted to run a highly complex, technologically advanced system where errors in judgment become costly and dangerous mistakes, as the industry learned at Three Mile Island in 1978.

Today, however, such individuals are trained in an identical model of the nuclear power plant's control room where they will work. This model control room was designed and built by Link Simulation Systems Division of The Singer Company, the leader in the simulation industry.

Link's industrial simulation business skyrocketed after the Three Mile Island accident, when the Nuclear Regulatory Commission recommended "plant-specific" models for individual control rooms at every plant. The firm also works with the military establishment, designing trainers for radar, sonar, and antisubmarine warfare. Link has been in Montgomery County since October 1967, but its antecedents date back over 50 years.

In 1929 Edwin A. Link founded the simulation industry in Binghamton, New York, when he developed an airplane trainer to teach aviation skills to young pilots eager to learn how to fly. Link's small blue box became famous during World War II, when naval and army aviators took to the air after extensive training on the simulator. The wartime success of the device encouraged the growth of competitors. One, Engineering and Research Corporation (ERCO) in Riverdale, Maryland, began simulation activities in the late 1940s.

ERCO initially produced tools and component parts for aircraft, but by 1949 had developed an all-electric flight simulator. Widely recognized as the standard by the aviation and simulation communities, ERCO's advancement in electronic simulation for radar and sonar in antisubmarine warfare looked particularly appealing to the Link Company, which had been absorbed by General Precision Equipment, Inc. (GPE), in the early 1960s. In 1965 the two organizations merged their

The Army Training Battle Simulation System (known as ARTBASS) provides real-time training for tactical operations through the use of a digital computer, mathematical model, and a data base. © Charles Feil, 1982.

simulation activities under the Link name.

The new firm moved from Riverdale in Prince Georges County in 1967 to a new building erected in the Montgomery Industrial Park in Silver Spring. About the time of the move, The Singer Company purchased General Precision and, later, split Link into two divisions. The Link Flight Simulation Division deals with moveable instrumentation such as aircraft, spacecraft, and tanks—"anything with wings and wheels." The Link Simulation Systems Division simulates everything else, including naval tactical and operational systems, command and control systems for military land operations, maritime ships systems for industrial process, and power generation systems.

Link Simulation Systems now employs 2,000 people, up from 800 in 1974. Approximately 60 percent of the company's employees are engineers, making Link SSD a member of the growing fraternity of high-technology engineering firms in Montgomery County.

The Link Simulation Systems complex in Silver Spring has been located in Montgomery County since 1967. © Charles Feil, 1982.

THE GEORGE HYMAN CONSTRUCTION COMPANY

George Hyman, founder of The George Hyman Construction Company.

His reputation as a frontiersman and an enthusiastic, reliable entrepreneur served George Hyman well when he began his Washington-area construction business at the turn of the century.

With $200,000 in savings in 1906, Hyman began his venture in the South Capitol Street area of Washington, D.C. Attuned to advances in industrial technology, Hyman introduced the steam shovel to the Washington construction industry. In 1927 he hired his nephew, Benjamin T. Rome, who had just graduated from Johns Hopkins University with a degree in civil engineering. Rome became a vice-president in 1929.

The George Hyman Construction Company survived the Depression, made a strong contribution to construction during World War II, and flourished in the 1950s. The firm completed 20 major military projects during the war and nearly the same number of projects for the University of Maryland in the 1950s.

George Hyman died in 1959. Benjamin Rome succeeded him as company president and 10 years later became chairman of the board, turning over the presidency to A. James Clark.

Clark saw that the company was easily capable of becoming one of the nation's largest contractors through expansion and diversification. His vision proved accurate as Hyman began to experience tremendous growth.

In 1968 the firm moved its headquarters to Bethesda because it needed room to expand and because many of its employees had moved to Montgomery County.

Responding to the major population shift south, Hyman opened regional offices in Atlanta, Georgia, and Richmond, Virginia, in 1970, and Miami, Florida, in 1979. In the early 1980s the firm experienced further expansion, opening regional offices in Boston in 1982 and Oakland, California, in 1983.

The Clark Building, built by The George Hyman Construction Company, is Bethesda's tallest structure. It is located at Old Georgetown Road and Wisconsin Avenue.

In Washington, Hyman's blue and white signs have been seen at hundreds of major construction projects such as Washington Square, National Place, International Square, and the Willard Hotel and Office Building.

Hyman began major construction in Montgomery County in 1961 with the Suburban Hospital addition, and later built such facilities as the first Air Rights Building in Bethesda, the Sherman Fairchild Technology Center in Germantown, and Lord & Taylor's White Flint Mall store. One of its major projects—and one that is particularly significant to Montgomery County—is the Clark Building at Old Georgetown Road and Wisconsin Avenue in Bethesda. Completed in 1984, the building now serves as Hyman's corporate headquarters.

From 1969, when Hyman moved to Montgomery County, to 1984, the business had grown from a $39-million enterprise to a $402-million nationwide corporation.

Indeed, like its founder, The George Hyman Construction Company of the 1980s is crossing new frontiers.

A. James Clark, president and chief executive officer since 1969.

OMNI CONSTRUCTION, INC.

Richard V. Caruso, president of OMNI Construction, Inc., since 1978 and chairman of its board of directors.

Who would think that in the late 20th century a multimillion-dollar company could be launched from a telephone booth? Yet that is exactly what happened with OMNI Construction, Inc.

In 1977 three people began OMNI by working out of a Washington town house that temporarily lacked a telephone. To conduct business, they had to cross a Foggy Bottom street and use the pay telephone booth opposite the building. Their first contract, however, was a choice one—the luxurious Four Seasons Hotel and Georgetown Plaza Office Building.

OMNI's parentage helped the venture on its way to such success. Officers of CEI Construction, Inc., realized that in order to satisfy their clients and continue to hold a strong share of the Washington-area construction market, a quality merit shop construction company was needed to complement their union construction operation. OMNI thus began and within six years contracted to build over $.75 billion of construction projects.

In 1978 Richard V. Caruso became president of OMNI, and the firm moved to Montgomery County because most of its key employees lived there, and because CEI, its parent firm, had its offices there. By 1979 the firm had completed the Air Rights III Building in Bethesda—a 570,000-square-foot office/retail structure.

Since its incorporation in 1977, OMNI has not only constructed modern buildings, but also participated in major historic restorations in both Washington, D.C., and Baltimore. In Washington it restored the Demonet Building and built a new office facility behind the restored structure. The new building's most striking feature is a large dome-shaped window matching the curves of the Demonet Building directly in front of it. OMNI also restored and reconstructed the B&O Central

An architect's rendering of the Bethesda Metro Center, now being built by OMNI Construction, at Old Georgetown Road and Wisconsin Avenue in Bethesda. The center is slated for completion in May 1985.

Building in Baltimore.

OMNI's construction projects in Montgomery County include the 8101 Connecticut Avenue Condominium; Woodmont Place, a Rockville office building housing IBM's government support service; and the 12-story, 1100 Wayne Avenue Office Building in Silver Spring. In 1985 the firm will complete construction of the Bethesda Metro Center, which will include a 17-story office building, a 12-story Hyatt Regency Hotel, and a shopping arcade integrated with both the bus and the subway. It is the largest private development in the county's history. OMNI is also constructing the Chevy Chase Metro Building at Wisconsin and Western avenues —a 12-story office and retail structure with bus and subway facilities; the Rolling Hills apartments at Northlake in Germantown; and an office building at 8484 Georgia Avenue in Silver Spring.

By 1983 OMNI Construction, Inc., has blossomed into an organization contracting $190 million annually with a regional office located in Orlando, Florida.

B.F. SAUL COMPANY

B.F. Saul, founder.

B.F. Saul II has headed the firm since 1969.

The severe depression that gripped the United States in the early 1890s closed factories throughout the nation. Hungry, unemployed workers lined up behind Colonel Jacob Coxey and marched on Washington, D.C. The times seemed hardly propitious for starting a real estate business. But that is exactly what B.F. Saul did in 1892.

The seeds for Saul's dream were rooted, appropriately enough, in nursery property held by his father. John Saul, a noted Irish horticulturist, had come to the United States from County Cork at the request of Andrew Jackson Downing, the famous landscaper of the Capital. The elder Saul helped landscape the area around what is now Walter Reed Hospital, the Smithsonian Institution, and Lafayette Square. Within a few years he became the first chairman of Washington's Parks Commission. Later, he opened 140 acres of nurseries in Washington, D.C.

In 1892 B.F. Saul inherited a portion of these properties from his father. He planned to subdivide the area and develop it in stages. Subsequently, he bought additional land, laid out plans, worked with home builders, and convinced the city to put in streets. To facilitate the sales of these lots, B.F. Saul took back notes from buyers and resold them to friends in Washington's growing community. The notes, which carried terms of three years, were secured, and B.F. Saul's solid reputation enabled him to place them easily. The Saul business world was quickly changing from flowers to finance.

By 1900 the firm prospered, and B.F. Saul founded the Home Savings Bank with its main office at Seventh and New York Avenue, Northwest. As he had sold notes to individuals, B.F. Saul sought to attract retail customers from small depositors. But he attracted large accounts as well, including that of Malcolm Gibbs, the founder of People's Drug Stores. In 1919 Saul merged Home Savings with American Security and Trust Company.

From its founding in 1892 until the 1930s, the B.F. Saul Company syndicated home mortgages by selling smaller notes to the public. Thus, a $5,000 mortgage, typical of the period, might have notes ranging in size from $100 to $1,000 issues against it. Saul's notes were interest bearing only and matured after three years. An investor generally received six-percent interest, an excellent return at a time when most banks paid little or no interest at all.

By the Roaring '20s, as Model T Fords kicked up dust in the company's new row house developments throughout Washington, B.F. Saul had about $60 million in outstanding notes. The firm also financed, constructed, and managed office buildings and apartment complexes throughout the District of Columbia. When B.F. Saul died in 1931, 38 years after forming his business, the company was in a strong enough financial position to weather the Great Depression and build upon the financial and housing reforms of the New Deal to emerge even stronger.

Although the enterprise actively participated in, and indeed spurred, the tremendous growth the Washington metropolitan area enjoyed after World War II and

The original B.F. Saul building was located at Seventh and New York Avenue, Northwest, in Washington, D.C.

the Korean War, it remained the same company, only larger. Another 38 years passed after the elder Saul's death before another B.F. Saul would introduce changes into the organization that would significantly alter its direction and growth.

Through the Real Estate Investment Trust, founded in 1962, B.F. Saul II allowed the Saul company to expand its real estate developments beyond the Washington area into the southeastern and southwestern parts of the United States. Taking the reins of the company in 1969, B.F. Saul II drove his financial team in several new directions, one of which was to found Chevy Chase Savings & Loan.

After nearly 80 years of operating in Washington, D.C., the firm moved in 1971 to a new headquarters on Connecticut Avenue in Chevy Chase.

The B.F. Saul Company is one of the oldest continuing developers in Montgomery County, having developed subdivisions such as Springfield, Walnut Woods, Windemere, and Bradley Hills. The firm is continuing to expand its role as a commercial developer, mortgage banker, property manager, and financial advisor. Employing over 3,000 people in 14 states, the B.F. Saul Company, as it approaches its 100th anniversary, has matured into one of the largest privately owned real estate finance and development businesses in the country.

The firm moved into its new headquarters on Connecticut Avenue in Chevy Chase in 1971. Photo by Nancy Jamieson.

BANK OF BETHESDA

When the Bank of Bethesda opened in 1919, it paid its depositors three percent interest. This rate remained stable for many years. Steady interest rates and a small-town atmosphere characterized the early years of Bethesda's bank business. In fact, according to Edward D. Sacks, current chairman of the board, horses grazed across the street from the institution in quiet pastureland as late as the 1930s.

Today the area is a busy city and the bank's present building, still on its original site, is dwarfed by a 17-story hotel and office facility over the new subway entrance. A blacksmith shop stood on the same site from 1910 to 1916, giving evidence that the property has been commercially valuable for many years. The institution is still locally owned and managed by the Sacks family, a heritage that helps the Bank of Bethesda keep its distinctive small-town flavor in the big city.

The Bank of Bethesda began business on December 1, 1919, with an elected board of directors, which included George P. Sacks, grandfather of the current board chairman. Within a month, the bank boasted $41,000 in deposits. Its first board of directors and early organizers recall prominent names in the development of Bethesda.

The "Gatehouse" building became the first bank's home, and within a couple of years a new addition was needed to accommodate its growing number of customers. A wooden counter, discarded by the Western Union Telegraph Company, stood opposite the tellers' windows, and iron gratings were added to the windows and doors.

A new bank building was constructed in 1926 of native

The Bank of Bethesda has seen a number of changes in its neighborhood since 1919, including the new 17-story office facility that was built next door.

stone from Stoneyhurst Quarries in Potomac. This structure was familiar to many Bethesda residents, but its 18-inch-thick walls are now refaced with concrete and its shape has changed.

During the Great Depression, the Bank Holiday of March 6, 1933, destroyed many neighborhood institutions, but the Bank of Bethesda remained in sound financial condition, perhaps reflecting the solidity of its foundation and the support of its community. It opened for business

as usual one week later. Months later it became a member of the Federal Deposit Insurance Corporation, invested its capital, and acted as service agent for the newly created Federal Housing Administration.

Over the next decades the Bank of Bethesda continued to grow, mirroring the explosive growth of southern Montgomery County. In the years following World War II, the bank expanded operations and opened 11 branches throughout the county. In 1982 it became a bank holding company, enabling it to diversify its business operations. It has also joined a network to share automated banking equipment, acknowledging that convenience is the hallmark of modern banking. The Bank of Bethesda has been able to combine risk-taking and prudence to adapt to the changing needs of the community and remains one of the foundations of the area.

The "Gatehouse," the Bank of Bethesda's first home, was in use from 1919 to 1926.

LEE BORD & SONS INC.

In Bethesda's pre-skyscraper days of the early 1960s, former Vice-President Hubert Humphrey, then a senator from Minnesota, burst through the door of Lee Bord & Sons jewelry store. "Fix them," he pleaded. "The people who presented these to me are coming to see me, and I must show them all clocks are in use!"

When Bethesda was still a small town 20 years ago, many members of Congress patronized Lee Bord & Sons, remembers Bernard Bord, co-owner of the family business with his brother, Bob. When watchmaker Moses Bord left Russia and came to the United States in 1899, he could not foresee that someday his grandsons would carry on his work and establish their own tradition as fine jewelers. Moses opened his watch and jewelry business in Washington, D.C., after first settling in Ohio. In 1945 Moses' son Lee left Washington to open a store in Bethesda. In the months after World War II, Bethesda was a small, sleepy town with a two-lane main street. In a narrow, open space between two taller buildings, at 7436 Wisconsin Avenue, near to the old Hiser Theatre, Lee Bord began business in 1946. While most jewelry firms today are operated in department stores or as branches of chain stores, Lee Bord & Sons is the oldest family-owned and continuously operated jewelry store in Bethesda.

In 1952, when adjoining space became available next to the small store, Lee knocked down walls and moved to larger quarters at 7440 Wisconsin Avenue. His oldest son, Bernard, joined the enterprise and later became a full partner with his brother, Bob, a graduate gemologist. The firm grew and the Bords opened a

Lee Bord & Sons Inc. moved in 1952 to larger quarters at 7440 Wisconsin Avenue in Bethesda.

branch in White Oak. Lee Bord & Sons operated a full-service jewelry business—selling, repairing, appraising, restoring, and engraving watches and jewelry. Previously, they carried china and silver, but now the Bords concern themselves exclusively with jewelry.

Lee Bord completely remodeled the store in 1967 during the Bethesda building boom. However, three years later, he learned that the entire block was to be leveled for subway construction. In order

to stay in Bethesda, where they had operated for almost a generation, Bernard and Bob, now partners after Lee's retirement, decided to move to spacious quarters in the Georgetown Square Center.

Active in many community organizations, Lee was a founder of the Bethesda Optimist Club. Bernard was a past president of the Greater Washington Jewelers' Association, the Maryland, Delaware and D.C. Jewelers' Association, and the Wheaton Kiwanis Club, and Bob has received the Diamond Certificate of the Gemological Institute of America. Thus, an immigrant's dream has been realized.

CHEVY CHASE LAND COMPANY

Senator Francis G. Newlands, founder of the Chevy Chase Land Company.

The history of the Chevy Chase Land Company began 3,000 miles away in San Francisco and is linked to two influential families —the Sharons and the Newlands. William Sharon journeyed to San Francisco as a forty-niner and struck it rich in the Comstock Lode in Virginia City, Nevada. Newlands went to the city to practice law, eventually met William Sharon, and began to manage Sharon's legal affairs— and also married his daughter.

As the executor of Sharon's estate, Newlands decided to invest some of its assets into eastern land. Coming from Nevada, a dry state, with little arable land and water resources, he was fascinated by land reclamation. Newlands and his family moved to Washington, D.C., in 1890 to organize the Chevy Chase Land Company and implement his ideas on land planning and reclamation. He wished to construct the ideal suburb and provide for all amenities and necessities in a beautiful, park-like setting with tree-lined streets.

Francis G. Newlands acquired 1,712 acres of farmland along what is now Connecticut Avenue, from Calvert Street in Washington, D.C., to Jones Bridge Road in Maryland for about one million dollars. In 1890 Chevy Chase was partly malarial swamp and farmland with cattle pastures, often referred to as "jungles" by Federal City residents.

Newlands' company graded Connecticut Avenue for the street railway and laid the track at a cost of one million dollars. The firm also built the bridge over Calvert Street to carry the car line across the Rock Creek ravine. The streetcar line hooked up with the Georgetown branch of the B&O Railroad. Here the land company dammed a small creek, known as Coquelin Run, to generate electricity to power the streetcar, create a water supply for the village, and provide recreation for all. Thus, Chevy Chase Lake, a body of water the size of a pond, was constructed. The Chevy Chase Inn (now the National 4-H Center), was built for visitors, and Newlands himself constructed a stately Tudor-style mansion at 9 Chevy Chase Circle. The trolley, lake, streets, and bridges were financed by the company and later turned over to local governments.

Both Chevy Chase, D.C., and Chevy Chase, Maryland, were created as attractive, self-contained communities with quiet, tree-shaded streets, spacious houses—some with servants' quarters—schools, churches, clubs, and shopping areas to house the growing number of government employees in relative comfort and ease, away from the inner city's oppressive summer heat. This was one of the first planned communities in the country.

Chevy Chase Land Company has recently acquired properties in Frederick, Maryland, and Richmond and Manassas, Virginia, and owns the land under such prime real estate as the Van Ness Center in Washington and Saks Fifth Avenue and other major stores in Friendship Heights, the community separating Chevy Chase and Washington. Land acquisition remains foremost; the company then leases the land to reputable builders, thus maintaining its income-producing capacity. Management looks to the future while remaining in the hands of the Sharon and Newland families, still united, and today Gavin Farr, great-great grandson of Senator Newlands, is president. Both the firm and the family have remained committed to the economic development of Montgomery County.

The Chevy Chase Land Company graded the land and laid the track for the Chevy Chase Circle trolley line, circa 1905.

M/A-COM DCC, INC.

The communications revolution has brought the world to local citizens through electronic communications and satellite technology. Events bearing good news and bad flash on television screens, voices from overseas speak clearly on the telephone, and data transmitted from international businesses to hometown stores reinforce the shrinking size of the modern world. M/A-COM DCC, Inc., located in Germantown, is a leader in innovative technology for satellite communications. The company's electronic equipment installed in earth stations provides the capability to process messages to satellites in orbit.

The firm's antecedents date to 1971, when the Digital Communications Corporation (DCC) was born. DCC was organized by eight individuals, six of whom were former engineers at Comsat Labs. The founders saw the need for a manufacturing company to produce equipment to satisfy the burgeoning com-munications industry. Their combined knowledge satisfied the demand. They were well-known experts in the international

satellite community; such recognition brought major contracts to the infant firm.

The bulk of early business came from international Post, Telephone, and Telegraph entities for countries such as Great Britain, France, and West Germany. However, this international business now constitutes only 35 percent of the company's work. The remaining 65 percent comes from U.S. firms such as AT&T, Western Union, and RCA, which provide communications service to customers. Within a few years DCC outgrew its Rockville offices and moved to a larger building in Gaithersburg. It also broadened its scope to include data and lightwave communication.

In 1978 DCC merged with Microwave Associates, forming M/A-COM Inc., a company consisting of eight subsidiary operations located worldwide. M/A-COM DCC is one of these divisions. In 1980 M/A-COM DCC moved into its new headquarters, a large administrative and manufacturing complex visible from I-270.

The corporation remained in

Montgomery County because its founders wanted to stay in the area, and because they believed the firm could more easily attract professionals and their families based on the area's fine schools, recreational facilities, and cultural offerings. Another contributing factor was the company's proximity to metropolitan Washington, D.C.—the focus of the nation's satellite communication industry. This decision has been rewarding, not only for M/A-COM DCC, but for Montgomery County as well. In a little more than a decade the firm has grown to become a multimillion-dollar corporation, employing 1,000 people and anticipating that its annual growth rate will remain at 30 percent for the next several years.

M/A-COM DCC, manufacturing state-of-the-art equipment for the telecommunications industry, has made its mark in Montgomery County, a high-technology imprint that serves the county, the nation, and the world.

M/A-COM DCC'S new headquarters, a large administrative and manufacturing complex, is located in Germantown.

CHEVY CHASE SAVINGS AND LOAN

In its first 15 years of operation Chevy Chase Savings and Loan grew from a one-room operation housed in a trailer to the largest savings institution headquartered in Maryland, with 800 employees and over two billion dollars in assets.

The company was founded by B. Francis Saul II, president of the B.F. Saul Company, a mortgage banking and real estate development firm that was founded in 1892 in the nation's capital. Saul saw the need for a savings and loan where the public could deposit funds at a better-than-market rate.

When the doors opened in 1969, customers were offered just one account—a 6 percent passbook account. At that time 6 percent was well above the passbook rate offered by banks and many other savings and loans, so area customers were readily attracted to the financial newcomer.

In 1971 the Chevy Chase Savings and Loan main office moved into the Chevy Chase Lake Building on Connecticut Avenue, near the Capital Beltway. Then,

Gathering for the fox hunt at the Chevy Chase Club, circa 1900. This is one of the historical drawings commissioned by Chevy Chase Savings and Loan in 1974.

in November 1972, the first branch was opened on Western Avenue in the Friendship Heights area, and by 1981 Chevy Chase Savings and Loan had grown to 18 locations throughout Montgomery and Prince Georges counties.

In November 1982 Chevy Chase acquired Government Services

Savings and Loan, and the combined branch network grew overnight to 26 locations.

Community consciousness and the desire to enhance historical awareness have been a part of Chevy Chase's activities from the beginning. When the savings and loan opened its Aspen Hill branch in October 1974, it sponsored a week-long arts festival entitled "The Arts and Aspen Hill." More than 5,000 area residents turned out to hear and see the Opera Society of Washington, the D.C. Youth Orchestra, the Festival Arts Orchestra under William Radford-Bennett, the Palisades Theatre Company, Adventure Theatre In-School Players, and two National Symphony orchestra groups. The program continued through the month of October with an art exhibition featuring eight paintings by Washington artists, loaned by the Corcoran Art Gallery. To further promote Chevy Chase Savings and Loan and the arts in Washington, new customers were offered a free membership in the Corcoran

Locust Grove, home of Samuel Wade Magruder, revolutionary patriot, before restoration by Chevy Chase Savings and Loan.

(worth $15) for opening an account with $250 or adding that amount to an existing account. The five-week Corcoran promotion brought 1,000 new members for the art gallery and an equal number of new savings deposits for the savings and loan.

In another 1974 cultural event, Chevy Chase Savings and Loan commissioned the work of a prominent local artist to create a series of 12 original pen-and-ink drawings capturing the colorful life and times of Maryland in the year 1875. These original prints, together with historically documented text, were brought together in a limited-edition 1975 calendar. The calendars were given out to new customers who opened a passbook savings account and were also given out to existing customers.

As a more recent community project, the institution has undertaken the restoration of Locust Grove, Samuel Wade Magruder's home near Potomac. One of Montgomery County's oldest surviving brick houses, Locust Grove was built in 1783 and remained in the Magruder family for 70 years. In 1853 it was sold at a public auction to pay off existing debts. No significant repairs were made to the house in the late 1800s, although the land was farmed and the sawmill and gristmill were kept operating. By 1890, following more penniless owners, the house was nearing collapse and one wall had to be shored up.

Locust Grove lay in disarray until 1972, when Chevy Chase Savings and Loan acquired it and opened a branch office nearby. The company plans to restore it

The interior of the firm's main office. Courtesy of Max Mackenzie.

as it was in Samuel Wade Magruder's day and will operate the branch in the restored home. After these renovations are completed, this imposing house should take its place beside other major historical sites in Montgomery County.

The key to the success of Chevy Chase Savings and Loan has always been its orientation toward the individual depositor, offering high-interest-bearing accounts while at the same time providing the advantages of a full-service financial institution. Today Chevy Chase Savings and Loan offers over 15 types of savings accounts, including passbook and statement savings accounts, interest checking, the insured money fund account, and certificates of deposit. A wide variety of consumer loans, home mortgages, and personalized investment services have also been introduced over the years.

The original main office of Chevy Chase Savings and Loan.

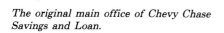

GENERAL BUSINESS SERVICES, INC.

Bernard S. Browning, president and chairman of the board of directors.

The present home of General Business Services, Inc., is located in Rockville.

The story of General Business Services, Inc., is a tribute to the ingenuity and inventiveness of one man—its founder, Bernard Browning, who foresaw a needed service that no one else offered. The idea began with the observation that the small businessman, whether just beginning or struggling for survival, often lacks the professional advice and services that are needed to ensure success.

GBS offers business counseling in six critical areas. The first is record keeping with great emphasis on keeping it simple. Browning has designed a unique copyrighted accounting and record keeping system called Dollartrack Systems. It provides financial controls without debits and credits

for non-accountants, and a bookkeeping system for non-bookkeepers. In recent years a proprietary line of pegboards, plus computer hardware and software have been added to meet more sophisticated requirements.

The second area is compliance requirements, both governmental and private, which continue to be a dangerous minefield for the small business owner, and counseling in this area is greatly appreciated for the peace of mind it brings. Various tax reports and income tax returns constitute the bulk of compliance counseling. Preparation of income tax returns, both federal, state, business, and personal, is a vital part of the services offered. GBS is believed to prepare more business income tax returns in one location than

any other organization in America.

Business planning, tax planning, personal financial planning, and management assistance are the other services offered by GBS. In the latter category, every GBS franchisee is trained to be a professional business counselor and to be a member of the small business owner's management team. Many of GBS's clients have used its services for over 20 years, unusual for any consulting firm. These services provide the tools and expertise to small business owners that have traditionally been available only to large corporations.

A small businessman himself, Browning owned and operated three small enterprises before helping to establish GBS in 1962 as a small business consulting firm. One year later the organization moved to Bethesda, where it remained until 1976. That year it became permanently housed in the GBS building in Rockville.

From modest beginnings, GBS now has 1,000 franchised representatives in 50 states, pioneering a new concept of business counseling. In Maryland there are 34 franchise operations, eight of which are in Montgomery County. The firm employs about 155 people on a yearly basis, although in tax season the work force swells to over 260. Over the past 22 years GBS has worked with over 150,000 different businesses.

General Business Services, Inc., forecasts new markets and provides services to the backbone of American commerce—the small business. The firm's growth is a testimony to the strength of small businesses nationwide, and the desire for sound economic advice and assistance.

DECATUR PRESS, INC.

The printing industry, once the largest industry outside of the United States government in Washington, D.C., reflects the American passion for the written word—whether it be in advertising, political persuasion, or general information dispensation. Part of that industry is Decatur Press, Inc., which began as a family-owned business in 1939, guided by the energies of three brothers: Richard, John, and Donald Price. The enterprise still remains in the hands of its founders. Richard Price, the firm's president, recalls that his oldest brother, a bookbinder, brought him a small printing press when he was young and thus stimulated his interest in printing. Now, 45 years later, he has seen his business grow from the basement of his father's house on Decatur Street to a 15,000-square-foot, custom-designed building in southern Rockville, its home for the past eight years.

After having outgrown its Washington quarters, Decatur moved to Bethesda in 1946 and rented a building on Old Georgetown Road for a year before building a small plant on Bethesda Avenue. In 1960 a new and larger facility was constructed on Auburn Avenue in the Woodmont Triangle. Each of these facilities was carefully planned to allow for new equipment and to provide space for future expansion.

The Decatur operation is best described as a general commercial printing company which handles all types of printing from business cards to books. This includes full-color brochures, business stationery, business forms, and high-quality social invitations.

More innovations have occurred in the printing industry in the

The present home of Decatur Press, Inc., is on Marinelli Road in Rockville.

decades after World War II than in the 500 years following Gutenberg's printing press. The composing room captures the evolution of printing. Two old hot-metal Linotype machines with their supporting type cases and foundry type, as well as the most modern computerized typesetting equipment, are included. The composing room, when combined with the latest camera, dark room, and plate-making equipment, gives Decatur the capability to do just about anything necessary to allow the paste-up and art departments to provide top-notch graphics.

The carefully regulated, humidity-controlled pressroom includes several sizes of offset presses as well as two old-style letterpresses which are used for speciality jobs such as numbering, perforating, and die cutting. From the pressroom, the work is moved to the small but efficient bindery,

which is capable of handling cutting, trimming, folding, collating, and carbon interleaving. A large part of Decatur's bindery work is sublet to larger commercial bookbinders.

A philosophy of keeping the company relatively small, well equipped, and staffed with well-trained craftsmen has produced excellent results. Decatur's 20 employees, with an average employment span approaching 20 years, have helped to make and keep the firm a profitable and enjoyable venture.

Civic and professional activities have been an integral part of Decatur's existence. Richard Price is on the board of directors of the Bank of Bethesda and is a member of both the Printing Industry of Washington and the Printing Industry of America. He is also a past president of the Bethesda Chamber of Commerce.

Richard Price and his brother, John, in front of their first print shop on Old Georgetown Road in Bethesda in 1946.

WESTAT, INC.

Westat began in 1961 as a partnership in Denver, Colorado, to do statistical research for private clients. Two years later that partnership became Westat, Inc. Winning a statistical services contract for the U.S. Patent Office convinced the firm that opportunities lay in the Washington area, and Westat moved to Bethesda in 1965. The corporation soon outgrew its headquarters there and moved to Rockville. At that time about 50 full-time staff members were employed. In 1970 the American Can Company acquired Westat as part of its Information Technology Group.

In 1977 an employee stock-ownership plan was established to purchase American Can's interest and return the company to employee ownership. Currently over 300 employees have a vested interest in the firm's stock, and employee ownership has played an important role in its success. The

number of full-time employees in Montgomery County has grown to 250. There are another 250 part-time workers and an average of over 150 field staff nationwide.

As the professional staff increased, Westat acquired broad experience in social science research, survey management, data processing, and specific government programs such as education, housing, training, and employment. Senior statisticians, who are internationally recognized authorities on sample survey design, joined the company. Westat developed a nationwide field-interviewing organization and built a large telephone survey research center with modern facilities for computer-assisted telephone interviewing.

The studies that Westat undertakes for governmental agencies mirror the broad spectrum of federal government priorities. They range from support for epidemiological medical research to energy consumption to military personnel recruitment and retention studies. While the federal government remains the principal source of research activities and growth, the

Telephone interviewing using computer-assisted terminals provides the primary data needed for many survey research projects at Westat, Inc.

organization continues to pursue the development of services in the private sector. Westat has recently acquired Crossley Surveys, a market research firm that specializes in custom studies of consumer products. The company has also developed training and consulting services in statistical process control that are being provided to major industrial clients as part of their quality improvement programs.

Westat's success symbolizes the development and progress of the growing field of survey research. Both business and governmental agencies, reflecting growing demands for information, are expanding the use of survey data in their research activities and in their program-monitoring and evaluation functions. Westat, Inc., as a contract research organization, is building from its strong reputation in survey research to provide a broad range of support services and special analyses.

The directors of Westat, Inc., are Dr. Edward C. Bryant (center), chairman and a founder of the firm; Morris H. Hansen (left), vice-chairman and international authority on sample survey design; and Joseph A. Hunt (right), president.

U.S. HOME CORPORATION

The Washington, D.C., division of U.S. Home Corporation constructs not just buildings, but communities, and provides housing for every segment of the housing market. Young, first-time home buyers, families with children, and successful business people looking for a home to reflect that success can all find a home and a community built by U.S. Home Corporation to fit their needs.

In 1959 a nationwide conglomerate of small home builders was formed, structured along the same lines as General Motors—central cash management with independent regional divisions comprised of small builders in local markets. Each division of the national organization tailors its building to the housing needs of the area. The result was U.S. Home Corporation, and the success of this concept in building has been phenomenal.

The D.C. division, formed in 1971, covers the Maryland and Virginia suburbs of Washington. By 1983 seven communities in Montgomery County had been completed: Cinnamon Woods, North Creek, Woodlake, and Shady Grove Village in Gaithersburg; Rock Creek Hills in Kensington; the first two phases of Timberlawn near White Flint Mall; and Beacon Place. There were five ongoing projects in 1984: Fernshire and Waters Landing in Gaithersburg; Mazza Woods in

Homes like this one are part of both the Naples and the Westfarm developments.

Potomac; and Naples and Westfarm in the Route 29 corridor of Silver Spring. These projects run the gamut of housing types, styles, and price ranges, from town houses beginning in the high $70,000s to magnificent estates on one to five acres selling for $300,000. One thing all of these homes have in common, according to Bruce Leinberger, president of the D.C. division, is that they are all high-quality, are 100-percent complete before the buyer moves in, and are homes one can be proud to live in. Most U.S. Home Corporation developments include amenities such as tot lots, "hiker-biker" trails, and all-purpose playing courts.

U.S. Home Corporation recognizes that there are a number of ingredients necessary for success in the housing market. The first is to accurately target areas of future growth in the county. Once a location is targeted, the company seeks available land in that area and does extensive development

studies. It generally takes one and one-half years from the time land is purchased until the first units in that new development are ready for sale.

The next important ingredient is identifying trends in consumer buying patterns in the local area. The 1980s witnessed a general desire on the part of consumers for open, spacious town homes and a demand for housing with two master suites with the capacity and flexibility for expansion.

Another important factor in building success is the ability to stay abreast of the latest developments in construction technology. Increases in building costs are pushing housing further and further out of the reach of young, first-time buyers. The firm feels that these problems will be addressed by an increase in manufactured housing. As always, however, consumers will vote with their dollars, and U.S. Home Corporation will continue to provide a great variety of high-quality housing in pleasant Montgomery County communities.

These town houses are part of the Westfarm community, a U.S. Home Corporation development, in the Route 29 corridor of Silver Spring.

211

GLEN CONSTRUCTION COMPANY INC.

Ralph J. Hubert, president and founder of Glen Construction Company.

The Glen Construction Company was founded in 1959 by Ralph J. Hubert and Frank B. Darcey, Jr. Hubert graduated from Catholic University in Washington, D.C., with a bachelor's degree in architectural engineering. He had spent 10 years gaining experience in the construction field before he and Darcey, a subcontractor, decided to start their own general contracting company. They borrowed capital, set up shop in Rockville, and won their first job, a $20,000 contract for a nursery day school, in 1960. That first year Glen Construction had six employees, worked out of a one-room trailer, and contracted jobs on two buildings for a value of less than $100,000.

By 1984 the number of Glen employees had grown to 216 with 14 jobs under way. The volume of completed work in the first 20 years rose dramatically from $1.5 million to $54 million in 1983. In 1981 the firm moved into spacious new headquarters in Gaithersburg. Although the company began in Maryland, it expanded its business to all of the Washington suburbs as well as to the District itself and to places as far away as Ocean City, Maryland; Virginia Beach, Virginia; and Nags Head, North Carolina.

Glen Construction is a general contracting company that erects commercial buildings as opposed to homes. The kinds of structures built by the firm during its first 20 years in business include schools, condominiums, shopping centers, courthouses, medical centers, hotels, motels, and even a wildlife preserve. This last project was probably Glen's most unusual undertaking; part of the job included unloading a hippopotamus.

One aspect of the business that has changed over the years is the method by which Glen Construction secures jobs. Originally, almost all jobs were won by competitive bids. Today nearly 95 percent of all projects are negotiated. This means that the company is selected by the developer while the project is in the planning stage and involves preconstruction services by the contractor. These services include conceptual cost estimates, design recommendations, updating the estimate, and project scheduling. The advantages of this type of arrangement are that it includes expert input from the builder during the project's planning stages, flexibility to update cost estimates, and preordering long-lead-time items.

Once the negotiated project is ready to begin, Glen Construction arranges the subcontracts and oversees the actual work. The development and preconstruction phase of projects averages about 6 months and the actual building time is generally about 12. The company does its own concrete work for foundations, curbs and gutters, and sidewalks, which it considers critical work. It also employs its own carpenters. The approximately 150 field people employed directly by Glen Construction also include its supervisory personnel. Approximately 25 percent of the actual work on a job is done by permanent Glen employees; the remaining 75 percent is subcontracted.

During the time the firm has been in business, there have been great changes in the mechanical and electrical designs of buildings to make them more energy efficient. Another change has involved climate control. In the early 1960s many buildings were not air conditioned, whereas 20 years later all facilities Glen constructed were. Also, as time progressed, a much higher percentage of the exteriors of buildings were glass as demonstrated by the common use

The Tycon Courthouse in Tysons Corner, Virginia, is another Glen project. The building is seven stories high and has a composite structural steel frame. Its parking structure is four stories high.

of curtain walls. The energy shortage, which began in the early 1970s, increased the costs of building construction by an estimated 25 percent.

Another situation that had a great effect on the building industry was the rise in interest rates in the early 1980s. This brought about a desire to reduce the amount of time needed in the construction schedule. As a result of this effort, the entire construction period was reduced approximately 10 to 15 percent from its 1960 level.

Glen is a completely computerized operation. It uses this capability to perform management-information functions, schedule jobs, solve engineering problems, and search out the latest and most cost-effective technical advances.

Along with all of the changes in the construction business from the 1960s to the 1980s, many things at Glen Construction have remained the same. The first is that the firm is a merit, or open, shop. This means that both union and nonunion subcontractors can be used. This has a number of advantages for everyone concerned. From the point of view of the labor force it eliminates the threat of layoffs and seasonal stoppages, as well as allowing for incentives and rewards for exceptional individual work. For the client it means that no work stoppages, restrictions, or picket lines will slow construction and add unnecessary costs.

The company was listed in the *Engineering News Record* top 400

Another Glen project is the 302-room Marriott Pooks Hill Hotel, with 200,000 square feet of gross area. This reinforced concrete structure is 15 stories high and has a dryvit facade and fan coil units for the mechanical system.

largest contractors in the United States for the first time in 1971 and has been listed on a regular basis ever since.

As Glen Construction Company continued its expansion in its third decade of its existence, it continued to be guided by its founder, Ralph Hubert. Although co-founder Frank Darcey left the firm in 1970, Hubert was joined in the business by his two sons —Steven P., marketing research manager, and Michael A., project manager. The senior Hubert was president of the Metropolitan Washington Chapter of the

Associated Builders and Contractors in 1973 and national president of the American Institute of Contractors in 1983-1984. C. Edwin Becraft, vice-president of sales/marketing, was president of the Metropolitan Washington Chapter for the Associated Builders and Contractors in 1981.

Glen Construction built the Bethesda Office Center on East-West Highway in the early 1980s. The structure has 178,914 square feet of space above grade and 142,785 square feet of parking space. The eight-story building is constructed of reinforced concrete.

BULLIS SCHOOL

Commander William F. Bullis, founder.

Attending the groundbreaking ceremonies for Founders' Hall in 1981 were Commander and Mrs. William Bullis (foreground), and Lawrence Bullis, current headmaster, (looking over the commander's shoulder).

Secure with a firmly established educational reputation since the 1930s, the Bullis School stands alone amid its playing fields, tennis courts, and open spaces not far from the burgeoning village of Potomac. While Potomac seeks to disguise its development behind a facade of quaintness and small size, Bullis openly acknowledges its use for open spaces with plans for future expansion. Viewed through stone gateposts from a country lane are a group of stark, spare buildings standing isolated in the midst of 100 acres of rolling hills in the Potomac highlands. During the 1970s debates about school funding, philosophies and missions of education, and declining academic standards contributed to educational unrest around the county. Bullis has kept to its tradition and consequently adds steadily to its student body each year.

Commander William F. Bullis, father of present headmaster Lawrence H. Bullis, began the school in 1930 for the express purpose of preparing one-year, post-high school graduates to attend the service academies. At present, 100 percent of the graduating classes gain acceptance to four-year colleges; a few still attend West Point and Annapolis. Bullis was incorporated as a nonprofit institution in 1935, and is accredited by both the Middle States Association and the Maryland Department of Education.

From its original location on New Hampshire Avenue below Dupont Circle, the school moved to Silver Spring in 1934 near Montgomery Blair High School where it remained until moving to Potomac in 1965 (although a portion of the school remained in Silver Spring until 1969). In 1934 the school enrolled 220 young men, including 18 boarders who followed an accelerated curriculum for one year prior to entrance into the academies. A family operation, the school was administered by Commander Bullis, who counseled the boys, raised funds, taught mathematics and science, and, in between, kept the buildings in repair. Mrs. Bullis was the school's dietician, secretary, and general factotum. She held this post until her retirement in 1968. Three additional teachers comprised the beginning faculty.

Commander Bullis, a 1924 graduate of the Naval Academy, taught at the school from 1930 until 1943, when he returned briefly to active duty during World War II. All four of his children have inherited his love of teaching—one teaches in Harrisonburg, Virginia; one teaches special education in California; and Lawrence (an alumnus) and a sister both teach mathematics at the school. Lawrence describes his entrance into the field and into the life of the school as "backing into it" by temporarily agreeing to teach at the school in 1964 while pursuing his graduate studies at American University. He also doubled as a baseball and football coach, intending to stay for only two years.

The commander retired in 1943, to be followed by two more headmasters, Al Grossman and Jack Dillon. By the time of his appointment as headmaster in 1976, Lawrence had had front-line experience, having been chairman of the mathematics department as well as coach, and was well qualified to lead the school into its fifth decade. Today he continues as a math teacher and is also head of the school under the direction of a highly interested and motivated board of trustees. Most of the trustees are parents of current or graduated students and many are themselves graduates of the school. One of the trustees, an architect for a well-known firm, designed the school's main building, Founders' Hall. Mrs. Lawrence Bullis is the current business manager, thus carrying on her mother-in-law's function as an integral part of the school.

The 1970s were years of great turmoil for private as well as public schools. Moves to liberalize the curriculum were appearing; operating costs skyrocketed as a result of the Arab oil embargo; drugs and alcohol claimed increasing numbers of students; and public confidence in education seemed to be eroding. The school was faced with the triple dilemma of declining enrollment, rising costs, and the appearance of more troubled students. Many parents, unable themselves to deal with their rebellious children, hoped that private schools could do the job.

However, the Bullis School chose to maintain its careful selectivity in admitting students, thus preserving its traditionally high standards while dismissing several students each year for breaking rules regarding drugs and alcohol. Simultaneously, Bullis and several other "old-line" area private schools decided to suspend boarding operations and admit only day students beginning in 1975. The underlying reasons were financial as well as administrative; there was the growing propensity of parents to conserve tuition payments for college rather than private

The Bullis School was located in Silver Spring from 1934 to 1965.

secondary schooling. Additionally, fewer faculty members were willing to give up a private life, including weekends, to live at the school and supervise students on a 24-hour basis. The transition was smooth, and today the students move about in a well-ordered, purposeful atmosphere with the school day ending at 4:15 p.m.

Reflective of the increasing importance of women's role in society, the headmaster, with the encouragement of the board of trustees, made a deliberate decision in 1977 to admit girls beginning in 1981. The school both led and reflected society's changing population—more women than ever are preparing for a professional life and entering fields traditionally reserved for men. Also, many families are headed by two working parents.

The entrance to the Bullis School in Potomac.

Planning for a smooth integration of girls into the school was vital. Therefore, when 30 girls were accepted in 1981, the institution had already hired more female faculty and added women's sports. Presently there are 110 girls in the upper school, grades 9-12. Twenty young women graduated in 1983, the first coeducational graduating class. The headmaster foresees an ideal student body of about 800 (it is now 600), with 60 percent males, 40 percent females, and 50 faculty members.

The Bullis tradition acknowledges there is no substitute for strong academic subjects, and the "basics" of math, English, science, history, and foreign languages secure the school's foundation ever more firmly, thus preparing students for a demanding and challenging 21st century.

WOODWARD AND LOTHROP

Samuel Woodward and Alvin Lothrop opened their first area dry-goods store in 1880 at 705 Market Space in Washington, D.C.

When the two New Englanders came to Washington, D.C., in 1880, they marveled at a city of tree-lined avenues and monuments and memorials saluting the nation's founders. The two young entrepreneurs viewed Washington as a vital city of the future; consequently, they chose the nation's capital to become the home of their department store, affectionately known as "Woodies," now an area institution for over 100 years.

Samuel Walter Woodward was born in Brunswick, Maine, in 1848. In the late 1860s he headed to Boston, Massachusetts, in search of employment. As the family's eldest son, he felt obliged to pay off his deceased father's debts. In 1870 Woodward secured a job at Cushing & Ames, a Boston dry-goods store. He learned the retail business during his three years with Cushing & Ames and also met his future

business partner, Alvin Mason Lothrop.

Lothrop was born in 1847 in South Acton, Massachusetts. When he was 18 he decided against working on his family's farm and eventually secured a clerk's position at Cushing & Ames in 1870. Within three years the two young men decided to open their own dry-goods store. They disagreed with the Cushing & Ames sales policy and wanted to put their own ideas into action. One particularly radical notion was the one-price plan. The usual practice had the store manager randomly selecting a price and allowing the sales clerk to ask any price above that he wanted. The clerk only negotiated reduction when a stubborn customer refused to buy the item.

The first Woodward & Lothrop store, located in Chelsea, Massachusetts, used the one-price plan. The company also allowed for merchandise exchange and return, and boldly offered periodic sales. The store did well, but Boston was too small and the competition was too strong for Woodward and Lothrop's expansionary vision. They sought new locations from Baltimore to Kansas City, but decided that Washington, D.C., was the place to be.

Woodward and Lothrop opened their first area dry-goods store in 1880 at 705 Market Space, in the heart of the city's business district. Named The Boston Dry Goods House, the store had 1,700 square feet of space and a staff of 35. Woodward and Lothrop continued innovative merchandising techniques and believed that a satisfied customer was their best advertisement.

The thriving business outgrew its first store within a year. With

200 employees and 4 delivery wagons, Woodward and Lothrop moved the Boston Dry Goods House to 921 Pennsylvania Avenue, Northwest, a three-story building with the first passenger elevator in Washington. The two owners stunned the community during the grand opening by displaying spring fabrics and colors throughout the store—in January, thus beginning the trend of early seasonal display.

By 1887 the company again sought larger facilities. The owners decided to move to F Street, believing that the area would become the city's business center. To many people, F Street was Washington's wilderness and was too far from the shopping district to attract customers. But the customers followed. The Carlisle Building opened on April 2, 1887, on the corner of F and 11th streets, Northwest, at a cost of $100,000. The new store, decorated with flowers and plants and illuminated with gaslight, formed the nucleus of the large facility. Woodward and Lothrop also purchased lots adjoining the building to add more space for the growing department store. The Italian Renaissance-style Carlisle Building provided shoppers a

Woodward and Lothrop in 1913, with new additions on each side of the Carlisle Building.

relaxed, yet elegant environment to spend their time and their money. The interior had French plate-glass windows, mahogany balustrades, light-blue and ecru ceilings, and terra-cotta walls. An information booth gave out train schedules and directions to public buildings and monuments.

In 1902 Woodward and Lothrop completed an annexation of the surrounding buildings, making it one of the largest department stores in the country. The company kept pace with the changes of the new century when it sold its 44 horses and wagons and bought automotive delivery trucks.

Alvin Lothrop died in 1912 and Walter Woodward in 1917. By that time their store had 12 acres of floor space, 1,500 employees, and an office in Paris with two resident buyers. Donald Woodward, Walter's son, ran the business from 1917 until his death in 1942; William Everett presided until 1947 when Andrew Parker, Walter's grandson, became president. A. Lothrop Lutrell, Alvin's grandson, became executive vice-president that same year. Edwin K. Hoffman became president following Parker's retirement in 1969.

Under the direction of these leaders, Woodward and Lothrop continued to grow and change, but kept its reputation as an innovator in the field. In 1926 a new structure replaced the Carlisle Building, and 11 years later Woodies moved its warehouse to the Washington Service Building to make for more selling space in the store. In 1946 Woodies purchased the Palais Royal department store, thereby

The present-day "Woodies"—a Washington, D.C., institution.

The Carlisle Building opened in 1887 on the corner of F and 11th streets, Northwest.

obtaining additional office and retail facilities. This became the North Building. That same year the company also acquired the Palais Royal's suburban outlets in the Pentagon and Bethesda.

Woodward and Lothrop followed metropolitan suburban growth in the years following World War II. Significantly, this transformed Woodies from an advanced main-store system into a multiunit system, where each store operates independently within the corporate body. The Chevy Chase, Maryland, store was the first suburban outlet planned and built entirely by the corporation. The store was renovated in 1978. A number of Woodward and Lothrop stores were located in Montgomery

County during the past 30 years, including outlets at Wheaton Plaza and the Montgomery and Lakeforest malls.

Woodward and Lothrop's strategies became multifaceted in the 1980s. Not only active in downtown real estate development, Woodies began aggressive sales promotion in 1982 to compete with the many retail stores opening in the area. In addition, the company is remodeling older suburban stores. Today the firm remains proud of its tradition and heritage begun many years ago by Samuel Woodward and Alvin Lothrop.

MONTGOMERY MUTUAL INSURANCE COMPANY

Montgomery Mutual Insurance Company's history is inescapably intertwined with the history of the small, proud Quaker community in Sandy Spring, Maryland. Founded as the Mutual Fire Insurance Company of Montgomery County by Edward Stabler in 1848, the business is the oldest insurance company in Montgomery County.

In the 1840s no firm would issue fire insurance policies in the area. After several years of planning, Stabler received a charter from the Maryland General Assembly in December 1847, and the following year the company began issuing policies. Stabler took out policy number one, which bore the corporate seal that was used for over 100 years. Mutual Fire's policyholders owned the company. Such an arrangement, the founders believed, permitted them to insure the community at a reasonable cost.

In its first year of business, Mutual Fire issued 120 policies,

showed a total of less than $200,000 in total insurance, and had assets of just $245.59. By 1928, the firm's 80th anniversary year, 83,000 policies had been issued, total insurance was approximately $43 million, with assets of $903,000. Today the company boasts over 53,000 policyholders, assets of over $30 million, and the highest-possible rating in Best's Key Rating Guide of Property/Casualty Companies.

The first, 13-man board of directors were the prominent men of the area, many of whose descendants are still residents of Sandy Spring: Edward Stabler, Robert Moore, Dr. William Palmer, George Brooke, William Farquhar, Joseph Gilpin, Richard Bentley, Joshua Pierce, Edward Lea, Samuel Ellicot, Henry Stabler, Francis Blair, and Caleb Stabler.

One of the chief policies of the board was to encourage and provide fire-fighting equipment in areas insured by their company. To that end they provided garaging for the Sandy Spring Volunteer Fire Department equipment in 1924.

In 1857 Mutual Fire appropriated $500 for the purchase of a lot and construction

of an office building, which was erected at the corner of Sandy Spring and Meeting House roads. In 1904 this modest structure gave way to a "statelier mansion" which was deemed more appropriate to represent Mutual Fire's prominence, prosperity, and reputation. This second building, with several additions, was the firm's home until it moved to its present location on an adjacent property in 1977.

By the mid-20th century the insurance business had begun to change, and Mutual Fire changed with it. The old, single-line fire insurance company began to offer extended coverage and complete home-owners' policies and packages that include liability and multiperil protection. The firm became the Montgomery Mutual Insurance Company, following a merger in 1967. It began to pursue a more aggressive approach toward marketing, expanding its coverage outside of the state of Maryland and offering complete multiline service in property and casualty coverage.

This handsome building has been the home of Montgomery Mutual Insurance Company since 1977. Located on Meeting House Road in the heart of Sandy Spring, it is adjacent to the property that had housed the firm since 1849.

The first permanent home of the Mutual Fire Insurance Company of Montgomery County, which later became Montgomery Mutual, was this modest structure, built in 1857.

NATIONAL GEOGRAPHIC SOCIETY

Verdant rolling hills and a pristine countryside—these were the ingredients that induced Gilbert H. Grosvenor, and later his National Geographic Society, to build in Montgomery County in the 20th century. The events that brought them to the area, however, began nearly 80 years earlier.

The society began in 1888 with 33 members. Gardiner Greene Hubbard, a Boston lawyer and philanthropist, served as its first president. From the outset the organization's interests encompassed a variety of projects. In October 1888 it issued the initial *National Geographic* magazine, a highly technical journal for 165 charter members. Two years later the society sponsored the exploration and mapping of Mount St. Elias, bordering Alaska and Canada. The goals of Hubbard, however, were even broader, for he wanted the organization's magazine to appeal to laymen as well as to geographers. When Hubbard's son-in-law, Alexander Graham Bell, became the society's

president in 1898, he helped to fulfill Hubbard's dream.

Bell wanted to increase National Geographic's membership by including anyone who wished to join, and he also wanted to popularize the magazine. He accomplished those goals by hiring Grosvenor, a 23-year-old schoolteacher, in April 1899. Grosvenor increased membership to 2,000 by 1900, and introduced color photographs 10 years later. The society also expanded its interests to include sponsorship of such ventures as the Robert E. Peary expedition to the North Pole and the Richard E. Byrd flight over the South Pole.

National Geographic gave a further boost to the science of geography in 1918 when it began adding maps as supplements to its magazine. Throughout the 20th century it continued to expand its educational work by producing television specials, as well as films, filmstrips, and kits on science and social studies for school reading programs. A variety of books on such subjects as national parks and wildlife were published by the society as well.

In 1965 National Geographic decided to build its membership center near Gaithersburg. The society purchased the 100-acre farm of unspoiled, rolling hills and a lake from Otis Beall Kent, a retired attorney, and opened the facility in 1968.

Meanwhile, the organization

continued to support such notable projects as the Leakey family searches for the remains of ancient man and Jane Goodall's field studies of chimpanzees. In 1975 the society began publishing National Geographic *World* for children ages 8 through 12, and in March 1984 it started issuing a new travel magazine, *Traveler.*

National Geographic magazine, along with its worldwide coverage, also produced features on Maryland, including Montgomery County, in December 1897, February 1927, July 1938, September 1943, and February 1972. The 1897 issue discussed the old Cabin John Bridge, and the 1972 edition showed the Kenwood cherry trees in full bloom.

In 1980 Gilbert M. Grosvenor became the 14th president of the National Geographic Society. Of the 28 society trustees and trustees emeritus from across the United States, seven lived in Montgomery County in 1984, including Dr. Melvin M. Payne, chairman of the board, and the trustees presided over 10.6 million members throughout the world.

Dr. Gilbert Grosvenor (left) is shown here arm in arm with his father-in-law, Dr. Alexander Graham Bell. © *Underwood & Underwood.*

Gathered around a world globe are three generations of the Grosvenor family, Dr. Edwin A. Grosvenor, noted author and historian (center), his son, the late Dr. Gilbert H. Grosvenor (right), and his son, Dr. Melville Bell Grosvenor (left), president and editor of National Geographic from 1957 to 1967. © *National Geographic Society.*

SOLAREX CORPORATION

Entering the 21st century, the world will not be dependent on heroes like Buck Rogers and Luke Skywalker to demonstrate the power of solar energy. The ability to generate electricity on Earth from the sun's rays is a 20th-century phenomenon—not a futuristic dream.

Solar energy technology has been brought to Earth and the 1980s by the Solarex Corporation, a Rockville-based firm founded in 1973 by Dr. Joseph Lindmayer and Dr. Peter Varadi. The founders, formerly scientists with Communications Satellite, Inc., recognized the need for solar energy for nonspace, or terrestrial, applications. They became dedicated to producing solar cells, which, as a group, could generate large amounts of electricity.

Solarex was created before the federal government or the public showed interest in solar energy. Cheap fossil fuel seemed to be in abundance. But the 1974 Arab oil embargo changed all that. Government support and public interest steadily increased as the industry began experimenting with the direct conversion of sunlight. Solarex enjoyed steady growth throughout the 1970s and into the 1980s.

Solarex has installed photovoltaic systems for the communications industry, for Third World village electrification, for navigational aids and irrigation systems, and for wilderness homes and solar toys.

The future of photovoltaics is even brighter. Company leaders believe that technological development, which results in significant cost decreases, will create ever-expanding market opportunities. The firm has advanced photovoltaic technology to such a level in 10 years that costs have dropped from $500 per peak watt to an estimated $8 per peak watt in 1984. As these prices are approached, photovoltaic power will become commonplace, even in areas where conventional power sources are readily available.

Solarex employs about 500 people in Montgomery County and in manufacturing facilities located in Hong Kong and Australia, in addition to an international marketing organization.

Solar energy is here to stay; the trick is to capture the rays and convert them to electricity. Solarex Corporation has made that a reality.

A variety of Solarex modules include single and semi-crystalline modules—the state-of-the-art technology in the mid-1970s and early 1980s.

The corporate headquarters of Solarex Corporation is located on Piccard Drive in Rockville.

JAFFE-NEW YORK DECORATING COMPANY

The Jaffe-New York Decorating Company is one of the oldest and most respected firms in Washington, D.C., and has become an institution in the political metropolitan area. Although the company has grown over the years, it has never lost its identity as a Jaffe family organization. As the firm approaches its 80th anniversary, it is evident that the history of the business and the history of the family are one.

In 1908 Benjamin Jaffe arrived in Washington from Schenectady, New York, where he owned and operated a small paint and papering company. In the early years Jaffe's newly acquired business used a horse and wagon to deliver the large barrels of paint to various jobs. His men could, however, take such materials as ladders and papering tables to their destination on the streetcar.

Four of the eight Jaffe children, Henry, Harry, Morris, and Bessie, joined their father in the business as they became old enough. Because of the quality of their work and the reputation they built, their business grew almost entirely by recommendation and referrals. They did both interior and exterior work on commercial and residential properties, and for many years did the vast majority of the decorating work on Washington's many embassies. A list of the firm's clients over the years is a real "Who's Who" of the creative and dynamic people in the Washington metropolitan area, including many outstanding legislators, judges, and executives, as well as such notables as Nelson Rockefeller, Averell Harriman, Henry L. Stimson, and Joseph H. Hirshhorn.

During the Depression the

Jaffe-New York Decorating founder Benjamin Jaffe (foreground), with sons (left to right), Henry, Harry, and Morris. Photo circa 1912. © 1984 Larry Jaffe.

company kept busy maintaining properties, many of which were for sale. At about that same time Jaffe's construction branch was founded. Originally begun as a maintenance operation, it soon became involved in renovation and in space change in office buildings.

One of the Jaffe Company's most noteworthy jobs was painting the exterior of the White House during Franklin Roosevelt's first term in office. After being invited to bid on this prestigious undertaking, the firm was awarded the contract and finished the job in a record one month for under $15,000.

Because the Jaffe Company was not, and is not, a union company, the episode was not finished with the last stroke of the paintbrush. A controversy developed in which Secretary of the Interior Harold Ickes insisted that workers on government jobs should not be paid less than prevailing wages. Secretary of Labor Frances Perkins sided with the Jaffe Company, saying that its wage position had been clearly spelled out in the contract. The Jaffe

position prevailed.

Congressional hearings were held partly because of this controversy and the outcome was the Bacon-Davis Bill, which requires that prevailing wages be paid on any job done for the federal government above a fixed amount.

In 1945 the Jaffe Company was working for Vice-President and Mrs. Truman in their home on Connecticut Avenue when Mr. Truman became President. Although the Trumans asked the firm to help redecorate the White House, Jaffe declined, just as it has declined invitations to bid on painting the Capitol and many other government jobs.

Having built a strong and widely respected company, Benjamin Jaffe went into semiretirement in the early 1930s. With the third generation of Jack and Larry Jaffe now in charge, and with the fourth generation coming forth the firm continues to be run on the same principles of personalized attention and pride of workmanship that have always been its hallmark.

The crew of Jaffe-NYD (with the Jaffes in the foreground) paused while painting the White House during Franklin Roosevelt's first term in office in the 1930s.

THE ARTERY ORGANIZATION, INC.

Northwood Forest, Plymouth Woods, and Concord Green suggest pastoral settings of trees and rolling hills—just the type of places Montgomery County residents might choose to live. And many have been able to do so because of The Artery Organization, Inc., a local land developer and builder founded in November 1959. Since that time the firm has built single-family homes, town homes, and apartments for home buyers and for renters, focusing especially on those looking for their first house or apartment. Artery has built an organization aimed at people "starting out," fulfilling the housing needs for young families in Montgomery County.

On November 1, 1959, Henry H. Goldberg and an associate purchased 10 lots and formed the Artery Construction Company. Goldberg, a University of Maryland graduate, became interested in home building when he worked on construction crews during his college years. They hired three employees and several contractors and began Connecticut Avenue Estates, the firm's first development, which consisted of

10 single-family homes. Alan Geller joined Artery Construction Company in 1966 as Goldberg's partner. The concern changed its name to The Artery Organization in 1968. Jack Luria joined the firm in 1971 and became a partner in 1976.

Throughout the early 1960s Artery continued to build single-family homes and expanded its operations to Prince Georges County to keep pace with the rapidly growing metropolitan area. The firm remained competitive while targeting the first-home-buyer market, designing large, functional homes that gave home owners more living space for their dollar. Artery also incorporated recreational facilities and open space for residents and kept pace with trends in exterior aesthetics. By 1966 Artery completed plans for an extensive $40-million building program, which included town homes and garden and high-rise apartments. Plymouth Green was the first Montgomery County phase of the plan to reach completion. Located off I-270 in Rockville in the Woodley Gardens section of town, the community contains Cape Cod, colonial, and split-level, single-family dwellings in addition to garden apartments and town homes. Artery also continued to build rental units in

the late 1960s.

By the early 1970s Artery had not only expanded its business to the entire metropolitan region but had expanded internally as well. The organization had added new associates and created additional divisions to handle specific project developments in various locations. Artery today includes five residential and two commercial divisions, a mortgage banking affiliate (Developer's Mortgage Corporation), and a financial-services group involved in acquisition, syndication, and financing. The firm's construction personnel, located at the division offices or in mobile trailers on the construction site, have dealt with every phase of development. They sample each part of the construction process, from walking knee-deep in mud, to talking with a construction foreman, to relaying messages to the corporate office. The founders believe that associates understand and appreciate the complexity of the business as a result of this integration of responsibility. The staff was kept busy in the 1970s, whether it was on-site or in the administrative offices, because

The Artery Organization built Peppertree Farm, an example of the company's garden apartments, in Silver Spring in 1974-1975.

Townes of Gloucester, 278 town homes in the final development stage in Montgomery County.

by 1979 Artery had its most financially successful year. Company chairman of the board Henry Goldberg attributed this to the associates' hard work and cooperation.

The Artery Organization, Inc., entered the 1980s encouraged by its success in the previous decade. The venture's first major step was to issue a five-year diversification plan, which included proposals to construct office buildings, neighborhood shopping centers, and mixed-use developments (self-contained communities mixing commercial and residential structures). At present, Artery is constructing a new office-retail complex at Wisconsin and Bethesda avenues in Bethesda, which will also house the corporate offices. Also under construction is a major commercial facility in Arlington, Virginia. The corporate officers decided to enter commercial construction to complete their role in the "total development picture." Artery also began rehabilitating older apartment dwellings.

Once the diversification plan went into effect, Artery moved its headquarters from the Chevy Chase Building on Wisconsin Avenue to the Park West on Friendship Boulevard in Chevy Chase. The firm will move into its

The Artery Organization's new headquarters will be built in 1984-1986. The complex will provide office, retail, and restaurant space at the Wisconsin Avenue location.

Bethesda facility in 1985.

In August 1983 Artery formed the Developers Mortgage Corporation (DMC), a full-service mortgage banking affiliate, which originates residential, commercial, and multi-family mortgages and sells those mortgages to others in the secondary-mortgage market.

The Artery Organization, Inc., which remains a privately owned corporation and is the largest private builder in the metropolitan area, is active in the community. Its directors, Henry H. Goldberg, Alan Geller, Tom Hall, Jack Luria, Robert H. Smith, and Robert Kogod, are involved as bank directors, they sit on advisory boards to educational institutions, and they support local theater and the arts. The firm has a large collection of paintings and sculpture, and hosted an art reception in early 1984 to share its collection with the public. Artery prides itself on building for the future, whether it be in real estate, in its associate programs and participatory style of management, or in supporting community activities. In building for the future, Artery does more than simply provide shelter. Well-planned, environmentally sound communities are the tradition of The Artery Organization, Inc.

Ground was broken in 1982 for Greenfields at Brandermill, 593 back-to-back town houses and villas to be completed by 1985.

CHEVY CHASE CHEVROLET

Chevy Chase Chevrolet, the only remaining automobile dealership opened in Bethesda before World War II, was founded in 1939 by Arthur H. Bowis, now retired, the father of the current owner and president, Fred Bowis. The elder Bowis had wanted to "be his own boss" and with the opening of the Chevy Chase Motor Company, as it was then called, this dream became a reality.

Chevy Chase Chevrolet began in a two-story facility on Wisconsin Avenue, originally built in 1938. Although the physical plant has been expanded and enlarged eight times, with the last addition completed in 1980, the original facility remains in use today and has been considered for historic preservation.

In February 1940 the company received a Chevrolet franchise, and during that same year young Fred Bowis wrote his grandmother, telling her that, "Daddy has sold nine cars and we think that is pretty good." That figure has increased to over 2,000 automobiles sold in 1983.

Business went along smoothly until Pearl Harbor. Suddenly there were no cars, no salesmen, and even more critical, no mechanics. Gasoline and tires were rationed. Men were needed for the war effort, and although the draft took many of the company's needed employees, Chevy Chase Chevrolet continued to operate throughout the war years, often with only skeleton crews. It was important to keep civilian automobiles already in use running, and the firm would often service these cars with homemade

or cannibalized parts, making do with whatever was available.

In 1946 Chevrolets became available again, but the postwar models were the same design as those manufactured before the war. At Chevy Chase Chevrolet many of the employees who had been drafted and fought during the war years were once again re-hired by the company. By 1949 Chevrolet factories rolled the first of the entirely new postwar cars off the assembly line.

Because of Arthur Bowis' experience as an automobile mechanic, he believed the most important aspect of Chevy Chase Chevrolet was its emphasis on customer service. Service excellence was a goal that was realized by the inauguration in 1948 of a safety inspection lane within its service area. Here school buses and taxicabs could come and be inspected free of charge. Fred Bowis has continued this tradition.

Another important feature of Chevy Chase Chevrolet is its relationship with its employees. Fred Bowis continues a policy begun by his father in which a percentage of the company's earnings are put into an employee profit-sharing program. The success of the firm's employee/ management relations is demonstrated by the fact that there are a substantial number of employees

with over 10 years of service with the company, and one with more than 40 years.

Fred Bowis has been involved in many civic and community organizations, but his membership on the executive committee of the Montgomery County Economic Development Advisory Board in 1978-1979 has perhaps given him his greatest satisfaction. It was during those years that the county became committed to a pro-growth environment. Today Fred Bowis believes that while progress points to high-tech development, nevertheless a commitment to protect the older, smaller businesses in lower Montgomery County remains a continuing concern and responsibility.

Chevy Chase Chevrolet, located on Wisconsin Avenue, in 1941 (right) and 1984 (top right). Although the plant has been expanded and enlarged eight times, the original building remains in use today.

SHADY GROVE ADVENTIST HOSPITAL

*The 224-bed, 4-story Shady Grove
Adventist Hospital was opened in 1979.*

On December 16, 1979, state and county officials, along with residents of upper Montgomery County, gathered for the festive opening-day ceremonies of the county's newest building. For a change, neither a new mall nor corporate offices would be celebrated, but rather the 224-bed, 4-story Shady Grove Adventist Hospital. The opening of the facility was prompted by the rapid increase in the population of the I-270 corridor area of upper Montgomery County. County officials, concerned about the population's health-care needs, had approached Adventist Health Systems' leaders and requested the development of the facility.

Because the hospital had no previous patient or physician base, success depended upon its ability to build a reputation of quality, up-to-date personal health care. "Offering health programs for all stages of a person's life as community needs arise" became the basic philosophy behind the development of the hospital's services. From the beginning, Shady Grove made the commitment to stand behind this foundation.

This philosophy, combined with a commitment to offer the most technically effective medical programs, is reflected in the hospital's nursing division. Shady Grove boasts an all-registered nursing staff. Since 1982 the facility has been recognized as a magnet hospital by the American Nurses' Association—one of the 41

magnet hospitals in the nation earning this status because of policies that attract and maintain professional nurses.

Shady Grove is also proud of its maternal/child-care unit, which provides patients with excellent facilities, flexibility, and modern medical techniques. In the obstetrics department, the emphasis is placed on the celebration of birth and total family involvement rather than the technical procedure. Families are also offered a short-stay option when the delivery is expected to be uncomplicated, allowing the mother and newborn to return home within 24 hours after birth. In addition to cutting costs, the short-stay option reunites the family as soon as possible, making the adjustment period less disruptive.

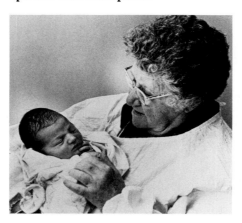

*One of Shady Grove's newborns with a
volunteer "grandmother." The facility is
proud of its maternal/child-care unit,
which combines flexibility with modern
medical techniques.*

Shady Grove's community health education programs are yet another example of the hospital's commitment to total health care. This emphasis is based on the premise that total, modern health care relies heavily upon prevention as well as treatment in fully caring for the individual. Therefore, health education is an integral part of the Adventist health-care philosophy, "A healthy body, a healthy mind."

Shady Grove offers various programs including weight control, stop-smoking, physical fitness, and prenatal classes. One of the hospital's most successful programs has been the Montgomery County KISS (Kids in Safety Seats). The hospital, along with other service organizations in the county, developed this extensive rental and education program.

Although the Shady Grove Adventist Hospital has a relatively short history, it looks forward to a bright future. The facility is already expanding its services in areas that match the community's health needs. Future plans include the physical expansion of the maternal/child-care unit, and construction of a nursing home. Overall, Shady Grove Adventist Hospital plans to keep pace with the growing community of which it is a part.

WASHINGTON ADVENTIST HOSPITAL

In 1903 Seventh-Day Adventist Church leaders purchased the 50-acre tract of forested land in Takoma Park as a building site for a new denominational headquarters, a college, and a sanitarium. Construction of the four-story Washington Sanitarium building, which stood in a rural setting on the shores of a man-made lake on Sligo Creek, began in 1906. Shortly after the sanitarium's opening in 1907, its governing board reported that it had 21 patients and was already meeting expenses.

Designed as an alternative to popular medical facilities found in the early 20th century, the sanitarium was not a tuberculosis clinic or mental asylum, but rather a limited-care hospital. In a spa-like atmosphere, it provided patients with instruction, recreation, and hydrotherapy. The governing board stated its philosophy in 1911 by saying, "Our aim is not merely to restore the sick to health, but to instruct them so fully in regard to the laws of health that they may continue to keep that which they have gained."

Undergoing a program of rest, diet, and exercise, patients stayed for weeks and often months at the retreat. The Adventists believed that this type of health treatment was more beneficial to patients than the medical treatments in

The original Washington Sanitarium, as it looked in 1907 in rural Takoma Park.

Both patients and staff enjoyed activities on the Washington Sanitarium and Hospital grounds in 1941.

vogue at that time. Patients enjoyed tennis, croquet, shuffleboard, golf, and boating. A gymnasium and swimming pool were later constructed, and a string orchestra was established for the patients' enjoyment. Because of its excellent facilities, the Washington Sanitarium gained popularity among government representatives and other wealthy clientele.

The sanitarium's transition from rehabilitative treatment to modern medical care was gradual. It began with physical expansion and the change of the institution's name. In 1918 an acute-care building was erected to house emergency

and surgery wards and an obstetrics unit. The facility then changed its name from Washington Sanitarium to Washington Sanitarium and Hospital.

Progress and expansion continued through mid-century with the completion in 1924 of a wing addition and a bakery. From 1940 to 1950 the hospital constructed two more large additions to accommodate patient rooms and the hydrotherapy department. In the late 1970s the institution began to expand again and started a major construction project. It was at this time that the original 1907 structure was razed to make way for both the construction and increased services.

Growth in the hospital's services kept pace with physical expansion. In 1967 the institution implemented the coronary-care unit. Two years later the alcoholism treatment program was begun. The 1970s saw the opening of the pulmonary medicine and cardiology departments, and Washington Adventist Hospital performed its first open-heart

Washington Adventist Hospital in 1984.

surgery in 1971.

In addition to these services, Washington Adventist formed the patient education department in 1972. Health education had long been an important facet of the institution's treatment program. It was not until 1972, however, that the hospital opened a department to carry out community health-education programs and classes on such topics as smoking, nutrition, and childbirth.

Through increased services and physical expansion, Washington Adventist Hospital has evolved into a full-service institution. Today the hospital offers procedures not found anywhere else in Montgomery County. The facility is the county's designated emergency cardiac-care center. It is the preferred hospital for heart-attack victims and other cardiac emergencies. It continues to be the only institution in the county performing open-heart surgery, radiation therapy, and cornea transplants—the only transplant operation performed in the county.

During its more than 75-year history, the Washington Adventist Hospital has grown from a sanitarium accommodating 40 patients to a modern, acute-care, 310-bed hospital with a staff of 1,300. The county's oldest hospital has grown along with the community and its expanding health-care needs. It now consists of 7 buildings on 13 acres of land and continues to offer skilled medical care and up-to-date health education, supporting the Adventist theory of healing the body as well as the spirit.

Washington Adventist Hospital offers full-service, up-to-date medical treatment.

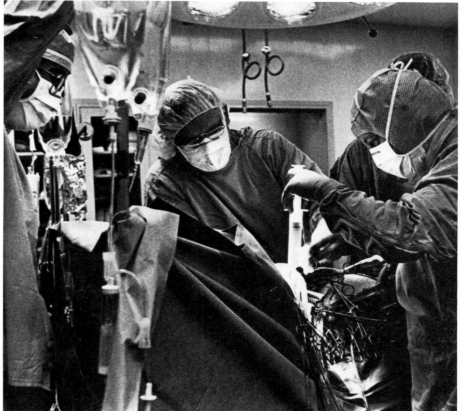

MONTGOMERY GENERAL HOSPITAL

Montgomery General Hospital was Dr. Jacob W. Bird's dream. That dream became a reality in 1918 when the citizens of Olney, then a rural community, decided to act to support a community hospital. Then, as now, community involvement and support has been the foundation on which Montgomery General Hospital is based.

Dr. Bird came to the Olney area in 1909 and established a medical practice in his home on a street that today bears his name. In the first decade of the 20th century, there was no place in Montgomery County for treating patients needing intensive care or surgery. Instead, patients had to travel by wagon or by the Baltimore & Ohio Railroad to a hospital in Washington, D.C. In 1917 Dr. Bird rented Wrenwood, a private home that still stands on the road between Ashton and Brighton, where he could more easily treat intensive care patients.

At Wrenwood Dr. Bird treated over 250 patients during a two-year period, although the hospital only had five beds. Almost immediately both the citizens of the rural community and Bird realized that the meager facilities at Wrenwood were inadequate to meet the expanding needs of the community. By 1918 Dr. Bird was able to assemble a

In 1971 the hospital's $9-million facility on Prince Philip Drive was opened.

Montgomery County General Hospital, the dream of Dr. Jacob W. Bird, was dedicated in 1918.

group of Olney citizens at a meeting where he described the pressing need for a community hospital. At first no one responded, but finally Robert H. Miller, a farmer living near Spencerville, Maryland, agreed to donate $100 if the rest of the gathering would do the same. By the end of the evening, Dr. Bird had enough pledges of support to assure that there would be a hospital for the community.

In 1918 the facility was dedicated and ground was broken. During the winter of 1919-1920 a devastating influenza epidemic struck the community, and although the new hospital building was not yet completely finished,

patients were admitted. But the hospital had to contend with inadequate facilities and insufficient equipment. There was also a lack of food and water. A blizzard complicated matters. The epidemic lasted for three weeks, and as Dr. Bird later recalled, "It was the worst time of my career."

Originally, Montgomery General Hospital had formed a stock company to raise money for the new facility and was able to raise $40,000. But the formation of a stock company also raised the issue of whether or not the hospital was a profit-making corporation. In an effort to eliminate the chronic problems that consistently arose over the hospital's tax status, in 1962 the board of directors tracked down the existing stockholders and voted to cancel all stock. The issue of the hospital's tax status was finally resolved. Throughout Montgomery General Hospital's long existence it has always relied on community support.

One of the major contributors to Montgomery General Hospital's financial independence has been its Women's Board, which was organized in 1919 by Miss Anna M. Farquhar. Since its founding the Women's Board has sponsored everything from preparing surgical dressings to operating the gift and thrift shops and running annual bazaars and suppers. The Women's Board has also contributed $1.5 million for nursing scholarships.

The building itself has grown rapidly since that grim winter of 1920. Erected at a total cost of $76,000, the original 28-bed facility soon began to expand. A maternity wing was the first addition to the original structure, followed by several other additions over the years. During the 1930s a nurses' home was built, and today this facility serves as the hospital's thrift shop. The final addition to the original building was completed in 1956.

At the 1937 kick-off dinner to raise the money for the nurses' home, Dr. Bird noted that the hospital had become a regional institution, with only 15 percent of its patients coming from within a five-mile radius. Today the hospital serves much of Montgomery and Howard counties, and occasionally receives patients from Prince Georges, Anne Arundel, and Carroll counties. But the facility has always been committed to its role as a community-oriented health facility. There has been, from its inception, a long-term commitment to the community. Its position as one of the largest single employers in Olney and Montgomery County also serves to make the hospital an integral part of the community.

By the early 1960s the board of directors initiated studies for a new hospital, and in the spring of 1971 the new $9-million facility on Prince Philip Drive was opened.

Today Montgomery General Hospital offers a full range of

health services and is fully accredited and licensed. Some of the services offered by the facility include emergency; X-ray and laboratory facilities; physical therapy; critical care; obstetrics; occupational therapy; general medical, surgical, and orthopedic care; anesthesia; a pharmacy; pediatric and adolescent care; medical and psychiatric social workers, combined with the Upper Montgomery Community Mental Health Center; and cardio-pulmonary and electro-

diagnostic services. Community, education, and volunteer services also provide the hospital and community with a full range of services.

Montgomery General Hospital's long-term community commitment has provided a unique balance of modern technology and health care at a reasonable cost.

Today Montgomery General Hospital offers a full range of health services, including obstetrics and surgical, and is fully accredited and licensed.

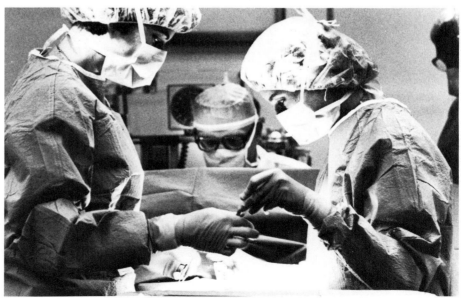

SUBURBAN HOSPITAL

Cows grazed in fields on the northern edge of the quiet village of Bethesda in 1943, when construction began for a much-needed medical facility. By the time Suburban Hospital opened its doors on December 13, 1943, thousands of new government workers had moved into the capital area, putting enormous demands on available medical resources. The resulting shortages threatened to endanger the community's health. The availability of federal funds for hospital construction in defense areas, however, pointed the way to a solution.

A citizens' committee, formed in 1942, planned the construction and organization of Suburban Hospital, but it was only through the efforts of hundreds of volunteers that the facility was furnished, equipped, and made to function. Volunteers worked to beautify both the inside and outside of "their" hospital by sewing drapes and slipcovers and by landscaping the gardens and grounds. They made, collected, and donated such needed items as silverware, bed sheets, diapers, surgical stockings, and towels. Once the patients arrived at the hospital, volunteers continued to supply badly needed services, which the staff, reduced by

Suburban Hospital's modern, five-story facility is located in Bethesda.

wartime shortages, could not provide. They served as nurse's aides, librarians, office assistants, and gardeners.

This hallmark of professionalism and dedication is reflected in today's volunteers even though the community and its hospital have changed in many ways. Just as the population expanded in Montgomery County, and the Bethesda area became an urban complex with excellent health research facilities and government offices, the hospital grew and changed. From the

A hospital team prepares to move a patient from an emergency helicopter to the county's only shock-trauma unit.

original four, single-story wings with 100 beds, Suburban evolved into a modern, five-story facility licensed for 375 beds. All of the original buildings have been replaced over the past 30 years as the hospital expanded its services through a comprehensive construction program.

Throughout its planning and building activities—from the A wing completed in 1956 to the D wing opened in 1979—the hospital has been sensitive to community needs. The facility is owned by the 420-member Suburban Hospital Association, a community group to which any Montgomery County resident can join by paying a small annual membership fee. The members provide input to the board of trustees regarding concerns and needs of the community. In response to articulated needs, the hospital has an outstanding ambulatory surgery unit and an outpatient cardiac rehabilitation program to help victims of heart ailments maintain recovery through exercise and special instruction. Lifeline, a 24-hour emergency response system, allows the frail, but mentally alert, older adult to remain independent at home, yet only a push-button away from help. An adult Day Treatment Center provides nursing supervision and social support for those needing medical attention or rehabilitation during the day.

Suburban Hospital is an area leader in providing crisis medicine —it has the county's only state-approved shock-trauma unit—and is once again turning to volunteers in order to renovate and expand its emergency facilities through a $5-million project. Thus, in its 41st year of operation, the hospital continues its tradition of looking to the local community for support and direction.

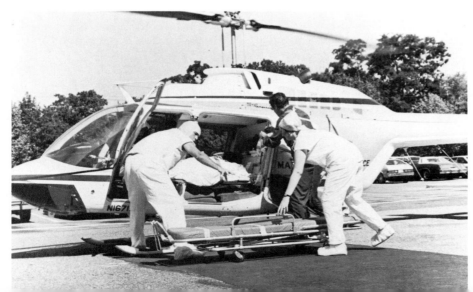

EISINGER, KILBANE & ASSOCIATES

Roger W. Eisinger, Jr.

John K. Kilbane

In the mid-1940s a 300-foot-wide strip of the Baltimore & Ohio Railroad freight line cut through Bethesda. The railroad not only dissected the heart of the city but became an eyesore as rubbish filled the pit below the embankment.

Roger Eisinger, Sr., wanted to cover the pit. He owned the Eisinger Mill & Lumber Company, located right next to the B&O Railroad. The notion of covering the pit sparked Eisinger's imagination and led to his negotiations with the B&O Railroad. He wanted to secure the air rights over the railroad to construct a modest two-story building, with the foundation on railroad property.

It wasn't until 1952, when his son, Roger Jr., reopened negotiations with the B&O, that the parties discussed terms of the lease. Terms were secured in 1954.

In 1960 Eisinger had joined forces with John "Tree" Adams, an ex-Redskin football player and home builder, and John K. Kilbane, an attorney and shopping center developer, to form a trio of expert commercial developers.

The trio then set about to acquire the rest of the block on

Wisconsin Avenue, and also acquire another block of air rights and real land immediately behind the first air rights lease. Rounding out their long-range plan, they began to slowly acquire properties that would eventually give them a third block, so that when it was all finished the initial air rights lease was the beginning of piecing together a three-block continuous connected area of air rights and real land in the heart of downtown Bethesda. It was the beginning of Bethesda's renaissance.

Since no private developer in the metropolitan area had erected a building over air rights before, many major problems had to be solved, including the type of structure to span the railroad tracks and the thickness of the crash walls to be erected so that trains could pass safely under the buildings.

No longer the modest two-story structure envisioned in 1947, the first 10-story Air Rights Building became a Bethesda landmark. Not only did the complex beautify downtown Bethesda, but it made Eisinger, Kilbane & Associates the first commercial real estate firm to risk purchasing air rights for profit in the country.

The firm began Phase II of the development in 1968, building it perpendicular and connecting it to the first Air Rights Building by way of an enclosed retail mall running through the center of the two buildings. Ten years later Eisinger, Kilbane & Associates started the final phase of the complex, Air Rights III, a 12-story, $100-million addition covering an entire block.

Eisinger, Kilbane & Associates has developed and owns areas of real estate development, including hotels, medical and many other office buildings, special institutional facilities, shopping centers, office and research parks for corporate users, a 110-acre industrial park, and an innovative apartment complex for the elderly which also will have complete social and health care facilities, as well as a retail office complex.

Roger Eisinger, Jr., and John K. Kilbane have received many awards, not only for the innovative ideas included in the design of their buildings, but also for their involvement in community activities.

Present at the Oliver Owen Kunn Award in 1964 were (left to right) John K. Kilbane; Roger W. Eisinger, Jr.; Stanley T. Lewis, architect; John "Tree" Adams; Roger W. Eisinger, Sr.; and Robert R. Furman, general contractor. The award was presented to the firm for the Air Rights Building, which was praised as being the "most significant addition to the business district."

AMERICAN SATELLITE COMPANY

Every morning millions of Americans receive *USA Today,* a national newspaper with a national focus. Delivered in cities across the country, *USA Today* is able to beam its news features via satellite from its large, gleaming silver headquarters in Rosslyn, Virginia, to its 22 printing plants around the country.

Satellite transmission is the crux of that newspaper's business. Speed and accuracy are essential to its survival, as they are to many of today's corporations. American Satellite Company (ASC®) has made such rapid data transmittal possible. Formed in 1972, ASC currently provides service to over 450 customers in private industry and government, including Federal Express, E.F. Hutton, and the Space Shuttle Program.

American Satellite's history is rooted in the 1970 Federal Communication Commission's decision to open the domestic satellite communications market to private industry. In response to that opportunity, Fairchild Industries, Inc., made the decision to enter the market through the creation of a subsidiary. By 1972 that decision became a reality, and American Satellite was formed.

By the end of the decade Fairchild reached an agreement with Atlanta-based Continental Telecom Inc., a firm with sound technological expertise, to help share the development and financing of the satellite business. Continental and Fairchild each own 50 percent of ASC and have representatives on ASC's management board.

American Satellite approached its business gradually, first leasing and subsequently purchasing capacity on other satellites rather than building its own. Within five years ASC owned and operated a national network of earth stations, and by 1983 signed contracts to have two satellites built. The first

An ASC satellite in orbit, transmitting communications across the country.

will be launched in 1985.

ASC offers two basic service options to its customers. The first is General Services, which supplies private lines on a shared network basis for voice, low-speed data, facsimile (printed material), and video teleconferencing communications to businesses with small to medium-size communication needs. The second option is Specialized Network service, a private network that provides on-site earth stations to large corporations with a heavy volume of communications. In addition, ASC offers government dedicated networks, providing private lines and special services to federal agencies such as DOD, DOE, and the armed forces.

American Satellite's growth can be attributed to the expansion of its nationwide earth station networks, a steady increase in space segment capacity, and an ability to penetrate new areas of communications technology. ASC shared Fairchild's Germantown, Maryland, facilities until 1982, when it moved into its new complex on Research Boulevard in Rockville.

American Satellite Company turned its first profit in 1982 and has since almost doubled its staff from 325 to 640 people. The firm's revenue stream is growing at a rate of 35 to 40 percent each year, not only a good sign for the company but for the communications industry as well.

American Satellite's headquarters, on Research Boulevard in Rockville, with a representative earth station.

PSYCHIATRIC INSTITUTE OF MONTGOMERY COUNTY

Founded on the principle that a psychiatric hospital should reflect the outside world and teach people how to take increasing responsibility for their own lives, the Psychiatric Institute of Montgomery County was opened in 1981 as one of the core facilities of the Montgomery County Medical Center. It has gone on to develop therapeutic strategies that are designed to put this principle into practice. The hospital is operated by the Psychiatric Institutes of America, a subsidiary of National Medical Enterprises, Inc.

Dr. John E. Meeks, a psychiatrist and the medical director for the 75-bed private hospital, was centrally involved in the planning of the institute, which treats both adults and adolescents who have psychiatric and/or chemical dependency problems.

Among the unique approaches taken by Dr. Meeks and the Psychiatric Institute staff is the development of a program for working with adolescents who have the dual problem of psychiatric illness and chemical dependency. This program, the Closed Adolescent Unit, is based on the premise that treatment of either the psychiatric illness or the chemical dependency alone will not guarantee recovery. Instead, for maximum success, both problems are treated simultaneously by a staff that combines the specialization of the medical community (psychiatrists, social workers, psychiatric nurses) with the experiential expertise of drug/alcohol counselors. Ado-

lescents suffering psychiatric illness are treated separately in the Open Unit.

A major component of the therapeutic process is the Developmental School, which all youngsters at the Psychiatric Institute must attend. The school is guided by the philosophy that all students can experience academic success and that self-esteem is built on successful learning.

The programs for adults, either those with psychiatric illness or chemical dependency, are designed to be a microcosm of real life, only much more focused and intense. Everyday challenges of life are dealt with in a structured, safe, and supportive atmosphere in which individuals' strengths can be developed and their difficulties confronted and understood.

At the Psychiatric Institute of Montgomery County, family therapy is a cornerstone of treatment. Learning and changing on the part of family members are seen as crucial to the achievement of long-term gains by the patient.

The Psychiatric Institute sponsors free programs aimed at community education on contemporary topics in the fields of psychology and mental health. In

A two-story skylight in the lobby of the facility echoes the hospital's hopeful philosophy. Photo by David Kasamatsu.

addition, there is a continuing education series for the mental health profession.

Situated in attractive surroundings, the Psychiatric Institute of Montgomery County tries to provide a healing atmosphere where patients can confront their problems and eventually learn to help themselves.

The natural beauty, openness, and light of the interior courtyard provide a therapeutic setting.

LINOWES AND BLOCHER

Almost every real estate developer and local government planning official in metropolitan Washington, D.C., knows Linowes and Blocher, a prominent real estate development, land use, and zoning law firm. Citizen and neighborhood associations are particularly acquainted with this prestigious group of lawyers because of proposed zoning changes that directly affect their properties.

The practice began small in 1956 with R. Robert Linowes, alone, sharing office space with an architect; Mrs. Linowes served as secretary and bookkeeper. Although today the firm has multiplied many times over and has two branch offices, one in downtown Washington and one in Prince George's County, its home base is still in the heart of Silver Spring, near its original location on Georgia Avenue. John Moore joined the practice two years later and was subsequently appointed judge to the Montgomery Circuit Court and then to the Maryland Court of Special Appeals. In 1965 Joseph P. Blocher became a principal partner, and in 1973 the firm became a partnership of six. The letterhead now lists 42 names of partners and associates and will have over 50 practicing attorneys by the end of 1984.

Many of the senior partners have served in state or local government posts, representing the state, county, or bi-county agencies. Linowes and Blocher is the largest firm in Montgomery County and the largest in Maryland outside of Baltimore. Currently there are 18 law clerks working for the firm, and, indeed, several of the partners and more of the associates began as clerks and today have a long history with the firm. R. Robert Linowes graduated from Hamilton College

Joseph P. Blocher, co-founder.

and Columbia University Law School and has led a distinguished career. He has co-authored several books, has served as attorney for the Federal Power Commission and the Department of Agriculture, and was assistant county attorney for Montgomery County in 1954-1955. He has served as chairman of numerous organizations, including the Greater Washington Board of Trade and the Greater Washington Research Center. Linowes also serves as a trustee of

American University. He is a member of the Montgomery County, Maryland, Federal, and American Bar associations.

Joseph P. Blocher graduated from St. John's College, Colby, and the University of Maryland. He has served as treasurer of the City of Rockville and as assistant and deputy county attorney for Montgomery County. He is also a member of the Montgomery County, Maryland, District of Columbia, and American Bar associations.

Acquisition of extensive knowledge through work with local government has enabled the firm to skillfully assist its clients through the complex maze of zoning regulations. Because of this, Linowes and Blocher settles many cases out of court, surely an accomplishment in these days of the litigious society. The majority of the cases that appear before the Montgomery County Planning Board (the zoning authority that makes recommendations to the county council and the local half of the bi-county Maryland-National Capital Park and Planning Commission) are represented by Linowes and Blocher. While the firm specializes in real estate law and developers' interests, the variety of clients served by the company reflect the broad range of groups that serve Montgomery County: shopping centers, banks, universities, development corporations, industrial firms, an urban renewal corporation, major restaurant chains, hotel chains, the National 4-H Foundation, the National Geographic Society, title insurance corporations, and home builders' associations.

R. Robert Linowes, co-founder.

The planned and orderly manner in which Montgomery County has achieved adulthood, growing from a largely agricultural county to a group of small towns after World War II, has been due, in large part, to the efforts of Linowes and Blocher. Montgomery County has been recognized locally, regionally, and nationally as a leader in comprehensive, innovative land-use planning; in the development of parks and the preservation of open space; and in controlling and multiuse zoning for commerce and residences.

Linowes and Blocher has participated in the growth of many of these carefully developed projects such as Montgomery Mall, Wheaton Plaza, Old Georgetown Village, Montgomery Auto Sales Park, and various apartment complexes. Since water, sewage, real estate development, and transportation cross jurisdictional lines, Linowes and Blocher advocates a regional approach in land-use planning. It cooperates with a business research group, the Greater Washington Research Center, which undertakes business comparison studies, as well as with the bi-county agency, Maryland-National Capital Park and Planning Commission.

Because Linowes believes that zoning and land-use regulations should be tools to facilitate development while simultaneously protecting the community interest and environment, the firm has been instrumental in urging local government to create different zoning categories. Cluster zoning of homes is an example that open space can be preserved. Another is the I-3 (industrial category), which combines industrial classifications with restrictive covenants, to establish a multiuse tract for a single industry or business. The Montgomery Industrial Park and Montgomery Auto Sales Park are models of this idea. The latter contains several car dealerships with complete services under one roof so that the car buyer can proceed from one to the other, and the businesses mutually support each other. The modern shopping mall is, of course, the ultimate embodiment of this idea. The firm has pioneered in this type of site use, a forerunner of the "high-tech park," as long ago as 25 years. The recently adopted Mixed-use Commercial Development Zone (MXPD) is yet another example of Linowes and Blocher's creativity.

As if to give meaning to its community orientation and belief in an improved quality of life, Linowes and Blocher has been a leader in Montgomery County affairs. The partnership has been active each year in assisting and contributing to various charities; it has undertaken *pro bono* work in Ken Gar, an urban renewal project in Kensington which dates from post-Civil War days. Besides Linowes, other senior partners have been presidents of the Silver Spring and Bethesda-Chevy Chase chambers of commerce. The firm also sponsors *Metro Week in Review,* a weekly public-affairs program on educational television.

The six partners of Linowes and Blocher are (left to right), R. Robert Linowes, Robert H. Metz, Charles G. Dalrymple, John J. Delaney, Andrew L. Isaacson, and Joseph P. Blocher.

CHESTNUT LODGE

"I knew the psychotic as a person long before I knew what the implications of the word 'patient' were," recalled Dexter Means Bullard, Sr., just before his death in 1981. Dr. Bullard was referring to the 15 years he spent as a child living on the grounds of Chestnut Lodge where his father was the medical director. Living with psychiatrically disturbed people during these formative years would later serve to convince Dr. Bullard that "psychotic people could be treated by psychotherapy and needn't be labeled and put on a shelf." It was this attitude that shaped the basis of his own ideas regarding psychoanalysis and today underlies the principles on which Chestnut Lodge Hospital operates.

The Bullard psychiatric family began with Ernest Luther Bullard, who started his medical career as a "horse-and-buggy doctor" in Waukesha, Wisconsin. Governor Robert M. LaFollette appointed Dr. Bullard superintendent of the Mendota State Hospital for the Insane. It was here that Dexter Means Bullard, Sr., lived as a small boy for two years, and where he first encountered psychotic patients, "who were my baby-sitters, my escorts, my playmates."

Meanwhile, the elder Bullard began looking around the eastern seaboard area for a suitable location where he could set up an institution of his own. He purchased a popular summer resort hotel known as Woodlawn in Rockville. After extensive renovation Dr. Bullard admitted the first patient in 1910 to the hospital he named Chesnut Lodge. The name was chosen because of the over 125 chestnut trees on the property.

After Ernest Bullard's death in 1931, Dr. Dexter Bullard began assembling a staff of medical students who helped him with night and weekend calls. In 1933 he recruited his first analytically trained psychiatrist, Dr. Marjorie Jarvis.

Two years later Dr. Freida Fromm-Reichmann came to Chestnut Lodge. In order to induce her to stay at the facility, against the urging of Dr. Karl Menninger who wanted to employ her, Dr. Bullard had a cottage built on the grounds where she lived until her death in 1957. One of Fromm-Reichmann's patients was Hannah Green, who wrote the book, *I Never Promised You a Rose Garden,* based on her stay at Chestnut Lodge.

In 1969 Dr. Bullard retired as medical director of Chestnut Lodge and was succeeded by his son, Dr. Dexter Means Bullard, Jr. Today Dr. Bullard continues the philosophy begun by his father that all people deserve care, understanding, and to be treated with dignity. In 1975 he added a child and adolescent division and

a therapeutic school. Dr. Anthony Bullard returned to the hospital in 1977 and now serves as its administrator.

Over the years many nationally known psychiatrists such as David Rioch, Harry Stack Sullivan, Mabel Blake Cohen, Harold F. Searles, Otto Will, Robert Gibson, and Alfred Stanton have been associated with the facility. In turn, Chestnut Lodge has been instrumental as a training center for men and women entering careers in psychiatry and psychoanalysis, both nationally and in the Washington, D.C., area.

Chestnut Lodge, circa 1910.

Chestnut Lodge in 1984.

Patrons

The following individuals, companies, and organizations have made a valuable commitment to the quality of this publication. Windsor publications and the Montgomery County Historical Society gratefully acknowledge their participation in *Montgomery County: The Progress of its Legend.*

Henry M. Abbot
Alberti Van & Storage Co., Inc.
American Satellite Company*
The Artery Organization, Inc.*
Florence Helen Ashby
Aspen Systems Corporation*
Bank of Bethesda*
W. Bell & Co., Inc.*
Lee Bord & Sons Inc.*
Bullis School*
Mr. and Mrs. John H. Carman
Chestnut Lodge*
Chevy Chase Chevrolet*
Chevy Chase Land Company*
Chevy Chase Savings and Loan*
COMSAT Laboratories
DANAC Real Estate Investment Corp.
Decatur Press, Inc.*
Mr. and Mrs. Rock E. Du Teil
Eisinger, Kilbane & Associates*
Eric L. Engelberg
John Fagen-J.B. McBride Dist. Inc.
The Robert R. Fredlunds
Walter and Carol Petzold

*Partners in Progress of *Montgomery County: Two Centuries of Change.* The histories of these companies and organizations appear in Chapter 9, beginning on page 176.

Bibliography

Andrews, Matthew Page. *History of Maryland: Province and State.* Garden City, N.Y.: Doubleday, Doran & Company, 1929.

Archives of Maryland, Vol. XV. Baltimore: Maryland Historical Society, 1896.

Atwood, Albert W. *Francis G. Newlands, a Builder of the Nation.* Washington, D.C.: Newlands Co., 1969.

Barfield, Jean, and Koch, Alice. "Madison House, Seat of Government for a Day." *The Montgomery County Story* Vol. 25 No. (Nov. 1982).

Betts, Maude Wilson. *Piscataway to Prince Georges Parish.* Rockville, MD.: The Author, n.d.

Boyd, Thomas Hullings Stockton. *History of Montgomery County, Maryland.* Baltimore: Regional Publishing Co., 1969 (reprint of 1879 edition).

Clarke, Nina H., and Brown, Lillian B. *The History of the Black Public Schools of Montgomery County, Maryland 1872-1961.* New York: Vantage Press, 1978.

Clarke, Eugene, and Clarke, Edythe. *The Spirit of Captain John.* New York: Carlton Press, Inc., 1970.

Cohen, Roger S., Jr. "The Civil War in the Poolesville Area." *The Montgomery County Story* Vol. V No. 1 (Nov. 1961).

Cohen, Roger S., Jr. "The Defenses of Washington Located in Montgomery County During the Civil War." *The Montgomery County Story* Vol. IV No. 2 (Feb. 1961).

Cohen, Roger S., Jr. Text of speech delivered at Montgomery County Historical Society meeting (typescript).

Cohen, Roger S., Jr. "The Glen Echo - Cabin John Area of Montgomery County." *The*

Montgomery County Story Vol. VII No (Aug. 1961).

Crook, Mary Charlotte. "The Men of the Hungerford Resolves." *The Montgomery County Story* Vol. 19 No. 2 (May 1976).

Desellum, John T., Manuscript of events in Montgomery County during the Civil War (handwritten).

Ecker, Grace Dunlop. *Portrait of Old Georgetown.* Richmond, Va.: The Dietz Press, Inc., 1951.

Ellenberger, William J. "History of Street Car Lines in Montgomery County." *The Montgomery County Story* Vol. 17 No. 2 (May 1974).

Farquhar, Roger Brooke. *Old Homes and History of Montgomery County, Maryland.* Silver Spring, MD.: The Author, 1962.

Ferguson, Alice L.L., and Ferguson, Henry G. *The Piscataway Indians of Southern Maryland.* Accokeek, Md.: Alice Ferguson Foundation, 1960.

Fishwick, Marshall W. *Clara Barton* (Illustrious Americans Series) Morristown, NJ.: Silver Burnett Company, 1966.

Fitzsimons, Neal. "The Maryland Line." *The Montgomery County Story* Vol. 19 No. 1 (Feb. 1976).

Fitzsimons, Mrs. Neal. "Montgomery County's Big Ditch and the Iron Monster." *The Montgomery County Story* Vol. XVI No. 2 (May 1972).

Fitzsimons, Mrs. Neal. "The Gold Mines of Montgomery County." *The Montgomery County Story* Vol XV No. 3 (May 1972).

Getty, Mildred Newbold, "Montgomery Blair." *The Montgomery County* Story Vol. VIII No. 1 (Nov. 1964).

Goetz, Walter A. *Maryland Gold Fever.* Bethesda, MD.: The Author, 1979.

Henson, Josiah. *The Life of Josiah Henson.* Dresden,

Ontario, Canada: Uncle Tom's Cabin Museum, 1965 (reprint of 1849 edition).

Humphrey, Robert L., and Chambers, Mary Elizabeth. *Ancient Washington: American Indian Culture of the Potomac Valley.* Washington, D.C.: George Washington University, 1977.

Jacobs, Charles T., and Jacobs, Marian Waters. "Colonel Elijah Veirs White" Part I. *The Montgomery County Story* Vol. 21 No. 4 (Nov. 1978).

Jacobs, Charles T. *Civil War Guide to Montgomery County.* Rockville, MD.: Montgomery Civil War Round Table, 1983.

Jewell, E. Guy. *From One Room to Open Space: A History of Montgomery County Public Schools From 1732 to 1965.* Rockville, MD.: Montgomery County Public Schools, 1976.

King, Leroy O., Jr. *100 Years of Capital Traction.* Dallas, TX.

Land, Aubrey C. *The Dulanys of Maryland.* Baltimore: Maryland Historical Society, 1955.

Levy, Benjamin. *Glen Echo Chautauqua on the Potomac.* Washington, D.C.: National Park Service, Department of Interior, 1967.

Lord, Walter. *The Dawn's Early Light.* New York: W.W. Norton and Company, Inc., 1972.

MacMaster, Richard K., and Hiebert, Ray Eldon. *A Grateful Remembrance.* Rockville, Md.: The Montgomery County Government and The Montgomery County Historical Society, 1976.

Manakee, Harold R. *Indians of Early Maryland.* Baltimore: Maryland Historical Society, 1959.

Marine, William M. *The British Invasion of Maryland 1812-1815.* Baltimore: Genealogical Publishing Co., Inc., 1977.

Markwood, Louis N. *The Forest Glen Trolley and the Early Development of Silver Spring.* Arlington, VA.: National Capital Historical Museum of Transportation and Montgomery County Historical Society, 1975.

McCreesh, Caroline. "The Secession Crisis of 1860-1861." *The Montgomery County Story* Vol. 20 No. 3 (Aug. 1977).

McSherry, James. *History of Maryland.* Baltimore: The Baltimore Book Co., 1904.

Nielson, Jon M. "Debacle at Ball's Bluff." *Civil War Times Illustrated* (Jan. 1967).

Nourse, Alice Darby. Reminiscences of Alice Darby Nourse (typescript).

Poole, Martha Sprigg. "Ninian Beall". Poole family file, MCHS Collection, n.d.

Poole, Martha Sprigg. "Maryland Constitutional Convention of 1776." *The Montgomery County Story* Vol. X No. 4 (Aug. 1867).

Poole, Martha Sprigg, and Malloy, Mary Gordon. "Montgomery County Courthouses." *The Montgomery County Story* Vol. XIII No. 3 (May 1970).

Radoff, Morris L. *County Courthouses and Records of Maryland* Part One: The Courthouses. Annapolis, MD.: Hall of Records Commission, State of Maryland, 1960.

Regional Publishing Co., 1968 (reprint of 1882 edition).

Rural Survey in Maryland. New York: Department of Church and Country Life of the Board of Home Missions, Presbyterian Church, U.S.A., 1912.

Sanderlin, Walter. *The Great National Project: A History of the Chesapeake and Ohio Canal.* Baltimore: Johns Hopkins Press, 1946.

Scharf, John Thomas. *History of Maryland from the Earliest Period to the present Day.* Vol. I Hatboro, PA.: Tradition Press, 1967 (reprint of 1879 edition).

Scharf, John Thomas. *History of Western Maryland,* Vol. I. Baltimore: Regional Publishing Co., 1969 (reprint of 1882 edition).

Scharf, John Thomas. *History of Maryland From the Earliest Period to the Present Day* Vols. II and III. Hatboro, PA.: Tradition Press, 1967 (reprint of 1879 edition).

Scharf, John Thomas. *History of Maryland From the Earliest Period to the Present Day* Vol. Hunt. New York: Charles Scribner Sons, 1906.

St. Mary's Parish. *Historic Saint Mary's, Montgomery County, Maryland, 1813-1963.* Rockville, MD.: The Parish, 1963.

Stabler, Esther B. "Cultural Activities in the Sandy Spring Area." *The Montgomery County Story* Vol. XI No. 1 (Nov. 1967).

Steers, Edward, Jr. "The Escape and Capture of George A. Atzerodt" *The Montgomery County Story* Vol. 26 No. 3 (Aug. 1983).

Steiner, Bernard C. *A History of Education in Maryland.* Washington, D.C.: Government Printing Office, 1894.

Stevens, Andrea Price. "Suburban Summer Resorts in Montgomery County, Maryland 1870-1910." (Master's thesis) George Washington University, 1980.

Thompson, Noma. *Western Gateway to the National Capital.* Washington, D.C.: The Author, 1849.

Walsh, Richard, and Fox, William Lloyd, Ed. *Maryland: A History* (typescript).

Wert, Jeffry E. "The Snic kers Gap War." *Civil War Times Illustrated* (July 1978).

White, Andrew (Father). *Relatio Itineris in Marylandiam.* Baltimore: Maryland Historical Society, 1874. Regional Publishing Co., 1969 (reprint of 1882 edition).

Index